Information Technology Management

IT Department
Siemens Microelectronics Ltd
Siemens Way
Silverlink
Newcastle Upon Tyne
NE28 9NZ
Ref: 0048

By the same author:

- *Network Analysis.* (1969). Prentice Hall.
- *Development of Information Systems for Education.* (1973). Prentice Hall, Inc.
- *Information Processing Systems for Management.* (1981 and 1985). Richard Irwin.
- *Information Resource Management.* (1984 and 1988). Richard Irwin.
- *The Computer Challenge: Technology, Applications and Social Implications.* (1986). McMillan Publishing Co.
- *Information Systems for Business.* (1991 and 1995). Prentice Hall International.
- *Management of Information.* (1992). Prentice Hall International.
- *Artificial Intelligence and Business Management.* (1992). Ablex Publishing Corp.
- *Information Systems: Analysis, Design and Implementation.* (1995). McGraw Hill Inc.
- *Knowledge-Based Information Systems.* (1995). McGraw Hill Europe.
- *Telecommunications and Networks.* (1997). Focal Press.

Information Technology Management

K. M. Hussain

and

Donna Hussain

BUTTERWORTH
HEINEMANN

Butterworth-Heinemann
Linacre House, Jordan Hill, Oxford OX2 8DP
A division of Reed Educational and Professional Publishing Ltd

⋐ A member of the Reed Elsevier plc group

OXFORD BOSTON JOHANNESBURG
MELBOURNE NEW DELHI SINGAPORE

First published 1997
© K. M. Hussain and Donna Hussain 1997

All rights reserved. No part of this publication may be reproduced in any material form (including photocopying or storing in any medium by electronic means and whether or not transiently or incidentally to some other use of this publication) without the written permission of the copyright holder except in accordance with the provisions of the Copyright, Designs and Patents Act 1988 or under the terms of a licence issued by the Copyright Licensing Agency Ltd, 90 Tottenham Court Road, London, England W1P 9HE. Applications for the copyright holder's written permission to reproduce any part of this publication should be addressed to the publishers

All trademarks referred to are acknowledged to be the property of their respective owners.

British Library Cataloguing in Publication Data
A catalogue record for this book is available from the British Library.

ISBN 07506 2656 9

Designed and typeset by ReadyText, Bath, UK
Printed and bound in Great Britain by
The Bath Press, Bath

Contents

1 Introduction — 1

  The emergence of computers — 1
  Applications — 2
  Information technology — 3
  Evolution of computing — 4
  Interrelationships with management of computing — 5
  The purpose of this book — 9
  Outline of this book — 9
  Conclusions — 11
  References — 11

2 Organization of Computing — 13

  Introduction — 13
  Location of computing resources — 14
  Equipment configurations — 17
  Micro–mainframe link technology — 20
  Rewards and risks of DDP — 21
  When to implement DDP — 22
  End-user computing — 23
  Summary and conclusions — 30
  Case 2.1: Organization at United Distillers — 32
  References — 33

3 Computing Services — 35

  Introduction — 35
  Remote processing — 36
  Consultants — 39
  Vendors — 43
  Facilities management — 44
  Information centres — 46
  Service bureaux — 52
  Computer utilities — 55
  Summing up — 57
  Case 3.1: Facilities management at EDS — 59

	Case 3.2: Choosing a consultant	59
	Case 3.3: Study of information centres	60
	Case 3.4: Survey of consultants	61
	Case 3.5: Barcelona 1992 Olympic Games	62
	References	62

4 Computer Personnel 65

Introduction	65
Staffing for an IT department	66
End-users	77
Hiring	78
Turnover	80
Career development	81
Training	82
Technostress	83
Summary and conclusions	85
Case 4.1: Personnel for XCON	87
Case 4.2: Technical education at the Bank of Boston	88
Case 4.3: Training at Abbey National	88
Supplement 4.1: Ways to reduce stress for IT personnel	89
References	89

5 Oversight of Computing 91

Introduction	91
A business within a business	91
Steering committee and subcommittees	92
Oversight role of top management	96
The role of the Computer Director	98
The new breed of computer managers	101
Hierarchy and adhocracy	101
Strains between corporate management and IT professionals	104
Summary and conclusions	108
Case 5.1: Study of CEOs and CIOs in the UK	110
Case 5.2: Oversight at a bank	111
Case 5.3: Selection of projects by steering committee	111
References	112

6 Development of an Information System 115

Introduction	115

Development strategies	116
SDLC for a development strategy	116
Critique of the SDLC	133
Prototyping	133
Structured methodologies	136
Automating the development process	137
Summary and conclusions	139
Case 6.1: Development of the SABRE/SABER system	141
Case 6.2: The development of R1/XCON	142
Supplement 6.1: Methodologies and techniques of development information engineering (IE)	144
References	146

Part 2: Strategies for Development — 149

7 Buy or Build Software Systems — 153

Introduction	153
The "buy" vs. "make" decision	154
Development of software	156
Prototyping and software development	163
Summary and conclusions	165
Case 7.1: 4GL at Hogg Robson Travel, Hong Kong	167
Case 7.2: Programming languages for XCON	167
Case 7.3: Software testing for the Metro in Paris	168
Case 7.4: Software at Societe General, Paris	168
Case 7.5: Software management at CTC (Canadian Tire Corp.)	169
Case 7.6: A vendor's perspective of software management	169
Supplement 7.1: Programming languages	170
References	171

8 Reuse — 173

Introduction	173
Component engineering	175
Component engineering and the SDLC	178
Management of reuse	181
Summary and conclusions	184
Case 8.1: Hewlett Packard Co.	186
Case 8.2: Hartford Insurance Group	186

Case 8.3: Success stories of reuse ... 187
References ... 188

9 Acquiring Computing Resources ... 189

Introduction ... 189
Request for proposals ... 190
Proposal submission ... 193
Validation of proposals ... 193
Choice of vendor ... 197
Approaches to financing ... 201
Contract negotiations ... 207
Contract implementation ... 209
Summing up ... 210
Case 9.1: Acquisition using the weighted-scoring method ... 214
Case 9.2: Acquisition using the cost–value method ... 215
Case 9.3: Rent vs. purchase ... 216
Case 9.4: Lease vs. lease/purchase ... 217
References ... 220

10 Outsourcing ... 221

Introduction ... 221
Nature and content of outsourcing ... 221
Risks and rewards in outsourcing ... 223
When to outsource ... 225
Factors in outsourcing contracts ... 227
Outsourcing and other approaches ... 229
Global outsourcing ... 230
Summary and conclusions ... 232
Case 10.1: Examples of outsourcing ... 234
Case 10.2: Outsourcing at General Dynamics ... 235
Case 10.3: Study of large firms using outsourcing ... 235
References ... 236

11 Reengineering ... 239

Introduction ... 239
Why reengineering? ... 239
When to reengineer? ... 241
Process of reengineering ... 246
Implementation and its monitoring ... 253

Success and failure factors	253
Summary and conclusions	254
Case 11.1: Reengineering at Texas Instruments (TI)	256
Case 11.2: Reengineering at Corning	257
Case 11.3: Reengineering at FAA	257
Case 11.4: BAI (Banca di la America e de Italia)	258
Case 11.5: Rank Xerox, UK	258
Case 11.6: Examples of reengineering	259
References	259

12 Humanizing Information Systems — 261

Introduction	261
Technostress	262
Human–computer interaction	262
Strategies for humanizing information systems	264
Natural language interface (NLI)	272
Hypertext and hypermedia	273
Summary and conclusions	275
Case 12.1: Graphic tools at Merrill Lynch	279
Case 12.2: Keyboard injury lawsuits	279
Case 12.3: Voice input in production	280
Supplement 12.1: Design of a workstation	281
Supplement 12.2: Preventing strain when using a keyboard	282
References	283

13 Maintenance — 285

Introduction	285
Software maintenance	285
Maintenance/redevelopment life cycle	286
Maintenance, reengineering, redevelopment and reuse	293
Software maintenance management	295
Software maintenance contract	296
Maintenance priorities	297
Summary and conclusions	298
Case 13.1: Some statistics on maintenance	299
Case 13.2: Study of software maintenance	300
References	300

Part Three: Technological Strategies — 303

14 Data and Knowledge Representation — 307

Introduction — 307
Representation of data — 307
DBMS models — 308
Database to knowledge base — 312
Knowledge representation — 313
Databases and knowledge bases — 321
Resources needed — 321
Summary and conclusions — 322
Case 14.1: Survey on methods of knowledge representation — 324
Case 14.2: Bringing a database to heel (heal) — 324
References — 325

15 The Client–Server Paradigm — 327

Introduction — 327
Components and functions of a client–server system — 329
Organizational impact — 337
Advantages of the client–server system — 339
Obstacles for a client–server system — 340
Cooperative processing — 341
Summary and conclusions — 342
Case 15.1: Client–server at the 1994 Winter Olympic Games — 343
Case 15.2: Citibank's overseas operations in Europe — 344
Case 15.3: Applications of client–server systems — 344
References — 345

16 Network Management — 347

Introduction — 347
Fault/problem management — 349
Performance management — 350
Security management — 351
Configuration management — 355
Account management — 355
Software for network management — 356
End-user management — 357

Development of networks		358
Resources for network management		361
Historical view		365
Summary and conclusions		368
Case 16.1: Networking Parliament		370
Case 16.2: Intrusions into the Internet		371
Case 16.3: Analyzers at a Honda car plant		372
Case 16.4: Citibank with its $200 billion a day business		372
References		373

17 Privacy and Security 375

Introduction	375
Privacy	375
Security	383
Security for advanced technology	395
Computer viruses	397
Organization for security	401
Summary and conclusions	404
Case 17.1: Cases in hacking	406
Case 17.2: Examples of malicious damage	407
Case 17.3: German hacker invades US defence files	408
Case 17.4: Buying the silence of computer criminals	408
Case 17.5: The computer "bad boy" nabbed by the FBI	409
Case 17.6: Case on virus offender caught and punished	410
References	410

18 Controlling Quality and Performance 413

Introduction	413
Identify what is to be evaluated	415
Establish evaluation criteria	416
Total Quality Management (TQM)	422
Quality control of operations	431
Summary and conclusions	433
Case 18.1: Quality control at Kodak	435
Case 18.2: Quality at CIGNA	435
Supplement 18.1: Causes for errors and their solutions	436
References	440

19 Project Management — 441

- Introduction — 441
- Selection of a project manger — 443
- Team structure — 444
- Team size — 448
- Project plan — 448
- Scheduling — 449
- Project reviews — 450
- Slippage — 451
- Project organization — 453
- Use of computer programs — 458
- Systems integrator — 461
- Critical success and failure factors — 463
- Rules for project management — 464
- Summary and conclusions — 465
- Case 19.1: Project failure at MVD, California State — 466
- Case 19.2: Project disaster at AMR — 467
- Case 19.3: Systems integrator at USAA — 468
- Case 19.4: Systems integrator at Mölnlycke — 468
- References — 469

Postscript: What Lies Ahead? — 471
Appendix: Glossary in Prose — 477
Index — 487

1 Introduction

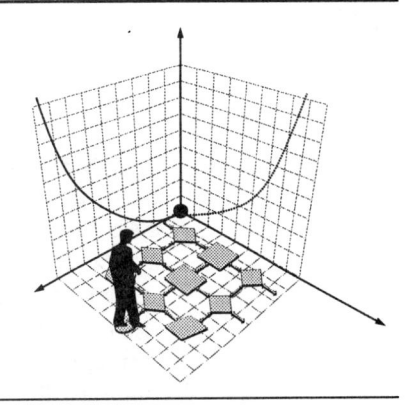

To live effectively is to live with adequate information.

Nobert Weiner

The emergence of computers

Computers are a world-wide, multi-billion pound industry. Every year, the number of installed computers is on the increase – as is the number of employees who need a working knowledge of computers to carry out their jobs. We are an information society with more than half of our workforce engaged in the production of information or employed by organizations that manufacture or sell information products. No wonder the development of computers – with the ability to process information on a large scale – has had such a revolutionary effect on the way business is conducted around the globe.

Modern information machines emerged during the Second World War. At that time, the emphasis in business and commerce was on data processing: the use of machines to reduce clerical costs and the volume of paperwork. Early computers processed business transactions primarily for financial applications. Their use was justifiable, economically speaking, because computers performed some of the functions of clerks and helped increase their productivity.

As performance improved with advances in technology and as equipment became cheaper, more robust, and portable, computer applications expanded. Companies began to use computers to process information related to production, marketing, inventory control, accounting, payroll, and other functions. With this expansion, focus shifted from systems that would simply save money towards computers that would improve operations. By the mid-1960s, when computers were miniaturized by solid-state logic technology and integrated circuits reached the market, the computer revolution was launched.

Today, the intense competition facing modern business is a force driving information technology (IT). It is now being used at higher levels of management for decision-making – as in *decision support systems* – and with expert systems using artificial intelligence. Most corporations recognize that information is an *asset* and can be a weapon to enhance the corporation's posture in local and world markets. Information can improve a firm's product and its service to customers. There are many ways in which information technology has helped suppliers of goods and services to become low-cost producers, to stake out a market niche, or to differentiate their products from those of their competitors. Some are discussed below.

Applications

Consider the following applications:

- In launching its new chocolate bar, *Wispa*, Cadbury orchestrated its strategy from one personal computer (PC) using *Delta* database products. To catch the competition off-guard, orders were generated and processed in almost total secrecy in each new market. The speed of order processing and the quality of information analysis that the computer system produced helped Cadbury win a market for *Wispa*.
- On days with few races, or in the evenings, the Tote (Horserace Totalization Board) earns extra revenues by using its computers and telecommunications equipment for a telemarketing bureau.
- The German television company ZDF, which developed its *Sphinx* system to store newsagency flashes and to respond to complex queries by journalists, is marketing its system to other news organizations with similar needs.
- British Airways plans to put PCs with touch-sensitive screens on the back of passenger seats to attract travellers to its flights. The PCs will allow people to order goods, rent a car, make a reservation at a hotel or theatre, and obtain information about their destination while still in the air.
- The Washington Hotel in Tokyo uses a robot to check-in its guests. Many tourists are drawn to the hotel because of its novel and efficient computer applications.
- Exxon is developing a debit-card network to give customers the convenience of a credit card but with the same discount given cash receipts. The cost of the purchase is immediately debited from the customer's bank account through the network.

Tracking jobs through the factory floor is not new to IT. What is new is the use of a chip attached to the shoe of a runner that would track him or her from the start of a race to the very end. But what if the racer–chip technology was used to track and trace every employee in an office or factory? What if every citizen was to be traced through his work and home? How will this affect the privacy of individuals and would they accept such surveillance?

E-mail has been the "killer" application of the early 1990s. Will it replace all internal communications in government and corporations? Will e-mail replace (even partially) the US post office, the Royal Mail and the PT&Ts?

Digital libraries with all reading material accessible to computers are technologically possible. What is not yet resolved is how the authors will be paid for their royalties and how this will be collected – especially from countries that do not respect intellectual property rights. But if these problems were resolved, could digital libraries be used by businesses for accessing information and, along with interactive video conferencing, improve their product design and reduce their product cycle? Will digital libraries assist firms in training their personnel? Will digital libraries transform publishing (of newspapers, journals and books) as we now know it? Will digital libraries assist distance learning and make education and training accessible to anyone anywhere as long as they have the resources of a computer and access to a LAN (local area network)?

Information technology

IT has grown at a rapid pace in its short lifetime. One view of this growth is shown in Figure 1.1. Within five decades we are already using fourth generation languages (4GLs) and we have progressed from the early electronic computing to the fifth generation computer systems (5GCS) using AI (artificial intelligence), knowledge-based systems, LANs (local area networks), and multimedia. Fortunately, a corporate manager does not need to know all the details of the technologies listed above – any more than a driver of an automobile needs to know all about the internal combustion engine. However, we may lose a human life if the driver does not know how and when to use the accelerator and the brake. Likewise, every user of a computer (that includes most of us citizens and almost all of corporate management) must understand the basics of computing and how it can be managed.

There are many questions of what technology will be feasible in the future and what implications they may have on the management of computing. Which of these technologies are desirable and what are their social implications?

Figure 1.1:
Evolution of computing

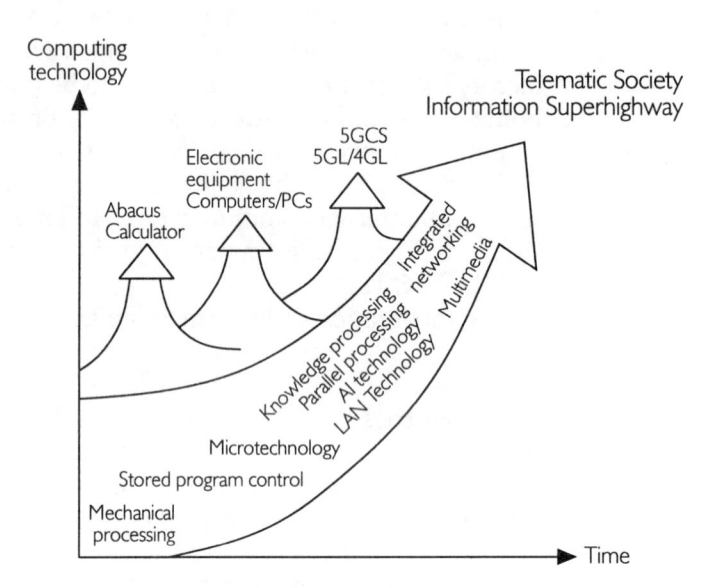

In this book we are concerned with a computing technology that must be managed and do not have the space to explore social implications. Organizations that do not implement and manage IT well are likely to lose customers and their markets. The challenges that business managers face is to utilize IT to improve the competitive position of their companies. One strategy is to anticipate and absorb the necessary computing technology despite its rapid growth and evolution.

Evolution of computing

One view of the evolution of computer systems is shown in Figure 1.2. Technology has evolved from a reliance on mainframe and centralized computing in the 1950s and 1960s; to minicomputers and shared distributed computing in the 1970s; to PCs, workstations and personal computing of the 1980s; to the client–server system, the Internet, collaborative computing and networking in the 1990s. We shall examine all these configurations later in the book.

The stages of evolution shown in Figure 1.2 are not mutually exclusive. Each department in a firm can be at different stages and levels of computing at any one time – depending on the resources available and the computing abilities of each department. They may operate independently or cooperatively. It is the function of computing management to keep them happy and comfortable with the level of technology that they desire and need.

Figure 1.2:
Evolution of computer systems

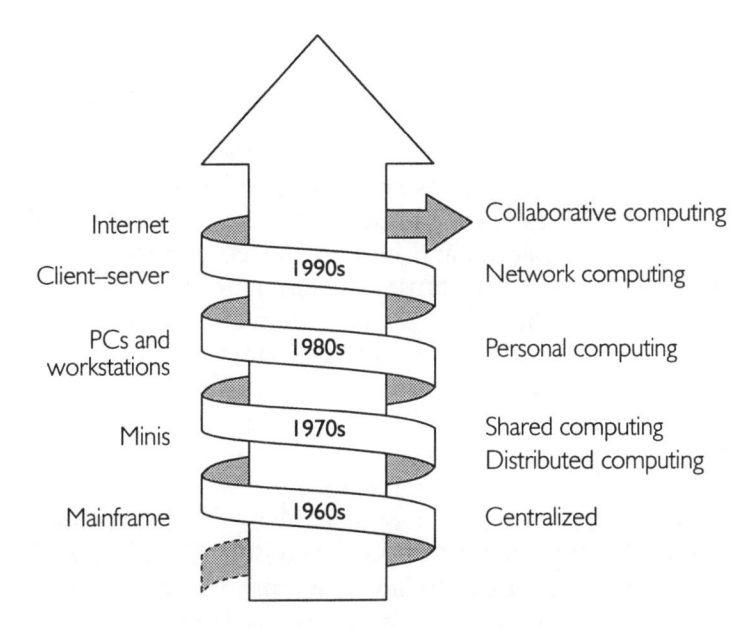

Internet		Collaborative computing
Client–server	1990s	Network computing
PCs and workstations	1980s	Personal computing
Minis	1970s	Shared computing / Distributed computing
Mainframe	1960s	Centralized

Interrelationships with management of computing

The client–server approach is perhaps the most promising paradigm for computing. In it, the *client* is a computer, even as small as a primitive PC, that is connected by telecommunications and a LAN to a *server*. The server is also a computer but is more powerful and one that "serves" computing resources to the "clients". These resources may be software, programming languages, applications, data and knowledge, or a specialized peripheral such as an optical scanner or a fast laser-printer.

The client–server paradigm is a good example of a technology-driven system. It is the technology of telecommunications, networking and the PC that made the client–server system technologically feasible. What made it organizationally feasible is the desire of the end-user (the ultimate user of computing, distinct from any intermediate user like a programmer) to be independent of centralized computing and the willingness on the part of the end-user to become more computer-literate and to take responsibility for the client system. We shall discuss the client–server system in greater detail in Chapter 15 but suffice to say that it has an important impact on computer management – as implied by Figure 1.3.

Chapter 1: Introduction

There are other interrelationships between end-users and computer management besides the desire for decentralized computing. These include a demand (or request) for more humanized and end-user friendly systems, easily accessible (yet secure) data/knowledge management facilities, as well as security and privacy of the computer system.

Besides impacting on computer management, end-users also have an impact on the computer industry. For example, they demand end-user friendly systems both in software and hardware. This means that technology supplied by the computer industry must be designed with ergonomics and human factors in mind. The computer industry also has relationships with the environment. This is more of a one-way relationship where the environment (the government, for example) may enact laws and regulations that impact on the computer industry. An example of one such law is the 1996 Telecommunications Act which deregulated the (US) computer and telecommunications industry to the point that the industry could well offer a one-stop integrated service that could include video/films-on-demand to any office or home. This raised the question of how much control the end-user has over content such as violence and pornography. The 1996 law then requires the computing industry to have the capability (also referred to as the "V chip") of controlling programmes considered undesirable by the end-user. Laws and regulations also affect computing management. For example, in 1996 the government of Singapore decreed that all providers (including cybercafes) of services on the Internet must register with the government and take "reasonable measures" against the broadcast of "objectionable" material.

Figure 1.3:
Interrelationships with the management of computing

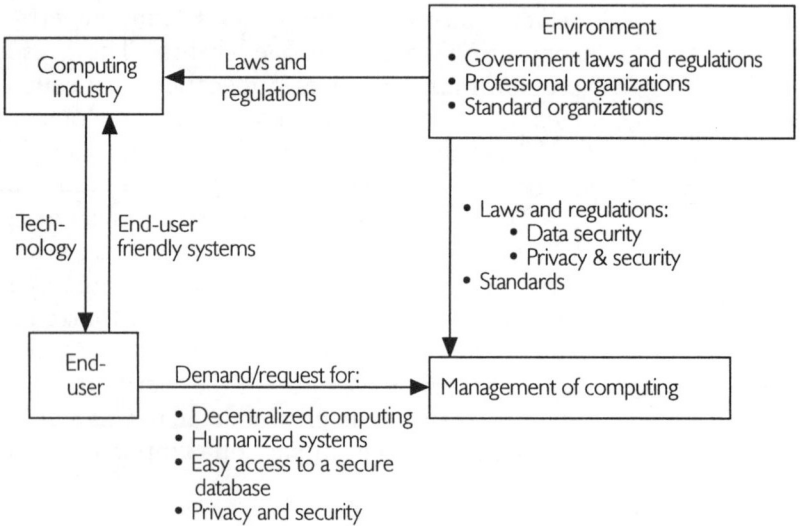

There are many other laws and regulations, especially in Europe, relating to data transfer, database construction, and privacy. In the US there is the 1974 Privacy Act which is restricted to government data but only on the assumption that private enterprise will have its own laws as they relate to privacy: a responsibility of computing managers and corporate managers. Standards are also a constraint on computing management and are formulated by professional, as well as international, organizations and cover wiring sizes and construction, display formats, hardware interfaces, programming languages, and even documentation. All these relationships are shown in Figure 1.3.

Another set of relationships are those which exist between corporate management and computer management. Some of them have been implied when discussing the end-user who is often represented (organizationally speaking) by corporate management if not by an "end-user's group". In addition, corporate management is also concerned with offering a service that is both effective and efficient.

Figure 1.4: *More interrelationships with the management of computing*

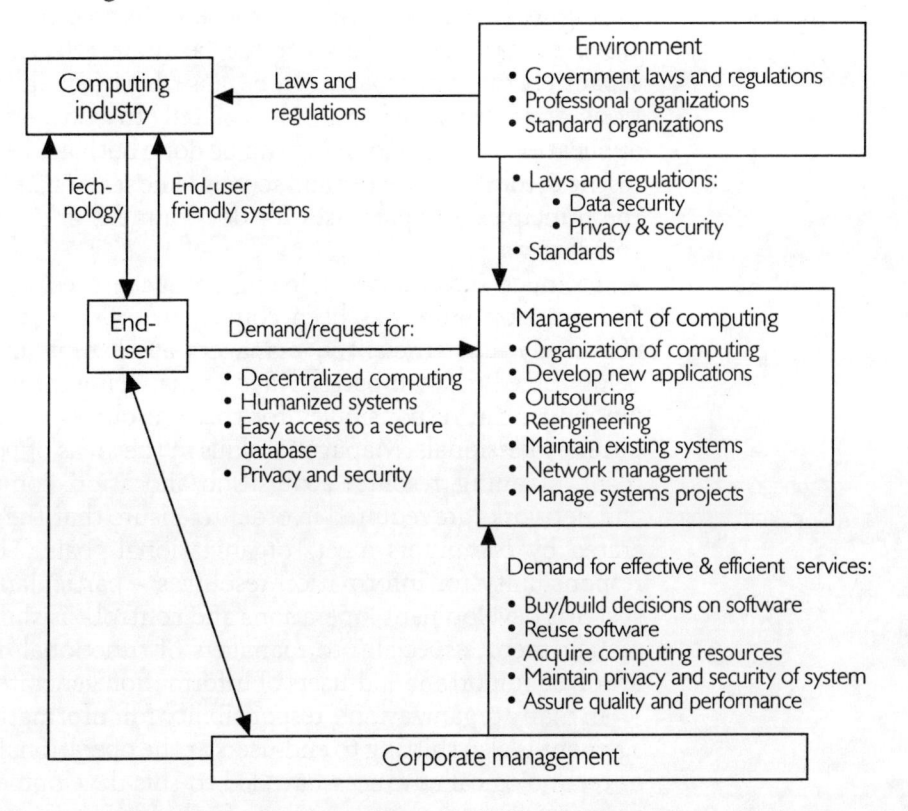

This implies strategies for the organization of computing; building in-house or buying-in of software; the reuse of software whenever possible; the acquisition of computing resources (mostly hardware and software); maintaining both privacy and security of information; and assuring the quality and performance of service offered.

In response to the demands of corporate management, computing management must organize and staff itself; develop new applications as needed and feasible; outsource (subcontract outside the enterprise) the development of software or services like network management or facilities management; reengineer (redesign and implement) an entire system, if necessary; maintain existing applications and services; institute, maintain and enhance telecommunications and networking; and manage projects which may be for new applications or enhancements to old applications. All these functions of computing management and their relationships are shown in Figure 1.4 (which is an overlay on Figure 1.3).

Note that the management functions reserved for centralized computing are best done for the enterprise as a whole. A good example is network management. This cannot be done effectively or efficiently separately for each department because departmental networking functions are interrelated and not isolated. In contrast, development of applications and outsourcing can be done both at the centre and at the distributed sites of clients and servers. The scale is different but many of the principles and processes for development and for outsourcing are common.

So much information is being produced these days that the term "information glut" has been coined. In order to utilize information effectively and efficiently, managers at all organizational levels are being forced to learn better ways of managing information resources. No longer can responsibility for these resources be delegated to computer professionals. Managerial skills in the areas of personnel management, planning, resource acquisition/allocation, computer application and networks are required in order to ensure that the information generated by computers meets organizational goals. This explains why responsibility for information resources – particularly in the areas of systems development, operations and control – is shifting to corporate management, especially to managers of functional departments who are often important end-users of information generated by computers.

In many organizations, responsibility for information resource management is also shifting to end-users at the operational levels. A number of technological advances have led to this development. For example, advances in telecommunications facilitate distributed processing and independence of processing nodes. The establishment of computer networks, improved end-user interfaces, the availability of database management systems, and the widespread use of PCs and microcomputers have contributed to the ability of end-users to manage information resources. Today, end-users frequently choose equipment, design and develop new systems, and handle their own local computer operations, especially at the client sites.

The purpose of this book

The purpose of this book is to help you, the reader, gain an understanding and appreciation of information resource management for your future role as a manager or user of information technology. You will discover that concepts applicable to the management of "things" and physical property do not apply to the management of information. For example, information, when used, is not depleted as are raw materials such as coal and iron. Information, when exchanged, does not become the exclusive property of one individual or department but is a shared asset. Information has a tendency to leak. To hoard or monopolize information is only possible in specialized fields and then only for short periods of time. Traditional hierarchies of power have been based on ownership, access, or control of physical resources. These hierarchies crumble when the resource is information. Clearly, many of the basic assumptions in the management of materials and manufactured goods do not apply to information. No wonder a course on "strategies of information management" – one that teaches how to manage computing resources using contemporary technology in an effective and profitable way – has been added to the curriculum of most schools of business and commerce and to many internal corporate management training programmes. This explains why so many corporate mangers and users of information are studying books such as this one.

Outline of this book

The topics discussed in this book are those shown in Figure 1.4. The chapter where each topic is discussed is shown in Figure 1.5, which is an overlay on Figure 1.4.

This book is in three parts. The organization of computing resources is the focus in Part One. The organization of computing is the subject of Chapter 2; services of computing offered is discussed in Chapter 3; computer personnel, including their hiring, training, and retention are examined in Chapter 4; and the oversight of this computing organization is the topic for Chapter 5. Chapter 6 covers the development of information systems.

Part Two is on strategies for development. These include the buying or building decision for software in Chapter 7; reuse of software and the trend towards the software factory in Chapter 8; the acquisition of computing resources (hardware, data and software) in Chapter 9; outsourcing in Chapter 10; reengineering in Chapter 11; humanizing information systems in Chapter 12; and the maintenance of existing systems in Chapter 13.

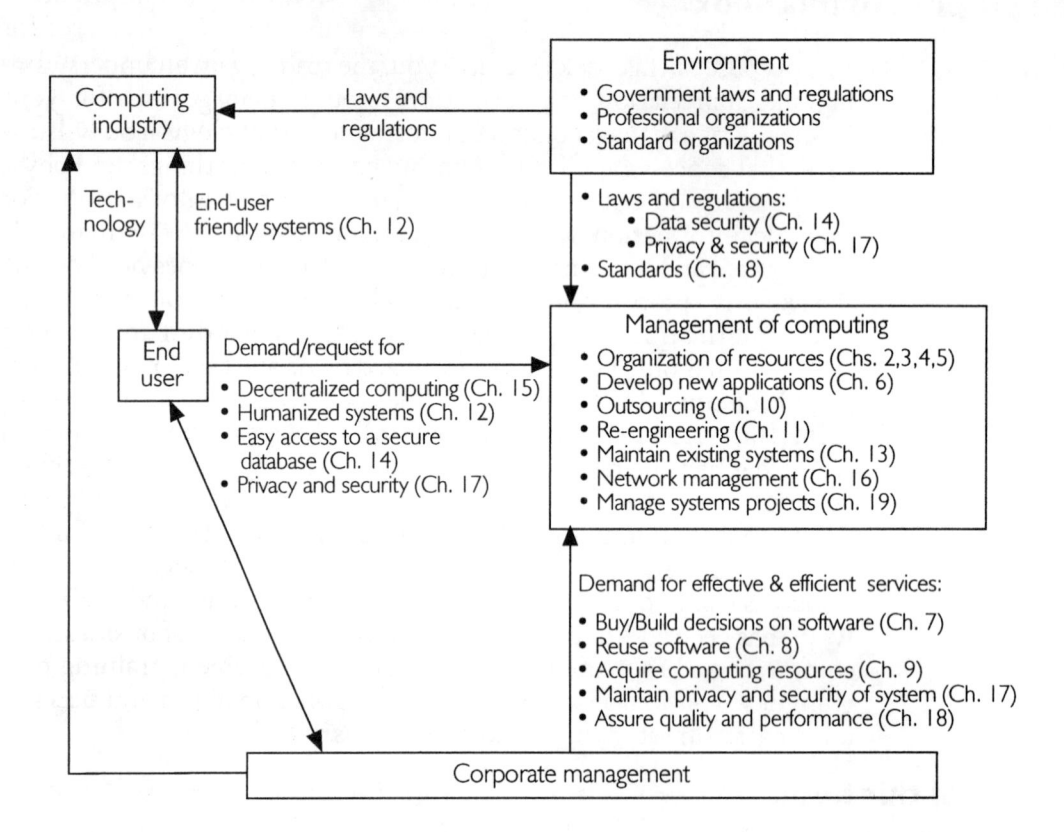

```
                                        Environment
                                        • Government laws and regulations
  Computing        Laws and             • Professional organizations
   industry        regulations           • Standard organizations

  Tech-     End-user                     • Laws and regulations:
  nology    friendly systems (Ch. 12)        • Data security (Ch. 14)
                                              • Privacy & security (Ch. 17)
                                          • Standards (Ch. 18)

                                         Management of computing
   End     Demand/request for            • Organization of resources (Chs. 2,3,4,5)
   user                                  • Develop new applications (Ch. 6)
           • Decentralized computing (Ch. 15)   • Outsourcing (Ch. 10)
           • Humanized systems (Ch. 12)   • Re-engineering (Ch. 11)
           • Easy access to a secure      • Maintain existing systems (Ch. 13)
             database (Ch. 14)            • Network management (Ch. 16)
           • Privacy and security (Ch. 17) • Manage systems projects (Ch. 19)

                                         Demand for effective & efficient services:
                                         • Buy/Build decisions on software (Ch. 7)
                                         • Reuse software (Ch. 8)
                                         • Acquire computing resources (Ch. 9)
                                         • Maintain privacy and security of system (Ch. 17)
                                         • Assure quality and performance (Ch. 18)

                         Corporate management
```

Figure 1.5: Outline of this book

Part Three starts with the management of data and knowledge systems in Chapter 14; the client–server paradigm of distributed computing in Chapter 15; network management in Chapter 16; privacy and security in Chapter 17, and the control of quality and performance in Chapter 18. For related activities that are costly, time consuming and important, they must be managed as a project. Management of systems projects is the subject of our last chapter, Chapter 19. For some predictions of the future of computing and its impact on management of computing, there is a postscript.

There are case studies for each chapter along with references to recommended supplementary reading.

Conclusions

In this book there is nothing on the *uses* of computers (because it is the subject of other books) and yet that is the "bottom-line" and *raison d'être* of all management of IT. Information is power. However, information can be innocent or it can be not so innocent. Information can be used for the benefit of the corporation (and society) or it can be misused and be harmful to the corporation (and society). To maximize the benefits of information and minimize the dangers of it being misused is the function of management of information and IT.

In this chapter (and in future chapters) there are references to IT management. Traditionally, this meant professional computer personnel. In the future, this will increasingly include all corporate managers and end-users for they now have the responsibility for managing their own local computer systems. To them this book is addressed and dedicated.

References

Ang, J. and Pavri F. (1994). "A Survey and Critique of the Impacts of Information Technology." *International Journal of Information Technology*, vol. 14, pp. 122–133.

Berleur, J., Clement, A. and Sizer, R. *et al* (eds.). (1990). *The Information Society*. Berlin: Springer-Verlag.

Cheng, T. C. E. and Kanabar, V. (1992). "On Some Issues of Information Resource Management in the 1990s." *Information Resource Management Journal*, vol. 5, no. 1 pp. 21–32.

Clark, J. and Thomas, D. (1992). "Corporate Systems Management: An Overview and Research Perspective." *Communications of the ACM*, vol. 35, no. 2, pp. 61–75.

Davenport, T. H., Eccles, R. G. and Prusak, L. (1992). "Information Politics." *Sloan Management Review*, vol. 34, no. 1, pp. 53–65.

Diebold, J. (1994). "The next Revolution in Computers." *The Futurist*, vol. 28, no. 3 (May–June), pp. 34–7.

Eaton, J. J. and Bawden, D. (1991). "What Kind of Resource is Information?" *International Journal of Information Management*, vol. 11, no. 2, pp. 156–65.

I/S Analyzer. (1991). "Critical Issues in Information systems Management." vol. 29, no. 1 (January), pp. 1–16.

References

Mathews, Peter. (1994). "The Future of the Fourth Framework Policy." *Managing Information*, vol. 1, no. 9, pp. 28–9.

Scarrott, G. G. (1989). "The Nature of Information." *The Computer Journal*, vol. 2, no. 3 (June), pp. 262–6.

Scully, John. (1990). "The Human Use of Information." *The Journal of Quality and Participation*, vol. 13, no. 1, (January/February), pp. 10–13.

Selig, Franz F. (1991). "Managing Information Technology in the Nineties." *Information & Management*, vol. 21, no. 5, pp. 251–55.

Seymour, Tom. (1992). "Information Technology and the Manager." Journal of Computer Information Systems, vol. XXXII, no. 3 (Spring), pp. 35–8.

Symons, V. J. (1993). "Impacts of Information systems: Four Perspective." *Journal of Information Technology*, vol. 33, no. 3 (April), pp. 181*ff*.

Tapscott, Don and Art Caston. (1993). *A Paradigm Shift: The New Promise of Information Technology*. N.Y: McGraw Hill, Inc.

Trauth, Eileen M. and Winslow, Christine. (1992). "A New Paradigm for IS." *Journal of Management Information Systems*, vol. 9, no. 2 (Spring), pp. 7–14.

Webster, Frank. (1994). "What Information Society?" *The Information Society*, vol. 10, pp. 1–23.

2 Organization of Computing

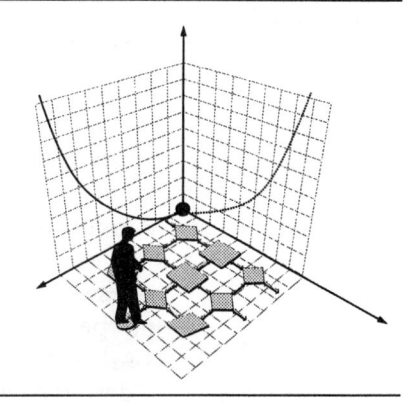

> You can't sit on the lid of progress. If you do, you will be blown to pieces.
>
> *Henry Kaiser*

Introduction

All organizations, whether they are business firms, manufacturing plants, government departments or agencies, service organizations such as hospitals and schools, research labs, or charitable groups like the Red Cross, generate information. In today's world, most depend on computer hardware and software to process this information. The location of hardware/software resources within the organization is one facet of the organization of computing. Another is the placement of people who operate or manage these resources in the group's organizational hierarchy.

This chapter traces the organization of computer resources from the 1950s – when computer facilities were commonly under the auspices of subdepartmental units – to the mix of organizational modes of the 1990s. You will learn that most large organizations today retain a department for computing services, commonly called an *information systems (IS) department*, the term we use in this text. Other names for this department are "management information system centre," "information processing centre," or some similar title. The IS department is usually assigned responsibility for planning and control of processing, the maintenance of hardware and software, the development of new computerized information systems, and the processing of applications that require the expertise of computer processing professionals. Decentralized processing options are also described, including distributed data processing and end-user computing.

In the 1950s, only those with computer expertise – including programming skills and knowledge of operations – could interact with computers. Today, many employees with little knowledge of computer science spend their work hours at computer terminals or depend on computer-generated information in their jobs. Conflicts often arise between these employees and computer personnel because of differences in outlook, training, and level of computer expertise. In organizing the computer function, managers must look for ways to keep such conflicts to a minimum and provide mechanisms for problem resolution as described in this chapter.

Misunderstandings may arise between corporate managers and computer processing personnel as well. Again, the cause may stem from differences in background and experience with computer systems. The way in which processing is structured can facilitate communication between these two groups, as you will learn.

Finally, this chapter looks at ways in which the workload of information workers has been changed by the dynamic nature of the computer industry. The continual introduction of advanced hardware/software products requires frequent reorganization of computing resources within a single organization.

Location of computing resources

Many locations for a computer are possible within the organizational structure of a firm. Six alternatives are shown in Figure 2.1. When computing was in its infancy, most businesses and industries used computers to process accounting and financial applications. At that time, a subdepartmental unit for *electronic data processing (EDP)* was common (see Case 1, Figure 2.1). Although companies might have several computers located in dispersed departments, no centralized authority coordinated their activities.

When more resources were devoted to computing and computers began to play a larger role in information processing, EDP rose in the organizational hierarchy of most firms. This placed computer processing personnel directly under a department head (Case 2) or a division chief (Case 3).

Later, as the need for expensive data processing resources grew and applications extended to all functional areas (for example, marketing and production), sharing of data and equipment across divisional lines was initiated to cut costs. This gave impetus to *centralized data processing*, the establishment of a single computer department reporting directly to top management (Case 4). Planning, computer operations, development of new computer systems, and control over hardware, software, and corporate data were consolidated. *Common databases* were established – pooled data integrated for shared use by computer professionals and employees dependent on information processing for their jobs. The expectation was that costs would drop. Indeed, studies showed that a single large installation was less expensive to run than small dispersed centres. It was also expected that information processing would become more responsive to management needs; that the speed of information delivery would increase; that redundancy in data collection, storage, and processing would be eliminated; and that security and control of information would be tightened.

Figure 2.1:
Alternative locations of EDP within a firm's organizational structure

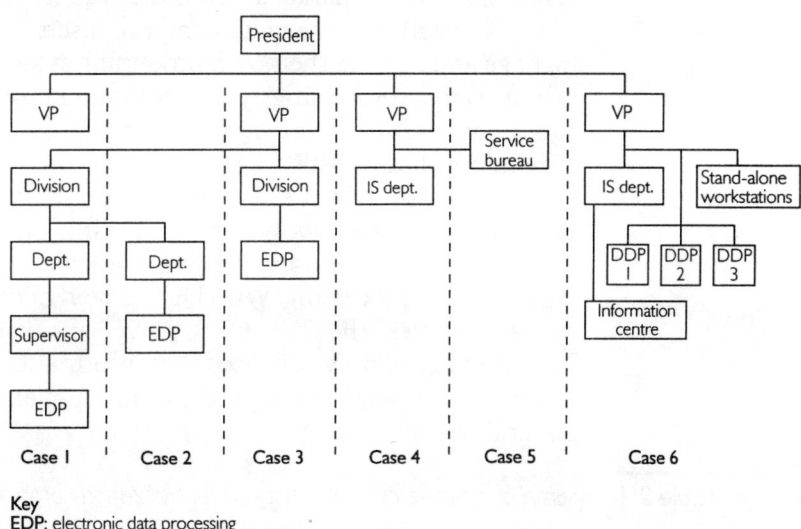

Key
EDP: electronic data processing
IS dept: information systems department
DDP: distributed data processing

Unfortunately, these expectations were not all realized. Lack of communication between information users and processing personnel continued under centralization. Information users resented the hours required to justify and document requests for computer processing services and felt isolated from computing facilities. They complained that centralized data processing was unresponsive to their needs, that the bureaucracy of centralization was inept at mediating conflicts. Computer professionals chafed at the criticism. They believed that the length of time required for the development of computer systems in response to information requests was simply not understood by users.

In spite of these problems, centralized computing is the organizational structure of many firms today. However, the name "EDP centre" has become outmoded since computer processing nowadays includes text and image processing as well as data processing. We now speak of "information systems (IS) departments" rather than EDP centres because the term is more inclusive. Many organizations supplement their internal computing capacity by contracting jobs with outside service bureaux (Case 5). In this context, a service bureau provides clients with computer equipment, software, or personnel.

However, in recent years a large number of firms, disenchanted with centralized computer centres, have once again decentralized much of their information processing (Case 6). A number of technological advances have made this an attractive option. Microcomputers and minicomputers with capabilities exceeding many former large computers are now on the market at low cost. In addition, experience with computer processing has given information users confidence that they can manage and operate their own processing systems. This has led to *end-user computing* (processing by non-computer professionals) and facilities to support end-users (for example, information centres) – subjects that are explored later in this chapter.

Furthermore, recent strides in telecommunications mean that computer processing networks can now link dispersed processing sites (called *nodes*) at low cost, making *distributed data processing (DDP)* a rapid mode of processing. With DDP, a worker sitting at a computer terminal can access the computing power of a distant computer facility. The argument is now advanced that information users are better served and computer applications more easily implemented and maintained under DDP.

Table 2.1 *Some alternative centralization–decentralization combinations*

Alternative	Development personnel	Equipment and operation	Development activities	Database	Planning
1	C	C	C	C	C
2	D	C	C	C	C
3	D	D	C	C	C
4	D	D	D	C	C

C = Centralized D = Decentralized

To centralize or distribute processing is not an either/or proposition. As shown in Table 2.1, a variety of combinations are possible. Alternative 4 has become increasingly popular in recent years with operations and development activities placed under local control, but planning and database control centralized.

Centralized computing

To fully understand the ramifications of the centralization–decentralization issue, you need to understand the jobs of computer professionals in each of these functional areas – something we explain in Chapter 4. For the purposes of this chapter you should recognize the complexity of modern computing operations. As you learn about problems with distributed processing and end-user processing in sections that follow, you will understand why some organizations decide that centralized control of their computing facilities is the best way to effectively utilize their computer resources, given the number of people and variety of skills required to meet information requirements of modern workers.

Distributed computer systems

Let us now take a closer look at distributed data processing (DDP). Among computer scientists, the definition of DDP is still evolving. For the purposes of this text, we shall define DDP as many separate computing processing centres all belonging to a single organization. Each node has computer facilities for program execution and data storage. Yet linkage between the nodes enables them to cooperate in processing tasks. A DDP network can be spread over a large or small area. Some DDP systems are global (for example, air traffic control systems). Others may be local, within a single room, building, or group of buildings.

The distributed computer concept applies age-old management principles to new technology. For example, DDP permits division of labour and the increase of productivity through parallelism. It incorporates the concept of specialization of labour, since computers (like people) vary in the tasks that they do best. Furthermore, DDP promotes the delegation of responsibility because management at remote nodes commonly controls hardware/software acquisitions, operations and the development of systems for local use.

Distributed computing is a simple concept but it is not simple to put into practice. DDP is more than relocating hardware from a centralized computer centre to dispersed locations. The design of the operating system, databases, and applications are affected. Job descriptions, departmental structures, the flow of corporate information, and relationships between management and workers are altered. So is the process of decision-making.

Equipment configurations

The difference between distributed data processing and dispersed processing of the 1950s is linkage: DDP involves a communication network to link decentralized processors. Figure 2.2 shows sample DDP network configurations. In a *star network*, failure of a central computer impairs the entire system. The *ring network* structure overcomes this problem because rerouting is possible should one processing centre, or its link, fail. A ring network allows interaction and *offloading* (transfer of processing from one site to another) without dependence on a central host.

Figure 2.2:
Sample DDP network configurations

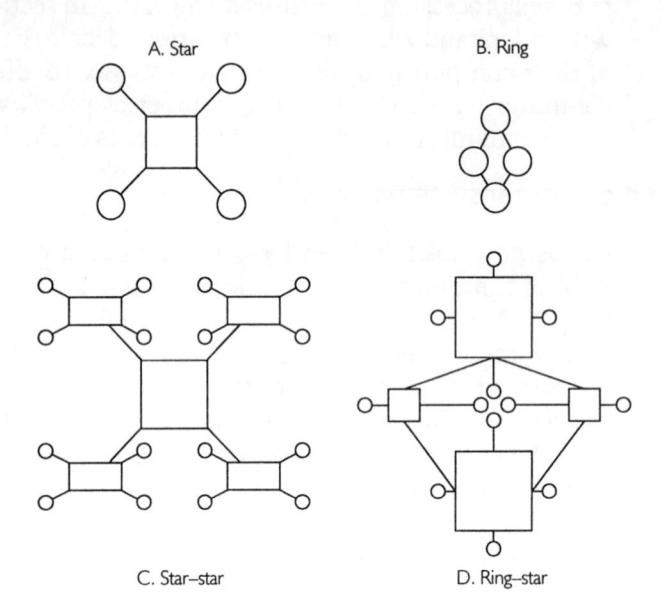

A. Star

B. Ring

C. Star–star

D. Ring–star

Both star and ring configurations are essentially horizontal systems. That is, each node processor is equal (although the hardware may be unique to each node), which means that not all computer resources in the organization are purchased from the same vendor. The advantage is that users can acquire hardware/software that incorporate the latest technology on the market. However, this flexibility has a negative aspect: it increases problems of linkage and compatibility between nodes.

Hierarchical distribution is the configuration that many firms prefer. This configuration has a central host computer and common database with minis and micros at dispersed sites. Generally, all equipment and software in hierarchical systems are supplied by the same vendor, minimizing problems of compatibility between nodes. Because many computers have either a *fail-safe capability* (ability to continue operations, in spite of breakdown, due to the existence of backup) or a *fail-soft capability* (the ability to continue with a degraded level of operations), a breakdown in the hierarchy should not incapacitate the entire system.

Distributed database configurations

With distributed processing networks, a decision also needs to be made regarding the organization of the company's databases. In such networks, should all data be centralized, or should processing nodes store database segments that they need for daily operations? Perhaps data stored centrally should be replicated for use at local sites. Options for data organization are discussed next.

Centralized database

Centralization of data is possible under DDP, but costs are high when all data must be transmitted to distributed nodes for processing. A centralized database is appropriate when infrequent access to that data is needed or when updating needs to be strictly controlled.

Segmented distributed database

The storage of parts of the database at local nodes is called *segmented distributed database organization*. The segments might be data from a function or data pertaining to the geographic area – data that allows the node to be virtually independent, although other nodes may also use the data as a shared resource.

Replicated distributed database

When more than one dispersed processor needs the same data, a common approach to database organization is to store the database at a central repository with duplicate segments needed for local processing stored at each node. A database organized in this fashion is called a replicated distributed database. The local bases used for processing, including online real-time operations, are then periodically used to update the centralized database. From the updated centralized base, the replicated databases at distributed sites are updated in turn.

Large regional banks frequently adopt this form of database organization. Central processing takes place after banking hours, and replicated distributed databases are then created for branch offices. These replicated databases consist essentially of working files used for local transactions – such as deposits and withdrawals. At the end of each working day, the central database is again updated by incorporating data on transactions conducted at the branches during the day. Then the cycle begins once again with the creation of updated databases for distribution to the branch offices.

In general, the centralized database includes all control and summary data, whereas transactional data and local data are in the replicated distributed databases. Branch offices still have to access the centralized data during the course of the day. This occurs if a customer of the bank wishes to cash a cheque at a branch that does not have a record of his or her account. In this case, the transaction has to be routed through the central database.

One advantage of replicated databases is that they provide backup. As a result, the system is less vulnerable should failure occur at the central location. An additional advantage is that systems are more responsive to local needs when data are managed locally (an advantage that applies to segmented databases as well). In particular, maintenance and updating of large and complex databases are more effective when portions of the database are under local control. Certain types of processing are also more efficient. For example, retrieval by indexes requires careful cross-indexing. Personnel on location with a need for the retrieved data will be more highly motivated to update and maintain indexes and retrieval software and are more knowledgeable about user needs than programmers at a centralized database.

A major problem with replicated distributed databases is redundancy. For efficient processing, no more data than absolutely necessary should be stored at remote sites. Unfortunately, the distributed centre's exact need for data is not easily determined.

Hybrid approach

Some firms both segment and replicate their databases. This is the *hybrid approach* to database organization. For example, a large national business may segment its database geographically, giving regional headquarters segments relevant to their operations. Replicated data from these headquarters are then distributed to branch offices within each region. Warehouse inventories are often controlled in this manner.

Micro–mainframe link technology

Although microcomputer use for stand-alone processing has been common in the business world since the early 1980s, recent advances in technology today make it feasible to integrate microcomputers (and minis) into distributed processing networks. Sales of *micro–mainframe link* products, including software, modems, and emulation boards are on the rise. The number of vendors for such products is also increasing.

The original impetus for linkage was the desire of users to download data from mainframes to micros. But today, uploading is viewed as a major application of the technology as well. In the future, mainframes may be used as database machines, while much local processing will take place on network microcomputers.

Many technological problems still must be resolved. Software to facilitate micro–mainframe communications is needed, as are ways to handle different people working on the database at the same time. Security is a major issue. Any proprietary corporate data downloaded on to portable floppy disks are in jeopardy. How can access to data (and disks) be controlled? The possibility that users may upload incorrect information processed on their microcomputers is also a concern. Ways to check and verify data before they are uploaded need to be devised. Other problems that affect microcomputer–mainframe linkage are:

- The cost of micro–mainframe products and the speed with which such products are developed for the marketplace.
- Problems of incompatible data formats. Data downloaded from the mainframe may require processing before they can be used for microcomputer applications.
- Lack of open-architecture links. At present, some micro–mainframe systems are based on proprietary architectures. The micro–host software will only access data residing on the same vendor's mainframe software.

Rewards and risks of DDP

Improved systems reliability is one of the primary functional advantages of DDP. The fact that work is modularized means that tasks are less complex and therefore less vulnerable to failure. Furthermore, natural compartmentalization can reduce the scope for errors, failure, and damage. Should one module fail, another can provide backup service.

A DDP system facilitates growth without disruption of service. System upgrades can take place in small increments. For example, modules can be replaced or modernized one at a time so that conversion can be easily managed. There is built-in flexibility that allows systems to meet new requirements, to bypass failed components, to integrate new services or new technologies, and to extend the system's life expectancy. What's more, throughput and response time are improved because communication delays and queuing are avoided when local nodes process local databases. Less complex software is required, a fact that reduces the cost of systems development, maintenance, and training.

With on-site processing, the need for communications with a centralized processor is lessened. This helps to reduce costs, as does improved systems response. Shared resources minimize the need for duplication of resources. Modularity can improve procurement competition and can likewise improve cost–performance ratios because of economies of specialization. (A system can cater to the needs of a particular group rather than service the complex needs of diverse groups.)

Certainly, this list of benefits should include increased motivation among distributed staff, resulting from greater independence and local control of processing. With a smaller user base, fewer political and priority conflicts need to be resolved. Staff can concentrate on systems optimization instead. There is also a psychological advantage when users find services tailored to their needs and have more voice in computing decisions, such as hardware and software upgrades. In addition, the geographical location of facilities is no longer an important factor.

In spite of these advantages, the initiation of DDP involves multiple risk. Among the more common are poor systems design resulting from inexperience, redundancy among nodes, interface problems, costs that are hidden or that escalate, and employee resistance to change. For example, distributed computing requires more planning than centralized systems. More attention must be paid to the efficiency of information flow and distribution. Standards for data elements and interfaces need to be designed, monitored, and enforced. Four thorny data distribution issues need to be resolved:

- Where to store data.
- How to efficiently find needed data.
- How to keep data synchronized and maintain integrity.
- How to protect data from security, privacy abuse and fraud.

Distributed architectures are still in the early stages of development. To date, most of the work has centred on how to connect hardware components. A number of issues, such as how to build a distributed network operating system, still need more research. Clearly, new technology means new potential yet also heightens risk. And designing a multiple-processor system is much more difficult than designing a single-processor system.

When to implement DDP

Distributed data processing is not applicable to all organizations. How does a firm decide whether it is appropriate? What *organizational considerations* are important in the decision? Unfortunately, no formula or precise decision rule exists to guide management in reaching a DDP implementation decision. However, firms with geographically dispersed outlets, firms with a matrix structure rather than functional organization, multinationals, project-based companies (such as construction firms), and conglomerates have organizational structures that lead naturally to decentralization and the distributed mode.

In less obvious cases, a grid analysis may help determine the appropriateness of DDP. A sample is shown in Table 2.2. Here, a hypothetical firm with sites A, B, C, and D has informational needs satisfied by Processes 1–3 and Files 1–3. The informational requirements of each site are marked on the grid. Since Process 1 and File 2 are required by all sites, centralization of their processing is indicated.

Table 2.2 *Illustration of grid analysis*

Needs \ Informational sites	A	B	C	D
Process 1	X	X	X	X
2	X			
3		X	X	
Files 1	X			
2	X	X	X	X
3			X	X

Since Process 2 and File 1 are needed by only a single site, they are clear candidates for the distributed mode. Process 3 and File 3 are possible candidates.

However, before implementation, management should assess DDP's impact on the firm. How will DDP affect corporate decision-making? Is DDP economically feasible? If a firm has centralized processing, a switch to DDP is usually not considered unless there is dissatisfaction with centralization. It is up to management to decide whether this dissatisfaction with operations can remedied by DDP and whether the benefits of DDP will be worth the cost and disruption that reorganization entails.

End-user computing

There are many terms that reflect the decentralized and distributed philosophy including disaggregation, demassification, unbundling, devolution, and federal decentralization. Whether centralized or distributed, in those early days of computing, the mainframe computers were expensive, large and demanded severe environmental conditions. In those days, the first air conditioning system installed at the US Space Center in Huntsville, Alabama, was not for the highly paid scientists and engineers assembled to prepare for the first journey into space, but for their computer system. Since then, computer technology has given us PCs and workstations that are not only small, robust and "inexpensive", but also just as powerful as the mainframe. Also, technology gave us telecommunications and networks that connected the PCs and workstations with databases, large computers, and exotic peripherals.

The PCs and telecommunications had software that made systems easy to use – unlike the mainframes that were accessed only by programmers who communicated in languages unlike natural human language and spoke in acronyms and computer jargon. This made for "noise" between the computer specialists and the ultimate user of computer systems, the end-user, and an increasing backlog of undeveloped jobs. Meanwhile, the end-users became computer literate, had their own computers, and started developing their own computer systems leaving the computer specialists to develop and maintain a computer infrastructure. Also, end-users lost most of their "technofear", which resulted in computers losing much of their mystique. Thus came about a dramatic shift in the computing paradigm shifting control (and responsibility) for computing from the computer professional to the end-user. This computing paradigm, known as *end-user computing* (EUC), is the subject of the rest of this chapter. In it we discuss the shifts of control and responsibility in end-user computing and identify the success (and by implication some failure factors) of end-user computing. First, however, we need to distinguish between the end-user and the user of computing.

Users and end-users

One approach to definitions is to look at the process of traditional transactional computing as illustrated in Figure 2.3. It often starts with a *manager* (or client) having a need for a report which is explained to a *systems analyst*. The analyst designs a system to meet the manager's needs and communicates it to a *programmer* who then writes a program to generate the required report. This program is submitted to the computer along with data prepared by a *data collector* (data clerk) and with instructions from a *computer operator* on what data to process and with a specific program. The programmer communicates through a computer program and the operator through some programming commands, as well as through physical machine communication such as buttons or keys on a computer console. The computer generates the desired report and it is given to the manager. Note that out of all the persons involved (identified above in italics) only the manager is the beneficiary of the end results of computing and is referred to as the end-user. The others involved: the analyst, the programmer, the data preparation clerk, and the computer operator, are intermediaries and are termed users. Historically, we did not make the distinction and hence have inherited such terms as "user-friendly" systems when an "end-user friendly" system is really intended. The user, like a programmer, does not need or want a friendly system, but the end-user certainly does. So the distinction is important.

Figure 2.3:
Computer–client interaction

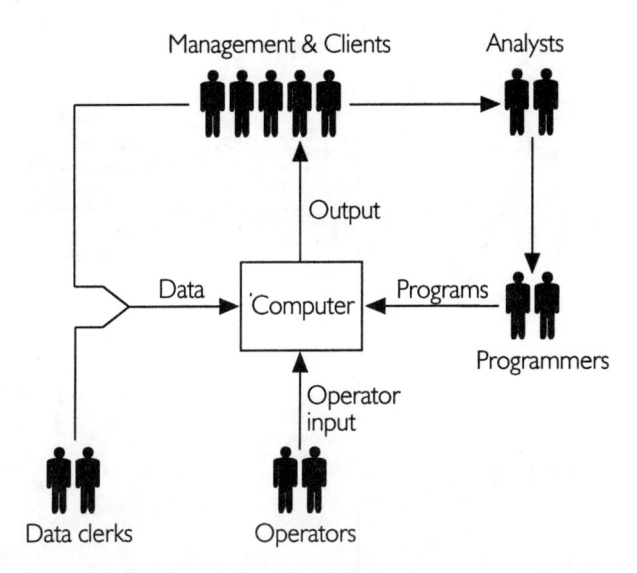

Formally, we can define users as those persons who interact (directly or indirectly) with an information system. In contrast, there are some users who are the ultimate users of an information system; these people are called end-users. They include the employees of the organization, customers, vendors, and others (including government agencies) that receive computer reports. They are the ultimate consumers of computer output. The end-user is often differentiated from the user, who like a programmer or an analyst, is only an intermediate user and transient recipient of many computer outputs, but not the ultimate user. The users include all computer personnel including programmers, analysts, computer operators, database personnel, and telecommunication personnel. Users also include the data clerks that may not belong to the computer department, but work on computer processing. In a sense, the data clerks are not ultimate users, but they are end-users for the task that they must perform. They use output to check their input and for reference purposes. The clients, like managers, are the real end-users.

There are cases when a user is also an end-user. For example, a programmer may receive a cheque for wages and is an end-user, but the programmer is also a user when debugging a program. (Does this raise special organizational security problems?)

Figure 2.4:
Users and end-users classification

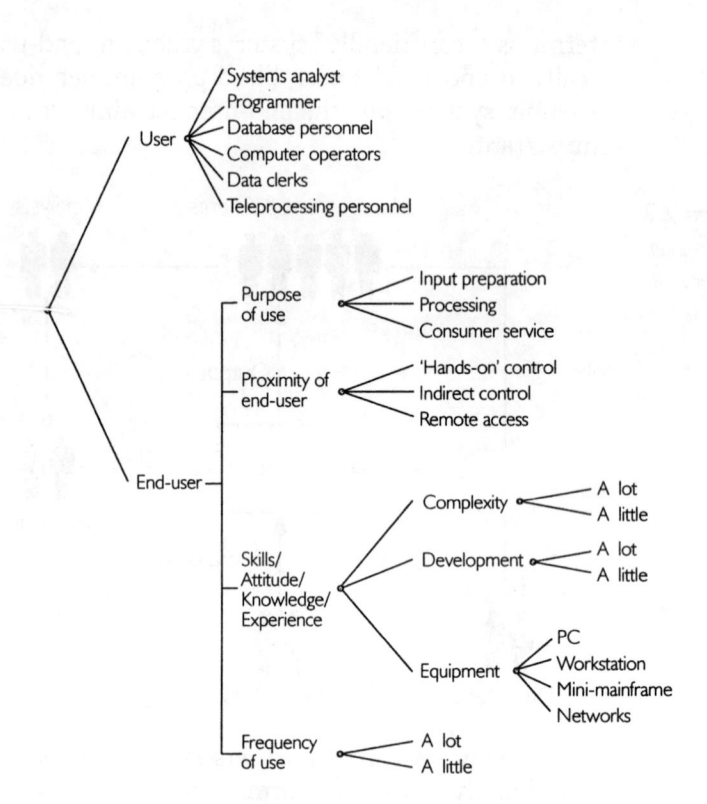

- User
  - Systems analyst
  - Programmer
  - Database personnel
  - Computer operators
  - Data clerks
  - Teleprocessing personnel
- End-user
  - Purpose of use
    - Input preparation
    - Processing
    - Consumer service
  - Proximity of end-user
    - 'Hands-on' control
    - Indirect control
    - Remote access
  - Skills/Attitude/Knowledge/Experience
    - Complexity
      - A lot
      - A little
    - Development
      - A lot
      - A little
    - Equipment
      - PC
      - Workstation
      - Mini-mainframe
      - Networks
  - Frequency of use
    - A lot
    - A little

There are many types of end-users. One classification is shown in Figure 2.4. The assertion by the end-users for autonomy as well as faster response time has largely led to end-user computing (EUC).

Features of EUC

We can define EUC with reference to Figure 2.5 which is the identification of relationships between humans and other humans or machines (as in Figure 2.3). We can soon see that the relationship of analyst with the end-user and with a programmer as well as the relationship between the machine and the programmer, operator and data clerk are all unnecessary in an EUC environment. There is, however, an extra relationship not seen in the transactional processing, that of the human–machine relationship which involves the end-user providing the computer with data and the necessary programs.

Figure 2.5:
Computer–client interaction in EUC (the shaded area identifies the relationships in transactional processing eliminated in EUC)

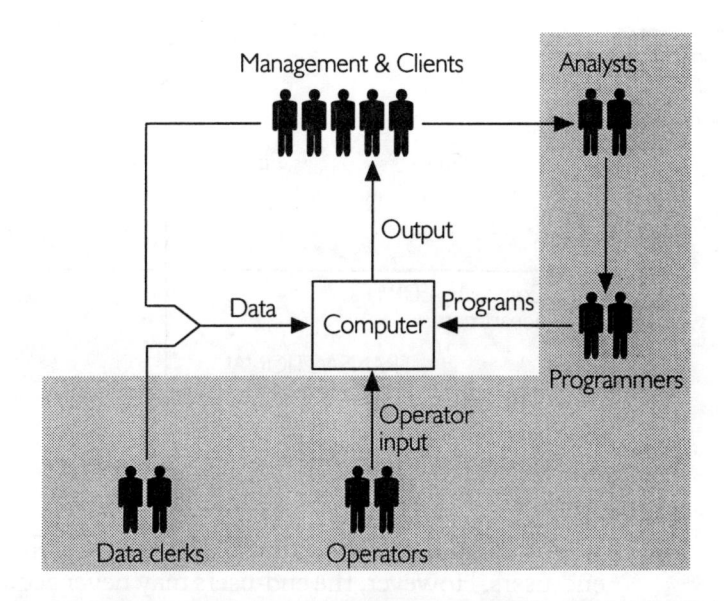

Perhaps the most important feature, and in fact the *raison d'être* of EUC, is the shift of control and responsibility for daily operations from the professional computer staff to the end-user. The end-user is also responsible for the development (design and implementation) and operation of local applications. All this requires skills and knowledge about computing that is much more than computer literacy. In fact, managing a computer system requires the knowledge contained in this book. It also requires the ability and willingness to accept the responsibility that goes with having to manage and control a computer system. Traditionally, it was the responsibility of computer professionals who designed, created, and maintained the database.

As data processing graduated from being data processing by EDP (electronic data processing) to information processing, we had more systems like the DSS (decision support system) for problem solving by middle management and an EIS (executive information system) for higher levels of management, but control sometimes resides with the EDP or IS (information systems) or IT (information technology) department. This was also the case with the shift from centralized to decentralized and distributed systems. However, with EUC daily operational control (including local systems development) shifted dramatically from the EDP/IS/IT department to the end-user. This included some DSSs that were controlled by the end-user. However, many DSSs and EISs serve corporate management who, for the most part, would rather have these systems maintained and controlled by computer professionals in the IS/IT departments. These shifts are illustrated in Figure 2.6.

Chapter 2: Organization of Computing

Figure 2.6: *Shifts in control of data/ information*

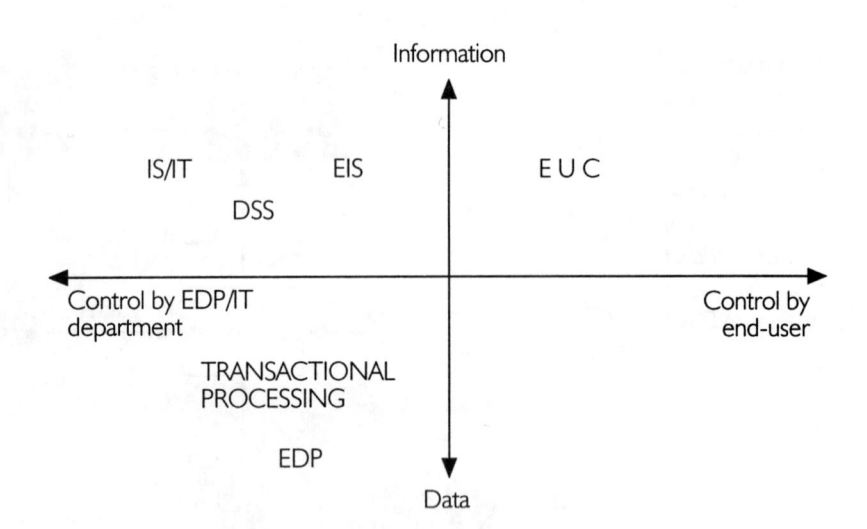

```
                        Information
                            ▲
                            │
        IS/IT      EIS      │      E U C
              DSS           │
    ◄───────────────────────┼───────────────────────►
  Control by EDP/IT         │           Control by
  department                │            end-user
                   TRANSACTIONAL
                    PROCESSING
                     EDP    ▼
                           Data
```

We mentioned earlier that EUC requires skills of computing by the end-users. However, the end-users may never acquire all the knowledge and skill necessary for developing or running a computer system of any complexity. Complex applications and applications that require the common corporate data/knowledge-base will still be done by the computer professionals at the centre who are also responsible for the infrastructure such as telecommunications, availability (acquisition and maintenance), and peripherals (expensive or not heavily used by some end-users).

End-users need support from the professionals which may come from external sources such as the vendor or consultants, or even *facilities management* (FM) for the running of a computer facility. Alternatively, the help comes from internal sources, such as the IS department or a special service offered to the end-user, like the *information centre*. Such support is the subject of the next chapter.

Besides support, there are other factors critical to the success of EUC. Such critical success factors (CSFs) are listed in Table 2.3. The list may seem long and confusing (one study of CSFs for EUC had 35 factors evaluated), but many of the factors will be discussed later. Factors discussed later include:

- Security problems: Chapter 17.
- Support needed for the acquisition of new computer resources: Chapter 9 and Chapter 3 – see the *Information centres* section on page 46.

Table 2.3 *Success factors for EUC*

- Providing adequate support and involvement from corporate management
- Developing a strategic plan
- Creating the "right" environment
- Knowledge of teleprocessing
- Ability to use prototyping
- Ability to use 4GLs (fourth generation programming languages) and packaged programs
- Choosing the right technology
- "Real" control residing with the end-user
- Availability of skilled personnel amongst end-users
- Initiation of applications by end-users
- Acceptance of new responsibilities by end-users

EUC also implies a shift in costs. An end-user wanting more than a PC on the desk will have to pay perhaps £10,000 for a workstation that is required for serious computing work such as the use of AI (artificial intelligence), some DSS modelling, and CAD (computer-aided design). But as we will see later with the client–server system, the shift from the mainframe to the end-user is a shift of costs from the central office to the distributed node and end-user. This shift implies that the end-user must also be responsible for the budgeting and managing of finances for local computing.

There is a substantial hidden cost regarding the use of EUC because now the end-user relies on professional peers versed and experienced in computing for help in running their system. This represents a cost to the organization (sometimes referred to as "peer support") because now the productivity of the professional help suffers. This hidden cost not only distorts the costs of EUC, but also hides the need for EUC support to replace peer support. Corporate management therefore needs to clearly define the domains of EUC and its support as distinct from corporate management responsibilities. We also need to link these responsibilities with organizational goals and the overall success of the organization.

Summing up on the EUC

EUC became popular in the mid-1990s. In 1993, there were 144 articles published on the EUC (Brancheau and Brown, 1993:479–482). This popularity came about despite shifting the costs to the end-user, a shift that corporate management welcomes even though the total costs will rise especially with end-users wanting more and more computing facilities at their desk. End-user computing does give end-users independence from the "tyranny" and delays of IS.

> IS management needs the end-user more than the end-user needs IS management. Users can go their own way without involvement of IS management ... until IS managers take the initiative and build the bonds that result in teaming.
>
> *Delligatta*, 1993:55

EUC is an extension of corporate computing, but also is a social learning phenomenon. As end-users learn to develop their own systems and manage them efficiently and effectively, they will take greater initiatives in accepting responsibilities for many computing tasks especially in the areas of DDSs and EISs. Transactional, legacy systems, and "mission critical" systems must still be developed and maintained by professional IT personnel. This will relieve the IT staff to develop integrated systems that cover the entire enterprise and at the same time include the strategic needs of the organization. The professional staff will now also have more time to plan and implement the applications portfolio as well as construct and maintain the corporate information infrastructure. They will also help the end-users in learning, maintaining, and adapting to the complex advances in computer technology as and when they appear. Some of these tasks can be performed by an *information centre* which provides support and liaison between the end-user and technical staff and is the subject of our next chapter.

Much research on EUC is still needed and is currently being done. We conclude our discussion on EUC with a quote on the significance of such research:

> Over the long run, the findings from EUC management research will increase our knowledge about managing organizational computing and improve our understanding of the interplay between the organizational and individual learning processes. For many organizations, these may be the keys to the survival in the next century.
>
> *Brancheau and Brown*, 1993:477

Summary and conclusions

Describing where a computer department fits into a firm's organizational schema is no simple task because technological advances have changed the nature of information processing over time and, as a consequence, altered the location of computer centres within the hierarchy of firms. In the 1950s, computers were generally found in subdepartmental units wherever processing was needed. As more resources were allocated to computing, centralization was favoured in order to take advantage of economies of scale and to ensure better integration, control, and management of computer facilities. Today, the trend towards centralization has reversed itself. Distributed processing and EUC are becoming very popular, with autonomy over development and operations of local applications. However, there are many activities that are still centralized like systems planning, standardization, corporate databases, and the availability of an infrastructure of computing resources.

The centralized configurations of Figure 2.1 are still viable today though they may no longer be EDP for data processing but IS/IT for information processing and information technology respectively. IS/IT must embrace not just data but text, images and even voice and multimedia.

Figure 2.7:
Organizational configurations

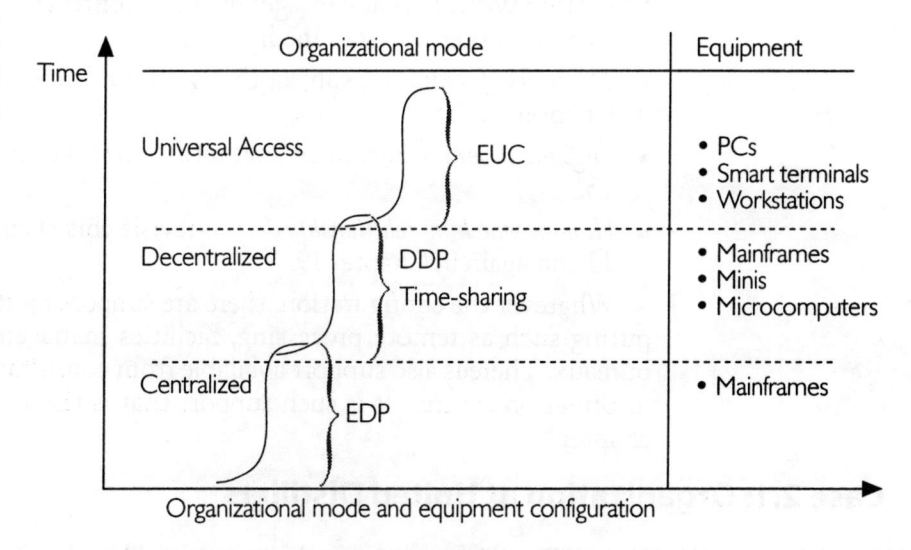

The organizational structure for computing evolved from being centralized with mainframes and telephone links to a decentralized and distributed structure allowing for time-sharing and sharing of resources which were largely mainframes and minis with some PCs. We now have universal access in EUC where there is connectivity between the end-users having PCs, smart terminals and workstations. This evolution is depicted in Figure 2.7.

The growth shown in Figure 2.7 is not represented in a spiral, but as a set of growth curves. These are the S-shaped curves proposed by Skinner to represent learning in humans and later adapted to represent growth in computing; these curves are known as *Nolan's growth curves*. The curve's shape does represent the important characteristic of learning in each of the organizational configurations: a very slow start, a fast

Chapter 2: Organization of Computing 31

adolescence, and then a flattening out, but then overlapped by an advanced growth curve.

The organizational configurations are not always mutually exclusive and, in fact, they may recycle from one to another. Thus, the centralized approach was replaced partly by a decentralized approach, but then re-emerged in the 1990s. Why? Partly because of the changing strategies of computer vendors. With centralization, the computer industry recognized that the important criticism was the high cost of computer equipment, so the industry (with help from advances in technology) dropped the prices of large computers, but increased the cost of licensing each program. Thus, a distributed system with many nodes now needs many licensed programs and so the total cost goes up. Why not go back to centralization with all its advantages of better control?

In this chapter, we examined:

- *The shifts of control* – a subject that we return to in Chapter 4 and Chapter 10.
- *Organizational configuration* – we return to this subject in Chapter 15.
- *Human–machine relationships* – we revisit this theme in Chapter 12 and again in Chapter 19.

Whatever the configuration, there are supporting strategies of computing such as remote processing, facilities management and service bureaux. There is also support available from consultants, vendors, and information centres. It is such support that is the subject of our next chapter.

Case 2.1: Organization at United Distillers

United Distillers produces whisky, gin and bourbon in 32 distilleries in Scotland. In each distillery, PCs collect data directly from casks – information on date, distillery, and characteristics of each barrel of whisky. This information is automatically loaded on to a corporate database. Nightly, data are downloaded to the distilling centre in Legion and eventually sent to the Edinburgh head office for mainframe processing. This system allows tracking of 7 million separate barrels, information used by masters responsible for the whisky blend. Each bottle of whisky that is blended at one of the United Distillers bottling plants may draw from 40 different malts stored in one of six warehouses throughout Scotland. The information also keeps the Customs and Excise department at bay. A heavy per-barrel fine can be imposed if the company cannot account for each and every one of its 7 million barrels.

Department computers, usually a Bull, DEC VAX, or a Hewlett Packard mini, act as file servers to access data in corporate mainframes for operating groups within the company. From there the data can be retrieved by individual PCs. This is to avoid the problem of a large number of people searching for information in the mainframes all at once.

Distributors worldwide are given "agreed autonomy" over computer systems in their local offices so long as rules in the areas of interconnectivity and communications are followed. Within the UK, however, there is standardization because this results in discounts from suppliers.

> In fact, the purchasing power we can exert has actually been more important in the UK than the need for communications compatibility.

says a company spokesman.

Source: *Which Computer?*, (April 1991), pp. 126–8.

References

Aggarwal, A. K. (1994). "Trends in End-User Computing: A Professional's Perspective." *Journal of End-User Computing*, vol. 6, no. 3 (September), pp. 32–3.

Brancheau, James C. and Carol V. Brown. (1993). "The Management of End-User Computing." *ACM Commuting Surveys*, vol. 25, no. 4 (December), pp. 437–482.

Choo, Chun Wei. (1994). "Beyond Stage Models for EUC Management." *Information Technology & People*, vol. 6, no. 4 (September), pp. 197–214.

Delligatta Ann, and Robert E. Umbagh. (1993). "EUC Becomes Enterprise Computing." *Information Systems Management*, vol. 10, no. 4, pp. 53–5.

Gillette, Dean. (1993). "The State of End-User Communications." *Information Systems Management*, vol. 10, no. 4, pp. 60–2.

Guimaraes, Tor. (1996). "Exploring the Relationship between EUC Problems and Success." *Information Resource Management*, vol. 9, no. 2 (Spring), pp 5–16.

Gunton, Tony. (1988). *End User Focus*. Hemel Hempstead: Prentice Hall International (UK), pp. 60–91.

Halloran, John P. (1993). "Achieving World Class End-User Commuting." *Information Systems Management*, vol. 10, no. 4, pp. 7–12.

Henderson, John C. (1990). "Plugging into Strategic Partnerships: The Critical IS Connection." *Sloan Management Review*, vol. 31, no. 3, pp. 7–17.

References

Igibaria, Magid and Karanti Toraskar. (1994). "Impact of End-User Computing on the Individual: An Integrated Model." *Information Technology & People*, vol. 6, no. 4 (September), pp. 371–92.

Moda, Jeff. (1994). "Welcome to the Virtual IS Organization." *Datamation*, vol. 40, no. 3 (February 1), pp. 32–5.

Suh, Kunsoo, Sanghoon Kim, and Jinjoo Lee. (1994). "End-User's Disconfirmed Expectations and the Success of Information Systems." *Information Systems Management Journal*, vol. 7, no. 4, pp. 30–8.

Tayntor, Christine B. (1993). "Customer-Driven Long-Range Planning: Integrating EUC into IS Planning." *Information Systems Management*, vol. 10, no. 4, pp. 13–20.

3 Computing Services

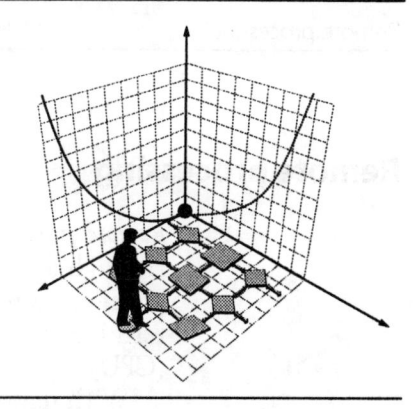

> If you want to make a long trip through a far wilderness, find a guide who has made the journey before.
>
> *Old proverb*

> Knowledge exists to be imparted.
>
> *Ralph Waldo Emerson*

Introduction

A large computing service industry has developed over the years to provide organizations with computer expertise to supplement and enhance in-house processing capability. For example, a company may contract with an outside firm for remote processing. Data will be transmitted by telecommunications to this outside source for processing. Another segment of the computing service industry provides consulting services. When the problem is lack of personnel to manage and run a corporate computing facility, a facilities management company can be contracted on a short- or long-term basis to operate the centre.

Firms with no computers of their own may turn to a service bureau or a utility for information processing. Such service firms are also used by companies that want access to computing power to supplement in-house capability and by those needing access to hardware or software that they lack in-house.

This chapter will discuss the advantages and disadvantages of each of the above types of computing services, stressing that these alternatives are not mutually exclusive. A variety of mixes is possible. For example, a firm with an in-house computer centre may assign certain jobs to a service bureau. Or a firm that contracts for facilities management may also use remote processing to access a utility's specialized database.

Remote processing

Remote processing is defined as the processing of computer programs through an input/output device that is remotely connected to a computer system. That is, jobs are submitted online to a computer from a terminal that is physically distant from the central processing unit (CPU).

With remote processing, a terminal may be used by an employee to access a company computer located in another room, on another floor, or in another company building. (The terminal will be connected to the CPU by in-house cable or by telecommunications.) Another type of remote processing is access to computing power from an external source, such as another firm with excess computing power or a utility that specializes in meeting the computing needs of clients. (Utilities will be described later in this chapter.) This latter type of remote processing is categorized as a computing service, the subject of this chapter.

Remote processing may be either *continuous processing* or *batch processing*. That is, data can be transmitted online as it is generated for instantaneous processing (*active online processing*) or can be stored upon receipt by the computer for later batch processing (*passive online processing*). An example of active online processing would be an airline system that allows a travel agent to ascertain seat availability for a given flight and to confirm a reservation for a client. An example of passive online processing is found in the automobile industry when a local car dealer sends sales data by remote job entry to headquarters for overnight batch processing with sales data from other dealers around the country. Reports based on information so processed are then transmitted back to the dealers to aid in management decision-making.

Active online processing may be subdivided into two parts: processing that does not require any updating of the database (*non-modifying*) and processing that does (*modifying*). A query to an existing database or processing of scientific input data are examples of non-modifying processing. Functional online real-time (OLRT) systems dedicated to process control, or transaction processing in banking or reservations, are examples of processing that modifies the database. Modification is also required in some general-purpose online computing, such as when a manager or production engineer wants to know the effect of a certain parameter change. *Time-sharing*, which is sharing a computer with other users (although the speed of response may give one the illusion of being the sole user), is another mode of remote processing in the business sector. Figure 3.1 shows the relationship of the modes of remote processing discussed in this section.

Figure 3.1:
Classification of modes of remote processing

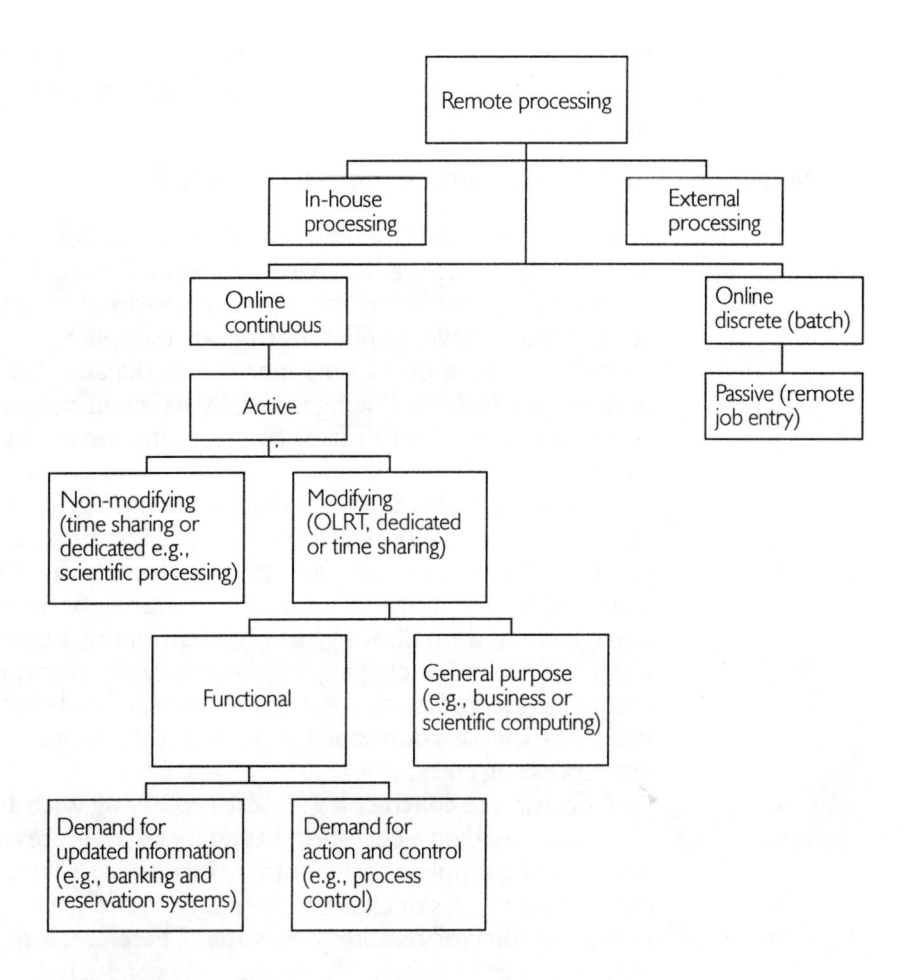

Why remote processing?

Remote processing is a time saver. It allows a person to input data for computer processing without having to go to the location of the CPU. Sometimes, a company uses remote processing to an external source to supplement its own processing capability, taking advantage of the storage capacity, specialized databases, or other processing services offered by the source. An additional reason to combine remote with local processing is to cushion surges in processing demand. When professional personnel and corporate management want the computational power of a large computer but need it only intermittently, remote processing may be the most cost-effective answer.

Other firms choose remote processing as an alternative to developing an in-house computing facility. They save space, equipment, and personnel resources that would otherwise have to be allocated to a computer centre. Still other firms utilize remote processing as an interim solution to their processing needs while developing an in-house processing capability.

Selection of an external remote processing service

Factors that should be considered when deciding whether external remote processing is advisable are listed in Table 3.1. Turnaround time, for example, may be critical, so benchmarks should test the response time of prospective suppliers during both supplier and user peak periods, as well as during hours with normal workloads. Teleprocessing costs may also be decisive. Pricing is usually based on transmission costs plus computing costs (per unit of connect time or per unit of computing time).

Most supplier firms have elaborate pricing algorithms that vary by as much as 200%. These algorithms are based on type of use and length of job. Adjustments may be made for guaranteed minimum usage, and discounts given according to number of terminals or other considerations. Charges may drop 20% by simply mentioning a competitor. To help users understand pricing algorithms, many suppliers provide users with accounting reports so that expensive jobs can be identified. Often, by redesigning the jobs or rescheduling them to non-peak periods, users can cut processing costs.

A decision to contract for remote processing with an external source should be based on a cost–benefits analysis, and care should be taken in selecting the supplier of this computing service. Over time, increases in transmission costs or changes in volume of service may reduce the economic viability of remote processing. Therefore, a financial review of remote processing should be periodically conducted.

Table 3.1 *Factors to be considered in deciding on external remote processing*

- Type of assistance needed:
    - Hardware
    - Software
        - Operating systems, DBMs, etc.
        - Applications packages
- Support
- Financial payoff
- Remote processing performance:
    - Turnaround and response time
    - Error rates and accuracy
- Effect on credibility and public relations when work is not done in-house
- In-house knowledge and experience with remote processing

Table 3.1 *Factors to be considered in deciding on external remote processing (continued)*

- Experience to be gained by contact with outside firm
- Telecommunications problems
- Possible loss of control over data
- Possible need to submit to outside standards
- Added vendor contacts and hassles
- Human factor considerations
- Organizational impact

Consultants

Using *consultants* is a thoroughly ingrained way of doing business. Few firms can afford to staff their companies with experts in all technical fields. As a result, they face problems from time-to-time that no employee within the firm is qualified or competent to handle. The expertise of a consultant is invaluable when in-house experience is lacking. What is more, consultants can bring an independent viewpoint to problem solving. They often serve as mediators in internal politics and act as spark plugs to get projects moving.

In the field of computing, the need for consultants is accentuated by the fast pace of technological development. The typical data processing department is struggling to fill backlogged user demands. There is no time for internal staff to develop expertise in technical areas such as micro to mainframe links, local area networks, office automation, telecommunications, information systems architectures, or general systems integration. Just to keep abreast of vendor trends in both hardware and software may require outside help. According to one observer, "The computer industry has been characterized by phenomenal change, and change creates uncertainty, and uncertainty creates the demand for consultants."

Even large firms with a wide range of specialists on the payroll often employ consultants. The need may arise because in-house personnel have ongoing commitments and do not have time to devote to new projects. Sometimes, a company wants the services of someone experienced in the problem at hand. For example, in applications development, a consultant who has had practical experience designing a similar system for another firm can be an invaluable member of a project team. Sometimes, the technicians a firm wants to hire are unavailable in the marketplace. Sometimes, a consultant rather then a full-time specialist is preferred because the latter's wage demands would distort the organization's wage and salary plan and create wage inequities.

An important advantage of consultants is that they are not a party to the internal power struggles within a firm and so can be more objective when seeking problem solutions. Their jobs and future promotions are not jeopardized by any recommendations they make. And by not being bound to a firm's traditions or precedents, they should be able to evaluate vendors and systems without bias.

The outside consultant, on the other hand, will not be acquainted with the personalities in the firm and will not understand how departments interact or how the firm functions. Recommendations made without taking time to gain familiarity with the firm's unique environment may prove inappropriate. What is more, the presence of a consultant may be viewed as an intrusion and hamper smooth working relationships. The large hourly salary of the consultant may be resented by in-house staff. In addition, ruffled feelings may arise from the fact that advice received from internal staff members may have been ignored by top management while the same advice is accepted from the consultant. The question of security also arises. Should sensitive data be exposed to consultants who have not demonstrated loyalty to a firm? The possibility exists that the information the consultant learns about the business might later be sold to competitors.

The need for an outside opinion can arise in all phases of development and operations. For example, consultants often participate in feasibility studies, decisions of resource acquisition, systems specifications, and the design of new systems. They may be hired to set standards, to establish privacy and security procedures, to help select personnel, or to run training programs. They have even been known to function as project managers for short-term, highly technical development projects. Managerial consultants may also help organize departments, assist in planning, or devise strategies to reduce resistance to change.

The broad range and critical nature of these activities require that consultants must be selected with care, with their qualifications and reputations carefully screened.

Selection

When searching for consultants, a good starting point is to ask professional associates to make recommendations based on their past experiences with consultants. Corporate executives may ask contacts at conferences or industry meetings to provide names of consultants with whom they have had successful dealings in the past. In addition, many professional organizations compile consulting lists. In the United States, the Independent Computer Consultants Association in St. Louis has a listing of more than 1,600 member firms representing more than 4,000 independent consultants. Other lists of consultants may be obtained from organizations such as:

- Association of Management Consulting Firms.
- JobNet Inc., Self Employed Professionals.
- Professional & Technical Consultants Association.
- Society of Telecommunications Consultants.
- Software Consultant Brokers Association.

Many consultants advertise in newspapers and professional journals. Academia is another mine for consultants. Unfortunately, no official governmental body regulates or certifies consultants, so the selection of a suitable candidate can be a risky proposition. Here are some guidelines that should help narrow the field and control the consultant's work:

- Examine the consultant's personal and corporate background through reference checks and financial reviews.
- Draw up a detailed written project plan and schedule for the work the consultant is to do. Make sure that the consultant understands the assignment and can demonstrate competence in this area of work.
- Build checkpoints or milestones into the project.
- Conduct regular review meetings between milestones.
- Thoroughly test the work of the consultant.

These recommendations are basic hiring and project management techniques.

Consultants may be hired by the hour or by the job. Rates are high. Well-known consultants command £3,000 to £6,000 per day, plus expenses. Consulting firms may charge from £50 to £150 per hour: independents command fees that range from £25 per hour to the rates cited earlier for superstars. Nevertheless, most firms feel the money is well spent.

Surprisingly, consulting firms find their clients mainly among successful companies rather than companies in trouble. As stated by Ira Gottfried, president of Gottfried Consultants, "The growing, profitable corporation recognizes its limitations and is able to spend the money to gain additional assistance from outside the company."

Chapter 3: Computing Services

Conclusions on consultants

The fast pace of technological advances in the computer industry suggests that consulting work should continue to be plentiful in the future. As in the past, corporations will undoubtedly call upon the services of consultants in order to keep up-to-date regarding developments in the computing field. However, many observers suggest that the more important role of consultants in the future will be to help corporations integrate and manage their information assets and resources in order to gain competitive advantage and improve quality and effectiveness of their IT operations. For example, corporations that have installed personal computers, local area networks, and telecommunication equipment will want to learn how best to integrate such technology in order to best meet their organizational objectives, information that no single vendor or technician can easily provide. Consultants will be valued for their computer knowledge plus their expertise and experience in industry and in business. A survey of 1,400 UK companies that used consultants concludes:

> The survey also provides an interesting picture of what IT managers do and do not want from a consultant. They want someone who is reassuringly credible, has the right interpersonal and technical skills, is accountable, can get to know the business quickly, does not upset the permanent staff, and who provides realistic, tailor-made (or at least individually packages) solutions. To get the best out of using consultants, client companies can clearly benefit from greater forethought....

> Looking at the areas in which consulting services are applied, they appear to divide into two halves: the provision of "hard" technical skills, such as networking or specific application skills, strategic planning, training, feasibility, and organization studies and marketing. This suggests two types of skills gap within IT in the UK that consultants are used to plug. Technical skills are quite understandable. It would not be cost effective for companies to try to cover all types of technical skill, some of which will only be required on a one-off basis. The rate of technological change also makes it understandably difficult for companies to keep all the necessary areas of technology covered. More worrying is that IT departments seem to need to call for help to cover some aspects of management. This may be linked to the lack of management training in general within the UK compared to the likes of Japan, Germany and North America...

> Unless the IT industry really gets to grip with its own problems of technical and managerial skills shortages, IT consultants are likely to be a visible feature of the industry for a long time to come.

Mingay and Peattie, 1992:348

Vendors

Vendors are often underutilized as a source of technical expertise. Unlike consultants vendors have a bias in favour of their own products, but this bias does not necessarily preclude sound advice on equipment and systems. (A company would, however, be wise to check the literature and consult other users for corroborative opinion.)

Vendors can often provide technical information on controls, security, and even installation of equipment. For example, when a computer centre is being planned, vendors frequently furnish an installation expert to help design the layout. The expert may supply tables and charts on clearances and power needs and even provide templates and sample layout diagrams. For microcomputers, many computer stores offer a range of services, from maintenance and support to seminars and consulting. A store that sells both hardware and software may be in a better position to know what is wrong and how to solve the problem than either hardware and software vendors, who tend to waste time blaming one another when something goes wrong. A classic example of vendor assistance with systems design was IBM's contributions to the first commercial airline reservation system for American Airlines.

Vendors commonly provide documentation and training on systems they supply. One vendor specializes in training programs featuring management games played at a country club, with golf interspersed between work sessions. This is good publicity for the vendor, while informative and fun for the trainee. Vendors often keep clients informed regarding industry gossip – such as who is in the job market and what new products are being launched.

Of course, not all vendors perform such roles, but many do offer valuable counsel. Establishing good rapport with vendors can speed up delivery dates of equipment, even result in visits by the vendor's analysts and engineers. Without doubt, most vendor representatives are knowledgeable in their respective fields, well supported by their companies, carefully trained, and well rehearsed. That they can be smooth talkers and high-pressure salesmen should come as no surprise. It is up to computer departments to be just as well prepared, know what questions to ask, and review responses critically, compensating for bias.

Sometimes, a vendor representative responsible for equipment maintenance is assigned to a given firm and is on-site daily. Such individuals become well acquainted with the staff and problems of the computer department and often act as informal consultants. On occasion, they take sides in disputes. Vendor representatives have even been known to appeal to corporate management to reverse computer department decisions and to win. Vendors have clout and sometimes use it.

Chapter 3: Computing Services

Facilities management

Facilities management (FM) is the use of an independent service organization to operate and manage the contracting firm's own data processing installation. Firms assign some or all of their computing to FM corporations for a variety of reasons. Some lack the technical personnel needed to run their data processing centre. Others do not want responsibility for operating computing equipment. Still others utilize facilities management because their firm's own computer department has been so badly mismanaged (dissatisfied users, missed deadlines, poorly utilized equipment, frequent time and cost overruns) that it must be reorganized, rebuilt, and restaffed. In the interim, the FM company is given responsibility for the centre. Some firms also decide on a long-term facilities management contract because they believe that their centres will be better managed under FM than by in-house staff.

Advantages and disadvantages

Few firms can match FM corporations in the quality of their computing staff. This is one reason why companies turn to FM for computing assistance. Good salaries and challenging work attract highly qualified personnel to FM. Computer professionals are drawn by the range of experience that helps them move quickly along their chosen career paths. Experts in fields such as teleprocessing, numerical control, and planning that use linear programming or simulation are also attracted to FM because they are able to concentrate on their specialties full-time in an FM job. In other firms, demand for their expertise might be limited, resulting in work assignments outside their fields of expertise.

Under facilities management, a computer centre can often be operated more economically than when managed by a corporation's own computing staff, partly because FM firms buy in quantity lots and obtain bigger discounts from vendors than do other firms. The highly trained professionals who work for FM companies also get better efficiency, reliability, and utilization from computer resources than the average employee in a data processing centre. What's more, FM employees can redesign systems, reorganize, and eliminate redundancies to achieve better performance in client firms without being encumbered by obligations to individuals or power blocks within that firm.

With FM, however, interface problems are compounded because computing is no longer organizationally in-house. The user must now interact with computer personnel whose primary loyalty lies with the FM company. New liaison procedures must be established, and new boundaries of authority and responsibility have to be defined between users and electronic data processing (EDP) personnel. Though obligations of the FM corporation should be detailed in the contract (see Table 3.2 for a list of subjects to be included in FM contracts), it takes time to develop smooth working relationships when an FM firm takes over management of a firm's computer centre. Considerable disagreement between users and FM staff regarding performance under FM may surface as well: evaluation of performance can be a highly subjective judgement. In such cases, relations are bound to be strained.

Table 3.2 *Subjects for inclusion in facilities management contracts*

Duration of contract	Standards
Availability of personnel	Input requirements
Availability of expertise	Documentation scope
Lines of reporting for personnel	Output portfolio and schedule
Liaison	Priorities
Ownership of equipment	Changes
Ownership of software	Payments
Security	Limitation and liabilities
Privacy of data	Right to audit FM firm's operations
Property interests	Contract termination procedures
Applications portfolio	Scope and level of effort of FM personnel and contracting firm
Extension of applications	

Another disadvantage of FM is that users lose control over their data and worry about privacy and security, particularly when the FM company is also servicing a competitor (FM companies must guard against legal violations in such cases). User flexibility is lost as well. And how can clients ensure that FM employees are motivated to act in the client's best interest? Designing contract incentives can challenge a client's lawyer.

When negotiating for FM services, the length of the contract period will depend on what type of service is required. Activities that have a long period of gestation, such as development of integrated systems or training programs, cannot be undertaken when the FM contract is short-term. (An FM company may prefer to omit training, since lack of training may extend the company's need for FM and hence create a dependency on FM.) A long contract period, however, may so entrench FM that it is hard for the client to take back management responsibility for processing. Most users do plan to manage their computer departments eventually, and they try to estimate the length of time needed to develop the technical expertise to do so, signing an FM contract for this interim period only. Indeed, many client firms find reliance on FM insulting to corporate management and believe their own personnel will be more responsive to internal processing needs than will FM staff. A compromise strategy is to take a short-term contract with an option to renew.

Cost

The cost of FM will depend on the size of the data processing configuration to be managed, scope of processing activities of the client firm, level of performance to be achieved, and ownership conditions. Contract length is also a factor (most run two to six years). The contract awarded to Bunker Ramo by the National Association of Security Dealers to run the nationwide stock market quotations and trading for over-the-counter securities is one example of what facilities management costs: $10.5 million for a three-year contract. Though this figure may seem high, many firms find that FM is less expensive than the cost of developing equivalent in-house expertise and capability.

Cost-plus contracts are sometimes negotiated for facilities management. The problem is defining the "plus" component.

Variations

FM contracts are based on user needs. Although most facilities management means processing is on the client's hardware, some FM firms will also contract for services on their own equipment. (One-third of a major FM corporation's 90 client firms, for example, use the FM company's hardware.) Advantages to the client include freeing equipment and personnel for other activities, and the creation of backup. Security and transportation are major problems in this arrangement. Another variation is a contractual agreement whereby the FM company selects equipment, installs it, and makes it operational, providing the client with a *turnkey system*. The client takes possession and manages processing once all problems associated with systems development, database implementation, programming, testing, and conversion have been resolved. This concept is popular in the Middle East, where technical expertise is in short supply but companies don't want outsiders, particularly Americans, responsible for daily operations.

Information centres

The concept of a computer support group to provide information workers with guidance and training in computer use, as well as with hardware/software tools, evolved during the 1970s and the 1980s as organizations looked for ways to maximize the efficiency and effectiveness of their computer processing. A number of terms have been used to describe this support, such as client service centre, solution centre, resource centre, and business systems support centre. However, the term *information centre*, coined by IBM Canada in 1976, is the name most widely used today.

Information centre services

Typically, information centres are designed to support end-users, not computer professionals. A survey on the current services offered by IT/IS managers in the US is summarized in Table 3.3. (Rainer and Young, 1993:56).

Table 3.3 *Services offered by information centres*

Services	%
Software support	81.1
Hardware support	78.8
Functional support	78.8
Data support	57.8
Training and education	57.0
Miscellaneous support	53.9

Here is a sampling of the type of services that may be offered.

Aid in problem resolution

User assistance usually begins by staffing a telephone hotline and a help desk. Requests for service may range from a simple query regarding the meaning of a message on a computer screen to an appeal for help when a system malfunctions or breaks down. When a problem cannot be resolved quickly, the user will be referred to a staff member with expertise in that area.

Consultation

Typically, the role of a consultant in an information centre is to help end-users plan for effective use of their computing resources, to advise them in ways to computerize their work, to evaluate proposed computer applications, to assist in product selection, and to answer specific questions regarding hardware and software.

Training

Computer literacy is the main objective of educational programs. Training may consist of self-study methods, such as computer-based training and audio-visual presentations, or be instructor led. Self-study is favoured when:

- Immediate training is required and the centre does not have time to plan and deliver a course on the subject.
- The schedule of the employee in need of training precludes class attendance.
- Training is needed at a remote site that instructors cannot reach.

Individualized instruction may be given when an employee needs to develop a specialized skill not needed by others. More commonly, workshops and classroom instruction are the teaching mode. Popular courses include word processing file creation, electronic mail, and how to use software such as *Lotus 1-2-3*, *Microsoft Word*, and *Pagemaker*. Classes may last half a day (for example, an introduction to the personal computer) or for as long as a week to 10 days (for example, application engineering to teach techniques in prototyping, data modelling and structured analysis).

Technical support

Technical assistance is provided by the centre when user problems are too large or complex to be solved without the aid of a technical specialist, but only if the solution is not an extensive modification of a large applications system or new systems development. (Those problems will be referred to persons in the IS department responsible for development projects.) "Fast-response report group" – a name some information centres give to their technical support team, helps explain the team's assignments. In addition to problem solving, staff may be asked to help audit systems performance, establish backup and recovery procedures, plan data access, assist with the design of security, plan projects or document user requirements. In effect, technical support is an extension of the centre's consulting service.

Product support

Software packages may reside at the information centre to provide end-users with services such as graphics, spreadsheets, decision support, modelling capability, financial analysis, fourth-generation query languages, database management, applications generators and so on. Staff may demonstrate how the software is used, perhaps by providing a sample problem solution walkthrough. In addition, they may help end-users interpret reference manuals, suggest tips and techniques for using the products and give debugging assistance if needed. Aid of this nature will also be given to end-users when they purchase new software.

Hardware access

Terminals, microcomputers, printers, plotters, microfilm and microfiche readers and other equipment may be available for use, or hardware may be on display to help end-users decide what equipment to acquire. Sometimes the information centre serves as an in-house computer store. End-users can try out equipment, receive advice about the relative merits of models produced by different manufacturers and then lease or purchase the equipment directly from the centre. This eliminates the lengthy acquisition procedures that are required when dealing with outside vendors. The centre offers "one-stop shopping", and the prices may be lower than those of retail stores. Furthermore, the centre can provide training, configuration assistance and maintenance after the lease or purchase.

Staffing
Some information centres provide backup assistance for end-users who have a temporary need for information processing personnel.

Computer resource planning and justification
The centre can help end-users analyze their workloads, make projections of future needs and prepare (and justify) requests for additional funding for computer resources. One of the more important roles of the centre is to nurture end-user awareness of the importance of standardization and integration of resources.

New-service evaluation
In order to provide better services to end-users, centre staff will keep abreast of user's needs. When new products (both hardware and software) come on the market, these products will be evaluated to see whether they will increase end-user self-sufficiency and productivity. If appropriate, the centre may then initiate a proposal to management for acquisition of the product.

Administrative services
This category of service commonly includes:

- Promotion and advertising of information centre activities (for example, a newsletter or bulletin board notices).
- Orientation workshops or open houses to introduce end-users to the information centre.
- New-product announcements.
- A library of computer-related materials.
- Equipment maintenance and service.
- Accounting billing for centre use.

Delivery of services

Most information centres are the responsibility of the firm's IS director, who monitors and controls the centre's usage and growth. The ways in which services are delivered varies from organization to organization.

In some centres, a person on the staff will work with an end-user from start to finish. That is, the staff member will analyze the user's problem and requirements, select appropriate packages, train the end-user if needed, and support the end-user in developing the problem solution. In this way, the staff member will have time to become thoroughly familiar with the end-user's environment (perhaps even be able to identify hidden problems) and will be able to develop a close working relationship with the end-user. The drawback is that a single individual may lack some of the skills needed to solve the problem.

At other centres, someone at the help desk may first analyze the end-user's problem, then pass the end-user to staff members who have expertise in that specific problem area. A number of specialists from the centre may work with the end-user over a period of time.

Most information centres being opened today are microcomputer oriented. But training is not limited to stand-alone computing: remote computing is supported as well, since microcomputers are often used as intelligent terminals when connected with minis or mainframes. Within the centre, computers may belong to a local area network or be networked with computers in other departments. An important role of many information centres is to promote the acquisition of computers with a set of data communication standards, so that linkage of all corporate computers will be facilitated in the future.

Future of information centres

Since the inception of information centres, a debate has raged in professional circles over the following question: Are the centres here to stay, or are they a temporary phenomenon? It is generally agreed that end-users will always need troubleshooting, training, and consultation in order to take full advantage of their computing resources. The focus of the controversy is whether such services will be the responsibility of departmental experts working in functional areas or whether they will remain in the information centre in the future.

Judging by the content (and number) of current articles on the subject, information centres are not likely to disappear soon. Centres may remain the central focus for guiding and supporting end-user computing, as long as centres keep up-to-date on new applications and technology, maintain quality staff and address issues of end-user concern.

Integration of information services

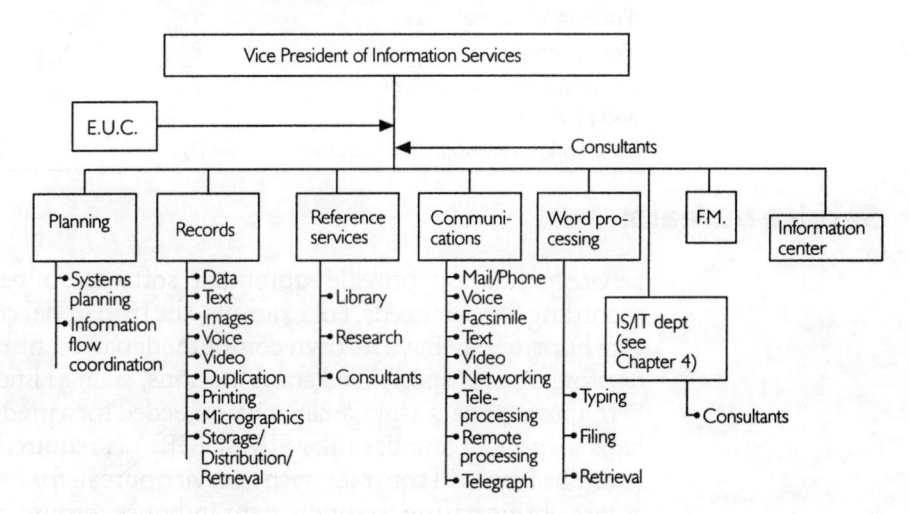

When information services are the responsibility of a number of departments, coordinating and integrating their activities becomes necessary. Many firms appoint a Vice President of Information Services to oversee this integration. (The exact title of this position may vary from firm to firm. Vice President of Information Resource Management is also frequently used.)

Figure 3.2 is an example of a sample organizational structure for *integration of information services*. Of course, not all firms are organized in this manner. Some will place record-keeping in the IS department, others will join word processing with reference services.

Figure 3.2:
Integration of information services

```
                          Vice President of Information Services
                                        |
        E.U.C. -----------------------→ |
                                        | ←----------- Consultants
        ┌────────┬─────────┬──────────┬──────────┬───────┬──────────┐
     Planning  Records  Reference  Communi-  Word pro-  F.M.  Information
                        services   cations   cessing           center

     • Systems  • Data    • Library  • Mail/Phone           
       planning • Text               • Voice       IS/IT dept
     • Information • Images • Research • Facsimile  (see
       flow     • Voice              • Text        Chapter 4)
       coordination • Video          • Video
                  • Duplication • Consultants • Networking
                  • Printing            • Tele-       • Typing
                  • Micrographics         processing
                  • Storage/            • Remote      • Filing  • Consultants
                    Distribution/         processing
                    Retrieval           • Telegraph   • Retrieval
```

Whatever structure is chosen will be temporary at best, because advances in computer technology will undoubtedly lead to the development of new computer applications in the future. Over time, it becomes necessary to restructure departments to incorporate new technology.

Critical success factors for an information centre

One study identified 26 critical success factors for an IC. What is interesting in this study is that the ratings of the end-users were often different from that of IC management. The results of this study (Magal and Strouble, 1991:32) for the first 10 of these factors is shown in Table 3.4.

Table 3.4 *Ratings of critical success factors for an IC*

Critical success factor rating	Rating by end-users	Rating by information centre management
A competent staff	1	1
Reliability of services provided	2	4
End-user training	3	5
Communication with users	4	2
Support software packages	5	11
Systems performance	6	22
Training for IC staff	7	7
Top management support	8	3
Understanding of user's business and problems	9	6
Respond to development requests	10	25

Service bureaux

Service bureaux can provide equipment, software, or personnel to clients according to their needs. For example, the firm under contract to the service bureau may have its own computer department but lack hardware or programs for specialized computations, such as linear programming. Perhaps more data storage capacity is needed for a prediction model. Perhaps a special compiler (like SIMSCRIPT) is required for a simulation run. The firm will contract with a service bureau for hardware/software access of this nature to supplement in-house resources.

Some bureaux provide access to specialized databases, such as the full text of court decisions or updated daily lists of stock market transactions. One service bureau has a database of extracts from Securities and Exchange Commission filing from over 12,000 publicly held companies; another has data on the Japanese economy, including a macro model and forecasts. Service bureaux can also prepare data, assist in data collection, consult, and even contract facilities management. A sample list of service bureau offerings appears in Table 3.5.

Table 3.5 *Services offered by a service bureau*

■ Contribute to one or more stage of development	■ Storage capacity
■ Provide specialized database	■ Facilities management
■ Prepare firm's database or assist in data conversion	■ Capacity for excess workload:
	※ Unexpected
■ Prepare data for an ongoing database	※ Seasonal
■ Provide programs:	※ Growth
※ Standard functional programs (e.g., accounting)	■ Handle processing when firm lacks:
	※ Capital for hardware acquisition
※ Programs for decision support systems	※ Space
	※ Personnel
※ Industry-specialized programs	※ Time
※ Customized programs	※ Processing capacity
■ Process data in a variety of modes:	■ Miscellaneous:
※ Batch	※ Data collection
※ Interactive batch	※ Output delivery
※ Online	※ Consulting
※ Online real-time	

Why service bureaux?

Many of the advantages of facilities management apply to service bureaux as well. Service bureaux can attract highly qualified personnel and specialists and can therefore operate at a higher level of efficiency and professionalism than the average firm. They can also operate at lower cost, taking advantage of economies of scale. For example, program development is less costly when shared by a large base of users. Because of this base, service bureaux can also maintain large computer installations, develop extensive databases, and offer all modes of processing (batch, interactive batch, online, and online real-time).

Firms that utilize service bureaux may not have the in-house capability of performing needed activities or may find it more economical to use a service bureaux than to gear up for the activity. Even large, well known firms, including Boeing, Chase Manhattan, Control Data, GE, GTE, Lockheed, New York Times, Time Inc., and Xerox Corporation are service bureau customers. In some cases, these same firms sell services to others and buy services concurrently (for example, Boeing and Control Data).

Selection

A firm considering the option of a service bureaux should first examine the economic feasibility of handling the activity in-house, then contact a number of service bureaux and compare their offering, because service bureaux differ in their fee structures. Some charge a flat rate. Others base fees on the amount of resources used, how they are used, and of what applications. Before a service bureau's contract is signed costs should also be compared with other alternatives (for example, facilities management or acquisition of minis and software packages).

But cost of services should not be the only criterion for selection of a service bureau. Table 3.6 lists other factors that should be considered.

Table 3.6 *Factors to be considered in service bureau selection*

■ Services offered	■ Hardware configuration
■ Reputation of service bureau	■ Arrangements for data transfer
■ Years of operation	■ Time involved
■ Experience with firm's industry	■ Convenience
■ Competence of personnel	■ Frequency
■ References	■ Availability for access
■ Financial stability	■ Benchmark results
■ Promptness record	■ Backup facilities
■ Quality of service	■ Pricing algorithms:
■ Errors	▪ Normal load
■ Reruns	▪ Offload
■ Integrity	▪ Reruns
■ Security and privacy record	■ Liability and damage conditions
■ Software portfolio	■ Discontinuation conditions
■ Compatibility	

The challenge facing service bureaux

The availability of inexpensive microcomputers has enabled many firms to keep work in-house that was formally contracted to service bureaux. The bureaux have also lost clients because the cost of software is down. Many companies can afford to purchase all of the programs they need, so software availability is no longer a major service bureau attraction.

With revenue dropping, service bureaux are consolidating and redefining their role. Some industry observers predict that by the 1990s the field will narrow to a few gigantic superbureaux that emphasize information management instead of processing. These bureaux will offer services such as time-sharing, on-site microcomputers, and turnkey systems. They will help to establish information centres and increase installation support and education. More emphasis may be placed on software-related consulting services. The companies may download software to customer microcomputers or act as distributors of small software developers. Electronic data interchange, the linking of buyers and suppliers, is a technology that may open new markets for service bureaux. Artificial intelligence and voice recognition may lead service bureaux in still other directions.

Change in the service bureau industry is nothing new. The industry today is radically different in appearance form that of the 1960s, when service bureaux were primarily hardware vendors. The industry has survived by meeting the evolving needs of clients, providing service that users have been unable to develop for themselves. According to the Yankee Group, a US (Boston-based) research and consulting firm, the future of service bureaux will lie in their ability to offer:

> A combination of access to processing power; application specific software, standalone, online, and hybrid; value-added services; intercompany computer facilities; micro-to-mainframe linked; variable bandwidth services; on-site hardware; and customized communications software.
>
> *Myers*, 1984:110

Computer utilities

A *computer utility* is a source of remote processing, selling computer time and services. Utilities offer unique processing features that distinguish them from service bureaux and other remote processing suppliers. Instead of contracting with a client for a specific service, time-sharing is available at any time, for as long as requested, to any user who can pay for it. The computer utility resembles an electric utility insofar as computing power, like electric power, must be continuously offered and be able to handle fluctuations of demand. This requires a grid or network, so that computing power can be accessed form a distant site if regional facilities are overloaded.

Figure 3.3 shows a sample utility configuration. Individual customers at home or business may be serviced by a utility node supported by a variety of resources (software, databases, and computers) as illustrated.

The node may draw on computing power from other nodes for special services or during peak periods of demand. Compatibility of hardware, software, and interfaces is therefore needed. Telecommunications and protocols to link utility nodes are also required.

A computer utility is an old concept, but because of regulation and networking problems, utilities offering comprehensive services are not too common. However, recent court decisions (in relation to AT&T and

IBM) that now allow the intersection of communications and computing may well spur the growth of this industry and foster fierce competition for customers. Conceivably, computer networks of the future may connect thousands of computers and service millions of users. They will undoubtedly carry both voice and video traffic, be fail-soft, and have sharing protocols for both terminal and file transfers.

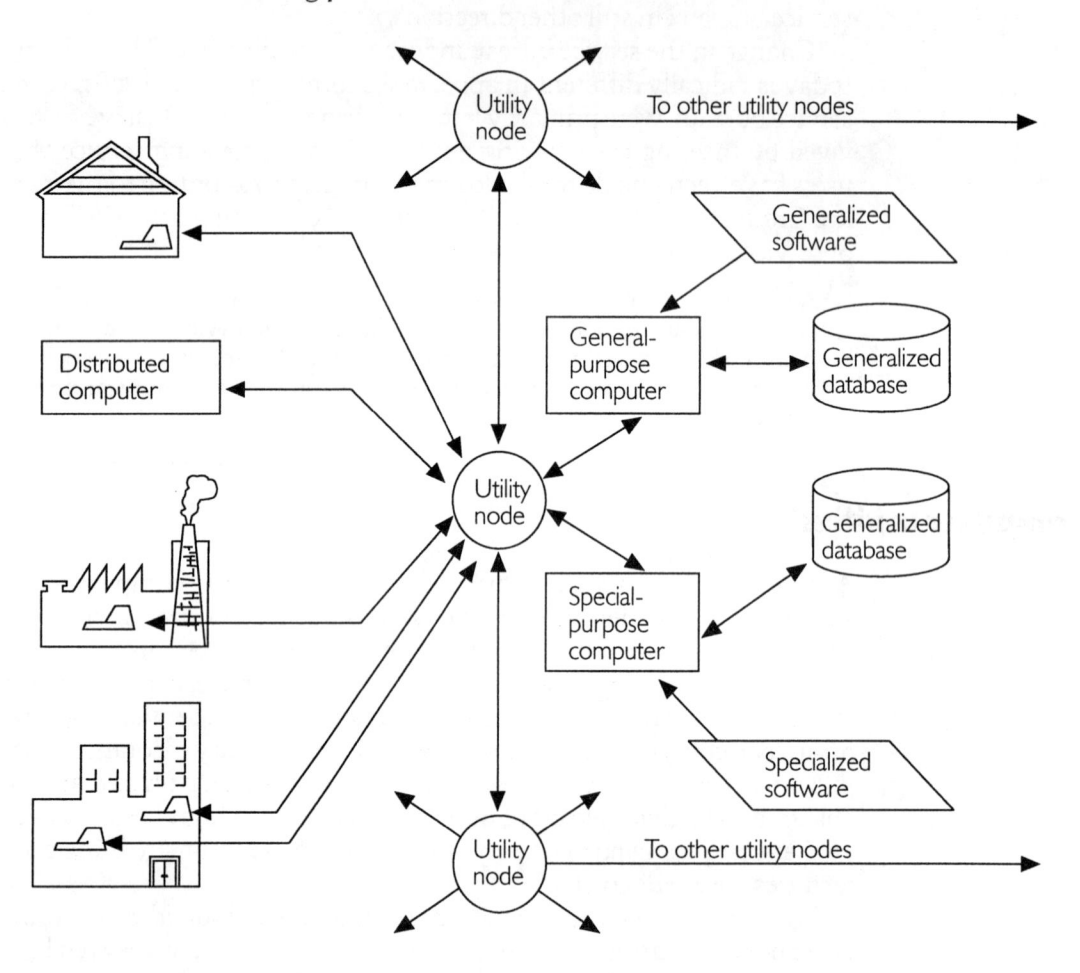

Figure 3.3:
Sample configuration of a utility

Public fears over data security and privacy issues may slow public acceptance and use of utilities. Will proprietary data be safe from unauthorized intrusion when processed by a distant utility? Will linked utility databases infringe upon individual privacy rights? How utilities should be regulated is also an unresolved question. The social implications of computer networks need now to be addressed by computer specialists as well as political and social scientists. The growth of utilities as a sector of the computer service industry will depend, to a large extent, on future legislation affecting network regulation and control.

Summing up

This chapter has described segments of the computing service industry. Both consultants and vendors offer professional services based on their technical knowledge and experience. Consultants are more objective, have a broader base of experience and wider range of knowledge. The services of vendors are usually free and, within narrow parameters, equally professional. Another difference between the two is that consultants may be hired to give advice to corporate management or the computer department, whereas vendors mainly counsel the latter and have a bias in favour of their own products, a difference illustrated in Figure 3.4.

Figure 3.4: *Relationship of consultants and vendors to the client*

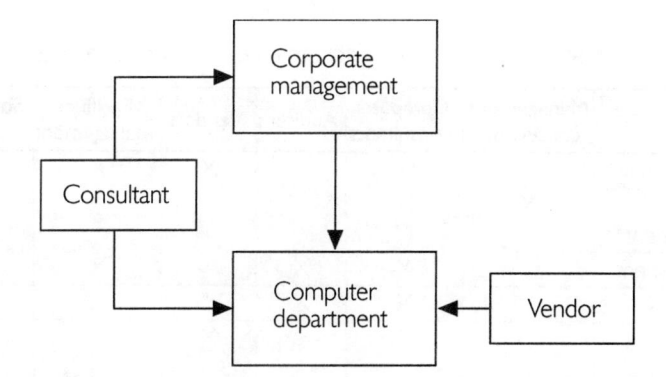

Facilities management is useful when a firm owns equipment but does not wish to operate it. The firm may have had a bad experience with ineffectual internal management of computing in the past, or the shortage of qualified candidates means personnel capable of managing high technology cannot be hired. FM can be a short- or long-term solution to computing problems for small and medium-sized companies. Large firms are usually able to attract or generate the management necessary for their computing operations and so use FM less frequently.

Remote processing, service bureaux, and utilities may be contracted for external processing. Remote processing is appropriate for firms that want access to hardware, software, or databases not available in-house, or that have occasional demand for a powerful computer. Remote job entry is also an alternative for firms that want to gain experience in computer processing before setting up an in-house processing facility.

Many small and medium-sized firms that want a full range of computer services are attracted to service bureaus. Two other sources of professional assistance not discussed in the chapter deserve mention. One is auditors. The other is software houses, sellers of standard packages, who can also develop customized software and will, if paid, provide programmers and analysts to assist in software implementations, including documentation. Table 3.7 summarizes, by source, professional sources available to computer departments. In selecting a supplier for computing services, cost–benefit studies should be conducted and bids from more than one vendor received, because pricing and services vary considerably. Alternatives should also be periodically reevaluated, since costs and benefits may change in time. For example, the availability of low-cost microcomputers means that many of the applications formerly contracted to outside service companies can now be done more cheaply in-house by many corporations.

Table 3.7 *Professional services available to computing departments by source*

Source	Management consultants	Computer consultants	Auditors	Vendors	Facilities management	Software houses	Service bureaux	Utilities
Planning for computing	X	X		X	X		X	
Organization of computer department	X	X					X	
Phases of development		X	X		X		X	X
Standards		X	X		X		X	
Program implementation				X	X	X	X	
Control systems design		X	X	X	X		X	
Audit of efficiency and performance			X					
Hiring of computer personnel			X		X			
Training			X		X	X	X	X
Planning for change	X	X		X	X			
Selection of computing resources		X					X	
Operations					X		X	X

In this chapter we discussed the integration of computing service as in Figure 3.2. In this diagram we identified the personnel for IS/IT as a set of personnel without any details. Now we are ready to provide the details. We referred to the IS/IT department because sometimes the IS department is the same as the IT department. In recent years, however,

IS is a subset of IT. IT is often organized to embrace not just IS but also record keeping, telecommunications, word processing, and all other activities related to information systems. It is the personnel for such an extended department of IT that is the subject of our next chapter.

Case 3.1: Facilities management at EDS

EDS stands for *Electronic Data Systems* which started in 1962 as a facilities management firm on a cheque of $1,000. In 1982 it was sold to GM, General Motors, for $2.6 billion. It is an autonomous unit in GM and its rate of growth has not slowed any.

EDS makes its money by taking advantage of economies of scale in the use of its technical services for managing computing facilities (including the acquisition of equipment) for other companies like the ten-year contract with Xerox corporation for running its computer and telecommunications network.

In 1994, EDS processed 43 million transactions a day; linked 411,000 PCs; had a storage capacity equivalent to 45 times that needed to hold the US Library of Congress; spent half its budget on telecommunications; and had a backlog of $32 billion in future business.

EDS is a US-based company but operates in 36 countries through its 78,000 employees, 2% of whom are American.

It has partnerships with Video Lottery Technologies and France's Telecom; is helping SpectraVision to provide digital videos-on-demand for 680,000 hotel rooms; working with Transaction Partners on interactive home banking; and chasing a $1.5 billion contract to run the Inland Revenue's computers.

EDS has made a shift to multimedia and from serving large customers to serving individuals whether they be in the office or teleworkers at home.

Source: *Economist*, vol. 333, no. 7891, (November 26, 1994), pp. 69–70.

Case 3.2: Choosing a consultant

Mercury Combinations has a computer system that takes responsibility for ensuring that all queries will be dealt with promptly and satisfactorily. In 1992 it decided to streamline its business process and boost its customer appeal. It wanted a consultant to help identify the best state-of-the-art practice. It selected Andersen Consulting for its $6 million system that linked its workers into a seamless web of electronic communications. The process of selection is of interest in this case study.

Mercury sent a two-page brief to all those interested in tendering with a request that they submit a maximum of five pages in response. On the basis of these responses, four consultancies were short-listed and asked to send quotes for the project.

Mercury had specific requirements. It demanded specific experience of the project manger, wanted to meet him (or her) in person, and an assurance that the project manager will be expected to stay with the job from start to finish. Mercury also demanded a guide on how the system was to be put together in addition to an assurance of skill transfer.

Roberts, at Mercury, advises to make the consultant share the risks as well as their rewards even if they have subcontractors on the project:

> They all say they do this anyway and talk a lot about mutual trust... But what they really mean is that they want to get paid even if they don't deliver.

Roberts is in favour of a prime contractor:

> The prime contractor is strongly motivated to do what you want, and you have the time to focus your energies on managing it.

In making the project specifications, Mercury told the contractors exactly what they wanted. Roberts adds:

> We let them talk to users and didn't consciously hold anything back. We even told them how their quote would be measured... Each of the acceptance criteria was weighted, so Mercury was able to decide the best very rapidly by multiplying scores against weightings and totting up the total.

Source: *Management Today*, September 1994, pp. 70–2.

Case 3.3: Study of information centres

A study of 115 information centres showed that all users got the same support whilst the needs of end-users varied with their computer sophistication. Recommendations by the authors to correct the situation is for the information centres to:

- Learn to identify differences among end-users, anticipate differential support needs, and address them on a proactive basis.
- Support services should be designed around needs of end-users.
- IC staff should put more effort into understanding the business functions of their end-users.
- Successful management of the EUC requires careful planning on their part.

- Allocation of adequate resources for their management of EUC is necessary to prevent dysfunctional consequences for the organization.
- The formation of user groups should be facilitated by the IC staff so that the users with similar support needs can assist each other.

Mirani and King, 1994:163

Source: Rajesh Mirani and William R. King. (1994). "Impact of End-User and Information Center Characteristics on End-User Computing Support." *Journal of Management Information Systems*, vol. 11, no. 1, pp. 141–66.

Case 3.4: Survey of consultants

A study of around 1,400 companies from a random list of 6,000 companies in Wales and the South West had the following main comments made about consultants:

- Too expensive.
- Anyone can set themselves up as a consultant, so there are no standards.
- They forget who is paying them sometimes.
- Failing to understand the client's problem and coming up with a standard solution.
- They rarely have an edge over permanent staff and often less knowledge of the business. Once their work is complete, they leave and the permanent staff have the pick up the pieces, which is resented.
- Too many bucket-shop consultant firms who offer misdirected and misguided advice at expensive rates.
- Upset permanent staff with high fees.
- Advice unrealistic when related to the business requiring their services.
- Long-term relationships are very expensive, short-term ones tend to be insufficient.

Source: Mingay and Peattie. (1992). "IT Consultants: Source of Expertise or Expense?" *Information and Software Technology*, vol. 34, no. 5, p. 348.

Case 3.5: Barcelona 1992 Olympic Games

Responsibility for organizing the information technology infrastructure for the 1992 Olympic Games fell under the jurisdiction of the Organizing Committee of Barcelona (COB '92). The philosophy adopted by the Committee was to decentralize the system as much as possible. They approved a systems configuration that revolved around IBM mainframes loosely connected with approximately 3,600 PS/2s located throughout the city of Barcelona. A local area network operated autonomously in each stadium, but data was sent to central mainframes for processing. Software applications for the Games were divided into four categories as follows:

- Management of total operations.
- Calculation and management of events.
- Management of city resources to support the Olympic family (including athletes, journalists, invited personalities, members of COB '92, and so on).
- Systems for internal use by COB '92.

Contracts for development of these applications were awarded to Sema Group PLC, Electronic Data Systems Corp., Gestio, and Apple Computer.

A number of factors contributed to the complexity of the design of the infrastructure. For example, the Games had a fixed starting date on which all systems had to work perfectly. Also, the buildings in which the PCs, telephones, photocopiers, and walkie-talkies were to be installed were only available two to three weeks before the opening ceremonies. Because of the last-minute installation, testing was limited to parts and components. No time was available for total systems testing or fine-tuning. A breakdown in telecommunications or the information systems would potentially be visible to 300 million people worldwide.

Source: Enrique San Juan. (1993). "Barcelona '92: The Technological Games." *Datamation*, vol. 36, no. 13 (1 July), pp. 107–8.

References

Bird, Jane. (1994). "Are You Being Served?" *Management Today*, (September), pp. 70–3.

Carr, H. H. (1992). "Are Information Centers Responsive to End User's Needs?" *Information & Management*, vol. 22, no. 2, pp. 113–122.

Healy, Paul. (1991). "Good Advice, Bad Advice." *Which Computer?*, vol. 14, no. 6 (June), pp. 76–88.

References

Khan, Emdad H. (1992) "The Effects of Information Centers on the Growth of End-User Computing." *Information & Management*, vol. 23, pp. 279–89.

Kirkpatrick, David. (1991). "Why Not Farm Out Your Computing?" *Fortune*, vol. 124, no. 7 (23 September), pp. 100–2.

Magal, Simha R. and Dennis D. Strouble. (1991). "A User's Perspective of the Critical Success Factors Applicable to Information Centers." *Information Resource Management Journal*, vol. 4, no. 2, pp. 22–34.

Mingay, S. and K. Peattie. (1992). "IT Consultants – Source of Expertise or Expense." *Information and Software Technology*, vol. 4, no. 5 (May), pp. 341–450.

Myers, Edith. (1984). "Here comes the Service Bureaus." *Datamation*, vol. 30, no. 16 (October 15).

Narcisco, John. (1992). "Confessions of a DP Contractor." *Journal of Systems Management*, vol. 42, no. 9 (September), pp. 33–35.

Piede, Duane L. (1996). "Restructuring Internal Services." Information Systems Management, vol. 13, no. 1 (Winter), pp. 12–17.

Ranier, R. Kelly, Jr. and Dale Young. (1993). "The State of Information Center Services." *Information Systems Management*, vol. 10, no. 1, pp. 54–58.

Ring, Tom. (1990). "Who's In Charge?" *Which Computer?*, vol. 13, no. 9 (September), pp. 40–6.

von Simon, Ernest M. (1990). "The Centrally Decentralized IS Organization." *Harvard Business Review*, vol. 68, no. 4 (July–August), pp. 155–62.

Wittenberg, Aviwah. (1990). "Europe's Age of Reason." *International Management*, (September), pp. 52–5.

4 Computer Personnel

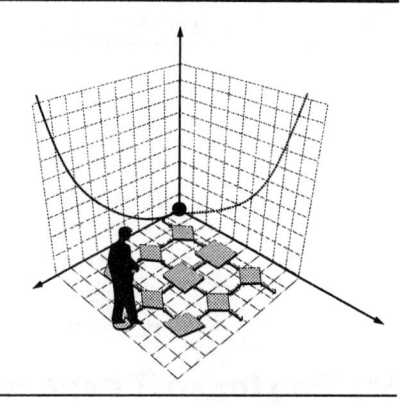

> The extension of man's intellect by machine, and the partnership of man and machine in handling information may well be the technological advance dominating the century.
>
> *Simon Ramo*
>
> There are three major problems in computer systems development: people, people, and people.
>
> *Derek Partridge*

Introduction

Although computerized societies are often pictured as machine dominated, with humans subservient to technology, computers exist to serve people and to aid managers in reaching decisions. And they cannot execute given tasks without the assistance of a large number of information technology (IT) professionals and support personnel.

For example, input – be it data, operating instructions, or application programs – is initiated by humans. It takes analysts to assess the needs of information by end-users and skilled programmers to convert these needs into bits, the only medium understood by computers. Collection and updating of data are an interactive human activity. Programmers are needed for the preparation of computer instructions, and many technicians are required for operating and servicing the computer system itself. Without analysts, programmers, operators, clerks, librarians, schedulers and other support personnel like telecommunications personnel, AI personnel (including knowledge engineers, and database personnel), computers are unable to produce the information end-users request and need. Newly emerging positions in IT include the Policy Analyst, the Technology Watcher, the CIO (Chief Information Officer) and the MOT (Manager of Technology). This chapter focuses on staffing of an IT department. First, the duties and responsibilities of computer personnel are described. Hiring, and turnover are discussed next. Since empirical studies have shown that computer people place a high value on professional growth, both career development and training are also discussed in this chapter. The chapter closes with a section on technostress and job stress in the computing field.

Staffing for an IT department

An IT department typically reports to a CIO (Chief Information Officer), MOT (Manager of Technology) or Director of IT which operates within a corporate organizational structure with its CEO (Chief Executive Officer). The organizational unit to which each group reports will vary greatly with systems departments within a large corporate structure. The organizational configuration is evolving as applications are being integrated and advanced applications are being implemented. For example, the emergence of a KBIS (knowledge-based information system) requires the working together of different personnel like OR/MS (operations research/management science) personnel and AI (artificial intelligence) personnel.

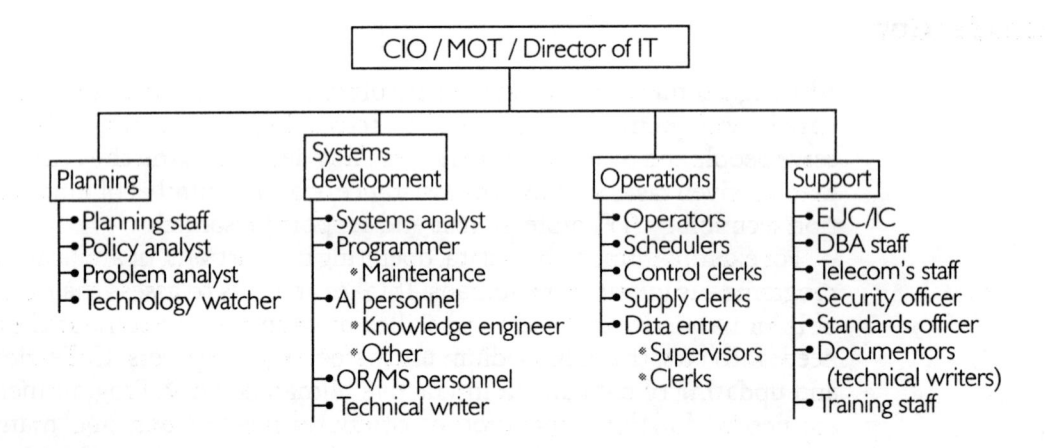

```
                    CIO / MOT / Director of IT
       ┌────────────────┬────────────────┬────────────────┐
   Planning         Systems         Operations         Support
                   development
   • Planning staff  • Systems analyst  • Operators        • EUC/IC
   • Policy analyst  • Programmer       • Schedulers       • DBA staff
   • Problem analyst    * Maintenance   • Control clerks   • Telecom's staff
   • Technology      • AI personnel     • Supply clerks    • Security officer
     watcher            * Knowledge     • Data entry       • Standards officer
                         engineer          * Supervisors   • Documentors
                       * Other              * Clerks         (technical writers)
                     • OR/MS personnel                     • Training staff
                     • Technical writer
```

Figure 4.1:
Organizational structure of an IT department

Many of these personnel are assigned to a project as the need for them arises and varies greatly with departments and their organizational culture. Meanwhile, for purposes of this discussion, we shall look at a configuration of systems personnel as shown in Figure 4.1.

The actual percentage of employees in each category varies from one company to another depending on the size of the company, the intensity of use of computers and information systems, the amount of resources devoted to information systems, and the manner in which the resources are organized. For example, a distributed processing configuration generally requires more operational and fewer support personnel at each node. A centralized information system has the opposite mix: more support and fewer operational personnel.

Even within a given facility, positions are not static, since needs are constantly changing. A salary survey by *Datamation* in the early 1950s listed 27 computer positions and in the 1980s it was 55. This growth in computer positions is attributed to the increasing complexity of information systems. Not all systems will have even 55 positions, however. Small companies may have far fewer positions, with a single individual filling several jobs.

Most of the personnel identified in Figure 4.1 will be discussed in this chapter. We start with the traditional systems personnel of systems analysts.

Systems analysts

A *systems analyst* is a technician who participates in the development, implementation and maintenance of information systems. The analyst studies a problem (or anticipates a potential problem) and decides which procedures, methods, or techniques are required for a computer solution to the problems. Analysts also gather and analyze data, document systems, design forms and procedures, and test systems.

In addition, analysts serve as the link between users (mostly end-users), and the IS department staff, interpreting client needs and formulating user specifications for systems development teams. Analysts are also responsible for explaining the capabilities and limitations of computing to users with no technical background. And analysts are the people who resolve complaints and serve as mediators in user–IS staff disputes. Indeed, the position of systems analyst was originally designed to bridge the gap between information (end-users) users and programmers in order to resolve the classic computing problem: how to develop computer systems when users (who want results) and programmers (who know how to make things happen) have difficulty communicating with one another. The idea was to train a computer professional with the knowledge of what computers can do, someone familiar with the jargon of programming, able to talk to and translate for end-users.

Figure 4.2 outlines the responsibilities of systems analysts in each phase of a computer system's development. During the feasibility study, analysts make cost–benefit estimates and advise the development team on the technological feasibility of proposals. During the user specifications phase, analysts take an active role in structuring the problem, quantifying objectives, and helping to synthesize and crystallize user desires so that system specifications can be prepared. When conflicting user interests arise, analysts must find a compromise.

Figure 4.2:
Roles of systems analysts in the development of a computer system

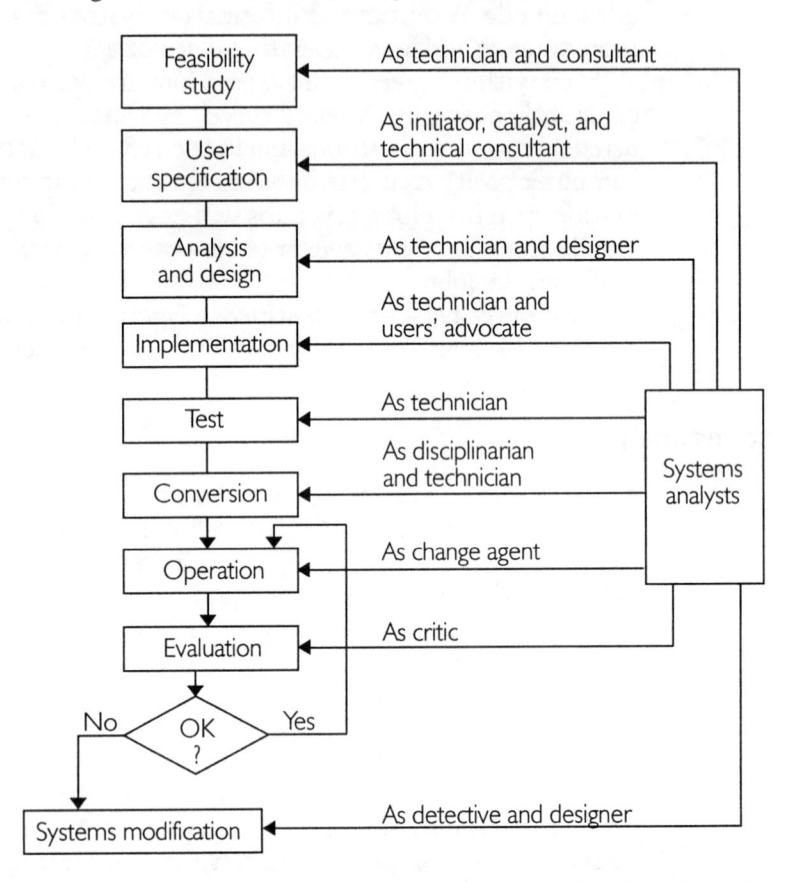

Feasibility study	As technician and consultant
User specification	As initiator, catalyst, and technical consultant
Analysis and design	As technician and designer
Implementation	As technician and users' advocate
Test	As technician
Conversion	As disciplinarian and technician
Operation	As change agent
Evaluation	As critic
Systems modification	As detective and designer

(After Evaluation: OK? No → Systems modification; Yes → continue)

When the design phase is reached, analysts have technical concerns: design specifications for output, input, files, forms, and procedures. In implementation, analysts become users' advocates, working with programmers for solutions that consider human factors. During conversion, analysts may seem to switch sides. Their job is to prod reluctant users procrastinating over conversion and to refuse user requests for late specification changes, working on behalf of the IS department to resolve technical problems and speed conversion.

Although most analysts are assigned other projects when a system is finally operational, some may assist management in planning and implementing strategies to reduce employee resistance to the new system. Analysts can advise management as to how new technology will affect daily operations, and they may be astute in gauging the amount of change an organization can comfortably absorb. Analysts may also assist in orientation and training programmes, effectively acting as change agents to promote favourable attitudes towards computing. Once systems are operational, analysts often participate in systems evaluation. They identify errors and recommend system modifications.

Most firms have a number of systems analysts so that no individual analyst would be assigned all of these functions. As a matter of fact, it is unwise for a single analyst to have prime responsibility for all stages of systems development. That would violate the principle of separation of duties, a management principle that stipulates that those who plan and design a system should not take part in testing and approval decisions. Since complex projects require the expertise of many analysts, this division of responsibility can usually be enforced. It is over the life of a number of projects that an individual analyst may be required to perform the spectrum of roles shown in Figure 4.2. However, small firms with limited personnel may require a single analyst to work on all phases of development.

The ideal systems analyst should have the characteristics listed in Table 4.1. One look at the list should explain why good analysts are in scarce supply. Because the ability to handle people is as important as technical competence and because knowledge of an organization, its power structure, policies and procedures is essential to analysts, many firms like to hire analysts from their organization's labour pool. Individuals who have demonstrated aptitude for systems analysis and have the right temperament are hired even if they lack some of the skills needed in the job. They are given appropriate technical training. It is thought by some that analysts hired and trained in this fashion are more quickly of value to the firm than analysts hired from outside who have technical qualifications but are unfamiliar with key personalities and how the company is run. Not everyone agrees with this viewpoint, however.

Table 4.1 *Desirable characteristics of a systems analyst*

- Technical expertise in systems analysis and systems design
- Working knowledge of hardware, software, databases, operating systems and telecommunications
- Detailed knowledge of a programming language, such as COBOL for business applications
- Creative mind
- Ability to think in the abstract, to work with symbols and problem logic
- Receptive to different approaches to problem solving, analysis and design
- Ability and patience to teach and train both professionals and non-technical users
- Good listening skills
- Project management skills

Table 4.1 *Desirable characteristics of a systems analyst (continued)*

- Enjoys working with people
- Sensitivity to people and knowledge about human factors
- Knowledge about clients, their business, and industry
- Sensitivity to the company's power structure
- Ability to work in non-structured, ill-defined, and conflict-prone environments
- Ability to function well under pressure, resolve conflicts and balance trade-offs
- Ability to work in a team
- Halo – if possible!

Programmers

The job of a programmer is to write and test the instructions that tell the computer what to do. Unlike analysts, who have to deal with the marriage between people and machines and often with unpredictable human emotions, programmers solve problems of logic in a more predictable environment – a machine environment. They first decide how to solve a problem, then prepare a logic chart, code instructions in a language the computer can understand, establish input/output formats, follow testing procedures, allocate storage, and prepare documentation.

Although some of a programmer's duties overlap with those of analysts, programmers do not require the social skills of analysts. Indeed, the typical programmer is reclusive, an individual who wants to work alone, without much social interaction or managerial direction. Many programmers are highly strung and overspecialized and reject externally imposed structure and routine. Most have no desire to enter into managerial or executive ranks. A large number of young, mobile, unmarried people with technical bents enter the field, which helps explain why programming is a high-turnover profession.

Sometimes, small firms that cannot afford a large staff merge the responsibilities of analysts and programmers in one position. Even large firms like the analyst–programmer combination, since it helps reduce the misunderstandings that often arise between the two professional groups and eliminates finger pointing and blame shifting when things go wrong. The problem is finding qualified personnel.

The development of special-purpose, high-level languages that make programming easier has contributed to a number of analysts doing their own programming, so the analyst–programmer may become more common in the future.

With regard to programming skills, there is great diversity among programmers. Some specialize in COBOL, FORTRAN, or other high-level languages. Others specialize in packages for decision support systems or languages for such support, like GPSS and SIMSCRIPT. Still others, schooled in operations research, focus on simulation. Systems programmers with expertise in hardware deal with low-level languages (assembler or machine languages). These programmers work more closely with operations than with applications development.

Operators

Since the early days of computing, the job of operator has changed greatly for both peripheral and computer operators. Formerly, operators loaded machines with tapes, disks, or cards and monitored relatively simple machine consoles. Vocational or junior college training was adequate for the job. Today's operators, because they operate sophisticated systems, must be knowledgeable about hardware, software, and databases. An estimated 80–90% of an operator's time is in software-related activities, where knowledge of the system's job control language is required in order to optimize the system's resources.

Operators have responsibility for the security and privacy of data and hardware as well. Operating errors can lead to damage of expensive equipment, necessitate reconstruction of the database, require costly reruns, or result in lost business due to delay or inconvenience to users.

Database administrator

The training of specialists to assist in systems development and implementation has arisen as information technology has grown more complex. For example, the position of database administrator (DBA) has emerged in recent years. This administrator is responsible for the coordination and use of data and knowledge stored under the control of a database management system. For example, it is the job of the DBA to minimize the cost of the machinery or hardware involved in data management and to minimize disk space and the time it takes to access data.

The position entails the upkeep of data (updates, additions, deletions, and database reorganizations), data maintenance (this may entail moving data from one storage media to another for quick and efficient access), maintenance of historical data (including modification of files when definitions of data elements and classifications change), and the purging of useless data. Any changes to the database, data directories or data element dictionaries must also be approved and supervised by the DBA. In addition, the DBA resolves conflicts when users dispute data classifications or who should create data, establishes policies for segmented or replicated databases and determines the distribution of data. The role of the DBA is both technical and non-technical: mainly, the DBA interacts with technical staff (analysts and programmers) and

Table 4.2 *Functions of a database administrator*

Database design
- Content
  - Create
  - Reconcile differences
- Dictionary/directory
  - Create
  - Maintain
- Data compression
- Data classification/coding
- Data integrity
  - Backup
  - Restart/recovery

Database operation
- Data element dictionary custodian/authority
  - Maintain
    - Add
    - Purge
- Database maintenance
  - Integrity
    - Detect losses
    - Repair losses
  - Recovery
  - Access for testing
  - Dumping
- Software for data element
  - Dictionary/data dictionary
  - Utility programs
  - Tables, indexes, etc., for end-user
- Storage
  - Physical record structure
  - Logical–physical mapping
  - Physical storage device assignments
- Security/access
  - Assign passwords
  - Assign lock/key
  - Modify passwords/keys
  - Log
  - Encrypt
  - Modify

- Retrieval
  - Search strategies
- Statistics
  - Access
  - Frequency of processing
  - Spare use
  - User utilization
  - Response time
- Operational procedures design
  - Access to database
  - Access for testing
  - Interfaces
  - Testing system

Monitoring
- Data quality/validity
- Performance
- Efficiency
- Cost
- Use/utilization
- Security/privacy
- Audit
- Compliance
  - Standards
  - Procedures

Other functions
- Liaison/communications with:
  - End-users
  - Analyst/programmers
- Training on database
- Consulting on file design
- Handling "knowledge" in addition to data, leading to knowledge bases and KBA (knowledge based administrators)

with end-users. Persons in this job need training in database management systems, physical and logical database design, data planning, relationship modelling, data standardization, data dictionaries, data security and operating systems.

Table 4.2 lists the numerous responsibilities of the DBA. Because of the scope of these activities, most large organizations provide DBAs with a staff including data specialists and analysts experienced in public relations and liaison with users. Usually, the DBA reports to the IS department director, but some firms give the position independent status, with the DBA reporting directly to a user committee.

Technical writers

Today, computers are in the hands of many people who have no training in information technology. As a result, an increased responsibility has been placed on the developers of both hardware and software to provide clear and complete descriptions of their projects and instructions for their use. Technical writers perform this role. In addition, they document computer and clerical procedures within an organization. This documentation helps to provide continuity when personnel turnover occurs and facilitates operations, programming maintenance and audits.

A new trend is to add technical writers to systems development teams. This helps the writer gain a clear knowledge of the product. In addition, the writer's skill as a technical communicator can be used to improve the quality of the writing in systems specifications, planning documents, and analysis statements prepared by analysts and programmers.

Knowledge engineer and other systems personnel

The popularity of the expert system has highlighted the emerging position of the knowledge engineer (KE). By academic training as well as experience, a KE is one who knows how to represent knowledge and write computer programs in AI languages that can make inferences and provide end-users and corporate management with expertise as found in expert systems.

A knowledge engineer is perhaps first and foremost a computer expert well versed in AI tools and techniques, but secondly he or she must also be able to interact effectively with the human domain experts and persuade them to articulate their expertise in a precise manner. The knowledge engineer must be able to translate the human expert's decision strategies into facts and rules of the appropriate form as well as translate problems with the functioning of the computer system into a form that the human expert can evaluate, giving results that the end-user can apply with ease and confidence.

There is a temptation to identify a KE with software engineers partly because they are both involved with software development. A study by Couger and McIntype done in 1987 concluded that there is no significant difference between knowledge engineers and software engineers in terms of their perceptions of the importance of task identity, autonomy and feedback from the job; but there were some significant differences in their perception of task significance and skill variety. These two groups are often considered part of the same breed partly, perhaps, because they are both professionally educated as computer programmers and computer scientists even though their functions are somewhat different. In the early days of expert system technology, it was naïvely thought that a human domain expert could simply explain the rules behind his or her expertise and the conventional programmer could then code them into an appropriate form for the knowledge base. We now know from experience of implementing expert systems that the domain experts are not particularly expert at articulating the reasoning behind their expertise. The knowledge engineers have to "extract" information from the human experts which may involve an understanding of psychology and group dynamics.

In addition, building a KBIS (knowledge-based information system) is not like programming a mathematical function – there is typically not a correct implementation to aim for in any absolute sense. The goal is usually to reproduce (and perhaps exceed) the performance of human experts – and the best of them are never perfect, but their behaviour provides the basic data for validating a KBIS. What this means, in practice, is that KBISs are never "finished" in the conventional software sense. It is a matter of first producing a system that is good enough to satisfy a real practical need, and then of continually working on the system to continue the long-term in-use validation process as well as to improve the system's expertise.

The MS/OR professional

A KE has much in common with a management science (MS) and operations research (OR) professional since both are problem-solvers. However, the areas of interest and the professional backgrounds are somewhat different. While the KE is interested in knowledge bases as in expert systems (ES) and knowledge-based information systems (KBIS), the MS/OR person is basically concerned with mathematical and statistical business solutions, though they differ somewhat in emphasis. The MS person is more concerned with implementation and the OR person is more concerned with modelling of decision-making. Both differ from the KE because they use a 3GL (3rd generation programming language) or 4GL (4th generation programming language) for finding a solution whilst the KE uses as AI language like PROLOG or LISP.

The KE and OR/MS persons are concerned with ill-structured and semi-structured problems. By way of contrast, the IT person in transactional systems is concerned with structured systems (with "certainty") and uses a 3GL. A comparison of the IT specialist in transactional systems with the OR/MS person and the KE is shown in Table 4.3.

Table 4.3 *Comparison of IT specialist, OR/MS practitioners and the KE*

Personnel functions	IT analyst	OR/MS practitioner	Knowledge engineer
Prime problem-solving environment	■ Transactional ■ Certainty ■ Structured	■ Decision-support system ■ Probabilistic ■ Ill/semi-structured	■ Knowledge-based system ■ Uncertainty ■ Ill/semi-structured
Application orientation	■ Business	■ Business/industry ■ EIS ■ DSS	■ Knowledge-based systems
Primary functional responsibilities	■ Transactional processing	■ Modelling ■ Decision-making	■ Knowledge acquisition ■ Knowledge representation ■ Knowledge systems programming
Programming languages used	■ 3GL	■ 3GL ■ 4GL	■ 3GL ■ AI languages 　■ PROLOG 　■ LISP
Mother discipline	■ Business ■ Computing	■ OR/MS ■ Decision science	■ Computer science

Policy analyst, problem analyst, and technology watcher

With the fast-moving technology of computing, it is incumbent on all large IS departments to keep abreast with the technological changes and recognize how these changes may offer new opportunities to their organization. One organizational position that addresses this need is the *policy analyst* who identifies potential technological changes (especially in IT) that may affect the organization's policies and operations. Another position is that of the *problem analyst* who anticipates and identifies problems that can possibly be addressed by computing. These positions can be fulfilled by someone in the corporate planning department but since this can be a technical task it is often the responsibility of a technical person such as a *technology watcher*. Sometimes, watching technology is assigned to the information centre.

Manager of Technology (MOT)

The importance of technology for IT watching and technology itself is reflected in the emergence of the position of the MOT, Manager of Technology. The MOT in some cases replaces the CIO (Chief Information Officer) and in some cases supervises the CIO along with other technologies.

Chief Information Officer (CIO)

A Manager of Technology for computing is sometimes called the CIO (Chief Information Officer). The position is being introduced in organizations where information plays a key role. In such organizations, the CIO is a senior vice president who acts as an information resource representative and computer technology adviser to the CEO (Chief Executive Officer) and other members of an Executive Board.

The job of the CIO is sometimes a staff position and should then best be called a technology facilitator. Such CIOs (and some MOTs) act as advisers and coordinators, relying on their ability to express and sell ideas to peers and subordinates to get things done. MOTs have a good technical background in computing and like the CIO have a good knowledge of the industry, and have management experience. The exact role will differ between one organization to the next, but the key functions that usually fall under their jurisdiction are information processing, office automation, communication and sometimes systems planning. A desirable profile of a CIO and MOT that will add value to IT are as follows:

Competencies

- Has IT knowledge
- Is a good communicator
- Is a facilitator
- Can act as a consultant

Experience

- Has been a manager in IS/IT

Behavioural pattern

- Is open-minded
- Is comfortable being a change-agent
- Is loyal to the corporation
- Is comfortable not getting compliments but only blame

- Can take a "global" view

Motivation
- Is goal-oriented
- Is idea-oriented
- Is systems-oriented

End-users

The end-user has gained great recognition (as well as great respectability) with the emergence of the expert system which makes a clear distinction between the interface for the end-user and the development interface for the system developer. The end-user is no longer the passive receiver of information dished out by the system. Instead, the end-user now can confront the system and demand an explanation or justification of what the system does.

This recognition of the end-user is partly the consequences of technological development like the robust PC (personal computer) and distributed processing. It is also the result of the end-user becoming more computer-literate, more willing to participate in computer processing and more able to manage computing resources. The objective of an information system should be to offer the end-user a system that is not only end-user friendly (from the point of view of ergonomics and human factors) but also a system that is understandable and credible.

Another evolution for the end-user is the transfer of responsibility from the computer professional to the end-user. An important reason for this shift to the end-user (and to end-user computing) is the desire for autonomy on the part of the end-user and a release from the "tyranny" of the computer kingdom which has resulted in many delays in the development and much "noise" in the development process. By assuming the responsibility, the end-user has nobody to blame but himself (or herself), and hence must be knowledgeable and literate in computing before taking such a responsibility in an information system environment. The shift to the end-user is actually an evolving process in the responsibilities of computing – as shown in Figure 4.3.

Figure 4.3:
Changing responsibilities of end-users and computer departments

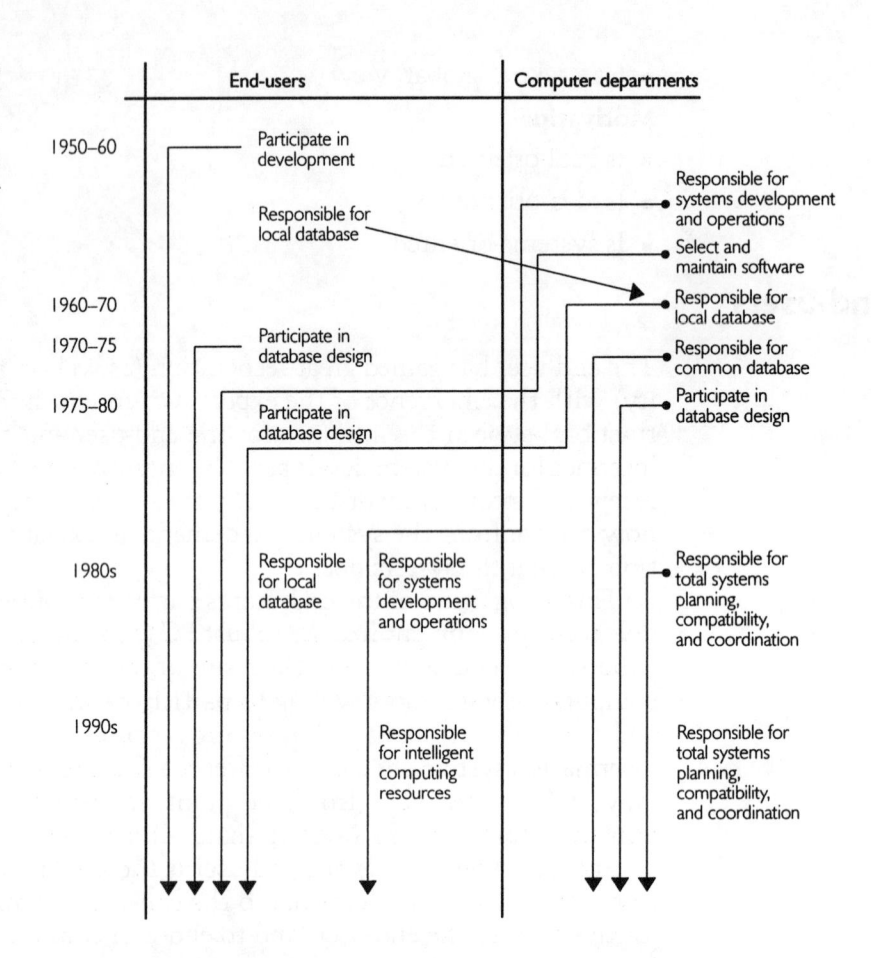

	End-users	Computer departments
1950–60	Participate in development	Responsible for systems development and operations
	Responsible for local database	Select and maintain software
1960–70		Responsible for local database
1970–75	Participate in database design	Responsible for common database
1975–80	Participate in database design	Participate in database design
1980s	Responsible for local database / Responsible for systems development and operations	Responsible for total systems planning, compatibility, and coordination
1990s	Responsible for intelligent computing resources	Responsible for total systems planning, compatibility, and coordination

Hiring

Computer personnel, especially those in professional classifications, are in demand. The shortage of qualified professionals is creating delays in the development of new computer systems and means large financial rewards for professionals who are willing to job-hop. To find experienced personnel, organizations engage in a variety of recruiting practices. Vacancies are advertised in "help wanted" sections of national newspapers, in professional journals and on the radio. Many companies send personnel representatives to recruit at universities and may also have members of their computing staff visit to explain what kinds of work they are doing. This sparks student interest and helps sow the seeds for future hiring. Other firms turn to recruitment agencies and search firms, even though the agency fees are high for a referred prospect who is subsequently hired.

Corporations with a large number of openings in many departments may hold an open-house for prospective employees. Sometimes, an IS director is looking for people with a more diverse educational background than computer science (someone with a qualification in accounting, finance, or engineering and with some computing experience is often preferred over the pure computer science graduate). The open-house setting allows the director to interview candidates who might not realize that their backgrounds qualify them for information processing positions.

Setting up booths at professional job fairs is another recruiting technique. Most people find that a fair is a non-threatening environment for job hunting and like being able to shop around and compare available jobs. Recruiters like the opportunity of meeting a large number of prospects face-to-face.

Some organizations have formalized internal employee referral services that have proven highly effective. They ask employees to inform recruiters when they learn of professional colleagues who have entered the job market. Succession planning, a form of internal recruitment, is another way to fill openings. It may be as simple as designating successors to key positions, or it can encompass detailed career planning and career ladders.

Because there are seldom enough qualified job applicants in computing, firms may have to hire inexperienced programmers and analysts or train people to fill openings. Unfortunately, predicting aptitude or potential is difficult for many computing positions. A few multiple-choice tests for programmers have been developed, but those in existence are used so often that applicants in the job market will probably be given the same test over and over. Before applying to firms of their choice, many try to gain experience with the test by first interviewing with companies low in their preference list. To make testing effective, a battery of tests is needed, or a large database of questions should be prepared from which a test can be generated at random.

As a result of the demand for qualified IT personnel and the shortage of suitable candidates, the already high salaries in IS departments are constantly rising. Personnel officers must guard against hiring new, inexperienced employees at a higher rate than the salary received by employees on the same job that were hired earlier. Compression, the reduction of salary differentials because of inflation, can also be the source of employee dissatisfaction if new employees are hired at high rates of pay. Salaries should synchronize so that employees who change to other occupational ladders (switching from operator to programmer, for example) do not experience loss of pay.

Sometimes, a fringe benefit package that will attract applicants is negotiated, or an appealing career path or promotion schedule is offered. Competition for applicants may be so keen that companies may even give bounties to employees who succeed in enticing (raiding) experienced IT personnel from competitors or other firms, although most managers consider this practice unethical.

Turnover

Because of the lack of qualified personnel in job markets, turnover is a major concern of IS directors. They try to create a work environment in their departments that will encourage employees to remain on the payroll. Research which tries to identify positive and negative motivational factors in the workplace is of great interest to them.

Although many studies have been done on employee motivation in the past, the question that needs to be addressed is whether IT personnel are different form other groups in the workforce. When Jac Fitz-enz asked 1,500 computer personnel to rank a list of job "satisfiers and dissatisfiers" (criteria drawn from an earlier study by Fred Herzberg whose work is still widely referenced in industrial training), he found that achievement, possibility for growth, work itself, recognition and advancement rated highest. Salary and status were much lower in the rankings than expected.

In another study, J. Daniel Couger and R. A. Zawacki compared the attitudes of 2,500 computer employees with the findings in a survey done by J. R. Hackman and Greg Oldman, using the same diagnostic survey instrument. The two main findings of Couger and Zawacki are that analysts and programmers express a greater need for personal growth and development than the 500 other occupational groups surveyed and they express a lower social need strength (desire to interact with others) than any other job category analyzed. More recent studies agree that computer people seek personal fulfillment and growth from their work and are less motivated by money and job titles than other employee groups. In acknowledgment of such differences, corporate managers have developed strategies to motivate and reward computer professionals other than the traditional rewards of pay, title and promotion. To reduce turnover, they:

- Keep on the leading edge of technology. Most computing people prefer to create new systems than to spend their time maintaining outdated ones.
- Provide challenges. Reduce routine.

- Pay attention to the needs and desires of individual workers. (When work tools are lacking, job-hopping may follow.)
- Make sure that each employee sees that the work he or she does is used and that it plays an important role in making a product (or project) successful.
- Provide training and educational opportunities.
- Create attractive career paths that allow for individual growth.
- Work together with IT staff to develop equitable ways to measure and evaluate performance.
- Establish informal lines of communication with coworkers and management.
- Decentralize the company's structure to allow for more individual autonomy and decision-making on the job.
- Recognize and reward contributions. (When a cash bonus or promotion is not appropriate, how about two tickets to a theatre show, a posh dinner, or a four-day weekend?)
- Involve employees in planning. This instills a commitment on the part of the employee to make the plans work.
- Provide work that increases the number of skills used on the job.
- Rotate unpopular assignments, such as systems maintenance.
- Move people from project to project to keep them from getting bored.
- Institute flexible working hours. Explore telecommuting.
- Offer stock-purchase plans or profit sharing as long-term incentives.

Of course, good personnel administration is also needed, the features of which are found in general business texts and will not be repeated here.

Career development

Since computer personnel place a high value on professional development, a computing facility should offer employees career paths that progress in responsibility, authority and compensation. These paths should allow employees to move from any position laterally or upward in the hierarchy of the IS department. (The possibility of a career track for technical employees that does not necessarily lead to promotion into management should be considered. Many IT specialists lack the interest in and aptitude for management.) The pipeline concept has been adopted by many firms: they encourage employees to prepare themselves for higher-level jobs and give employees first consideration for positions as they open up.

Training

Many computer departments sponsor training programmers to provide employees with the background knowledge, skills, and up-to-date information needed to support the firm's hardware and software. The programmes may also be designed to promote career development of personnel. The justification for the expense of the career programmes is that they help reduce turnover, improve productivity, instill cooperation and loyalty to the firm, attract applicants, and also help retrain at less cost than firing/hiring when new computer applications upset the job structure of the firm.

Table 4.4 *Sample training status report*

Name	Karen Dallenback
Current title	Programmer
Manager's name	Marion Latch
Interests	Working with people
Personal dislikes	Documentation
Future job	Systems analyst
Training needs	
Internal	Courses on systems analysis
	Basic course in accounting
	Assignment to development projects – especially accounting-oriented projects
External	Computer auditing
Other recommendations	Courses on DBMS
Target date of achievement	1999
Last date of update	5/2/97
Date of run	12/6/97

The approaches used by corporations in training IT personnel are much the same as those used to train employees in other departments of a firm. Programmes range from on-the-job training, briefings and seminars to course work that rivals degree programmes at many universities. Many software houses and manufacturers of hardware provide training materials, such as programmed instructions that come in manuals or packages for a terminal or PC. The primary advantages of computer-based training over formal classwork is that the course is self-paced and can be scheduled at that employee's convenience. (Unfortunately, many people lack the self-discipline required to take a course of this nature.) Vendors may also sponsor training programmes of their own at reasonable cost for their corporate clients.

Some firms organize training by setting up an educational matrix that identifies groups of employees and courses needed by those groups, scheduling courses on the basis of the matrix. Other firms build courses around jobs, scheduling courses needed for becoming a programmer or manager, for example. Still others provide counselling to employees, customizing the training for individual career development. Table 4.4 shows a sample training status report of one employee under such a programme. The company draws up a list of training needs prepared from the status reports and then plans and schedules courses accordingly.

Although training based on individual needs is expensive, it may prove the solution to firms otherwise unable to fill openings due to the low supply of, and high demand for, qualified IT personnel. Also, such training may be the only way to get needed specialists, such as employees trained in computer-aided design or in languages such as APT that are used in numerical control.

Technostress

Before closing this chapter, a few words are in order on the impact of stress (mental, emotional or physical tension) on workers in computer-related professions. Although moderate levels of stress can motivate and challenge, the negative effects of stress are becoming increasingly apparent in the computing field. Too often, stress is associated with low morale, decreased efficiency, hair-trigger tempers, ulcers, heart disease, nervous conditions, neuroses and job-hopping.

Some stress can be attributed to physical discomforts in a computer environment. For example, eyestrain may result form screen flicker or from terminal glare. Backache may be triggered by poorly designed or positioned equipment. Many people are sensitive to the cold temperatures of computer installations and to the loud noise of may peripherals, such as high-speed printers.

Other stress factors are attributed to the fast pace of the computer industry. Innovative products and technologies are continually emerging; IT professionals must keep abreast of advances in the field and adapt to them. Frequently, new procedures must be learned and new hardware mastered. The scope of computer jobs has to be altered and information processing departments reorganized. The tension that accompanies such change is often compounded by unrealistic management and user demands, heavy workloads, and backlog pressures. Furthermore, many computer installations are run in a day-to-day crisis mode. Technostress, a "disease that results when the delicate balance between people and computers is violated", may also result from inadvertent disk erasure, system breakdown, slow response time, or similar frustrations associated with computer use.

An important role of management in a computerized organization is to identify the causes of stress and to initiate programmes that will reduce it. For example, planning can help minimize strain during periods of heavy workload. Contingency planning and well-tested recovery procedures can lessen turmoil during and following system breakdown, while careful planning for project development should prevent unrealistic time schedules. It is no longer uncommon for firms to use the services of industrial psychologists and psychotherapists when planning social structures to relieve strain in the workplace.

Many companies also help employees learn how to alleviate stress. (For stress symptoms, see Table 4.5).

Table 4.5 *Stress signs*[†]

Rapid breathing
Heart rate increase
Nervousness and tiredness
Energy level lower or higher than usual
Headaches
Pain or irritation in neck, jaw, lower back, or outer body regions
General tension of body muscles
Changes in sleeping and eating patterns
Feeling of fear, anger and sadness
Circular thought processes
Excessive preoccupation with a single problem or situation

[†] Although the listed symptoms may occur when people are in stressful situations, no single sign is a good stress indicator. Consider the context in which these signs occur and remember that the presence of injury or disease may cause many of these same signs.

Source: *National Employee Services and Recreation Association.*

They offer seminars in stress control that teach time management techniques and physical remedies, such as special exercises. At career workshops, employees may play-act stressful situations and be counselled on ways to cope with job tensions. Since exercise is a good way to relax, firms may provide recreational facilities for their employees and sponsor sports teams.

The first step in alleviating computer-related stress is to acknowledge that the problem exists. Rather than debate whether information processing is more stressful than other professions, the focus should be on planning programmes to control and alleviate pressures associated with computer use

Summary and conclusions

In the 1950s, when firms first introduced computing, a single employee may have acted as a programmer, analyst and operator. As computing grew, more positions were added to computing departments. This is graphically portrayed in Figure 4.4.

Figure 4.4:
Correlation of temporal and size evolution in computing personnel configurations

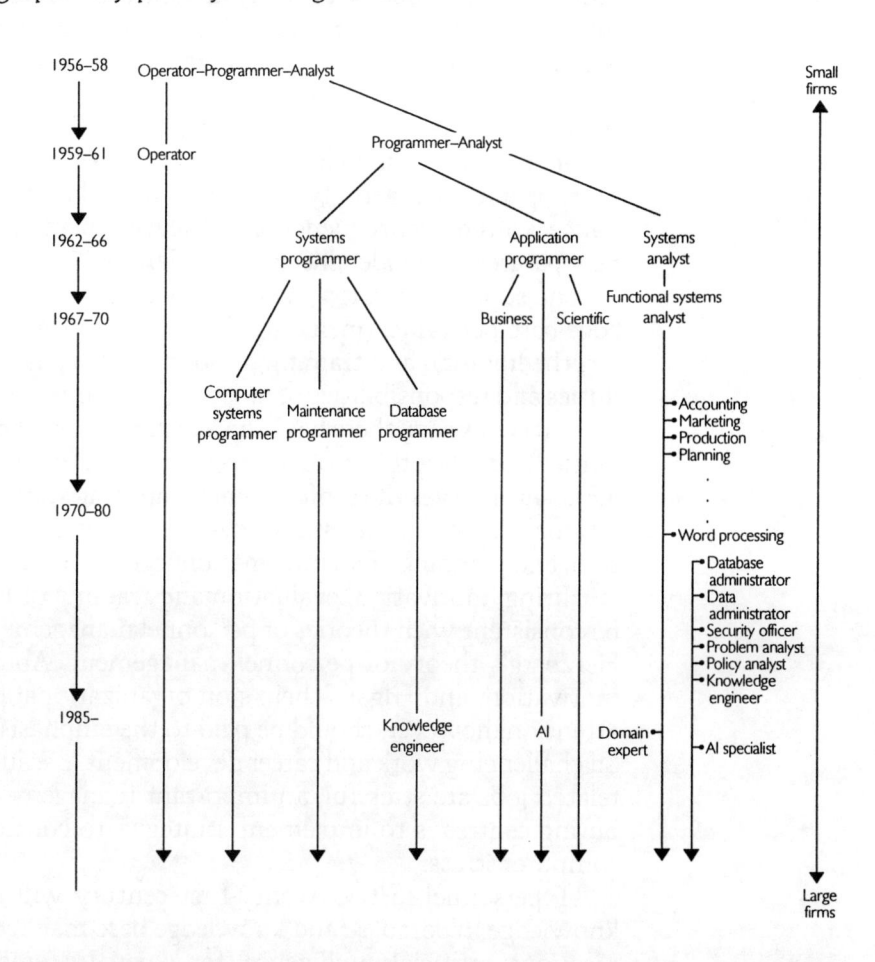

Note that the temporal evolution of computing corresponds with growth in firm size and that some new jobs were introduced in the

Chapter 4: Computer Personnel   85

1970s and 1980s. These include database administrator, security officer, word processing specialists, problem analysts (who might be compared to earlier time-and-motion experts tracing back to Taylor), and policy analysts (who evaluate information processing input and output for policy implications). Yet companies and departments with limited electronic processing equipment today may still retain the computing structures of the 1950s, consolidating operations, programming and analysis.

Computer personnel can be grouped into at least three basic categories: systems development, operations and support, leaving planning to perhaps the corporate planning department. The systems development group consists mostly of analysts and programmers concerned with information systems projects. Operations concern daily production activities. Maintenance programmers, production personnel, and operations often fall into this category, though this may vary. For example, maintenance programmers may report to the systems development department because maintenance is more of a developmental, rather than operational, activity. However, it could be argued that maintenance is often a consequence of bad development and hence they should be separate to provide "checks and balances".

The support function includes systems programmers, data/knowledge base personnel (including the DBA), security and standards officers, the librarian and training personnel. This chapter has outlined the duties and responsibilities of most of these employees.

In recent years, there has been a distinct shift of duties and responsibilities from the professional computing staff to the end-user (see Figure 4.3). This relieves the professional computing staff of some of their traditional responsibilities and allows them to spend more time on integration, and planning of an information infrastructure for the firm.

Hiring, motivation, evaluation and training of IT personnel should be consistent with theories of personnel management, such as the Fred Herzberg's theory of personnel management, Abraham Maslow's on motivation, and Edgar Schein's on organizational psychology. Special attention, however, should be paid to the emphasis IT personnel place on challenging work and career development. Because many computer-related jobs are stressful, an important management concern in computing centres is to implement strategies to control job tensions and computer stress.

IT personnel in the twenty-first century will need the skills and knowledge in database and knowledge base management, telecommunications, artificial intelligence (for expert systems, image processing, voice processing and natural language processing), fourth generation programming languages, and ergonomics (including human factors) – to name just a few areas where new technology relevant to information systems is being introduced. This need will exacerbate shortages of qualified personnel, although increased levels of computer literacy in schools and universities should lead to more people entering the computer field. Unions for computer personnel may well be in the offing, demanding higher salaries, shorter workweeks and more employee participation in job-related decisions. Management must therefore be constantly watching for such changes as well as for changing satisficers and dissatisficers for computer personnel. Management must also recognize factors that lead to success and failure of information systems in order to ensure relevance, effectiveness, and efficiency of the organization using information systems. Managing an IS/IT department in the future should be quite a challenge.

Some of the problems and issues mentioned above will be discussed later in this book. One of these issues is the overseeing and oversight of management of computing. This is the subject of our next chapter.

Case 4.1: Personnel for XCON

The model for development personnel for the expert system XCON reflected a broad perspective of involvement. It is a model of functions not individuals and with each individual playing one or more roles. The roles played were:

- The champion.
- The sponsor.
- The program manager.
- The technical team.
- The knowledge engineer.
- The software systems integration engineer.
- The domain experts.
- The end-users.

The integration of XCON into the manufacturing process at DEC was achieved by people with no previous experience of developing expert systems. DEC had to employ personnel from outside the company despite the fact that DEC is a computer company and presumably many different sorts of computer technologists were on hand. Outside personnel commentators and DEC itself were quite surprised by the need to set up a support group of knowledge engineers – people with expertise that was significantly different to that which they already had available.

There was a formal training program to ensure a supply of qualified AI engineers to maintain their AI systems.

Students are first given a fourteen-week introductory course in AI, which is taught by both DEC personnel and university AI researchers. They then enter a nine-month apprenticeship in building expert systems at either a university or a DEC AI group. The aim of this program is not to produce AI researchers, but rather to provide a pool of people familiar with AI who can support the systems DEC develops.

Source: Stephen Polit (1985). "R1 and Beyond: The Technology Transfer at DEC", *AI Magazine*, vol. 5, no. 4 (Winter 1985).

This article (as well as the other articles on R1 by McDermott and Barchant and McDermott) is printed in Robert Engelmore, (Ed.). *Readings from the AI Magazine*, Volumes 1–5, 1980–1985, Menlo Park: American Association of Artificial Intelligence, 1988, pp. 635–8.

Case 4.2: Technical education at the Bank of Boston

The Bank of Boston has around 1000 people working for their information system's operations and development. Their technical education programme includes over 40 course offerings where individuals can learn at their own pace using a PC or Macintosh computer, video or audio, and self-instructional manuals. They also offer formal lecture courses in their educational centre that has multiple conference rooms, 3 fully equipped PC classrooms and four self-study learning carrels. The strategic approach to technical training includes:

- A commitment from top management.
- A long-range vision.
- An educational plan that links IT to long-range business plans.
- Education of both IT and non-IT personnel.
- A commitment that does not waver in tough economic times.
- An education plan that is linked to corporate career paths.

Source: *I/S Analyzer*, vol. 30, no. 9, (September 1992).

Case 4.3: Training at Abbey National

Abbey National believes that company success depends on a well-rounded, well trained staff. Indeed, training is at the very heart of company strategy, says Julian Wakely, manager of the firm's distance learning group. Included in the contract of every member is a clause stating that the employee will receive training.

Recently, the company began the process of installing a new Olivetti financial system in its 687 branches. Managers and staff members of each branch are being sent on a three-day seminar which begins with a video to introduce the new system, followed by hands-on tutorials. A supplementary computer-based training package, written by Mr. Wakely's department, is available for use once back at local branches. (Each branch has one terminal available at all times for staff training. Mr. Wakely's department sends out 2,000 copies of training packages when new applications are introduced.) In addition, training programmes are embedded in new systems to serve as help tutorials on the job.

Source: *Which Computer?*, vol. 15, no. 5 (May 1991), p. 72.

Supplement 4.1: Ways to reduce stress for IT personnel

- Keep in touch with end-users. Nip problems in the bud.
- Be open to change. Accept the fact that nothing in an IT department stays the same for very long.
- Remember that you are not a solo act. Use support resources that the IT department offers.
- Accentuate the positive. Some pressure can add colour and excitement to your work.
- Realize that you've got plenty of company. Long and late hours are found in other professions.
- Get more training if you find yourself falling behind. In IT, you must upgrade and upgrade all the time.
- Plan your career. Explore other career options if you fear being "burned-out".
- Look for the "right" company. Make sure that the corporate culture matches your personality.
- Learn to play politics. Just doing a good technical job is not enough. You must develop good working relationships with management and end-users.

References

Couger, D. and R. A. Zwacki. (1980). *Motivating and Managing Computer Personnel*, New York: John Wiley & Sons.

References

Das, Amit and Shobha Das. (1993). "Supporting Diversity in Technology: The Role of MIS Managers." Proceedings of the International Conference on Information Systems, pp. 315–320.

Davies, J. Eric. (1990). "Professional Development and the Institute of Information Scientists." *Journal of Information Science*, vol. 16, no. 6, pp. 369–79.

Feeny, David F., Brian R. Edwards, and Keppel M. Simpson. (1992). "Understanding the CEC/CIO Relationship." *MIS Quarterly*, vol. 16, no. 4 (December), pp. 435–48.

Fougere, Kenneth T. (1991). "Role of the Systems Analysts as Change Agents." *Journal of Systems Management*, vol. 24, no. 11 (November), pp. 6–9.

Grover, Varun, Seung-Ryut Jeong, William Kettinger, and Choong C. Lee. (1993). "The Chief Information Officer." *Journal of Management Information Systems*, vol. 10, no. 2 (Fall, 1993), pp. 107–130.

Igharia, Magid and Jeffrey H. Greenhaus. (1992). "The Career Advancement Prospects of Managers and Professionals: Are MIS Employees Different?" *Decision Sciences*, vol. 23, no. 2 (March/April), pp. 478–99.

McLean, Epharaim R., Stanley J. Smits and John R. Tanner. (1991). "Managing new MIS Professional." *Information and Management*, vol. 20, no. 4 (1991), pp. 257–63.

McCusker, Tom. (1990). "Why Business Analysts are Indispensable to IS." *Datamation*, vol. 36, no. 2 (January 15), pp. 76–8.

Morrison, Mike, Joline Morrison, Olivia R. Liu Sheng and Kunihigo Higa. (1992). "Environment Selection, Training, and Implementation in High-Level Expert Systems Environments: Experiences and Guidelines." *Journal of Systems Software*, vol. 19, no. 2 (October), pp. 147–52.

Stokes. Jr., Stewart L. (1991). "The New IS Manger for the 1990s." *Information Systems Management*, vol. 8, no. 1 (Winter), pp. 44–50.

Swanson, N. E., W.R. Cornette and N. K. Keith. (1991). "Dogmatism and Systems Development Personnel Performance." *Decision Sciences*, vol. 22, no. 4 (September/October), pp. 911–922.

Trauth, Eileen M. (1993). "The IS Expectation Gap: Industry Expectations Versus Academic Preparation." *MIS Quarterly*, vol. 17, no. 3 (September), pp. 293–307.

Wood–Harper, A. T. *et al.* (1996). "How we Profess: The Ethical Systems Analyst." *Communications of the ACM*, vol. 39, no. 3 (March), pp. 69–77.

5 Oversight of Computing

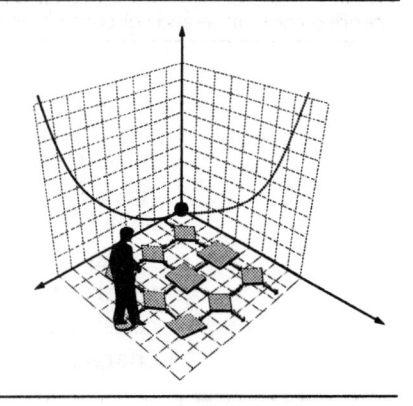

> All the time the Guard was looking for her, first
> through a telescope, then through a microscope, and then
> through an opera-glass. At last he said,
> "You are travelling the wrong way"
>
> Lewis Carroll, *Through the Looking-Glass*

Introduction

Computer departments have often been called "a business within a business". But for reasons described in this chapter, they are under the direction of corporate management. User departments also exercise a measure of control over computer departments through their representatives on steering committees and project development teams. The sections that follow will describe the many ways in which activities of computer departments are subject to supervision and how steering committees, top management, users and computer department directors interact in their oversight roles.

Each firm has a unique environment. Although this chapter describes how the *oversight function* is typically carried out, companies vary considerably regarding supervisory practices.

A business within a business

Within the organizational framework of a firm, a computer department is merely one of many departments. In structure, however, it resembles an independent business. Indeed, the department can be compared to a manufacturing concern, since it operates as a job shop (in batch mode) or a continuous-production shop (real-time processing) to provide a product (information). There is a correlation in specific activities as well, as shown in Table 5.1. For example, facilities planning in manufacturing could be compared to computer configuration and network planning, tooling might be compared to programming, and a product line resembles the department's applications portfolio. The primary difference is product disposal: computer departments do not have to rely on market mechanisms for pricing or selling. Their product is often for a captive market (when sold to other departments in the company) or considered as a service when provided to user departments without charge.

Table 5.1 *Parallel computer centre and manufacturing business activities*

Manufacturing business	Information processing centre
Product planning	Information systems planning
Facilities planning	Computer configuration and network planning
Market research	Computing demand forecasting
Product research	Keeping abreast with computer technology
Market development	User education
Product design	Systems design
Problem analysis	Systems analysis
Tooling	Programming
Production scheduling	Job scheduling
Production	Computing and operations
Production control	Production/operations control
Inventory control	Supplies inventory
Quality control	Input/output and information quality control
Consumer survey	User satisfaction survey
Consumer services liaison	User liaison
Personnel management	Personnel management
Administration	Administration
Product for sale	Information (sold or as a service)
Product line strategy	Applications development strategy
Product cost analysis	Applications project estimation
Pricing policy	Charge policy

Nevertheless, computer departments do seek to provide a product that is competitive with outside information processing centres. To do so, they must be managed with efficiency and effectiveness. Usually, a steering committee plays an oversight role.

Steering committee and subcommittees

A *steering committee* might be considered a board of directors for computing: it ensures that computing strategy is in line with corporate strategic planning objectives. That is, the steering committee usually establishes corporate policy toward information systems, makes long- and short-range plans for the computer department, sets data processing (IT) priorities, and allocates computing resources. It may also set standards and performance levels; schedule, monitor, and control operations; approve acquisitions; evaluate interfunctional applications; and resolve conflicts concerning user (as well as end-user) needs.

See Table 5.2 for a summary of the responsibilities of a typical steering committee. These functions can be classified in five general areas:

- *Direction setting* – links corporate strategy with computer strategy.
- *Rationing* – reconciles the commitment of corporate resources to information systems with commitments to other business activities.
- *Structuring* – settles the centralization versus decentralization issue and charters various organizational units.
- *Staffing* – selects top computer managers.
- *Advising and auditing* – assists in problem solving and checks to ensure that the department's activities are on track.

Top management should be represented on steering committees, as should management representatives from user groups. Sometimes, consultants will be added to a committee to ensure a balance between technically oriented members and those knowledgeable about the goals, objectives, and policies of the organization.

A balance between line and staff representatives is also advisable, as is a balance between planners, production personnel, and individuals from accounting and finance. With such representation, committees become a forum for computer management and user departments to express their views, air their problems, and reconcile their differences with regard to information systems.

Table 5.2 *Functions of a typical steering committee*

- Establishes corporate policy for information systems
- Formulates strategy to reach corporate objectives
- Assures coordination of information systems policy with corporate goals, objectives, and policies
- Approves strategic, tactical, long- and short-range plans
- Recommends to top management the allocation of resources (budgetary decisions)
- Designs organizational structure to ensure effective use of computers within the company

Chapter 5: Oversight of Computing

Table 5.2 *Functions of a typical steering committee (continued)*

- Evaluates and approves proposals for resource acquisition and development of projects
- Reviews and monitors milestones of major development projects
- Establishes criteria and levels of performance for computing operations
- Establishes evaluation procedures
- Monitors and controls operations and schedules
- Resolves and arbitrates conflicts on priorities and schedules
- Formulates standards, guidelines, and constraints for both development and operations
- Allocates scarce resources
- Exercises funding discipline over major expenditures
- Oversees staffing
- Provides communication link between computer centre and corporate management
- Provides forum for feedback from users

Some steering committees are more successful than others. (Many data processing mangers consider them bureaucratic nonsense, rubber-stamp committees of little value.) Those that function effectively do so because they involve senior management as well as EDP personnel and users. Indeed, most steering committees today are chaired by a corporate manager, and it is probable that as information technology becomes more intertwined with corporate strategy, the trend toward top management chairmanship will continue. Another characteristic of successful steering committees is that they make long-range plans instead of approving projects singly. Furthermore, they involve users in project planning and require them to justify their requests for information services.

According to some observers and practitioners, steering committees that meet too frequently get bogged down in details and find that they do not have enough knowledge to deal with the issues. Quarterly meetings that focus on strategic issues work best. The ideal committee size seems to range between 5 and 10 members. Larger committees often result in one-way communications, not an open discussion of problems.

Organizations with a small computing facility may find that a single steering committee suffices. But organizations with large computer departments that offer complex services will undoubtedly require a hierarchy of lower-level steering committees. For example, a project review committee may be given responsibility for project development, while a tactical steering committee has responsibility for operations.

Other common subcommittees and their reporting units are listed in Table 5.3.

Table 5.3 *List of committees and their reporting units*

Committee	Responsible to:
■ *Standing committees*	
▪ Steering committee	Top management
▪ Tactical steering committee ▪ Operating committee ▪ User's committee for operations ▪ Project priority committee (for development, maintenance, and redevelopment) ▪ Resource planning committee	Steering committee
▪ Database committee	Steering committee or director of systems
■ *Ad hoc committees*	
▪ Resource selection committee • Hardware committee • Software committee ▪ Resource acquisition and implementation committee ▪ Security advisory committee ▪ Privacy advisory committee ▪ Control advisory committee	Steering committee
▪ Project team	Project manager and project review committee

The function of standing committees differs from that of *ad hoc* committees, which are created to solve an immediate problem, then dissolved after a solution is reached. The former have ongoing responsibilities.

At times, the steering committee may act as a crisis centre. Ideally, however, problems should be brought to the attention of the committee before reaching crisis proportions. Computing activities should be constantly monitored by steering subcommittees. Feedback and control systems (such as exception reporting) should alert committee members to problems. In addition, the Computer Director has the responsibility of bringing problems to the committee before they get out of hand.

Oversight role of top management

Let us now focus on *senior management oversight* of computer departments. As explained in the preceding section, representatives from senior management serve on steering committees. Although user representatives and EDP (IT) personnel are also on the committees, two factors add weight to management's importance: (1) usually, the chair is drawn from senior management and (2) corporate management oversees the steering committees themselves. That is, the function of steering committees is decided by corporate managers, and they are the people who appoint committee members in the first place.

Figure 5.1:
Management's oversight role in development

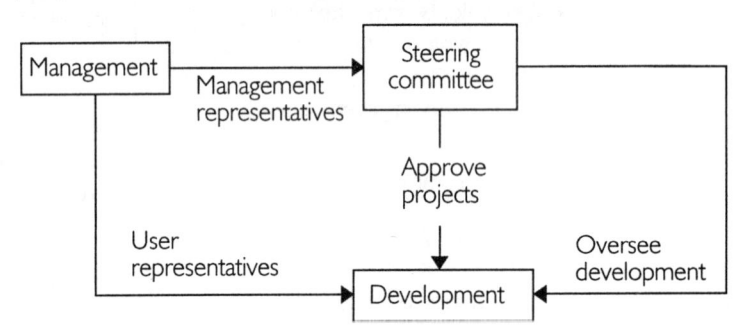

Since corporate managers are also users of information systems, representatives from the top echelons of the firm participate in the development activities of many projects. Managers, for example, as future systems users, will participate in feasibility studies and help draw up system specifications when new applications are initiated. They will help evaluate testing to see that systems that are developed do, in fact, meet managerial needs. As illustrated in Figure 5.1, senior managers have an oversight role in computing through development team membership as well as through steering committee stewardship.

Furthermore, corporate management has budgetary control over development activities. It makes go/no-go decisions following feasibility studies, selects methods of financing projects, and approves major resource acquisitions. This can be seen in Figure 5.2, which also clarifies the relationship of top management and computer centre staff to each stage of development. With regard to daily operations, management again has multiple supervisory roles.

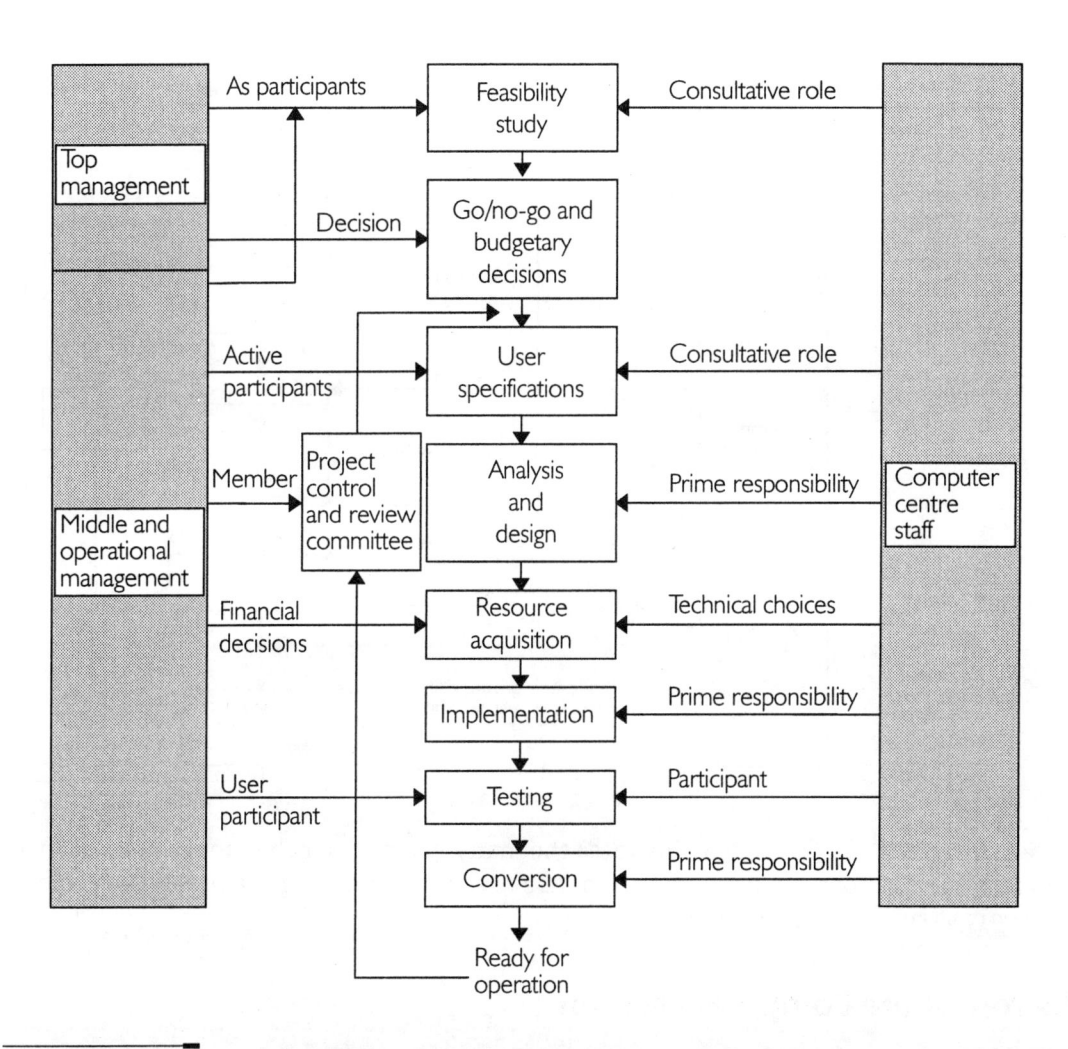

Figure 5.2: *Role of management and EDP (IT) staff at various developmental stages*

As a user of information services, management can exercise a measure of control by refusing to accept output that fails to adhere to system specifications. Through membership in the steering committee, management will appoint auditors to evaluate efficiency and effectiveness of daily operations. Approval of maintenance or redevelopment and the setting of priorities are also responsibilities of the steering committee, which gives management control over operations. Finally, management supervises the activities of a computer department through the budgetary process. Expenditure for ongoing operations require the approval of the financial officers of the firm. By holding the purse strings, top management controls operations.

Chapter 5: Oversight of Computing

The role of the Computer Director

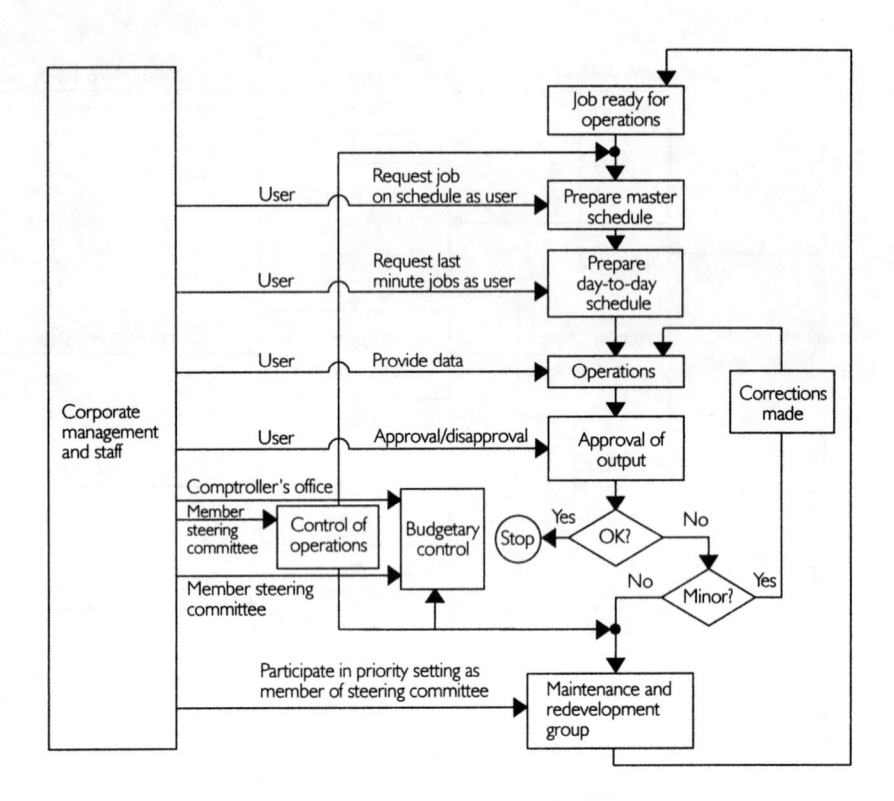

Figure 5.3: *Corporate management's role in computer operations*

Figure 5.3 illustrates the many ways in which management participates in daily operations as a user while engaging in a supervisory role at the same time.

The role of the Computer Director

The *Computer Director* (also called an IT Manager/Director) is responsible for daily operations of the computer department. In some companies with a steering committee, the Computer Director is hired/fired by the committee and may approach top management only through the committee. In others, the director is directly responsible to senior management, reporting to a vice president of information services or some similar officer.

Like other departmental managers in a firm, the Computer Director must plan departmental activities, prepare and control budgets, schedule work assignments, monitor work in progress, and select, hire, train, and evaluate personnel. The personnel roster of a computer department includes individuals with a wide range of skills: from clerks engaged in repetitive tasks and having hourly deadlines and a short-term outlook to highly trained professionals engaged in experimental systems design with long-term vision. Such diversity complicates management. So does the fact that many of the people working in high-tech fields are task-oriented, creative individuals who like working alone, dislike interruptions and small talk, and work with a sense of urgency that makes them insensitive to the status quo.

It is up to the Computer Director to establish a work environment that provides freedom of creative expression, yet promotes orderly organizational processes at the same time. The director has to command the technical respect of employees and be responsive to innovative ideas. Yet, the manager's knowledge must extend beyond technology to people, equipment resources, user relations, and budgeting and capital expenditures. At the same time, the director needs to understand the corporate environment outside of the department, be comfortable in relationships with senior management, and be knowledgeable about the industry to which the company belongs. The director should be prepared to make and stand behind a decision, willing to get involved in risky projects or play the role of a change agent.

Clearly from this list, the director needs both behavioural and technical skills. Unfortunately, many Computer Directors have been promoted from systems engineering ranks and have no managerial training other than on the job. Only recently have universities begun to add information management to their master of business administration programs.

The relative importance of behavioural and technical skills on the job is determined to some degree by the size of the applications portfolio that a Computer Director must oversee. When the portfolio is limited (a small budget and few computer employees), the director's job is more technical and less managerial. As the size and complexity of applications increases, technical tasks will be delegated to analysts and specialists: thus freeing the executive for managerial concerns associated with an enlarged staff and budget. Figure 5.4 shows that the skill requirements of a director's job are a function of portfolio size and complexity.

The position of Computer Director is very stressful and has a high turnover. This can be attributed largely to the element of risk in the job. Technical risks are run when trying to incorporate the latest computer advances in new systems. Financial risks are high due to the probability of time and cost overruns in systems development. Security of computer resources and privacy of data are vulnerable to assault, while reputation and credibility depend on user satisfaction.

Figure 5.4:
Required Computer Director skills as a function of application portfolio size

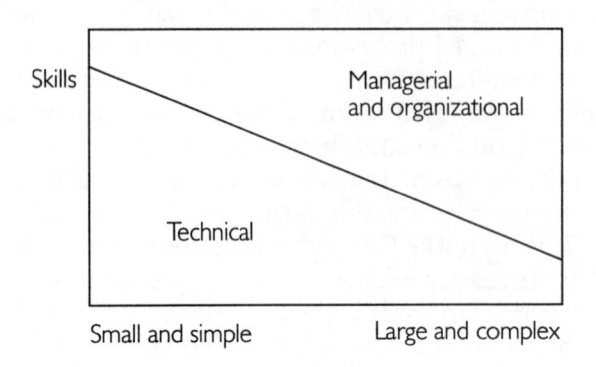

Tension in the job can also be attributed to the fact that computer technology tends to upset traditional organizational and operational patterns, sending disruptive reverberations throughout the firm. It is the Computer Director who is responsible for orchestrating the introduction of new computer applications, for setting up interface committees to interpret technology to users, and for smoothing conversion to new systems. Hostility may be exhibited toward the computer department, and toward the Computer Director in particular, by persons who resent the intrusion of computers in their work spheres.

The Computer Director cannot seek solace from other department heads, who may themselves harbour resentment against the computer department. They are piqued that computing is given favoured status, yet produces no tangible product or benefit of ascertainable market value. They are embittered that the failure rate accepted in computer projects would cost them their jobs.

A strain may also exist in the relationship between the Computer Director and corporate management. This strain is based, in part, on differences in their backgrounds, technical orientations, and objectives but can also be traced to problems in communication. Technical jargon and computer acronyms are not always understood outside the computing field. "Talking down" to senior management is also inappropriate, for management is becoming increasingly knowledgeable about computer capabilities. A genuine dialogue should be sought: corporate management sharing its vision of the firm's future, the Computer Director explaining in nontechnical terms how computer advances (such as microtechnology, telecommunications, networking, office automation, computer-aided design and manufacturing, and robots) can further corporate goals. Corporate management can help moderate the pressure on the Computer Director by being accessible for counsel and by establishing a fair approach to evaluation of the director's performance.

The new breed of computer managers

Because of the large funds involved in computer processing and the long lead time required for equipment delivery and systems development, planning has always been a major concern of Computer Directors. "What can the computer department do for you?" was the question traditionally asked of end-users. Today, however, the style of computer management is becoming more aggressive. Directors, as change agents, offer innovative ideas instead of waiting for service requests, saying: "Here is what we can do and should do for you."

The new breed of Computer Directors is more political, able to recognize power bases and win converts. Such directors are also integrators, able to merge computers, communications, and databases into effective delivery systems. But not all have the same outlook regarding the primary function of their computer departments. Some endorse the concept that computer departments should be profit centres and that users should determine what services are offered by their willingness to pay. Others view their departments as service agencies. They are less concerned with departmental profits than with developing systems to improve corporate performance. Perhaps, the ideal Computer Director would be a combination of the two: a profit-conscious, service-oriented manager.

Hierarchy and adhocracy

Hierarchy is the traditional organizational approach to direction and control. Orders pass from top to the relevant bottom level and the relevant operational information flows from the bottom levels to the top level going through the appropriate levels of supervision and control. This is a faster way to reach those directly concerned with the information they need rather than flush all in the system with all the information and let them filter what is relevant and what is irrelevant. However, in a hierarchy there is no direct lateral communication and there can be no response to unexpected changing conditions at the bottom unless there is a direction and authority from the top to act. Also, the top nodes can become information-overloaded and therefore unable to react to changing conditions or to consider enough information about certain issues that are complex and need lots of information. The bottom is relieved of responsibility of decision-making and problem solving, but those involved may feel left out and therefore be less motivated to take responsibility.

One alternative to a hierarchy is to have lateral communication and to disperse the data-filtering responsibility. Also, this alternative allows responses and actions to changed conditions at the bottom and lower levels of the hierarchy. This is what occurs in most open market systems and in an organization: it is called *adhocracy*. The term was coined in the book *The Future Shock* by Alvin Toffler:

> The organizational geography of super-industrial society can be expected to become increasingly kinetic, filled with turbulence and change. The more rapidly the environment changes, the shorter the life span of organizational forms. In administration structure, just as in architectural structure, we are moving from long term enduring temporary form, from permanence to transient. We are moving from bureaucracy to Adhocracy.
>
> *Toffler*, 1970:122–3

Adhocracy can have many interconnections. This is illustrated in Figure 5.5, where adhocracy is compared with a hierarchy of a simple structure of two levels in the middle and four nodes at the bottom.

Figure 5.5:
Hierarchy vs. adhocracy

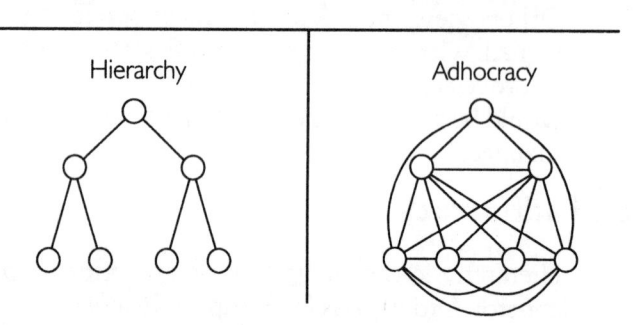

Now, imagine a realistic situation with many levels and many nodes at each level. The number of interconnections and cross currents will increase far more than linearly and soon become unmanageable. What is needed are new strategies of filtering, cooperation, and coordination among the many nodes. Fortunately, computer technology can help. It offers equipment configurations that enable quick and fast lateral communication as in the client–server configuration (to be discussed in Chapter 15).

It also offers tools to facilitate lateral communication without overloading the centre, such as e-mail (electronic mail), bulletin boards and teleconferencing. Computer networks can provide the desired information selectively and facilitate coordination and cooperation among the nodes. The nodes at the bottom are now better informed and more able to respond to changes which, in turn, results in better decisions. The decision-making and responsibility are better distributed.

The many cross-connections due to a large number of people interacting will affect productivity. Productivity rises for an increase in the number of people working together in a group but then productivity trends to drop.

The productive time, P, can be calculated by the formula:

$$P = KT\left(C - 0.0001\left\{\frac{K(K-1)}{2}\right\}\right)$$

where:

P = Productive time
K = Individual number of people working together in a team
T = Individual employee hours per work period
C = Percentage of calendar week that is productive

For T = 40 and C = 55 we calculate P for different values of K and plot them as shown in Figure 5.6. It is interesting to note that the productivity peaks around a team size of 60 and that the productive time for 20 is about the same as for 90.

Figure 5.6:
Productive hours according to team size

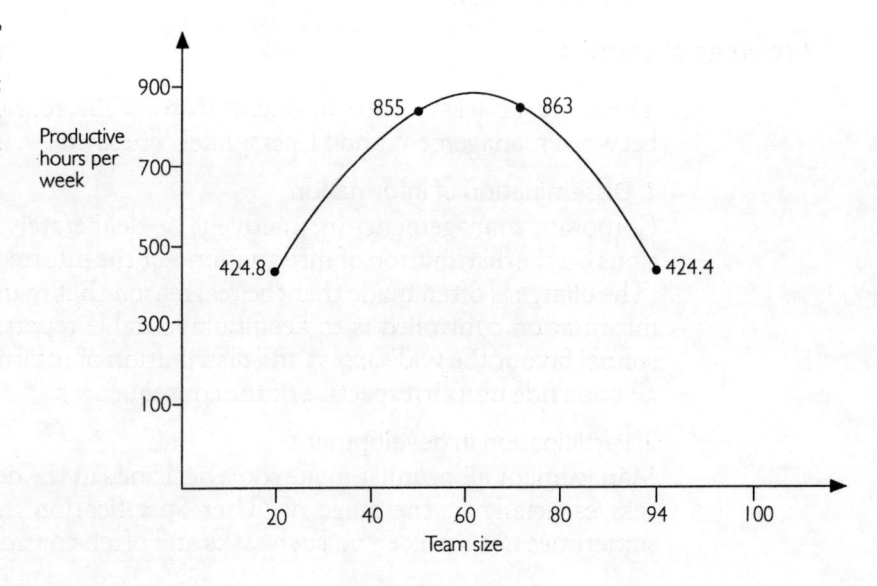

Of course the shape of the curve will vary with the type of people working together and the tasks being performed. But the peaking of productivity has been observed by many commentators in the IT field including Fred Brooks, the author of *The Mythical Man-Month* and the manager of the IBM 360 software system.

Strains between corporate management and IT professionals

Whether hierarchy or adhocracy, for corporate management to oversee IT personnel it is important that corporate management understand IT personnel and that IT personnel have confidence in corporate management to be able to perform the task of overseeing. Unfortunately, this is sometimes not the case. There is often much stress in the relationship. Part of the reason is that the two have different backgrounds. Corporate management are, generally speaking, generalists with managerial skills while the IT personnel are specialists with analytical and technical skills. Corporate management seek stability while IT personnel are committed to change. Indeed, change and motion are viewed as constants in the field of computing. From the computer specialist's point of view, stability within change is a viable concept and not a contradiction of terms. Also, corporate management may oppose change brought about by computerization because they feel threatened and may loose their jobs or have different jobs that they may not like. As a consequence, there is often tension and lack of trust if not hostility between the two groups. Often, there is also a lack of communication and a high level of frustration.

7 sources of conflict

There are at least seven different reasons for tension and conflict between management and IT personnel. These are:

1. Dissemination of information
Corporate management, instinctively or deliberately, favour restrictions on the distribution of information lest the information is misused. (The charge is often made that the real reason that management wants information controlled is to keep unfavourable reports quiet.) IT personnel favour the wide access and distribution of information (valid) to all bona fide users irrespective of the consequences.

2. Participation in development
Management alone must make some decisions in the development process especially in the stage of "User Specification". Management is sometimes not too keen on such tasks and often consider them second-

ary. If management is pressed for time, as they often are, the development responsibility is neglected. Systems personnel, facing project deadlines, make the decisions instead. This can be dangerous because computer programs can contain the rules of how a corporation is directed and controlled. Systems personnel are neither prepared for nor want to make such decisions, but when they are made by default the decision-making is implicitly delegated to IT. They want corporate management to be involved in development and take responsibility for their important role in development and not delegate it to them (knowingly or by default).

3. Time horizon

The time horizon of corporate managers in terms of computer applications is much more short-term than for IT personnel. Managers do not get their output soon enough because IT personnel are planning for the long term taking a "holistic" and integrative approach. Many of the projects take a long time and have a long gestation period. Thus, there is a certain amount of unhappiness at the pace of development.

Sometimes the data for deliverables is set too early and are not realistic. Changing them is not politically possible. As a result, IT personnel are pushed to a deadline that they cannot meet and so they cut out some of the functions to be performed. Corporate management does not always appreciate the problem but complain about the loss of functionality.

Another bone of contention in the development process concerns the user specification. For corporate management this may be a slow process of evolution which may require changes in the specification even after the user specification has been agreed upon. This is a nightmare for the analyst and programmer for it can be very disruptive to the development process since it is the basis for all applications. Besides, changes in user specification can lead to delays (and "patching" of programs) in the project completion which the corporate manager will not understand or tolerate.

4. Accountability of IT

Many of the benefits of IT are intangible such as the speed and timeliness of information that is available and of information that is available that would otherwise not be available. These benefits are not always appreciated by management as much as IT personnel would like. The benefits of IT are often illusive to corporate management. For example, integration of a data/knowledge system has advantages in the eyes of IT personnel and is sometimes very time-consuming and difficult to achieve, but is not always appreciated by corporate management.

Many a corporate manager would like IT to be a cost centre. One problem with IT being a cost centre is that the concentration is on reducing costs even if it is to the detriment of the end-user and the organization. In contrast, some IT personnel would prefer IT to be an investment and profit centre which instills a market approach to managing IT and focuses on revenues as well as costs. The IT department should then be encouraged to have its own policies and to go after additional outside tasks as long as there is unused capacity (physical and human capital).

5. Control of systems

It is often contended by corporate management (and end-users) that they must conform to the computer system rather than have the computer systems conform to corporate needs. Too often, one must do what the computer system requires even if this does not seem to be the most efficient or effective way. Corporate management contends that computer systems should bend to the needs of business and serve management, not the other way around. Computer systems should reflect the corporate management vision and needs, not what the IT personnel think that corporate management should want. Corporate management do not wish to see IT shape their wants, but rather have IT respond to their needs. IT must be in harmony or at least in step with organizational goals and objectives instead of corporate management bending to IT demands and requirements. The relationship between corporate management need not be one of master and slave, but of two parties working together for the common organizational goal fully utilizing IT's capacity and potential.

6. Evaluation of IT personnel

Resentment against corporate management is fuelled because of the manner in which performance of IT management is often judged. The evaluation is often based on budgetary and quantitative measures (budget variance, for example), and general efficiency measures that poorly reflect important performance characteristics of IT management. When embarrassing mistakes are made, IT is blamed but IT rarely gets any credit when computer systems function well. At least, this is the perception of many people in IT. The belief that their services are unappreciated and undervalued is a source of much tension that exists in their relations with corporate management.

7. Recognition of IT management

Friction between corporate management and IT management can often be attributed to the belief that corporate executive do not give IT executives the recognition or status that is their due. Rarely are IT managers included (as are other department heads) in key decisions on new products or budgets, although information processing can contribute to the decision-making and problem-solving process for such determinations. Too often, the road to executive positions is blocked for IT managers, creating a dead-end career path in the organization. Computer managers are seldom promoted to managerial echelons of the firm because corporate executives see them as computer technicians uninformed about business and the industry of the business, and in the process disregard managerial skills of IT management.

Given the reasons for tensions and mistrust that exists between the two groups, how can the relationship be improved? The first step in improving the working relationship between corporate management and IT managers is to identify and recognize the sources of friction. Only then can steps be taken to resolve misunderstandings. Although the actions taken will depend on the nature of the problems, many companies look toward educational programs for answers. Presumably, an understanding of IT (and IS – information systems) by corporate management and an understanding of management of business (and the industry it is in) will promote harmony between the two groups.

Because it is easier and faster to educate and train corporate management on computers than to educate and train technicians to acquire the prerequisites for managing a firm, most companies provide in-house educational programmes on computer technology for corporate management (including top management) sponsoring group seminars, or video programmes in their home communities. Others organize pilot studies, demonstrations, and briefings at work. Another method of keeping management technically up-to-date is to circulate selected pertinent literature.

What is needed is an intellectual (and social) bonding between corporate management and IT personnel. One approach is collocation, that is seating IT personnel full-time during a project with a corporate manager related to the project. Both parties see the same problem, and often differently. Understanding and appreciating each other's perspective can greatly contribute to a better understanding of each other's point of view. This may seem to be a relationship confined to just two people, but done many times and with different people at different levels in the organization will increase the bonding between the two groups. It also gives corporate management better appreciation of issues in IT. Some of this happens in prototyping of DSSs and EISs, but the prototyping interaction is often too short and confined to a specific function. A broader and longer exposure to each other's viewpoint is necessary.

IT should no longer be an island in the corporation. Despite the PC, which has made the corporate manager more independent of the IT technician, there is still a great deal of dependence: the dependence of IT on its corporate clientele as well as the dependence of IT for support from corporate management. There is a need for mutual understanding and integration of each other's point of view.

All of the approaches of education and collocation attempt to soothe communication between corporate management and computer personnel. When the two groups use the same vocabulary and when corporate managers have enough vocabulary and a frame of reference to understand computing, relations between the two groups generally improve. Improved relations should speed the resolution of computer-related problems and raise employee morale, leading to higher IT productivity. IT would also help identifying more acutely when computers should be used and not used. The technological approach is not a substitute for business acumen and entrepreneurial skills, but rather an enhancement of business decision-making and problem solving. The danger lies in corporates "stepping back" from involvement in IT, and not:

> Making informed decisions about IS. IS has moved into a vacuum, not out of conscious desire to grab power but to get those decisions made. As part of the process, IS has planted many of its values and beliefs within the organization. Managers need to understand that these changes will be the real impact of computerization on the organization and to ask themselves if they are really willing to pay the price for lack of involvement. If their answer is no, then they must begin to make a conscious effort to reassert business leadership in the use of IS technology.
>
> *Smith and McKeen*, 1992:63

Summary and conclusions

Computing involves a web of relationships between corporate management, end users (who are sometimes not corporate management) and computer personnel. This chapter has focused on committees that provide formal structure for interaction between these groups in the oversight of computing as shown in Figure 5.7, which diagrams a sample configuration of oversight relationships, the computer centre (or IT) director reports directly to a steering committee.

The steering committee also receives reports on performance from subcommittees that oversee developmental activities and operations. Some committees require that all computing be done in-house. Others allow end-users within the firm to request bids for jobs, placing in-house computing facilities in competition with outside service centres. These service centres may be facilities management, service bureaux or remote processing. In addition, committees may seek expert advice from consultants, vendors or peer groups in the industry. Alternatively, the committees may offer consulting for the end-users in their organization through information centres.

Figure 5.7:
Sample configuration of a steering committee and subcommittees in relation to corporate management and the computer director

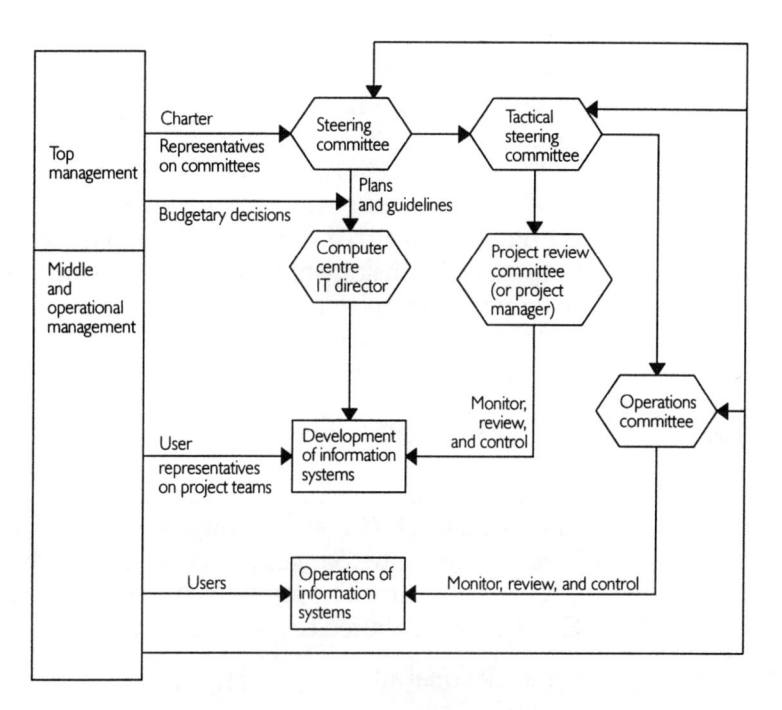

Top corporate management controls computing by charting the steering committee, making budgetary decisions, and serving with other end-users as members of the steering committee and subcommittees. Corporate management is also a receiver of computing services and so participates in development projects as a team member and critiques output, just as other end-users do.

End-users are found at all levels of an organization, from data clerks to company presidents. The steering committees and the IT director need a method of determining whether the services offered meet end-users' needs. Many firms conduct their own end-user surveys for this purpose. These surveys can be conducted using questionnaires, or through in-depth interviews, or a combination over time. In such cases, questions must be designed to avoid or at least minimize bias.

New responsibilities are continually being added to the department of IT. An expansion of the applications portfolio, increasing complexity of applications, the addition of office and factory automation, the movement towards distributed and client–server systems, all require technical expertise and business skills that the former head of EDP/IT

Chapter 5: Oversight of Computing

did not need when computing was a mere back-shop operation. The future IT director (CIO or MOT) needs to be an information manager who takes the initiative in business information planning, one who discovers opportunities (plays the roles of a problem analyst and policy analyst) for improving the effectiveness of information utilization and "sells" these options when appropriate and beneficial, to the organization.

IT directors, CIOs, and MOTs, that have demonstrated proficiency in managing computing resources have a management talent that should not be wasted. Their jobs should not be a dead-end job. This can be avoided by the organization having a career path for them that leads to corporate management.

Whatever the structure of computer personnel, they must develop information systems, the subject of the next chapter.

Case 5.1: Study of CEOs and CIOs in the UK

An in-depth interviewing of CEOs (Chief Executive Officers of corporations) and CIOs (Chief Information Officers) in 14 large organizations based in the United Kingdom was done to study the quality of the CEO/CIO relationship. The study identified the attributes of the CEO and CIO that contributed to a successful relationship. These are:

Organizational attributes

- Personal/informal executive style.
- CIO accepted as part of the corporate executive team.
- Workshops are held on strategic issues.

CEO attributes

- Background in general management or marketing.
- Orientation in change management.
- Attend IT "awareness" programs.
- Experience successful IT projects.
- Perceive IT as critical to business.
- Position IT as agent to business transformation.

CIO attributes

- Background and orientation of an analyst.
- Integrates IT with business planning.
- Accurately perceives CEO's views on business and IT.
- Profile stresses consultative leadership and creativity.

- Contributes beyond IT functions.
- Promotes IT as agent of business transformation.

Source: Feeney David F., Brian R. Edwards, and Keppel M. Simpson. (1992). "Understanding the CEO/CIO Relationship." *MIS Quarterly*, vol. 16, no. 4 (December), pp. 435–439.

Case 5.2: Oversight at a bank

In a regional bank in the US, management was dissatisfied with the bank's computer processing, as were departmental end-users within the bank. The bank officers were concerned about the data processing budget. End-user departments felt that data processing should be of greater service but weren't sure how. Computing management worried about staff turnover and how best to allocate computing resources. There was general agreement that the bank needed an organizational body to provide direction and control of computing.

The first step in setting up a guiding body was to establish objectives for such a group. It was agreed that the group would be responsible for setting data processing directions and services, and for the establishment of priorities for data processing activities and development.

As Executive Steering Committee (ESC) was then chartered. It asked a consulting firm to assist the bank in evaluating the bank's data processing. Systems maintenance and enhancements were found to be inadequate, and efficiency pressures had gone too far, resulting in damage to many systems and resources. The ESC then formulated a data processing funding evaluation strategy and established new funding directions for the bank's data processing. In time, the committee broadened its scope to include more technical oversight of data processing. The ESC has proved effective in its oversight role. One key to the committee's success is that the ESC members have developed (1) a working relationship with employees, and (2) analysis procedures that lead to consensus regarding the current status of data processing issues, and resolution of problems. They are also able to communicate this consensus in business language and business structure to bank officers.

Source: Richard Nolan (ed.). (1982). *Managing the Data Processing Function*, 2nd ed., pp. 381–3. St. Paul, Minn: West Publishing.

Case 5.3: Selection of projects by steering committee

The selection of projects to be developed determines the content and profile of the applications portfolio. Because of the importance of the selection process, it is sometimes done by a Corporate Steering Committee. A study of 92 projects selected from 32 organizations shows that such a selection does result in a strong bias of the projects chosen. The study suggests the favouring of:

- Large projects (in terms of man-hours to develop and total number of users).
- Projects with little vertical integration.
- Lower-level projects (clerical to supervisory level).
- Projects with formal proposals complete with written cost–benefit analysis.
- Projects which can demonstrate both tangible as well as intangible benefits for the organization.

Source: J. D. McKeen and Tor Guimaraes. (1985). "Selecting MIS Projects by Steering Committee." *Communications of the ACM*, vol. 28, no. 12 (December), pp. 1344–1351.

References

Boynton, Andrew C., Jacobs, Gerry C. and Robert W. Zmud. (1992). "Whose Responsibility is IT Management?" *Sloan Management Review*, vol. 33, no. 4, pp. 32–38.

Malone, Thomas and John Rockart. (1991). "Computers, Networks and the Corporation." *Scientific American*, vol. 265, no. 3 (September), pp. 128–35.

McKeen, J. D. and Tor Geimaraes. (1985). "Selecting MIS Projects by Steering Committee." *Communications of the ACM*, vol. 28, no. 12 (November), pp. 1341–51.

McLean, Epharaim R., Stanley J. Smits, and John R. Tanner. (1991). "Managing new IS Professionals." *Information & Management*, vol. 20, no. 4, pp. 257–63.

Meiklejohn, Ian. (1990). "Whole Role for Hybrid." *Management Today*, (March), pp. 137–8.

Ryan, Hugh W. (1991). "The Third Wave: User as a Producer." *Journal of Information Systems Management*, vol. 8, no. 1, pp. 71–4.

Smith, H. A. and J. D. McKeen. (1992). "Computerization and Management: A Study of Conflict and Change." *Information & Management*, vol. 22, no. 1, pp. 53–64.

Stokes, Jr., Stewart L. (1994). "Networking with a Human Face." *Information Systems Management*, vol. 11, no. 3, pp. 34–40.

Straub, Detmar W. (1996). "Partnering Roles of the IS Executive." *Information Systems Management*, vol. 13, no. 2 (Spring), pp 14–18.

Toffler, Alvin. (1970). *Future Shock*. New York: Random House.

Watson, Richard T. (1990). "Influences on the IS Manager's Perception of Key Issues: Information Scanning and the Relationship with the CEO." *MIS Quarterly*, vol. 14, no. 2 (June), pp. 217–31.

Wolman, R. (1990). "Managing Technical Professionals." *Information Center*, vol. 6 (March), pp. 9–11.

6 Development of an Information System

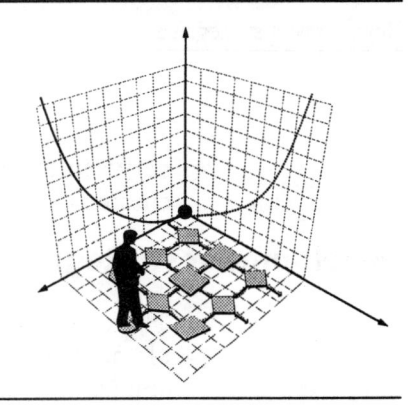

> We build systems like the Wright brothers built the airplane – build the whole thing, push it off a cliff, let it crash, and start all over again.
>
> *R. M. Graham*

> The sooner you start programming, the longer it takes to finish.
>
> H. F. Ledgard in *Programming Proverbs*.

Introduction

Development in the context of an information system is the process in which the needs of an information system are specified, the system is designed, implemented (including programming), tested, and made ready for operation.

There are two main approaches to development: one is the SDLC (systems development life cycle); and the other is through prototyping. The SDLC is appropriate for the more comprehensive information system and is the focus of this chapter. It is a set of activities that must be followed in a prescribed sequence. In contrast to an SDLC (where the activities are distinct and formally separate) prototyping has many of the activities intertwined. Thus in prototyping the design and implementation may be performed at one time or the design may evolve from a user specification that is also evolving in an interaction between the end-user and the systems analyst. Thus prototyping is very appropriate for certain subsystems and will be discussed later in the context of an appropriate application environment. In this chapter, we will focus on the SDLC which is often appropriate for the larger information system and for some subsystems. For the SDLC, we shall identify and describe its many activities and discuss the nature and importance of sequencing between them. We shall, however, start our discussion by briefly discussing the nature of an SDLC as a development strategy.

Development strategies

There are many development strategies. Some are summarized in supplements to this chapter. The earliest and most successful commercial applications are discussed as cases: SABRE, an airline reservation system and XCON, an expert system, both are benchmarks for all large commercial information systems. Comparing these methodologies we find different terms used but the same basic stages of development as in a traditional SDLC.

Therefore, we will stay with the traditional SDLC whilst recognizing that this does not preclude the possibility that components of an information system can be developed using prototyping but all within the framework of an SDLC.

SDLC for a development strategy

An overview of the development of an information system development is shown in Figure 6.1. It all looks very sequential but in reality there is much iteration and repetition amongst activities. Thus the design activity may be repeated many times before a design is agreed upon. In addition, repetition of an activity may cause reassessment of one or more previous activities. Thus one design may suggest a revised user specification or even a revised feasibility study. Such complex interaction is not shown in Figure 6.1 in order to keep it simple.

It may also be necessary to repeat an entire SDLC for an information system by using one SDLC as a demonstration prototype for other progressively more complex and comprehensive ones making the information system progressively more effective and useful. Or the repetition of an SDLC may result from redevelopment of a system after one has served its purpose and a new one is required. This spiralling of the SDLC is illustrated in Figure 6. 2. Whether spiralling or not, we have a set of main activities that will now be examined. The first important activity to be discussed is a feasibility study which follows the preparation of a systems plan.

SDLC for a development strategy

Figure 6.1:
Development of an information system (its SDLC)

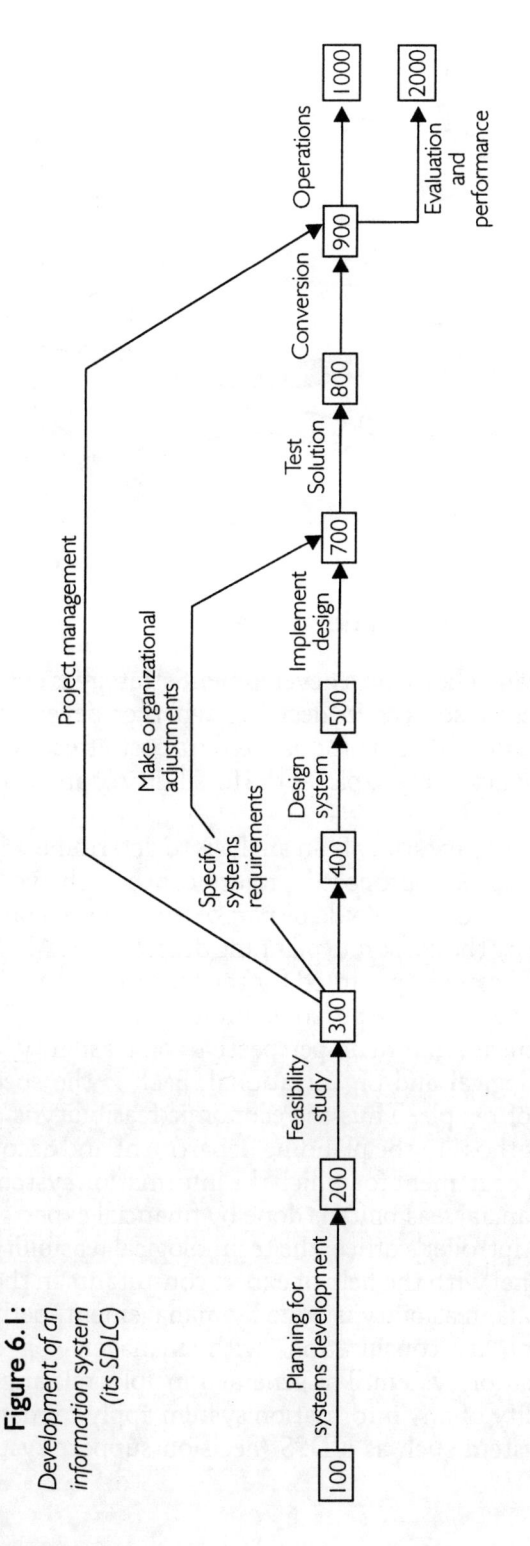

|100| Planning for systems development → |200| Feasibility study → |300| → Specify systems requirements → |400| Design system → |500| Implement design → |700| Test Solution → |800| Conversion → |900| Operations → |1000|

From 300: Make organizational adjustments → |700|

Project management: 300 → 900

|900| → Evaluation and performance → |2000|

Chapter 6: Development of an Information System 117

Figure 6.2:
Spiralling of an SDLC

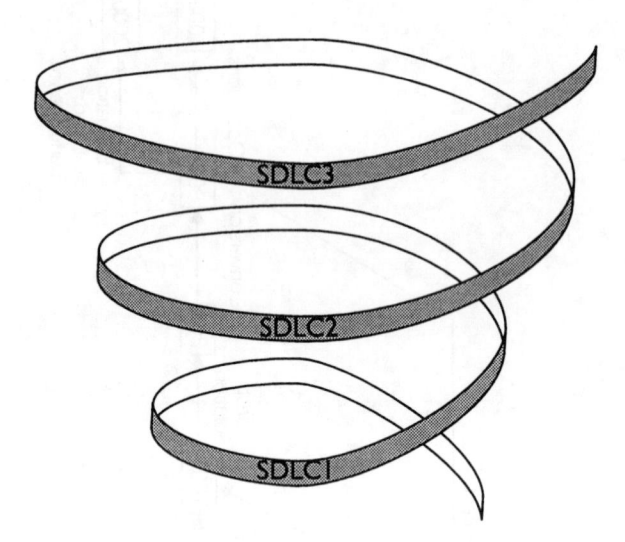

Feasibility study for an information system

Before any choice on a development strategy is contemplated, it is wise to invest resources in deciding whether development of a proposed information system promises to be a cost-effective exercise or not. This preliminary study explores the feasibility of an information system proposal.

A feasibility study is an analysis to determine whether or not desired objectives of a proposed project can be achieved within given constraints. The study could be part of the planning process and can be conducted by the corporate planning department. Alternatively, a committee in IT can be appointed for the task, consisting of management that are interested in the proposed project's results.

There are four main perspectives on feasibility: economic, financial, technological and organizational. Each is the specialty of a different group of people. Thus the economic feasibility is done by economists such as those in the planning department and accountants in the functional department for which the information system is being developed; the financial feasibility is done by financial experts and personnel from the comptroller's office; the technological feasibility is done by systems personnel with the help of expert consultants in the field; and the organizational feasibility is done by management, perhaps corporate management in consultation with managers of computing and of information system. The general principles relating to the process of the feasibility of any information system apply to many types of information system such as a DSS (decision support system), EIS (executive information system), ES (expert system), and even a subsystem like software. All these activities are summarized in Figure 6.3.

Figure 6.3: Flowchart for feasibility study

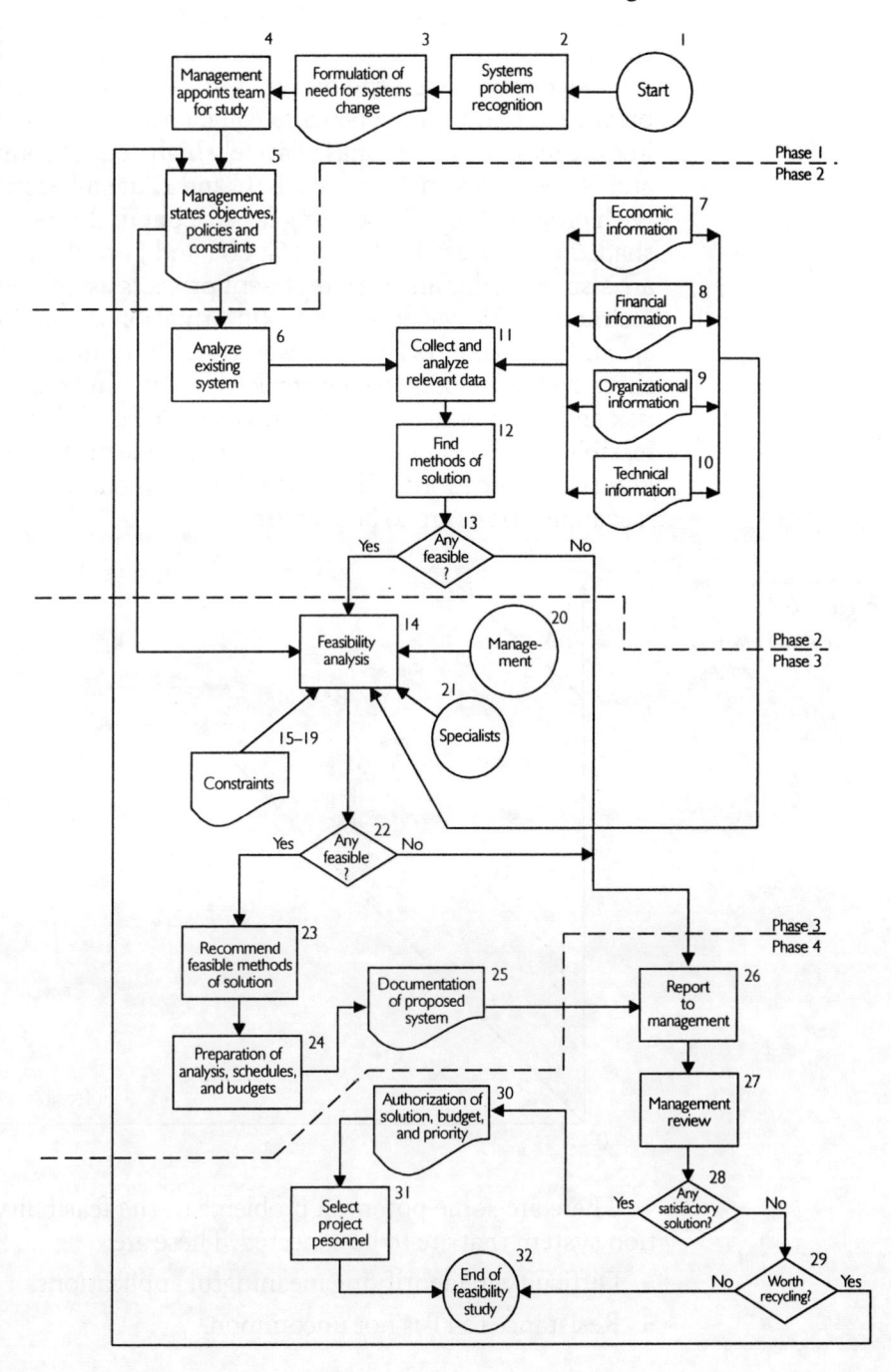

And what if there were many information system projects that were all economically feasible and there was more than one information system project that could be implemented? Then one would select those that represented least risk. This can the illustrated in Figure 6.4 where the diagonal through the origin O (dotted-dashed line) represents the breakeven point where benefits equal costs. Points above the diagonal line are feasible. Point A has relatively high benefit compared to its costs and is the lowest risk project. B, C and D are all economically feasible with projects E and F also being feasible but in the high-risk area (shown shaded in Figure 6.4). Projects G, H, I and J are all unfeasible. E´ and F´ are also infeasible and may represent projects using traditional software technology. However, using IT (information system technology) they are shifted to points E and F respectively but into the high-risk area. Of these two, F is closest to the breakeven point and represents the highest risk and must only be implemented at the bottom of the economically feasible list. Thus within the area of feasible problems, both high- and low-risk applications will occur. Clearly, when all else is equal, the low-risk applications are to be preferred.

Figure 6.4: *High-risk and low-risk zones.*

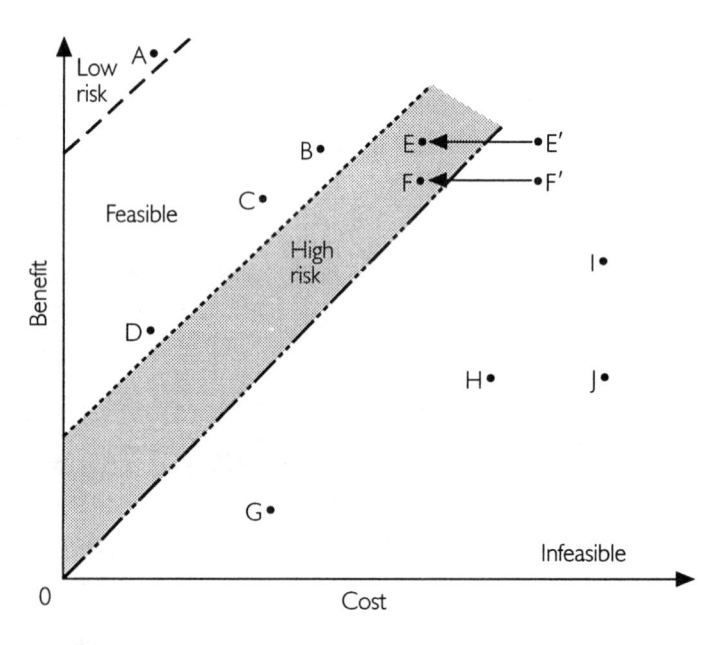

There are some potential problems in the feasibility of an information system that are to be expected. These are:
- Difficulty in identifying meaningful applications.
- Resistance to IT is not uncommon.

- Unrealistic expectations of end-users.
- Difficulty in integrating an information system with existing information systems.
- Lack of skills required for an information system implementation.
- Gaining commitment of:
  * Senior/top management.
  * Operational management and end-users.
  * Specialists such as domain experts, as in the case of a KBIS (knowledge-based information systems including expert systems).

User specifications

Once it has been determined that an information system project is feasible (in relation to a set of constraints), then it is time to determine, as precisely as possible, what the proposed system should (and should not) do. This is the requirement and specification stage.

Problem specification, also referred to as user requirements, user specification, or systems specifications, can vary from a one-line statement on the cognitive tasks to be performed to a detailed manual that may even specify which systems analyst or knowledge engineer should be assigned to the project. In cases of doubt it is better to overstate than understate. To illustrate the problem, consider the following case study. An application was delivered by a programmer to the supervisor who looked at the coding and asked why PL/1 was chosen when it was not the only language appropriate for the application and besides it is a language not maintained by the organization. The answer was: "I know that PL/1 is not maintained here but I have never used the language and thought it will be fun to program an important application in it." But the programmer soon left the company, as is to be expected in a profession with a high turnover and high mobility, with the result that the entire application had to be redeveloped. However, this time the problem specification was constructed to conform to standards which included the specification of the menu of programming languages to be used. A lesson was learned the hard way.

It is important not to over-specify in the specification stage because this reduces the flexibility open to the designer and developer. It is also important that the system is not under-specified. The specifications should be complete and well articulated with no ambiguities to be misinterpreted by the designer. And what should be articulated? The objectives and constraints for the system. Or else the system may well be delivered with unstated constraints being violated and objectives not being met because they were not specified.

Table 6.1 *Some factors to be specified in the user specification stage*

Output	Backup
■ Format	■ Items needing backup
■ Content	■ Procedures
■ Availability	**Security**
■ Response time	■ Define unauthorized access
■ Retention time	■ What is to be controlled?
Processing	■ Control of access
■ Inference mechanism	■ Procedures
■ Inference and decision "rules"	■ Auditing
■ Approach to data/knowledge acquisition	■ Internal or external or both
■ Approach to data/knowledge representation	**Maintenance**
■ Uncertainty management approach	■ When to maintain?
■ Programming language/shell/ environment to be used	■ When to redevelop?
	■ Mechanism to maintain
Input	**Personnel**
■ Sources	■ Specification of domain experts
■ Media	■ Number
■ Procedures	■ Who?
■ Validity checks	■ Training
Testing	■ Who?
■ Approaches to testing	■ What?
■ Content of testing	
■ Who performs the testing?	

Who makes the specifications? The ultimate source is the end-user of course, helped perhaps by the corporate manager (if not the same person) and perhaps by the project sponsor who may well be from another department and at a higher level of management. But the systems analyst and the knowledge engineer can also make significant contributions. They can ask questions about possible objectives and constraints based on their past experience with similar projects. They must persuade the end-users to make specifications that are complete and operational. It is not sufficient to say the one wants "more" and "better" information or an "effective" and "efficient" system unless these terms are defined operationally.

This is difficult to do because end-users who are managers are busy people and have crises (e.g. in functional operations) to attend. However, they must be convinced of the importance of the specification stage because it is crucial to a successful final system. Another person who can help in the end-user and problem specification is the domain expert, either from within the organization or from outside. And the outside domain expert, as a consultant, could bring experience from other information systems and can, of course, offer objectivity – especially to an organization that is inwardly oriented. Part of end-user specifications may be left to the design stage but factors that may be specified in the user specifications stage may include those listed in Table 6.1

Another approach to the contents of an end-user's specification is taken by Ince (1990:261). Ince lists the properties that every software system specification should exhibit:

- It should be unambiguous.
- It should be free of design and implementation directives.
- It should enable the developer to reason about the properties of the system it describes.
- It should be free of extraneous detail.
- It should be partitioned.
- It should be understandable by the customer.

Design and user specifications

Design is the stage between the stages of problem specification and implementation.

Figure 6.5:
Overview of design showing the preceding and succeeding activities of a partial waterfall model of development.

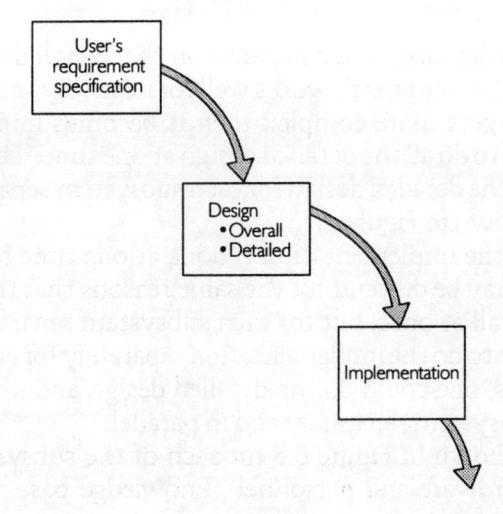

Much of what is done in the design stage depends on the completeness and detail of the user specification stage. Design is, in part, the elaboration of the user specification stage and, in part, the stating of the remaining necessary specification details. Design is the stage that precedes the implementation stage. This is reflected in Figure 6.5 in which each activity or stage of development flows into another which gives it the name of the "waterfall" model.

In Figure 6.5 we merely show one part of the total waterfall of development. Here, the design stage includes both the overall and the detailed design. As the system gets complex, the detailed design is separated from the overall design as shown in Figure 6.6.

Figure 6.6:
Detailed design and implementation in a partial waterfall model.

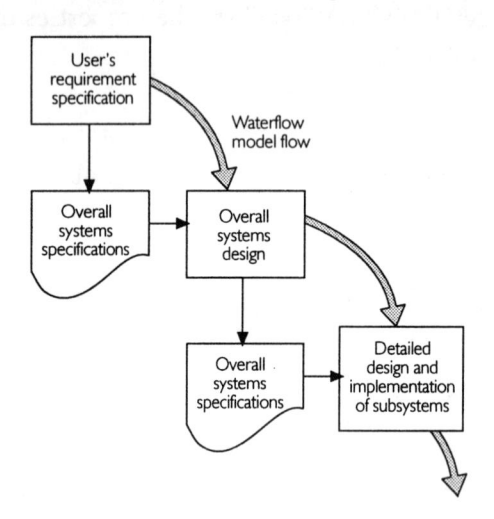

Here the detailed design depends on the overall design specification document. This approach works well for relatively small systems but as the system gets more complex then it becomes impractical (perhaps impossible) to do all the detailed design at one time. Then it makes more sense to do the detailed design for each subsystem separately. This alternative is shown in Figure 6.7.

Here all the implementation is done at one time for the whole system. This may be difficult for the same reasons that the detailed design is not done all at once, but for each subsystem separately. Thus it also makes sense to do the implementation separately for each subsystem. In other words, one could do the detailed design and its implementation for each subsystem separately and in parallel.

This is shown in Figure 6.8 for each of the subsystems of facilities (such as hardware and personnel), knowledge base, inference engine, and interfaces.

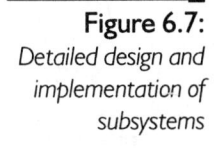

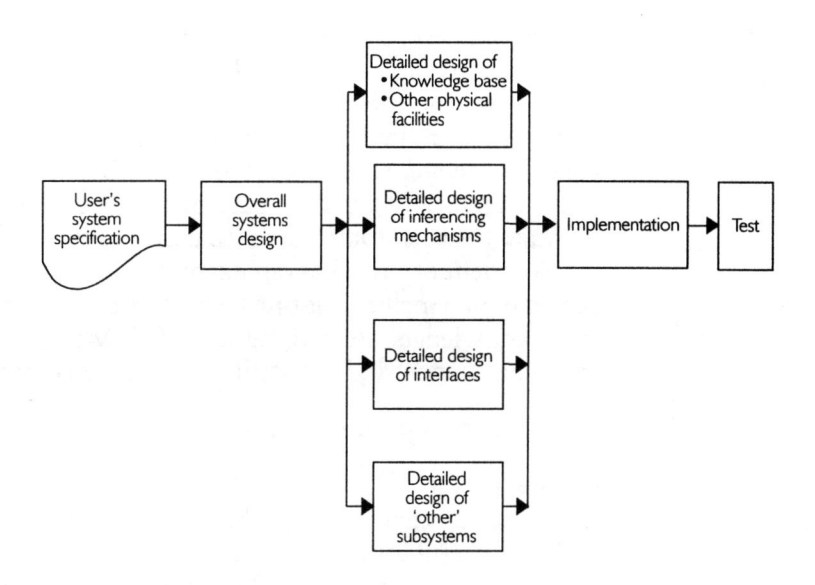

Figure 6.7:
Detailed design and implementation of subsystems

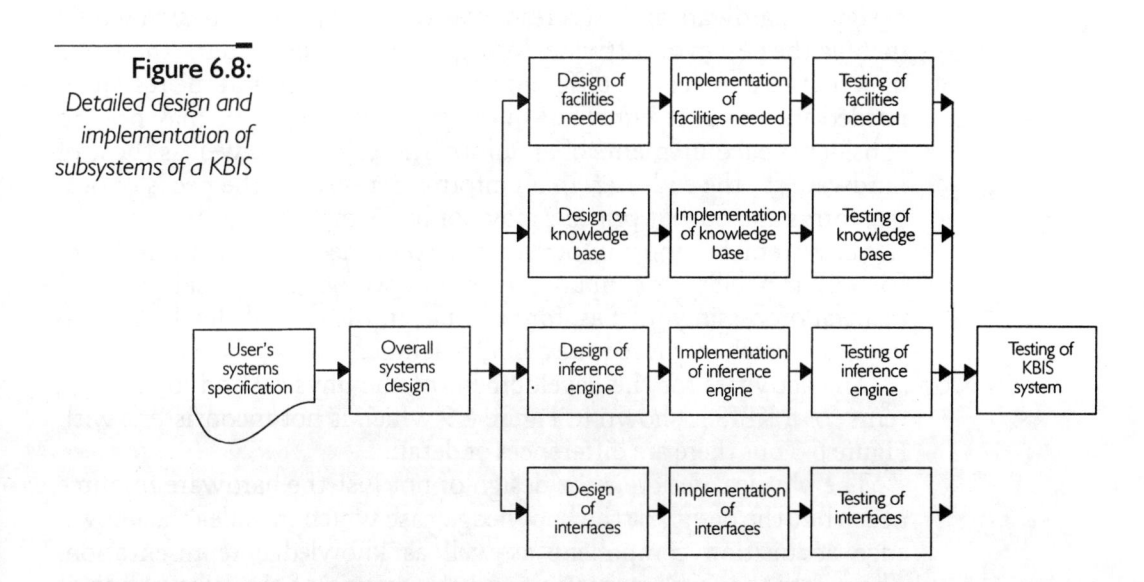

Figure 6.8:
Detailed design and implementation of subsystems of a KBIS

This makes sense since each subsystem requires a different set of personnel, tools and techniques and even programming languages. This subsystems approach is also appealing from the pedagogical point of view because it is easier to discuss and explain. It is therefore the approach that we will follow in this text whilst recognizing that there are other approaches to combining design with implementation.

Integration of the subsystems of an information system is just one of the problems of integration. The other integration problem is that of integrating the information system with other information systems and subsystems in the organization – assuming such integration is desirable. Such systems or subsystems must be identified and strategies for their integration must be part of the overall systems design which becomes the basis for the detailed design of subsystems. We consider the development of a KBIS as our example since it is a comprehensive application which includes not just a database of a transactional system but also a knowledge base and the use of OR/MS (operations research/management science) and AI (artificial intelligence) for a DSS and EIS.

Activities of design and implementation

Physical design

An approach that distinguishes between physical design and logical design is useful for it separates activities that require different human and technological resources. Thus the physical design would include the design of hardware and data resources whilst the logical design would include the design of software. In large and complex systems these sets of activities may require different types of personnel, and the resources needed are also different. Thus in the physical design, one may need to consider the requirements of an information system as well as those of hardware for the end-user. In an information system the needs of output forms and output printers may not be so important as in a transactional system, but most information systems need a good and end-user friendly capability for input. Sometimes we need a specialized CPU (central processing unit) as, for example, in the case of the decision to use LISP which might require a LISP machine.

The activities for the development of the physical and logical systems for a KBIS is shown in Figure 6.9 which is not inconsistent with Figure 6.8 but there are differences of detail.

The physical design is the design of not just the hardware resource needs but the design of the knowledge base which includes the knowledge acquisition component as well as knowledge representation. Thereafter the implementation and the testing of the subsystems of hardware and of the knowledge base are carried out (often by different sets of personnel). Only after the subsystems are tested satisfactorily are they ready to be tested with the outcome of the logical design. These subsystems are to be discussed in great detail in later chapters.

Figure 6.9:
Development of a KBIS

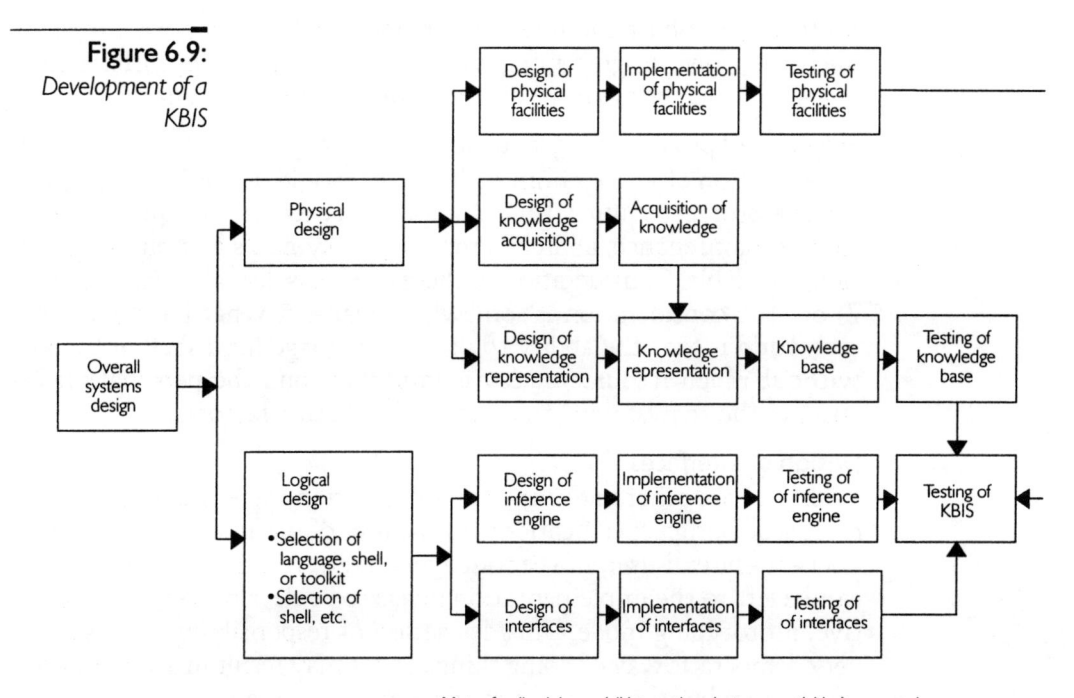

Note: feedback loops (all interactions between activities) are **not** shown

Logical design

The logical design of an information system as shown in Figure 6.9 is in parallel to the design of the physical system. We start with the overall logical design which includes decisions about the selection of a language as opposed to an environment, a shell or a toolkit. There are issues of integration as well as of security and control that must be resolved. There are also specifications of resources, operations, testing and even output and input formatting that may need to be explicitly stated. In addition, there is the overall design of both the inference engine and the interfaces. This overall system design is followed by detail design, implementation and testing of each subsystem. Again, as with the physical design, these subsystems will be discussed in later chapters. It should be noted though that the activities of logical design and implementation can be viewed as activities of software development which we will discuss further in a later chapter

Inference making

The software for the inference making is often developed in parallel to that of the software for interfaces. Why the separation? Because the nature of the software is different in the two cases, and they require different approaches to development (interface development may require prototyping whilst the inference engine usually does not). These are likely to involve programming in different languages. Why different languages? Which brings us to the problem of selecting languages.

Selection of programming language

The selection of a programming language would depend of factors like internal storage required, time (compile and execution) required to run, ease of maintenance, ability to manipulate symbols and built-in functions available. Consideration of these factors is desirable, (see Chapter 7) but full consideration is somewhat idealistic. What happens in the real world is that the ability to use the language (or a shell or toolkit) without much resource outlay is important and the personal preferences of the analyst will often supersede all other factors.

Design of interfaces

Interfaces are other modules of an information system that need to be designed. Design specifications for each set of interfaces, for the developer and the end-user, can be stated separately. Alternatively, the design can be left to the implementation phase to be developed in an interactive, prototyping mode. This delegation of responsibility may seem a very democratic way of doing things and it may result in a very responsive system but there is the great danger that the resulting system may not be standard or portable. In a large organization, the system may have to be used at different, geographically separate, sites of the organization and the system needs to be portable. It also needs to be portable in a small organization since users will vary over time. It may therefore be deemed desirable and even necessary to specify certain minimum standards of performance and user-friendliness for the interfaces rather than customize them to whoever happens to be user at the time of the initial system development.

Interfaces are necessary for making the system end-user friendly and is a subject discussed further in Chapter 12.

When does development end?

We have discussed the activities that led up to the implementation of the subsystems of an information system. But the implementation of this set of subsystems does not imply that the system is complete even if the subsystems are tested satisfactorily. There are activities that concern all subsystems that must be designed and implemented. These activities are shown in the overview diagram in Figure 6.1. Sometimes, all the activities after design (until the system is operational) are lumped as "implementation" (somewhat different to the disaggregation shown in Figure 6.1).

The most important of the activities not yet discussed is that of organizational changes which includes the activities of orientation and training. And then all these activities and subsystems need to be tested as a system (activity 700–800 in Figure 6.1). Only when the system receives a satisfactory acceptance test by the end-user is the system ready for conversion (800–900) and ready for operations (900–1000). Only then can the system development process be considered as finished. Meanwhile, all these activities must be coordinated and managed by some technique of project management (300–900) which must be documented as part of the final documentation of the system. It is these topics that finish the project which are the subject of the rest of this chapter. We start with organizational changes (300–700) necessary for implementing and operating a information system.

Organizational changes

The organizational changes required for an information system (activity 300–700 in Figure 6.1) would include training and education of personnel, detecting and overcoming resistance to information systems, and even making structural changes to the organization. New systems may result in some new jobs being created while other jobs are eliminated. Some personnel may have to be displaced from their old jobs and retrained for their new jobs. All these changes require careful consideration of how the changes may affect morale and productivity.

Testing

Testing, when performed on a component, function or a subsystem as a unit is referred to as *unit testing*. In a small system, components and functions (and sometimes all subsystems) are treated as a unit for the purposes of testing. Once the subsystem is satisfactorily tested and all other subsystems are satisfactorily tested, then they are ready for the systems test. This test is performed by the technical personnel and later by the end-user and management. Once they are satisfied the system is accepted and ready for operations. Such testing is referred to as *acceptance testing*. The acceptance test being completed, the system is ready for conversion (figure 800–900 in Figure 6.1), that is of course only when an old system is being phased-out into a new system. It is then that old knowledge, programs and procedures must be purged out of the system and new ones instituted. This is also a period of "danger" in the sense that every one is relaxed and a potential intruder can slip-in a code which will allow unauthorized access later on. Therefore, some end-users may lock-up the source code after the acceptance test until such time that it is used operationally.

Approaches to testing

There are many approaches to testing: pilot testing, parallel testing, simulation, systems testing and functional testing. Each approach is appropriate in a specific problem environment. For an information system, especially a large complex system, it is often best to consider functional testing where each function is tested before each set of functions in a subsystem is tested. In a complex environment one may go one step further and test for each component and then the set of components in a function. This schema is represented in Figure 6.10. The important rationale for this type of testing at different level of aggregation is that it is much easier to detect and correct an error at (or close to its point of origin) before it propagates through the system which is likely to happen if we go straight to the system test. The other advantage is that at each level it is possible to bring the relevant expertise to check for errors and correct them.

Figure 6.10: *Levels of testing*

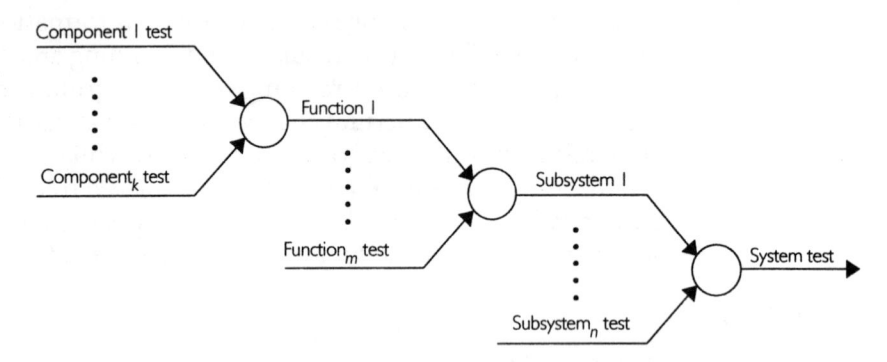

Final testing is often performed in two stages. First comes the systems test which is concerned with verification and validation and is performed by the technical personnel such as an outside specialist who also participates in the final testing in order to provide some objectivity and not take assumptions for granted. Also, such cross-project testing provides backup training for each project. More objectivity to the final testing can also come from a consultant who could also bring knowledge and experience not available in the organization. Once the systems test is performed successfully, the system is now ready for the second stage of testing by the end-user(s) who may be joined by the project manager and the project sponsor and any manager assigned to the task of testing by top corporate management. A consultant may also be used to provide objectivity, knowledge and experience in representing the end-user's viewpoint. But once this group approves of the project then the development team is released of further responsibility since the system has been implicitly "accepted". Hence the term *acceptance* test.

Interaction in testing

The discussion thus far and the diagrams showing the activities in development may give the impression that all the activities are neatly sequential. This is not the case. It is seldom sequential especially the testing activity. Seldom is the first test satisfactory. There is much repetition needed. Another view of interaction in testing is given by using a flow chart as in Figure 6.11.

Here we can see explicitly what triggers the repetition. In this case, the interactive loop goes back to the design stage, which may be the overall design or detailed design stage. Alternatively, (and not shown) are the possibilities of repeating an activity previous to the design stage.

Figure 6.11:
Recycling in testing.

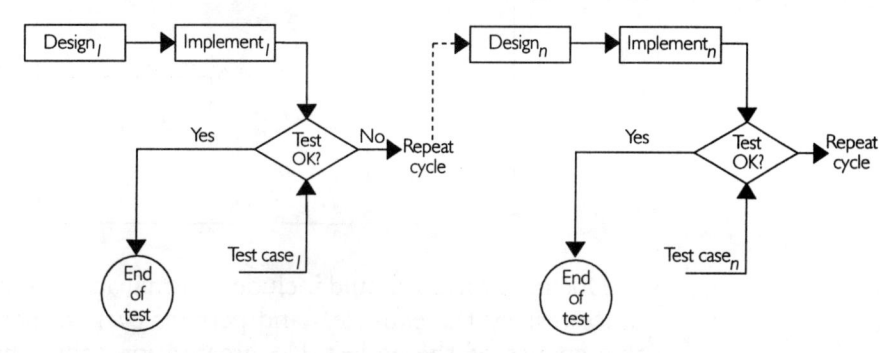

Documentation

Documentation is a most neglected activity in many an information system. Documentation is important during the development process as depicted in Figure 6.12.

For example, documentation of systems specifications are used in the overall design process and the documentation of the overall design is used for the detailed design and implementation activities. In a small system, such documentation is replaced by word of mouth but in a complex system and one that involves many people, this can be hazardous. People do not always say what they mean. People do not always remember what they have said. People change their minds. It is in the best interests of both the analysts and the end-users to document all commitments, explicit or implicit. It is sometimes necessary to document not only actions but intentions such as what would have been done if specific resources were available or certain constraints were not imposed. Such documentation could also be most useful during maintenance and enhancement of the system.

Figure 6.12: *Flow of documentation in different stages of development*

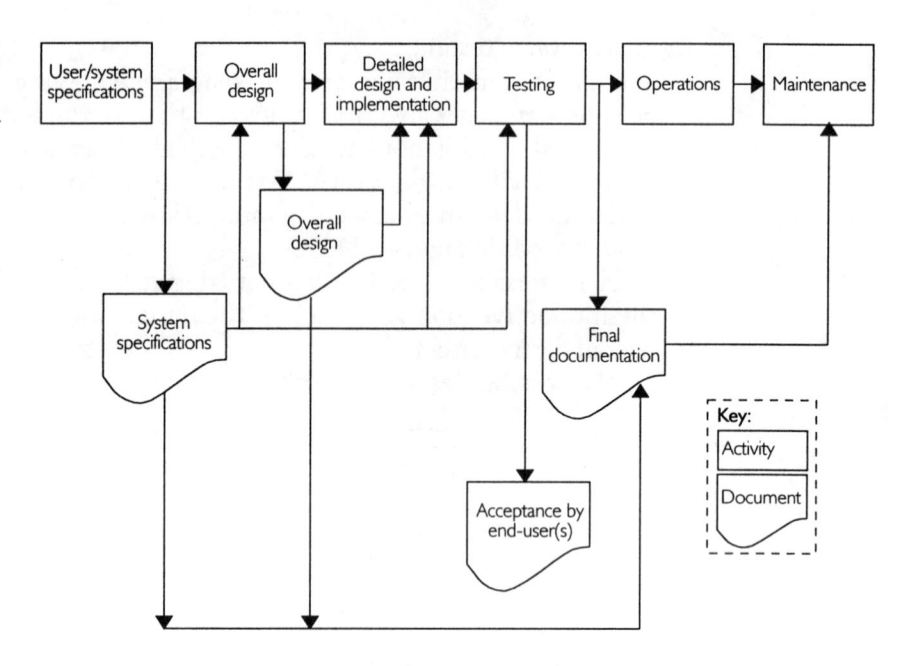

Documentation should include a formal acceptance after the acceptance test by the end-users and perhaps even corporate management that sponsored the project. Documentation should be progressive and not left to the end for then it may never be completed nor available when needed during the development process. Finalizing documentation is perhaps the very last activity in the life of a project. This includes documentation of the project itself which could include a description of lessons learned in project management and, perhaps, a record of the original time estimates for each of the project activities.

Because documentation is not a popular activity amongst analysts and knowledge engineers, documentation is sometimes contracted to a consulting company or one that specializes in documentation. The problem with contracting outside is that the knowledge acquired by documenting is lost to the organization. This loss is especially important when the documentation could have been done by someone other than the analyst responsible for the job who is then available for evaluation, maintenance and backup. The problem with documentation is that it tends to become bulky. There is too much paperwork involved. Werner von Braun, a space scientist and project manager of the US space program, once said: "Our two greatest problems are gravity and paperwork. We can lick gravity, but sometimes the paperwork is overwhelming."

Critique of the SDLC

Because the SDLC is formal, systematic and detailed, it is inherently cumbersome, rigid and slow. The long lapse time taken for an SDLC was tolerated in the early days of computing but as the demands for applications increased faster than our ability to implement, there developed a backlog of unfulfilled demand and unhappiness among the end-users.

The long time required for completion also meant that the user's specifications were frozen for a long time, in fact, sometimes they became outdated by the time the project was completed.

The SDLC is often the province of technical personnel on the project with little interaction with the end-users except when they are explicitly involved. This has two important consequences. One, it tends to isolate the project personnel from the real world environment including the end-user's needs which may be changing. Two, the SDLC does not have the involvement and commitment of the end-users. The end-users are then not morally bound to accept the product.

The SDLC has a reputation for overruns both in cost of the project and the time taken for the completion of the project. This is partly due to time taken in stabilizing the end-user's need and partly because of poor project management. Also, many a completed project was either irrelevant to the real problems at hand (because of poor articulation of end-user's need), or too difficult to comprehend, use and maintain. Many of these limitations of the SDLC are the strengths of prototyping, our next topic.

Prototyping

Prototyping can be represented in Figure 6.13 as being one big activity of user specification, design and implementation.

Figure 6.13: *Prototyping*

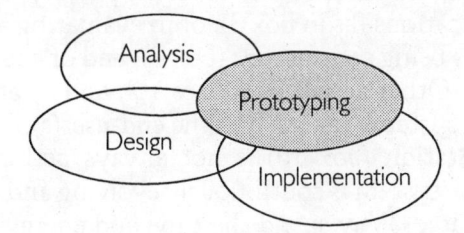

This is a simplification in the sense that each of the activities of user specification, design and implementation are in one sense performed separately. This is better shown in Figure 6.14.

Chapter 6: Development of an Information System

Figure 6.14: *The process of prototyping*

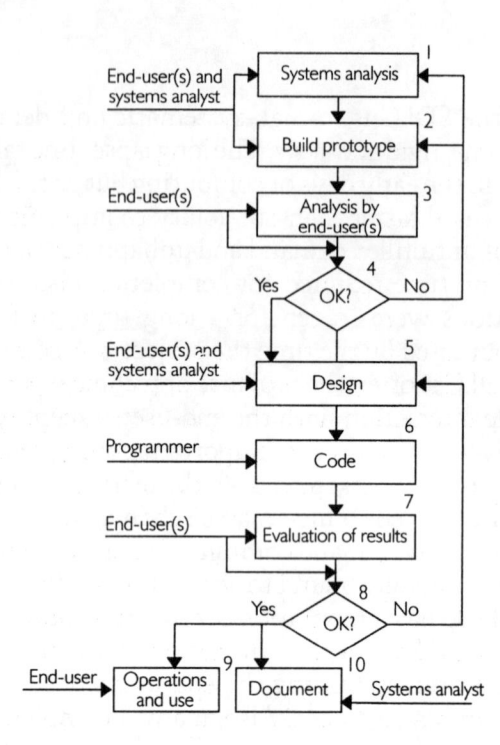

Here we have the end-user specification, i.e. systems analysis (box 1) through the prototype construction evaluated in (box 3) being repeated if the decision on it being OK (satisfactory) is "No" (shown in box 4). Likewise, design (box 5) through the analysis of the coded product (box 7) may be recycled ("No" exit in box 8), typically 3–5 times, until the end-user is satisfied. Note also that different activities are performed by different personnel. Thus the programmer does the coding (box 6) but the end-user is the primary decision-maker when it comes to reaching a satisfactory result, whether this is on the prototype expressing the end-user's specifications (as in box 3), or in evaluating and determining the deliverable as being satisfactory (box 7), and of course in using the system (box 9). Other activities (boxes 1,2, and 5) are performed collectively by the systems analyst and the end-user(s).

Documentation (box 10) is not always performed because some think that the system is continuously evolving and any documentation is soon outdated. Why spend the time and energy on it? This may be what happens in an *ad hoc* DSS or an EIS, but it should not happen for situations like the development of an interface for an ES. Even with some other prototypes, it is desirable to perform the other activities of an SDLC, not just documentation but also conversion and acceptance testing. One of the strong criticisms of prototyping is that these "back-end" activities of an SDLC are not performed or not performed well. For example, the testing process in a prototype even when done by the end-user may not be very thorough.

However, when the system is tested by the systems analyst in an SDLC, it is expected to be thorough. The analyst is trained and experienced in what to look for, such as exceptional values and boundary conditions. An example of checking of boundary conditions would be $x=5$ in the condition $x<5$. This the end-user may or may not do depending on the pressures of time, knowledge, and experience in development. The implications of this role of the end-user will depend on the nature and importance of the activity being prototyped.

There is one other potential problem that the decision-maker must be aware of. It is the role of the analyst (systems analyst). The analyst in the development of an *ad hoc* DSS serves as a model builder (and prototype builder) but it is corporate management who states the assumptions, identifies relationships and provides the parameters (box 2 in Figure 16.14). However, if management does not play its proper role then by default the analyst becomes the decision-maker and the results may not be what the decision-maker expected or wanted. This danger also exists in an SDLC but less so because the implementation is not rushed as in most prototypes.

Prototyping when used in the systems analysis phase is used iteratively to converge on a user specification acceptable to the end-user. Thereafter the prototype is thrown away. Such prototyping is aptly called the *throw-away prototype*. There are other prototypes:

- The *partial prototype* is for demonstrating procedures for input and output.
- The *breadboard prototype* is concerned with the temporary nature of the intermediate design.
- The *pilot prototype* is attempted on an isolated pilot case before it is used for all other cases.
- The *staged prototype* attempts a stage after the previous stage has been satisfactorily prototyped.
- *Rapid prototyping* entails the selection of a partial system, its prototyping quickly, its testing, iterative refinement and enhancement, followed by further development if necessary. Also, rapid prototyping sometimes results in identifying the user interfaces early in the requirements analysis phase, then constructing the system behind it.

Prototyping is being used in many business systems to focus on end-user interfaces specifically screens and reports. These can be done with "screen painters" commonly available on PCs with a minimum of resulting throw-away software. The justification of prototyping and its characteristics and advantages are summarized in Tables 6.2 and 6.3 respectively.

Table 6.2 *When to use prototyping?*

- When the system is small and a simple or a partial subsystem like the design of a screen in an end-user interface for an expert system, DSS or EIS
- With an online system being used by an end-user for quick output and input
- When a system needs a few computing resources, like the use of a PC with a GUI (graphical user interface)
- When a system is dynamic and changing with time
- When the system has many end-user dialogues and interactions
- When the end-user cannot articulate or react in the abstract

Table 6.3 *Characteristics and advantages of prototyping*

- Speed of development, not necessarily the efficiency of the process
- End-user participation resulting in:
    a. credibility of the resulting system
    b. less "noise" in communicating the user's needs
    c. vested interest of end-user in the resulting system
- Interactions resulting in enhanced systems
- Uses workbench tools like 4GLs, screen or report generators, dictionaries, statistical packages and online help
- Resulting system is easy to learn and use
- Low level of effort on the part of systems analysts and programmers and hence reduced development costs
- Allows for experimentation by end-user
- Results in "right" system at least as perceived by end-user

Structured methodologies

In the 1960s there was a view held that programming productivity could be greatly increased by separating the analysis and design process from the programming and coding process. These techniques were collectively referred to as structured techniques and part of structured methodology. More specifically, structured analysis and structured specification focused on *what* the application was required to do and silent on how that could be accomplished; structured design has the philosophy of using reusable procedures and broke down difficult and complex problems into smaller problems and modules that were simple to solve and manage. Structured programming is an approach to programming with restricted program control structures and requiring a top-down design.

Structured methodology encompasses top-down decomposition, modelling, modularization, and iteration. Structured methodologies is a subject of more than one course in computer science departments and the subject of many books. We will not discuss the subject further except to say that there are numerous techniques for each of the development stages of analysis, design and implementation and some like SADT (Systems Analysis and Design Technique) that attempt to integrate more than one phase of development. Different phases of development use different diagrammatic tools like the dataflow diagram, program flowcharts, structure charts, structured English, pseudo code, HIPO (Hierarchy plus Input-Process-Output) charts and the Warnier–Orr method.

Automating the development process

Both the SDLC and structured methodology were criticized for being labour intensive. What was needed was to automate the development process. One early approach was by Hoskyns in the UK, who produced a workable code in the COBOL language. In the US, the emphasis was on automating the entire development process through ISDOS (Information System Design and Optimization System). Another optimization technique is SODA (System Optimization and Design Algorithm). However, neither SODA nor ISDOS became operational or went commercial. Perhaps the development process was too subjective and "ill-structured" to be modelled, programmed and optimized. But the need (and desire) to automate did not die.

There are still attempts at automating the entire development process like the RAD (Rapid Applications Development) by the James Martin Group and the IEF (Information Engineering Facility) by Texas Instruments. IEF is an attempt to integrate CASE (computer-aided software engineering) tools in the development phase. Meanwhile, CASE is also being implemented to automate different and distinct parts of the development process.

There are many CASE tools on the market. Lindholm (1992) has a list of 272 CASE tools. They perform over 100 distinct functions. One list of these tools by functions performed is shown in Table 6.4. The tools are sold by a large number of vendors which creates two problems: one is the selection of the right tool, and the other is the selection of the best vendor. There are no good guidelines let alone infallible rules for selecting the right tool for the occasion. It depends entirely on the systems analysts involved: on their knowledge and experience. They may get advice from a consultant but the final decision is theirs. The second decision, that of selecting a vendor, requires preparing a matrix of factors to be considered in the selection and the vendors. The cells of this matrix would then have a score for each vendor for each factor of selection. A study by Shafer and Shafer (1993:21–2) has a list of 73 factors with three vendors. Assuming that there are three people scoring, that comes to 657 individual decisions. This can be overbearing for most systems departments especially for the many tools that can be bought out of the annual departmental budget. In practice, the selection process is much more practical. It is based on a system analyst's personal choice based on experience, knowledge or bias. This practice is not recommended for important and expensive tools where the weighted-scoring method (which uses a weighted score for each factor in selection) should be used but with a smaller list of factors to be considered.

Table 6.4 *Functions performed by CASE tools (adapted from Alavi, 1993:16)*

Analysis
- Check inconsistencies in definitions and models
- Check inconsistencies between data model and process model
- Check for existence and redundancies in model construction
- Identify impact on production schedule or design

Representation
- Represents relationships between information
- Represents requirements and organizational goals
- Make compatible the conventions used
- Aggregate processes and entities when possible
- Convert high level to detailed representation
- Represent design in terms of data model and data flow

Transformation
- Convert logical to physical specifications
- Generate executable code from screen image
- Generate executable version for evaluation and testing
- Provide necessary documentation
- Perform reverse engineering
- Perform reengineering

Coordination
- Provide project management tools
- Provide messaging and communication tools
- Provide calendering facilities
- Provide scheduling facilities

Once a tool is selected, financed and acquired, there is the matter of preparing the Systems Department for the change. A lack of adequate preparation is perhaps responsible for the low usage of CASE tools:

> ...only 25% of organizations in the US have acquired CASE tools and that only 4% of these are sustained users of CASE innovation
>
> *Alavi*, 1993:20

The main problem is that CASE brings with it a unique set of definitions, structures, representations and processes and there needs to be a compatibility between CASE and the computing environment, work patterns and procedures of the Systems Department. This requires training on CASE for the Systems Department personnel. This cannot be done exclusively by attending a course in a junior college, polytechnique or Technischehochschule. Nor can the necessary knowledge be gained from reading the CASE manuals. Many software houses have the bad reputation of having poor documentation on the grounds that they will train systems personnel in on-site training sessions for the specific institutional problem, and for a hefty fee of course. And so training can be costly and time-consuming. There is also often an unexpected resistance to CASE. The profession of computing is used to complaining of the need to manage change and resistance to IT by the end-user. But with CASE, there is a need to manage resistance and manage change within the Systems Department if CASE is to be successfully implemented and used. In implementing CASE, there is not just the cost of the CASE tools but perhaps a higher cost (monetary and organizational) of implementation.

Summary and conclusions

In this chapter we have discussed the development of an information system. The first activity discussed is the feasibility study. In it one needs to spend considerable time in considering the many unique factors relating to the feasibility of an information system. Why? Partly because information systems is a new field and we have relatively little experience in the area of assessing the benefits and risks involved. And partly because an information system is very resource-consuming: resources of equipment, software, and time of specialized personnel.

Once the feasibility study is performed there may still be a problem when the number of projects that are feasible cannot all be implemented because there are not enough resources. Then all the feasible projects must be evaluated, scored and weighted. (Laufmann, *et al.* 1990). Some of the factors already considered, such as profitability may be reconsidered along with factors such as opportunity, contribution to organizational goals, task appropriateness, risk inherent in the project, aversion to risk by decision-maker, time required for implementation and even political factors. The latter may involve the consideration of the project sponsors and end-users. The status of these personnel is important. Are they high in the hierarchy of the organization? Do they shout loud and long? Do they hold the purse strings? Thus the choice of a project may start as being very rational, scientific and even mathematical but may end up being shaped by political and subjective decisions.

A feasibility study is followed by the activities of user specification, design, implementation, testing, organizational changes and documentation in accordance with the diagram in Figure 6.1.

In evaluating the SDLC, it has been found to be slow, expensive, cumbersome, rigid and adding to the backlog of pent-up demands. The methodology of prototyping that claims to overcome the limitations of the SDLC has its own problems. A list of the conditions that affect the choice of prototyping is presented in Table 6.2. A summary of the characteristics and advantages of prototyping is listed in Table 6.3. This list is also a reflection of many of the limitations of the SDLC which in practice is still the best methodology for many a large and complex development project.

In between the initiation of the SDLC some four decades ago and the common use of prototyping, there were numerous other tools, techniques and methodologies that were used, prominent among them being the structured methodology. Also, in parallel have been many attempts at automating the development process. In the US, an early attempt at automating the entire life cycle was ISDOS. It was perhaps too early for its day and did not succeed though components like PSL/PSA still have many supporters and users. The more recent attempts are RAD (Rapid Applications Development) and IEF (Information Engineering Facility). IEF is an integrated CASE environment with numerous CASE tools being used independently for specific tasks. In Europe, methodologies of SSADM, Multimedia, Merise, and JSD have been used successfully and extensively. These methodologies along with other selected ones are summarized in a supplement at the end of this chapter.

Another methodology for AI applications uses programming languages like LISP and PROLOG. Yet another emerging methodology causing considerable excitement is the *object-oriented* (OO) methodology. According to Yourdon, the Dean of structured methodologies, the OO approach will soon replace the structured and other approaches. The evolution of the development tools and methodologies is summarized in Figure 6.15.

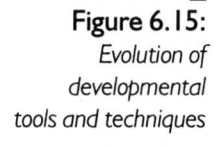

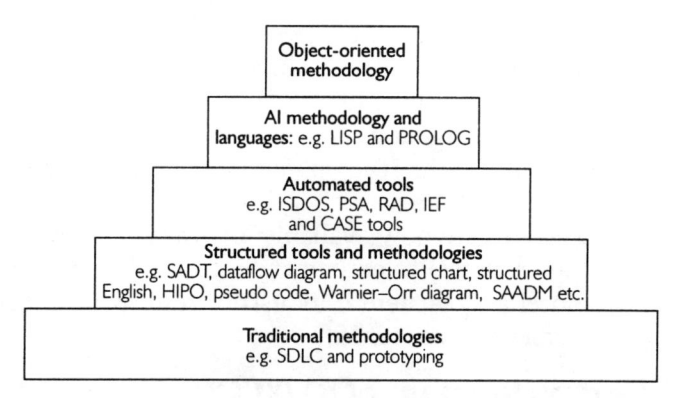

Figure 6.15:
Evolution of developmental tools and techniques

- Object-oriented methodology
- AI methodology and languages: e.g. LISP and PROLOG
- Automated tools e.g. ISDOS, PSA, RAD, IEF and CASE tools
- Structured tools and methodologies e.g. SADT, dataflow diagram, structured chart, structured English, HIPO, pseudo code, Warnier–Orr diagram, SAADM etc.
- Traditional methodologies e.g. SDLC and prototyping

Case 6.1: Development of the SABRE/SABER system

Back in 1954, American Airlines took the first step towards developing a computerized information system for reservations. The airline was finding it increasingly difficult to maintain accurate and timely manual records for passengers. In addition, the conventional system of assigning quotas to travel agents was unsatisfactory. When local agents sold out their seat allotment quotas, passengers were often lost to the airline because of delays in locating a seat held by an agent in another part of the country. Lost revenues resulted. It took 10 years and more than $30 million and a joint effort of the airline and IBM to develop the desired central reservations system. The chronology of the development was as follows:

Preliminary study	1954–8
Precontractual analysis	1958–9
Contract negotiations	1959
Functional requirement and program specifications	1960–2
Program coding	1961–4
Single path testing	1961 onwards
Equipment arrival	January 1962
Package testing	1961–2
Final checkout	October–December 1962
Test city parallel operation	December 1962 to March 1963
First firm cutover	April 1963
Several more cities cutover	April 1963
Several more cities cutover	May 1963
Further cutover delay pending addition to memory to 7090	June–November 1963
Remainder of cities added	November 1963 to December 1964

SABER is a museum piece both literally and figuratively. A Washington DC museum has SABER on display along with recorded experiences of these who operated and used the system. The experience gained from this first large commercial online real-time information system has contributed to the development of many advanced systems especially in the reservation areas such as hotel, car rental and theatres. Many of these systems are now available "off-the-shelf". An attempt (also by American Airlines) to extend the information system for the airlines to the hotel and car rental industries resulted in a colossal failure. It is discussed in Chapter 19.

Case 6.2: The development of R1/XCON

In 1980, XCON became the first large expert system to be used. It was developed by Digital Corporation, a manufacturer of computer minis. XCON used a customer's purchase order to determine what, if any, substitutions had to be made to the "typical" configuration of 50 to 100 components for the system to be complete and consistent with the needs of the customer. The system was originally called R1 in its formative stages that started in 1978 by John McDermott and associates at the Carnegie Mellon University. Ever since the system has been under continuous development, the experimental version being known as the R1. As has been commented:

> If R1's supporters had not emerged when they did, R1 could have easily sunk out of sight. But for R1 to survive, not having enemies was as important as having some strong supporters. R1's place in Digital was tenuous enough that if a few people had believed that exploring R1's potential was a serious mistake, the exploration would have stopped.

Three factors stopped the all-persuasive caution turning into hostility:

1. The degree of difficulty was just right for the VAX 11/780s, the computer then sold by Digital.
2. The number of people involved were quite small and grew very gradually.
3. The people who were the spokesmen for the project worked hard to manage people's expectations to ensure that no one would count on more than it could deliver.

Once developed, XCON soon became part of the manufacturing process at Digital Corporation (DEC). With XCON, DEC was able to configure equipment accurately 98% of the time compared to 65% by the manual system. Manufacturing operations benefited from accurate systems configurations because of:

1. Better use of materials in inventory.
2. Increased throughput order rate.
3. Fewer shipment delays because of fewer configuration errors.
4. Faster response time to orders.
5. Greater user satisfaction.
6. Reduced cost of manufacturing and assembly.

The development of XCON has seen more than one SDLC. Its growth from 1980 to 1984 is shown in the table below:

	1980	1984
Average rules per subtask	7.6	10.3
Average rule firings	1056	1064
Percentage of knowledge frequently used (%)	44	47
Number of parts in the database	420	5481

The organization of XCON in subsystems has remained essentially the same and is as shown in the figure below.

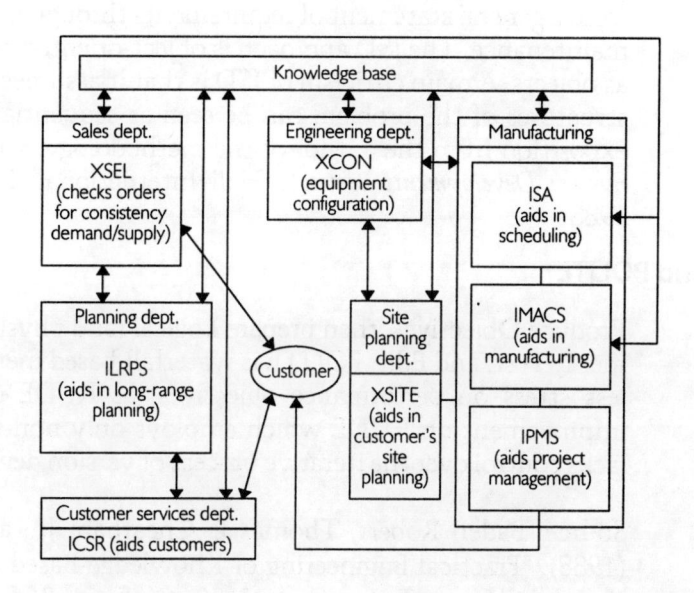

Sources: Judith Barchant and John McDermott. (1984). "RI Revisited: Four Years in the Trenches." *AI Magazine*, vol. 5, no. 3, pp. 177–88. John McDermott. (1981). "R1: The Formative Years." *AI Magazine*, vol. 2, no. 2, pp. 21–9.

Supplement 6.1: Methodologies and techniques of development information engineering (IE)

IE is the application of technology:

> ... to the development of an information systems which support the mission, strategic objectives, decision processes, and day-to-day operations of an enterprise...
>
> *Richmond*, 1991:41

IE emphasizes data sharing, modelling closely to the business, use of AI, multimedia and the automation of the development process especially through CASE.

Source: Richmond, Ken. (1991). "Information Engineering Methodology: A Tool for Competitive Advantage." *Telematics and Informatics*, vol. 8, nos. 1&2, pp. 41–57.

Jackson structured design (JSD)

JSD addresses most of the systems development life cycle, extending from a general statement of requirements through implementation and maintenance. The JSD approach is object-oriented, identifying entities as objects. A main criticism of JSD is that it assumes that all important structures of the problem can be seen as sequential processes. For an exposition from the author of the methodology, see Michael Jackson, *System Development*. Prentice Hall International, Hemel Hempstead: 1983.

RUDE and POLITE

Produce **O**bjectives, then prepare **L**ogical (and physical design), **I**mplement, **T**est, and **E**dit. POLITE is waterfall-based methodology and lays less stress on performance objectives, as RUDE does. But it is an improvement on RUDE which employs only non-heuristic rules and lacks control over the iterative process of version development.

Source: Bader, Robert, Thomas E. Cheatham Jr., and Cordell Green. (1988). "Practical Engineering of Knowledge-Based Systems." *Information and Software Technology*, vol. 30, no. 5, pp. 266–77 and Derek Partridge (1992). *Engineering Artificial Intelligence Software*. Oxford: Intellect.

Multiview

Multiview combines the work on structured techniques by Yourdon with a socio-technical approach, emphasizing the social aspects of systems development that most other approaches ignore. This involves a great amount of information gathering. Multiview does explicitly include the activities of testing, training, maintenance and enhancement but ignores the activities of conversion, cut-over and modifications.

Source: Avison, D. E., Shah H. U., Powell, R. S. and Uppal, P. S. (1992). "Applying Methodologies for Information Systems Development." *Journal of Information Technology*, vol. 7, pp. 127–40.

Merise

Merise is the approach to information systems development in France, both in the private and the public sector. Merise is based on the traditional systems life cycle but excludes the planning and implementation phases. The approach consists of addressing three levels: conceptual, logical and physical.

Merise is used extensively in the French-speaking countries and is one of the contenders for the European methodology for information systems development. An excellent text on Merise in French has been translated into very readable English by M. A. Avison. More accessible perhaps is Quang, Pham Thu and C. Chartier-Kastler. (1990). *Merise in Practice*. Macmillan Education, London.

Object-oriented methodology

Object-oriented (OO) methodology implies the existence of objects, inheritance, encapsulation, and polymorphism. The environment results in higher productivity of programmers and lower maintenance costs of programs. It can handle complex real-world problems – especially interactive environments.

The OO system has its own design methodology and its own programming languages (OOP languages). It is matured to the point that it has its own journal (*Journal of Object Oriented Programming*) and its own annual professional meetings (OOPSALA).

Source: Oscar Diaz. (1996). "Object-oriented system: A cross discipline overview." *Information and Software Technology*, vol. 4, no. 1 (January), pp. 45–57.

Structured systems analysis and design method (SSADM)

SSADM like Merise, is restricted to the middle stages of the systems life cycle. It has 3 phases and 8 stages. Phase 1 of Feasibility Study has stages of Problem Definition and of Project Identification. Phase 2 of Systems Analysis has stages of Analysis of Operations and Current Problems, Specification of Requirements, and Selection of Technical options. Phase 3 includes phases of Data Design, Process Design and Physical Design.

SSADM is well documented by numerous books and has been extensively implemented in the UK in both by the government and the private sector. Source: Downs, E., Clare, P. and Coe, I. (1988). *SSADM: Structured Systems Analysis and Design Method*. Prentice Hall International, Hemel Hempstead.

References

Aaen, Ivan. (1994). "Problems in CASE Introduction: Experiences from User Organizations." *Information and Software Technology*, vol. 36, no. 11 (November), pp. 643–54.

Alavi, Maryam. (1993). "Making CASE an Organizational Reality." *Journal of Information Systems Management*, vol. 10, no. 2, pp. 15–20.

Avison, D. E., Shah, H. U., Powell, R. S. and Uppal, P. S. (1992). "Applying Methodologies for Information Systems Development." *Journal of Information Technology*, vol. 7, pp. 127–40.

Bersoff, E. H. and Davis, A. M. (1991). "Impacts on Life Cycle Models on Software Configuration Management." *Communications of the ACM*, vol. 34, no. 8 (August), pp. 104–16.

Boehm, B.W. (1988). "A Spiral Model of Software Development." IEEE *Computer*, vol. 21, no. 5 (May), pp. 61–72.

Boehm, B.W., Gray, T.E. and Seewaldt, T. (1984). "Prototyping versus Verifying: A Multiproject Experiment." *IEEE Transactions on Software Engineering*, vol. 10, no. 3 (March), pp. 290–302.

Cameron, J. R., Campbell, A. and Ward, P. T. (1991). "Comparing Software Development Methods: Example." *Information and Software Methodology*, vol. 33, no. 6 (July–August), pp. 306–401.

Carey, J. M. (1990). "Prototyping: An Alternative systems Development Methodology." *Information and Software Technology*, vol. 32, no. 2 (March), pp. 119–26.

Checkland, P. B. and Scholes, J. (1990). *Soft Systems Methodology in Action*. Chichester: Wiley.

Downs, E., Clare, P. and Coe, I. (1988). *SSADM: Structured Systems Analysis and Design Method*. Prentice Hall International, Hemel Hempstead.

Iavari, Juhani, (1996). "Why are CASE Tools Not Used?" *Communications of the ACM*, vol. 39, no. 10 (October), pp. 94–103.

Ince, D. (1990). "Z and System Specification" in D. Ince and D. Andrews (eds.). *The Software Cycle*. London: Butterworths, pp. 260–277.

Lindstrom, Daniel. (1992). "Five Ways to Destroy a Development Project." *IEEE Software*, vol. 10, no. 5 (September), pp. 55–58.

Mayhew P. J. and Dearnley, P. A. (1990). "Organization and Management of Systems Prototyping." *Information and Software Technology*, vol. 32, no. 4 (May), pp. 245–53.

Modha, J., Gwinnett, A. and Bruce, M. (1990). "A Review of Information systems Development Methodology (ISDM) Selection Techniques." *Omega: International Journal of Management Science*, vol. 18, no. 5 (May), pp. 473–90.

Myer, B. (1985). "On Formalism in Specifications." *IEEE Software*, vol. 2, no. 1, pp. 6–26.

O'Connor, Ad. (1992). "Soft Systems Methodology." *Australian Computer Journal*, vol. 24, no. 4 (November), pp. 130–38.

Olerup, A. (1991). "Design Approaches: A Comparative Study of Systems Design and Architectural Design." *The Computer Journal*, vol. 34, no. 3, pp. 215–24.

Partridge, D. and Hussain, K. M. (1995). *Knowledge Based Information Systems*. McGraw-Hill Book Company Europe, London.

Plyler, Robert W. and Young-Gul Kim. (1993). "Methodology Myths." *Journal of Information Systems Management*, vol. 10, no. 2, pp. 39–44.

Richmond, Ken. (1991). "Information Engineering Methodology: A Tool for Competitive Advantage." *Telematics and Informatics*, vol. 8, nos. 1&2, pp. 41–57.

Ryan, Hugh W. (1993). "User-Driven Systems Development." *Information Systems Management*, vol. 10, no. 3, pp. 56–65.

Shafer, Linda L. and Donald F. Shafer. (1993). "Establishing a CASE Tool Box." *Journal of Information Systems Management*, vol. 10, no. 1, pp. 15–23.

Sobol, Marion G. and Kagan, Albert. (1989). "Which Systems Analysts are More Likely to Prototype." *Journal of Information Systems Management*, vol. 6, no. 3, pp. 36–43.

"Special Issue on CASE." *Information and Software Technology*. vol. 33, no. 9 (November 1991), pp. 610–732.

Swartout, W. and Blazer, R. (1988). "On the Inevitable Intertwining of Specification and Implementation." *Communications of the ACM*, vol. 25, no. 7 (July), pp. 438–40.

References

Walls, J. G. (1992). "A Methodology for Developing Dependable Information Systems." *Omega: International Journal of Management Science*, vol. 20, no. 2, pp. 139–48.

Part 2: Strategies for Development

The greater the power at our disposal the greater the number of insolvable problems that we can solve

Jacques Stern

Introduction to Part Two

Having discussed the organization of computing in Part One, we are now ready to discuss using such organizations to develop information systems. With software development, the choice is between buying packaged software or constructing software in-house. The pros and cons of both strategies are discussed in Chapter 7.

As an applications portfolio increases, one soon finds that there are modules of some systems and subsystems that can be reused in new software. Such reuse is not only a saving in development costs but also a great saving in time required for development. The strategy of reuse is the subject of Chapter 8. When software cannot be reused or built in-house then software must be acquired. The principles of "buying" software also apply to the acquisition of other computing resources especially hardware. These are discussed in Chapter 9.

Sometimes there is another cost-effective alternative to buying or constructing software in-house: subcontract the software construction to another firm whether in the country or abroad. This subcontracting is called outsourcing and is an applicable strategy not just for software but also for data preparation and even the management of computing resources. Outsourcing is examined in Chapter 10.

Buying software packages, constructing them in-house, or outsourcing computing work is a short-term proposition. After a while the system may have to be completely overhauled and redesigned. In other words the system has to be reengineered. Reengineering of information systems is the subject of Chapter 11.

Reengineering is often an occasion when the system is humanized, that is it is made to be end-user friendly. Ideally, all information systems should be end-user friendly from the start, but sometimes the need and strategies of making the system end-user friendly are only apparent after the system is used and operated for a while. Humanizing information systems is discussed in Chapter 12. Whether reengineered or not, a system has to be maintained much as our car and house have to be maintained if they are to serve us effectively and efficiently. Such maintenance is the subject of Chapter 13. If the system is beyond minor repairs and maintenance (as is the case with our cars and even houses) then the system has to be redeveloped, the subject discussed earlier for Chapter 6 when we examined the systems life cycle. And so we complete the loop of recycling and conclude Part Two.

One last comment: you will note that there are more than four chapters on software but only part of a chapter on hardware (Chapter 9 on acquisition of resources). If this book were being written in the 1970s, the emphasis would have been exactly the reverse. This change in emphasis is also reflected in the percentage of an IT budget spent. In the US in 1979 35% was spent on hardware and only 6.2% on software. In 1993, on the average in the US, 19% of the budget was spent on hardware and 16.6% on software. The budget share for software will further increase in the future because we need to lash together the various computing hardware ranging from PCs to parallel processors into an integrated enterprise system. In these enterprise systems any end-user (bona fide ones only) can access any data/ knowledge and any applications program from any platform (hardware or operating software) for individual or cooperative processing with anyone from any part of the world.

There is another reason for the emphasis on software in this book which is targeted to the corporate management audience. Hardware is not within the control of management in that it cannot be customized at will. We are often at the mercy of what the hardware manufacturers offer us. Software, on the other hand, can and is often customized. Software development is an endogenous (internal) variable and a decision variable for management (IT and corporate management). It is important then that management must be more aware of software alternatives and their cost implications.

7 Buy or Build Software Systems

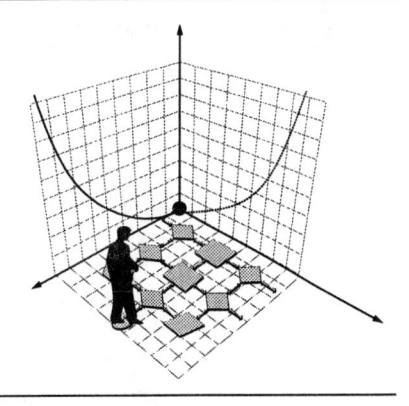

Software design technology is a system – not a secret.

Lawrence Peter

Futurists warn that if software is not made truly friendly, lucid, error free, fail-safe, and easily accessible, that computer technology will suffer protracted pains of maladjustment.

Anon.

Introduction

In this chapter we will be concerned with software for information systems, especially those for business and industry. There are common elements in the development of all software systems, such as the need to develop software that is correct and fail-proof. But there are also differences. For example, with business systems the development must be a cost-conscious process, unlike systems for research that are more open-ended on costs, and systems for defence that are mostly developed on a cost-plus basis. Also, business systems (like defence systems but for different reasons) are very security conscious and not all business applications place priority on performance as do operating systems software. But business systems have requirements of their own: they must be programmable by business-oriented programmers, and from the point of view of the end-user, the resulting system must be truly end-user-friendly. The concept of end-user friendliness is a complex one and will be discussed later in Chapter 12: *Humanizing Information Systems*.

The development of software is much like software engineering, which according to the working party of the British Computer Society and The Institution of Electrical Engineers: "requires understanding and application of engineering principles, design skills, good management practice, computer science and mathematical formalism." Software engineering is so important and complex a subject that it is the core of many a masters and doctoral programme in computer science. Many doctoral dissertations have been written in the area including the development of business systems software. However, not all this knowledge is necessary for the corporate manager or end-user of an information system even though they now increasingly have to manage their own computing resources. They, however, need to know about selected activities involved in software acquisition and development and the presentation of this necessary perspective will be attempted in this chapter.

Construction of software is only required if the solutions needed are unique. There are, however, many cases when the necessary software is available as a packaged program, in which case no project for software development is necessary except perhaps to enhance or modify the packaged software. Thus the first decision that must be made is whether or not we need to develop and "make" new software or to "buy" it in a packaged form. This make/buy decision is the next subject for discussion. If the decision is to make the software, then the making can be done "in-house" or contracted outside i.e. outsourcing. We shall discuss all these alternatives in this chapter.

The "buy" vs. "make" decision

Not all software for an information system under development has to be written in-house. Some ready-to-use software already packaged is available on the market, the purchase or lease of which may speed software development and save money because the expense of development is shared by many customers. Such packaged software can be used independently or as a module with customized software that is developed in-house.

Importance and uniqueness of software are major considerations when choosing between packaged or in-house developed software. As illustrated in Figure 7.1, a software project that falls in the three cells on the SW corner of the matrix (low to medium importance and low uniqueness in addition to low importance with low and medium uniqueness) are applications most appropriate for packaged programs. Applications that fall in the NE corner of the matrix (combinations of high importance and medium to high uniqueness along with medium importance and high uniqueness of application) are appropriate for "making" and constructing customized software in-house. Examples would include an industry-specific application that would not have wide sales or a simulation model used for a DSS in a specialized environment. These applications would qualify for high uniqueness and high importance and hence candidates for in-house development. Programs of this nature are not sold as packages. Important and unique applications usually have high performance requirements that general purpose packages cannot meet. Cost, time and the availability of computer processing talent (How many skilled programmers can be assigned to a development project?) are other factors that will influence a software acquisition decision, especially for those cells on the diagonal ("question mark" cells) of the matrix in Figure 7.1.

Figure 7.1:
"Make" or "buy" matrix for software

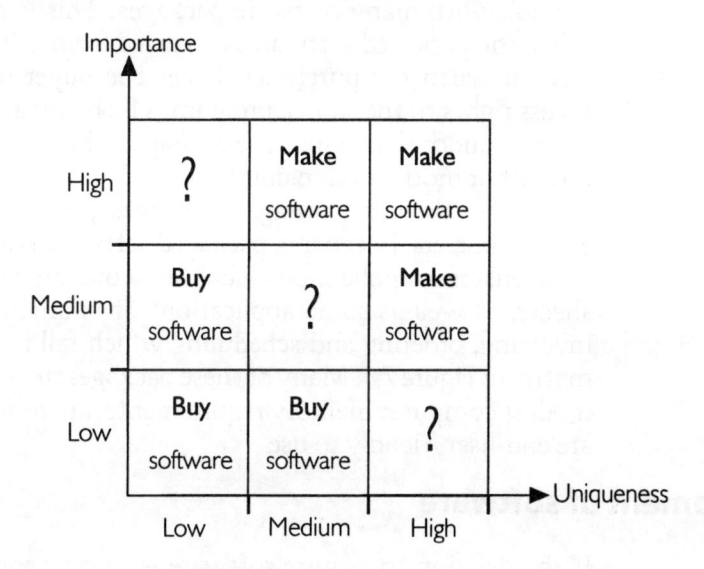

Importance	Low	Medium	High
High	?	Make software	Make software
Medium	Buy software	?	Make software
Low	Buy software	Buy software	?

Uniqueness →

In-house development can sometimes cost ten times as much as packaged software and require a long development period whereas software packages on the market are relatively cheap and immediately available (though they may need some customization). Many organizations have a shortage of analysts and programmers which limits the amount of customized software they can develop at any one time.

However, the availability of new programming languages with powerful instruction sets that are easy to learn means that there are many end-users writing their own programs, adding to the institutional pool of programmers.

On the other hand, some organizations have cumbersome authorization and acquisition procedures. It may actually take less time to develop a customized system than purchase a package, especially if the packaged program requires substantial tailoring. An additional benefit is that the company will "own" the software and won't need to worry about unauthorized copying and other legal issues. Nor will the company be at the "mercy" of an outside vendor to provide support. Also, reliance on commercial off-the-shelf packages means that in-house personnel fail to develop software expertise that will be useful to the firm in the long run in other application areas. Employees will not gain experience in software development that may be needed for other projects especially those that involve integration. Furthermore, acquiring software packages results in loss of control for the buyer. As an organization grows, advances technologically, or shifts its operational mission, software improvements may be desired. Yet no in-house modifications are possible with many software packages. This is the case, for example, when the packaged software is accessed from a dial-up timesharing service, or when the purchaser denies the buyer modification rights or access rights to the source program. The buyer and user must then rely on the vendor to enhance the package, which the vendor may have no interest or motivation in doing.

Despite the disadvantages, packaged programs do have their users and supporters. In general, packaged software is a good option for standard business applications, such as word processing, e-mail, spreadsheets, as well as some applications of billing, equipment inventory, invoicing, ordering and scheduling which fall in the SW corner of the matrix in Figure 7.1. Many of these packages run on a PC, have relatively modest computer memory requirements, are robust, easy to install and are end-user friendly to use.

Development of software

If the decision to acquire software is that of constructing it in-house then a methodology for development must be chosen.

Figure 7.2: *SDLC for software development*

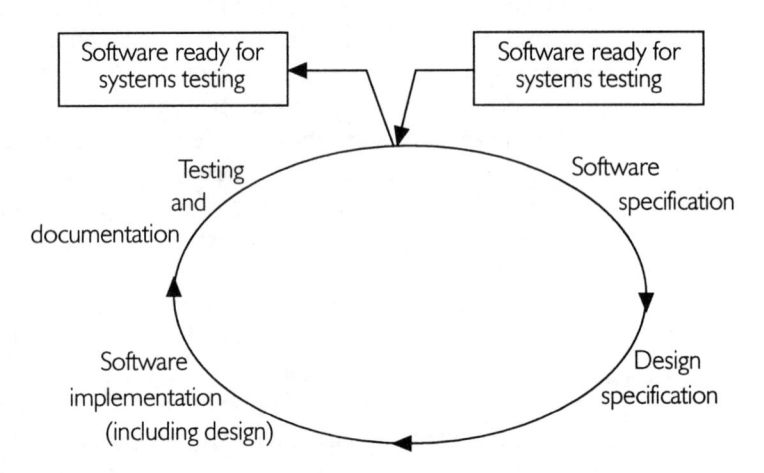

Software ready for systems testing

Software ready for systems testing

Testing and documentation

Software specification

Software implementation (including design)

Design specification

If the system is small and simple as for an *ad hoc* DSS or an EIS, or if the software were for a partial system or subsystem such as the interface for an end-user, then prototyping would be the most appropriate. However, for other systems, such as transactional systems and DDSs involving models, an SDLC will be necessary.

The activities of such a SDLC are shown in Figure 7.2. Note that we have chosen the cyclic representation to emphasize the life cycle of software development. The cycle is repeated either for redevelopment or for maintenance

SDLC for software development

The SDLC for software may look the same as that for an information system but there are many important differences. The software SDLC does not start with a feasibility study because the feasibility has already been determined in the SDLC. Also, the specification activity is different: the system specification is for the user's needs and is stated by the end-user. In software development, the specification is for software and is made by the systems analyst. As for the design of the software, that is determined by the user's need specification and will involve an appropriate model. The implementation of that model will involve programming in a language appropriate for the model – such as GPSS for a queuing model. And finally, there is the testing of software. This should be done for the subsystem of the software and ready for testing as part of the overall system. This strategy will help to isolate problems before they compound. Also, software testing may require a different methodology than systems testing. It is done by different personnel. The system is tested by the end-user for meeting the user's need specification. The different activities of software development will now be discussed in some detail but only in terms of considerations that are of interest and importance to the end-user, and so are also important for the management of software development.

Activities for software development

Specification

The specifications of the system's end product is already specified in the user specification document. This may be detailed to the point of specifying the output and stating requirements for input constraints, response time, levels of security, backup, recovery, and privacy considerations. An alternative to specific requirements may be a general statement of the type of output desired and then the analyst in the detailed software specification stage must provide the details.

In addition, there are many technical details that must be specified. These could include standards for software development, special features such as modularization, and even testing specifications. Programming standards might specify the programming language and tools of analysis and design to be used. If these are not already specified, then this must be done in the design stage.

The specifications for software also need to be analyzed and tested for feasibility even though an analysis and a feasibility study has been done for the system as a whole. It is quite possible that the system as stated in the feasibility stage has changed (from the software development viewpoint) in going through the end-user need-specification stage. The desired adjustments must be negotiated with the end-user(s). Perhaps the constraints can be relaxed or perhaps the requirements reduced. Once the software specifications are stabilized, the software system design can begin.

Design

Design of applications software has some design objectives in common with all software design, e.g. being correct, well debugged and safe to run. Some software, business software, has one particularly important requisite: it must be end-user friendly because some end-users are not necessarily computer-oriented or even computer literate. Also, business software need not be most efficient but it must be easily useable.

It is well recognized that some software generates needs for particular hardware, data/knowledge and procedures. If these have not been previously stated, or if these have been stated but change because of the design of software, then these particular needs must be specified and the relevant personnel so informed. Also, problems of linking, compatibility and portability must be considered in as far as they affect software development.

The design stage of software will depend on the processing to be performed which could involve transactional processing, an OR/MS model, an AI application, or some combination. The design will be done by professionals knowledgeable of the model and stated in a form and format that can be used by a systems analyst and programmer. To facilitate this communication, there are numerous forms, charts and techniques for design and some for analysis and design. These are part of the tools of the trade of the systems analyst and are the subject of courses and many books on systems analysis and design and hence beyond the scope of this book (see Hussain and Hussain, 1996).

Implementation

Implementation of software is mostly coding. The important decision before coding starts is the selection of the language to be used. This may be done in the design stage or it may be part of the programming standards. Sometimes this decision is left to the implementation stage. It is a difficult decision because of the proliferation of programming languages. In the early days of computing, there were two groups of languages: the scientific languages like FORTRAN, that were compute intensive but processed little data as input/output; and then there were the business oriented languages like COBOL, which involved simple processing but much handling and manipulation of masses of data and large volumes of input and output. In modern computing systems, this distinction is not always relevant. Business programming often involves complex mathematical and statistical models and masses of data/ knowledge stored in complex representations. For such environments a mix of programming languages are used.

For transactional processing there is COBOL, for DSSs there are a variety of appropriate languages, including 3GL (third generation procedural languages). Then there are specialized languages including simulation languages appropriate for a simulation model for a DSS, and AI languages for knowledge bases and expert systems. There are also many multiple-purpose languages such as SIMSCRIPT used for simulation but which also has many of the features of the 3GL FORTRAN and the business procedural language, COBOL. Some procedural languages are multipurpose: FORTRAN, for example, is excellent for number-crunching numerical data but can also be used for some transactional processing and for some simulation applications. We also see the coming of logic programming, declarative languages and object-oriented languages. The evolution of the different generation of these languages is shown in Figure 7.3.

4GLs and higher level languages have a comparative advantage over 3GLs including COBOL. One study showed that the:

> Effort for the 4GL implementation vs. the estimates for a comparable COBOL implementation favored the 4GL approach by 400%. If feasibility and requirements were factored out (because the time to do them should not be dependent on the language chosen), then the savings was 530%.
>
> *Glass*, 1991:131–2

Figure 7.3:
Generations of programming languages

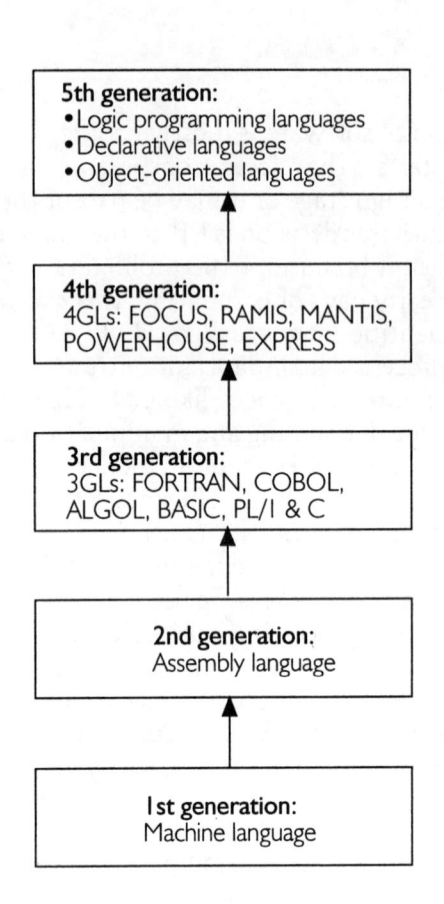

```
5th generation:
• Logic programming languages
• Declarative languages
• Object-oriented languages
        ↑
4th generation:
4GLs: FOCUS, RAMIS, MANTIS,
POWERHOUSE, EXPRESS
        ↑
3rd generation:
3GLs: FORTRAN, COBOL,
ALGOL, BASIC, PL/1 & C
        ↑
2nd generation:
Assembly language
        ↑
1st generation:
Machine language
```

However, the 3GLs have some comparative advantages too. This has been borne out by numerous empirical studies comparing a 4GL with COBOL. One study showed that a 4GL source code was 29 to 39% smaller in length but 50 times slower.

The chances are that during the professional lifetime of managers and end-users in business, they will use not just one but many programming languages and sometimes several of them simultaneously. It is therefore necessary to have a comparative appreciation of programming languages (the more the merrier!) in order to be able to select the appropriate language(s) for any given application and to participate meaningfully in the development, maintenance and management of software.

The problem is one of selecting the best language for the problem at hand. Unfortunately, the choice is not always a rational one. If left to the programmers, they will often opt for the language that they are most familiar and comfortable with. In one case on record, a programmers elected PL/1 for no reason other than wanting to try out the language. Soon thereafter, the programmer resigned leaving no one with

PL/1 knowledge or experience to maintain the program. As a result, the program had to be rewritten. Clearly, the selection criterion in this case did not serve the purpose of the firm. Many language options exist, from machine language to high-level procedural languages, query languages, and 4GLs. The most efficient to run in terms of computer time is machine language, but this language is difficult and complex to learn. Languages closer to natural language, i.e. high-level language, take more processing time, but are easier to master and faster to write. And the resultant programs are easier to understand and hence to maintain and enhance.

Because skilled programmers are an expensive and scarce resource whereas memory is cheap and computer run-time inexpensive, inefficient but high-level languages are favoured and usually preferred today for new systems. Even operating systems are no longer written in machine language. End-users have always preferred high-level languages, the higher the better, although not all end-users agree on how to rank programming languages. Some of the factors to be considered in program language selection are:

- Purpose of program/system.
- Built-in functions available.
- Internal storage required.
- Ability to manipulate:
    - data
    - strings
    - graphics
- Time to:
    - compile
    - execute
- Special features.
- Ease of use and user-friendliness.
- Ease of maintenance.
- Documentation available.
- Availability of technical staff.
- Compiler of language to be around for five to ten years.

It is the function of the analyst and the Project Manager that such choices are based less on personal preferences and biases and more on sound economic and technical considerations.

Testing

One approach is the *walkthrough* which is primarily an attempt to control the quality of a unit of software where errors might well occur. It is performed by the author of the program to be walked-through by the analyst or the programmer, stepping through the logic. This is done before a group of people who are knowledgeable of the field of the program domain as well as knowledgeable about software development. They are in a position to provide constructive and supportive critiques. The group is often three to five in size so that the dialogue is intensive and constructive. Those participating in the walkthrough may be peers, supervisors, end-users and others appointed by the project manager. It is a technical review to ensure that the task has been performed thoroughly, nothing important has been deleted or overlooked, and no obvious or potential errors exist. A walkthrough identifies errors before they compound and then become difficult to detect or correct. The correction is not part of the responsibility of the walkthrough session nor does it guarantee that the resulting system is correct and flawless. But the chance that the system is effective and even efficient is increased. However, there is a price to pay. The experience can be devastating to one's ego. The "author" must have the strength to face the scrutiny and criticisms of fellow professionals and even end-users.

A walkthrough is not testing in the conventional sense that you compare actual results with expected and desired results. Instead, it is a peer review that should identify potential errors before they occur. The later the errors are detected and corrected the more expensive it gets. Thus, errors caught in coding are almost twice as expensive as errors caught in a walkthrough and almost 40 times as expensive when caught during operations (source: *IEEE Spectrum*).

A walkthrough can be very threatening to an "author". To control the group dynamics and problems of group decision-making, variables of meetings such as their timing, their frequency, and the people attending the meetings must all be carefully managed. This is often done by a "coordinator" or "facilitator", who enables the author to come away from the walkthrough with the feeling (or at least a perception) that the discussion was constructive and supportive.

Documentation

Once the software has been tested as units, it is then ready for the systems test. There is one last activity left and it is that of documentation. This may start earlier than shown in Figure 7.2 but it should be completed before delivery of the system for operations. If not, then there may well be serious problems when it comes to the maintenance or enhancement of the system. Unfortunately the documentation is seldom completed on time, if at all. It is perceived to be uncreative and hence is an unpopular activity. There is procrastination and the excuse that the software cycle will be documented after the system has stabilized and more often than not the system stabilizes after the programmer or analyst in question has left for another job. One solution to this problem is to have standards on how documentation is to be prepared (including content, format, and specifying who performs the documentation and when) and who enforces the standards. The other alternatives are to subcontract documentation or to hire only conscientious and disciplined systems personnel who are aware of the importance of documentation.

This later alternative actually happened in one recorded case. An analyst was being interviewed for a job. In the final stages of the successful interview, the dialogue went as follows:

Manager: "How soon can you join us?"
Analyst: "Not before the end of November."
Manager: "Can we somehow persuade you to come earlier?"
Analyst: "No."
Manager: "Why is that?"
Analyst: "Because I have just completed a project and will not be able to complete the documentation before the end of November."

The analyst was hired on the spot and on his terms. Someone with such conscientiousness and an awareness of the importance of documentation is, unfortunately, a rare breed.

Once the system is satisfactorily tested (including the documentation) and ready for delivery, the cycle of software development is complete.

Prototyping and software development

Prototyping can be used effectively when "experimenting" with different approaches in both the development of "new" software or the modification of bought (or "old") software. It is especially appropriate when there is more than one end-user involved who do not have "fixed" views on say the output format. This often happens in the development of an EIS or DSS.

There is some empirical data available pertaining to the implications of prototyping as opposed to formally specifying the user's needs in an SDLC. The existence of good empirical data is a not a common occurrence in this area and thus we should not ignore it. Boehm, Gray, and Seewaldt (1984) conducted an experiment to compare prototyping and specifying as techniques for software development. Seven teams each tackled the same 2–4K source code lines project. The specifying teams were constrained to produce a requirements specification and a design specification before any implementation. And the prototyping teams had to produce a prototype by week five (the midpoint of the overall project). The seven versions of the final system were compared both quantitatively (e.g. lines of code and pages of documentation) and qualitatively (e.g. maintainability and ease of use). Because of the small number of small teams involved and the use of limited subjective evaluation, the results should be thought of as no more than suggestive, certainly not definitive. But with this disclaimer in mind, it may be useful to examine the major conclusions.

1. Prototyping tended to produce a smaller product, with roughly equivalent performance, using less effort – almost half the size from almost half the effort. The specifiers often found themselves overcommitted by their specifications: "Words are cheap" they remarked somewhat ruefully.
2. Prototyping did not tend to produce higher "productivity" (measured as delivered source-code instructions per man hour). However, when "productivity" was measured in equivalent user satisfaction per man hour, prototyping was superior.
3. Prototyping did tend to provide expected benefits such as:
   - Better human–machine interfaces.
   - Always having something that works.
   - Reduced deadline effect at the end of the project.
4. Prototyping tended to create several negative effects such as:
   - Less planning and designing, and more testing and fixing.
   - More difficult integration due to lack of interface specification.
   - A less coherent design.

The authors comment that these last negative effects from prototyping will become particularly critical on larger products. In summary, the three authors conclude that both prototyping and the SDLC approach have valuable advantages that complement each other, and that for most large projects a mix of these two approaches is the best strategy.

Summary and conclusions

The advantages and limitations of software packages are listed in Table 7.1.

Table 7.1 *Advantages and limitations of software packages*

Advantages
- Cheaper (than developing customized software)
- Faster to acquire, often available off-the-shelf
- Does not require from the buyer the commitment of scarce personnel (systems analysts, programmers, telecommunications experts, data specialists)
- Problems debugged and software validated
- Documented
- Often regularly maintained and upgraded by vendor
- Often represents state-of-the-art technology

Limitations
- Not available for specialized applications but only for generalized ones
- Not appropriate for complex applications especially integrated ones
- Most require some fine-tuning and tailoring to meet local needs
- Some require long and sometimes painful administrative procedures
- Can lead to legal problems in copying what is legally owned by the vendor
- User must conform to format and procedural constraints and demands of the packaged software
- No "learning" experience of development by buyer
- No transfer of technology of application development to other applications

The process of software development is shown in Figure 7.2. An alternative to such development is outsourcing, a subject discussed in detail in Chapter 10. The initial activities in acquiring software are summarized in Figure 7.4. An early decision in software development is whether or not to acquire a software package. Only if packaged software is not used ("No" exit in box 2), and if the outsourcing strategy is not selected ("No" exit in box 4), and prototyping is not used ("No" exit in box 6), is it necessary to think about developing software using an SDLC "in-house" (box 8).

The activities of an SDLC for software development are much the same as the activities in an SDLC for an information system discussed in Chapter 6.

Chapter 7: Buy or Build Software Systems

Figure 7.4:
Strategies for software development

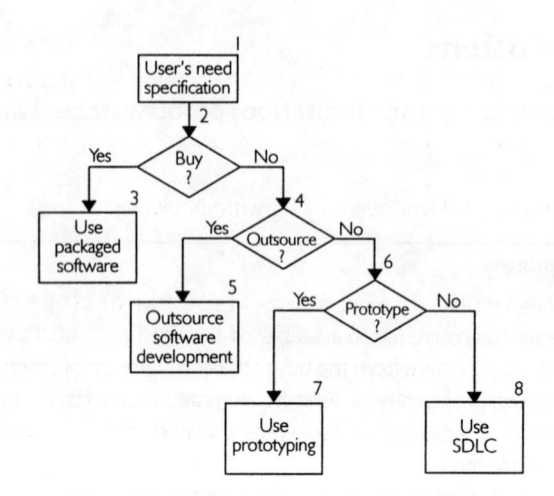

Software development requires many tools and techniques including structured walkthroughs used for testing software. A summary of the advantages and disadvantages of a walkthrough are listed in Table 7.2.

Table 7.2 *Summary of advantages and pitfalls of walkthrough*

Advantages
- Detects errors before they propagate
- Requires software personnel to justify their approaches
- Offers different opinions of approaches
- Avoids overlooking functions that have to be performed
- Permits fine tuning of system
- Improves "quality" of software
- Improves communication between systems personnel as well as between them and end-users
- Offers an avenue for reviews from experienced personnel and end-users
- Can be a "learning" experience for all involved – especially the author

Pitfalls
- Can be time consuming and expensive
- Requires a certain type of person to accept reviews and criticisms from peers, supervisors and end-users
- Requires an understanding of group dynamics
- Can result in conflict and bad feeling between systems personnel as well as with end-users
- Criticisms can go beyond professional critiques and become personal. This could be bad for the morale of systems personnel and discourage greater use of walkthrough
- Walkthroughs should not be viewed as any guarantee that the system is correct or of best quality. Other efforts at improving quality and efficiency as well as reducing errors should also be pursued

Once the software is ready, it is tested to the satisfaction of software personnel. It is then ready for being tested as part of the whole system to be tested for the end-user's satisfaction. There is another alternative to "buying" software outside "building" in-house: reuse of software within an SDLC or even within prototyping – the subject of our next chapter.

Case 7.1: 4GL at Hogg Robson Travel, Hong Kong

In November 1988, the management at Hogg Robson Travel determined that they needed a computerized system to enable currency dealings by placing kiosks in their 200+ branches. They had to have the system online in five months in order to benefit from the traditional holiday booking. The system had to verify and control the transactional data from its branches, control "in transit cash", maintain robust audit trails, and report stocks for balance sheet purposes.

Management also recognized its limitations: it had no in-house experience in programming such systems and did not know of any consulting firm for computing that had the experience with its business. Nonetheless, management decided to go-ahead and using a 4GL. The system was delivered on time and within budget.

Source: Mortimer, Andrew. (1991). "A 4GL success Story." *The Computer Bulletin*, Series 1V, vol. 3, (Part 1, February), pp. 18–20.

Case 7.2: Programming languages for XCON

The programming languages used for the different components of the XCON application of computer systems configuration at DEC were:

BASIC User interface and related mechanisms
C   Component database access
LIST   Component database access and creation
Pascal Batch control
SCAN   Pre-specified selection
OPS5   Variety of tasks such as counting, sorting and various numeric conversions were performed by routines written in traditional languages and called by OPS5.

Source: Barker, Virginia E. and O'Connor, Dennis E. (1989). "Expert Systems for Configuration at Digital: XCON and Beyond." *Communications of the ACM*, vol. 32, no. 3 (March), pp. 298–318.

Case 7.3: Software testing for the Metro in Paris

The RATP, part of the Metro (underground/subway) system in Paris had a two-minute separation between trains. To allow for the traffic of 60,000 passengers/hour, RATP wanted to reduce the separation time to 30 seconds. A project to accomplish this was conceptualized in 1979, finished in 1982 and fully deployed in 1989. The hardware was new for the 9,000 lines of program code which was first tested in part by the Hoare method. Later, a mathematician and consultant, Raymond Abrial, was hired to help perform an external evaluation. Abrial used his B-method which helped control the project's coherence. End-user communication was good and there was good rewriting of the specifications. The stages of testing as part of total testing was as follows:

Formal proof = 32.4%
Module testing = 20.1%
Functional testing = 25.9%
Respecification = 21.6%

The B-method proved so successful that it has been used by academic groups including Oxford University; some governmental groups; a transportation system in Calcutta, India; and by the French Railways.

Case 7.4: Software at Societe General, Paris

Societe General has 2,500 branches and representative offices in its international network headquartered in Paris. In mid-1990, the company launched a new business venture in Guaranteed Investment Contacts which had security as a crucial aspect of its operations. The company began looking for a 4GL when it saw an advertisement for CorVision and compared favourably with the 4GLs because it:

> ...could generate applications that interface seamlessly and easily with their existing applications, such as foreign exchange, money market and general ledger.

CorVision was adopted and in the first phase:

> ...there were 608 function points, 41 data sets, 30 screens and 23 reports. The application has been revised about half a dozen times, and is now in release 2.3.1. Today, there are 65 datasets, 90 screens, 50 reports, 65 queries and 40 windows. Traders now have online query capabilities, and the system provides better support for the back-office and automatically adjusts the portfolio on an as-needed basis.

Source: *I/S Analyzer*. (1992). vol. 30, no. 7 (July), pp. 8.

Case 7.5: Software management at CTC (Canadian Tire Corp.)

Canadian Tire Corp. is a $3 billion integrated supplier of automotive, home and leisure products in Canada. It recently had a merger and its biggest problem of the data centre consolidation was software licensing. After eight months of negotiation with the provider, CTC came out rather unhappy with the results but had learned valuable lessons in software management. These were:

- Do not trust the statement: "Just sign these order forms and everything will be taken care of, and you can go on with your reorganization." This open-ended authority hides situations like: "If CTC put in two physically separate CPUs next to each other and attached them by cable, there would be no upgrade, transfer or license fee. But if they put in one CPU and used LPAR to partition the machine and ran two images, since it was on the same machine, they would have to pay the transfer fees even though they weren't changing the use of the software."
- A close relationship between the legal department and IS needs to be fostered.
- It helps to develop, with a consultant, a standard contract dealing with software, maintenance, escrow, and evaluation. These could favour the corporation and is a good starting point for negotiations with the vendor who has a standard contract template that favours the vendor.
- CTC saved a great deal of money (about 25%) by not paying for redundant software, allowing to downsize software, eliminating extra vendors (for example, of compilers), and opening new negotiations with vendors. One must look at the total cost not just the initial cost. Thus a $50,000 cost of software with a 10% discount may look good but hidden is the $60,000 cost of maintenance. This is a business issue and not an IS issue but cannot be looked at separately.

Source: *I/S Analyzer*, vol. 31, no. 7 (July 1993), p. 5.

Case 7.6: A vendor's perspective of software management

Digital Equipment Corporation (DEC) has "taken a series of actions that brings to life the user–vendor relationship in its most positive form." DEC got the SSAM (Strategic Software Asset Management) Award in 1992. The criteria for the SSAM Award is: licensing, contract, relationship building, counsel and tools.

Supplement 7.1: Programming languages

DEC uses a management model that has six phases: evaluation and selection; acquisition order placement and receipt; software distribution and installation; access control/inventory; asset optimization/resources tracking and reporting; and user support. Technologies like client/server have complicated software management to the point that vendors have the responsibility of supplying the right tools to manage distribution, version control, and configuration control. Early versions of these tools are starting to hit the market.

DEC recognizes that end-users, other users, developers, and systems vendors do not all have the same needs of software:

> Part of DEC's strategy is to be able to quickly offer innovative license terms to respond to changing market needs.

Source: *I/S Analyzer*, vol. 31, no. 7 (July 1993).

Supplement 7.1: Programming languages

Figure 7.5 shows the spectrum of high- and low-level languages.

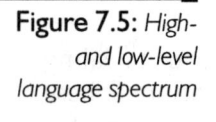

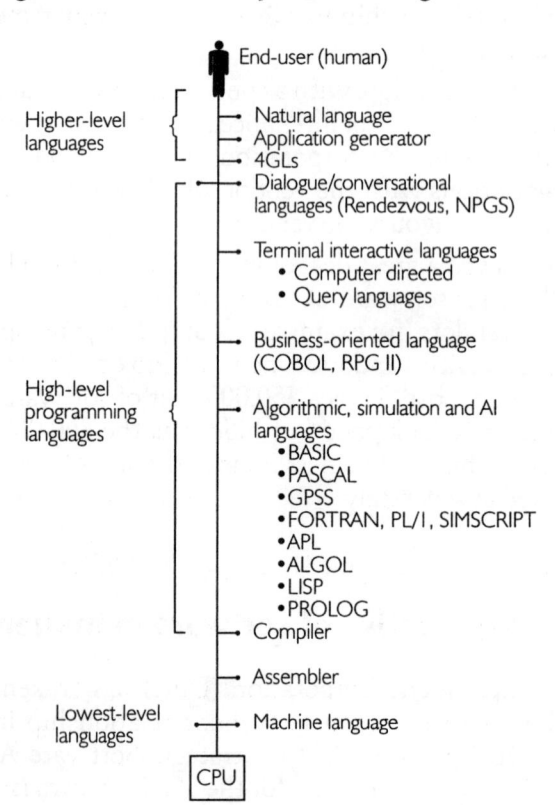

Figure 7.5: *High- and low-level language spectrum*

Higher-level languages:
- End-user (human)
- Natural language
- Application generator
- 4GLs
- Dialogue/conversational languages (Rendezvous, NPGS)
- Terminal interactive languages
  - Computer directed
  - Query languages

High-level programming languages:
- Business-oriented language (COBOL, RPG II)
- Algorithmic, simulation and AI languages
  - BASIC
  - PASCAL
  - GPSS
  - FORTRAN, PL/I, SIMSCRIPT
  - APL
  - ALGOL
  - LISP
  - PROLOG
- Compiler
- Assembler

Lowest-level languages:
- Machine language
- CPU

References

Abdel-Hamid, T. K. (1990). "The Elusive Silver Lining: How We Fail to Learn from Software Development Failures." *Sloan Management Review*, vol. 32, no. 1, pp. 39–48.

Abel, D. and Rout, T. P. (1993). "Defining and Specifying the Quality Attributes." *Australian Computer Journal*, vol. 25, no. 3 (August), pp. 105–12.

Bliss, Marian. (1993). "Software Configuration Management." *Journal of Information Systems Management*, vol. 10, no. 3 (September), pp. 35–47.

Brooks, Frederick P. (1987). "No Silver Bullet: Essence and Accidents of Software Engineering." *Computer*, vol. 20, no. 4 (April), pp. 10–20.

Cockburn, Alistair. (1996). "The Interaction of Social Issues and Software Architecture." *Communications of the ACM*, vol. 39, no. 10 (October), pp. 40–6.

Galletta, D., King, Ruth C. and Rateb, Dina. (1993). "The Effect of Expertise on Software Selection." *Database*, vol. 26, no. 2 (May), pp. 7–20.

Glass, Robert L. (1991). "4GLs and CASE: What is the Payoff?" *Journal of Systems and Software*, vol. 14, no. 3, pp. 131–2.

Grudin, Jonathan. (1991). "Interactive systems: Bridging the Gap between Developers and Users." *Computer*, vol. 24, no. 4 (April), pp. 59–69.

Heineman, G. T., Botsford, J. E., Galdiera, G. *et al.* (1994). "Emerging Technologies that Support a Software Process Life Cycle." *IBM Systems Journal*, vol. 33, no. 3, pp. 501–529.

Hussain, Donna and Hussain, K. M. (1995). *Information Systems, Analysis, Design, and Implementation*. New Delhi: Tata McGraw-Hill Publishing.

IEEE Software. (1994). "Special issue of Software Development." vol. 11, no. 1 (January), pp. 16–68.

Iivari, Juhani. (1990). "Implementability of In-House Developed vs. Application Package Based Information Systems." *Database*, vol. 2, no. 1, pp. 1–9.

Information and Software Technology. (1991). "Special Issue on Information and Software Economics." Vol. 33, no. 3 (April).

Ince, Darrel and Andrews, Derek, (eds.). (1990). *The Software Life Cycle*. Oxford: Butterworth.

Nooteboom, Bart. (1992). "Information Technology, Transaction Costs and the Decision to Make or Buy." *Technology Analysis and Strategic Management*, vol. 4, no. 4, pp. 339–52.

Perry, William E. (1992). "Quality Concerns in Software Development." *Information Systems Management*, vol. 9, no. 2, pp. 48–52.

References

Pfleeger, S. L. and J. C. Fitzgerald, Jr. (1991). "Software Metrics Tool Kit: Support for Selection, Collection and Analysis." *Information and Software Technology*, vol. 33, no. 7 (September), pp. 477–98.

Sasserath, J. D. (1990). "Buying Packaged Software? Caveat Emptor." *Industrial Management and Data Systems*, vol. 90, no. 2 (1990), pp. 11–3.

Snell, Ned. (1992). "Quality Tools for Quality Software." *Datamation*, vol. 38, no. 1 (January 1), pp. 53–6.

Welch, James A. (1992). "Strategic Sourcing: A Progressive Approach to the Make-Buy Decision." *Academy of Management Executive*, vol. 6, no. 1, pp. 23–31.

Welke, Richard J. (1994). "The Shifting Software Development Paradigm." *Data Base*, vol. 25, no. 4 (November), pp. 9–17.

8 Reuse

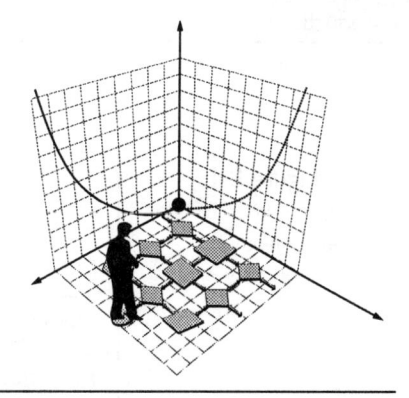

> Reuse should complement automation, not compete with it... The defining characteristic of good reuse is not the reuse of software per se, but the reuse of human problem solving.
>
> *Barnes and Bollinger, 1991*

Introduction

Packaged software may require modification. Custom-made software can become too expensive in time and money. There may, however, be an alternative: to supplement custom-made software with software previously used and now *reused*. Some of this reuseable software may come from a library of reuseable software and the rest can be bought off-the-shelf. The reuse concept is illustrated in Figure 8.1. This reuse is for finished software itself, but one could reuse parts and products such as: requirement specifications, designs, test data, customized tools, and even problem-solving techniques. Such reuse will not only improve productivity in the development process but because the reusable parts are well tried and tested, they are reliable and will reduce maintenance costs. Reuse also reduces the time required for development, and so increases productivity. Many success stories of reuse are summarized in cases that appear at the end of this chapter.

Reuse is the use of existing components and artefacts in the construction of another system. It avoids having to start from scratch and reinvent the wheel. Reuse is not a new concept. It was introduced into the automobile industry at the turn of the century when all the cars were custom built just as much of our software is generated today. But then Henry Ford decided to standardize parts and reused them as part of good engineering practice.

Introduction

Figure 8.1:
Comparison of development with and without reuse of components

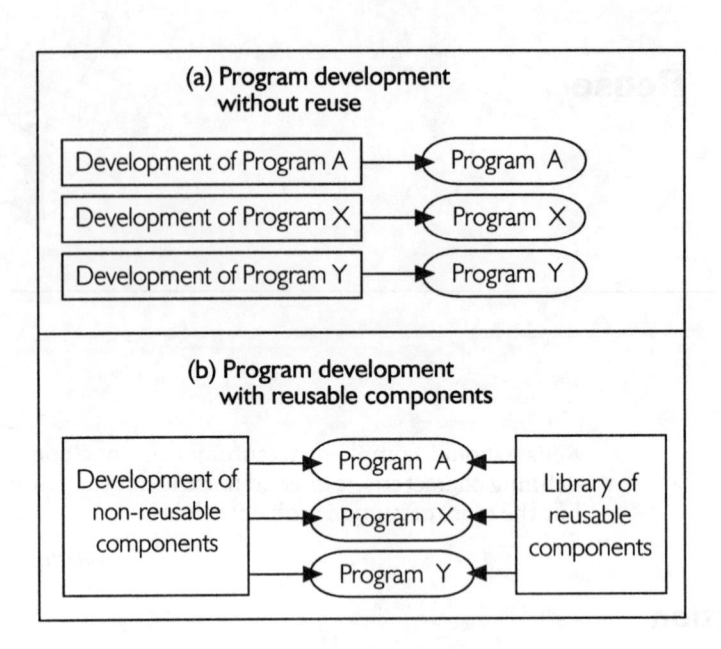

(a) Program development without reuse

- Development of Program A → Program A
- Development of Program X → Program X
- Development of Program Y → Program Y

(b) Program development with reusable components

Development of non-reusable components → Program A, Program X, Program Y ← Library of reusable components

Since then, the state-of-the-art in production has come to the car industry with increasing choices in colour, style and accessories but there are a number of parts like the chassis, axle and steering mechanism that can be reused in different models. Such industrialization of production has not yet taken place to any large extent in the software development industry, and this is the subject that we will explore in this chapter. Reuse is viable if one has a large number of related products. This is now becoming possible in software development especially in business computing. But as the reuse increases so does the problem of managing the reuse: the standardization of parts; certification that parts are reusable; the protection against piracy; the encouragement of reuse through incentives; and the management of resistance to reuse. These are subjects that we will examine. First, however, we will discuss the process involved in reuse: an analysis of the application domain; the calculation of risks and benefits involved; the determination of what to reuse and what to custom build; what reusable components can come from the corporate library and what have to be imported; and the relationship of reuse production to the SDLC. We then examine the production and management considerations of reuse and conclude with an examination of the concept of mass-producing software in a software "factory". First, however, we start with the consideration of production of components.

Component engineering

We use the term "component" which would be a "module" in a software system, an "object" in the OO methodology, or a user specification or documentation in the development of an information system. The first problem is determining which components can be reused and which cannot. To illustrate the problem we consider a simple set of components for a simple reuse problem: development of a software program as shown in Figure 8.2.

Figure 8.2:
A representation of components of a software program

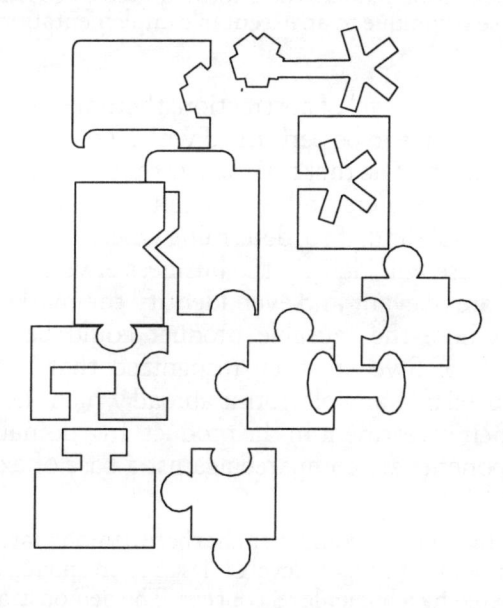

Here, the components can be any of the following:
1. Reusable part that is available in the reusable library.
2. Reusable part that must be imported (not necessarily form abroad).
3. Part that must be custom made.
4. Part that provides the "framework" or "glue" that holds the rest of the components together.

The problem now is to determine the optimal mix of the above types of components from the point of view of feasibility, risks, benefits, and costs (initial cost of development and running cost of maintenance). Fortunately, there are many tools that help us in this task of configuration. They include: browsers, builders, generators, and specific systems such as Matisse, and HP SynerVision. The tools to be used will depend on the level of abstraction.

> Abstraction plays a central role in software reuse. Concise and expressive abstractions are essential software artifacts are to be effectively reused. The effectiveness of a reuse technique can be evaluated in terms of cognitive distance – an intuitive gauge of the intellectual effort required to use the technique. Cognitive distance is reduced in two ways:
>
> 1. Higher level abstractions in a reuse technique reduce the effort required to go from the initial concept of a software system to representations in the reuse technique, and
> 2. Automation reduces the effort required to go from abstractions in a reuse technique to an executable implementation.
>
> Krueger, 1992:131

Whatever the level of abstraction, there are tasks of component engineering that have to be performed which starts with the formulation of a reuse strategy. The first task here is that of performing a domain analysis, where we understand the domain to be programmed to determine if reuse is viable and, if so, determine where to focus our attention. The analysis phase will identify the business environment and product factors that are relevant and even identify the market (both at home and abroad) where the reusable product could be sold. In the case of NobelTech of Sweden, they recognized that the reused application could be used in many platforms abroad which allowed the company to recoup their investment in the product. In a domain analysis, all potential components are compared against a base of existing reusable components:

> ...until a candidate component has been demonstrated. It is then possible to abstract to the higher level of description and replace the component discovered by a higher level concept. The demonstration that a component is present could be very formal, involving proof techniques, or it could involve the execution of code against some critical test case that will confirm or refute the hypothesis...
>
> Hall, 1992:246

Prieto-Díaz discusses domain analysis further:

> Domain analysis is the key to systematic, formal, and effective reuse. It is through domain analysis that knowledge is transformed into generic specification, designs, and architectures. Generic templates will be the basis for creating components that are easy to reuse.
>
> Prieto-Díaz, 1993:66

One key problem is the identification of the related elements of reuse.

> The gathering into one routine of all the connecting links between a program and some function it will need at many points, so as to form a single standard interface between the two. A typical subject of modularization in this sense is an I/O package, which accepts all input/output

requests from a program in a machine-independent form, and generates from them calls on the hardware or operating system functions that actually provide the needed service.

Halpern, 1990:139 (quoted in *Partridge*, 1992:115)

Another related problem is that of sequencing.

...we never want to reuse ALL of some previous derivation sequence. So clearly, such sequences cannot be recorded as a monolithic block and replayed whenever required. Derivation sequences will have to be structured in such a way as to mesh with a control strategy that selects, deletes, substitutes, etc. appropriate elements to generate the new (and perhaps quite similar) derivation sequence.

Partridge, 1992:116

Another task in formulating a reuse strategy is to determine the ability of the corporation to undertake the reuse program. This task is performed by a reuse capability model which identifies the process and organizational factors necessary for the reuse alternative.

Figure 8.3:
SCERT-like simulation of component configuration

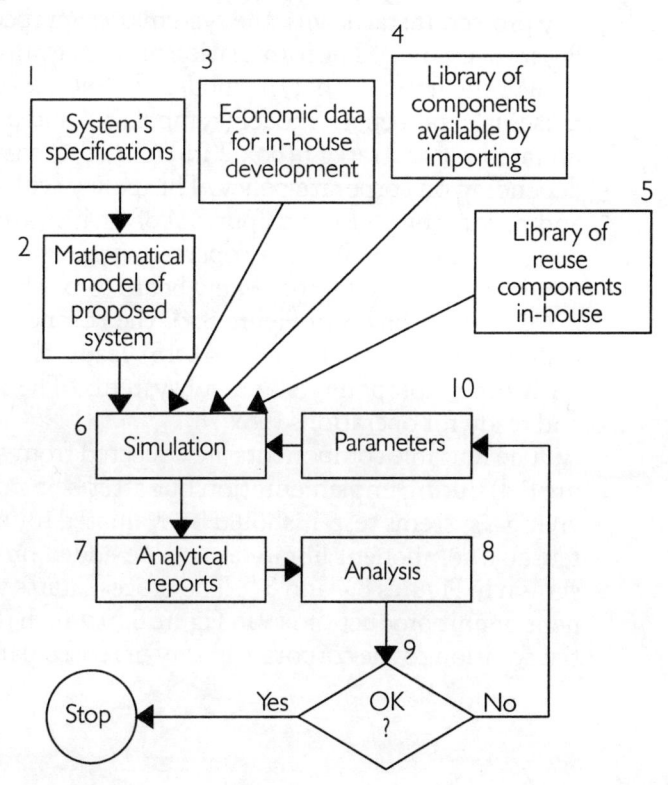

Chapter 8: Reuse

Yet another task to be performed is to determine the benefits and risks involved in reuse. This is done by the reuse economics model which could be a spreadsheet that determines the economic feasibility of reuse; or it could be a simulation in a model like SCERT (System and Computer Evaluation Review Technique) that computes the consequences of different component configurations. The overview of such a SCERT program is shown in Figure 8.3. Here, a simulation of components is run (box 6) for a mathematical model (box 2) of the proposed system using components from libraries of components outside the organization and in the organization (boxes 4 and 5 respectively). If the analysis of the solution is not satisfactory (box 9 in Figure 8.3), then the parameters of the choice of components is made (box 10) and another simulation is made ("No" exit in box 9), until a satisfactory solution is reached ("Yes" exit of box 9).

Component engineering and the SDLC

Component engineering is the implementation phase of the SDLC for any project. It starts with the systems design specifications as shown in Figure 8.4 (box 1). The formulation of strategy may need the use of models like the domain analysis model, the reuse capability model and the reuse risk and benefit model (symbols 3,4 and 5 respectively). The formulated reuse strategy (box 2 in Figure 8.4) may have to be approved depending on corporate policy. This policy will vary with corporations and may require a formal approval of each strategy for reuse by a reuse review board (box 6) or may operate within guidelines formulated (and regularly updated) by the review board (box 6 to box 2). Once approved ("Yes" exit of box 7 in Figure 8.4), the components are collected, unit tested and then assembled (box 13) ready for the systems test along with other components and subsystems. The system is documented and ready for operations (box 18).

The reusable components are collected from a library (box 11 in Figure 8.4) during implementation but after being product tested and surviving a systems test, it should be evaluated for possible addition to the reusable component library as a value-added product. This is a process shown in Figures 8.4 and 8.5. The process starts with the tested component or unit product (box 9 in Figure 8.5) which is considered as a potential addition to the corporate library of reused parts (box 1 in Figure 8.5).

Figure 8.4: *Reuse component engineering*

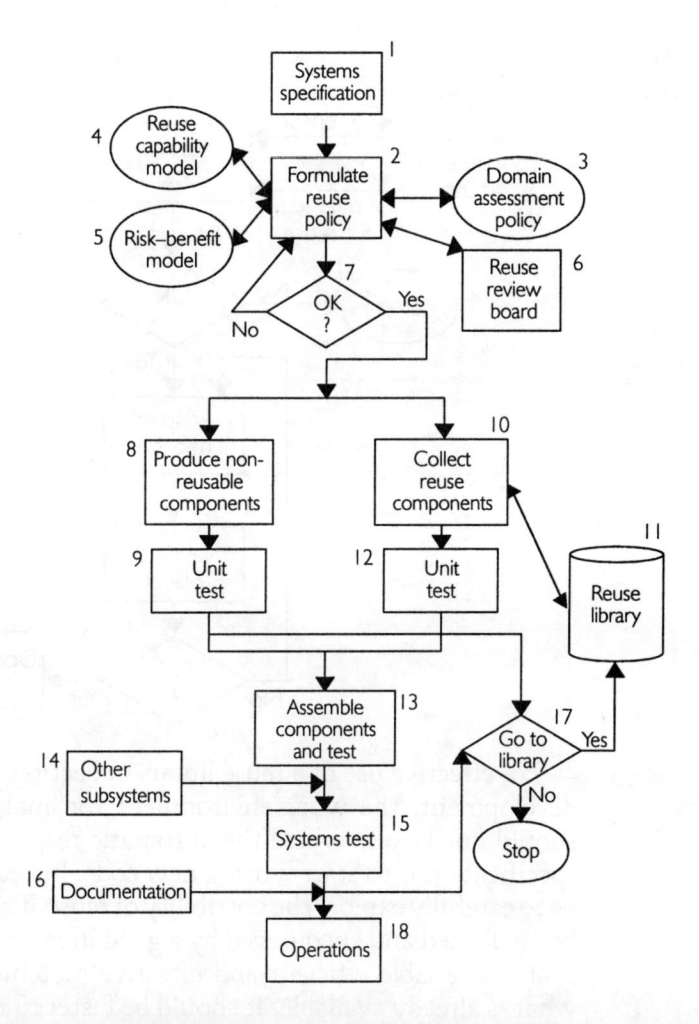

The reuse potential is often discovered by someone either as a response to an incentive (or without an incentive) who then becomes a sponsor and shepherds the part through the reuse review process. The review board will consider the part and the sponsorship. An approval may be given subject to some modification. Once that is done ("Yes" exit, box 3 in Figure 8.5, and box 17 in Figure 8.4) the component is modified and adapted and passes the requirements of the corporation's standards requirements ("Yes" exit, box 7 in Figure 8.5), the part is certified and documented for reuse (box 8) and gets added to the reuse parts library (box 9) for potential use by the next development process.

Component engineering and the SDLC

Figure 8.5: *Reuse library adoption procedure*

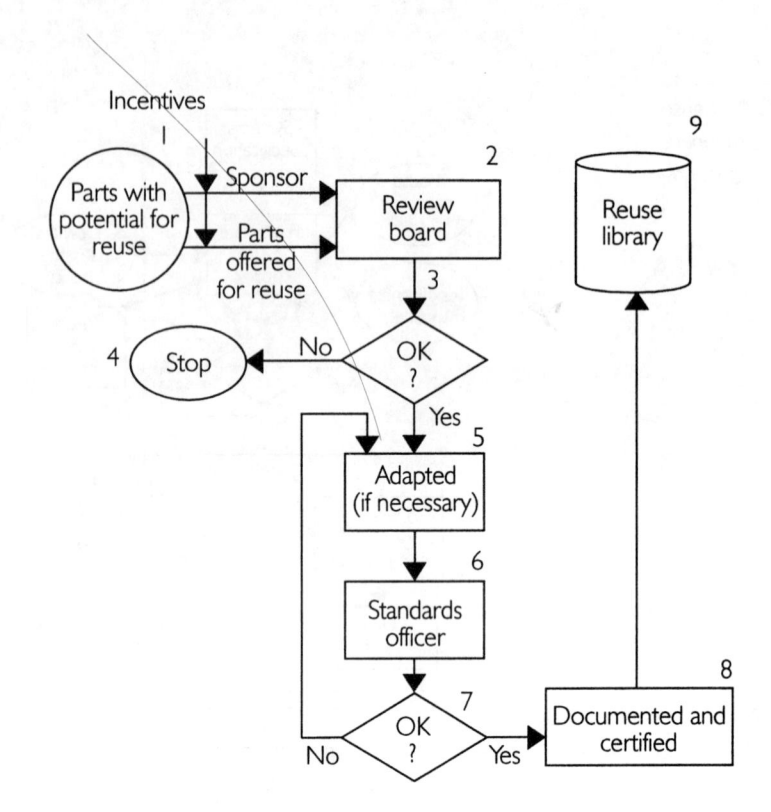

[Flowchart: Parts with potential for reuse → Parts offered for reuse; Incentives → Sponsor → Review board (2); 1 = Incentives; 3 = OK? (No → Stop (4); Yes → Adapted (if necessary) (5)); 6 = Standards officer; 7 = OK? (No → back; Yes → Documented and certified (8)) → Reuse library (9)]

For effective use of a reuse library collection, in context of software development, the work environment for analysts and programmers should not be one where the automatic response to a systems design specification is to start writing new code. Instead, the response should be to carefully explore the possibility of reuse. This use of reuse parts can be facilitated and encouraged by a good inventory of the reusable parts that will enable efficient and effective matching of new needs with what is already available. It should be faster to retrieve a part for reuse that to rewrite it. Often, a programmer tends to rewrite a program module because the original cannot be quickly retrieved. Thus the reusable part must be classified to facilitate retrieval. In addition to information on the consequences (costwise and otherwise) of the reuse part being used, we need information on:

- What it does.
- The underlying concepts and principles.
- The level of testing carried out.
- Its reuse and revision history.
- Who was the sponsor, if any.

Such information should all be recorded before certification (box 8, Figure 8.5). If the part was produced using reverse engineering, then the component from which it was extracted should be cross-referenced.

Libraries for reuse can vary from tens to thousands of parts that are all well-tried and tested. The ADA and Smalltalk libraries each have a few thousand. Corporations with a diverse applications portfolio will have thousands of reuse components which can be classified into the following types:

- "As-is" components.
- Structured collection.
- Unstructured collection.
- Structured collection of generic components.
- General purpose building blocks (of stacks, lists and queues).
- Domain-specific building blocks.
- Code skeletons.
- Front-ends.
- Front-ends with multilevel generics.
- I/O packages.
- Design scavenging.
- Software schemas.
- Documentation packages.
- Application generators.

A future development is what Bary Boehm and William Sherlis have called *Megaprogramming*. It would (Prieto-Díaz, 1993:66) be the integration of reuse technology with its tools, techniques and libraries into a:

> ... systematic framework of industrialized reuse. It has the potential to establish a new development paradigm that is domain specific, reuse-based, and process driven.

Management of reuse

Establishing a reuse library is only one function of the management of reuse. Another function mentioned was the use of a review board. There are other support facilities needed for reuse management including reuse engineers and specialists in econometrics, in financial modeling, in reuse architecture and design, in standards for reuse, and in the certification of reuse. (Some of these specialties may be in one person.) Also important is the protection of intellectual property represented in the reuse library and in the marketing of some reusable parts. A summary of

Chapter 8: Reuse

some of the functions of reuse management is shown in Figure 8.6 which is mostly self-explanatory.

Figure 8.6:
Organization for reuse

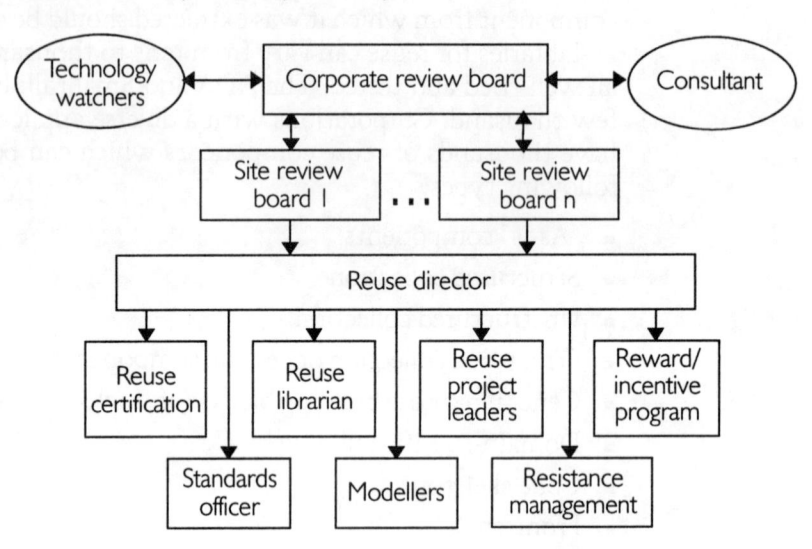

Also needed are non-technical personnel like the human-factors engineer who identifies resistance to reuse and implements strategies to overcome them. Resistance is not uncommon in information systems but this comes from the end-user side. In contrast, the resistance to reuse often comes from the computer professional. There are some programmers who do not want to be bothered with reuse and would always rather write their own programs. Also, they think that they can write programs that are better than the "true, tried and tested" reuse programs. This may be arrogance but unfortunately such attitudes do exist. One way to overcome this problem and to encourage others to contribute reusable programs and to reuse unmodified programs (or else the maintenance goes up) is to offer incentives. One firm (Hartford Insurance in the US) offers a cash bonus of $300 for each reuse part accepted by the library. This program can be justified to management as a royalty or a license fee. Another firm (Pacific Bell in the US) offers a mug for every program that gets into the library. The mug may seem to be a gimmick but it worked. It became a status symbol and no programmer was worth anything unless they displayed an array of reusability mugs, one for each year of contribution. Soon every one has a reuse mug and the status symbol lost its allure. However, by then reuse had become an intrinsic part of the development culture even though it had been a slow and difficult goal to reach. It must evolve and not be achieved by edict from the top, i.e. it is best if this cultural change comes from the bottom-up. Meanwhile, there are other incentives that include recognition, salary raises and promotion.

Offering incentives is one factor that can bring success. Griss identifies 48 factors relating to reuse (Griss, 1993:554). Of these, the important success factors are a good reuse parts library that is easily accessible and has good instructions on use; education, advice and consulting on reuse; good strategies and policies for reuse; good quality and progress control; competent project managers; and a high standard for the quality for reuse artefacts.

From library to factory

If a corporation has most (if not all) the success factors for reuse, it is then approaching what is often referred to as a *software factory*. The basic concept was first suggested by Dough McIlroy in 1968 who envisioned software being produced *en masse* and offered by catalogue. Since then there have been many other versions including the term "software factory" being registered by Systems Development Corp. in 1974; the terms *experience factory* and the *knowledge factory* coined to emphasize the learning aspect of reuse; *the new software factory* that emphasizes the domain-specific nature of reuse; and the *workstation software factory* that highlights the desktop nature of software production. One scenario that identifies the basic functions performed in a software factory is shown in Figure 8.7.

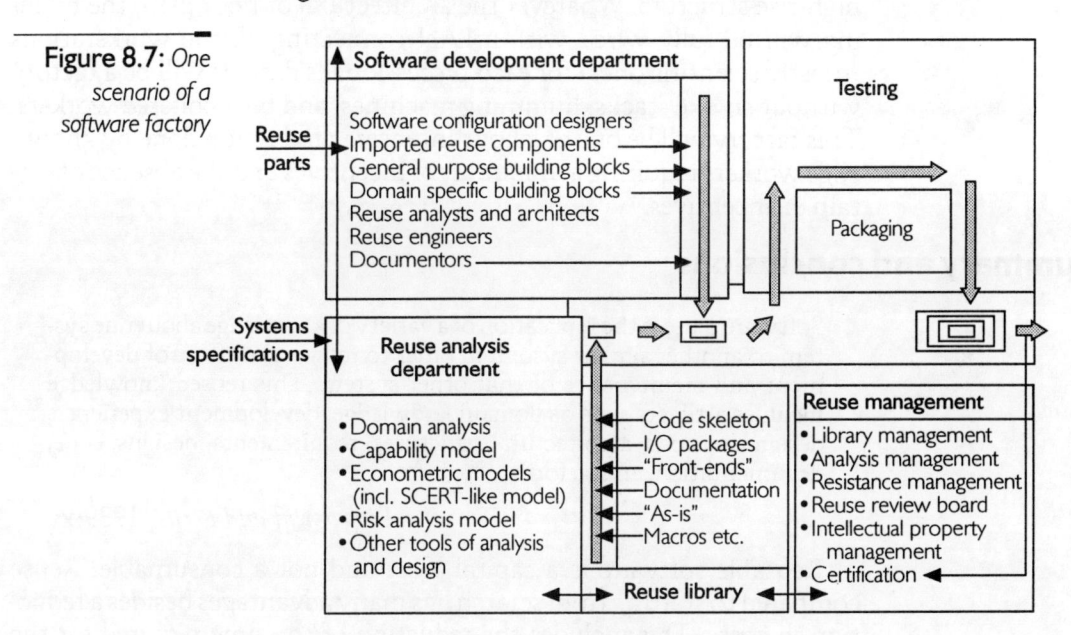

Figure 8.7: One scenario of a software factory

The flow towards a complete software product starts with the design specifications received by the *reuse analysis department* that performs the component analysis using various models, tools and techniques. The determination of what to reuse and what not to reuse is then sent to the library and the *software development department* (names of these administrative units will of course vary with firms and countries). Each will contribute and add value to the product: the *library* by contributing the reuse components needed and the *software development department* by producing programs that are domain-specific not reused.

This process includes the acquisition of reuse components that must be imported, and contributions by the many other professionals including the software configuration designers, reuse analysts and architects, reuse engineers and the documentors. The different building blocks and specialized software is then unit tested and added to the product on the "assembly line". The product having received all the "value added" needed is then ready for the systems test and packaging department. Just before being shipped, a copy of the product or its newly produced subsystems is sent to the *certification department*. If selected for addition to the corporate *library of reuse components*, it is then sent to the *library* and the process for one software product is complete.

The architecture of our software factory will vary with its location. In California, each window may well look over a garden, a lawn, a lake, or a fountain. In cities with a premium on land the building will be a high-rise structure. Whatever the architectural or floor plan, the building will be fully wired with a LAN connecting all the workstations (mostly scientific ones) for each professional's desk. It will be a factory without smoke stacks, humming machines, and blue-collared workers. This factory will be one of labour-intensive production done by knowledge workers requiring a unique set of incentives and the absence of certain disincentives.

Summary and conclusions

> Software reuse is the replication of a variety of knowledge about one system to another similar system in order to reduce the effort of development and maintenance of that other system. This reused knowledge includes artifacts such as domain knowledge, development experience, design decisions, architectural structures, requirements, designs, code, documentation, and so forth.
>
> *Biggerstaff and Perlis*, 1989:xv

Reusable software is a capital asset and not a consumable. Reuse compared to starting from scratch has many advantages besides a reduction in costs. This includes the reduction of the time required for the project; breaking the bottleneck in software development; the use of well tried-and-tested components; and even, perhaps, another product for sale.

Figure 8.8:
Approaches to reuse

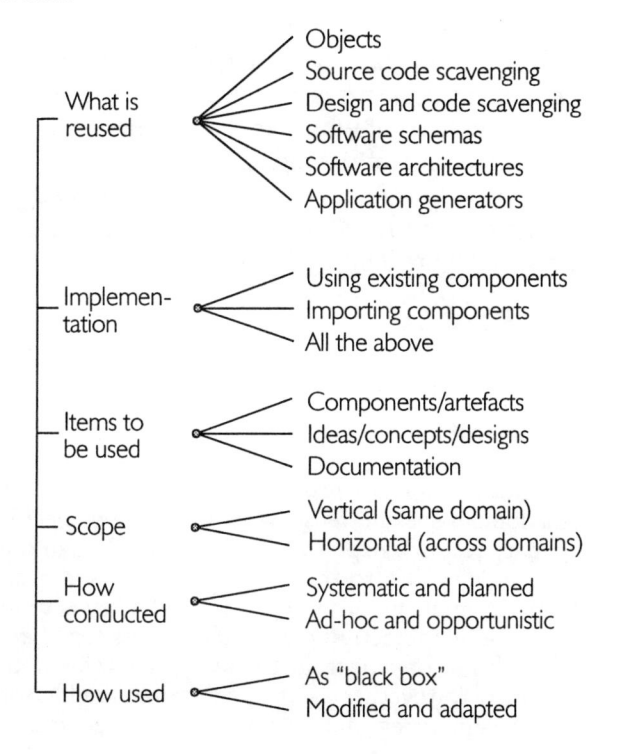

- What is reused
  - Objects
  - Source code scavenging
  - Design and code scavenging
  - Software schemas
  - Software architectures
  - Application generators
- Implementation
  - Using existing components
  - Importing components
  - All the above
- Items to be used
  - Components/artefacts
  - Ideas/concepts/designs
  - Documentation
- Scope
  - Vertical (same domain)
  - Horizontal (across domains)
- How conducted
  - Systematic and planned
  - Ad-hoc and opportunistic
- How used
  - As "black box"
  - Modified and adapted

Most of the reuse currently is in software and this constituted only 15% of all programming in 1983. Thus 85% of all programming (in 1983) was generic and a potential candidate for reuse. Reuse of generic programs will increase as our applications portfolio continues to enlarge and as the demand increases for rationalizing of development operations through downsizing. Also, reuse components may use other reused components. These components could be objects which will fit naturally with the OO methodology, a methodology that is now fast replacing structured methodology. Even without the OO methodology, the concept of reuse is intuitively appealing and easy to grasp. It may soon become part of the thinking in all software development. The implementation of reuse involves the selection, specialization, and integration of artefacts with each implementation emphasizing one phase or another. Matching and adapting reuse components to needs of the moment is still a major problem. Searching for high-level abstractions is another which is a critical step followed by the use of the domain analysis model, the reuse capability model and the econometric model for reuse. Currently, software development is popular and effective because it is at the software component level where elements can be easily standardized and generalized. However, higher levels of abstraction, like subroutines, macros and functions, promise greater gains in productivity. This is important when we realize that typically around 40% of a development project's cost is in software. The rest is in design, testing and documentation which are areas where reuse is the least developed. The combination of the high potential of reuse and the need for economizing on software development costs does suggest great promise for reuse in the future. A summary of the different approaches to reuse appears in Figure 8.8.

Case 8.1: Hewlet Packard Co.

Hewlett Packard has:

> ...initiated a multi-faceted corporate reuse program to help introduce the best practices of systematic reuse into the company, complemented by multidisciplinary research to investigate and develop better methods for domain-specific, reuse-based software engineering... The multidisciplinary research department includes experts in organizational design, anthropology, software process modeling, and business as well as software technologists and engineers... the key is to integrate several factory and manufacturing derived concepts together to understand how the cultural, organizational, people, management, technical and process issues play together as an organization builds software by creating, using, supporting, and evolving domain-specific kits.
>
> *Griss*, 1993:548,561

Reuse is very important for Hewlett Packard because 70% of its engineers perform software development and 50% of its research and development involves software development.

Source: M. L. Griss. (1993). "Software Reuse: From Library to Factory." *IBM Systems Journal*, vol. 32, no. 4, pp. 548–66.

Case 8.2: Hartford Insurance Group

The Hartford Insurance Group started its reuse program in 1981. Its reuse product library is maintained on a Wang computer and accessible to the staff of 1,200 systems development personnel. The library has 35 tested and documented COBOL code modules consisting of 15 programs and 20 subroutines.

- Another 45 items reside in the "use as is" section of the library, which contains modules that have not got certification.

- Programmers search through the reusable library using a function index, which can be searched from any workstation. The full inventory is indexed and cross-indexed according to data processing and business functions.
- To track company-wide reusability, Hartford's 14 application development divisions are required to file monthly reports showing what percentage of reusable code comprises new systems.

Perhaps, as a consequence of this managerial control, 30–40% of all its code comes from the reusable library.

Source: Edward J, Joyce. (1988). "Reusable Software." *Datamation*, vol. 34, no. 18 (September 15), pp. 98.

Case 8.3: Success stories of reuse

- AT&T, with 30 staff in their reuse program, has reduced development costs by 12% and the time-to-the-market from 18–24 months to 6–9 months.
- ESPIRIT in Europe has numerous industrial–academic collaborations in reuse technology including ITHACA, KNOSOS, PRACTITIONER, REDO, REBOOT and SCALE.
- The European Space Agency has a reuse project that emphasizes organizational and contractual issues.
- GTE Data Services had savings of US $15 million for 1987 with a reuse factor of 14%. It has a library of 136 components consisting of 168,000 LOC (lines of code) available to its 700 programmers.
- Hartford Insurance realized a net saving of 225 person-days per month in their support and maintenance costs and 30–40% of all its code comes from its reusable library.
- Through reuse, Hitachi of Japan reduced (in 1984) its number of late projects from 70% in 1970 to 12% and its defects to 13% of its 1974 level.
- NobelTech in Sweden realizes up to 70% reuse saving US $20 million in one program alone.
- REBOOT in Europe focuses on OO technology for reuse
- The US Naval Surface Warfare Center in Virginia achieved a reuse of 89–99%, a three-fold reduction in defects, and an 8- to 20-fold increase in productivity.

- Toshiba of Japan realized productivity rates higher than 20,000 LOC per person-year as a result of reusing designs achieving 13–48% reuse levels in its power plant systems business.

References

Biggerstaff, T. and Perlis, A. J. (eds.). (1989). *Software Reusability*, vol. 2.

Cusumano, Michael A. (1991). *Japan's Software Factories*. Oxford: Oxford University Press.

Davis, E. (1994). "Adopting a Policy of Reuse." *IEEE Spectrum*, vol. 31, no. 6 (June), pp. 44–8.

Griss, M. L. (1993). "Software Reuse: From Library to Factory." *IBM Systems Journal*, vol. 32, no. 4, pp. 548–566.

Hall, P. A. V. (1992). "Overview of Reuse Engineering and Reuse." *Information and Software Technology*, vol. 34, no. 4 (April), pp. 239–251.

Isoda, S. "Software Reuse in Japan." (1996). *Information and Software Technology*, vol. 38, no. 3 (March), pp. 165–72.

Krueger, Charles W. (1992). "Software Reuse." *ACM Computing Surveys*, vol. 24, no. 2 (June), pp. 131–83.

Partridge, D. (1992). *Engineering Artificial Intelligence Software*. Oxford: Intellect.

Pfleeger, Shari Lawrence and Bollinger, Terry B. (1994). "The Economics of Reuse: New Approaches to Modeling and Assessing Cost." *Information and Software Technology*, vol. 36, no. 8 (August), pp. 475–84.

Poulin, J. S., Caruso, J. M. and Hancock, D. R. (1993). "The Business Case for Software Reuse." *IBM Systems Journal*, vol. 32, no. 4, pp. 567–94.

Prieto-Díaz, Rubén. (1993). "Status Report: Software Reusability." *IEEE Software*, vol. 10, no. 6 (May), pp. 61–6.

Rada, Roy. (1994). "Software Reuse: An Introduction." *Intelligent Tutoring Media*, vol. 5, nos. 3&4 (December), pp. 149–52.

9 Acquiring Computing Resources

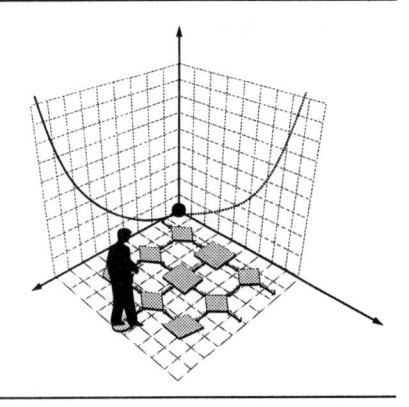

Better one safe way than a hundred in which you cannot reckon.

Aesop

Introduction

During the design phase of the development of an information system, a list of computing resources (hardware, software, and personnel) required for the new system is prepared. Some of these resources may already be available "in-house". For example, the firm may have an IT centre with many of the required peripherals and computing equipment. But should the firm lack the necessary software or should the mandated equipment be fully committed to other projects, acquisition of resources will become necessary.

This chapter describes the steps in the acquisition process. Included are sections on how to translate needs into vendor proposals, how to evaluate alternative proposals and vendor claims, and criteria for selection of vendor. There is also a discussion of method of financing, contract negotiations, and liaison with vendors during installation of acquired resources. Figure 9.1 outlines the sequence of the acquisition process.

In large businesses and commercial organizations, procurement procedures may be formal requiring a full-time staff. In government agencies bidding may be necessary. In smaller firms, acquisition decisions are often made informally, even secretly at times, by one individual. But in all cases, the steps in the procurement process described in this chapter apply (explicitly or implicitly) since the principles involved are not related to corporate size or degree of formality in the decision-making process for acquisition.

Figure 9.1:
Procurement process for computer resources

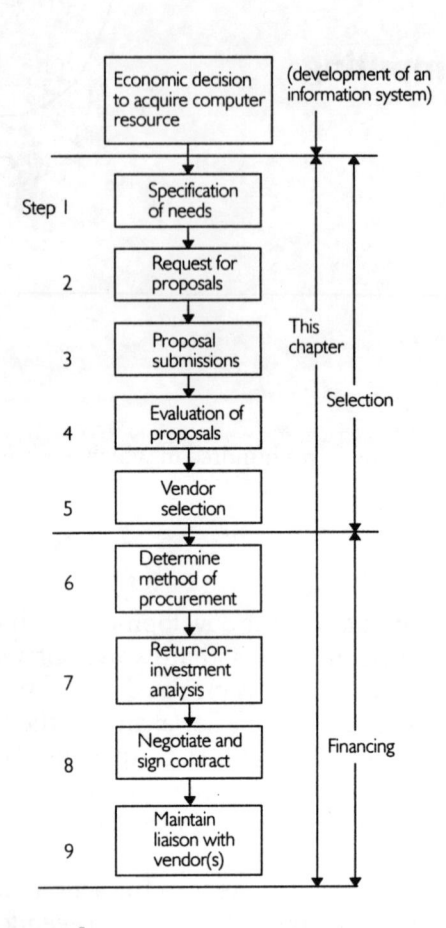

```
                    ┌─────────────────┐  (development of an
                    │ Economic decision│   information system)
                    │ to acquire computer│
                    │ resource        │
                    └────────┬────────┘
                             │
    Step 1           ┌───────▼─────────┐
                     │ Specification   │
                     │ of needs        │
                     └───────┬─────────┘
         2           ┌───────▼─────────┐
                     │ Request for     │
                     │ proposals       │         This
                     └───────┬─────────┘         chapter
         3           ┌───────▼─────────┐
                     │ Proposal        │
                     │ submissions     │         Selection
                     └───────┬─────────┘
         4           ┌───────▼─────────┐
                     │ Evaluation of   │
                     │ proposals       │
                     └───────┬─────────┘
         5           ┌───────▼─────────┐
                     │ Vendor          │
                     │ selection       │
                     └───────┬─────────┘
         6           ┌───────▼─────────┐
                     │ Determine       │
                     │ method of       │
                     │ procurement     │
                     └───────┬─────────┘
         7           ┌───────▼─────────┐
                     │ Return-on-      │
                     │ investment      │
                     │ analysis        │
                     └───────┬─────────┘         Financing
         8           ┌───────▼─────────┐
                     │ Negotiate and   │
                     │ sign contract   │
                     └───────┬─────────┘
         9           ┌───────▼─────────┐
                     │ Maintain        │
                     │ liaison with    │
                     │ vendor(s)       │
                     └─────────────────┘
```

Request for proposals

The first step in procuring computer resources is the preparation of a document that outlines specifications for needed hardware or software. This document, called a *request for proposals* (RFP), is similar to (and an extension of) user specifications drawn up in the development cycle of an information system. It is important that the buyer lists requirements in clear, unambiguous terms so that the vendor cannot misinterpret the specifications or manipulate the buyer into purchasing an inappropriate product.

Who decides what specifications are to be included in the RFP? That will depend on the resource to be procured and the size and structure of the firm. If only a small peripheral for exclusive use by one department is needed, the department head alone may write the specifications. At the other extreme, specifications for a major acquisition affecting many users and requiring a large capital outlay (a database management system, for example) would probably be made by a team including user representatives, technical personnel, a financial officer, and someone from the upper levels of corporate management. Often, outside consultants are included as well.

When specifying needs in the RFP, the buyer should indicate mandatory features (for example, minimum capability in a computer) that must be included in the bid. These requirements should not be so restrictive that no vendor has a product that qualifies or so lax that a large number of vendors respond. Processing proposals is a time-consuming task: three to six submitted proposals is optimal.

Consulting with vendors is often helpful when drawing up mandatory requirements, although firms should be cautious of vendor bias. Vendors can also indicate whether their companies would be in a position to submit a bid. This, in effect, acts as a preselection process, reducing the number of RFPs that need to be sent.

Table 9.1 *Vendors' ability to meet mandatory requirements*

Vendor →	1	2	3	4	...	15	16
Capability to meet current needs in one shift and 5-year future needs in three shifts	X	X	X	X	...	X	X
Real-time response of 35 seconds for 95% of the time	X	X	X	X	...	X	
Communication facilities	X		X	X	...	X	X
COBOL and FORTRAN IV compiler	X		X	X	...	X	X

Canvassing vendors can be done informally (on the telephone, for example) or by a document called *request for information* (RFI). On the basis of the information collected, a matrix (such as the one in Table 9.1) can be compiled to show which vendors have the capability of meeting requirements requested. If, upon examination of the matrix, it is noted that most vendors fail to qualify, requirements can be relaxed. If too many qualify, additional mandatory features can be added for ease in processing proposals.

Once mandatory requirements are set, non-critical but "nice to have" features should be determined – for example, many users want terminal screens to have a colour capability. Some features have a functional value, others may be wanted "to keep up with the Jones". Buyers should distinguish between these two categories when evaluating proposals with optional features. Sometimes, requirements show a bias toward one supplier that other vendors consider unfair. Complaints may be strong enough to force buyers to reevaluate mandatory requirements. To avoid ill will, clients should not write their specifications to fit the product of a particular vendor but instead should require minimum acceptable values for parameters that more than one vendor can meet.

Other components of the RFP

Although a major portion of the RFP is delegated to need specification, information should be given on procedures, schedules, and the user environment. In addition, required documentation should be explained. Table 9.2 is a sample list of contents showing what items an RFP should include.

Table 9.2 *Sample contents of an RFP*

1. Needs specifications	10. Procedural details:
2. Mandatory features	▪ How to handle questions
3. Desired features	▪ Liaison
4. Performance data wanted	11. Schedule:
5. Cost data needed	▪ Bidder's conference
6. Information needed on vendor	▪ Proposal due date
7. Documentation required from vendor	▪ Award date
8. General information on buyer	12. General comments
9. Request for vendor demonstration	

General information on the buyer (item 8) needed to help vendors understand the environment in which the product under consideration will operate, should consist of:

- Résumé of firm and product(s).
- Projected rates of growth.
- Data volumes – maximum, minimum, and average.
- File characteristics.
- Input/output characteristics.
- Response time – maximum, minimum, and average.
- Constraints.

Table 9.3 *Information to be supplied by vendor*

1. Experience of firm with computer resources:
   - Recent mainframe and micro technology
   - Inquiry and response capabilities
   - Communication capabilities
   - Graphics
2. Systems development expertise and experience:
   - Design
   - Implementation
   - Human engineering
3. Technical assistance available:
   - Systems support
   - Nature
   - Experience
   - Response time
   - Maintenance
4. Training to be provided:
   - Facilities
   - Courses
   - Materials
   - Instructions available
   - Media used
5. Research and technical programs of firm:
   - Human engineering
   - Education and training
6. Names and addresses of recent customers
7. Financial summary statement on assets and liabilities
8. Annual report (optional)

Table 9.3 is a further elaboration of item 6 of the RFP sample contents. It lists the data that the vendor should supply to help the buyer evaluate whether the vendor is reliable and has the necessary expertise and support facilities to back up a bid.

Proposal submission

Vendors, upon receipt of an RFP, will prepare their bids. During this preparation period, it is useful for the buyer to keep in close contact with the vendor in order to answer questions and clarify the RFP if necessary. Sometimes, the RFP will be altered during this period as a result of vendor comments or objections. If so, all vendors receiving the RFP should be so informed.

This liaison and dialog with vendors can be very educational for the acquisition committee. It can teach them about advances in the computer industry and help them identify and weigh the importance of various features. Such knowledge will prove of value when proposals are later evaluated.

Validation of proposals

When the acquisition is a minor piece of equipment, validation of proposals can easily be done by technicians in the user department. But when a large computer or computer system is to be purchased, checking proposals and validating vendor claims may take an acquisition team many months. There are two basic approaches to validation: a literature search and a study of vendor justifications. When performance is crucial, hand timing, benchmarks, and simulation are also useful tests.

Literature search

With reference to validation of proposals, a literature search does not mean a book survey, because the time lag in book production means books cannot keep current with computer advances. Rather, publications such as DataWorld (published by Auerbach) or DataPro (by McGraw-Hill) should be studied. In a service similar to that of consumer bulletins, magazines provide up-to-date evaluations of computer resources, especially peripherals and packaged software.

Literature searches are time consuming. One needs to locate relevant articles and to find a common basis for comparing equipment (or software) described in articles written by different authors. Another limitation is that a literature search can only be done after a product has been on the market for some time. Should the acquisitions committee be interested in recently developed computer resources, enough time may not have elapsed for evaluation of these resources to reach print. (Risks in acquiring new technology should not be underestimated. Hardware may still have bugs, delivery may fall behind schedule, software may prove unavailable, etc.)

One can supplement a literature search by asking other customers of the vendor how they evaluate the vendor's products and services. For this reason, a list of customer names is requested in the RFP. Usually, only the names of satisfied customers will be supplied, but those customers may refer the buyer to dissatisfied firms, which should be consulted as well.

Vendor justification

Another technique used by acquisition committees to validate vendor proposals is to ask vendors to appear before the committee or to submit documentation to justify their proposals. When using this approach, the committee must be careful that it is not swayed by a slick sales promotion instead of carefully evaluating the merits of the vendor's proposal. Many managers are "satisficers" and prefer to deal with vendors who have proved reliable, helpful, and satisfactory in the past.

Such managers are particularly receptive to this method of proposal validation. "Optimizers", those who attempt optimization, usually choose the more time-consuming literature search and validation (which require more technical expertise as well).

Hand timing

In hand timing, the engineering time to perform each set of operations is multiplied by the number of these sets in each applications program in order to determine run time. This calculation is matched with the vendor's proposal. Hand timing is feasible in simple processing but is beyond present capabilities for complex processing configurations, such as parallel processing or multiprocessing.

Benchmarks

A benchmark test measures hardware or software performance under typical conditions, using a small set of programs selected to represent the work stream. The problem is in defining "typical" conditions. In a bank, the number of transactions processed on a single midweek day might be a fairly accurate sample of transactions throughout the year. But in a manufacturing plant, the workload may vary from day to day or week to week. The choice of a representative workload must, therefore, be made with care. The set of programs selected for the benchmark should include all important functions of processing, such as sorting, matching, updating, and queries.

Table 9.4 *Factors to be considered when preparing a benchmark*

■ Representative workload:
     ▪ Current
         * Normal
         * Peak
     ▪ Future
         * Normal
         * Peak
 ■ Representative equipment requirements:
     ▪ Memory
         * Internal (core)
         * External
     ▪ Input/output channels
     ▪ Communication equipment
     ▪ Peripherals
	■ Representative time requirements:
	     ▪ Compile
	     ▪ Execute
	     ▪ Input/output
	 ■ Representative processing:
	     ▪ Files
	     ▪ Functions and types of processing:
	         * Sort/merge
	         * Update
	         * Computing:
	             Matrix
	             Simulation

Table 9.4 lists some of the factors to be included in a benchmark. Note that not only time, equipment, and processing must be representative but that current workload and future projections should be considered.

One can allow for growth by multiplying test-run time by a multiplier called an *extension factor*. This factor varies according to each class of programs.

Benchmark testing may mean running the test programs on several different computers for the purpose of comparing execution speed, throughput, and so on. If the buyer doesn't have the equipment, this means arranging with others for the testing. The problem is to find a firm willing to lend its hardware for testing, one with the exact combination of CPU features, peripherals, and software needed for the testing. Vendors may assist buyers in locating equipment for benchmark tests. They may contact clients (on contract to provide testing facilities) on the buyer's behalf or allow use of their own equipment for testing, as does IBM at its regional centres.

Another problem with benchmark testing is that the application programs in the benchmark (programs in current use) may be in a different language than the system to be evaluated. For example, the benchmark programs may be in COBOL, whereas the new system under consideration uses APL. In such cases, new programs must be written for test purposes. Although preparing special benchmark programs has a high learning value, the effort is not trivial. The time spent on programming can be quite costly.

Simulation

An alternative to benchmark testing is to lease or purchase a special simulation program, such as SCERT, CASE, or SAM, that can be run on equipment already available in-house to simulate workload processing on equipment configurations under consideration. Or a computer service organization can be contracted to run the simulation.

A simplified representation of the flow of a SCERT simulation can be seen in Figure 9.2. This figure does not show all the stages within each phase, nor does it show all phases necessary for complex modes of operation, such as multiprogramming or real-time processing. However, the basic logic of the simulation is illustrated.

The first phase of simulation is to develop a mathematical model of the desired information system (box 2), based on data that define the environment, system, and files (1). In parallel, a mathematical model of the hardware and software systems under consideration is developed (5), based on the configuration to be tested (4) and on information on resources capabilities stored in SCERT's factor library (3). The simulation is then run (6). The output (7) will include not only information on utilization of each main hardware component but information on core requirements, software performance, and costs as well. When output proves unsatisfactory (exit 9), changes can be made to the resources in the configuration (4) or to the model itself (5), and the simulation will be rerun (6).

Figure 9.2:
Simplified flow of SCERT

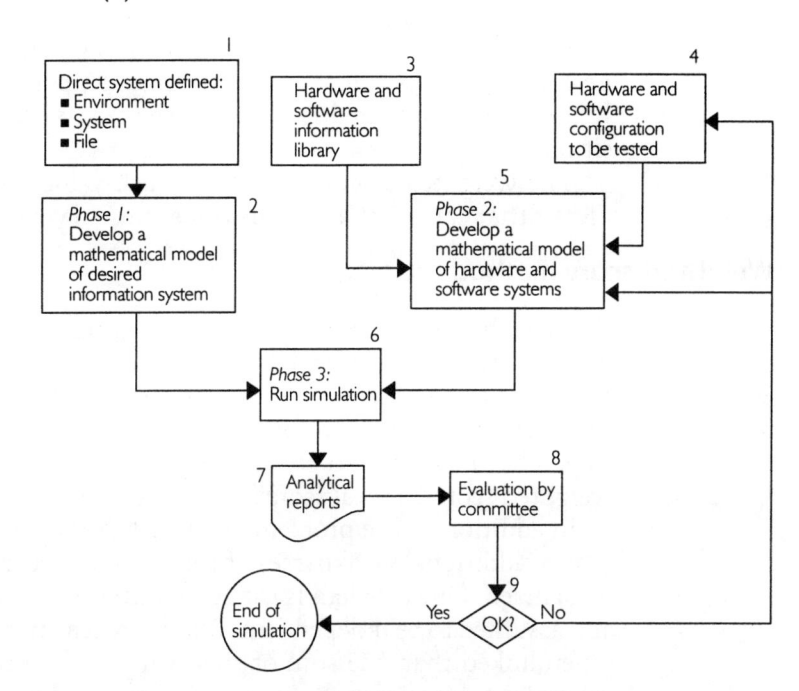

By definition, simulation will not give an optimal solution. It only provides information on different alternatives. The committee needs to exercise judgement when deciding which configurations (and how many) to test, since simulation runs are expensive. In making a choice among alternatives tested by simulation, the committee should be sure that no constraints have been violated. For example, a desirable solution may cost more than can be allocated to the system. The most satisfactory solution may turn out to be one vendor's central processing unit (CPU) combined with another vendor's peripherals.

Simulation is useful when validating a vendor's claims, but a significant difference generally exists between predicted and actual levels of performance. To minimize error in predicted performance levels, updated, correct, and complete information on equipment and software capabilities must be included in the simulation run.

Choice of vendor

For simple equipment, a quick review of proposals may suffice when choosing a vendor. Even when purchasing complex equipment, many buyers are tempted to avoid a long, formal selection process. They opt instead to deal with vendors with whom they have had satisfactory dealings in the past, as long as the vendors submit proposals that meet objectives. However, a formal review of proposals would lead to the "best" choice, resulting in a system with high efficiency and effectiveness. For this reason, formal evaluation of proposals is often firm policy. It may even be required by law, as is the case with governmental acquisitions.

The weighted-score method and cash-value method are two techniques that can assist an acquisitions team in vendor selection.

Weighted-score method

The weighted-score method is used to evaluate all vendors that meet mandatory requirements. In this system, desired features are weighted, and each vendor is scored (from 1 to 10) according to how well each feature meets buyer expectations. A vendor's score on a feature is then multiplied by its weight to give a weight score per feature. By adding all weighted scores, a total score for each vendor can be derived.

In addition to the problem of subjectivity in assigning weights and scores, additional weaknesses of the weighted-score method should be recognized. One problem is that each criterion is given a separate value and assumed to be independent. But many features have a greater value when linked than the sum of their values when separate. The classic example of this used in economics concerns beehives and fields of clover. The higher yields due to synergism when bees and clover are brought into proximity can be compared to the higher productivity of computers when features (such as telecommunications and minicomputers) are connected. The weighted-score method may not take this causality into account, although there is no reason why telecommunications and minicomputers cannot be listed as required features.

Another major weakness is that the assignment of weights does not include cost considerations, such as those listed in Table 9.5. The vendor receiving the highest weighted-score may not have the best proposal when cost–benefit ratios are analyzed. A lower weighted-score may, in fact, give more value per monetary unit. One solution is to use the weighted-score method only when evaluating proposals with the same total cost. In practice, however, proposals identical in cost are rarely submitted. Those that vary slightly in price seldom include exactly the same features.

Table 9.5 *Cost elements of proposals*

One-time costs	Recurring costs
■ Cost of computer resources to be acquired	■ Personnel
■ Cost of auxiliary resources to be acquired	■ Program development
■ Site preparation:	■ Operations
※ Electricity	■ Maintenance
※ Facilities, such as false floor	■ Supplies
※ Security facilities	■ Communication
■ Transportation:	■ Insurance
※ Freight	■ Backup
※ Insurance	
※ Installation	
■ Conversion:	
※ Programs	
※ File	
※ Personnel	
※ Documentation	

Cost–value method

The cost–value method attempts to equalize bids of features so that costs can be compared. Costs of desired features not included in proposals are added to each vendor's bid.

Table 9.6 *Value template for the desired software (for one vendor only)*

Developing the software in-house	£12,000
Maintenance for life of system	4,000
	16,000
Development of software by software company	15,000
Maintenance for life of system	4,000
	19,000
Cost of doing without the software (i.e., degraded system and decreased efficiency)	12,000

The cost of each feature is based on the lowest cost estimate of acceptable alternatives available when making the calculations. A monetary value should also be calculated for operating the system without the desired feature, and this figure used if it is less than the cost of the feature itself. Total costs are then compared, selection being based on the bid with the least cost.

For example, suppose a proposal is submitted that does not include a software feature that the buyer wishes to have. This software can either be developed in-house or purchased. To this initial expenditure, the cost of maintaining the software for the life of the system is added. In Table 9.6, a value template shows figures for this hypothetical software omission: the cost of developing the software in-house plus maintenance would be £16,000; the cost of software purchased and maintained, £19,000. The buyer estimates £12,000 as the cost of degraded service without the desired software. Of the three figures £12,000 is the lowest, so this figure is the amount to be added to the basic price of the vendor's bid when the alternative bids are compared during the vendor-selection process.

Table 9.7 *Value template for delivery dates*

Vendor	Delivery date	Value
A	June	£0
B	September	+£4,000
C	March	−£2,000

Sometimes, a value can be subtracted when a requirement is overfulfilled. If June is the specified delivery date, a vendor who promises delivery in March, three months early, is given credit. A vendor who can't deliver until September is penalized. In the value template in Table 9.7, the buyer estimates that the March delivery will result in £12,000 in savings to the company. This value is then subtracted from Vendor C's proposal cost. Late delivery (September) is assessed as costing the company £4,000, a figure added to Vendor B's bid.

The cost–value method does away with weighted-value judgements and scores. It takes into consideration costs and feature interactions. But the problem of subjectivity still remains when estimating the life of a system, the cost of degraded service as a result of lack of features, or the benefits to be gained from overfulfilled requirements. Nevertheless, fewer subjective judgements are required than for the weighted-score method.

A major disadvantage with the cost–value approach to vendor selection is that it requires much time and effort to complete the evaluation. The DBMS selection effort cited in Case 9.2 took three and a half manyears of effort for a team of seven (head of information systems, consultant, three systems programmers, two applications programmers). Note that no representative of corporate management was on the team.

In this case, management delegated selection responsibility because the choice of DBMS requires considerable technical expertise. Other firms commonly include a management representative in the selection process, regardless of the technical nature of the acquisition decision.

Review of acquisition recommendations

When a large investment is involved, the final decision on the acquisition of information resources rests with top management. Usually, the recommendations of the acquisition committee are followed. However, it is the responsibility of management to ensure that proposed acquisitions are, indeed, in the best interests of the firm and consistent with the corporate strategic plan. Before acquisition approval is given, management should receive satisfactory answers to the following questions:

- Does the acquisition meet all essential system and user requirements?
- Is the acquisition appropriate, given the priorities stated in the corporate and data processing strategic plan?
- Are technical staff available to implement the acquisition? Did the staff participate in the decision process and recommend acquisition?
- Is the vendor reliable? Does the vendor have the ability to provide required support services?
- Will users accept the new acquisition?
- Can the company absorb the new technology? Will there be organizational disruption? How will conversion be managed?
- How long will it take before the acquisition can be put to use? Will it survive as long as needed?

The cost of proposed acquisitions should also receive close scrutiny by top management before acquisitions are approved. Once management accepts the committee's recommendations, financing and contract arrangements can be made.

Approaches to financing

How should acquisitions be financed? Rental, purchase, or lease? A decision on financing computer resources differs from conventional acquisition decisions because unique pricing patterns have evolved in the computer industry over the years.

The industry was monopolistic at the beginning, with rental the only option. This changed in the 1950s, following antitrust litigation in the US. At that time, the Justice Department set price guidelines and prodded IBM to offer users a purchase choice. But users continued to favour rentals because of the continual improvement in performance and the decrease in price of new models reaching the market. In effect, the high technology of the industry discouraged users from investing in the purchase of equipment that would quickly become obsolete.

Leasing became an alternative in the 1960s. IBM, pressured by the government to lease equipment, began to do so but at a high price. Other computer manufacturers soon followed suit. Recognizing a business opportunity, entrepreneurs stepped in and formed leasing companies of their own. These entrepreneurs first purchased equipment, then leased it to users at a lower cost than the manufacturers asked. The new leasing companies were able to compete by depreciating equipment over a longer lifetime than computer manufacturers, relying on the premise that equipment could be leased to a sequence of users. The favourable investment climate of the early 1970s also fostered the growth of leasing companies. Leasing firms are thriving, although their market is volatile. The introduction of each new family of computers, for example, tends to disrupt the market, at least temporarily, as users wait for new equipment instead leasing the old.

In this section, the advantages and limitations of rental, purchase, and lease options will be discussed. Numerical examples will illustrate the computations to be made when considering each alternative.

Rental

In the early days of computing, rental was the only user option. Today, the rental option is used by companies that want data processing equipment for only a short period of time (usually less than 12 months). Rental is also advantageous when user demand is unstable or uncertain. (In most cases, only 30 days notice to the vendor is required to return equipment). However, the vendor charges a premium for the flexibility of a rental contract, as much as 20–30% higher than an operating lease. One reason for this high cost is that the vendor must allow a margin to cover reconditions or relocation of returned equipment.

Rental payments are tax deductible, an additional benefit to rental clients. Many vendors offer their clients a purchase accrual option that enables them to apply rental payments to purchase of their rented equipment. Another advantage of renting is that the vendor usually assumes responsibility for maintenance and insurance. However, the price of rental is high, so that renting for more than two or three years will cost more than the purchase price. Another drawback is a customary charge for overtime use beyond a specific number of hours a month, as much as 40% higher than the regular rental fee.

Purchase

Many users hesitate to purchase computer equipment because they fear obsolescence. This fear is justified. Computers have made quantum jumps in speed and performance in recent years, and competitive pressures often require firms to take advantage of the latest technology available.

The continual drop in computer prices is another reason many users are hesitant to buy. Indeed, the price–performance ratio has improved dramatically over time. An industry rule-of-thumb is that prices drop arithmetically while performance increases geometrically. No wonder many companies are unwilling to commit themselves to a major capital outlay when they know that the capability they need will cost considerably less in the future.

Still another reason why many firms are reluctant to purchase is that computer resources are limited: competing projects may be given funding priority. Furthermore, many firms choose to rent (or lease) because the bureaucratic procedures required to make a purchase are so involved that hardware can become outdated or obsolete before a purchase transaction is completed.

In spite of these problems, many considerations make purchase more attractive than rental or leasing. For example, purchasing equipment has an impact on a company's balance sheet. The purchased equipment is recorded as an asset, while the financing is recorded as a liability. There are also tax benefits to be considered. The purchaser might be eligible for investment tax credits (depending on the existence of such credits under current tax law) as well as interest expenses from financing the purchase, depreciation expenses, and maintenance expenses.

The fact that new computer technology is continually being introduced to the market does not make all systems in use obsolete. Some computer equipment has a useful life of up to 10 years in the United States and even longer abroad, which justifies the purchase price. (Useful life can be operationally defined as the time period during which the required workload can be economically processed by the equipment in question.) After all, not all firms require the latest technology. Even when equipment must be upgraded, firms can capitalize on the salvage value of discarded hardware, which is sometimes as high as 40% of purchase price.

At first glance, purchase is also very much cheaper than rental. A £1.6 million computer might cost £593,244 in rent per year, making three years of rental cost more than the purchase price. Such a comparison is simplistic, however, because it does not allow for tax advantages and maintenance depreciation, which benefit the purchaser; nor does it discount for the present value (PV) of cash flows for each of the years of useful life. (The discounted rate used for calculating present value is the average rate of return on investment.)

Other factors that have a bearing when comparing the advantages of purchase versus rental are:

- Life expectancy of the computer resource.
- Time expected until next generation.
- Reliability of resource (tried and proven?).
- Expected hours of usage.
- Stability of applications and usage.
- Likelihood of modification or updating of resource.
- Borrowing rate.
- Discount rate.
- Deprecation method.
- Property tax rate.
- Corporate tax rate.

The rent–purchase comparison in Case 9.3 is just one example. In another case, the cutover point might be two to three years. Variables also differ from one situation to another, although purchase is always less than rental over a period of five years, even when maintenance costs are included. Many of the variables affecting the calculations are exogenous (external) – that is, beyond a firm's control. Borrowing rates, tax rates, or investment tax credit rates fall in this category. Other variables, although internal, are not always easy to estimate or manage. For example, demand for applications and debugging programs may mean more run time is spent than anticipated, raising rental costs because of overtime fees. When this occurs, the cutover period is affected.

Usually, a stable demand for a computer resource over its calculated payback period is needed before purchase (instead of rental) can be economically justified. There is obviously no point in buying unnecessary equipment or software. Sometimes, firms are able to rectify purchase errors by passing inappropriate or redundant resources to other departments or subsidiaries. Sometimes, vendors allow clients to modify or upgrade purchased hardware that fails to meet user needs because of environmental change or because equipment is outgrown.

In brief, clients should have a solid understanding of both their present and future information processing needs before a purchase decision is made. The purchase of a computer system is less costly than rental (or lease, as will be described in the next section) for long-term use. It represents a solid investment that can be capitalized and amortized over time. The purchaser may benefit from tax advantages, pride of ownership, and ready access to known hardware resources. On the other hand, the purchase of a computer system is a major financial commitment that ties up capital and involves a certain amount of risk (potential obsolescence, uncertain resale). Another disadvantage is that once an ownership contract is signed, the purchaser has no way to pressure the vendor for upgraded service or support.

Leasing

Computer systems can be leased as well as rented or purchased. As with rental, ownership of a leased system is retained by the vendor. The main difference from a rental is the length of time the lessee is committed to the system: usually from 12 to 36 months for an operating lease or from four to seven years for a financial lease. Monthly payments depend on the length of the lease: the longer the term of the lease, the lower the monthly payment.

Leasing hedges against obsolescence. At the end of a lease period (or sooner if the lease contract has a cancellation clause), the lessee can switch resources to take advantage of new models that have been introduced to the market. (However, some leases have a penalty for early termination, typically a percentage of the monthly fee for each month remaining in the lease.) Although this same benefit exists with a rental, an operating lease is generally less expensive than renting when the contract is for more than a year. And few firms choose to switch systems yearly. Most find that it takes longer to develop an information system and to learn how to use the system effectively. If they switch systems after a short period of time, they face the trauma of conversion before being experienced with the equipment at hand. Most computer personnel favour three to four years to develop a system before a change in equipment is made. For the length of time, leasing is more economical than renting.

Leasing is also advantageous when a company lacks the cash or the credit required to purchase necessary hardware, or wants to conserve capital. Often, a lease with the option to buy can be arranged so that firms that have limited funds or are uncertain of the demand for the resource can postpone a purchase decision, yet not be greatly penalized by this postponement. The lessee makes monthly lease payments for a specified period or up to a given amount and then can decide whether to continue leasing or take title. Normally, this approach costs little more than a straight lease. Sometimes, it costs even less.

Another benefit of leasing is that less time and effort are generally needed for approval of a lease than for the purchase of equipment. Furthermore, equipment can usually be obtained without a long wait. Unlike rentals, a leased computer can often be used 24 hours a day without penalty. Some lease contracts allow upgrading of equipment with no penalty by simply adding the new amount onto the existing lease.

In addition, leasing vendors differ in their charges. Rates will be higher if a vendor has both developed and manufactured the equipment to be leased because it will be necessary to recover research and development costs. Rates are also affected by the payback period and how often lease equipment is updated. The lowest rates are charged by third-party leasing firms which purchase equipment directly from a manufacturer. They set a low rate structure (made possible, in part, by the tax benefits they derive from the purchase) and operate at a low profit margin. Rates are usually based on computer lifetimes between 8 to 12 years and the expectation that equipment will be leased to three or more consecutive users. (Manufacturers calculate a shorter life, approximately three to five years.)

The third-party lessor gambles on the firm's marketing ability to find users for older models in addition to users for up-to-date equipment. The lessor knows that firms are allocating an increasing share of revenues to computer processing and that the pool of potential customers is growing. Because of advances in technology, new equipment is becoming increasingly modular, flexible, reliable, and upwardly compatible. This makes it easier for leasing companies to find clients for their equipment and reduces the risk of unused inventories.

Unfortunately, in recent years, a number of leasing scandals have received publicity. As a result, many IT managers are wary of the leasing option. But common sense, careful scrutiny of vendor promises and reputation, and legal expertise when negotiating a contract should help companies avoid leasing problems. For example, it is important to deal with respected leasing firms that have the financial standing and the business reputation to back up their lease obligations. A company that is planning to lease should review audited and certified financial statements of the lessor, check its credit rating, and choose a vendor that is likely to survive competitive leasing wars. Proposals from a number of competing vendors should be requested and compared. Legal counsel should carefully review contracts, especially for penalties for early termination of the lease and purchase options at the end. When negotiating with a third-party leasing firm, it is wise to have a clear understanding of the actual equipment price paid to the manufacturer for the equipment being leased. Lessees should understand payment calculations and should consider the option of leasing certain system components but renting or buying others to reduce costs.

In addition, lessees should be suspicious of a deal that is "too good to be true". Before signing a lease that appears to be a bargain, consider how the leasing company can make that kind of offer. Perhaps the vendor will be unable to deliver what is promised. Perhaps the favourable terms mean that the system is not technologically up-to-date. Short-term and flexible leases should be given special scrutiny. The economic and competitive conditions in the leasing industry are such that users should be alert for deceptive marketing ploys.

Contract negotiations

Objectives

Negotiations should begin the moment the acquisition process is set in motion, not when lawyers sit down to prepare a written contract. If a company selects resources and commits itself to a vendor before beginning to negotiate terms, leverage in obtaining meaningful contract concessions is lost. The purpose of negotiations is to identify problems and forge consensus before the contract is drawn up.

During negotiations, both parties will try to improve their economic position. A vendor trying to break into the market may have to accept less favourable terms than a well-established vendor and may come out the loser in a zero-sum game (buyer gains at the expense of the vendor). But it is possible for both negotiating parties to settle on a mutually advantageous contract. For example, a firm may inform a third-party leasing company of its interest in particular equipment, which the leasing company then purchases.

The client should control the negotiation process to again maximum concessions from a vendor. The best way to do so is to:

- Form an interdisciplinary negotiating team that includes people with contract experience.
- Use a well-designed *request for proposals*.
- Maintain multivendor competition.
- Set the negotiating agenda. Do not user the vendor's standard agreement form as the basis of negotiations. (The vendor is generally a professional in such negotiations and such an agreement may be weighted in the vendor's favour.)
- Refuse to negotiate with vendor representatives who do not have final negotiating authority.

Contracts ultimately depend on the goodwill of both sides, but skilled negotiators and legal advice (either in-house lawyers or consultants experienced in computer acquisition contracts) are recommended.

Having computer technicians and financial personnel on the negotiating team is also useful. Many buyers take the initiative and prepare a contract well in advance to be used as a basis of discussion during the negotiations. They recognize that vendors are experienced adversaries who may not include in their contract proposals all the clauses the buyer considers mandatory. At best, negotiations are a bargaining dialogue. Confrontation is in the interest of neither party.

Contents

Misunderstandings sometimes exist in vendor–client relationships because the two parties have dissimilar backgrounds and use different terminologies. A primary objective of a contract is to specify in legally binding, unambiguous terms the rights and obligations of both vendor and client. Detailed specifications will help to produce a workable and enforceable document and also help avoid disagreements that can lead to ill-will or litigation.

Contracts will vary according to the nature of the product (hardware or software), the complexity of the system, and the personalities and past experiences of the negotiators. The basic contents of an acquisition contract should include the following:

- Requirement specifications.
- Critical commitments implied in demonstration and presentations.
- Acceptance criteria.
- Remedies for vendor non-performance.
- Penalties.
- Arbitration provisions.
- Warranties.
- Guarantees.
- Performance bonds.
- Maintenance provisions.
- Services:
    - Training.
    - Documentation.
    - Systems and engineering help.
- Financing.
- Payment schedule.
- Patents/proprietary rights.

- Limitations and disclaimers.
- Insurance.

In addition, the contract should specify the date and method of delivery and the vendor's responsibility with regard to site preparation, installation, documentation, training, security, and confidentiality of user's data. The contract should also clarify what the user will do regarding provision for electric power, a proper environment (for example, air conditioning), qualified staff.

When the acquisition is software, the contract should address the issue of software ownership. Is acquisition merely a license to use the software, or is the client purchasing proprietary rights? If the former, is the license perpetual or for a limited term? Who controls assignment and sublicense rights? Can the software be moved from one location to another? Does the client have the right to let others use the software? To avoid future disputes over extra site or user charges, the contract must fully document all restrictions on use.

Because the development of custom software is generally plagued by delays and cost overruns, three key elements should be included in a software contract: price, timing, and quality. Realistic acceptance procedures should be specified: tests should be designed both separately for modules or subsystems and collectively as a system. The agreement should also include warranty and maintenance provisions that provide for ongoing software performance, including routine and critical fixes, enhancements, and upgrades.

One cannot generalize on the level of detail or specificity required in the contract. Even definitions of terms may be subject to misinterpretation. It is a good idea to attach to the contract a copy of the *request for proposals* (RFP), incorporating it by reference.

Contract implementation

Once a contract is signed, its execution requires close liaison between buyer and vendor. When multiple vendors contribute to a computing system, liaison increases in complexity. Although a one-vendor proposition simplifies the acquisition process and eases detection and correction of malfunctions, the system will generally cost more than when components are supplied from a number of competing firms. Indeed, the unbundling decision by IBM has resulted in the establishment of many companies offering components and peripherals at a lower price, with better performance and more features, than many giant corporations offer. As a result, buyers today commonly contract with several vendors even though interfacing resources can add considerable time and effort to conversion and increase stress in the buyer–vendor relationship. For example, the end-user often gets caught in the crossfire between vendors when there are systems failures during installation and testing.

Fortunately, the computer industry is moving toward plug-compatible machines, especially for IBM equipment. This means that a plug-compatible manufacturer is able to replace an IBM computer with one of their machines without affecting systems software, applications, or peripherals. A few bugs may develop, but in principle, plug-compatibility reduces liaison headaches that formerly plagued buyers of multivendor computer resources.

Summing up

Although the computer industry did not grow during the 1990s as fast as predicted by pundits at the start of the decade, the computer industry is still accelerating the introduction of new, advanced-technology products that make old products obsolete. In addition, software for an expanded range of applications is on the market, and prices for computer resources are continuing to drop, bringing the computer revolution to the doorstep of an ever-growing number of organizations. The acquisition of necessary computer resources remains one of the major responsibilities of management in business and industry.

Acquisition decisions are often made by a team, appointed by corporate management, that determines need specifications, sends out RFPs, evaluates returns, and selects vendors. The network diagram in Figure 9.4 traces this process. This diagram is consistent with Figure 9.1 but has greater detail.

Validation of proposals may include a literature search and vendor justification. Hand timing, benchmark tests, and simulation are techniques for verifying performance claims. Two procedures for evaluating proposals have been explained in this chapter: the weighted-score method and the cost–value approach. Once a decision is reached, all vendors submitting proposals should be notified of the choice.

At all stages in the acquisition process, judgemental decisions are made, and they are subject to error. One cannot state future computer needs with certainty nor predict a company's growth with accuracy. Assigning values to developmental costs or desired features is difficult at best. However, the procedures outlined in this chapter should help reduce the risk in acquisitions and should help firms reach cost-effective procurement decisions. Vendor selection is a time-consuming activity requiring technical expertise. Constantly changing technology and the large number of possible hardware configurations available complicate the problem of choosing the best vendor proposal. The acquisition process does not end with vendor selection, because there are financial decisions to be made and contracts to be negotiated. In this chapter, the advantages and limitations of rent, purchase, and lease alternatives have been discussed. Possible alternatives are chosen in Figure 9.3. Modifications of these basic choices are also offered by many firms.

Figure 9.3: *Rent, lease and purchase alternatives*

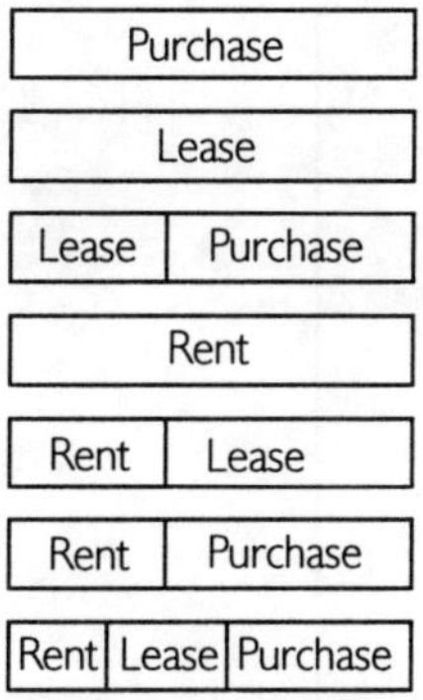

Purchase

Lease

Lease	Purchase

Rent

Rent	Lease

Rent	Purchase

Rent	Lease	Purchase

Table 9.8 *Comparison of purchase, lease, and rent alternatives*

Factors	Rent	Purchase	Straight lease
■ Separate maintenance contract necessary?	No	Yes	No
■ Depreciation possible?	No	Yes	No
■ Rent/lease payments tax deductible as expense?	Yes	Not applicable	Yes
■ Useful life	1–2 years	More than 5–6 years	6 months to 6 years
■ Capital outlay needed?	No	Yes	No
■ Total cost for period of 5–6 years or more	Highest	Lowest	Higher than purchase

The decision of whether to rent, purchase, or lease is complex because many factors such as those in Table 9.8 must be considered. What is best for one firm will not necessarily be appropriate for another. As illustrated in Figure 9.5 trade-offs have to be made.

Summing up

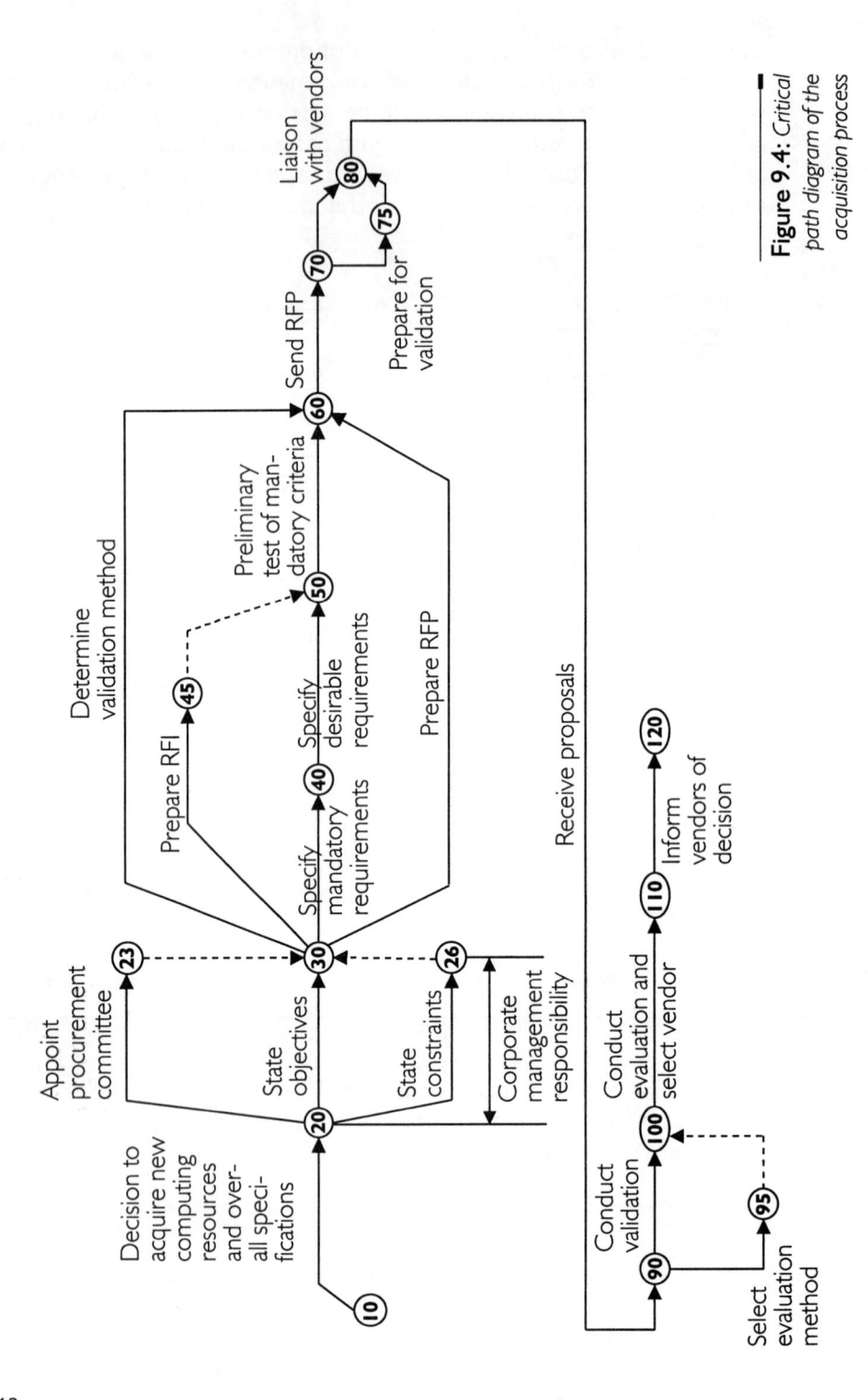

Figure 9.4: *Critical path diagram of the acquisition process*

Figure 9.5:
Comparison of equipment cost and upgrading flexibility for purchase, lease, and rent

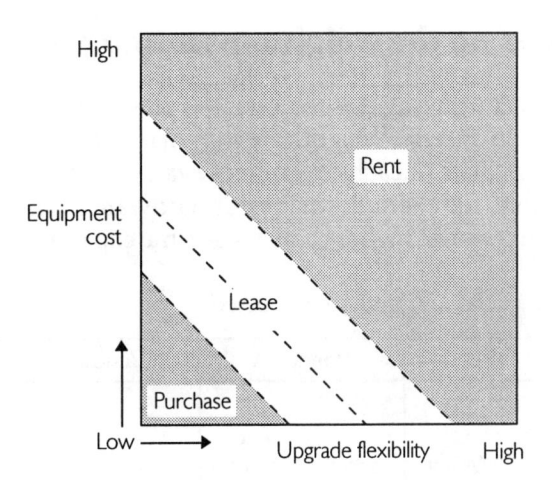

The purchase of a resource gives a buyer less flexibility in upgrading equipment than rental or lease. However, the latter cost more. Each firm, after studying its environment, should base its acquisition choice on:

- *Financial climate.* This includes availability of funds, both internal (opportunity costs) and external (banks and lending institutions); governmental policies on depreciation; and property taxes on purchase.
- *Anticipation of technological advances.* Will more reliable, compatible and cheaper computer resources soon be released? Will new innovative systems have a longer useful life, increasing their residual value to the lessor?
- *User demand projections.* These include current and future user demand projections as well as predictions on the secondhand usefulness of the resources to other units in the organization when the original user updates.
- *Ability to maintain equipment.* If the firm lacks maintenance knowledge and experience, rental or lease options may be advisable.
- *Decision-making structure.* Renting or leasing may be expedient (though not necessarily economically sound) if firms have cumbersome procedures for letting bids and making acquisition decisions.

Negotiation of acquisition contracts requires technical and legal expertise. When implementing contracts, close liaison with vendors may reduce the stress of conversion. Fortunately, interfacing equipment is becoming less of a problem with the introduction of plug-compatible machines.

Case 9.1: Acquisition using the weighted-scoring method

A worksheet utilizing this technique is present in Table C9.1. Column 1 lists decision criteria. Weights are shown in column 2 that reflect the relative importance of each criterion as evaluated by the acquisition team. In this table, for example, ability of hardware to meet growth needs is ranked three times higher than a real-time capability.

Table C9.1 *Worksheet for the weighted-score method*

		Vendor A		Vendor B		Vendor C	
(1)	(2)	(3)	(4)	5	(6)	7	(8)
			Wtd.		Wtd.		Wtd.
Decision criterion	Weight	Score	Score	Score	Score	Score	Score
■ Hardware							
■ Meets need of growth	3	7	21	7	21	5	15
■ Throughput/£	5	8	40	6	30	5	25
■ Communications	2	4	8	8	16	6	12
■ Real-time capability	1	1	1	5	5	3	3
■ Storage	2	8	16	6	12	7	14
• Input/output interface	2	6	12	6	12	6	12
• Site restrictions	1	4	4	6	6	8	8
■ Reliability	3	9	27	6	18	8	24
■ Ease of use	1	6	6	8	8	6	6
Total for hardware			135		128		119
■ Software							
■ Monitors	5	8	40	9	45	4	20
■ Compilers	4	7	28	9	36	3	12
■ Multiprogramming	1	8	8	8	8	6	6
■ Query capability	1	7	7	6	6	5	5
■ Data management	3	7	21	9	27	4	12
■ Reliability	3	8	24	9	27	6	18
■ Packaged software	2	8	16	9	18	5	10
■ Utility software	2	8	16	9	18	6	12
■ Documentation	4	7	28	7	28	8	32
Total for software			188		213		127
■ Other							
■ Cost	40	4.5	180	3	120	9	360
■ Engineering support	3	9	27	7	21	3	9
■ Systems support	4	9	36	6	24	1	4
■ Education	5	7	35	7	35	5	25
■ Reputation and stability	2	10	20	7	14	5	10
■ Delivery date	1	6	6	5	5	9	9
Total for other items			304		219		417
Total for each vendor			627		560		663

Assignment of weights is subjective and may cause disagreements among team members given the responsibility for calculating the table. Should top management intervene when a stalemate is reached? Have veto power? To reach consensus, long and heated discussions may sometimes take place, with arm-twisting and power politics playing a role. The next step is scoring vendors. For example, according to Table C9.1, Vendor A's hardware rates an 8 for storage capacity, whereas Vendor B's system is only given a 6. Scoring is also a subjective activity, sometimes even more difficult than assigning weights. Often an individual or group with expertise on a given feature will be given responsibility for scoring that feature. When newly developed systems are being evaluated, fair scoring may require considerable effort, involving literature searches, calculations, and customer satisfaction checks.

The weighted-score for each vendor for each criterion is calculated by multiplying the values in the weight column (column 2) by the values in each vendor's score column (column 3 for Vendor A, column 5 for vendor B, column 7 for Vendor C). The total score for a given vendor is calculated by adding all of the values in the vendor's weighted-score column. According to Table C9.1, Vendor C has the highest score.

Case 9.2: Acquisition using the cost–value method

Table C9.2 shows the cost–value method applied to an actual case: acquisition of a database management system (DBMS). This case demonstrates that the cost–value method, usually applied to hardware acquisition, is equally valid for software, and it lists the features many companies seek when choosing software. The costs are realistic, although the table has been simplified for use in this text. (For example, 36 features have been consolidated into 10.)

Table C9.2 *Cost calculations for selection of a DBMS (£000s)*

Cost items	Vendor A	Vendor B
▪ Cost of vendor proposal	£208	£102
▪ Interface to a higher-level language (i.e., BASIC)	42	18
▪ Natural language query facility, including communications interface	20	50
▪ Equipment interdependence (52k/machine)	51	104
▪ Data element dictionary	–	57
▪ Supporting equipment necessary	–	20
▪ Inverted file	–	70
▪ Recovery procedures	–	55
▪ Security	55.5	5
▪ Conversion of database	34	95
Total	£410.5	£596

Case 9.3: Rent vs. purchase

Note that Vendor A's proposal price is twice that of Vendor B but that when the value of omitted features is added, the total cost of A's system is lower than B's system. Also notice the high cost of conversion listed in the table. Conversion costs should be considered when acquiring new hardware, since existing application programs may have to be altered to run on the new equipment. The most efficient hardware may turn out to be unacceptable because of such conversion costs.

Case 9.3: Rent vs. purchase

Calculations for rental and purchase of a medium- to large-sized computer that take into consideration some of the variables cited above are shown in Table C9.3.

Table C9.3 *Purchase versus rent calculations*

A. Data on which purchase calculations are based

1. Purchase basic price	£1,600,000
2. Estimated useful life	5 years
3. Maintenance contract	£3,040 per month
4. Property tax	12,960 per year
5. Investment tax credit	10%
6. Depreciation (ACRS*)	Taken over 5 years, annual rates of 15%, 22%, 21%, 21% and 21%
7. Discount rate	10%
8. Tax rate (state and federal)	50%
9. Salvage value at end of fifth year	£500,000
Maintenance per year	£36,480
Tax savings per year at 50%	£18,240
Net cost on maintenance	£18,240 per year

* ARCS = accelerated cost recovery system

B. Calculations for purchase (inflows in parentheses)

		Year 1	Year 2	Year 3	Year 4	Year 5
Original purchase price	£1,600,000	£ 0	£ 0	£ 0	£ 0	£ 0
Maintenance contract	0	18,240	18,240	18,240	18,240	18,240
Property tax (net)	0	6,480	6,480	6,480	6,480	6,480
Cash savings from deprecation	0	(120,000)	(176,000)	(168,000)	(168,000)	(168,000)
Investment tax credit	0	(100,000)	0	0	0	0
Salvage value	0	0	0	0	0	(500,000)
Total cash outflow	£1,600,000	(£255,280)	(£151,280)	(£143,280)	(£143,280)	(£643,280)
Present value (PV) factor	1.0	.9091	.8264	.7513	.6830	.6209
PV of cash outflow	£1,600,000	(232,075)	(£125,018)	(£107,646)	(£ 97,860)	(£399,412)
Total PV of cash outflow for five years:		£637,988				

Table C9.3 continued ▸

Table C9.3 (continued)

C. Calculations for rental (inflows in parentheses)

	Year 1	Year 2	Year 3	Year 4	Year 5
Rental	£593,244	£593,244	£593,244	£593,244	£593,244
Tax savings from rental (50%)	(296,622)	(296,622)	(296,622)	(296,622)	(296,622)
Total outflow	£296,622	£296,622	£296,622	£296,622	£296,622
Present value (PV) factor	.9091	0.8264	.7513	.6830	.6209
PV of cash outflow	£269,659	£245,128	£222,852	£202,593	£184,172

PV of cash outflow for 5 years: £1,124,406

Data on which the calculations are based appear in the first section of the table. Calculations for purchase and rental are then shown. In these two sections, each column represents one year of transactions. A positive number indicates outflow or cost; a negative number (in parentheses) indicates inflow or savings. The total net outflow equals the sum of costs less inflows

To represent future costs as a present value so they can be compared with the present purchase price, the totals must be multiplied by a present value factor (as shown in the table). The present value of purchase and the present value of all other related costs after income tax are then totalled. The sum of £637,988 represents the PV of purchase outflows. This figure should then be compared with cash outflow for rentals over the same time period, discounted to their present value. In Table C.9.3, rental equals £1,124,406. Purchase, therefore, costs £486,418 less than rental in present value terms. According to the table, the cutover point is about three years. That is, if the useful life for the system is longer than three years, buying would be cheaper than renting.

Case 9.4: Lease vs. lease/purchase

A decision to lease, with or without the option to buy, should be based on a discounted cashflow analysis. Calculations showing costs for a straight lease for a period of five years appear in Table C9.4. A lease/purchase decision (purchase after a one-year lease) is shown in Table C9.5. The calculations are similar to those made earlier when comparing rental and purchase (Table C9.3), although more variables are involved in leasing (see Table C9.6). Again, each column in the tables represent a year of transactions, with costs discounted to present value. Straight lease has a PV of £1,202,562 (Table C9.4), compared to the lease/purchase alternative costing £638,077 (Table C9.5).

According to these calculations (given the assumptions of the problem), lease/purchase is the better alternative, with a saving of £564,485 =£(1,202,562 − 638,077). However, note that calculations of present

Case 9.4: Lease vs. lease/purchase

value may lead to erroneous conclusions when comparing different kinds of equipment with different useful lives. In such cases, the total cost of equipment alternatives should be converted to annuities over the lives of the respective alternatives and a comparison made of these annuities.

Table C9.4 *Calculations for lease*

A. Data on lease environment

1. Lease payment	£600,000 per year
2. Period of lease	5 years
3. Maintenance	£24,000 per year
4. Property tax	Lessee pays
5. Investment credit	Tax benefit to lessor
6. Depreciation	Tax benefit to lessor
7. Discount rate	10%
8. Marginal tax rate	50%
Lease payments	£600,000 per year
Tax savings (50%)	300,000
Net lease cost	£300,000 per year
Maintenance	£24,000 per year
Tax savings (50%)	12,000
Net cost on maintenance	£12,000 per year

B. Calculations

After-tax cash outflow	Year 1	Year 2	Year 3	Year 4	Year 5
Lease	£300,000	£300,000	£300,000	£300,000	£300,000
Maintenance	12,000	12,000	12,000	12,000	12,000
Property tax	5,265	5,265	5,265	5,265	5,265
Total outflow	£317,265	£317,265	£317,265	£317,265	£317,265
Present value factor formula	$\frac{1}{(1.10)^1}$	$\frac{1}{(1.10)^2}$	$\frac{1}{(1.10)^3}$	$\frac{1}{(1.10)^4}$	$\frac{1}{(1.10)^5}$
PV factor	.9091	.8264	.7513	.6830	.6206
PV of total after-tax cash outflow	£288,426	£262,188	£238,361	£216,692	£196,895
Total PV of cash outflow for 5 years:	£1,202,562				

Some of the variables used in these two sets of calculations differ from the rental–purchase variables in Table C9.3 (for example, the depreciation rate has been altered). This is to show the reader that calculations are not always made on the basis of the same variable. Indeed, in an actual case, few of the variables or values of the variables listed may be applicable because a change in government can affect tax laws, discount rates, and useful life allowances. Also, the length of the lease period will affect calculations.

Table C9.5 Calculations for lease/purchase

A. Data on environment

Lease payments	£600,000 per year
Period of lease	1 year
Maintenance	£24,000 per year (note difference from purchase year)
Property tax	£10,530 per year after purchase
Investment credit	10% claimed on purchase
Deprecation	Straight line on five years after acquisition
Discount rate	10%
Tax rate	50%
Useful life	5 years
Portion of rentals deducted from purchase price	£320,000
Purchase price	£(1,600,000 − 320,000) = £1,280,000
Resale value at end of 5 years	£300,000

B. Calculations (inflows in parentheses)

Cash outflows	Year 1	Year 2	Year 3	Year 4	Year 5
Lease	£300,000	£0	£0	£0	£0
Purchase price	0	1,280,000	0	0	0
Maintenance	12,000	12,000	12,000	12,000	12,000
Property tax	0	5,265	5,265	5,265	5,265
Tax savings from depreciation	0	(160,000)	(160,000)	(160,000)	(160,000)
Investment tax credit	0	(128,000)	0	0	0
Resale value	0	0	0	0	(300,000)
Total outflow	£312,000	£1,009,265	(£142,735)	(£142,735)	(£442,735)
Present value (PV) factor	.9091	.8264	.7513	.6830	.6209
PV of cash outflow	£283,639	£834,057	£107,237	£97,488	(£274,894)
Total PV of cash outflow for 5 years:	£638,077				

Table C9.6 Variables in leasing

- Lease payments
- Leasing period
- Maintenance cost
- Discount rate
- Tax rate
- Costs for installation
- Cost for shipping
- Costs for system checking and integration
- Conditions for upgrading and updating
- Conditions for renewal
- Depreciation rate
- Investment tax credit rate
- Recipient of investment tax credit (either lessor or lessee)

References

Auer, Joe. (1993). "Negotiating a Better Deal with Vendors." *Information Systems Journal*, vol. 10, pp. 66-8.

Hillard, B. L. (1985). "Techniques for Negotiating a Computer System Acquisition." *Computers in Auditing*, vol. 1, no. 4, pp. 41-4.

Loud, James F. (1985). "Software Selection for Non-DP Senior Management." *Bank Administration*, vol. 61, no. 1 (January), pp. 34-40.

Nelson, P., Richmond, W. and Seidmann, A. (1996). "Two Dimensions of Software Acquisition." *Communications of the ACM*, vol. 39, no. 7 (July), pp. 29-35.

Pollis, Richard. (1985). "The Oath to Successful Procurement." *Infosystems*, vol. 22, no. 11 (November), pp. 72-7.

Schreiber, Richard. (1995). "Middleware Demystified." *Datamation*, vol. 41, no. 6 (April 1), pp. 41-5.

Tardy, Jean E. (1993). "Strategies for Software Acquisition." *Journal of Systems Software*, vol. 18, no. 3 (July), pp. 281-3.

Weiner, Hesh. (1984). "Lessons on Leasing." *Datamation*, vol. 30, no. 7 (May 15), pp. 103-11.

Weiss, Stephen E. (1994). "Negotiating with the 'Romans'–Part 2." *Sloan Management Review*, vol. 35, no. 3, pp. 85-100.

Welch, James A., and Ranganath Nayak, P. (1992). "Strategic Sourcing: A Progressive Approach to the Make-Or-Buy Decision." *Academy of Management Executive*, vol. 6, no. 1, pp. 23-31.

Yates, John C., and Henry W. Jones III. (1985). "Computer Acquisitions: The Role of Due Diligence." *Computer Negotiations Report*, vol. 8, no. 9, pp. 1-4.

10 Outsourcing

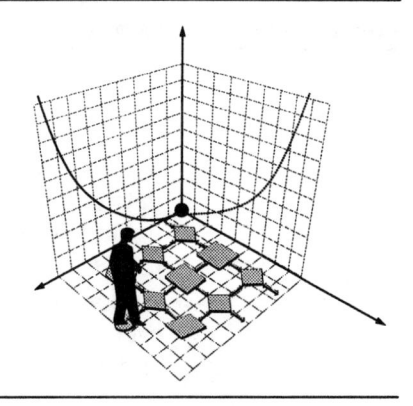

> We see the success of the company as doing core things well. It is not an accident that the rest is outsourced.
>
> *An Executive*

Introduction

Outsourcing is the subcontracting of IT activities. It originally started with data preparation but now extends to programming, maintenance of PCs, teleprocessing services, and special projects. In the case of programming, if the decision is not to "make" and construct software "in-house" but to contract it outside, then we have outsourcing. In the case of facilities, the contracting is similar to FM (facilities management). The main difference between FM and outsourcing is that FM is concerned primarily (and historically) with operations of IT while outsourcing is primarily concerned with programming and with the use of advanced computer skills like teleprocessing. When there are economies of scope (in addition to economics of scale), then FM and outsourcing are very similar. In this chapter, we examine outsourcing by looking at the risks and rewards in outsourcing; the situations when outsourcing is desirable (and equally undesirable); factors to be considered in outsourcing and in contracts with the outsourcing vendor; a comparison of outsourcing with other organizational approaches; and finally, global outsourcing. We conclude with some very short cases to illustrate the scope of outsourcing in terms of content and benefits. We start with the nature of outsourcing and its content.

Nature and content of outsourcing

Historically, outsourcing was exclusively for data preparation. The firm would send data on coded sheets and this would be converted to machine readable form, mostly on cards. This was a very structured situation and outsourcing relieved the firm of repetitive work done by unskilled labour. Some firms considered their data to be too proprietary therefore one would see rooms with a total area of about half a football field with key punchers and verifiers working three shifts a day. However, with technology data preparation moved away from cards to tapes and disks; from offline peripherals to online point-of-sale terminals; and from key operators to terminal operators and mark-sensors, optical scanners, image, and voice processing. Developed countries with large-scale data-preparation needs hardly have a visible formal function for data preparation anymore. But the need for outsourcing did not disappear. It merely shifted from data preparation to programming. The programming specifications in selected applications were sent to the outsourcing vendor and programs were delivered in return. However, the nature of the work became more complex and contracts became more important and involved more funds.

Outsourced programming often includes maintenance work. Why maintenance? Partly because maintenance is perceived to be not very creative and hence not too popular when there are new programs that have to be written. Also, it is somewhat a structured situation in that the system has already been designed and implemented; now it has to be modified. This task can well be contracted out, i.e. outsourced. One problem with outsourcing maintenance is that if it may involve an unspecified design for modifications, making the estimation of costs somewhat difficult. This difficulty is overcome partly by "cost-plus" pricing where the vendor is paid costs plus a mark-up. The problem is now one of controlling costs. We will discuss costing of outsourcing later in this chapter.

As firms became confident with contracting services via outsourcing and facilities management, other services are outsourced. Some of these services may be one-time activities like the installation of an image processing system. Or, it could be a one-time installation plus its ongoing maintenance. One such set of services are for telecommunications and networking. Why telecommunications and networking? Because this is a state-of-the-art field that seems to be ever-changing. It is technical and crucial. It needs to be in the hands of professionals. If a firm does not have the resources or confidence to manage such work internally then it is outsourced.

We can see that outsourcing has a wide range of activities. These are summarized in Figure 10.1. They involve risks and benefits which we will now examine.

Figure 10.1: *Outsourcing*

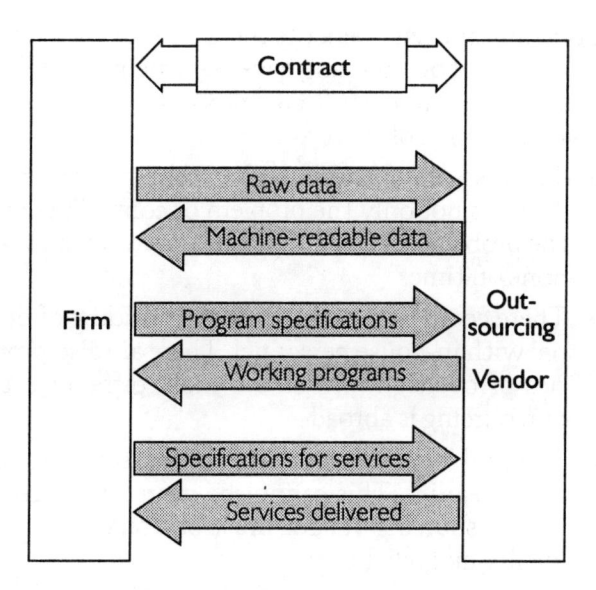

A diagram showing the relationship between a Firm and an Outsourcing Vendor, connected by a Contract. Flows between them include: Raw data → ; ← Machine-readable data; Program specifications → ; ← Working programs; Specifications for services → ; ← Services delivered.

Risks and rewards in outsourcing

There are rewards and risks in outsourcing. First, the rewards and benefits. These are:

- Cost reduction and cost containment are perhaps the most important benefits. The savings in cost must, however, be offset against the cost of entering into an outsourcing agreement which requires the specification of pricing, procedures, performance, and the invoking of penalties in the event of non-performance. Also, there is a cost of measurement and monitoring of performance which is not always an easy task nor are the legal aspects of contracting – especially when foreign countries are involved.

- Outsourcing, especially of programming of subsystem's development, can reduce the backlog of applications development and reduce the time of development if it were done in-house. It enables the reallocation of computing resources to other high value-added strategic activities.

- Outsourcing could be a solution to the problem of scarce resources since it enables access to a pool of highly skilled personnel (including globally) not just in programming, but also in data/knowledge bases and telecommunications. Such use of resources could help in balancing the workload especially when the workload is seasonal. It saves the overhead costs of the logistics of hiring, firing, and the managing of high-tech personnel.

Chapter 10: Outsourcing

Concomitant with benefits there are costs and risks involved. The overhead costs of outsourcing have been mentioned. There could be running costs such as line costs for teleprocessing. There are other costs and risks involved. Some of these are:

- The loss of control is perhaps the greatest risk in outsourcing. There is not only the problem of controlling operations, but also the problem of controlling quality and ensuring that the tasks get done on time.
- There could be a problem of the blending of outsourcing personnel with in-house personnel. There are also problems of the logistics of oversight which are more difficult especially when the outsourcing is abroad.
- The problems of negotiating an outsourcing contract was mentioned earlier. This cannot be overemphasized. The selection of the outsourcing vendor must be done with great care to ensure quality and reliability.

The concern with control is a subject that came up when discussing EUC (end-user computing), with all the control of processing information going to the end-user. We also identified the traditional control of data and its processing shifting from under the control of the IT (EDP or IS) department to the end-user. In the case of centralized and decentralized/distributed processing, we saw the control of information still retained by the IT department. This is also the case with outsourcing, except perhaps in some cases the control migrates to the end-user. Also, with a foreign vendor the *de facto* operational control will go to the vendor, but the IT department will retain formal control through a contract. These locations of control are shown in Figure 10.2 which is really a superimposition of outsourcing on the diagram of control discussed in Chapter 2.

Back to costs and benefits. In balancing costs and benefits, there is a problem of determining intangible benefits. For example how does one assess the benefits for any of the following:

- Being relieved of the hassle of the maintenance of PCs?
- Having more time to spend on planning the infrastructure and integration?
- Having access to state-of-the-art technology and the research and development resources of the outsourcing vendor?
- Shifting the potential political problems of making enhancements and doing maintenance to the outsourcing vendor?
- Not having to worry about peak and erratic loads?

Figure 10.2: Shifts in control of data/information

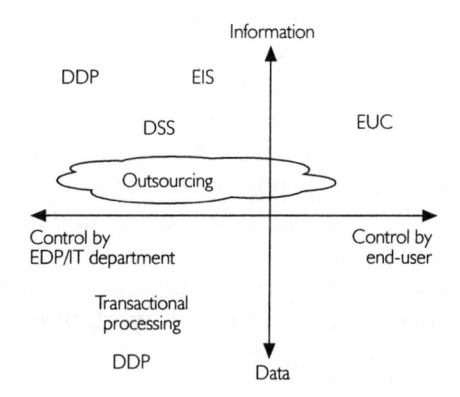

One solution to such problems may be the assignment of net-benefits. But the problem of assigning values to intangible benefits is the same as those faced in a feasibility study of any complex information system: to compare benefits in their abstract and intangible form and compare it with tangible costs. The corporate manager then must decide whether or not the benefits are worth the costs entailed. In other words, we must use the ordinal approach of ordering rather than the cardinal approach of assigning specific values.

When to outsource

Vital or proprietary work of high strategic value and high cost–benefit ratio is often not outsourced. However, a computing task that is of low strategic value and low cost–benefit ratio is outsourced. The gray area in between may or may not be worth outsourcing and should be examined on a case-by-case basis. The matrix of decision-making in outsourcing is shown in Figure 10.3. There are many factors other than strategic value and cost–benefits that must be considered. Some factors that favour outsourcing are listed in Table 10.1.

Figure 10.3: When to outsource

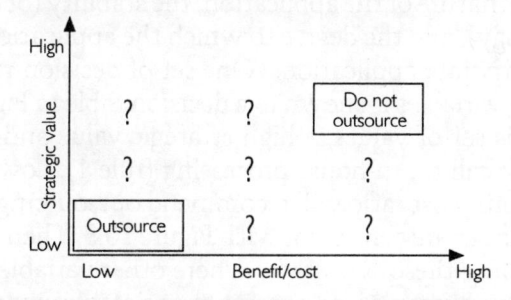

There is a large "gray area" as represented by "???" in Figure 10.3. This area includes situations like a project that is well structured and well defined, requires skills in short supply, has a fluctuating demand, does not have a tight time-schedule and need not be controlled too closely. Or a situation where there is a complex system involving systems integration that may point towards the option of not outsourcing but the outsourcing vendor has a long record of competence and reliability. In this latter case, corporate (and IT) management may be quite comfortable with the outsourcing vendor and many decisions on outsourcing are personal and intuitive decisions. However, it helps to think through the decision rules (in the context of a decision table) for outsourcing by considering most of the important variables.

Table 10.1 *Factors that favour outsourcing*

- High benefit–cost ratio (low cost–benefit ratio)
- Low strategic value
- Positive effect on competitiveness
- No proprietary information involved
- Security and confidentiality of:
  - Data/information
  - Programs
- No or little infusion of technology and transfer of technology involved
- Need to stabilize costs from erratic and peak loads
- Need to relocate computing resources
- Shortage of IS talent locally
- Availability of resources with outsourcing vendor for:
  - Computing
  - Personnel
  - Telecommunications
- Control and auditing of outsourced operations
- No or little danger of disturbing morale of local personnel

One set of variables may be the strategic value, benefit–cost ratio, the technical nature of the application, the stability (of the business and the technology), and the degree to which the application is integrated with other corporate applications. One set of decision rules for outsourcing for these variables is shown in a decision table in Figure 10.4.

In this set of values, a high strategic value and a high benefit–cost ratio will call for in-house processing (rule 1). Low strategic value and low benefit–cost ratio will recommend outsourcing (rule 2).

Both rules are consistent with Figure 10.3. Then there is a whole area surrounding these two states where other variables are relevant (rules 3–11). One example is the presence of a stable environment, the nature of the application was technical, but the answers to other questions in the decision table are negative. In this case, outsourcing would be viable (rule 5).

Figure 10.4:
Decision table on when to outsource

	1	2	3	4	5	6	7	8	9	10	11	Else
Strategic value?	Y	N	Y	Y	N	N	N	N	N	N	N	
High benefit–cost ratio?	Y	N	N	N	N	N	N	N	N	N	N	
Stable?	-	-	Y	Y	Y	Y	Y	Y	N	N	N	
Of a technical nature?	-	-	Y	Y	Y	Y	N	N	Y	Y	N	
Highly integrated?	-	-	N	Y	N	Y	N	Y	N	Y	Y	
In-house	X			X		X		X		X	X	
Outsource		X	X		X		X		X			
Examine carefully												X

Factors in outsourcing contracts

There are many factors to be considered in selecting an outsourcing vendor such as experience with outsourcing, reputation in cost-effective and reliable outsourcing, availability of desired talents, and business connections with a competitor. Once a vendor is selected, attention should be paid to drawing-up a contract.

The general cautions in making contracts for outsourcing are the same as any contract made for IT resources like hardware and software discussed earlier. The contracts for outsourcing could be very comprehensive including the transfer of technology and assets (buildings, hardware, software and personnel). There are also some special conditions that are important and relevant for outsourcing. They include penalties on non-compliance of performance, or deadlines for dates of delivery, or violations of other clauses in the outsourcing contract. The clauses must be specific yet not too rigid to allow for unexpected conditions. These factors are fairly self-evident and are listed in Table 10.2.

There are considerations not listed in any contract but are of concern to the firm after having outsourced its tasks. These include policies and procedures for implementing the contract and meeting obligations under the contract, monitoring the compliance by the outsourcing vendor, blending the outsourcing personnel into the organization to the extent needed, and maintaining a working relationship with the vendor. These indirect cost factors must be considered before entering into any contract.

There are many types of contract. The simplest is the fixed fee for a contract that is tightly written and a structured environment with little or no uncertainty. In contrast, there may be situations where there is high uncertainty and the contract cannot be tight or structured. Examples will be new applications for an organization such as a client–server system, a sophisticated telecommunications system, or an advanced application such as a intelligent image system.

Table 10.2 *Factors to be considered in an outsourcing contract*

- Scope and responsibilities of contractor and vendor (contact points may be defined and formalized)
- Metrics of quality
- Performance measures and date of their achievement
- Penalties for non-performance at each important stage and milestone
- Service levels to accommodate mergers and acquisitions
- No hidden costs passed on by the outsourcing vendor
- Confidentiality of data/information and penalties on infraction
- Ownership of intellectual property, assets and services, and the transfer of assets
- Auditing of costs, performance, confidentiality, and quality
- Training (scope, content, approaches and timing)
- Terms and conditions of payments including to staff "on loan" from firm to outsourcing vendor
- Termination of contract. Options for renegotiation, renewal and revision of contract. Too long a contract should allow for lower cost because of technology advances to be passed down to the firm
- Settlement of disputes and interpretation of contract

There are cases where the risks and rewards are shared between the outsourcing firm and the vendor in a risk/reward contract that has some uncertainty and a low contractual definition. There are also situations where there may be high certainty (low uncertainty) but a loosely written contract. This is open to abuse and therefore not recommended. The other extreme would be high uncertainly with a tightly written contract. Here there is little flexibility for the vendor with changing conditions of technology. This may be too constrained for the vendor and not recommended from the vendor's point of view. Where there is low uncertainty and a high content definition, a fixed contract is indicated. These combinations of certainty and contractual definitions are shown in Figure 10.5.

There are many points outside the areas discussed. These may be covered by other types of contracts, such as fixed fee plus variable costs, fixed fee plus a management fee, or a fixed fee and an incentive scheme.

Alternatively, there may be no contract at all. An example would be point A in Figure 10.5, where there is high certainty and the possibility of a fixed fee contract in a tightly written contract. But this may not be the choice of the firm making the contract, or the choice of the vendor. Both may prefer no contract at all. They may argue that the relationship should be one of trust and hence there is no need for any contract. Besides, they may argue for an informal agreement where decisions are made by mutual consent based on goodwill and common sense and adaptive to changing conditions.

Figure 10.5: *Type of contract for outsourcing*

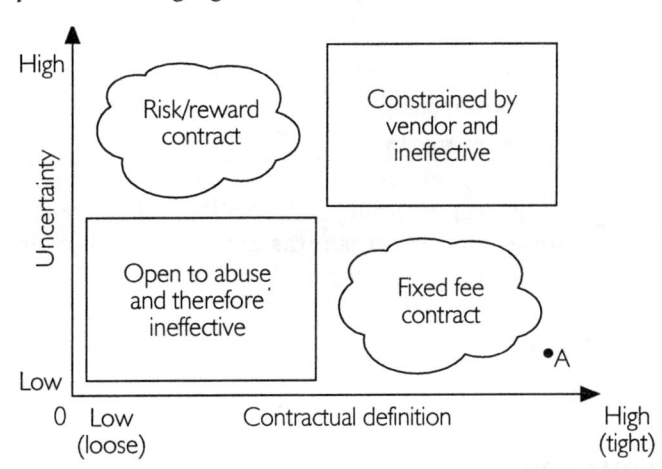

One can only wish good luck to such parties that have trust and faith in human nature. Often, this is the road to misunderstandings and even court cases especially if the two parties come from different organizational cultures and different national cultures in the case of global outsourcing.

Outsourcing and other approaches

We mentioned the difference between outsourcing and the EUC in terms of control. There are other differences in terms of type of processing performed, structure of tasks, location of responsibilities involved, and skills required. We will now compare outsourcing with EUC and traditional transactional processing for each of these factors.

Tasks are highly structured for transactional processing as with outsourcing but ill-structured or unstructured with EUC. Control of data/information and equipment for the enterprise as in transactional processing is still the responsibility of IT which shifts to the end-user in EUC and may stay with the IT department or with the end-user in the case of outsourcing.

Chapter 10: Outsourcing

Figure 10.6:
Comparison of transactional processing with end-user computing and outsourcing

	Transactional	End-user computing	Outsourcing
Structure	High	Little/none	High (mostly)
Control by IT centre	IT	End-user	IT
Responsibility:			
▪ Development	IT	End-user	IT
▪ Computing	IT	End-user	Vendor
Skills required by	IT	End-user	Vendor

The responsibility for development is with the IT department in transactional processing as with outsourcing, unlike that of EUC where the responsibility lies with the end-user. The responsibility for operational computing and skills required in computing is with the IT department in transactional processing, with the end-user in EUC, and with the vendor in outsourcing. A summary of these differences is shown in Figure 10.6.

Global outsourcing

One strategy for outsourcing is to go global and take advantage of the lower wage levels in developing countries. Subcontracting labour-intensive activity makes sense for developed countries because of the wage differentials between workers at home and workers in developing countries. For example, a data clerk earns between $3,000 to $5,000 per annum in Barbados or Jamaica while a comparable job commands a salary between $14,000 to $18,000 in the United States. Santa Lucia is one country that supports local data preparation with an acceptable turnaround time by using a digital earth station with telecommunication links to the US, Canada, and Europe. Many countries do data processing for foreign banks handling electronic data transfer and other financial transactions. The Cayman Islands, Naura, Vanuatu, the Cook Islands, Maldives, the Marshal Islands and Micronesia are other examples.

However, the outsourcing of data preparation in the developing countries is on the decline because of advances in data preparation technology (like optical scanning and voice processing). On the other hand, subcontracts for software development are on the rise. In 1989, an Irish programmer earned approximately $15,000. In the US, a programmer of matching skills earned twice that amount. No wonder American firms like to contract their programming abroad.

Taiwan, South Korea, and Singapore are major exporters of software. India has declared software development as an economic goal and has the scientific manpower to implement it. At present, most of India's software exports are to the US and are largely through bodyshopping, a practice of sending engineers abroad to develop software for customers. Bodyshopping has proved an easy way to get business, but travel costs are high and the risk is great that nationals posted in America and Europe may find more lucrative jobs abroad and not return home, resulting in a so called "brain-drain" from developing countries.

China is another country that is a competitor in the software business which is one of its modernization priorities. Chinese bid low for software so that outsourcing to China can be very cost effective for Western firms but the lack of English speakers in China is a disadvantage. Many software contracts are lost to India as a result where English is widely spoken. The language factor is also relevant in the case of Russia and Eastern European countries where IS talent is available, but communications are difficult.

The downsides of software outsourcing from the point of view of corporate management in developed countries is unpredictable social, political, and legal conditions in developing countries and the danger of software piracy. Software piracy may prevent a company from recouping its investment in computer projects and may even undermine its competitiveness. No wonder firms want guarantees that outsourced software be secure. These firms favour contractors in countries that have a legal framework for the protection of intellectual property and computing resources and legal remedies if project security is breached.

In an international context, the protection of software (and other computing resources) is a very complex issue because of conflicting domestic laws on copyrights, patents, trade secrets, and crime. These laws, if applicable to information (many are not because they are written to protect tangible property and software is not universally recognized as "tangible"), quickly become outdated because of the speed with which the computer revolution is changing and the way that business and commerce is now conducted. Even in countries that have participated in the computer revolution from the start, people are only now beginning to address the question of what constitutes ethical conduct in computerized business operations. With the world becoming smaller through trade and the flow of information across borders, there is a growing need for international standards, treaties, and laws relating to information technology. The lack of such an environment impedes the transfer of technology and outsourcing to the third world.

Global outsourcing raises many new factors that must be considered in determining whether or not to go global and if so, to make sure that the firm is protected in its contract. Special factors to be considered in the global outsourcing decision include foreign exchange, reliability of the telecommunications infrastructure, time-zone differences, and changes in national laws and salary structures. Other factors that are not within the firm's preview but must be negotiated between countries (and sometimes through international agreements like GATT) are the problems of transfer of technology, transborder flow of data, the emerging problem of brain-drain, and the problem of protecting intellectual property.

Summary and conclusions

Summarizing the discussion on outsourcing, it must be said that outsourcing is not for every firm and for every country. It must be approached with caution. A rigorous cost analysis must be supported by proper consideration of technological and strategic factors. Also, the outsourcing vendor must be chosen carefully for proven reliability and quality of work.

A summary of the advantages and disadvantages of outsourcing are shown in Table 10.3. These must be weighed before any decision to outsource is considered. From the feasible list, one may purge projects that have high strategic value, involve proprietary information and have a high cost–benefit ratio as well as consider disadvantages such as those listed in Table 10.3.

Table 10.3 *Summary of advantages and disadvantages of outsourcing*

Advantages
- Use pool of scarce resource of knowledgeable and experienced IT personnel available elsewhere
- Reduce applications backlog and meet peak and erratic loads
- Easy to work with
- Carry no "baggage" of:
    - Hiring and firing costs
    - Having to negotiate with unions
    - Following national and state laws
- Economical in terms of:
    - Total costs
    - Fringe benefits packages may not be needed
- Share risks in advanced projects
- Outsource in IT areas of your weakness
- Appropriate for applications that are:
    - Structured and well defined
    - Not too complex
    - Not "vital" or critical
    - Not involving propriety information (e.g. trade secrets)

Table 10.3 *Summary of advantages and disadvantages of outsourcing (continued)*

- Fluctuating loads and overloads
- No strict timetable required

Disadvantages and limitations
- Loss of "in-house" expertise and experience
- Require control and monitoring of:
  - Quality of software
  - Adherence to standards
  - Confidentiality and security
  - Project management requirements
- Must have a vendor that is reliable
- Danger of "hidden" costs
- May require training of vendor personnel on industry and organization culture

Also, to be excluded from the list of feasible projects are IT functions that are strategic and "mission critical," the development of business-specific and strategic applications, and the support of important and critical applications. There is a lot left over including data preparation, run-of-the-mill programming and maintenance, and services that may include maintenance of PCs and telecommunications services. The running of a data or computer centre can also be outsourced but this has traditionally been the jurisdiction of FM (facilities management). Work that is not crucial to the firm, work for which there are no local skills easily available, or work that is not desirable to its staff, should also be candidates for outsourcing.

Once the decision is made to outsource, a vendor must be chosen and a contract drawn with great care in considering changes in the demand and cost curves. Failures in outsourcing have often been attributed to a poor or loosely written contract. The trick in having a good contract is that it is specific and yet flexible for adaptation to changes in technology. The cautions (mostly generic) in vendor selection and contract preparation which must be followed when acquiring any computing resource have already been discussed. There are, however, some special matters that are unique to outsourcing and are listed in Table 10.2. Additional factors must be considered in global outsourcing. One must look at the country of the vendor for stability (economic, social, and political), the infrastructure (especially in telecommunications), the availability of skilled IT talent that speaks your language, and the stability of policies relating to the protection of intellectual property and the transborder flow of information.

Case 10.1: Examples of outsourcing

- In 1993, CSC (Computer Science Corporation) agreed to be the outsourcing vendor for the operations of the Inland Revenue: over a ten-year period and a for a fee of $1.5 billion. CSC had previously won an outsourcing contract with British Aerospace for $1.34 billion. CSC agreed to a transfer of 1,250 IT employees from British Aerospace.
- EDS contracted with Meritir Savings Bank for 10 years in a downsizing effort to fend off bankruptcy. EDS did the data and cheque processing as well as data and voice networking.
- EDS, along with Texas Air, formed a joint venture to provide the reservation system. EDS paid $250 million to Texas Air for the assets of Systems One reservation system subsidiary. The expected savings were to be $25–45 million with a cap on the expenditures of information systems of 3% a year.
- IBM, AT&T, and Hughes got a joint contract from Chevron for its networks connecting the 2,000 service stations. IBM is to manage the SNA network, AT&T the private voice network, and Hughes the point-of-sale network.
- ISL (Information Solutions Limited, an outsourcing subsidiary of IBM) signed up with Equifax, a consumer credit data supplier in the UK. The CEO remarked: "One of the benefits of our agreement is that we will have access to IBM's state-of-the-art systems and technology."
- MCI contracted with Merril Lynch for $150 million to cut operating costs by $100 million in 5 years. IBM was the subcontractor for network management.
- Northern Telecom contracted with Bankers Trust for 6 years and $40 million to provide network integration, network administration, maintenance, engineering, and recovery services.
- IBM's Integrated Systems Solutions Corporation signed a $415 million contract with Southern Pacific to handle data processing and help in boosting the efficiency of the business.
- US Sprint contracted with Sears (Technology Services) for the management of a voice network with virtual net bulk services and enhanced switched services for interface with IBM computers.

Sources: Takac (1994:147); *Computer Weekly* (18 November 1993, p. 1); *IW* (November 15, 1993:14); and *IW* (November 29, 1993).

Case 10.2: Outsourcing at General Dynamics

In 1991, General Dynamics entered into a $3 billion outsourcing contract with Computer Science Corporation (CSC). 2,450 of its employees were transferred to CSC; 800 software designers for the cruise missile and space launch vehicles were retained; 75 were assigned to office staff for planning and control; and the remaining 75 retired or were transferred to other jobs. Of the office staff, two or three performed budgeting, planning, and prioritization tasks while two or three acted as program managers to see that the IS needs were identified and satisfied.

The positions that stayed were end-user positions, that is to say, they were "people who were as important to business functions as they were to information systems."

The supervisor of information resource management explains the intent of outsourcing:

> ...was to focus pure (information technology) and separate that from people who had the business knowledge... Now we rely on CSC to help figure out how to put technology into solving problems. There are fewer gray areas as to who does what.

Source: *Computer World*, May 16, 1994, pp. 92–3.

Case 10.3: Study of large firms using outsourcing

500 of the largest firms in the US were studied and got a 22% response. The results are partly reported below:

Reasons for outsourcing	% of respondents
Personnel cost savings	49
Increased flexibility	48
Focus in-house IS in core functions	47
Improved quality of IS services	35
Increased access to new technology	32
Provide alternatives to in-house IS	29
Technology savings	25
Stabilize IS costs	21
Reengineer process	10
Reduce technological obsolescence risk	4

Chapter 10: Outsourcing

Reservation noted	% respondents
Loss of control of IS	56
Loss/degradation of internal IS service	53
Corporate security issues	47
Qualification of outside personnel	44
Cost/benefit unclear	42
Ability to terminate arrangements	39
Corporate strategic issues	19
Loss of IS strategic planning capability	17
Existing union/labour agreements	6

Source: Collins, J. and Stephanie and Robert A. Millen. (1995). "Information Systems Outsourcing by Large American Industrial Firms: Choices and Impact." *Information Resource Management Journal*, vol. 8, no. 1, pp. 5–13.

References

Apte, U. (1991). "Global Outsourcing of Information Systems and Processing Services." *The Information Society*, vol. 7, pp. 287–303.

Altinkemer, K., Chaturvedi, A. and Gulati, G. (1994). "Information Systems Outsourcing: Issues and Evidence." *International Journal of Information Management*, vol. 14, pp. 252–68.

Fitzgerald, Guy and Willocks, Leslie. (1994). "Contracts and Partnerships in the Outsourcing of IT." *Proceedings of the 15th. International Conference*, December 14–17, pp. 91–98.

Gurbaxani, V. (1996). "A Two-Level Investigation of Information Systems Outsourcing." *Communications of the ACM*, vol. 39, no.7 (July), pp. 36–44.

Jones, Caper. (1994). "Evaluating Software Outsourcing Options." *Information Systems Management*, vol. 11, no. 4, pp. 28–33.

Judenberg, Joseph. (1994). "Applications Maintenance Outsourcing." *Information Systems Management*, vol. 11, no. 4, pp. 34–8.

Kelter, K. and Walstrom, J. (1993). "The Outsourcing Decision." *International Journal of Information Management*, vol. 13, pp. 449–59.

Lacity, M., Hirschheim, Rudy and Willocks, Leslie. (1994). "Realizing Outsourcing Expectations." *Information Systems Management*, vol. 11, no. 4, pp. 7–18.

Lacity, M. and Hirschheim, R. *Information Systems Outsourcing: Myths, Metaphors and Realities*. (1993). John Wiley & Sons.

Loh, Lawrence. (1994). "An Organizational Economic Blueprint of Information Technology Outsourcing: Concepts and Evidence." *Proceedings of the 15th. International Conference*, December 14–17, 1994, pp. 73–90.

Myer, N. Dean. (1994). "A Sensible Approach to Outsourcing." *Information Systems Management*, vol. 11, no. 4, pp. 23–27.

Pickering, Bobby. (1992). "Passing the Buck." *Which Computer?*, vol. 15, no. 6 (June), pp. 68–75.

Takac, Paul F. (1994). "Outsourcing: A Key to Controlling IT Costs." *International J. Of Technology Management*, vol. 9, no. 2 (1994), pp. 139–53.

Willcocks, L. and Fitzgerald, G. A. (1993). *Business Guide to IT Outsourcing*. London: Business Intelligence.

11 Reengineering

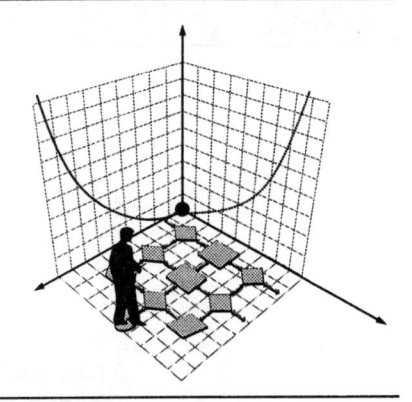

Law of Increasing Entropy: The entropy of systems (their unstructuredness) increases with time, unless specific work is executed to maintain it.

Belady and Lehman, 1976

Introduction

Reengineering lies somewhere between maintenance (minor modifications) and redevelopment (for major modifications). It is emerging in importance as old transactional systems become outdated or too complex for economical operations. We will examine the nature and reasons for the increasing complexity of systems, and also define when a change and modification is minor or major along with a more formal definition of reengineering (also spelled "re-engineering").

We will also discuss the process of reengineering and examine the eight distinct stages of its methodology. We conclude with a listing of the success and failure factors of reengineering.

Why reengineering?

There are many reasons why an organization may want, or need, reengineering and some of these reasons are reflected in the examples discussed as cases at the end of this chapter. Many of the objectives of reengineering are reflected in the results and success stories of organizations that have been through the reengineering process. Some specific reasons for undertaking reengineering could be:

- To reduce the cost of maintenance. Often, maintenance is no longer feasible because of the unexpected consequences of additional changes. There is the ripple effect of local changes that may result in unexpected maintenance, induced bugs and "bad

fixes" that may kill a critical system. Also, there may be little documentation that is still valid, the intellectual grasp of the system may be lost, and the system is no longer understandable or manageable, and so gets out of control.
- To introduce new technology: the stacking-up of ageing programs in the applications portfolio that were developed with old technology. The new technology may be as simple as an e-mail capability, or as fundamental as the introduction of AI and inference-making capabilities. Or it may be the use of graphics, imaging and voice processing. In some cases, the new technology could be from a batch system to an OLRT (online real-time) system. This could mean faster response times and easier access made possible by telecommunications and easy-to-use programming languages like the 4GLs.
- To achieve the necessary integration, not just horizontal and vertical integration, but integration of technologies like multimedia and teleprocessing into functional everyday applications.
- To affect organizational change. Changes in the attitudes and knowledge of users will make modes like DDP (distributed data processing), client–server, and end-user computing emerge as viable and feasible options.
- To accommodate information not hitherto available.
- To achieve efficiency and cost effectiveness. Many systems are developed haphazardly and have "patching" of programs which results in "spaghetti" code that may become inefficient to maintain, *and* ineffective. Reengineering will not only make the systems more efficient but also easier to use and maintain. It could, at least, "contain" the cost of operation and maintenance.
- To satisfy the desire to automate, improve quality, and reduce the complexity of the system may necessitate reengineering.
- To accommodate restructuring of the database and using knowledge bases (or even a relational base) may suggest the need to consider reengineering.

There are many side-effects of reengineering. It will improve (and in some cases provide for the first time) good documentation of the system. It may recover lost data and information. It may identify problems (current or potential) in the logic of the system. And most important, it could raise the level of abstraction to a higher platform to facilitate more advanced applications and the use of newer technology. It could well be the opportunity to salvage and even reshape, revise and revamp the system as well as enhance the informational architecture and infrastructure of the organization. It is an opportunity to change the large and unmaintainable existing system and make it closer to the ideal system.

When to reengineer?

As a system ages, it tends to get large because of all the additions and "fixes" added to its working code. It may even no longer be viable or responsive to the changing needs of information and knowledge despite its complexity. The complexity also increases as the end-users increase and as communication between groups of end-users breaks down, and sometimes actually conflicts. This is especially true of transactional systems that tend to be large and serve multiple end-users and organizations. Take a customer billing system which can be 75,000 lines of code or an insurance company in the US that has 4 million lines of code in 1300 program modules operating on 7,500 items. Such systems quickly get complex and unwieldy with costs of maintenance going up.

Figure 11.1:
Costs as a function of system complexity

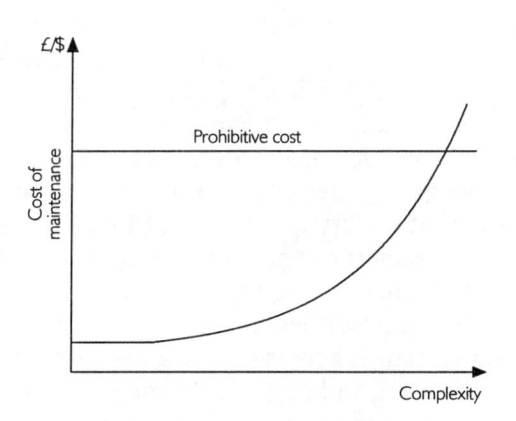

This increasing-cost curve is shown in Figure 11.1 where there comes a point at which the system is no longer tenable: it hits the prohibitive-cost line. The saviour for such systems is reengineering. The trick is to anticipate the prohibitive-cost line in time to install a reengineered system with a smaller size and lower complexity of program code. The reengineered version is not only low in maintenance cost but has higher functionality and quality along with the other advantages of reengineering. We now come to the "when" question. When should a system be reengineered? When does the problem need a minor change that can be handled by the maintenance staff, and when does the problem require a major redesign and thus needs to be reengineered? The decision to reengineer depends on the balancing of benefits with cost and risk.

Chapter 11: Reengineering

Factors to be considered are:
- Cost of reengineering compared to the cost of maintaining the old system, redevelopment and reinventing.
- Benefits of redevelopment, both tangible and intangible.
- Risks involved in reengineering.
- Time involved in reengineering and the remaining life of the system.

When and by whom should this decision be made? It is often made as part of an ongoing evaluation process by a group responsible for maintenance and operations.

And now we come to the final question about "how" reengineering is achieved. Unfortunately, there are no standards for the reengineering methodology. There are some tools for reengineering that facilitate restructuring and automation like the CASE (computer-aided software engineering) tools. There is, however, no single tool that will solve all reengineering problems. An analysis of the problem should identify the best tool available for the problem at hand. Many firms have established their own internal standards against which the final product is measured for quality and performance. These standards could ensure that reengineering is performed as few times as possible; that good code, data and knowledge are preserved; problem areas are identified and contained; and that quality is enhanced. Much of this cannot be measured by quantitative metrics and so the process is still very subjective and hence all the more challenging. It is equally difficult to always capture and quantify business rules and objectives so that they are met in the reengineered system. There is clearly a need for a methodology to facilitate understanding and to guide the modification process. It is difficult to predict the escalating and exploding results of changes made to a system. As one IS manager is quoted as saying: "There is no such thing as a small change." It is important for managers to appreciate that, and so there is a need for educating managers and end-users about maintenance, reverse engineering (to be discussed later), and reengineering.

The decision to reengineer a system is shown in Figure 11.2. In an evaluation caused by a problem or during regular maintenance, the need for a modification is determined ("No" exit for box 1). If the system cannot be tolerated any longer and cannot be left "as is" ("No" exit for box 2), then maintenance must be considered. If the change is beyond maintenance ("No" exit for box 3), then the modification is large. If it is large enough ("Yes" exit from box 5) then the system is replaced by a redeveloped system or else the system is a good candidate for renovation of the system through reengineering ("No" exit from box 5). The Yes/No decisions are often not quantitative and must be made by a maintenance committee that will consider not just the technological and economic factors but organizational factors as well.

Figure 11.2: *The decision to consider reengineering*

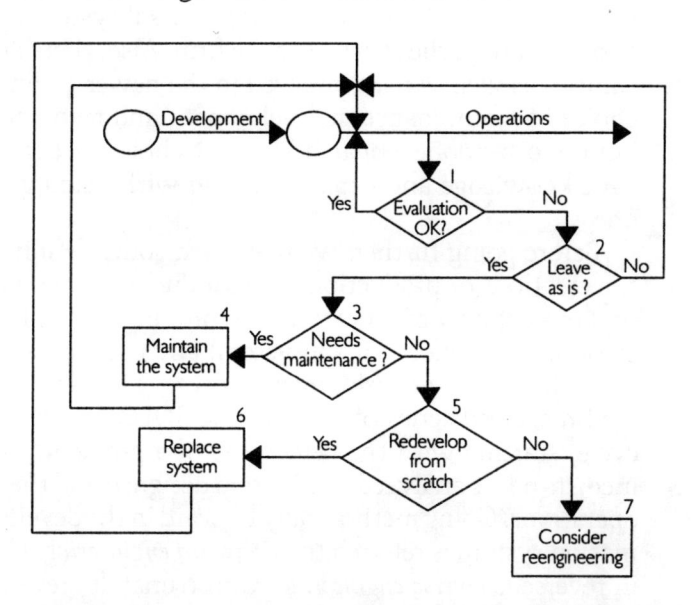

The subject of maintenance is discussed in another chapter and is a relatively easy decision compared to box 5 where one has to decide whether to redevelop or reengineer. For example, is a new image processing system, or a client–server system or a KBIS (knowledge-based information system) appropriate for reengineering? In practice, a KBIS is a candidate for redevelopment whilst the image system and the client–server system are appropriate for reengineering. Thus reengineering is an economically sound compromise between doing nothing (status quo), and starting all over again from scratch (redevelopment) despite the costs and risks of reengineering.

The decision to maintain, redevelop or reengineer is not, in principle, too different from many of the day-to-day decisions that we make. An example would the replacement of an old car with a new or newer car. We replace the old car when the cost of maintenance and inconvenience is higher than the cost of replacement. But there is a middle ground, that of overhauling the engine (reengineering) and increasing the life of the car assuming that the rest of the car is in good condition. There is still the risk that the car will breakdown at night, or in the middle of a deserted road, or even not start in the morning. And there is also the possibility of inconvenience when the car is being repaired. Thus the choice between maintaining, reengineering and replacing is still a balancing of the tangible factors (savings in cost of maintenance) and the intangible factors (the cost of inconvenience and the risk of breakdowns). In the case of information systems, the magnitudes of risks involved are much higher. A failure in a critical system or subsystem can stop operations and even affect the survival of the firm. Also, there are potential opportunities as well as risks involved in the newer techniques of IT. So the choice of maintenance, redevelopment and reengineering is a difficult but important one. Fortunately, such choices get easier with more relevant knowledge and experience, and with reading books such as this one.

Before going further, we may need some definitions. *Engineering* is the creation (or production) of a product starting with an idea or concept or a detailed specification. The product in the IT environment is the information system (or subsystem) and the engineering process is the equivalent of the development process. The development process is a well rehearsed series of steps in the SDLC (systems development life cycle) starting with the perception of a problem, its feasibility examined, its needs analyzed, the system designed and then implemented for operations. Going methodically forward in the development of an information system is referred to as *forward engineering*. Going backwards or in reverse is *reverse engineering*. Unfortunately, reverse engineering has acquired a bad reputation in some developed countries. Products that are researched and developed, often at great expense, are copied (component by component) in developing countries and the (sometimes enhanced) product is sold back into the developed country at a lower price – often outselling the original product in its own market. Reverse engineering can be a perfectly legal practise in the market economies with firms copying their competitor's product unless, of course, it is copyrighted or the basic idea has been patented.

Reverse engineering is also practised within a firm with its own information system. Now this may seem odd to have a firm find out what they have started themselves. But this happens with systems that grow over the years with modifications implemented and maintenance carried out without any documentation. Such a system acquires an identity of its own having adapted to the ways of the corporate culture and the realities of the world around it. It is therefore necessary to learn the real "decision rules" of the system by reverse engineering. These rules are then adopted in a renovated version of the system which is now more multifunctional and goes deeper into the business processes. This renovation is termed *reengineering*. It is the redevelopment of a product in existence or of a product that is external to the firm (even that of a competitor). To produce the new product we need the basic ideas and concepts, and these are sometimes provided by *reverse engineering*, a process going from product to idea or concept, which reengineering then uses to produce another product. The resultant product may have enhanced functionality, or be more efficient in operation, or be more efficient to maintain and enhance in the future.

Other objectives of reengineering may be the improvement of quality and reliability of the product while at the same time reducing its dependence on other resources (programs and hardware).

Figure 11.3: *Some definitions in graphics*

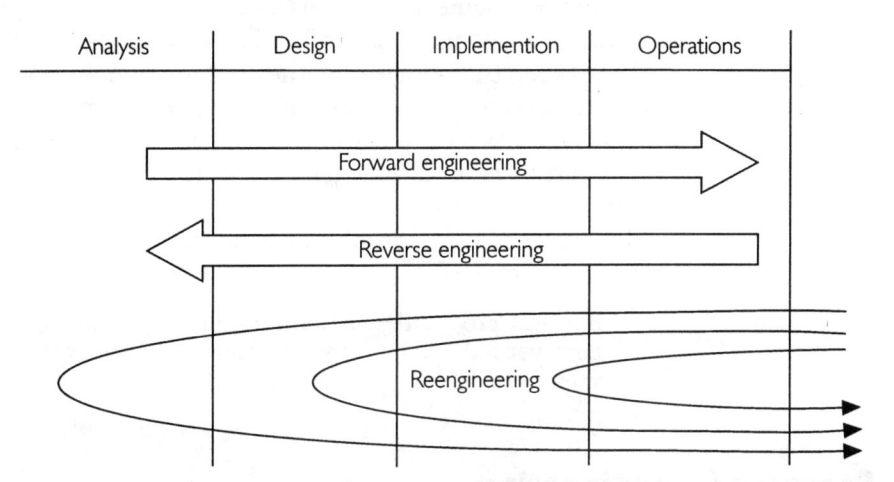

Analysis	Design	Implemention	Operations

Forward engineering →

← Reverse engineering

Reengineering

To achieve these objectives, reengineering uses the latest technology (not available perhaps when the original system was developed). And sometimes one wants what a competitor has: in which case the reverse engineering process of capturing the design, structure, and content of the complex system to be copied is much more difficult. Reverse engineering is the analysis part whilst reengineering is the production process. They are a complementary pair. It is in reverse engineering that we expose the pattern of the logic underlying the program. In reengineering we build on this logical framework to produce working code and an operational system. These interrelationships between related terms are displayed in Figure 11.3.

Reengineering is sometimes viewed as part of maintenance. While traditional maintenance is the "fixing" of errors and making minor changes, reengineering is a more radical change in design (and, perhaps, of the user specification). It sits somewhere between minor maintenance of "fixing" errors and developing again or redevelopment and the spiralling of the SDLC.

Thus far we have examined the term reengineering in the context of IT. The term is also used in the macro sense for an entire business enterprise in which case it will involve all the functions of product development, manufacturing, marketing, etc. This may require overhauling the entire process from top to bottom in order to achieve the objectives of speed, efficiency and consumer satisfaction. These objectives are the same as those in reengineering for IT. The scope, however, is different.

Reengineering in IT is sometimes confined to software which in many cases is the most important component of an information system. Thus reengineering of IT is a subset of reengineering of an organization. Reengineering is thus a supporting technology for a more global structural change. The staff of IT are often called in to help and sometimes even to take a lead in the organizational reengineering effort, but reengineering of the organization may be the prime goal.

The term reengineering (as well as rightsizing) were buzzwords of the early 1990s. They originated in the management literature. Many managers perceived that IT could help with reengineering problems. They turned to IT for solutions and so it was that reengineering became a buzzword in IT.

> Business process design and information technology are natural partners, yet industrial engineers have never fully exploited their relationships.
>
> *Davenport and Short*, 1990:11

Process of reengineering

We are now ready to discuss the life cycle of reengineering. An overview is shown in Figure 11.4. Each stage in the life cycle will be discussed in detail below.

1. Plan for reengineering

A plan for reengineering (box 1 in Figure 11.4) must identify the important processes involved where each process in a business is a set of activities that must be performed to achieve a business objective. The processes selected for reengineering must be vital and critical to the organization and have a high potential impact on business objectives. They may be interorganizational and span more than one internal and external organizational boundary or they may be interfunctional and interpersonal. This makes it difficult to identify (let alone isolate) these relationships for analysis and alignment with organizational goals. The plan in the early stages may well be more visionary than analytical as with analysis in modelling for a DSS (decision support system) or with making a cost–benefit analysis. The plan is a statement of overall business philosophy and provides a sense of high-level direction. However, the plan should be stated (or discussed in brain-storming sessions) in as many operational terms as possible, not be too nebulous or imprecise, so that it is a helpful guide to the designers of the reengineering effort.

Figure 11.4:
Overview of the reengineering process

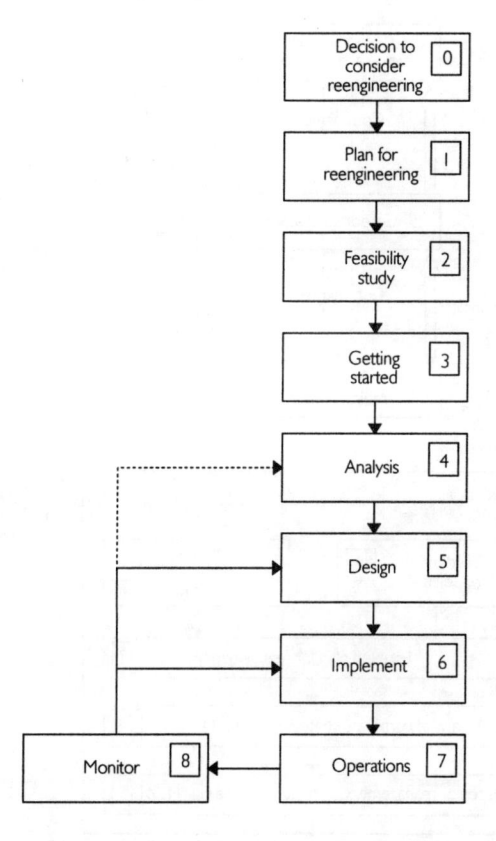

```
        ┌──────────────┐
        │ Decision to  │ 0
        │  consider    │
        │ reengineering│
        └──────┬───────┘
               ▼
        ┌──────────────┐
        │   Plan for   │ 1
        │ reengineering│
        └──────┬───────┘
               ▼
        ┌──────────────┐
        │  Feasibility │ 2
        │    study     │
        └──────┬───────┘
               ▼
        ┌──────────────┐
        │   Getting    │ 3
        │   started    │
        └──────┬───────┘
               ▼
  ┄┄┄┄▶ ┌──────────────┐
        │   Analysis   │ 4
        └──────┬───────┘
               ▼
   ────▶ ┌──────────────┐
        │    Design    │ 5
        └──────┬───────┘
               ▼
   ────▶ ┌──────────────┐
        │   Implement  │ 6
        └──────┬───────┘
               ▼
┌─────────┐  ┌──────────────┐
│ Monitor │8◀│  Operations  │ 7
└─────────┘  └──────────────┘
```

Planning for reengineering is the stage when top management support for the reengineering plan must be obtained. Getting such support is easier than for many other IT projects because top management recognize the organizational interests involved. Without their support reengineering would never have been possible. Nevertheless, the commitment of top management is important, even essential, for any successful reengineering effort because reengineering may require a totally different way of problem solving and doing things. People (top management included) tend to resist change and having to do things differently.

In summary then, one can visualize an idea coming from the organizational goals and objectives, qualified by corporate strategy, and result in the reproduction (or reengineering) of an information system. This top-down flow is quite consistent with a bottom-up feedback and information about the opportunities and risks involved in the reengineering

Chapter 11: Reengineering 247

using state-of-the-art technology. These information flows and the aligning with corporate goals and policies are shown in Figure 11.5, and are part of the related activities of planning as shown in Figure 11.6.

Figure 11.5:
Reengineering related to corporate goals, vision, objectives and strategies

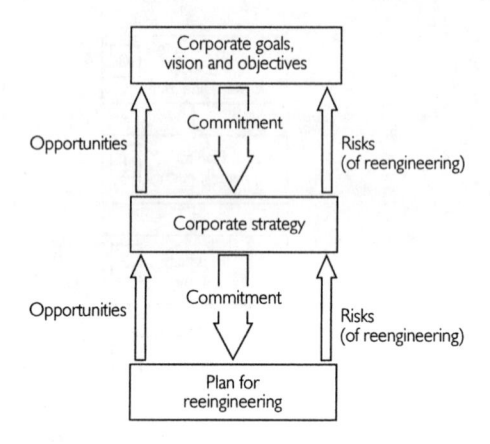

Figure 11.6:
Planning for reengineering

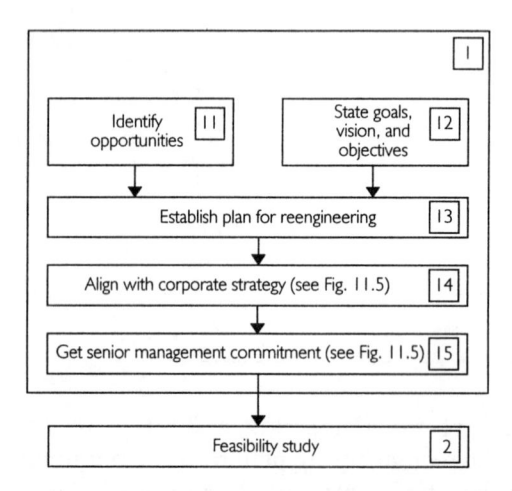

The final result of all the flows should be a plan with definite organizational and performance goals and with agreed metrics for measurement of performance. The goals, the scope and the commitment of top management should be communicated to all employees. To carry out the project of reengineering, a director or project manager for reengineering (or systems integrator – see Chapter 19) must be appointed whose first task would be to conduct a feasibility study.

2. Feasibility study

A feasibility study for reengineering has many commonalties with feasibility studies for other information systems projects. There are intangible benefits: perhaps more so in reengineering because the potential outcome of reconfiguring the system (and the subsequent impact on business) is extremely difficult to assess and quantify. A risk analysis in reengineering is also more difficult because we are often dealing with new technologies. Assessment of technological deficiencies in addition to a technology-mismatch problem or a technology/organization mismatch is often very difficult. Assessing complexities does pose problems of uncertainty because the nature and scope of technology changes so rapidly. Predicting the "correctness" of reengineered software is also difficult because we know little of the immediate and eventual effects of the many new interrelationships. The ripple effect of changes inherent in reengineering will be especially difficult to predict with any degree of accuracy. The risks of reengineering must be weighed against the risks of doing nothing. One cannot easily predict when the current system will go out-of-control, or whether or not we can maintain the current system at all. (One large, current, transactional system has all its code in assembly language: this poses real maintenance problems because it is difficult to find assembly language programmers).

One important component of risk, and the price of doing nothing, may well be higher maintenance costs. There is some data available on the potential savings in maintenance costs resulting from reengineering but the benefits are mostly intangible. The final weighing of benefits and costs would be subjective and judgemental, resulting in an ordinal rather than cardinal, and thus subjective, decision. The expected benefits must be justified by anticipated costs.

3. Getting started

Like any other project, to start reengineering one needs a team. This is not a new concept whether for IT or many other business organizations. It was practised as early as the 1950s in teams for OR (operations research) projects. Its composition should have a balance between the idealists and the pragmatists, the quantitative and the qualitatively oriented, the efficiency expert and the humanist, the old-guard stewards and fresh blood, the status quo and the iconoclasts who challenge the status quo, and finally the technologist (like the technology watcher) and a conservative IS staff member. Fortunately, a single team member can have more than one desirable characteristic and different team members represent different levels of management, another desirable characteristic. Also, the reengineering team must be representative of the critical functions of the organization.

If the reengineering is to be very cross-functional, which can well change the organizational culture, then the task should not be taken lightly. In which case, the project should earn the participation of high levels of management on the reengineering team and/or a project manager is warranted.

Another person on the reengineering team may be a reengineering analyst. As distinct from an analyst of a traditional information system, the reengineering analyst must combine state-of-the-art technical knowledge with knowledge of the business as well as knowledge of systems structure. Combining all these traits in one person may be difficult but the task of reengineering is also not easy.

4. Analysis

Once the feasibility of the reengineering project is established, one should proceed with a detailed analysis of the specifications of the project (box 4 in Figure 11.4). This activity is sometimes called analysis, the diagnostic phase and sometimes called the system's specification. Whatever the name, it is a diagnostic phase where the goals and objectives as well as the constraints on the project are stated in operational terms. As an example, the goal of faster claim-processing may now be stated as: "90% of the claims must be satisfied in the first phone call from the claimant." Specifying end-user satisfaction is more difficult. The metrics of measuring end-user satisfaction must be stated in order to provide an objective measure of system performance. Also, one must try never to overspecify or underspecify. The former amounts to an unnecessary restriction on the subsequent process, and the latter leads to unwanted latitude. The specifications may have to be partitioned and derived by stepwise abstraction. Whatever the approach, the specifications must be unambiguous, free of extraneous detail, and free of implementation directives that may limit and constrain the designer and implementor. Thus the task is not easy. It is often identified as one of the most difficult activities in systems development. It is also a task that must be done by management and not delegated or left to the analyst who then by default becomes the decision-maker. A task that may involve business fundamentals and organizational goals should not be delegated by corporate management (especially top management), or left by default to others – especially not to the reengineering analyst and designer. Much depends on the breadth and depth of reengineering that is envisaged. These dimensions are represented in Figure 11.7.

Figure 11.7:
Dimensions of reengineering

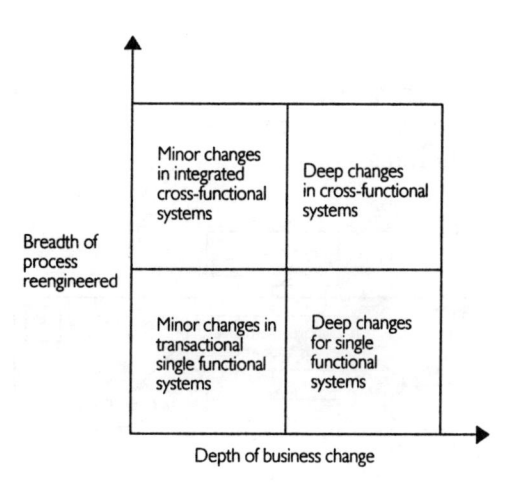

Minor changes in integrated cross-functional systems	Deep changes in cross-functional systems
Minor changes in transactional single functional systems	Deep changes for single functional systems

Breadth of process reengineered (vertical axis)

Depth of business change (horizontal axis)

The south-west corner represents a single activity within a single functional transactional system. A reengineering project may be well beyond this stage and would at least want an interfunctional and cross-functional integrated system which puts it into the north-west corner. Most likely, the greatest productivity gains would not only stem from the breadth of cross-organizational and cross-functional workflows and processes, but also from looking at the business' operations in depth for the most critical operations of the corporation (north-east and south-east corners of Figure 11.7 respectively). This may involve restructuring the cross-organizational boundaries, the roles and responsibilities of personnel (including management), objectives of processes, incentives offered, and the sharing of information technology. The north-east corner is where:

- Most benefits and dramatic process-cost reductions will be derived.
- The restructuring will be the most severe.
- The problems of integration and the management of resistance will be the most difficult.

But all this *is achievable* and a study by Hall, and others, identified 6 firms (including 2 European banks, a US hotel chain and bank, and a European computer manufacturer) that are now in the north-east corner of Figure 11.7. Reduced costs reported from reengineering were between 15 to 50% (Hall, Rosenthal and Wade, 1991). The final product of this task and activity is a specification that is the basis for the design of reengineering (box 5 in Figure 11.4).

5. Design

An overview of the design phase is shown in Figure 11.8. One of the earliest activities is to research on what has been done both in terms of successes and failures.

Figure 11.8:
Process of design for reengineering

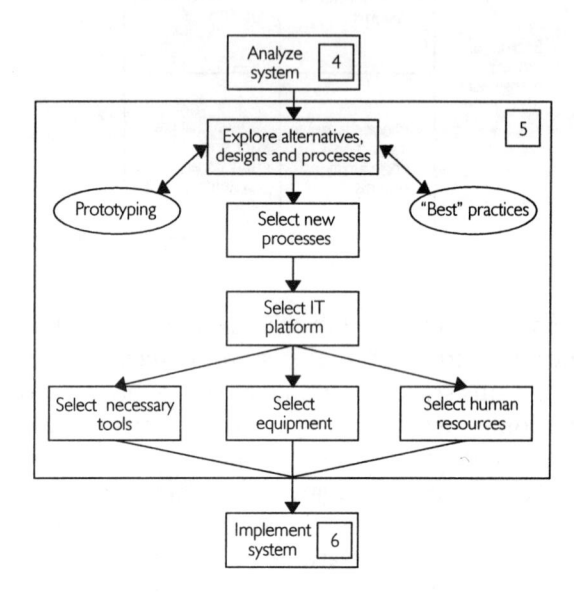

One can learn to avoid the failures and adopt or adapt success stories. This approach to best practices can select one of many ideals: the ideal company, the ideal industry, the ideal service, the ideal system or even the Year 2005 ideal. Alternatively, or in addition, one can have brainstorming sessions, or simulate alternative consequences for different sets of variables and parameters until one finds a solution that is "satisfactory". Finding an ideal or optimum is rarely possible, perhaps it is impossible? This simulation can be done in the prototyping mode which enables a quick-and-dirty solution for the end-user to look at and approve or disapprove, which then starts the development process again.

The dangers and advantages of simulation or prototyping will not be discussed here, but only to comment that prototyping (discussed in Chapter 6) is one of the methodologies of development and in this case it is appropriate. This activity and other activities in reengineering will most likely have to be within the framework of an SDLC (systems development life cycle) which provides a structured way of developing large and complex projects.

The design in reengineering can be the result of:

> ...a fundamental analysis of the organization and a redesign of organization structure, job definitions, reward structures, business workflows, control processes, and in some cases, a reevaluation of the organizational culture and philosophy.
>
> Guha et al., 1993:14

The design may also envision reconfigurations including networking across functions designed around business processes rather than functional hierarchies in order to support parallel processing, higher quality, better service and more innovative ways of integration, ease of migration and adaptability to changing technologies. To facilitate such design there are special tools that make the design for reengineering possible (Klein, 1994:31–3). These tools, however, are still evolving including CASE tools that build linkages whilst also performing other important functions.

Having selected a design and a set of processes one must then select an IT platform with its unique configuration of equipment, software tools and human resources and, if need be, to transform part of the old system derived from reverse engineering to the new IT platform. This platform may be an OO methodology, LAN-based, or enterprise IT architecture. We are now ready to discuss implementation.

Implementation and its monitoring

Implementation as a concept will be examined in Chapter 13 but it should be mentioned here as part of the reengineering process – see box 6 in Figure 11.4. What is interesting is the monitoring during operations (boxes 7 and 8 in Figure 11.4) which may involve the repetition (recycling in US-English) of some activities. This recycling is not the recycling done in the testing phase as part of the implementation activities but a recycling for minor modifications necessary as a result of operations of the reengineered project. The recycling may even go back as far as the analysis activity as shown by the dotted arrows in Figure 11.4. Recycling gives us the right to call this set of activities a part of the life cycle of reengineering. The recycling will not be as often as required in maintenance activities – unless the reengineering project is not done well or the environment changes dramatically.

Success and failure factors

We conclude with listings of success and failure factors in reengineering (Bashein et al., 1994). We start with the success factors even though the probability of success in reengineering is much less that the probability of failure, because a discussion of success factors may encourage corporate managers to create an environment with these factors. They are:

- Top management commitment.
- Management support at all levels.
- Strong sponsor.
- Realistic expectations.
- The anticipation and management of resistance.
- Focus on opportunities.
- Project vision shared with employees.
- Adequate project resources.
- Project personnel assigned sufficient time for the project.
- Trained project personnel, if needed.
- Reengineering workshops conducted for management.
- Effective communication that will build a consensus and create a cadre of champions for reengineering.

For every success in reengineering, there is approximately two failures (7 in 10 is quoted by Bashein *et al.*, 1994:7). Failure factors are often the mirror image of success factors – such as the absence of top management support and commitment. There are many failure factors:

- The wrong sponsor.
- Cost cutting or other narrow focus.
- Too many concurrent improvement projects.
- Reengineering in parallel with the system to be renovated operating in parallel.
- Fear and lack of optimism.
- Animosity towards the project by IS staff.
- Inadequate training and lack of positive attitude for reengineering.

Summary and conclusions

The life cycle of reengineering is summarized in Figure 11.9. It is a summary of our discussion which is, in turn, a summary of the many activities involved. One author lists 54 different activities (Klein, 1994:34). The life cycle and some of its activities are ill-structured or unstructured.

Summary and conclusions

Reengineering is contextual. It's a function of how an organization behaves, its belief system, its position in the market place, the character of its people. It is absolutely impossible to have a structured approach.

Klein, 1994:31

Figure 11.9:
Summary of the reengineering process

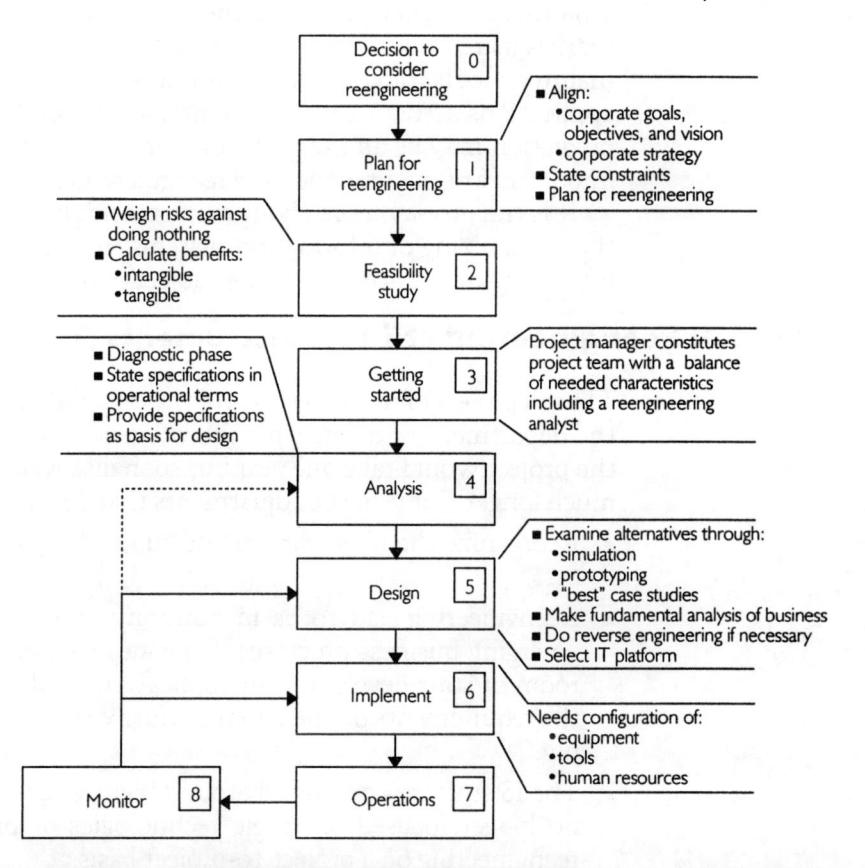

```
                            ┌─────────────────┐
                            │ Decision to  │0│
                            │ consider     │ │
                            │ reengineering│ │
                            └────────┬────────┘
                                     │         ■ Align:
                                     │           • corporate goals,
                                     ▼             objectives, and vision
                            ┌─────────────────┐  • corporate strategy
                            │ Plan for     │1│   ■ State constraints
                            │ reengineering│ │   ■ Plan for reengineering
                            └────────┬────────┘
   ■ Weigh risks against             │
     doing nothing                   │
   ■ Calculate benefits:             ▼
     • intangible            ┌─────────────────┐
     • tangible              │ Feasibility  │2│
                             │ study        │ │
                             └────────┬────────┘
                                      │         Project manager constitutes
   ■ Diagnostic phase                 │         project team with a balance
   ■ State specifications in          ▼         of needed characteristics
     operational terms        ┌─────────────────┐ including a reengineering
   ■ Provide specifications   │ Getting      │3│ analyst
     as basis for design      │ started      │ │
                              └────────┬────────┘
                                       │
                                       ▼
                              ┌─────────────────┐
              ┈┈┈┈┈┈┈┈┈┈┈┈┈┈▶│ Analysis     │4│
                              └────────┬────────┘
                                       │         ■ Examine alternatives through:
                                       │           • simulation
                                       ▼           • prototyping
                              ┌─────────────────┐  • "best" case studies
                         ────▶│ Design       │5│  ■ Make fundamental analysis of business
                              └────────┬────────┘  ■ Do reverse engineering if necessary
                                       │           ■ Select IT platform
                                       ▼
                              ┌─────────────────┐
                         ────▶│ Implement    │6│
                              └────────┬────────┘  Needs configuration of:
                                       │             • equipment
                                       ▼             • tools
                  ┌──────────┐ ┌─────────────────┐   • human resources
                  │Monitor │8│◀│ Operations   │7│
                  └──────────┘ └─────────────────┘
```

For reengineering we need an infrastructure of process change groups that learn to persuade rather than instruct, convince instead of dictate, make employees share rather than resist, and facilitate rather than rule by edict. This infrastructure must take advantage of the emerging technologies as they appear. The infrastructure personnel should be triggered and driven by opportunity not by crises. They should align reengineering with the corporate vision and objectives. They should strive for greater productivity in development and less maintenance costs in operations. This can come from customer-driven processes which rely less on hierarchy and more on cross-functional communication and cooperation with greater decision-making at lower and middle levels of management.

The need for reengineering is becoming clear as the applications portfolio increases, ages, and needs changes beyond the traditional maintenance of "fixing" errors. The "fixing" part of maintenance is estimated at around 20 to 30% of all maintenance which leaves 70 to 80% of all maintenance to reengineering. And the share of maintenance in all systems work is increasing. Owen predicts that the growing burden of software maintenance is going to overwhelm the average IS organization until no applications activities except maintenance occurs (Owen, 1991). This prediction may be an exaggeration but it does emphasize the growing importance of maintenance and reengineering.

It is time to say more about maintenance but first we must discuss the humanizing of information systems that is relevant to reengineering and maintenance. This is the subject of our next chapter.

Case 11.1: Reengineering at Texas Instruments (TI)

TI has a project of reengineering for the material procurement process in the department of defence for the US government. TI estimated that the project would take one year but soon discovered that it would take much longer. Some of the adjustments that TI had to make were:

- Reorganize the IS department to support the reengineering process.
- Reengineering had to be in harmony and "in sync" with the emerging business processes: "The idea that you don't leave the room or start developing an application until you have 100% of the requirements defined up front just won't work in reengineering."
- The IS staff was organized around "centres of excellence" which no longer focused on single technologies or platforms but on reengineering on a project-to-project basis.
- Think of business processes rather than automating the existing ways of doing business.
- Work with process owners rather than department heads and end-users.
- Train IS workers for new technologies.
- Evaluate IS workers on their breadth of technical knowledge and offer bonuses based on their performance (measured in business results) on specific reengineering projects.
- Publicize reengineering company-wide identifying the role of the IS department in the process.

Source: Moad, Jeff (1993). "Does Reengineering Really Work?" *Datamation*, vol. 39, (August 1), pp. 22–8.

Case 11.2: Reengineering at Corning

In 1989, CAV (Corning Asahi Video) Products won Computer World's Annual Reengineering Team of the Year Award. The team had just completed a 15-month project costing $570 million for halving the fulfillment time and slashing per-order ordering costs for CAV by 75%. The five project team members were asked to offer advice to other reengineering projects. Their one-liners are:

1. Pick the best people.
2. Keep roles defined, yet fluid.
3. Look for front-line leaders.
4. Sell and tell.
5. Don't fear conflict.
6. Consider purchasing software.
7. Expect resistance.
8. Keep focused.
9. Get ready for blood, sweat, tears – and long days.
10. Hang in there.

Source: Maglitta, Joseph. (1994). "Glass Act." *Computer World*, vol. 28, no. 3 (January 17), pp. 80–88.

Case 11.3: Reengineering at FAA

In 1986, the US Federal Aviation Administration (FAA) awarded a small contract of approximately $2.5 million to Data Transformation Corporation, IBM and Pailen-Johnson Associates to reengineer part of the New York TRACON software in a high-level language. The FAA was interested in determining:

> If a 20 year old, real-time system could be effectively reengineered into a commercial platform – including commercial hardware, commercial tools and languages, and commercial operating software – while retaining the behavior of the application.

The project was completed in 9 months and within budget. The team converted over 53,000 lines of ULTRA to 83,000 lines of Pascal/VS (62% comments). The evaluation showed that:

> ... the reengineered tracker was functionally equivalent to the original source... The results and conclusions indicate that reengineering the software of an existing system may be preferable to reinventing it.

Source: Britcher, R. (1990). "Reengineering Software: A Case Study." *IBM Systems Journal*, vol. 29, no. 4, pp. 551–566.

Case 11.4: BAI (Banca di la America e de Italia)

The management at BAI approved a project for reengineering that would give the retail bank a strategic advantage largely through being a paperless bank. Two of its teams worked in parallel with the authority to freely redesign the systems from scratch without any constraints and without any requirement to continue with current practices. They then streamlined some 300 processes with 64 activities, 9 forms, and 14 accounts into 25 activities, 2 forms and 2 accounts. Fifty branches were brought online simultaneously.

> Tellers underwent a five-day training period. In addition, branches were restructured to eliminate all back-office space, and the manager was placed directly out in front of the customer. Finally, a new security-officers position was created, so that BAI could increase its share of securities transactions. As a result, securities customers increased 306% from 1987–1991. Revenue of the bank doubled from 1987 to 1992 (24% of that increase has been attributed to the reengineering effort).

Source: *Harvard Business Review*. November/December 1993, pp. 124–6.

Case 11.5: Rank Xerox, UK

In 1985 David O'Brien became the division's managing director. He initiated an IT-driven process redesign study. In 1987, a senior management team began:

> ... identifying high level objectives and creating task forces to define information and other resource requirements for each process. It created career systems revolving around facilitation skills and cross-functional management, rather than hierarchical authority.

Of the 18 "macro" processes and 145 "micro" processes, the senior management team prioritized 7 macro processes as having:

> ... particular importance: customer order life cycle, customer satisfaction, installed equipment management, integrated planning, logistics, financial management, and personnel management.

The company emerged from:

... stagnation into a period of 20 per cent revenue growth... Jobs not directly involved with customer contact were reduced from 1,100 to 800. Order delivery time was, on average, reduced from thirty-three days to six days.

Source: *Sloan Management Review*, Summer 1990, pp. 21–22. The original source was the Henley Management College case study, September 1988 and interviews of Rank Xerox management.

Case 11.6: Examples of reengineering

- CIGNA RE Corp. saved $1.5 million a year in operational costs in addition to improving access to its data and knowledge base by a reengineering effort that cost $3.2 million.
- Digital Equipment Corp. eliminated 450 jobs by a reengineering project that consolidated 55 accounting groups into only five.
- Siemens Nixdorf Service at BAI (Banca di la America e de Italia) created a paperless office and attributed it to its reengineering program.
- C.R. England & Sons reduced its costs of sending an invoice to $0.15 compared to the average cost in 1989–91 of $5.10.
- Progressive Insurance reduced its claims settlement time from 31 days to 4 hours.
- Florida Power & Light Company reduced its power outage per customer to 32 minutes compared to 7 hours by its competitor.

References

Bashein, Barbara J., Markus, M. Lynn and Riley, Patricia. (1994). "Preconditions for BPR Success and how to Prevent Failures." *Information Systems Management*, vol. 11, no. 2, pp. 7–13.

Davenport, Thomas H. and Short, James E. (1990). "The New Industrial Engineering: Information Technology and Business Systems Redesign." *Sloan Management Review*, vol. 31, no. 4, pp. 11–26.

Friedlander, Philip and Tootham, William. (1994). "Reengineering done Right." *Information Systems Management*, vol. 11, no. 1, pp. 7–15.

Guha, S., Kettinger, W. J. and Tang, T. C. (1993). "Business Process Engineering." *Information Systems Management*, vol. 10, no. 3, pp. 13–22.

Hall, G., Rosenthal, J. and Wade, J. (1993). "How to make Reengineering Really Work." *Harvard Business Review*, vol. 61, no. 6 (November/December), pp. 119–131.

References

Hammer, Michael and Champy, James. (1993). *Reengineering the Corporation: A Manifesto for Business Revolution*. Cambridge, Mass.: Harper Business.

Kennedy, Carol. (1994). "Re-engineering: The Human Cost and Benefits." *International Journal of Strategic Management*, vol. 27, issue 5 (October), pp. 52–63.

Kim, Bonn-Oh. (1994). "Business Process Reengineering: Building a Cross Functional Information Architecture." *Journal of Systems Management*, vol. 45, no. 12 (December), pp. 30–7.

Klein, Mark M. (1994). "Reengineering Methodologies and Tools." *Information Systems Journal*, vol. 11, no. 2, pp. 30–5.

Lin, F. (1993). "Re-engineering Option Analysis for Managing Software Rejuvenation." *Information and Software Technology*, vol. 35, no. 8, pp. 462–67.

Lucas, H. C. Jr. "A Reengineering Framework for Evaluating a Financial Image System." *Communications of the ACM*, vol. 39, no. 5 (May), pp. 86–96.

Prieto-Diaz, Ruben. (1993). "Status Report: Software Reusability." *IEEE Software*, vol. 10, no. 3 (May), pp. 61–4.

Ross, Randy. (1993). "The Real Trick to Reengineering." *PC World*, vol. 11, no. 7 (July), pp. 54–6.

Sneed, Harry M. (1991). "Economics of Software Re-engineering." *Software Maintenance: Research and Practice*, vol. 3, pp. 163–82.

Zvenginzov, Nicholas. (1991). "Re-engineering." *Software Maintenance News*, vol. 9 (February), pp. 12–9.

12 Humanizing Information Systems

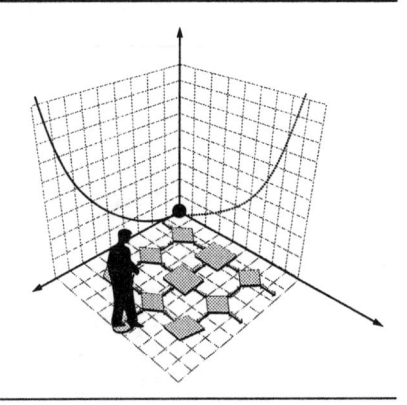

> More than machinery, we need humanity.
>
> *Charlie Chaplin, in the film* Modern Times
>
> ...we so often focus on the technical rather than the human side of work not because it is more crucial, but because it is easier to do.
>
> *T. Demarco and T. Lister*
>
> The real cause for dread is not a machine turned human, but a human turned machine.
>
> *Franz F. Winkler*

Introduction

We can define humanizing information systems as being the elimination or at least the reduction of technostress for the end-user. This is an awful definition, because it introduced two terms that need to be defined: technostress and the end-user. The end-user we have discussed at length in Chapter 2. The term technostress we will define soon. These definitions will provide a good basis for discussing the humanizing of information systems. We shall see that a computer system is not a machine system but a human–machine system with not just human–machine relationships but also human–machine–software and software–machine–human relationships. For all these relationships to contribute towards reducing technostress, we need to design and implement humanized output, humanized input and humanized procedures. Strategies for doing so are all discussed. Mention will be made of voice processing and image processing as strategies for humanizing information systems. Discussed in greater detail will be the design of dialogues and human interfaces including the design of an interface to justify what is being done by the computer system and explain how it is done through an explanation and justification interface such as those used originally in expert systems.

Technostress

Planning to alleviate technostress involves consideration of "human factors" and ergonomic factors. Ergonomics is the consideration of physical factors as they relate to computing whilst "human factors", as a separate discipline, is more concerned with the psychological aspects. In practice, the two are not considered as separate and distinct but are treated as one.

In the United States there is considerable concern about human factors and ergonomics especially as they relate to RSIs (repetitive strain injuries) like *carpo-tunnel syndrome* which results from using a keyboard and injures the wrist. An American agency, the OSHA (Occupational Safety and Health Administration), that administers ADA, Americans with Disabilities Act, requires "reasonable accommodations" for people afflicted with RSIs. OSHA has almost 12,000 complaints on-file with most being settled out of court with companies agreeing to follow recommendations made by the employee's doctor.

Human–computer interaction

There is a common perception that computerized information systems are machine systems. However, in most computerized information systems the computer (and even computer technology) is a small component of the total system. The large and important component is the human. The human is involved in all stages of developing and operating the system. This can be seen from Figure 12.1 where we can identify three types of interaction.

Going clockwise from the stage of end-user specification (top right-hand corner of Figure 12.1) between end-user (corporate manager and clients) and the analyst, we have a human–human interaction as is also the relationship between the analyst and the programmer. Then we have human–machine interaction with the programmer, the operator and the input clerk interacting with the computer.

Finally, we have machine–human interaction between the computer and the end-users and the closing of the loop. Each of these interaction types will be examined as to its nature and what can be done to make the system end-user friendly and more human.

Figure 12.1:
Human–computer interaction

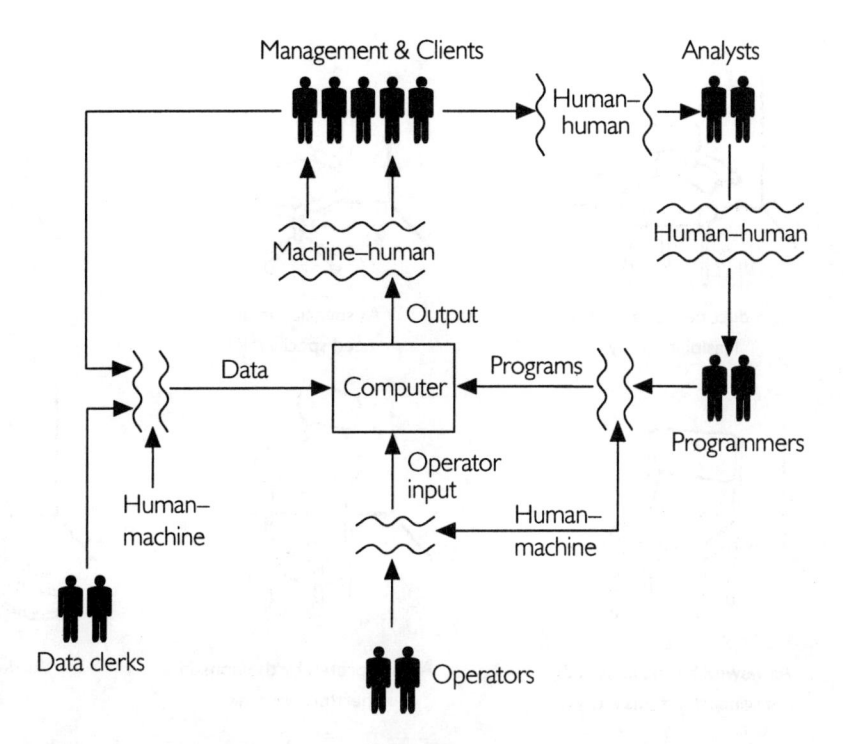

The existence of misunderstandings between people is as old as the human race itself. Such difficulties can be exacerbated (with unintentional results) when communications take place between users and analysts: the two groups have different backgrounds and even different motivations. It does not help that the analyst likes to talk in acronyms and computer jargon which the end-user may not understand and is not always ready to admit. The end-user may have a jargon and terminology of his (or her) own which the analyst does not understand.

Even between the analyst and the programmer there is often a misunderstanding because the jargon and terminology are not standard and the approaches and technological background of the two groups may be somewhat different.

A common (and sometimes serious) consequence of communication difficulties is that misunderstandings soon develop. These may stem from, or before, the time that the intentions and needs of the end-user are passed from manager to analyst and may carry on through to the programmer. This problem may be illustrated by a cartoon such as Figure 12.2.

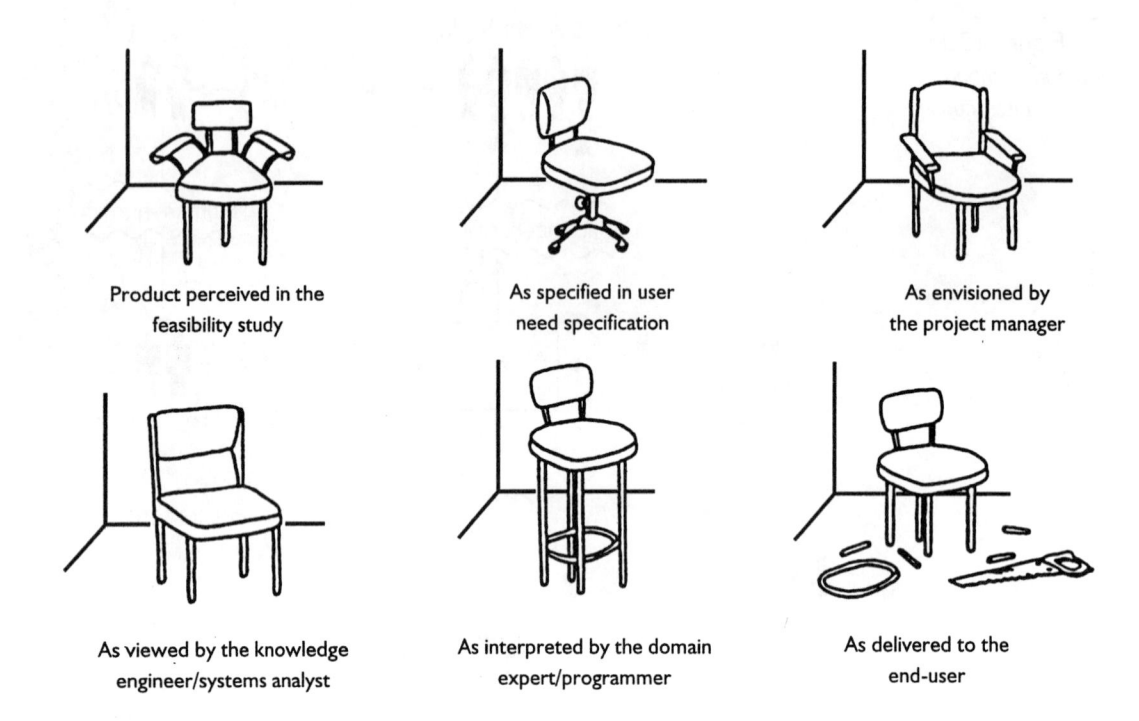

Product perceived in the feasibility study	As specified in user need specification	As envisioned by the project manager
As viewed by the knowledge engineer/systems analyst	As interpreted by the domain expert/programmer	As delivered to the end-user

Figure 12.2: *Different perspectives of a project for development*

It is difficult to draw a picture of a business organization and so a common object like a chair is used to represent an organization and one can see the distortions that occur in each level of communication. This problem of communication is perhaps one of the most important and unsolved issues of development. Note that this is a human issue, not a technological one.

Strategies for humanizing information systems

We have seen different interactions between humans and computers in Figure 12.1. That was the human point of view. Now we take the impersonal computer perspective. This is shown in Figure 12.3.

The machine is accessed by software through a computer program (area A). The software is written by programmers and end-users of computers (areas B and D). However, computers are sometimes directly accessed by humans in human–computer interactions (areas C and D) but mostly through a combination of hardware (machine) and software programs (area D). These two latter interrelationships (areas C and D) involve an end-user.

Figure 12.3:
Relationship between humans, machines and software

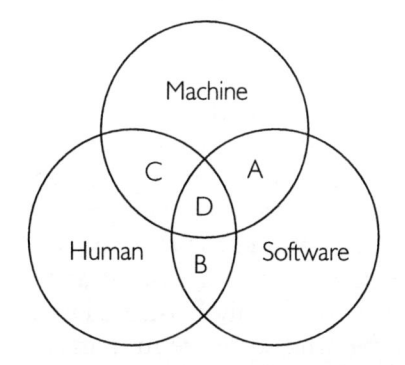

Area A = Machine–software interface
Area B = Human–software interface
Area C = Human–machine interface
Area D = Human–machine–software interface

Traditionally, the end-user as a data clerk or even a professional would use a machine to enter data (area C). Such data would then be loaded with a software program (area A) to produce results. The input machine could be a keypunch or even a terminal connected online to a computer. But this terminal was dumb, as distinct from a terminal that had processing capability and hence referred to as the opposite of dumb, i.e. intelligent. This is an unfortunate term since later in time we saw the emergence of AI and terminals that acted with significant "intelligence". Intelligent terminals and intelligent systems act more like humans and are more end-user friendly. But back to our terminal that was used as an input device. It was later replaced by a desktop computer or PC. The PC system received input from the human, processed it using its software, and produced output for the human. This interaction of machine hardware, software and humans is area D in Figure 12.3. This three-way relationship is becoming more common, and so it is important to humanize information systems. To do so, we must humanize all the components: hardware, output, procedures used and input. We shall discuss each of these in turn.

Areas B and D in Figure 12.3 are often identified as being the jurisdiction of the programmer. Technically-speaking it is true, but end-users are increasingly acting as their own programmers. This is largely due to programming languages that are becoming more end-user friendly. An example is the terminal interactive language which has computer-directed or computer-promoted queries to assist end-users in data entry and information retrieval. Many fourth generation languages and DBMS (database management system) languages (discussed in Chapter 7) have this capability. Instead of having to memorize instruction sets and codes, the end-user interacts with the computer responding to requests for information that appear on the screen. For example, end-users may be asked to select a choice from a menu on the screen, yes/no questions, or fill-in blanks (by entering requested information on the keyboard).

Interactive information systems are becoming end-user friendly but they still have some way to go and the pace of development could be quicker. For example, the author recently purchased one of the most popular desktop graphics packages, read the manuals and still could not get the package to work. A dedicated, 848-page book shed little light; still, the graphics package refused to work correctly. Thus, a powerful software package remains unused, but not for lack of motivation or education. In addition, there is a highly-frustrated user. But there are compensations. For example, the software in question provides icons for common operations and also allows an end-user to customize icons, thereby avoiding the need to navigate through menus that may be two or three levels deep. For this, and other conveniences, one has to pay the price of coming to terms with the complexity of using modern software as well as continually learning new jargon and ways of working.

Even with messages there is much to be done. At one time, the author had a file named after a person called *Afsur*. I got a message:

```
You have your file names sometimes as Afsur and sometimes as
Afsar, a highly inexcusable error but a common human error.
```

The user was impressed by the detective work and the personalized message but the unfriendliness of the system was not funny. And yet, this is progress. Some years ago, your author wrote a programming instruction in FORTRAN and forgot an crucial comma. He promptly got a syntax error message: `You forgot your comma, you silly little fool`. Now that was hardly an end-user friendly response by any standards. So we have a long way to go in making our systems end-user friendly but we are heading in the right direction.

Another example of an unfriendly message comes from a 1994 version of a popular PC operating system: `200142897 bytes free`. At a glance you do not know if this is approximately 200 million bytes, 20 million bytes, or even 2 billion bytes. The correct answer would be clear if one used commas as in 200,142,897 or even spacing as in 200 142 897.

Now there is nothing you, as an end-user, can do with messages from operating systems that are developed by software houses. But such unfriendly messages should not be tolerated in systems developed in-house. The end-user and management can demand end-user friendliness by stating it as a requirement in the system's specification stage and by checking for it in the end-user-acceptance stage of testing, or even looking for the appropriate attitude whilst hiring systems personnel. The interaction between humans and computers can be improved by strategies of humanizing information systems, topics that we will now address. We start with voice and image processing followed by output design, input design, justification interfaces and explanation interfaces.

One approach to end-user friendliness is having a voice processing capability.

Voice processing

Have you ever heard someone (including yourself) talk to a computer? If so, you have heard a very normal response to a computer. We would much rather talk to a computer than have to communicate through a keyboard or a pointer device (e.g. a mouse). Input by voice is not only natural but faster and even quicker, though not cheaper. You are no longer restricted to the computer but can (theoretically) communicate from the convenience of your sofa or while driving a car. However, there is often a stringent demand for good articulation – if the command is not said in just the right way, it may not be understood by the computer. There is also a psychological reason for using voice input, at least for corporate managers. There is much empirical evidence that corporate managers do not like keying input because they associate it with the work of a secretary.

And how about receiving output by voice processing? Again, that would be more convenient and faster (especially for slow readers) and certainly more natural. And the quality of voice output is much better than the early robot voices with greater control of pitch and resonance. A spoken output is also useful because it adds the hearing sense to the senses of seeing and touching commonly used in clerical and production work. However, all voice processing, whether it is analysis (input) or synthesis (output), is currently expensive and has some accuracy problems. But it is certainly one of the important strategies for making systems more end-user friendly.

Image processing

As an output format, an image is often preferred by most end-users: *a picture is worth more than a thousand words,* or so the saying goes. A pictorial output of graphs, bar charts and pie diagrams is valuable for communication – especially if they are in colour. Powerful, reasonably-priced graphics software is readily available.

Images as input can be "friendly" but not for all end-users. Some may choose to use a "scissors" icon to activate "deletion" whilst other end-users would rather use a key on the keyboard. It seems to be a matter of preference as determined by the end-user's background and profile.

An end-user who has used a typewriter extensively might, perhaps, prefer to use a keyboard while the stranger to the typewriter may prefer pointing the mouse to the appropriate icon (like scissors). Whatever mode of processing is chosen, it is important that the communication is clear and unambiguous. This requires that output is designed carefully, partly because output, in the context of an interactive system, initiates input. So if the output is bad then the resulting input is bad, and thus we may have a cycle of bad output–input–output. To prevent this, there are principles of output and input design that can be observed. These will now be examined.

Input–output facilities

Besides straightforward textual questions there may be questions that need to be intermixed with graphics or spreadsheets or even results from some DSS (decision support systems) model. Also, the graphics may be straightforward high resolution display images or they be moving results from a simulation. The output facility should be able to cope with such non-standard modes of output.

Output sometimes needs to be controlled for security purposes. Control for security can be at the level of the data type or the type of access or could be at a much lower and deeper level such as at the data-element level. This is technologically possible but then there is an increase in processing time and response time. The cost may be worth paying because in some knowledge-based systems the output can be very valuable to a competitor who may well try to penetrate the system as part of industrial espionage. Unauthorized access or misuse of output must be carefully controlled and even audited. Sometimes, security control would be the responsibility of the systems interface or it could be at the end-user interface, or both.

An interface for input should allow for online and sometimes even real-time run input. Keeping such input within the bounds of format constraints is not as difficult as it is for input entered by a human. The human may need a great deal of "hand-holding" compared to an input clerk in a transaction system. In contrast to the transactional input clerk, the person providing input for a knowledge-based system is not always trained in input preparation: they might be a professional in a non-computer field and a casual user of computers. Such a person needs assistance through "help" routines, cases, examples and tutorials. Tutorials and documentation are important with input interfaces and a shade less important for output interfaces.

There are some requirements for interfaces that apply to input and output with equal importance. One is the word processing and editing capabilities of the interface. With the increasing popularity of PCs, almost everyone is now acquainted with (and even addicted to) the

WIMP (windows, icons, menus and pointers) environment; "pointers" means pointing-devices like the mouse. Without the WIMP capability an interface will most likely be considered "unfriendly" by many end-users of an information system. And even within the WIMP configuration there will be additional demands such as pull-down and pop-up menus.

On-screen editing is often necessary, along with the need to accept default options and operate error-checking facilities. Thoughtful screen-design for various input/output options may be desirable and the designer should try to keep the screen-image layout, format and procedures consistent with those used for the hard copy that the end-user is accustomed to working with. Following such design guidelines can help reduce the stress felt by end-users as they adapt to change. Features of the input/output interfaces are summarized in Figure 12.4.

Messages

Messages could be audio ones like the alarm, bell or even music on a microcomputer with sound capability. These are binary and express the existence or not of a certain condition. Most messages, however, concern multiple possibilities and these are written ones. The early messages were coded and cryptic like "error XJ337". The user then had to search the manual to identify the error. Some messages were not very helpful like the one which when looked-up said "no specific error".

These days messages are more friendly and often appear on the screen. A message in this context is the means of communication from the computer system to the end-user. Messages may be prompts, information messages, references, cryptic encoded diagnostics, or requests for clarification.

Explanation and justification facilities

An end-user may ask many questions about a system being used such as "why" questions (for relevance), "how" questions (for reasoning path), and the "what" questions (for semantic clarification). Examples of "what" questions occur when the end-user asks for a clarification such as: "What is the meaning of the question being asked?" or, "What are the facts for this rule?" Note that the "what" and "how" questions are for explanation whilst the "why" question is for justification. The module answering the "what", "why" and "how" questions is for both explanation and justification but more for explanations; hence, for brevity, it is often referred to as the "explanation interface".

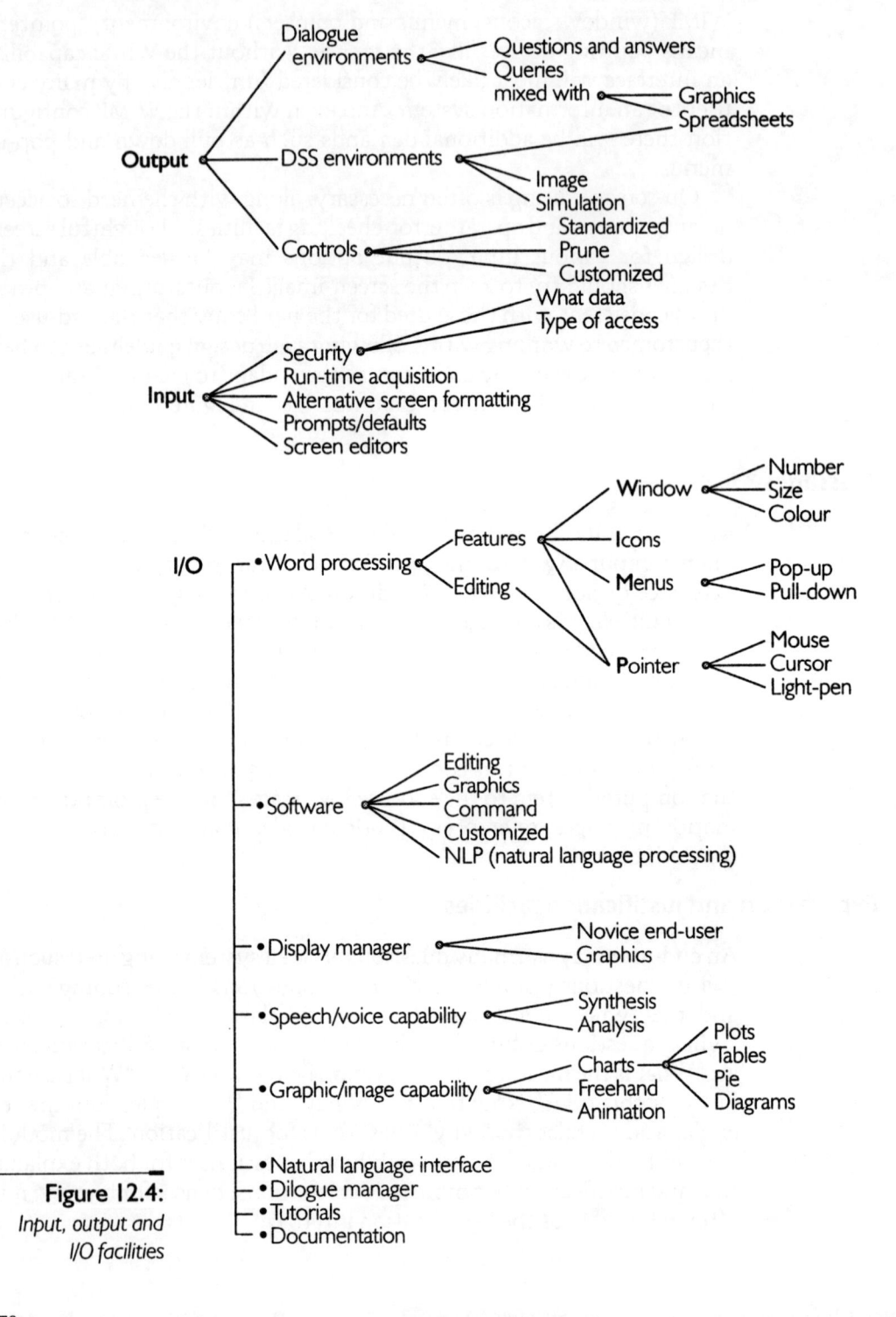

Strategies for humanizing information systems

Output
- Dialogue environments
  - Questions and answers
  - Queries mixed with
    - Graphics
    - Spreadsheets
- DSS environments
  - Image
  - Simulation
- Controls
  - Standardized
  - Prune
  - Customized

Input
- Security
  - What data
  - Type of access
- Run-time acquisition
- Alternative screen formatting
- Prompts/defaults
- Screen editors

I/O
- • Word processing
  - Features
    - Window
      - Number
      - Size
      - Colour
    - Icons
    - Menus
      - Pop-up
      - Pull-down
  - Editing
    - Pointer
      - Mouse
      - Cursor
      - Light-pen
- • Software
  - Editing
  - Graphics
  - Command
  - Customized
  - NLP (natural language processing)
- • Display manager
  - Novice end-user
  - Graphics
- • Speech/voice capability
  - Synthesis
  - Analysis
- • Graphic/image capability
  - Charts
    - Plots
    - Tables
    - Pie
    - Diagrams
  - Freehand
  - Animation
- • Natural language interface
- • Dilogue manager
- • Tutorials
- • Documentation

Figure 12.4: *Input, output and I/O facilities*

270

Other questions that may well be asked are:

- The "what-if" question for simulation where one may change a whole set of parameters, variables or relationships.
- Questions relating to sensitivity analysis where the end-user is concerned with the sensitivity of one parameter or variable.

One interesting feature that is often desirable is the ability to change previous decisions and answers without having to rerun the entire problem all over again and then comparing the results before and after the changes. In such cases, as well as situations of simulation and sensitivity analysis, it is important to have the ability to save results, a feature often found in an explanation interface.

In receiving results, explanations or justifications it is desirable that the responses are customized. This will help to reduce the alienation caused by the perception that computer systems are impersonal. The customized response is greatly appreciated by end-users especially the casual user. For example, the name of the end-user could be used when the end-user logs on and is recognized by the system with its responses addressed to the end-user by name. A good profile of the end-user stored as part of the dictionary would tell the title and sex of user which would make the personal addressing acceptable. Also, the text may be personalized to meet the end-user's preferences and even idiosyncrasies.

It is important to recognize that for a presentation interface, the end-user will not always be a technical person. The end-users will often be a mix of professionals with a strong mathematical and computer background as well as people who are novices in those disciplines and casual users of the computer system.

This mix of capabilities (and even attitudes) is important when using the word processing capabilities. The users of the presentation interface (end-users of the system) can be a heterogeneous group. Some of these end-users want default values and detailed menus at many levels whilst other end-users will object to too many defaults and long menus unless they have the ability to jump around in the menu. Thus the needs and preferences of the end-user can vary greatly and any interface for such end-users must be very flexible in relation to the end-user. The same problem applies to "help" routines which must anticipate the need for help on all sorts of problems – technical as well as mundane. A really end-user friendly system will only assume that you know how to switch the system on, and thereafter it will size-you-up and respond at your level for your needs.

Tutorials and documentation are important. The documentation must be at a level that will not insult or bore the professional and yet be understood by the layman.

A summary of the capabilities of an "explanation and justification" interface is shown in Figure 12.5.

Figure 12.5:
Explanation and justification facilities

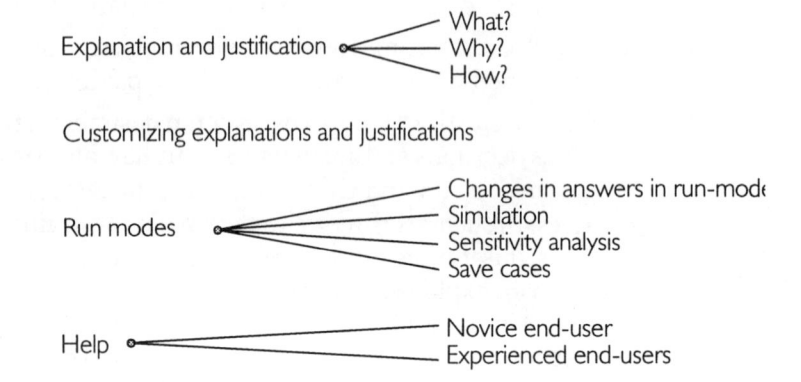

Explanation and justification
— What?
— Why?
— How?

Customizing explanations and justifications

Run modes
— Changes in answers in run-mode
— Simulation
— Sensitivity analysis
— Save cases

Help
— Novice end-user
— Experienced end-users

Another important interface is the *natural language processing* (NLP) capability. NLP is not yet a common capability but it has great potential. There is a great need for a natural-language interface for any information system. NLP is not so important for the development interface but it is of great importance for the end-user who may be highly trained and educated in the domain but does not have the appropriate attitude for computers, especially in preparing inputs. An NLP interface for natural language input, also called the NLI (natural language interface) is not as sophisticated as some would like but it is constantly improving and is applicable in a variety of applications. NLP in an NLI is really speech understanding which is an advance over voice processing.

Natural language interface (NLI)

NLI is an interface with other computer systems that allows communications (one or both ways) in a natural language like English. This can be of great economic significance to an end-user, business, or an office but in addition it makes the use of computers easier and more accessible. If the NLI had voice processing capability then the commands could be given verbally. If NLI were interactive, it would be more end-user friendly. Even without these additional features, an NLI can be used to communicate with smart products at home, get up-to-the-minute flight information at an airport, give the latest price of your stocks, communicate with a bank's ATM (automatic teller machine – also known as a "cashpoint machine"), provide access to data/knowledge bases, operate equipment including computer peripherals, etc. The NLI could be used in factories and financial institutions and could be of special significance in an office or business because the workers and corporate managers may have more computer anxiety and technostress than, say, the bank personnel or factory workers who are more technical and quantitatively oriented. NLI could also be used by programmers and end-users writing and using computer programs. They will save time by not having to manually enter programs and data needed for processing.

NLI assumes NLP (natural language processing) and NLP can be looked upon to have two parts: NLU (natural language understanding) also referred to as *natural language recognition*, and NLG (natural language generation). The goal of NLG is to encode into natural language information to be transferred, and the goal of NLU is to extract the information from the natural language text (i.e. decode it). In functions performed, an NLU is an analyzer while the NLG is the synthesizer. For the analyzer we emphasize issues of syntax, while in synthesizing we are obliged to also consider matters of content, intention, belief, etc. prior to planning the syntactic form of the text that has to be generated.

NLP is concerned with processing of a natural language and so its implementors must understand the structure of a natural language. This in turn requires the understanding of syntax, semantics, grammar and parsing where:

- *Syntax* concerns itself with the sentence structures permitted within a language.
- *Semantics* is concerned with meaning.
- *Grammar* is the description or even formal specification of the allowable or legal structures in a language.
- *Parsing* is the process of resolving a portion of the text to yield its grammatical constituents – its syntactic structure.

All this is part of the discipline of linguistics but must be confronted and mastered by the computer scientists if they are to use the natural language as a communication medium between a user and a computer. This is the subject of much ongoing research as part of AI (artificial intelligence).

Hypertext and hypermedia

A new emerging aid in information retrieval for an office is hypertext. It is the chaining of relevant material which may be scattered all around in a database or knowledge base. Instead of the linear search so common in our traditional ways of searching – especially in our book culture – we now have alternate paths through a set of information spaces by way of designated links. A search then becomes not just fast and efficient but also less painful.

And what if the relevant information is scattered in different media? Then we need hypermedia which links related information in different media such as numerical data, textual data, diagrams, photographs, sound (speech or music), animation and film.

Hypertext and hypermedia are very memory-intensive. This means the need of additional storage in the form of CD-ROM which can be an add-on to existing computer systems.

Related to hypertext and hypermedia is a *hypercard*, which is an authoring environment and information organizer.

We often see the use of hypermedia, hypertext, and hypercard in context of the office searching for a document but they could also be used in a manufacturing plant where blueprints, numerical calculations and user specifications stated in text are all retrieved with a few clicks of the mouse buttons. Hypermedia and hypertext are also used by many professionals such as architects, doctors, and lawyers. Its potential is only now being recognized for education and training as well as advertising and marketing.

An example of hypertext and hypermedia as being end-user friendly and very useful at the same time, is the WWW, or World Wide Web – or Web for short. The Web has been formally defined as:

> A wide-area hypermedia information retrieval initiative aimed to give universal access to a large number of documents.

Hypertext browsing on the Web is more popular than *Gopher* which also searches the Internet but in a hierarchical fashion. To access documents with Gopher, one has to navigate up and down the hierarchical tree structure. With the hypertext and hypermedia Web, one can hop around from one server site to another for the subject you are interested in. If the server has sound or images you can retrieve them, along with the text, simply by clicking at the relevant point on the site's menu. These "hyperfeatures" make the Web more end-user friendly and faster to use than Gopher. However here, as elsewhere, end-user friendliness is a somewhat subjective concept. What is friendly to you may not be friendly enough for me and vice versa.

Back to the basics of the explanation, presentation and justification interface. Whether there is an NLI or not, the presentation and justification interface does perform many important functions. It does offer definitions of terms and concepts besides clarifications and elaborations via the "help" routines. On request, it identifies facts and heuristics and paths of reasoning that lead to each set of conclusions thereby increasing the confidence of the end-user in the integrity of the system and the soundness in its reasoning strategies.

The presentation interface also keeps the end-user informed, when requested, of the status of the system at all times including where the system is in its computation sequence. Knowledge of the system's status and the end-user's ability to question the system (for explanations and justifications) give the perception that the end-user is in command. This feeling of self-assurance can be very important to many end-users.

Another function of the presentation interface is to transfer information about the system and that is why it can be used very successfully for both the training of a new end-user and of an analyst who may be new to the system. The interface has been found to be surprisingly helpful during maintenance, especially when enhancing the system.

These functions of the presentation and justification interface are summarized in Table 12.1.

Table 12.1 *Functions performed by the presentation and justification interface*

- Through "help" routines, provides definitions on:
    - Terms
    - Concepts
- Identifies facts, heuristics and strategies that led to conclusions
- Identifies reasoning paths
- Helps understanding by providing examples
- Increases confidence in the integrity of the system and the soundness of reasoning capabilities
- Increases confidence in the use of knowledge-based systems
- Increases acceptance of system
- Informs the end-user of the current status of system operations
- Gives the end-user the perception of being in control of the system
- Used for transferring information about the system, i.e. used for training of:
    - End-user
    - Knowledge engineer
- Facilitates maintenance of the system

Summary and conclusions

In the early days of computing, end-users had to do what the computer system required of them, and this was often very demanding, inconvenient and sometimes even seemed like harassment. There were many occasions when the end-user did not have the option of taking what seemed an easier way to navigate in the system because the computer system just would not allow it. Well, all that is changing and changing fast. Perhaps it was the backlash from the end-user, perhaps it was the increasing capability and flexibility of the computer system, but partly it is due to a change in the attitude of the computer industry. It is now generally recognized that systems should be developed for the end-user and not require that the end-user mould to the computer system. Information systems must now be "end-user friendly" and tolerant of common end-user errors. Systems must also be physically convenient and comfortable to use which leads to ergonomically designed systems. They should also be psychologically easy to use which has lead to the discipline of *human factors*. Ergonomics and human factors are converging in their practices but the objective is the same: to make computer systems easy to use and eliminate, or at least reduce, computer anxiety and technostress for the user. This anxiety and technostress can be partly reduced by making the work environment and equipment safe, comfortable and not contributing to fatigue. The height of the chair, the angle of the computer screen, the distance of the screen from the chair, and the level of the arm when entering data, can all be adjusted ergonomically to make the work area comfortable and less exhausting.

Analysts should keep abreast with ergonomic and human factor research and try to "humanize" any systems they design. They should take the lead in educating corporate management and other computer personnel regarding the importance of strategies to make information systems end-user friendly. In input design, human factors should be a consideration when choosing data entry hardware and design software for human–machine interaction (such as messages, menus, screen displays and "help" routines). Although design is the prime responsibility of analysts, the views of the end-users should be solicited regarding design features and their preferences should be taken into account when making design decisions. A system that is self-instructing to comprehend, tolerant to errors, easy to use, and comfortable to operate should be the goal of all information systems development.

Another attempt at humanizing information systems is to have effective explanation and justification interfaces. This type of interface engineered by AI through its development of expert systems technology is very important in that it has increased the credibility of reports from an information system in particular, and problem solving in general. In conventional systems, like a DSS (decision support system), EIS (executive information systems) and ES (expert systems), and even in transactional systems the system was treated as a black box either because the modeller was unable to explain or justify the model and its assumptions, or because the end-user was unable (or perceived to be unable) to understand what is being explained. Now this has all changed. The end-user is now encouraged to ask any question of the system and demand any explanation or justifications, and to do so without any inhibitions or pressures from the overbearing technical analyst. A tracing routine has given the end-user the ability to trace the path of a solution and see the results as they develop. This capability is especially useful in simulation models where more than one variable or parameter can be changed and the consequences cannot otherwise be easily isolated and appreciated. Systems of problem solving such as an EIS, DSS, expert system or a knowledge-based system, can now be explained or justified – this will:

- Greatly increase confidence in such systems.
- Remove much of the mystique surrounding them.
- Decrease the alienation of such systems.
- Increase the chances of acceptance of the system.
- Increase the comfort level of the end-user in using an information system.

Another strategy for humanizing information systems is to build-in ergonomic and human-factor considerations:

- During the design of input and output.
- When selecting the type of VDT screen.
- Within messages, menus, defaults, closure, system tolerance, response times, manuals and online help.

An extension to the definition of an end-user friendly and humanized information system is that there must be an ease and pleasure in using it. The system should not *only* be a way to save time and money and do required tasks, but should also give the end-user control and power over the system. Why should an end-user not feel the same power and pleasures as those who play computer games? Developers must learn to ratchet the level of difficulty incrementally upwards ensuring that the end-user is always challenged but never overwhelmed. The end-user must be encouraged to experiment and explore without the fear of loosing data, or anxiety of not knowing what is happening. The end-user must enjoy using the system with each step forward being greeted with colourful and helpful screen displays. The end-user, as in a computer game, must be posed with new challenges, hard enough to keep the processing interesting without it becoming unpalatable. This can bring pleasure and even excitement by supplementing the human mind. The potential for computer-induced enjoyment – like that for human creativity – is essentially boundless. Despite all our conscious attempts, there are many reasons why interfaces are ineffective. Some are summarized in a fishbone diagram of Figure 12.6. One important reason for interface ineffectiveness is lack of training on the interface. This could result from a lack of resources or from poor instruction (e.g., use of inappropriate instruction media or an ineffective instructor).

Figure 12.6:
Causes for the ineffectiveness of interfaces

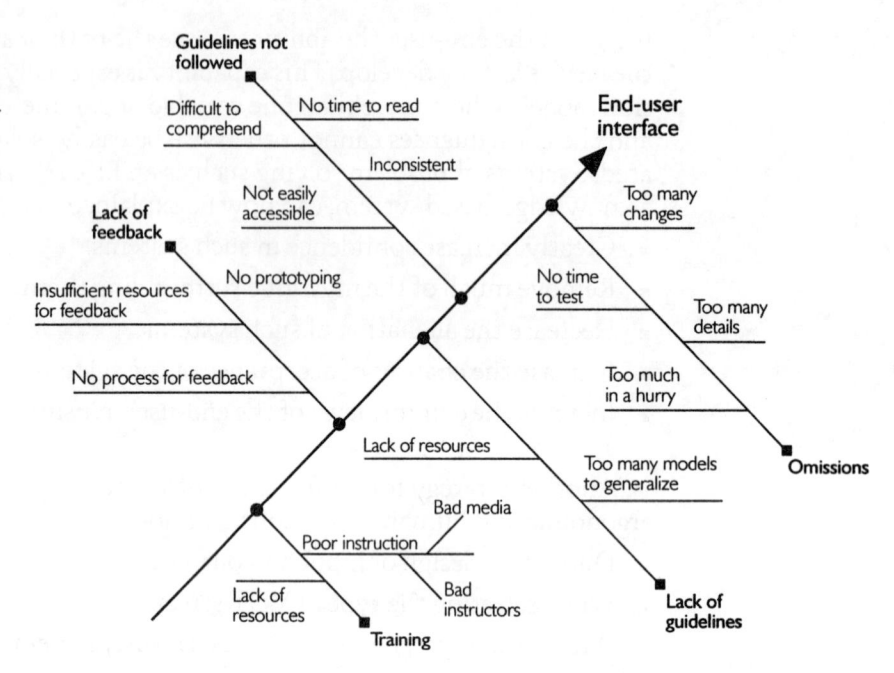

The main thrust of this chapter has been the consideration of interfaces and a work environment which would make information systems fun and friendly to use. Factors such as the desire of end-users to be in control of computer systems, and the relief people get when tasks have been completed should be considered by analysts when designing information systems. Ben Shneidermann, who has written extensively on human factors, (Shneidermann, 1987 and 1992) suggests that eight underlying principles should govern all interface design:

1. Strive for consistency of format, terminology and commands.
2. Enable frequent users to use short cuts such as abbreviations, function keys, and macro facilities.
3. Provide feedback to the user on the effects of actions initiated.
4. Design dialogues to yield closure.
5. Offer simple error handling.
6. Permit easy reversal of actions.
7. Give users the sense of control.
8. Design displays with short-term memory load in mind.

One could add to Shneiderman's list of design considerations the following:

- Design messages carefully.

- Design menus that are not too detailed nor too short.
- Provide appropriate defaults.
- Design systems procedures that are tolerant.
- Design response times that will not annoy the end-user.
- Design dialogues that are end-user-friendly.
- Have a presentation module with tracing, explanation and justification facilities.

Case 12.1: Graphic tools at Merrill Lynch

In 1993, Merrill Lynch saw demonstrations of commercially available graphics tools that make the system more end-user friendly and also dramatically reduce the time to build prototypes. The system was announced but not yet commercially available.

> Merrill Lynch saw advantages to incorporating Unify Vision into its development methodology. Unify Corporation saw advantages in having a customer as visible and influential as Merrill Lynch for its new product. It appeared to be a clear win–win situation. Unify sent Merrill Lynch a beta version of the product and a Unify development engineer for on-site support at no charge.

A pilot application was built by two Merrill Lynch developers. One of them, commented:

> We prototyped the user interface and the database access in three days. Vision's toolset allowed us to "paint" the user interface and much of the code required to access the data was automatically generated based on the structure of the GUI. Significantly, it wasn't throw-away. We've refined it. It's now one of our production support applications.

Source: *I/S Analyzer*. (1994). vol. 33, no. 5 (May), pp. 2–5

Case 12.2: Keyboard injury lawsuits

Suing a keyboard manufacturer for an RSI (repetitive strain injury) resulting from using the keyboard could be a very common occurrence except that winning against the large computer companies is not easy. This happened when Compaq won its case against RSI in 1993. But this did not discourage 31-year-old Nancy Urbanski from suing both Apple and IBM for $50,000 because of her condition resulting from using keyboards since high school. Her attorney claimed that: "She can't work at anything that requires her upper extremities. She can't tie her kids' shoes, and she can't chop or cook."

In 1995, Apple settled out of court because of a legal error on its part that opened it to punitive damages. IBM stayed defiant and claimed:

> We have diligently researched and kept abreast of most current medical and scientific data and are confident that keyboards pose no risk to users.

In court, IBM claimed that the use of a screwdriver could injure the user. The burden lies with the user who must understand the risks involved. The court agreed. Case dismissed. Many with RSI (including your author) were disappointed but all shareholders of IBM (including your author) were elated and relieved.

Source: *San Francisco Chronicle*, February 28, 1995, pp. D1–2.

Case 12.3: Voice input in production

In the early 1980s, voice input was being used in industry. One example was the acquisition of a $2,500 Votan VPC–2000 voice recognition system by Carra Donna Provision Co. The system was to help employees who worked at refrigerated loading docks scribbling information on paper with near-frozen fingers. This information was later manually entered into the corporate computer. Input in this manner was inefficient and error-prone.

With the voice system, the stock handler communicated directly with the computer via a headset, which leaves both hands free for unloading tasks. The handler uses their voice to input stock serial numbers as crates are unloaded. The system's vocabulary consists of numbers 0–9 plus several basic editing and function commands. The computer itself is installed behind a glass widow next to the loading dock where input is displayed on a colour video screen visible to the handler. This allows the handler to verify input accuracy. If the voice recognition system fails to recognize a command or word, a command can be given to the system to edit one or more entries. The handler can also tell the unit to stop listening if the handler needs to speak to a co-worker.

There is general consensus that voice input is end-user friendly compared to the written word. The problem of tone and inflection of the voice is not too relevant. This, however, is not true for a voice input/output system where the reception and acceptance of voice output can be very subjective and it is a challenge to construct a voice system that is perceived to be end-user friendly for different types of end-users.

Supplement 12.1: Design of a workstation

Physiological, psychological and training factors are considered when computer hardware (and software) is being designed. The purpose is to ensure that humans interface efficiently and effectively with computer systems. Two fields of effort concerned with ways to improve human–machine interaction are *human factors* and *ergonomics*. Historically, ergonomics has placed an emphasis on physiological rather than psychological considerations.

For example, eye fatigue when using computer terminals is a human factors problem. Eye fatigue may be caused by the angle at which light hits the computer screen. Sometimes eye fatigue is caused by the screen image itself. Many experiments have been done with colours, fonts, size of image, blinking and flickering in order to determine which factors produce eye strain. The results have influenced screen design. To accommodate differences between users, some manufacturers provide a choice of screen designs.

One early microcomputer had small keys placed close together. Users made many errors on this keyboard, striking the wrong keys because finger position was unnatural and uncomfortable. It is this type of problem that can be avoided when attention is paid to human factors. Noise levels can affect user concentration, operational procedures can affect user patience, and emissions from the machine may affect user health. (Whether the latter is true or not is a highly debated issue.) Vague or ambiguous error messages can hamper effective system use.

Standards for computer design and use are beginning to be developed based on human factors research. For example, a 12° slope of the keyboard and a 15° tilt for a twelve-inch monitor are standard in terminal design. Other standards common in the design of input terminals are as follows:

1. The European recommendation for the height of the home row keys is 28¼ to 29½ inches. The US military standard is 29¼ to 31 inches.

2. The viewing distance should be between 17¼ and 19¾ inches, with a maximum of 27½ inches.

3. Generally, the centre of the screen should be at a position somewhere between 10° and 20° below the horizontal plane and the operator's eye-height. One researcher recommends that the top of the screen be below eye height, another that the top line of the display be 10 to 15° below the horizontal, with no portion of the screen at an angle greater than 40° below the horizontal.

Supplement 12.2: Preventing strain when using a keyboard

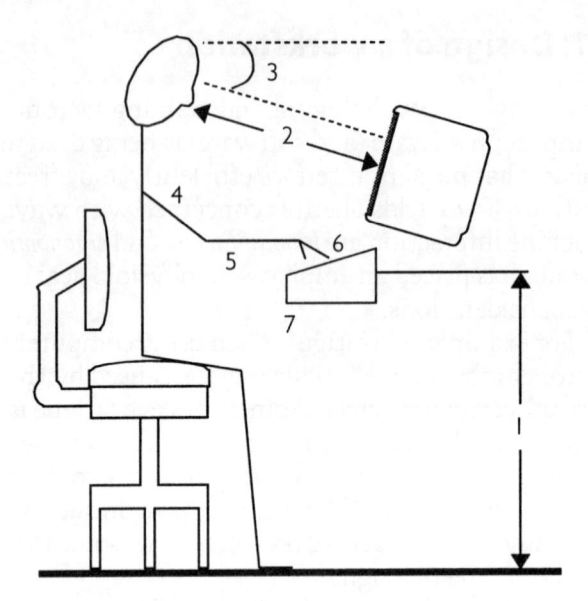

4. One researcher recommends that the angle between the upper and lower arms be between 80° and 120°.
5. The angle of the wrist should be no greater than 10°.
6. The keyboard should be at or below elbow height.
7. Don't forget enough room for your legs.

Source: *Potential Health Hazards of Video Display Terminals.*

Supplement 12.2: Preventing strain when using a keyboard

Keep your wrists straight
- Do not flex your wrist.
- Do not extend your wrists.
- Do not twist your wrists.
- Sit up straight.
- Do not flex your back.
- Do not extend your back.

Check your posture
- Hold your head up.
- Touch your keys lightly.
- Keep your feet flat.

Adjust your workstation
- Adjust the keyboard tray or desk height so that the hands are straight while typing.
- Adjust screen height so that the top is level to your eye-level.
- Adjust the chair height so that your wrists are straight.

Adjust workstation props
- A lower-back pack may prove helpful.
- A wrist-rest may help.
- A copy stand should be at the same height as the screen.
- A telephone headset is useful with dictation.

Exercise
- Hands and wrists: stretch, rotate and shake.
- Body: reach high, roll shoulders and shake body.

References

Benbasat, I., Lim, Francis J. *et al.* (1992). "The User-Interface in Systems Design." *Informatica*, vol. 1, no. 1 (December), pp. 62–95.

Blattner, Meera M. (1994). "In Our Image: Interface Design in the 1990s." *Multimedia*, vol. 1, no. 1, pp. 25–36.

Brod, Craig. (1984). *Technostress*. Reading: Addison Wesley.

Genter, D. R. and Grudin, J. (1996). "Design Models for Computer-Human Interface." *IEEE Computer*, vol. 29, no. 6 (June), pp. 28–36.

Gerlach, James H. and Feng-Yang Kuo. (1991). "Understanding Human-Computer Interaction for Information Systems Design." *MIS Quarterly*, vol. 15, no. 4, pp. 527–49.

Harrison, M. and Thimbleby, H. (eds.). (1990). *Formal Methods in Human Computer Interaction*. Cambridge: Cambridge University Press.

Hartson, Rex and Deborah Boehm-Davis. (1993). "User Interface Development Processes and Methodologies." *Behaviour & Information Technology*, vol. 12, no. 2, pp. 98–114.

Hix, Deborah and Shulman, Robert S. (1991). "Human Interface Development Tools: A Methodology for Their Evaluation." *Communications of the ACM*, vol. 34, no. 3 (March), pp. 67–87.

Hoang, Tien H. (1990). "Human Factors in Decision and Control: Nonstandard Modeling and Information Processing." *Information Sciences*, vol. 51, pp. 13–59.

Kinney-Wallace, Geraldine. (1992). "On Mind Over Matter: The Information Challenge to Human Software." *The Canadian Journal of Information Science*, vol. 17, no. 4 (December), pp. 46–57.

References

McCarthy, John C. and Andrew F. Monk. (1994). "Evaluating User Interfaces; 1: Software." *Behaviour and Information Technology*, vol. 13, no. 5 (September–October 1994), pp. 311–20.

Molich, Rolf and Nielsen, Jakob. (1990) "Improving a Human–Computer Dialogue." *Communications of the ACM*, vol. 33, no. 3 (March), pp. 338–48.

Preece, Jenny and Kleller, Laurie (eds.), (1990). *Human-Computer Interaction*. Hemel Hempstead: Prentice Hall International.

Shneiderman, B. (1987 and 1992). *Designing the User Interface: Strategies of Effective Human-Computer Interaction*. Reading: Addison Wesley Publishing Co.

Sibert, John and Machionini, Gary (eds.). (1993). "Special Issue: Human-Computer Interaction Research Agendas." *Behaviour & Information Technology*, vol. 12, no. 2 (March–April), pp. 1–146.

Woodhead, Nigel. (1991). *Hypertext and Hypermedia: Theory and Applications*. Winlow, UK: Addison-Wesley Publishing Co.

13 Maintenance

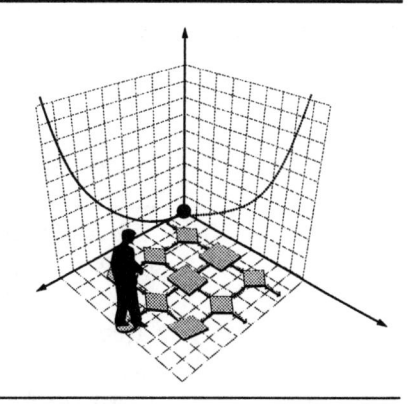

> Maintenance is not a problem, it is a solution.
>
> Unknown

Introduction

Maintenance can be of two kinds: hardware and software. Very large systems do have their own hardware repair and maintenance department but most systems managers cannot afford that option. Most likely, managers do not want to be bothered with the logistics of maintenance especially with computer equipment that changes often to the point of being obsolete soon after it is acquired. In such cases the solution is to subcontract maintenance, often to the vendor of the equipment. Maintenance of software is different. It is undertaken locally by maintenance programmers and is seldom outsourced. It is the responsibility of the IS/IT (information systems/information technology) department and so it is the main thrust of this chapter. In it we examine the maintenance life cycle, the reasons for maintenance, types of maintenance, and management practices needed for maintenance.

Software maintenance

Maintenance is costly. It is estimated that maintenance work constitutes more than half of the work of the typical information systems department; that 50% of the IS budget is allocated to maintenance; and that the annual, world-wide, maintenance spend is around £50 billion. The problem is not always the nature of software but current programming practices and tools that programmers use. Many experts believe that more effort should be spent during systems development to make software reliable and modifiable. They stress the need for improved modification techniques as well. For example, a methodology is needed that permits code reuse without risk, and the separate storage of unique and reusable code so that each can be maintained independently.

Many corporations are replacing software that has "aged". One reason is that old software systems are written in languages that are no longer commonly used by programmers. The software may use outdated programming and design practices, factors that complicate maintenance. Programs may have been extensively "patched" with changes poorly documented, or they may have increased in size beyond the limits that their structure was originally designed to cope with. Few people who worked on the original systems may be available to answer questions, explain how the program works, or help understand the existing documentation. One might compare an old information system to an old car that becomes increasingly unreliable and costly to maintain with age. Besides, most end-users want the latest technology. They favour the use of software that takes advantage of streamlined facilities and standard routines. They may even chose to redevelop software before the replacement of old systems can be economically justified.

Maintenance/redevelopment life cycle

Every firm needs a maintenance policy and procedures to identify when redevelopment is needed. In general, maintenance is defined as a change that affects few end-users and does not require much effort or many resources (not more than two weeks of a programmer's time, for example). Redevelopment, on the other hand, requires a major allocation of resources and personnel. A committee generally decides when maintenance or redevelopment is required.

Figure 13.1 illustrates that the maintenance redevelopment life cycle is similar to that of in-house systems development. First, the need for maintenance or redevelopment is identified. When change is under consideration, end-users should participate in discussions to ensure that proposed modifications meet their needs and that the final system will be accepted. When analysts are new to the organization and unfamiliar with the software that requires maintenance or redevelopment, the end-user can often save time for maintenance personnel by explaining how the system works and what problems to expect.

A feasibility assessment should be the next stage of the life cycle, including a cost estimate of the effort required to complete the change. Following management approval of the maintenance/redevelopment project, the job is scheduled and assigned to maintenance personnel. After analysis and design, the system is implemented. The system is then tested to verify that it performs as expected. When both end-users and managers approve the test results, documentation must be completed, and the old system is replaced with the modified system. The system is used in operations and evaluated. If changes are to be made the nature of the changes are determined. If the changes are minor, the system is maintained, or else it is redeveloped (or reengineered).

Figure 13.1:
Development and maintenance/ redevelopment cycle

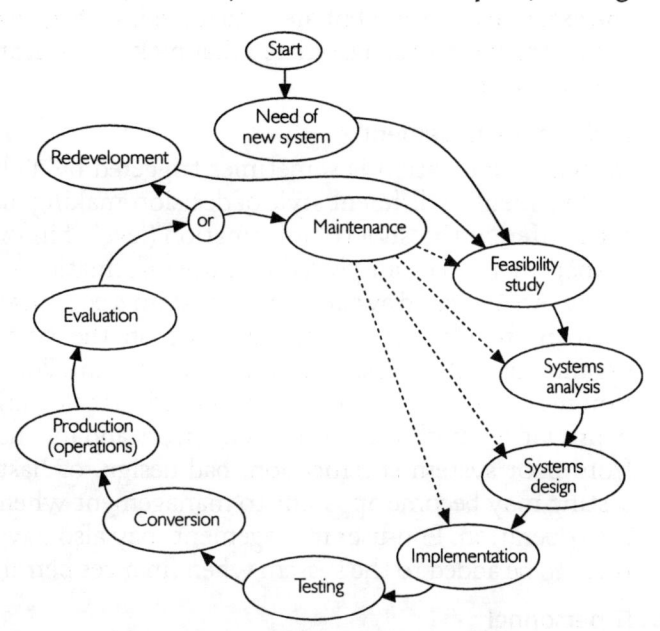

The principles of systems development and project control, discussed elsewhere, apply to software maintenance as well as to systems development and daily operations. The privacy of data/knowledge needs to be protected, computing resources should be kept secure, and the performance of individuals working on maintenance should be monitored and periodically evaluated to ensure quality work within budgetary constraints.

What triggers software maintenance?

The inputs for software modification may come from a number of factors; some of these are discussed below.

Error in output
Debugging of a program during a system development can never reveal the absence of errors, only their presence. Dijkstra, from Holland, puts this succinctly: "Testing shows the presence not absence of errors." Many errors in design are not revealed until a program has been in use for some time. When a previously working system ceases to function properly, maintenance is called for.

Chapter 13: Maintenance

External environment
New laws and changed government regulations are two reasons why systems are often modified. Also, competitors may so alter market conditions that system redesign must be initiated. When regular changes in the external environment are anticipated, such as revisions of tax rates, flexible programs can be written that make modification part of routine maintenance.

End-user management
System modification is sometimes triggered by a change in corporate management. A different style of decision-making may lead to the need for a different threshold of information (level of information detail). Or management may simply learn to use information systems more effectively. An increased awareness of a system's potential often causes management to place increased demands on the system. Policies of an organization often make demands on a system. Policies of an organization may change, requiring new methods of calculations – such as new depreciation methods. Or frequent errors and inconsistencies resulting from poor system specification, bad design, or hasty and incomplete testing may become apparent to management when the system is put into operation. End-user management may also have a wish list of features to be added to the system when finances permit.

IT personnel
Systems generally require modification when new equipment is acquired. For example, more secondary storage would allow a larger database, and increased processing would be feasible. The pace of technological change and innovation in the computer industry is legendary. Organizations adopting new technology or merely expanding their systems with more sophisticated computers will find that their information systems need modification. Once systems are operational, analysts may detect errors from poor design and implementation or invalid assumptions, errors that contribute to processing inefficiencies or reduce effectiveness.

Computer personnel, like end-users, may also have a wish list not included in the original development because the design was frozen or because development resources were lacking at the time. The list might include reorganization of data, new output form design, or even new programming solutions. Generally, these ideas were conceived and documented during development. Once the system is made operational, the suggestions are reevaluated.

Reasons for maintenance listed above (and some others) are summarized in Table 13.1.

Table 13.1 *Reasons for maintenance*

Wanted by decision-maker/manager
- Change in management
- Changes in decision-making style
- Changes in corporate goals/objectives/procedures
- Changes in growth patterns

Imposed by environment
- By tax and revenue department/ministry
- By regulatory agency

Required by computing/processing centre
- Changes in hardware (CPU, telecommunications and peripherals)
- Changes in software (compilers and application software)

Needed by computer personnel
- Changes in code and file structure
- Changes in design
- Better tools and development techniques

Types of maintenance

For each set of maintenance needs there is at least one type to maintenance. A classification of maintenance approaches are summarized in Figure 13.2.

Figure 13.2: *Classification of maintenance*

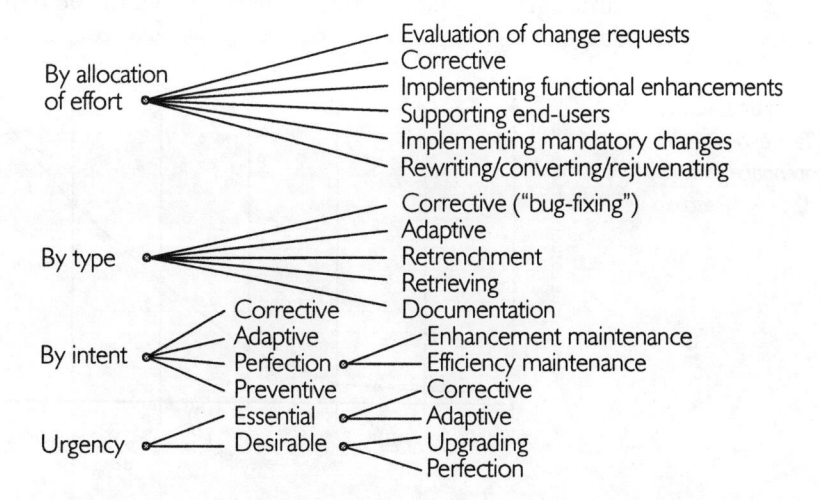

By allocation of effort:
- Evaluation of change requests
- Corrective
- Implementing functional enhancements
- Supporting end-users
- Implementing mandatory changes
- Rewriting/converting/rejuvenating

By type:
- Corrective ("bug-fixing")
- Adaptive
- Retrenchment
- Retrieving

By intent:
- Corrective — Documentation
- Adaptive — Enhancement maintenance
- Perfection — Efficiency maintenance
- Preventive — Corrective

Urgency:
- Essential — Adaptive
- Desirable — Upgrading
- Perfection

The list is not mutually exclusive but there are types that are generally accepted as being important. These are:
- *Corrective*: to correct faults and errors.
- *Adaptive*: upgrading to changing or advanced technologies.
- *Perfective*: in response to changes in the end-user requirements.
- *Preventive*: in anticipation of future problems in maintenance.

The distribution of the above types of maintenance is part of the results of a survey by Lientz and Swanson of 487 data processing organizations in the late 1970s (Bennet, 1991:75) is as follows:
- Perfective   50%
- Adaptive   25%
- Corrective   21%
- Preventive   4%

The lowest percentage for preventive maintenance may well increase as the need and importance of preventive maintenance is recognized. (A stitch in time saves nine!) Also increasing in the future (in percentage and in absolute terms) will be corrective maintenance. As the software portfolio inevitably enlarges and software gets more complex, the need for corrective maintenance will increase. This type of corrective maintenance is important because unlike perfective and adaptive maintenance, corrective maintenance can be greatly reduced if errors are detected in the early stages of development. It has been shown (Gabel, 1994:41) that the cost of errors corrected in operations is some 30 to 40 times greater than if they were corrected in the requirements or design stages.

Figure 13.3:
Effect of design on maintenance (not to scale)

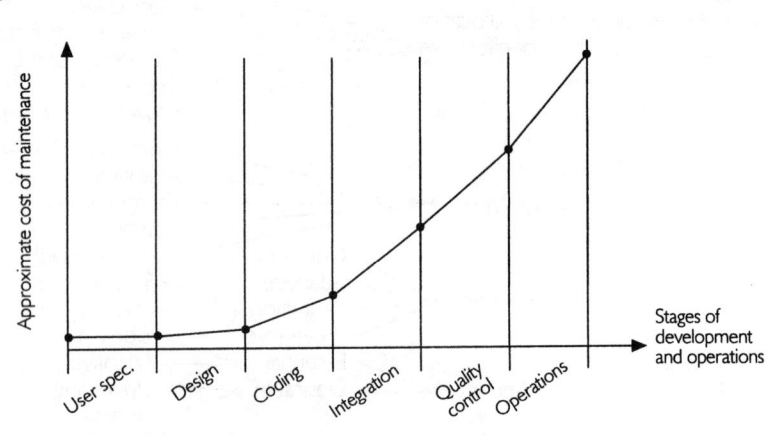

Source: adapted from Gabel (1994:41)

Cost of maintenance

Figure 13.3 reinforces the dictum well known to the software engineering profession: *the earlier the error is detected the lower the cost of maintenance*. This means that errors should be detected at least in the design stage and that *deliberate* attempts should be made to detect errors early in the development of software. This can be done by intensive walk-throughs, testing during design and testing at all later stages (unit testing of coding, systems testing of integration, and testing of quality assurance). The cost of maintenance increases depending on:

- Changes in the needs of end-users.
- High programmer turnover.
- Lack of knowledge of the environment and of the system.
- Ineffectiveness of existing programs.
- Poor existing documentation.
- Lack of adequate time for the project.

The cost of maintenance also depends on the type of maintenance. A matrix of maintenance costs occurring for different cost factors is shown in Table 13.2 (Gorla, 1991:67).

Table 13.2 *Cost factors affecting maintenance types*

Maintenance category / Cost factor	Corrective	Enhancement	Efficiency	Preventive	Adaptive
Lack of end-user knowledge of system		X			
Programmer ineffectiveness	X	X	X	X	
Poor programming and documentation practices	X	X	X		
Programmer under time pressure	X	X	X		
Inadequate processing resources					X

There are many tools used in maintenance. One matching of tools for different types of maintenance is shown in Figure 13.4 (Gorla, 1991:67).

Maintenance/redevelopment life cycle

Figure 13.4:
Types of maintenance tools.

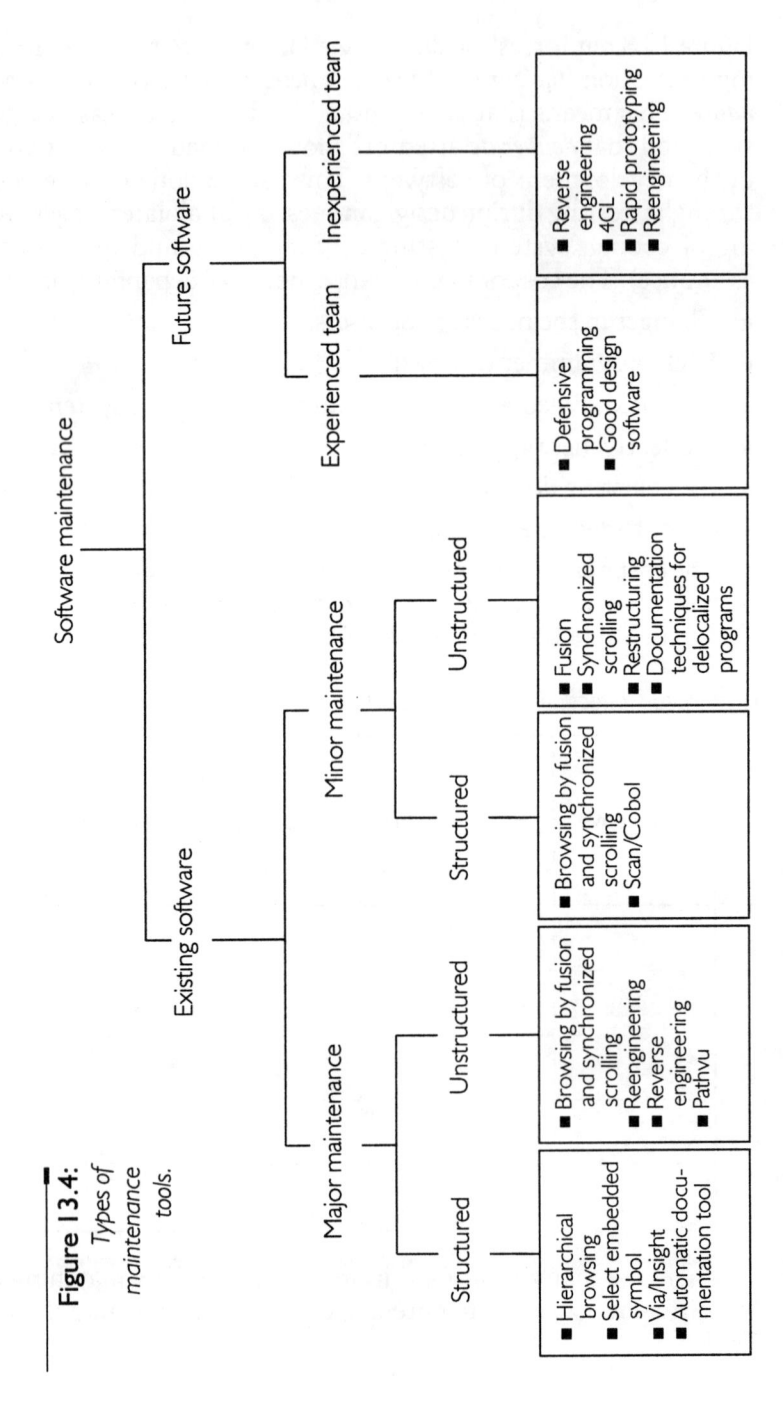

```
                                    Software maintenance
                                    ┌──────────┴──────────┐
                            Existing software        Future software
                    ┌──────────────┴──────────────┐     ┌──────┴──────┐
              Major maintenance              Minor maintenance   Experienced   Inexperienced
                                                                    team          team
          ┌────────┴────────┐            ┌────────┴────────┐
    Structured         Unstructured   Structured      Unstructured
```

- Hierarchical browsing
- Select embedded symbol
- Via/Insight
- Automatic documentation tool

- Browsing by fusion and synchronized scrolling
- Reengineering
- Reverse engineering
- Pathvu

- Browsing by fusion and synchronized scrolling
- Scan/Cobol

- Fusion
- Synchronized scrolling
- Restructuring
- Documentation techniques for delocalized programs

- Defensive programming
- Good design software

- Reverse engineering
- 4GL
- Rapid prototyping
- Reengineering

Source: adapted from Gorla (1991:72). Used with permission of Butterworth-Heinemann.

Maintenance, reengineering, redevelopment and reuse

One approach to maintenance work is to allocate all minor modifications to maintenance and all major modifications to reengineering and redevelopment. The problem is that of determining what is a minor and what is a major modification. It is considered easier by some to use the reverse logic: first determine what is a major modification (for reengineering and redevelopment) and what remains is a minor modification for maintenance. This residual approach makes the choice easier, at least for the IS/IT department, because major modifications are decisions first made by top management.

If top management decides to reengineer the business, then IS/IT follows. They have no choice. Also, if management decides to redo the user requirement specification, again IT must follow. An IT department may secretly even encourage a respecification or reengineering in order to have an opportunity to use more advanced development technology and design a higher performance system. Also, reengineering and redevelopment would involve a separate budget allotment and not burden the operational IT budget. What is not reengineered or redeveloped is residual maintenance. This approach is illustrated in Figure 13.5.

Figure 13.5:
Relationship of maintenance to reengineering and redeployment

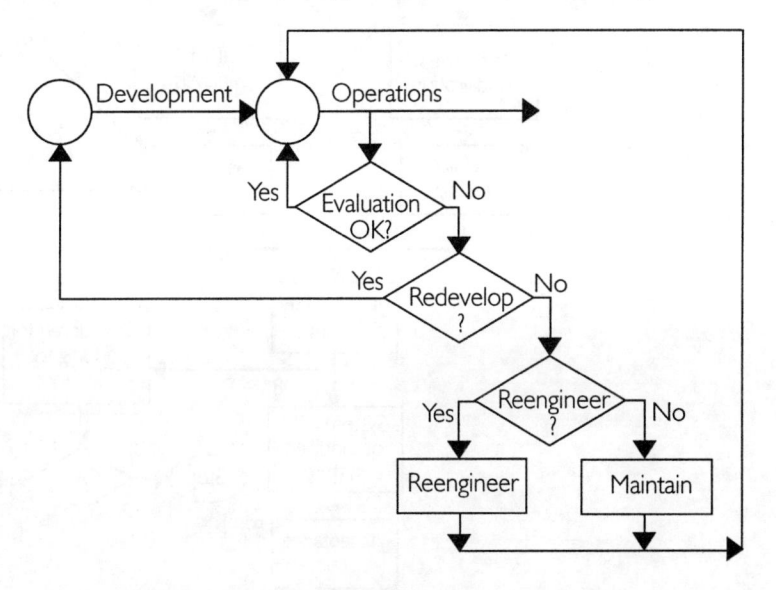

Whatever approach to maintenance (or reengineering or redevelopment), there is potential for reuse of parts and components. Some of these parts may come from the corporate *reuse library*, and others imported form outside "reuse vendors".

Chapter 13: Maintenance

Maintenance, reengineering, redevelopment and reuse

The part of software modifications that cannot come from reuse must be programmed as shown in boxes 5 to 9 in Figure 13.6. The reused parts are shown in boxes 10 to 13. If, however, the modified product is worth adding to the corporate reuse library, it is analyzed for suitability and, if accepted, documented and added to the library (boxes 14 to 16).

Figure 13.6:
Maintenance with reuse

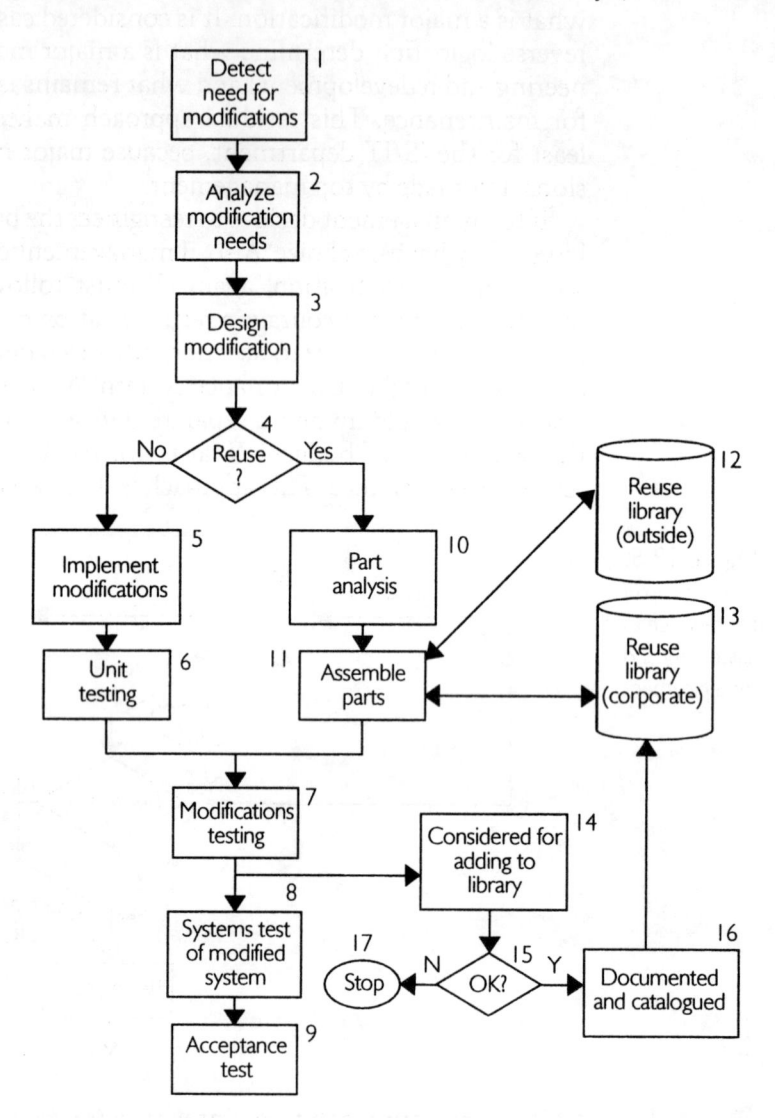

294

Software maintenance management

All companies that rely on information technology need to plan for software maintenance and to manage and control the process. Maintenance management entails a number of considerations as discussed below.

Personnel

In spite of the large share of the IS budget that is consumed by software maintenance, few companies are making a serious effort to reduce maintenance. It has earned the reputation of a second-class job and is typically delegated to junior programmers and programming trainees, not to the qualified senior-level programmers and analysts whose analytical skills are often needed in maintenance. Surveys reveal that maintenance work has only one-half to two-thirds of the motivating potential of other programming/analysis work and that the job is regarded as non-creative and non-challenging. People assigned to maintenance tasks seldom receive status or professional recognition for their contributions to maintenance. One indication of this fact is that few companies have even established the job classifications of maintenance analyst, maintenance programmer, or maintenance manager. Indeed, of all of IS technical personnel, the systems maintenance person is most prone to unhappiness and inclined to job-hop.

Performance

An IS/IT director might improve systems maintenance productivity by:

1. Hiring people with a flair for detective work and a preference for systems maintenance work over other analysis/programming tasks.
2. Enhancing maintenance jobs so that the motivational level and work status are comparable to those of new systems development.

Since the first suggestion is often impractical because of the lack of candidates, let us focus on the second strategy. Five variables (or job dimensions) typically motivate IS personnel: skill variety, task identity, task significance, autonomy, and feedback from the task. The job of management in organizing systems maintenance is to design the work to enhance as many of these dimensions as possible. For example, maintenance jobs may be rotated so that individuals work with a variety of software instead of specializing in software for one system. This will promote skill variety by the job. Also, management should require quality work, perhaps with monetary compensation. A career track should allow for professional advancement. Maintenance analysts and programmers should be challenged to apply new technology to their jobs and to try new maintenance methodologies.

Software maintenance contract

Software maintenance is not always an in-house activity. A company may enter into a licence agreement for a software product, including maintenance. Key provisions of the contract that will affect costs are:

- End-user responsibility for escalation of charges.
- Overtime and travelling charges.
- Unsupported service or extras.
- Response time to maintenance requests.
- On- or off-site maintenance.
- Termination rights by end-user/management.
- Payment terms.
- End-user rights to source code.

Chargeback policies

The way in which maintenance costs are assessed and charged to end-users can be a source of ill-feeling. If systems modifications are performed without charge by a computing centre, end-users may be tempted to demand more maintenance than necessary. End-users may also fail to include maintainability in their specifications for custom software or to approve maintenance features in the design of new systems because of their added costs.

On the other hand, a fair assessment of charges is difficult in an integrated system in which more than one end-user benefits from maintenance. Questions also arise about where fault lies when maintenance is required:

- Is the problem due to a technical or organizational condition?
- Are maintenance costs resulting because of circumstances that stem from the jurisdiction of computing or from the jurisdiction and responsibility of end-users?
- Is it fair to charge end-users for program modifications that are needed because the computer centre installs a new operating system or institutes new procedures that benefit the end-users?

Computer centres vary in their charge structures. A decision regarding which structure to adopt is the responsibility of the IS/IT management.

The microcomputer environment

Software for microcomputer users in a business is often purchased as a package. In this context, microcomputer maintenance may be little more that showing the user how the system works and providing help and a "hotline" when the user (including the end-user) is unable to understand terminal messages or unable to generate expected output. Alternatively, microcomputer maintenance could include updating and timely preventive maintenance of the software along with online help and training whenever needed.

Maintenance may result from microcomputer end-users who write their own programs. The development of non-procedural languages, such as query languages, report generators, and very high level languages, means that end-users now have tools that allow them to construct their own systems which may need maintenance. Sometimes, end-users use software packages and wish to modify or tailor them; this can result in maintenance requests.

To give end-users maintenance assistance, many firms have established information centres staffed by IT professionals. One role of the centre may be to train end-users in program modification techniques. For example, information centre personnel may give courses on a particular fourth generation language. After teaching how to write software using that language, the instructor might then ask: "Suppose the conditions of the original problem changes?" By doing exercises in rewriting the code for changed conditions, end-users can gain maintenance experience and, in the process, will learn ways to write programs so that they can be easily maintained.

Maintenance priorities

Usually, a committee composed of the DBA (database administrator), an auditor, and end-user's representative assigns priorities to maintenance requests, reconciles conflicts between end-user departments, and settles jurisdictional problems of maintenance when they arise. Ideally, maintenance priorities should be decided on the basis of cost–benefit and benefit–performance ratios. The availability of personnel is, of course, an important consideration.

Since most analysts and programmers prefer new systems development, personnel with the skills and interest in maintaining old systems may be in short supply. Some firms base maintenance priorities on the worst-first rule, clearly a subjective judgement because this requires a judgement on what is "bad" and what is "worse". Too often, the assignment of priorities is based on corporate politics (for example, preference given to the boss or to the person who shouts the loudest and longest), not on economic or technological grounds.

Summary and conclusions

Software, when aged through enhancements, has the possibility of capturing unstated rules of decision-making and problem solving and even the culture of the enterprise. Such software represents years of experience and effort and becomes an important organizational resource, and should continue to be maintained to further increase its useful life. Unfortunately, the modifications necessary are not always minor ones that can be handled by maintenance procedures. Then the software must be reengineered or redeveloped. Whichever development path is taken, parts and components of the old software may be reused. We say little about maintenance of hardware for that is often under a contract (usually negotiated at the time of purchase) with the vendor.

Software is under the control of management. It often requires continuous attention through maintenance. Such development should follow the stages of an SDLC for any initial development and should be based on a formal user's maintenance requirement specification. Sometimes, the current system with its revisions and releases is often not adequately documented (if at all) and so reverse engineering may become necessary.

Control over maintenance activities is exceedingly important, since empirical data shows that security violations often occur during maintenance procedures. There is also a tendency to cut corners in maintenance work to get to more exciting projects. Control procedures should ensure that one job is completed before the next one is begun.

Maintenance is very costly and takes a large share of effort, compared to the effort spent in the initial development of information systems. Managers should recognize the strong correlation between high standards in the original development process and low maintenance. To reduce the need of maintenance, systems developers should plan ahead for equipment and software compatibility, test thoroughly for system weaknesses, and maintain high standards of documentation so that the effort needed for future maintenance is minimized.

One major problem of software maintenance management is finding and retaining personnel with the skill, patience, and dedication needed to trace errors and weaknesses of programs. Detecting, correcting, testing, and documenting changes is often less interesting work, from the analyst's point of view, than working on a new project.

For every maintenance project, the possibility of reuse must be carefully examined. Reuse not only saves time and money but it involves the use of parts that have proven to be reliable. Thus reuse must be made part of the thinking of all maintenance work. Also, the importance of maintenance must be recognized. It should *not* be made the exclusive territory of young/inexperienced (or trainee) programmers; nor should it be the dumping ground of programmers who are thought to have lost their creativity and productivity. Instead, maintenance work must be recognized as difficult – especially in the diagnostic stages of maintenance. The image of maintenance work being undesirable, uncreative, unrewarded and going-nowhere should be corrected.

Job enlargement, assigning maintenance responsibilities to systems analysts, and job rotation are approaches to maintenance management. Rotation has advantages: a pool of maintenance analysts provides a sort of "systems backup" resource and brings a variety of approaches and fresh solutions to maintenance problems.

Maintenance must be integrated in the design stage of every SDLC so that every information systems product is maintainable. This feature should also be part of all systems requirements.

Case 13.1: Some statistics on maintenance

- In 1988, software maintenance in the UK ranged from 5.3% to 90% of the software life cycle costs; whilst in 1986 it was 10 to 70% (Gorla, 1991:65).
- Applications cost 200% more to maintain than to develop (Gibson and Senn, 1989:347).
- Maintenance is reported to consume more than 50% of all life cycle resources (Rombach, 1991:86).
- In an NASA/SEL study, it was observed that the relationship between the modified and the newly developed modules was about 50:1...

    More that 50% of the completed maintenance requests were found to be corrections; however, they were less complex than other changes consuming little more than 28% of the overall maintenance resources.

    Rombach, 1991:90

- In a study by Peat Marwick (consulting in the US), of more than 60 million lines of code to be maintained in COBOL 80% of it was structured (Gibbon and Senn, 1989:348).
- Enhancements exceed repair of errors by a factor or three to four. *Journal of Systems Software*, vol. 23 (1993), p. 209.

Case 13.2: Study of software maintenance

A study by S. M. Deklave (*MIS Quarterly*, vol. 3, no. 2 (1992), pp. 355–72) found that modern maintenance methods lead to:

1. More reliable software.
2. Less frequent software maintenance.
3. More total maintenance time.

Robert Glass, editor of the *Journal of Systems and Software* comments on point 3, the increase in the total maintenance time:

> ... the software user, discovering that these new products are less costly to change, comes up with a whole new flock of changes ... The increasing maintenance cost effect doesn't kick in immediately after the software is put into production, Dekleva's data shows, for the first year of use, these modern-method-built systems actually incur lower maintenance costs. That probably correlates with the reduced frequency of repair mentioned above. It is only after the users get used to the system, flush out its early errors, and begin to realize what additional capabilities they wish the system had, that the maintenance workload begins to increase.

Source: *Journal of Systems and Software*, vol. 23, no. 2 (1993), pp. 209–210.

References

Bennett, K. H. (1991). "Automated Support of Software Maintenance." *Information and Software Technology*, vol. 33, no. 1 (January/February), pp. 74–85.

Capretz. M. A. M. and Munro, M. (1994). "Software Configuration Management Issues in the Maintenance of Existing Systems." *Journal of Software Maintenance*, vol. 6, no. 1 (January/February), pp. 1–14.

Dekleva, Sasa M. (1992). "The Influence of the Information Systems Development Approach to Management." *MIS Quarterly*, vol. 16, no. 3 (September), pp. 355–372.

Gabel, D. A. (1994). "Systems Engineering." *IEEE Spectrum*, vol. 31, no. 1 (June), pp. 38–41.

Gibson, V. R. and Senn, J. A. (1989). "Systems Structure and Systems Maintenance Performance." *Communications of the ACM*, vol. 32, no. 3 (March), pp. 347–58.

Gorla. N. (1991). "Techniques for Application Software Maintenance." *Information and Software Technology*, vol. 33, no. 1 (January/February), pp. 65–73.

Nicoll, Bill. (1992). "Buying Maintenance from Independent Organizations". *Data Processing*, vol. 24, no. 2 (December), pp. 6–8.

Parikh, Garish. (1986). *Handbook of Software Maintenance*. New York: Wiley.

Rombach, H. D. (1991). "Software Reuse: A Key to the Maintenance Problem." *Information and Software Technology*, vol. 33, no. 1 (January/February), pp. 85–92.

Schach, S. R. (1994). "The Economic Impact of Software Reuse on Maintenance." *Journal of Software Maintenance*, vol. 6, no. 4 (July/August), pp. 165–84.

Schatzenberg, Doreen R. (1993). "Total Quality Management for Maintenance Process Improvement." *Software Maintenance Research and Practice*, vol. 5, nos. 1–12, pp. 1–13.

Zvegintzov, Nicolas. (1994). "Immortal Software." *Datamation*, vol. 30, no. 9 (June 15), pp. 170–80.

Part Three: Technological Strategies

Civilization advances by extending the number of important operations which we can perform without thinking of them

Alfred North Whitehead

Introduction to Part Three

Having discussed the organization of computing and the strategies for development, we are now poised for a discussion of the strategies for operations and management of computing.

We start with the subject of data and knowledge. They are accessed and processed by software. But once they are collected they must be represented in a form that can be accessed by software and used to make inferences and provide desired information. This is the subject of Chapter 14. This chapter may be somewhat technical. If so, then the reader is advised to absorb as much as possible and come back later for a better appreciation of data and knowledge representation.

Data and knowledge are stored in a local data/knowledge base or on a "server" to be shared by users who use "client" computers. This computing paradigm is known as the *client–server system* and is the subject of Chapter 15. The clients and the servers are all distributed. What enables them to communicate with each other is being *networked* via telecommunications.

The alternative to the client–server approach is some centralized computing which also needs telecommunications and networks to communicate with others: whether to exchange data files or send letters by e-mail. The management of such networks and telecommunications is the subject of Chapter 16.

While telecommunications and networks are a great boon to humanity they do raise problems of management. One such problem is security. But security is also a problem for computing resources that are centralized and even physically locked up. They still face the danger of unauthorized access, propagation of computer viruses and computer crime. These dangers and attempts to protect against them are the subject of Chapter 17.

Security is part of control in an information system. But there are other considerations of control especially those of controlling quality of information generated and the control of performance. The variables are identified and defined, and the control of information systems are examined in Chapter 18.

Our final chapter in this part of the book is on project management. Projects in computing are required for most information systems development. But even after a system is developed and is operational, project management is needed as in reengineering and even maintenance and redevelopment.

Introduction to Part Three

In this section we are only concerned with selected topics in the management of computing. Other topics like the management of computer personnel have been discussed in earlier chapters and other topics like causes for success and failure of systems and the management of change will be discussed in other books. First, however, we will discuss the nature and representation of data and knowledge.

14 Data and Knowledge Representation

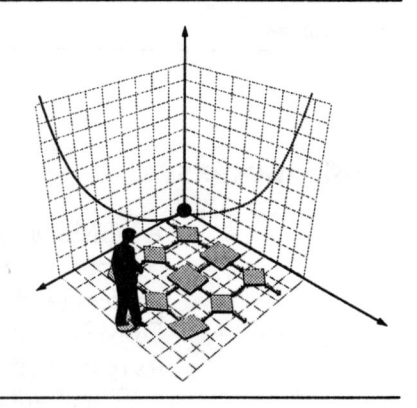

> Abstraction is a crucial feature... of knowledge, because in order to compare and classify the immense variety of shapes, structures, and phenomena around us we cannot take all their features into account, but have to select a few significant ones. Thus we construct an intellectual map of reality.
>
> Fritjof Capra in *Tao of Physics*

Introduction

In this chapter we examine the many ways of representing data and knowledge. We examine the sources of data and knowledge, and their many representations for an information system. For data, we look at the evolution of data and the different representations of data. For knowledge we examine the many ways of representing knowledge in a knowledge base including rules in decision tables, frames, prepositional logic, and the semantic network. We conclude by examining the computing resources needed for both data and knowledge representation.

Representation of data

The smallest unit of data representation from the end-user's viewpoint is a *record*, which is set of related data elements. As records grew larger, they were organized in *blocks* and a set of logical blocks constituted a *file*. As files got larger and their numbers grew, there came the need to integrate the files so as to reduce redundancies and inconsistencies, and also improve the efficiency of processing the data. This integrated set of data was called a *database*. As databases increased in number and complexity, there emerged a problem of having to manage the databases. To make this process efficient and effective, we needed a DBMS: a *database management system*.

DBMS models

A DBMS is software that provides the interface between data stored in computer readable form (e.g. on tape or disk) and people who want to process (add, delete, update, or retrieve) data. There are many types of DBMSs, each designed for a specific logical data model (framework) of its representation of data.

There are three basic data models for logical organization in widespread use: the *hierarchical* data model, the *network* data model (also known as the CODASYL model), and the *relational* data model. Each will now be described in turn.

Hierarchical data model

A typical business organization chart is shown in Figure 14.1. This same inverted tree structure with nodes and branches can be used in the organization of a database, a structure called the *hierarchical data model*. In this model, a node representing a file, record or data element with dependent nodes is called a *parent* (or owner), while each subordinate node is called a *child* (or member).

Figure 14.1:
Organization chart

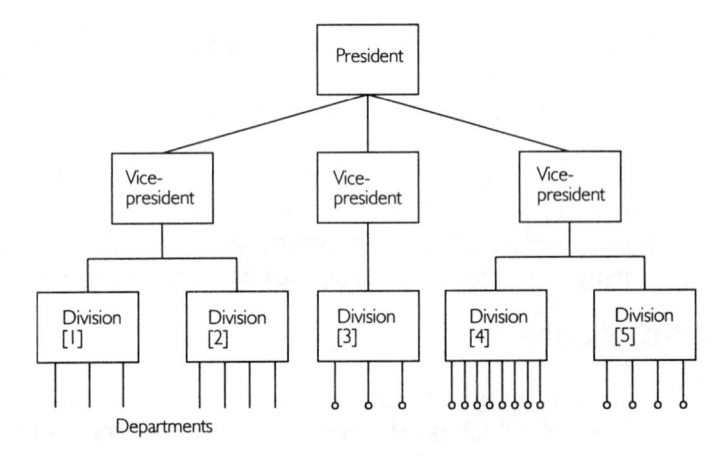

To illustrate, each node in level 3 is a child of a node in level 2 in Figure 14.2, but at the same time may be a parent of nodes in level 4.

A database organized in this hierarchical structure is shown in Figure 14.3. Note that every node has to be accessed through its parent (except, of course, the root). A DBMS that supports this logical organization of data follows established paths under program control in searching for an item – it does not have to search the entire forest.

The problem with this model is that analysts must spend much time working out data relationships when the logical structure of the data-

DBMS models

base is being designed. With a poorly structured database, some of the data may be difficult to access. Another problem is that new links must be forged when new kinds of data are added to the database. Care must be taken to ensure that these new links do not invalidate or corrupt existing connections.

Figure 14.2:
Hierarchical data model

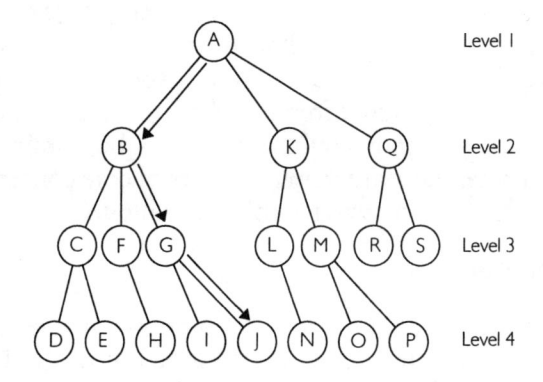

Node C is the child of B, but the parent of D and E. Node J can only be reached through the path A to B to G to J.

Figure 14.3:
Hierarchical database

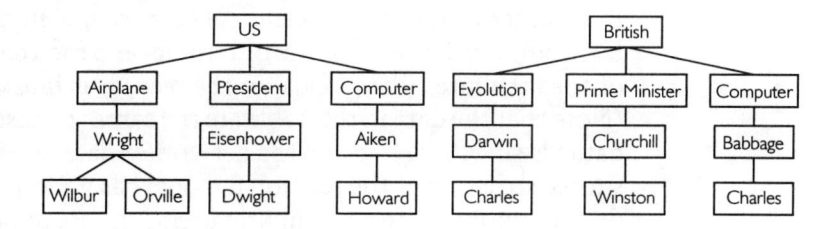

Network data model

The network data model resembles the hierarchical data model with one important exception – a child can have more than one parent. In Figure 14.4, which restructures the data in Figure 14.3, you will note that there are lateral connections as well as top-down connections within the database.

Figure 14.4:
Network database

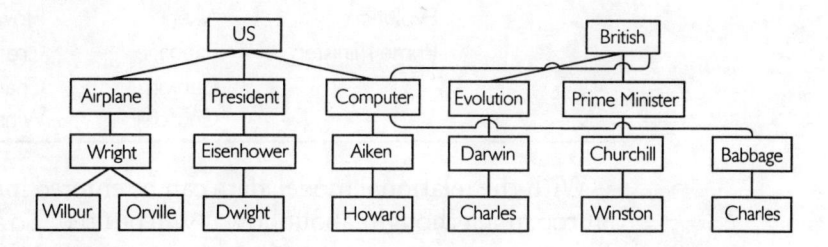

Chapter 14: Data and Knowledge Representation

This structure complicates database design and modification, but the model offers flexibility in searching for data without much loss of speed. The network data model was developed in 1971 by a working committee of CODASYL (Conference on Data System Languages), the group that developed the language standards for COBOL. But the reception of the model has been lukewarm despite the authoritative source of its design. One reason is that the model is complex and somewhat incohesive. Complaints have been made that decisions regarding the model's design were often based on group politics, not technical merit. Because agreement could not always be obtained in the CODASYL committee, there are many variants of core concepts that create confusion among those who try to use the model.

Relational data model

The relational data model, first proposed in the early 1970s by Dr. E.F. Codd of IBM, but not fully developed until the 1980s, is based on the mathematical theory of sets and relations. In this model, data relationships are represented in tables. (Although the relational databases can be conceptualized as a collection of related tables, it is formally a mathematical set of tables. A table is called a *relation* in mathematics.) Each horizontal row describes a record (tuple) and each column describes one of the attributes (data fields) of the record, as illustrated in Table 14.1 (Note that the data in this table are the same as those in the hierarchical database in Figure 14.3 and the networked database in Figure 14.4). The simple structure of the relational model has widespread appeal and has drawn supporters from computer users who are unhappy with the hierarchical network data models.

Table 14.1 *Relational database consisting of three tables*

Nationality	Fame category	Surname	First name
US	Airplane	Wright	Wilbur
British	President	Wright	Orville
	Computer	Eisenhower	Dwight
	Evolution	Aiken	Howard
	Prime Minister	Babbage	Charles
		Darwin	Charles
		Churchill	Winston

With the relational model, data can be entered into a database without too much thought about how it will be used. To add new data is like adding a new column of attributes or a new row at the bottom of the table. Programs can be written to manipulate or extract data from the database using relational algebraic operations such as AND, OR, NOT, *Join*, and *Project*. For example, the *Join* command will combine two tables to produce a third. *Project* will extract columns from one table and combine them into a new table. The power of relational systems is ascribed to this flexibility.

However, to find a particular item, a search of all the tables may have to be made by the computer system. In effect, each row in each table is searched sequentially until the item is found. Clearly this search process will be slow when databases are large. Moreover, every time that information is needed, the same search path takes place even though the same data may be needed hundreds of times a day in the processing of applications programs.

Although fast hardware may reduce search time, the cost of such hardware may raise the cost of processing. Speed may also be gained through programming effort. For example, an index can be prepared of common search paths with index pointers to frequently sought items. Then the computer can be programmed to scan this index as the first step of any search. The disadvantage is that this will lengthen search time for non-indexed items. Also, an index uses up computer storage space.

Which model is best?

Data experts have, for some time, been debating which DBMS data model is best. The answer depends, in part, on philosophical orientation. The hierarchical model is the oldest, and hierarchical DBMSs have long been the most popular on mainframes. People who think that the user or programmer should be able to have some control over the details of storage allocation and search paths often prefer a DBMS that supports network data organization. Those who believe that users should be isolated from the mechanisms used to access data, and those who assign high priority to a model that is easy to understand and construct frequently favour relational systems. Academics like the relational model because of its mathematical foundation. However, few DBMSs are fully relational. Instead they graft relational features onto a basic hierarchical/network structure.

A relational database differs from hierarchical and network data organization in two important ways: an explicit relationship between records in the database need not be defined and processing need not be done on a one-record-at-a-time basis. Consequently, relational databases allow flexible query and report generation. Use of the relational model is appropriate in generating answers to *ad hoc*, unstructured questions, like those that managers ask. The model is not appropriate for large batch processing used in functional applications such as payroll, accounts receivable and balance sheet generation.

Object-oriented DBMS

So much for the traditional DBMSs. An entry in the 1980s is the OO DBMS based on an object orientation. The system is based on the elemental data of an *object* which is an abstraction of the real-world system. An object models the composite units of activity and structure. An object can be a combination of data and chunks of code that can range in size from a small subroutine to a large application. Such objects, not algorithms, are the fundamental building blocks of an OO system. An object-oriented database has chunks that are not passively stored, manipulated and retrieved, but are active objects (see Partridge and Hussain: Chapter 16).

Database to knowledge base

Databases are adequate for transactional processing and DBMSs provide interactive dialogue languages (like the 4GLs) for accessing and querying the database. But all such processing involves the arithmetic manipulation of data.

Figure 14.5:
Content of knowledge

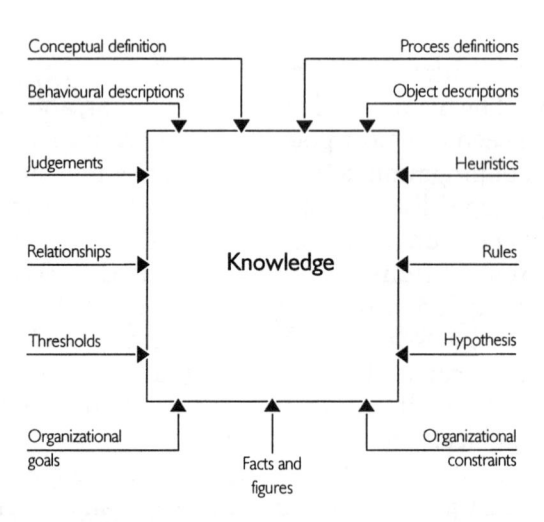

[Diagram: A box labeled "Knowledge" with arrows pointing inward from the following inputs: Conceptual definition, Behavioural descriptions, Judgements, Relationships, Thresholds, Organizational goals, Facts and figures, Process definitions, Object descriptions, Heuristics, Rules, Hypothesis, Organizational constraints]

What is also needed is the ability to make logical inferences such as those made by a human expert to generate new data and information from old ones, i.e. logical manipulation of data. To do this, what is needed are programming languages that can efficiently and effectively implement a mechanism of inference. To facilitate such making of inferences we need knowledge which is more than just straight data items. Knowledge includes facts, theories, heuristics, relationships, attributes, observations, definitions, and other types of information about a problem area gleaned from one or more experts in a given field, and supported by the literature, such as books and manuals, in that field of study. Content of knowledge is shown in Figure 14.5. Such knowledge is represented in a way that facilitates reaching an inference or a conclusion based on the knowledge available. Such representations of knowledge can take the form of either rules, frames, semantic networks, O–A–V triplets, logic or objects. Each of these representations will now be discussed.

Knowledge representation

Rules

Knowledge representation for use in making inferences (as do human experts) is the *rule*. It is used extensively in expert systems (ES) where the rule is applied to knowledge to reach a conclusion (or activate an action). These rules can be stated in an IF...Then (or IF...Then...Else) format are included in the knowledge base.

To facilitate the implementation of these rules for reaching a conclusion or activating an action, we need knowledge that must be represented such that it can be easily used by a programming language. For example, in the case of detecting a systems fault the rule is of the form:

IF condition(s) exist
Then take specific actions (or reach specific conclusions)

The above format of relating conditions to a conclusion (or action) is referred to as a *production rule*. It is extensively used in rule-based expert systems. It has the great advantage of being readily understood by domain experts as well as end-users.

Basically, a production rule has an antecedent and a consequent. The antecedent is the set of conditions. The consequent could be an action in which case the satisfaction of the antecedent is equivalent to scheduling an action for execution. Alternatively, the consequent could be a conclusion, in which case the satisfaction of the antecedent would lead to a conclusion such as an expert's opinion in an expert system.

This form of statement is easily programmed by many a procedural 3GL (third generation language) like FORTRAN, PL/1, Pascal or other language inheriting the ALGOL IF...Then... Else structure. The rules

Knowledge representation

can be expressed in a set of questions or answers as expressed schematically in Figure 14.6: determining whether an animal is an elephant or a tiger. This may seem a very trivial problem but in structure it is similar to a decision tree commonly used in decision-making for a DSS (decision support system).

Figure 14.6:
Dialogue with an expert system and rules to identify an elephant and a tiger

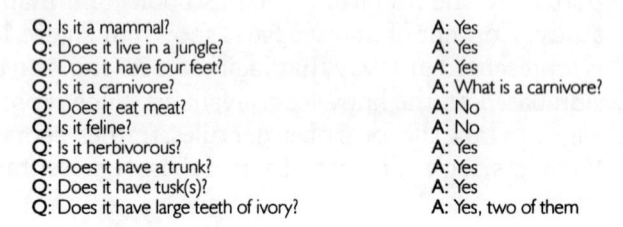

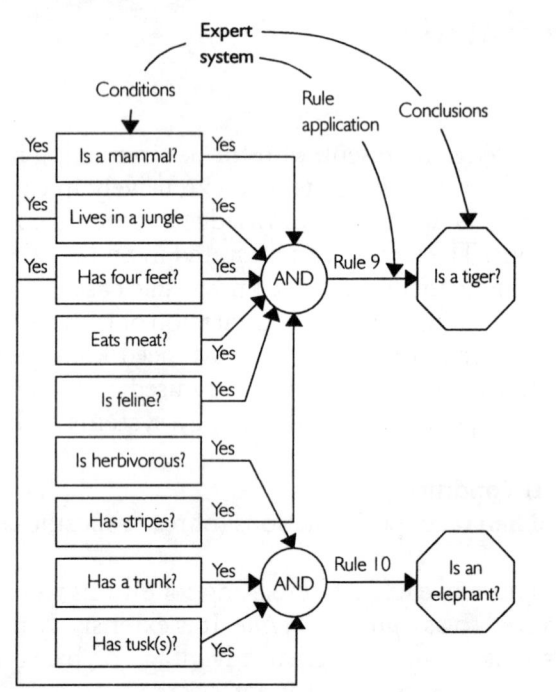

Q: Is it a mammal?   A: Yes
Q: Does it live in a jungle?   A: Yes
Q: Does it have four feet?   A: Yes
Q: Is it a carnivore?   A: What is a carnivore?
Q: Does it eat meat?   A: No
Q: Is it feline?   A: No
Q: Is it herbivorous?   A: Yes
Q: Does it have a trunk?   A: Yes
Q: Does it have tusk(s)?   A: Yes
Q: Does it have large teeth of ivory? A: Yes, two of them

It can be expressed as an equivalent in a decision table as is shown in a partial decision table in Figure 14.7. The conditional stubs that are relevant to an action or decision, the equivalent of the IF part of the statement, appear in the left-hand upper quadrant; action stubs, the equivalent of the THEN part of the statement, appear in the lower left-hand quadrant. Each decision rule is a column to the right of the vertical double line. Thus rule 9 in Figure 14.7 says that *IF* the object being examined is a mammal, *AND* lives in a jungle, *AND* has four feet, *AND* is feline, *AND* is not herbivorous (a plant-eater), *AND* has stripes, *AND* has no

314

trunk, *AND* has no tusks it is *THEN* a tiger. Rule 10 says that *IF* the object is a mammal, *AND* likes jungles, *AND* has four feet, *AND* does not eat meat (is not a carnivore), *AND* is not feline, *AND* is herbivorous, *AND* does not have stripes, *AND* has a trunk, *AND* has tusks, *THEN* that object is an elephant.

Figure 14.7: *A partial decision table showing rules 9 and 10 for the elephant and tiger example*

	...	Rule 9	Rule 10
Is it a mammal?		Y	Y
Lives in a jungle?		Y	Y
How many feet?		4	4
Does it eat meat?	:	Y	N
Is it feline?		Y	N
Is it herbivorous?		N	Y
Does it have stripes?		Y	N
Does it have a trunk?		N	Y
Does it have tusks?		N	Y
It is a tiger	...	X	
It is an elephant			X

Y = yes, N = no, X = conclusion

Although the above rules seem adequate at first glance, baby elephants lack tusks as do some mature female elephants, while some male elephants lose their tusks in fights. Therefore, the identification of an elephant should not depend on the presence of tusks as rule 10 states. In many subject domains, only experts have the necessary knowledge and knowledge engineers have the experience to state complete, unambiguous and unique rules.

Rules have the advantage of being able to readily capture problem-solving knowledge in a standardized representation format which facilitates checking and coding. The great disadvantage of rules is that they cannot be modified incrementally without unpredictable interactions with other rules. Also, with a large number of rules, the system becomes unwieldy to validate and difficult to maintain – the structure is too flat and diverse.

The rule representation is often appropriate for an expert system, and a 3GL for can be used for programming it. However, some expert systems and many other AI applications use another form of representation. One such early data representation was the *frame* which will now be discussed.

Frames

A frame is a knowledge representation proposed specifically for work in artificial intelligence by one of its pioneers Marvin Minsky. Similar structures are found in cognitive psychology as models of human memory. A frame is a data structure for representing a stereotyped situation. Attached to each frame are several types of information including information on how to use the frame. This information "attached to each frame" is in a slot, which is an extension of a field in a record or file in that it goes beyond merely holding a value. These slots define an event or a concept at each node (a point where an item links to another item or branch). A slot can contain information on rules, pointers to other frames, default values, as well as procedures. The procedures could be of many kinds, like the "IF-added" procedure to be executed when new information is placed in the slot; or the "IF-remove" procedure to be executed if information is deleted from the slot. These procedural attachments are incorporated in what would otherwise be a declarative representation. Also, frames can allow inheritance by appropriate linking.

Ideally, a frame is a small chunk of information that is easy to understand as well as easy to modify. This latter characteristic is important because a frame is a dynamic representation in short-term memory, memory actively used during a problem-solving session. As the system acquires more facts or there is a changed environment, the frame changes accordingly.

Frames are very useful when the content of information is important in problem-solving as in pattern-recognition of speech or visual screens of pictorial representations, where changes in slots may cause a change in a pictorial representation, called "active value" slots. Thus, frames allow for a very rich representation, but they have the disadvantage of being difficult to maintain because the interactions between frames are often not clearly defined. Also, there are many relationships between frames preventing modularity in a frame system.

Figure 14.8:
Example of a frame

```
Frame: Elephant
Superclass: Mammal
Subclass: Circus elephant

Value slot:
  Habitat: Jungle
  Colour: Grey
  Size: Very large
  Feet: Four
  Tusks: Default: two
  Food: Vegetation
  Rule slot: If a herbivorous mammal has
    a trunk and tusks, then it is an elephant.
```

Figure 14.8 is a sample frame containing descriptive information about an elephant. It would facilitate a knowledge-base search for rules and relevant data necessary to answer user queries of Figure 14.6 since all relevant information on an elephant is organized in a logical grouping. This frame has a default value of two tusks. Since some elephants may not have two tusks (because of deformity or loss of a tusk in battle), two tusks are a default value. Specifying a default allows us to assume the most obvious value unless otherwise specified. We also have (in Figure 14.8), an upward pointer to a superclass, a mammal, which makes an elephant a mammal by inheritance and gives it all the characteristics of a mammal. There is also a downward pointer to a special case, a circus elephant, which has a frame of its own with the peculiarities of a circus elephant stated in there. Thus the frame structure allows linking in an inheritance hierarchy as well as a representation of a concept in isolation of class of objects, or individual instances which are components of objects.

Semantic network

Another option to organize knowledge is the *semantic network*. Here we need to define the two terms: semantic and network. Semantic refers to "meaning" and network is a structure with "connections". A semantic network then is a structure of interconnected nodes that represent some logical meanings. The nodes represent objects, events or activities as well as descriptors that further describe the nodes – much like adjectives describe a noun. The interconnections are links referred to as *arcs*, which represent relationships between objects. The arcs can be one of many kinds:

1. "Is a" link: short for "is a", as in "an elephant is an animal".
2. "Has a" link: short for "has a" as in "an elephant has a trunk".
3. Definitional link: as in "an elephant is a very large herbivorous animal". A definitional link may be found in a specialized dictionary.
4. Heuristic link: captures heuristic information, like in "an elephant normally lives in a jungle because it must eat large quantities of leaves".

Figure 14.9:
Semantic network representation of an elephant

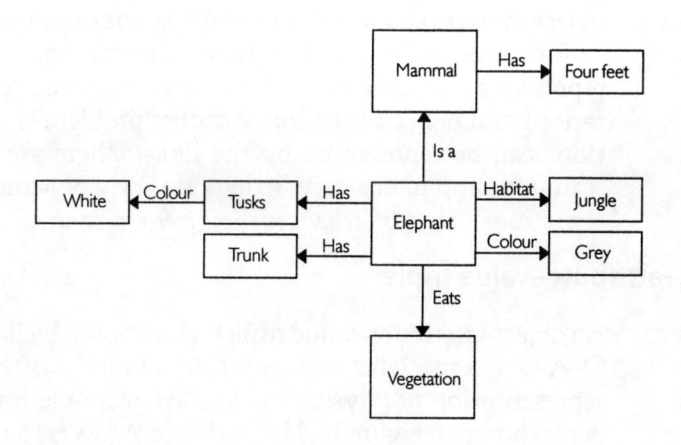

An example of a semantic network for an elephant is shown in Figure 14.9 containing information about an elephant that would facilitate a knowledge-base search for the type of questions raised in Figure 14.6

since all the information relating to an elephant is organized into a logical grouping.

We have persisted with the elephant case in order to provide some continuity and comparison with examples for other representation structures. But for diversity, let us consider another example, that of a car, as shown in Figure 14.10.

Figure 14.10:
Semantic network example

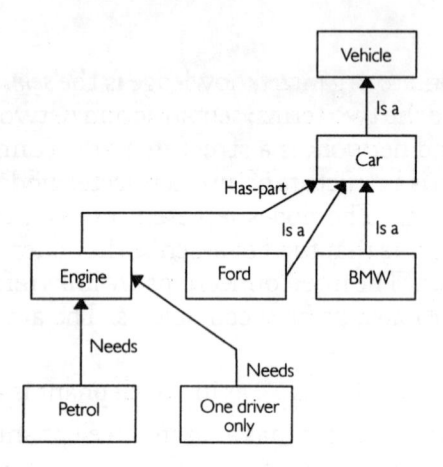

In it, a car has an engine, needs petrol and needs one driver only. Now we have the "is a" link connecting a Ford and a BMW to a car. Now the Ford and the BMW inherit all the characteristics of the car (has an engine, etc.). We do not need to repeat these characteristics. We merely add an "is a" link from the new object to the object class and the new object inherits characteristics of its parent object class.

One problem with semantic nets is that the "is a" relationship can represent a class or a relation or an instance leading to multiple interpretations and hence confusion. Another problem is that a variety of relations can be represented by the links. There are no widely accepted standards and hence very little portability of semantic network representations. Everyone devises their own network.

Object–attribute–value triplet

An object–attribute–value triplet, also known by its acronym OVA or as O–A–V, is a special case of semantic nets and is often used in knowledge representation of physical objects. An example for selecting a dog as a pet is shown in Figure 14.11. The bottom row is the set of attributes that are the input, the higher levels are attributes that are inferred.

Figure 14.11:
Object–attribute–value triplet for selecting a dog

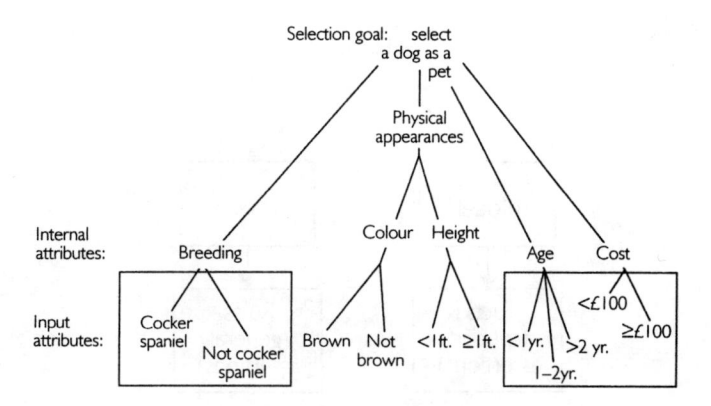

When all attributes are inferred according to the rules of what values of attributes are acceptable, then the final goal (in this case, the selection of a pet dog) is reached. Thus it may be necessary to associate values to attributes by giving an object–attribute–value triplet of information. For instance, using the dog/pet example, suppose that the selection criteria was a dog that had to be brown, a cocker spaniel, less than 1 ft (0.3m) high, between 1 and 2 years old, and had to cost less than £100. Constrained values, when violated, are rejected. A dog with attributes satisfying all conditions on its values is accepted.

The OAV method is more structured than the semantic nets but as the number of objects increases, the attributes associated with the objects also increases, making the OAV method conceptually complex. This is often the case with large organizations. In such cases we may wish to consider logic representations.

Logic

One type of logic is propositional logic, where a statement as a proposition may be either true or false. Statements can be linked together into compound statements by the connectives AND, OR or NOT. A truth table will give the true or false value of a compound statement. Thus if X is true and Y is false, then X AND Y is false but X OR Y is true. A more complex type of logic is predicate calculus, where statements or assertions about objects are called predicates. Thus "is animal (elephant)" is an assertion that the "is animal" predicate is true of the object "elephant" – i.e. it is stating that an elephant is an animal. A specific assertion is then a fact used by a model whilst a general assertion is a rule and may be part of a theory. Both model and theory are part of logic as shown in Figure 14.12.

Chapter 14: Data and Knowledge Representation

Knowledge representation

Figure 14.12:
Rules, facts, and logic

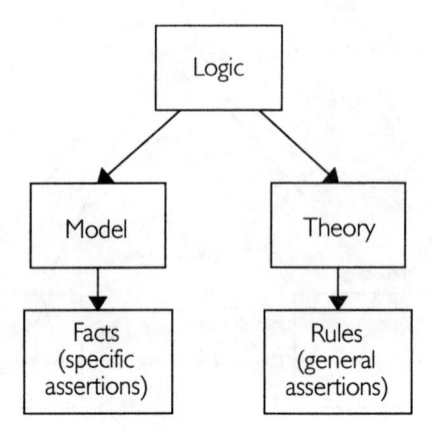

```
            Logic
           /     \
       Model    Theory
         |        |
       Facts    Rules
     (specific) (general
    assertions) assertions)
```

An example of the use of logic in a query situation in order to arrive at an answer is shown in Figure 14.13.

Figure 14.13:
Logic example

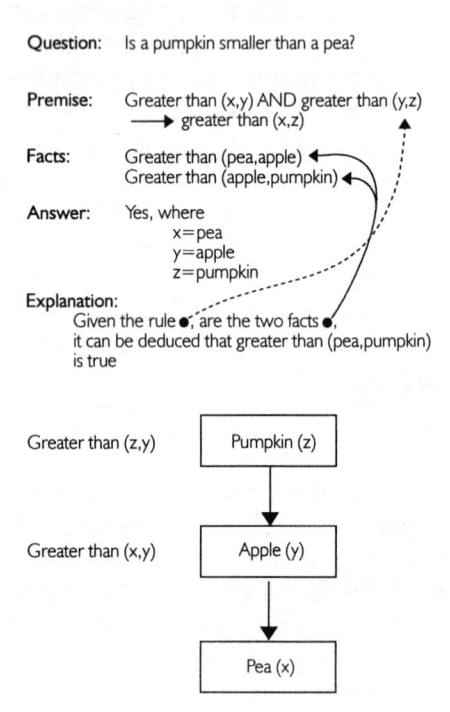

Question: Is a pumpkin smaller than a pea?

Premise: Greater than (x,y) AND greater than (y,z) ⟶ greater than (x,z)

Facts: Greater than (pea,apple)
Greater than (apple,pumpkin)

Answer: Yes, where
x=pea
y=apple
z=pumpkin

Explanation:
Given the rule •, are the two facts •,
it can be deduced that greater than (pea,pumpkin) is true

Greater than (z,y) | Pumpkin (z)

Greater than (x,y) | Apple (y)

| Pea (x)

Note the possible ambiguity in the example of a pumpkin being larger than a pea. In it there was an assertion that a pumpkin is larger than a pea. But is it possible that a small pumpkin is smaller than a large apple? If so, then the ambiguity must be resolved by making assertions about small pumpkins and not just any pumpkin or else the knowledge base using logic will not arrive at an answer that is always true.

Databases and knowledge bases

We made the statement earlier that databases are not usually appropriate for situations where we need to make inferences. Having just discussed the knowledge base, we can now confirm that statement and appreciate the differences between the conventional databases and knowledge-based systems. There are also many differences in terminology and there are many equivalencies. These are listed in Table 14.2. There are other differences. One important distinction is that the conventional database supports procedural programming languages while knowledge-based systems are typically declarative (If A is true then B is true) and are supported by AI languages like LISP and PROLOG.

Table 14.2 *Similarity mappings of a database to a knowledge base*

Databases	Knowledge bases
▪ Data	▪ Knowledge
▪ Input preparation	▪ Knowledge acquisition
▪ Output devices	▪ Presentation module
▪ Data representation:	▪ Knowledge representation:
▪ File	▪ Rule
▪ Hierarchical	▪ Frame
▪ CODASYL	▪ Semantic network
▪ Relational	▪ Logic
▪ Object orientation	▪ Object–attribute–value
▪ Database management system	▪ Knowledge-based management system

Conventional databases and knowledge-based systems are distinct but they may well come together. In fact there are currently many attempts at extending the heavily logic-oriented relational model to include knowledge bases. There is the advantage that there already exists a standard for the relational query language, SQL. Other attempts are in favour of object-oriented databases, with the continuing debate over whether it should be grafted on top of the relational model or developed entirely separately.

Resources needed

Of the resources needed for data and knowledge representation the main element is the *human resource* because the processes involved are human-intensive. However, there may be equipment consequences as a result of the selected representation structure. In the case of a database, if a DBMS is selected then there is the cost of the DBMS software and the need of a CPU to run the software. In cases of small and simple databases, the CPU needed would be a PC and most likely will not represent an incremental cost. But selecting the data model and the DBMS for a large and complex system would require additional resources (hardware and software) and could be costly. It is also a very important decision because it cannot be revoked or changed very easily or without much pain and disruption.

The choice of a knowledge representation schema may also have resource implications. As an illustration, consider a rule-base system being chosen. In this case, a procedural language with an IF... Then structure will most likely represent no incremental cost. However, the selection of a frame or a semantic network may need an AI language like PROLOG or LISP. And if LISP is used extensively, then a LISP processor may be necessary although LISP processing if often possible on a scientific workstation.

Human resources are also needed for knowledge representation including the knowledge engineer (KE) who is crucial and important to any knowledge-based system (KBS). The KE plays an important (and even dominant) role in the development of a KBS. In this chapter we discuss the KE very briefly, identifying the characteristics necessary for the knowledge representation function to be performed.

A knowledge engineer is perhaps first and foremost a computer expert well versed in AI programming languages, AI tools and techniques including knowledge bases and knowledge structures. Also, the KE must be able to interact effectively with the human domain experts and induce them to articulate their expertise in a complete and precise manner. The knowledge engineer must be able to translate the human expert's decision strategies into facts, rules and heuristics of the appropriate structure. The KE must also be able to translate inferences emanating from the knowledge structure into a form that the human expert can evaluate, giving results that the end-user can apply with ease and confidence.

The human resource needed, other than the KE, is for data representation. For systems involving an institutional database, this is the function of the DBA (database administrator).

Summary and conclusions

The 1970s and 1980s saw a dramatic growth in corporate databases. Beyond the 1990s, growth may slow (relatively speaking) but still be substantial. One manager recently reported an estimated 312 billion bits of data are delivered to his desk each month. The growth in database size is shown in Figure 14.14.

Figure 14.14:
Growth of corporate databases

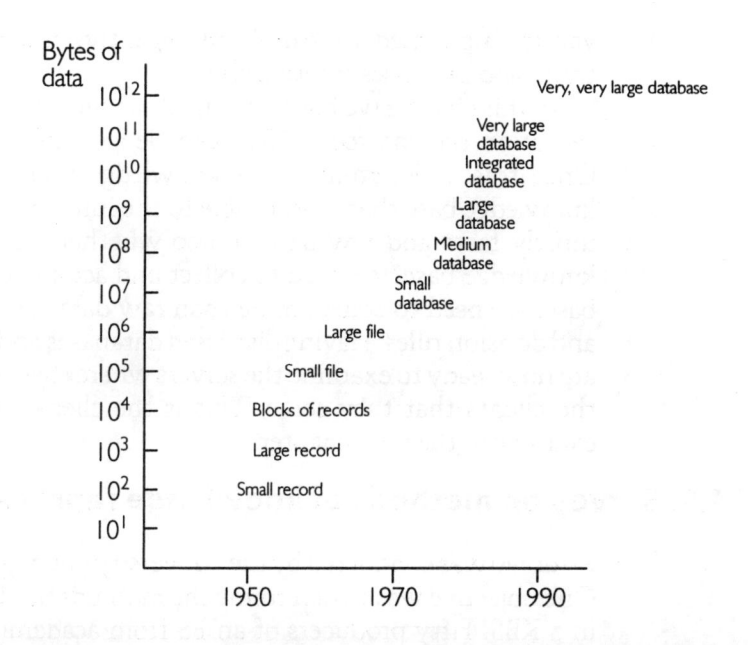

Bytes of data:
- 10^{12} — Very, very large database
- 10^{11} — Very large database
- 10^{10} — Integrated database
- 10^{9} — Large database
- 10^{8} — Medium database
- 10^{7} — Small database
- 10^{6} — Large file
- 10^{5} — Small file
- 10^{4} — Blocks of records
- 10^{3} — Large record
- 10^{2} — Small record
- 10^{1}

(x-axis: 1950, 1970, 1990)

The growth has been facilitated by advances in technology for example, the development of inexpensive random access memory (RAM) chips, making it practical to store large databases in computer memory; the manufacture of disk drives combining megabyte (million byte) to gigabyte (billion byte) capacities with fast access times; and the availability of DBMSs (database management systems) to assist in the creation, maintenance, and utilization of integrated databases.

There are three important representation schemas for a database: *hierarchical*, *network* (CODASYL) and *relational*. These models are still important to transactional systems and even some DSSs but not to many AI applications. Hence the need for knowledge-based representations (rules, frames, semantic nets, O–A–V, and logic) for knowledge-based systems and the emergence of object-oriented systems. One view of the evolution of these databases is shown in Figure 14.15.

Figure 14.15: *The evolution of databases and knowledge bases*

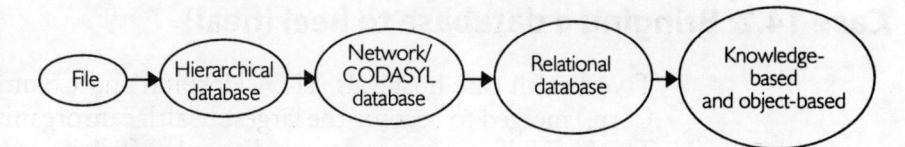

File → Hierarchical database → Network/CODASYL database → Relational database → Knowledge-based and object-based

What is not shown is the possible evolution of an "intelligent" database. Such a database would be able to process complex transactional (as well as DSS) environments. It would also processes knowledge with varying input media and do so intelligently – much as the human beings think and processes information.

In this chapter we have examined the selection of a knowledge representation schema for a KBS (knowledge-based information system). Once this is determined, the knowledge must be coded to create a knowledge base that is accessible to the inference engine. Knowledge is mostly facts and raw data and so whether we have a database or a knowledge base, we need to collect and acquire data. For a knowledge base, we need to collect more than raw data: we need facts, heuristics and decision rules. Having discussed databases and knowledge bases, we are now ready to examine the servers where these bases often reside and the clients that they serve. This is the client–server system that we examine in the next chapter.

Case 14.1: Survey on methods of knowledge representation

A survey was conducted by the University of Loughborough in 1987/88. One objective was to determine the methods used in making inferences in a KBS. Fifty producers of an ES from academia, industry and commerce were interviewed in depth. The results for methodologies used in knowledge representation were as follows:

Form of representation	%
Rules	56
Everything	17
Frames	10
Semantic nets	7
Decision trees	5
Object-oriented programming	5

Source: O'Neill, Margaret and Morris, Ann (1989). "Expert Systems in the United Kingdom: An Evaluation of Development Methodologies." *Expert Systems*, vol. 6, no. 2 (April), pp. 90–1.

Case 14.2: Bringing a database to heel (heal)

Two health care hospitals (HCA Hospital and Columbia Health Care Corp.) merged to become the largest health care organization in the US. The $5.7 billion merger expected to gain efficiencies from the merger. An assistant VP for systems support commented:

> The mergers real story from the IT perspective is the database. Having such a large volume should give them strategic advantages. They have a

tremendous opportunity to analyze a huge amount of data on patient care... The question now is whether HCA/Columbia management understands the challenge... In the health care industry, particularly on the provider side, the real shortfall is having senior mangers who know how to ask the right questions... As a result, the data has been locked up and has not been used for strategic advantage.

Source: *Information Week*. (October 11, 1993), p. 15.

References

Baugh, P., Gillies A., and Jastrzebski, P. (1993). "Combining Knowledge-Based and Database Technology in a Tool of Business Planning." *Information and Software Technology*, vol. 35, no. 3 (March), pp. 131–138.

Boulanger, Danielle and March, Salvatore T. (1989). "An Approach to Analyzing the Information Content of Existing Databases." *Database*, vol. 20, no. 2, pp. 1–8.

Eddison, Elizabeth B. (1988). "How to Plan and Build Your Own Database." *Database*, vol. 11, no. 3, pp. 11–5.

Kellogg, Charles. (1986). "From Data Management to Knowledge Management." *Computer*, vol. 19, no. 1 (January), pp. 75–83.

Kelner, Art. (1989). "Reflections on Database Design." *Personal Computing*, vol. 13, no. 11, pp. 109–12.

Hedberg, Sara. (1993). "New Knowledge Tools." *Byte*, vol. 18, no. 8 (July), pp. 106–111.

Parasaye, K., Chignell, Mark *et al.* (1990). "Intelligent Database." *AI Expert*, vol. 5, no. 3 (March), pp. 38–47.

Robinson, A. E. (1990). "Current Ideas in Knowledge-based Management Systems." *Information and Software Technology*, vol. 32, no. 4 (May), pp. 266–273.

Silberschatz, Michael Stonebraker and Ulman, Jeff. (1991). "Database Systems: Achievements and Opportunities." *Communications of the ACM*, vol. 34, no. 10 (October), pp. 110–20.

Stein, Richard Marlon. (1994). "Object Databases." *Byte*, vol. 19, no. 4 (April), pp. 74–83.

Subramanian, Girish H., Nosek, John *et al.* (1992). "A comparison of the Decision Table and the Decision Tree." *Communications of the ACM*, vol. 35, no. 1 (January), pp. 89–104.

Thuraisingham, Bhavani. (1989). "From Rules to Frames and Frames to Rules." *AI Expert*, vol. 4, no. 10 (October), pp. 30–9.

Yoon, Y. and Guimaraes, T. (1992). "Developing Knowledge-Based Systems: An Object-Oriented Organizational Approach." *Information Resource Management Journal*, vol. 5, no. 3, pp. 15–32.

15 The Client–Server Paradigm

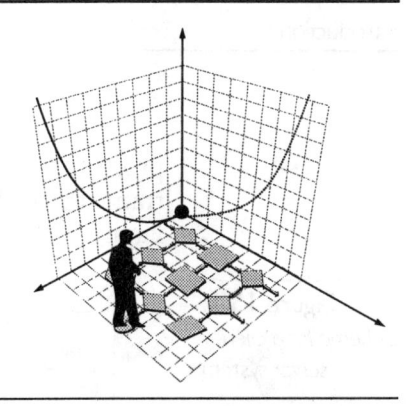

> In the 21st century, it will no longer be sufficient to put computers into environments. They must be part of the environment.
>
> Bill Joy, VP of *Micro Systems*

Introduction

In the early days of computing, computers were expensive and computer personnel were scarce. Development and operations were centralized. Soon, there was a backlog of applications and a lot of "noise" between the end-user and the computing providers. A reaction was towards decentralization into distributed processing where computing was decentralized while much of the centralized computing shifted to the nodes and later to the end-user. Meanwhile, there were two important technological developments. One was the arrival of the PC in the early 1980s with the promise of performance/price ratios higher than the mighty mainframe and yet small enough to stay on the desktop. But, the PCs were isolated from other computing resources like the expensive peripherals and the corporate database. In the mid-1980s came the second computing development which was the LAN (local area network). This enabled PCs (and other computers) to "talk" to each other and share the scarce resources of peripherals and databases. A LAN provided interconnectivity. What was also needed, however, were computer processors that would facilitate the sharing and serve out these resources. Thus the *server* came about. The *file server* was for sharing data and the *printer servers* were for sharing printer resources. But soon this was not adequate. The number of PCs rose dramatically with a resultant increase in the number of end-users and clients. Processors ranged widely: more power at a lower price. Peripherals became more versatile, requiring not just printer servers, but also *image processing servers*, and *voice processing servers*. These servers, with the database and application

Introduction

programs residing on them, were accessible to any PC, mini, or mainframe through a bus or a LAN. Such a client–server system is shown in Figure 15.1.

Figure 15.1:
Schema for a client–server system

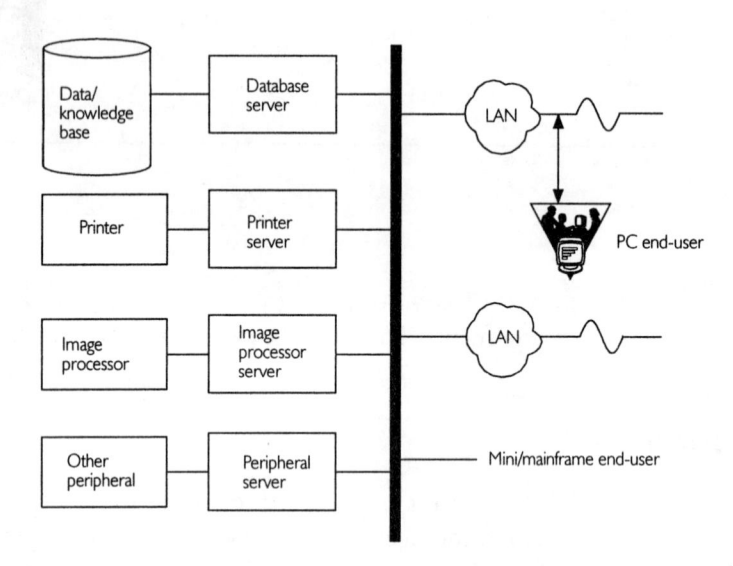

There were many limitations to the PC-centric approach. One was the lack of adequate administrative control and systems management tools. Also, there was a high cost of data swappage and network traffic as well as the inefficient use of the processors both at the end-user end and at the server end. A solution was to distribute the load and responsibilities between the processor at the front-end, called the *client*, and the back-end, called the *server*. Thus the *client–server* paradigm was born. It is the focus of this chapter. We start by examining the resources of a client–server system:

- Hardware (processor and user interfaces).
- Software.
- Communications facilities.
- Human resources.
- The organizational environment necessary for the client–server to be successful.

We will also examine the concern of corporate management with "downsizing" and "rightsizing", examine the advantages of the client–server paradigm and discuss the obstacles involved in its implementation. We conclude with a discussion of the client–server paradigm as used by many end-users for cooperative processing.

Components and functions of a client–server system

An overview of the client–server approach is shown in Figure 15.2. It is compared with the earlier configuration with a host acting as "master" and the connected PCs (or minis) acting as "slaves".

Figure 15.2: *Host computing vs. the client–server system*

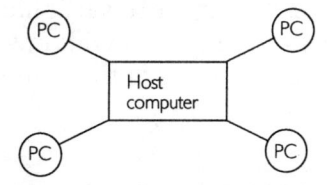

Host computing with master–slave orientation

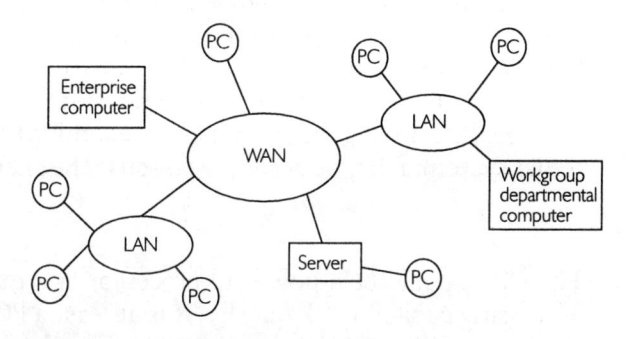

Distributed networking with client–server orientation

Figure 15.3: *Components of a client–server system*

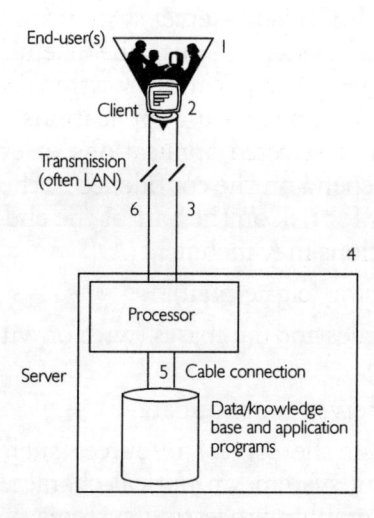

With the client–server approach, each PC is independent for local processing and sharing the centralized equipment (especially servers)

Chapter 15: The Client–Server Paradigm

through a LAN. In the case of widely dispersed clients and servers, the access could be through a MAN (metropolitan area network) or a WAN (wide area network).

The corporate database and enterprise-wide application programs typically reside with the server and are accessed by the end-user through the client processor, the LAN, and the server as illustrated in Figure 15.3. Each of the components of the system will now be discussed in turn. (The section numbering corresponds to the numbers in Figure 15.3)

1. The user

The user is typically the end-user, who accesses the client for service. The end-user could be a corporate manager, a professional or employee of the corporation or it could be a customer. Here is where some confusion can arise. The customer in business and commerce is called a client, but this client is a human, not to be confused with the client in computing which is a processor. We shall have more to say about the user and end-user later in this chapter when we examine the impact of the client–server system. First, however, we discuss the client.

2. Client

The client could be a powerful processor or a dumb terminal with no processing capability. Typically, it is at least a PC with its own operating system. Most of the processing is often done by the server and the division of work is determined by a computer program, which is why programs designed for a client–server system are different from a traditional transactional system. Thus, the client–server system is an enabling technology with applications written specifically for it. Sometimes this means rewriting existing applications. Whether this needs to be all applications or selected applications or even "mission critical" applications will depend on the confidence in the client–server system and the propensity for risk on the part of the end-user and IT management. The applications may include:

- Message processing (e.g., e-mail).
- Accessing local files and databases (with or without a DBMS) for local computing.
- Computing on server-supplied data.
- Sharing (through the server) resources such as the corporate image processing system, an optical character recognition system, advanced graphic processing systems, a colour plotter, or just a fast laser printer (note that these peripherals may all be produced by a variety of vendors).

Given a well designed application, a powerful server and a fast, well-tuned network, one can have quick results. The entire system behind the client may be totally invisible and transparent to the end-user who does not need (or may not care) to know where or how the processing is done.

To facilitate the query processing from a client, most client–server systems use a *structured query language* (SQL) which is a high-level dialogue language competing in its end-user friendliness with many 4GLs. SQL is compared with its equivalent in English in Figure 15.4.

Figure 15.4:
Sample query processing instruction compared to one in English

English: Find the employees working for Mr. Smith who make under £40,000 annually.

Query: For a client processor:

```
SELECT NAME
FROM PERSONNEL
WHERE MANAGER='SMITH'
AND SALARY <40000
```

SQL, along with its relational database (residing with the server), is almost a *de facto* standard for client–server systems, though more recent semantics of the language are increasingly object-oriented. Meanwhile, SQL does allow access to multiple database servers providing access to a wide range of decision-making information and knowledge residing in remote and dispersed locations.

An important component of a client processor is its UI (user interface), through which the user communicates. For a user such as a programmer, the UI need not be very user-friendly, but for an end-user it had better be end-user friendly or else it may not be used at all. A GUI, (graphical user interface) is usually preferred because it enables end-user access via graphical icons rather than (often verbose) commands.

In the future, GUIs may be able to accept and deliver information not just in terms of numbers and text but also graphics, voice, video, images, and animation; thereby becoming a multimedia terminal.

However, the more facilities, the more powerful the client processor needs to be. For simple data manipulation, even a laptop would suffice, but for more complex and large amounts of processing, a workstation may be appropriate. However, a workstation can be three or six times as costly as a PC depending on the "bells and whistles" (features) attached. However, a workstation is faster, has more memory and access to more programming languages (depending on what functions have to be performed). If it is a general purpose workstation, the most popular business programs would be the word processor, the spreadsheet, e-mail, DBMS processing, and business graphics.

For a DSS (decision support system), greater speeds, computing power (e.g., for business simulations) and access to programming languages (including simulation languages like SIMSCRIPT) are required. For a KBS (knowledge-based system) like an expert system, AI languages like PROLOG and LISP will be necessary. For an engineering workstation one needs not only computing power, but powerful graphics capability for applications like CAD (computer-aided design) and systems simulation.

A solution to the expensive workstation is to have an *X terminal*, which is essentially a workstation without a disk. It is designed specifically for the type of processing and functions of a client–server system with the focus on network communications, graphics performance, and an end-user friendly interface. The X terminal is actually an "application-specific" workstation optimized for running the X protocol. The X windows protocol:

> ...can support any number of windows with any type of font or window size. Also, the X terminal's bitmapped screen allows the application to display all sorts of data formats (text, images, drawings and so on) simultaneously, enhancing the user's productivity.
>
> *Socarras*, 1991:52

An X terminal can be connected directly to a LAN, through a workstation by cable, or with more than one X terminal attached to one workstation. The X Windows system is the *de facto* standard for the larger machines in the UNIX environment. For the PC, the *de facto* standard is Microsoft Windows. These *de facto* standards provide network transparency so that an application run on a server thousands of miles away will appear on the screen of the client and would appear to be running on the local client processor.

> Ironically, the X terminal's greatest virtue is the lack of functionality. By having no programmability, no local diskette drive, it is impossible for anyone to introduce unqualified software at the desktop. As a result, all software on the application sever is installed under the quality assurance of the IS organization. In addition, the inability to download files and copy them to a diskette, improves the data security of the network.
>
> *Connor*, 1993:52

3. Network and transmission

The server and the client can be connected together by hardwire. However, when they are dispersed, they must be connected to a LAN, which in turn is part of a MAN or WAN. This enables a corporation to have an enterprise network that may be strung around the country and yet operate individually, in a workgroup, or at a departmental or local level. For this to occur, it is important that there is interoperability, i.e., the operation and exchange of information in a heterogeneous mix of equipment using the network. Interoperability also implies an open network architecture. The earliest architecture was the SNA (Systems Network Architecture) by IBM, but this was not open to all vendors. Some, especially those in Europe, objected and supported the OSI (Open Systems Interconnection) proposed by the ISO (International Standards Organization). IBM has been manoeuvred by its European customers into accepting OSI, which (along with TCP/IP used by the Internet) is now the *de facto* communications standard even though there are many diehard SNA supporters around – especially in the US. The OSI model defines a basic set of rules and conventions for each of the seven functional layers of the OSI model (physical, data link, network, transport, sessions, presentation, and applications).

The essence of openness is that there is interchangeability of components of the system and therefore the vendors have to compete with better products and better service. Both customers and vendors benefit from this competition.

One very desirable feature of a client (and a server) is that it has an open architecture which ensures *interoperability*: hardware and software can operate interchangeably on each other's equipment despite being non-homogeneous. This is not the vendors' preference because they would like you to acquire all your equipment and software from them and have a captive market. In conflict to the vendor, it is in the interest of the customer to have the flexibility to mix-and-match components of the client–server system.

4. Servers

Connectivity, though very important, is not all that is needed for efficient and effective sharing of computing resources. This was recognized with the increase in the number of PCs when each manager of a PC could not afford the database and peripheral resources needed. The importance of resource sharing became obvious. This was achieved in the mid-1980s with servers, which is a hardware–software system that enables and controls fast and easy access to databases and application programs.

Databases evolved into knowledge bases and increased not just in number but greatly in types of model and complexity. Also, there was often the need to share software; not just application software, but language compilers such as one for SIMSCRIPT 2: for the occasional user of simulation.

There was also the need to download some of the applications from the minis and mainframes to the client PCs. All this included an increased recognition of the importance of the end-user and the importance of the client, who demanded not just fast and easy access, but also a user-friendly environment that facilitates and even encourages the sharing of resources.

The new paradigm of sharing computing resources has its own demand of specialized, ancillary-support resources: it requires a network server OS (operating system), multiple-user interface, sometimes a GUI (graphical user interface), a dialogue-oriented client–server language (such as a version of SQL), and a database architecture. Because the resources are distributed, not just across one nation but internationally, there is the need for fast and reliable telecommunications and interconnectivity. All this must be implemented while the hardware/software platform and communication technology being used is transparent to users.

The user must pay too by following the procedures and protocols required by the systems. The users must also learn and observe some of the rigidities for using the standard user interfaces and interface languages.

Much of the software required is available from vendors and software houses and the client–server systems vary greatly in emphasis and capabilities. They may be mainframe-centric, PC-server-centric, or may have an emphasis on data/knowledge bases distinct from being communication-based. But, despite the availability of software packages, there is often a need for in-house software development. There is also the need to integrate the client–server systems with existing information systems and to use the system not only independently as an end-user but also to use the system to work cooperatively and collaboratively among groups of end-users.

The server is a processor and in some aspects it is much like the client processor; in other ways it is very different. For one thing it does not have a UI, let alone a GUI. It is designed for networking, database processing, and applications processing. The server may act as a repository and storage of information in which case it is a *file server*, or it may perform data retrieval in which case it is a *database server*.

Which type of server is desirable depends on the needs and objectives of the system. In any case, the server must be able to do multitasking (perform multiple functions simultaneously), use multiple operating systems, be portable, have scalability, (being able to upgrade upwards without loss of software performance), and have a fast response time despite the time required for teleprocessing.

Because of these capabilities, well-specified servers are *much* more expensive than a client processor: somewhere in the range of £10,000 to £30,000 or more. Why are servers so expensive? Because they perform so many functions. These functions include:

- Network management.
- Gateway functions, including access to outside access and public e-mail.
- Storage, retrieval, and document management.
- File sharing.
- Batch processing.
- Bulletin board.
- Fax transmission and receipt.

The platform for a server processor are PC-LAN servers with the mainframe and minicomputer as alternatives. The server platform and issues relating to the servers are hidden from the end-user. These issues include: internetworking, disk space utilization, data management, gateway and other access control, backup and recovery, and fault tolerance. Another important issue is the management of data (and knowledge if any).

5.1. Database processing

By processing data at a server instead of at a mainframe there are some principles of processing data that are applicable. These include the integrity of the enterprise data that is a corporate resource and needs to be unified and integrated; that access to data must be controlled to maintain security; and that recovery be possible after systems failures. This should be done without affecting the access for legitimate sharing and without an uncontrolled proliferation of islands of data cropping up everywhere. Access optimization, security utilities and I/O (input/output) handling might vary with servers manufactured by different vendors, but should not impact on the consistency of data and the responsiveness for the end-user. This improved responsiveness is important, especially for a query which could now be a fraction of a second instead of 3–5 seconds under a mainframe, thus allowing the processing of customized "wild" queries. Most of the processing, however, is data entry and could still be done in batch with updating done in the day and processing done at night and transmitted by LAN for use in the early morning at the local client end. This enables multiple end-users (such as say small businesses or professionals like doctors) that cannot afford their own processing to use a client processor.

Much of data management (and resource sharing) is automated. Some of this is done through a DBMS that resides with the server which controls access between multiple processing systems (and even multiple distributed databases) and integrates data access with network management.

5.2 Applications processing

Data is used by application programs and most of these reside with the server. The number of off-the-shelf client–server applications available is increasing, as is their scope. Still, however, many applications must be painfully developed from scratch. Application tools and lower prices have made client–server systems development more competitive in terms of cost/performance when compared to mainframe and minicomputer development. However, client–server application development differs from traditional software development in some significant ways, including:

- Processing functions are distributed between client and server. The front-end client portion is run by end-users using languages like SQL that have simplified data request protocols and extract data from wherever it might be located, whatever computer stores it, and whichever operating system controls it.
- Use of a UI and more often a GUI because end-user friendliness is still very important.
- Uses advanced networking, mostly LANs.
- 4GLs, and code generators are used extensively though OO methodology is being increasingly used.
- Development tools like SQL Windows, FLOWMARK, Progress, ObjectView, and Uniface for OS/2 are emerging.
- CASE tools are being used with rapid prototyping.

6. Server back to client

Once the applications are processed and data retrieved as per request by the client, the results are sent back the way they came, through the LAN and to the client processor. There the application results may have to be formatted for better display or the data retrieved has to be processed. All this is done by the programs residing at the client. This is then given to the user through the UI (user interface).

Organizational impact

The end-user, unlike a user who may be a computer programmer, may well be less-than-enthusiastic with the client–server paradigm. Why? Because the programmer is concerned (justifiably or not) about the loss of control over development, processing, and use of information. Also, like the DBA (database administrator), the programmer is concerned about the loss of integrity and security of data. The programmers and the DBAs are supported by the manager of IT, but for an additional reason. The manager is concerned about a loss of power through a reduction of span of control and a loss of control over the acquisition of resources, powers, and responsibilities that now gravitate to the department administrating the client node.

While the professional computing personnel (including IT management) may not be enthusiastically in favour of the client–server system, the corporate management is enthusiastically in favour. Why? Because there is an opportunity of reducing costs at the centre. Some cost components increase and some decrease, but the net result is a decrease of overhead costs of computing at the centre.

The client–server paradigm is largely minicomputer- or microcomputer-centric and is competing well with the mainframe-centric systems where most of the "mission critical" applications reside. However, the *total* cost of the client–server system is higher than that of the mainframe, although *initial* costs are lower. In an American study (Semich, 1994:37) the annual cost per user in the fifth year (with 3,584 mainframe users) came to $1,484 for the mainframe and $2,107 for the client–server system. This is largely due to the client wanting more resources at the client end.

There are other organizational consequences of the client–server systems: the downloading of computer processing from the mainframes (and minis) is referred to (by corporate management) as *downsizing*. It is the decreasing of their overhead costs and is downsizing for them. Downsizing, in management parlance, also means a reduction in the labour force and the firing or displacement of personnel. This is popular in recessions and bad economic times while upsizing and expansion is popular in good economic times. The "right" size and "right" timing is referred to as *rightsizing*. But, in terms of computing resources, there need not be any change in labour force. There is a reduction of overhead computing costs at the centre, but not necessarily a reduction of total cost. What we have instead is a shift of costs and responsibilities to the client nodes. Althought this shift is welcomed by corporate management they do share the concerns with IT of losing control over the development and processing of information.

Support for the client–server system comes from the end-user who can see the reduction of time and "noise" and an increase in responsiveness in the development of systems. The end-user gains greater control over the system. End-users are now more computer literate and experienced and no longer fear the computer which is becoming more robust and friendly. They are willing to take the responsibilities of controlling the client-end and leave the server-end to the centralized processing centre. This coalition of corporate management and end-user with help from the computer industry in the delivery of appropriate systems, will overcome any resistance to the client–server system which is being increasingly implemented throughout business and industry.

There are three alternatives in implementing a client–server system. One is to go vertically and implement all the levels of implementation, but for only one business at a time. However, implementing just one business unit, for example, will not make much sense since this unit cannot benefit from the many advantages of interconnectivity. The other approach is to implement horizontally, i.e., the LAN, the server, the clients, applications, and the end-users (i.e., their training). This approach is also flawed in that some resources lay idle while others are being developed. The third alternative is to do all at once, horizontally and vertically simultaneously.

It is likely that the third approach is not feasible because of the high investment necessary in money and skilled personnel. It is also highly risky. The less risky approach is to implement vertically and do so on a pilot study basis. The first implementation may be very costly, as was the case of a $2 million implementation but then the next implementation of similar scope was almost half the cost. So, there is a learning curve involved. Also, in implementing a pilot study, it is desirable to select an application that is less risky, low cost, and has low visibility.

Bad economic times and recession are allies for the client–server system. Management wanting to downsize and reduce their centralized overhead will be more willing to give up some of their centralized control to the client, the server, and the end-user.

It will be sometime before IT personnel and corporate management are fully comfortable giving up their centralized processing, which in many cases is fairly well stabilized with its security regime, its backup and recovery practices, its fault-tolerance mechanism, and an experienced IT staff running the development and operations of their information and knowledge base. However, end-users are taking the initiative and accepting the responsibility. They want more control over their operations and application development.

Downloading to the end-user's desk is perhaps inevitable, especially with increasingly open architectures in hardware, open systems in telecommunications, and the refinement of multimedia equipment. The technology will work in favour of the end-users and the corporation and make the computer industry more competitive and responsive to the end-user's needs.

Advantages of the client–server system

The advantages of a client–server system is context-sensitive and depends on your vantage point. If you are a corporate manager you will be thrilled with the advantages of downsizing and the reduction of costs at the centre. If you are an end-user you will be pleased with getting control of the system even though it may mean that you cannot blame computer personnel for things going wrong and instead have to take certain responsibilities for the system (at the client-end).

Table 15.1 *Advantages of a client–server system*

- Reduction of responsibilities and cost overhead at centre
- Better local cost control of operations and development (original and modifications)
- Faster response time to requests for processing
- Greater access to corporate data and knowledge otherwise maintained in a highly protected and centralized data structure. The client–server system strips data off transactional systems and stores it in the server to be shared for analysis and even local manipulation
- Enables distribution of processing from centralized to desktop computing
- Offers cooperative processing between individuals and group departments across organizational boundaries, geographies and time zones
- Rewriting systems for the client–server system is often an opportunity to purge obsolete software from the application portfolio and to consolidate, integrate and make the system more efficient
- Offers more friendly interfaces for end-users – especially knowledge workers and customers
- Greater involvement of end-users in IT implementations
- The open architecture and open systems offer flexibility in choosing different configurations of hardware, networks, and DBMS from multiple vendors
- There is greater possibility for expansion by adding hardware (even laptop computers) to networks without replacing existing hardware. The plug-and-play possibility applies (at least in theory) when parts of a system can be replaced without impact on the rest of the system

If you are one of the computer personnel, especially at the management level, then you will be somewhat happy at your reduced responsibilities for the system but you are now concerned about the integrity and security of the system, especially that of the data/knowledge base. On the whole, viewing the system from the point of the enterprise, there are more advantages overriding the disadvantages, risks and limitations involved. These advantages are summarized in Table 15.1.

Obstacles for a client–server system

In achieving the advantages, there are some obstacles and risks. Some have been implied in the discussion of the organizational implications: problems associated with downsizing and the need for greater co-ordination and cooperation among the end-users of the system. There is also the problem of resistance, which must be expected of all new technological changes. There are also problems of conversion, especially the need to train personnel in the use of the new system.

Table 15.2 *Obstacles in the way of a client–server system*

- Organizational:
    - Lack of personnel skilled in the client–server system and in networking
    - Resistance to change and new technology
    - Risks of downsizing
    - Costs of conversion
    - Need for greater coordination and control of more end-users
- Technological:
    - Need of LAN/WAN infrastructure
    - Lack of skills and equipment resources
    - Lack of methodology/experience in planning for a client–server system
    - Lack of client–server products and tools of development
    - Lack of client–server applications
    - Lack of national and international standards for the client–server paradigm

Training may be considered a technological obstacle. End-users have to be trained not only on using the client and knowing the functions of the server, but end-users need to be educated about networking and trained in navigating across the LAN and perhaps even the Internet. Other technological obstacles are the lack of tools of development and products of the client–server system; the lack of methodologies for the development of client–server systems; the shortage of experience in the planning and implementation of a client–server system; and the lack of national and international standards relating to the equipment and operations of such systems. These, and other, obstacles have been summarized in Table 15.2 and can be overcome only by close cooperation between IT personnel, corporate management, and end-users.

Cooperative processing

The client–server system was originally designed to facilitate communications between the end-user (i.e., client) and the computer processor through a server. But how about communications between end-users still using the same database(s) and server(s)? This configuration could improve processing horizontally between colleagues, customers, suppliers, and other relevant personnel in organizations. It could also help decision-making within a firm or corporation by making the decision-making process online whilst sharing enterprise resources of computing as well as data and knowledge bases.

Such processing is facilitated by software known as *groupware* and the processing known as cooperative processing, or *groupworking*, or *group-scheduling*. Such processing involves multitasking instead of the single-task processing. It utilizes client–server computing, but facilitates interaction among end-users in addition to the dissemination and routing of the necessary shared data/knowledge from groupware servers as well as application and file servers. Groupware binds the separate activities of end-users and decision-makers into an ensemble of cooperative processing for the enterprise. It retains the advantages of distributed processing and downsizing.

Groupware is possible because of the many electronic tools used on a LAN that may or may not use a server but facilitate horizontal communications. These tools include:

- Group-calendering and scheduling, which enables the scheduling of meetings and travel, thus facilitating concentration on other productive tasks.
- Group document-handling, including groupwork software utilities and development tools.
- More intensive use of e-mail messaging.
- Group-meeting and teleconferencing. This enables contact and instantaneous reactions which, unlike video teleconferencing, can be spontaneous, taking place any time and at any place.
- Group decision-making and problem solving support through downloading of some decision-making from the boardroom to the desktop. Cooperative processing captures the flow of ideas (and discussions in teleconferencing) and creates a continuous database and knowledge base of all information relevant to decision-making and problem solving.

Personal productivity programs such as e-mail, spreadsheets, and word processing can still be used along with a DSS and EIS but seamlessly integrated with groupwork and without any special commands and procedures.

Cooperative processing will not be the best substitute for interpersonal relations of face-to-face meetings and the telephone, but it can reach a much larger audience responding to specific questions. It can overcome the barriers of time and place and offer a continuous communications at one's need and convenience. It facilitates many people working collaboratively irrespective of where they may be. This could improve product design and reduce product development time.

Cooperative processing has many advantages discussed and implied above, but it also has organizational implications that can be far-reaching: it can affect the structure of traditional decision-making and lead to adhocracy as discussed in Chapter 5. A comparison between cooperative processing and traditional processing is shown in Table 15.3.

Table 15.3 *Cooperative processing compared to traditional processing*

	Traditional processing	Cooperative processing
■ Tasking	Single	Multiple tasking with human interaction
■ Architecture	Open	Closed
■ Software	Software on client and server are independent	Software on client and server are integrated
■ Applications	Distributed	Host-based and enterprise-wide
■ Control	Resides with workstation	Resides with host or server computer
■ Security and integrity	A problem because of the distributed control	Has better integrity and security control because it is centralized
■ Path	Hierarchical	Many cross-currents leading to problems of cooperation and collaboration
■ Time and place	Same time and same place, i.e. face-to-face meetings Same time and different places, i.e. video conferencing	Same time and different places Different times and different places

Summary and conclusions

Alok Sinha has described the client–server system well:

> ... one or more clients, and one or more servers, along with the underlying operating system and interprocess communication systems, form a composite system allowing distributed computation, analysis, and presentation.
>
> *Sinha, 1992:78*

The resources and infrastructure needed for the client–server paradigm are displayed in Figure 15.5, where we see that an end-user navigates through the client facility, the network infrastructure, the server facility, and then the applications and data/knowledge base. Having done the computing, the reverse path is taken back to the end-user.

Figure 15.5:
Navigation in a client–server system

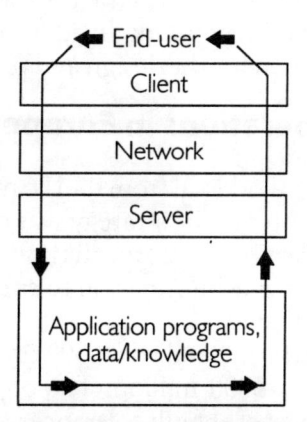

```
         End-user
        ┌────────┐
        │ Client │
        └────────┘
        ┌────────┐
        │Network │
        └────────┘
        ┌────────┐
        │ Server │
        └────────┘
   ┌──────────────────┐
   │Application programs,│
   │  data/knowledge  │
   └──────────────────┘
```

The end-user can do some local processing on a local database at the client facility and also use the many software productivity tools such as word processing, spreadsheets, and e-mail. Some of these productivity tools, like e-mail, will be used more intensively in cooperative processing which connects the clients horizontally and improves horizontal communications.

Collaborative and cooperative processing with groupware programs enable real-time computing amongst workers who may be dispersed and distributed. However, cooperative processing does increase the cross-currents between end-users and thus raises new problems of collaboration and cooperation in intercommunications and may lead to adhocracy.

Case 15.1: Client–server at the 1994 Winter Olympic Games

IBM installed a client–server system for the Winter Olympics in 1994. It was designed to serve 100,000 potential users that included 50,000 accredited personnel, 2,000 athletes, 8,000 media representatives and over 100,000 visitors per day.

The application was "mission critical" and reliability had to be absolute since there would be no second chance to capture, say, a ski slalom race. And what if the results were inaccurate? That would not only cause a flurry but bring many an athlete and relatives to tears!

There was a token ring LAN connecting PS/2 (PC computers) at 16 sites with clients and servers at over 3,000 sites. The network architecture used was IBM's SNA whilst the PS/2 handled all the accreditation and games management. The OS/2 graphical user interface (GUI) offered easy access to all users accessing a client. There was also an IBM ES/9000 mainframe which served as a central database with over 250,000 files available for the network. In addition, there was the RISC System 6,000 that was used for the design and planning of the games.

Case 15.2: Citibank's overseas operations in Europe

Citibank started moving workload from its 176 mainframes in 17 countries to a client–server system. The strategy was one of reengineering to have a more open and flexible platform that would support an object-oriented network and provide information to enhance decision-making and lead to higher productivity.

The client–server platform handled 30,000 transactions per day with a value of approximately $200 million. The objectives of the system were to have a very high level of fault tolerance, good contingency and a platform that would be scalable to the required processing power. Citibank runs Window NT on Compaq servers. They deliver transactions to other banks, do bookkeeping, accounting, MIS, reporting, drafts, DSS support, and cheque writing. It is planned, that all locations in Europe will be linked by a wide area network and document imaging system tied directly into the new platform, delivering transactions in an electronically structured format.

Case 15.3: Applications of client–server systems

- Morning Star group used the client–server approach to downsize from a 15-year-old mainframe system and achieved a faster response of time-to-market and greater productivity. It used the Hewlett Packard HP 9000 Business Server.
- Heinz Pet Products used the client–server paradigm to increase productivity and improve customer service.
- Electronics Distributor built its client–server system incrementally for tracking marketing information, increasing productivity, enhancing decision-making support, improving customer service and reducing the time taken to bring products to the market.
- Bank of Montreal in Canada with assets of $116 billion reengineered its operations to provide innovative and timely solutions.

The bank worked with Digital Equipment using an integrated suite of software products for enterprise information delivery developed by SAS Institute.

- Motorola, a $3.5 billion manufacturing enterprise, reports its rightsizing effort to result in halving its costs under a mainframe. (Connor, 1993:56).
- GE in one application showed a one-year payback for its start-up cost through its downsizing effort using a $6,000 PC.
- Unisys cut its IS costs by 1/3 and improved service to end-users by implementing client–server technology.

References

Cameron, K. S. (ed.), (1994). "Special Issues on Downsizing." *Human Resource Management*, vol. 33, no. 2, pp. 181–298.

Connor, William D. (1993). "The Right Way to Rightsize." *UNIX Review* (May), pp. 45–55.

Datamation. (1993). Cover story: *Client/Server Computing*, vol. 37, no. 20 (October 1), pp. 7–24.

Friend, David. (1994). "Client/Server vs. Cooperative Processing." *Information Systems Management*, vol. 11, no. 3, pp. 7–14.

Jeffery, Brian. (1996). "Enterprise Client/Server Computing." Information Systems Management, vol. 13, no. 4 (Fall), pp. 7–18.

Journal of Information Technology. (1994). Special issue: *Organizational Perspectives on Collaborative Processing*, vol. 9, no. 2 (June), pp. 71–136.

Levis, John and Schilling, Peter von. (1994). "Lessons from Three Implementations: Knocking Down the Barriers to Client/Server." *Information Systems Management*, vol. 11, no. 2, pp. 15–22.

Liang, Ting-Peng, Hsiangchu, Nian-Shing Chen, Hungshuing Wei, and Meng Chang Chen. (1994) "When Client/Server Isn't Enough." *Computer*, vol. 27, no. 5 (May), pp. 73–79.

Miranda, Max H. and Tellerman, Naomi A. (1993). "Corporate Downsizing and New Technology." *Information Systems Management*, vol. 10, no. 2, pp. 32–8.

Muller, Nathan J. (1994). "Application Development Tools: Client/Server, OOP, and CASE." *Information Systems Management*, vol. 11, no. 2, pp. 23–7.

Orfali, R., Harkey, D. and Edwards, J. (1995). "Intergalactic Client/Server Computing." *Byte*, vol. 20, no. 4 (April), pp. 108–22.

Semich, J. William. (1994). "Can You Orchestrate Client/Server Computing?" *Datamation*, vol. 10, no. 16 (August 15), pp. 36–43.

References

Sinha, Alok. (1992). "Client–Server Computing." *Communication of the ACM*, vol. 35, no. 7 (July), pp. 77–98.

Socarras, Angel E., Cooper, Robert S. and Stonecypher, William F. (1991). "Anatomy of an X Terminal." *IEEE Spectrum*, vol. 28, no. 3 (March), pp. 52–5.

Schultheis, Robert A. and Bock, Douglas B. (1994). "Benefits & Barriers to Client/Server Computing." *Journal of Systems Management*, vol. 45, no. 2 (February), pp. 12–15.

Wright, Tim. (1992). "Group Dynamics." *Which Computer?*, vol. 15, no. 7 (July), pp. 38–48.

16 Network Management

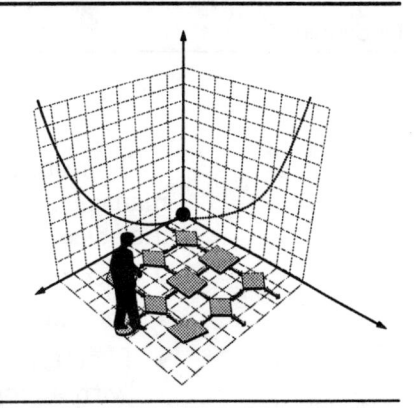

Introduction

In the 1980s, we witnessed the strong emergence of PCs (personal computers) as stand-alone computers on desktops. With trends towards decentralization and deregulation of the telecommunications industry in the US, innovation increased and prices dropped, especially the prices of PCs. As PCs became more robust and end-user friendly, the number of PCs on desktops of most corporations increased. However, many corporations were no longer able to afford the desired peripherals, databases and computing power that they needed. They had to pool and share resources. Many of these resources were dispersed and had to be connected. The solution to the connectivity problem was networks: LANs for local area networks, MANs for metropolitan areas, and WANs for wide area networks. In this context, a *network* is a set of nodes connected by links and communication facilities that have both physical and logical components. You need to manage and control networks where zipping...

> ...across your network are thousands of packets of information. Information that's vital to your organization. Losing even some of that data can cost your company millions of dollars.
>
> *Derfler*, 1993:277

The increase in the number and use of PCs led to the need of interconnectivity just as their physical dispersion within an organization led to the complexity of networks. There were bottlenecks in message flow, concurrent access, defective devices, devices that flooded networks with junk signals and slowed systems performance, loose connections, overloaded components, and incorrectly connected components resulting in crashes of networks.

Introduction

To restore order to this chaos, there was need for organizations to manage their networks and try to achieve most, if not all, of the following objectives:

- Increased productivity of end-users.
- Facilitate cooperative work between end-users.
- Function smoothly, continuously, efficiently and effectively without loss of integrity and security of system.
- Be robust against errors and misuse.
- Detect fraudulent activity but verify and account for selected legitimate activities.
- Monitor system to identify potential fault conditions and "fix" faults in real-time with minimum loss of performance.
- Provide statistics (on the system and its components) necessary for planning and system control.
- Perform maintenance when needed and preventive maintenance to avoid, or at least reduce, breakdowns of system.
- Plan hardware/software configurations for growing needs of applications and information.
- Control devices remotely if necessary – as in cases of failure.
- Implement/enforce security zones around sensitive resources.
- Be able to effectively integrate within the corporate information system.

Achieving some of the above objectives is the function of network management. It is the subject of this chapter. In it, we shall examine the functions of network management identified by ISO (International Standards Organization) as:

1. Fault/problem management.
2. Performance management.
3. Security management.
4. Configuration management.
5. Accounting management.

In addition, we will examine the software necessary for network management, managing the human element (end-users), the development of networks, and the acquisition of resources needed for network management. We will examine how our networks can be safe and conclude with a look at future trends in networks and network management.

Fault/problem management

Perhaps the most important and certainly the most urgent function of network management is to detect and fix problems on a network. These problems could be a loss of performance, impaired transmission, or a systems crash. This could immobilize an organization and any problems must be detected as soon as possible and corrected without delay.

Fortunately, we have many aids and tools to help identify and trace a problem and to provide statistics for maintenance and planning. These tools include pollers, monitors, and analyzers. A *traffic poller* sends echo packets to a specific device to check if there is any fault in the transmission line. A *traffic monitor* is concerned with actively checking for faulty devices. In contrast to the poller, a traffic monitor is passively "listens in" while displaying histograms of traffic patterns. Then there is the *analyzer*. One type of analyzer is the packet analyzer which identifies the device that is clogging the network. Like the traffic monitor, the analyzer is passive, but provides more information about the packets. The analyzer for a network, sometimes called the LAN/network analyzer, provides more information and for the entire network. They can search for duplicate network addresses, isolate failing nodes, identify probable cause of failures, and collect clues on how the network can be improved.

There is a wide range of services offered by a network analyzer. On the low end, we have the software analyzer that will be adequate for a low density of traffic (around 50% of capacity), troubleshooting between two network nodes, one or two protocols, and with limited functionality. But for more complex systems, one needs the hardware–software platform handling high density traffic which may be around 140 different protocols blazing across the network at any one time. Such analyzers can perform remote monitoring and control, and a slew of predefined filters. A filter allows you to sift through traffic for a selected set of parameters such as addresses, frame types, and even devices by different manufacturers.

Analyzers can be specialized like the protocol analyzer which can trigger a specific action when a preset threshold is exceeded. Some analyzers are portable ones and are dispatched to a trouble-spot. This may not be adequate in a continuous process production line especially with a high-value-added product in which case the analyzer is dedicated to a function or process and resides in a probe attached to the LAN, providing frequent or continuous information to the central network management. If the analyzer uses a distributed client–server architecture, its tasks (of monitoring, filtering, analyzing, offering graphic representations of data, and alerting errors to the operator) can be distributed between the embedded analyzer and the software manager at the centre.

In addition to the tools discussed above, there are other facilities for fault management such as the *trouble ticket*. It records the time, date, place, operator, alarm or action taken, with each problem that occurred. Also recorded is the equipment involved and its vendor. Such information is not only useful in tracing the cause of the problem, but in helping maintenance and in trying to ensure that the problem does not occur again.

In addition to the trouble ticket and analyzing tools, there are many pieces of information necessary for fault management. These include aggregated and disaggregated statistics on errors counts, traffic densities, network performance, as well as notices, alerts and alarms generated. This information should be available in an easy-to-digest format in addition to graphical map representations of the network to locate problem areas.

The network administration staff in testing the system and reactivating it, may need control over the network, its links and devices so that they can be initiated, closed down, or restarted remotely from the central console. They should also be able to divert traffic from failing lines and devices without the end-user being inconvenienced or even knowing about it.

The problem of detecting faults can become complex because many network systems (an organization may have more than one) not only has many different devices, but many of these devices may be from different vendors. Each hardware device is associated with specific network software and protocols, as well as specialized techniques to interpret the alarms and reports generated before other appropriate diagnostics and tests are performed. However, through the use of loopbacks and tests some faults can be isolated all the way down to a particular segment of a network, modem, or other device on the network. Also, invalid configurations and front-panel tampering on various types of equipment can be detected, often remotely from the central network management console.

Performance management

The management of performance involves measuring, monitoring, and metering of variables relevant to operations, maintenance, and the planning of a network. The variables include:

- *Network (and its components) availability* – which is the mirror image of system downtime.

- *Response time* (the time elapsed from query to output).
- *Utilization of devices and resources* – both *hardware* (like CPU, disks and other memory devices, bridges, gates, routers, communication cards, buffers, repeaters, modems, multiplexers, switches, clients, and servers) and *software* (like OS, software utilities, and application programs).
- *Traffic density* – by segment of the network.

Such statistics, when properly analyzed, can identify bottlenecks (current and potential), other potential problems, identify areas that need expansion or contraction, and help predict future trends for planning and budgeting of future systems.

Metering and monitoring is not just "big brother" snooping on end-users but provides data and statistics necessary for operations. For example, statistics on software used by each end-user can be very helpful in deciding how many copies of each licence to acquire rather than support clients with licensed software that may never, or seldom, be used.

Monitoring can be selective and activated by a set of thresholds. For example, the monitoring of a file system may start when it is 80% full, or for a printer when the print queue is longer than five. Likewise, licensed software can be monitored when, for example, 85% of its privilege has been exceeded.

Security management

Many of the problems of security (and their solutions) are common to IT, as are the cases of controlling access to a database, an applications program, or even a device and peripheral. The principles of security are discussed elsewhere in this book. There are, however, special problems of security that arise in telecommunications and networking because of the exposure of messages during transmission. Messages are vulnerable to wire-tapping: the electromagnetic pickup of messages on communication lines. In addition, there may be eavesdropping, passive listening, or active wire-tapping involving alteration of data – such as piggybacking (the selective interception, modulation, or substitution of messages). Another type of infiltration is reading between the lines. An illicit user taps the computer when a bona fide end-user is connected to the system, but while "thinking" leaves the computer idle and unattended. This is a tempting occasion for penetration of the system, which along with other unauthorized uses of computer time, can be quite costly to the organization.

One method of preventing message interception is to encode or encrypt data in order to render it incomprehensible or useless if the message is intercepted. This is *encryption*, derived from the Greek root "crypt" meaning "to hide" and can be done by either transposition or substitution.

In transposition, characters are interchanged by a set of rules. For example, the second and third characters might be switched so that 5289 becomes 5829. In substitution, characters are replaced. The number 1 can be 3, so that 514 reads 534. Or the substitution may be more complex: specified number might be added to a digit, such as a 2 added to the third digit, making 514 read 516. Decryption restores the data to its original value. Although the principles of encryption are relatively simple, most schemas are highly complex. Understanding them requires mathematical knowledge and technical expertise. An illustration of encryption appears in Figure 16.1.

Figure 16.1: *Encryption and decryption*

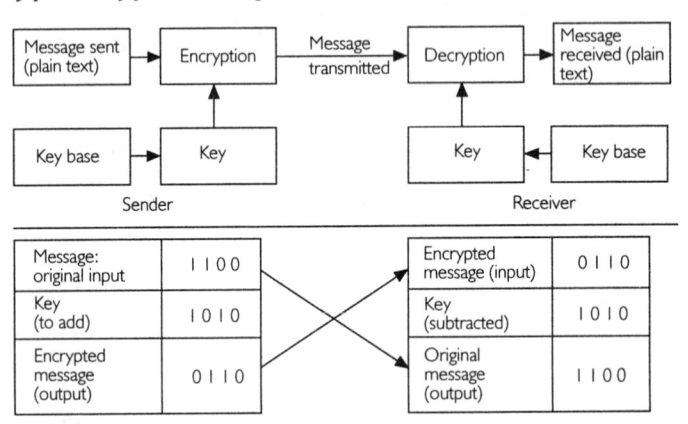

Message: original input	1 1 0 0		Encrypted message (input)	0 1 1 0
Key (to add)	1 0 1 0		Key (subtracted)	1 0 1 0
Encrypted message (output)	0 1 1 0		Original message (output)	1 1 0 0

Example in binary numbers

A key is used to code a message, a key that both sender and receiver possess. The coded message could be a random-number key or a key based on a formula or algorithm. As in all codes, the key must be difficult to break. Frequent changes of the key adds to the security of data, which explains why many systems have a key-base with a large number of alternate keys.

In the past, the transportation of the encrypted key to authorized users has been the Achilles' heel of system security. An additional problem is that there is sometimes insufficient time to pass the key to a legitimate receiver. One solution is to have a multiple-access cipher in a public key cryptosystem. The system has two keys, a public encryption key "E" used by the sender, and a secret decryption key "D" used by the receiver. Each sender/receiver has a set of D and E keys. To code data to send to firm X, for example, a business looks up firm X's E key, published in a public directory, and then transmits a message in code over a public or insecure transmission line. Firm X alone has the secret key for decryption. This system can be breached, but not easily, since a tremendous number of computations would be needed to derive the secret of D. The code's security lies as much in the time required to crack the algorithm as in the computational complexity of the cipher because much of the data's value resides in its timeliness. Often, there is no longer need for secrecy once a deal is made, the stock market closed, or a patent application filed. Cryptography, in effect, serves three purposes:

- *Identification:* helps identify bona fide senders and receivers.
- *Control:* prevents alteration of message.
- *Privacy:* impedes eavesdropping.

With the increased reliance of businesses (and governments) on teleprocessing and networks, much research is being done on cryptographic systems. However, experts disagree about how secure even the most complex codes should be. Some claim that people bent on accessing encrypted data will be able to break all codes, using the power, speed, and advanced technology of modern computers. Others maintain that the work factor required to decipher a doubly-encrypted message would require a degree of effort that would make it cost-ineffective. The illustration in Figure 16.1 is a very simple case of cryptography.

There are many algorithms designed in both the private and public sector. There are at least 114 different cryptography algorithms (Schneier, 1994). In the early 1990s, the US Government was in favour of a national standard cryptographic system so that it alone could access any messages at any time for purposes of national security. The civil libertarians have cried foul and so the debate rages.

Meanwhile, a common approach is the handshake sequence where a user provides a password to a modem before making a call. When the receiving modem responds, it asks for the password from the calling modem before the modems make their connection.

Other approaches include the dial-back or call-back control where the user calls the device and hangs up. The device checks for legitimacy of the caller (by password or location or both) and, if legitimate, calls the user back at the calling number stored in the network directory.

Security management involves the definition of the jurisdiction of network zones, which are available to everyone or only to users in selected zones. This capability, for example, prevents the users in one department from using an optical scanner and printer in some other department.

Another approach to security management in networks is to build a "firewall". This is a term taken from fire fighting for preventing a fire from going beyond a line of defence. We do that in business when we need to restrict access to certain buildings. One approach would be to demand an identification and logging of all those visiting the building. A more secure approach would be to page the person being visited who would then escort the visitor in the building at all times. A still more secure approach would be to not permit the visitor to enter, but to leave a message (or package) at the front desk. In networking, all these approaches in building "firewalls" are used. The control is of access, especially at the connections between networks such as a proprietary network and a public network.

Security management is also responsible for backing-up the system in the event of a failure or a disaster on the network and to do so quickly and without loss of valuable data/knowledge. Another problem is with viruses. Viruses are not a new issue in IT; they arise even with stand-alone systems that do not use networks. If a virus gets on a network the contamination can be severe because networks enable the virus to quickly spread over over a large area. Most network software is able to scan for known viruses. However, the population of "unknown" software is increasing and it seems that a network system is never completely secure so it is essential that network managers are increasingly vigilant.

Empirical data shows that a virus often infects a corporate database through a corporate end-user swapping floppies, especially an end-user who has a computer at home and swaps floppies from home to the office. Other common viruses on networks are the boot sector virus, the file-infecting virus, and the memory resident virus. Fortunately, there are numerous virus-detection software products with different types of scanners (including signature scanners), memory resident activity monitors, and immunizers. In addition, there are many protective procedures that should be adopted against viruses. These include: not putting executable files on the server in directories where end-users can change them, restricting dial-in access, and not leaving the computer on and unattended all night or during the lunch break.

Another responsibility of security management is to record all information that may be useful for security management in the future. This means that careful logs must be kept of all failures, intrusions, and unauthorized access, and qualifying each with identifiers that will trace each problem and help avoid them or at least minimize risks of security infringement in the future.

In security management, it is important not to overspecify or underspecify. If security is lax, then a security breach is just "waiting to happen". If security is too tight, then it is not only unnecessarily expensive to implement, but also has a high psychological cost of alienating the end-user who may then either bypass the system, ignore systems procedures (such as being careless with the passwords), or just not use the systems as much or not use them at all.

Configuration management

All network systems need to be initialized and then reconfigured. Reconfiguring may mean the addition, withdrawal, or modification of an existing configuration. In practice, to configure a device means assigning it a zone number and network number for routing purposes. These numbers are then used in collecting statistics on device operation.

Reconfiguring a system is also necessary when one needs to reroute network traffic through different links and connections or through different permutations or combinations of devices.

Another function of configuration management could be the reconfiguration of the application programs and their updates. In the early days of computing, a network manger went around each office cubicle with a computer installing new software packages or their updates. Fortunately, there is now network software that does the distribution automatically across all legitimate workstations and clients. This is a great saving in time and energy. Also, the programs loaded onto each client node automatically draws updates from the server.

Reconfiguration can also include the rerouting or bypassing of traffic from overloaded or failed (or failing) links or congested devices to other configurations that have excess capacity. When the quality improves, the original configuration is restored. This automatic rerouting is very important for "mission critical" applications where unnecessary delays and outages cannot be tolerated. Routers needed for reconfiguration are protocol-specific, which means that more than one router is often required. New technology, however, is delivering multiprotocol routers which are capable of routing several protocols simultaneously.

Account management

This is not accounting in the financial and auditing sense but an accounting of network assets in the sense of inventory control – both hardware and software. The accounting of each asset should be by physical location as well as by ownership so that each asset can be located quickly when needed (as in the case of a system crash) and for purposes of planning and operating the system.

Accounting of software may also be important when the software is under licence. Such systems will keep track of use under the licence so that violations are avoided or at least kept to a minimum. This tracing of licences is important for the purpose of ensuring that no legal requirements are violated. It is therefore sometimes necessary to enforce the limitations of use and this is often done by warnings when thresholds are repeatedly violated.

Accounting of assets is also important for financial accounting where the use of resources may be charged back to the user for payment toward maintenance and upgrading.

Software for network management

We have discussed the many functions of network management. But how are they implemented? In the early days, much was done manually. Nowadays, almost all such work is done by network software. Selected features of network management software are displayed in Table 16.1.

Table 16.1 *Selected features of network management software*

■ Diagnostic analyzers	■ Hardware and software inventory
■ Server monitoring and reporting	■ Allows setup of license limits
■ CPU utilization	■ Reports
■ Memory utilization	■ Predefined
■ Log-on and security	■ User-defined
■ Provides configuration information	■ Filtered
■ Network traffic monitoring	■ Automation and scheduling of tasks
■ Application metering	■ Client automation
■ Enforces blocking when licence is exceeded	■ Server automation
■ Queues users when license is exceeded	■ Remote control of client PCs
■ Application distribution	■ Software support
■ Notification and alerting	■ Integration
■ Virus protection	■ User interface
■ Server	■ Database
■ Client	■ Free technical support
■ Software distribution	

Some of these features are available in stand-alone packages. Some features are "bundled" in other packages. And some suite packages have most of the features. These features match most of the features in the list of functions discussed above (though not in the same order) as being part of the functions of network management. However, the functions needed by any one network will be unique. It is therefore up to the network management personnel to select one or more software package or to acquire a suite of integrated programs which may be more expensive, but more comprehensive.

Choice of software is not unique to network management. Every user of a PC has to face the decision of buying the best software package for each function like word processing, spreadsheets, database management, and even networking. Alternatively, users can buy an integrated package that has all the desired features plus much more. The suite choice is expensive and not optimal for each function, but it does avoid some of the problems of making the different packages compatible with the operating system available and with each other. Furthermore, the format for each package is consistent and one does not have to learn a different set of commands and icons for each package. This is the equivalent problem faced by network managers: acquire a suite that does all or most of what you want and pay more, but do not have the hassle of packages being incompatible and having to learn more instructions and formats.

End-user management

Besides hardware and software, there is another important element in every network system: the end-users. Some of them are professionals with considerable knowledge of computers and telecommunications. There are, however, many who have little or no knowledge of computers or of telecommunications. They have to be trained and educated. For some, use of networks can be a cultural shock. Take for instance an office with a large volume of interdepartmental mail that was traditionally delivered manually by a messenger. Now this is to be replaced by e-mail. The advantages do not appear instantly nor are they obvious, but the immediate problem is having to learn about telecommunications and networks and having to change a life style at the workplace. All this on top of having to give up the typewriter (In 1995, Smith-Corona, the largest typewriter manufacturer in the US filed for bankruptcy having lost all its business to the word processor).

End-users need to be trained in not only accessing and navigating networks, but also on the policies and procedures of handling data files; on troubleshooting and recovering from a crashed system; on the nature of network maintenance and network security; on protocols (rules and procedures that must be followed in transmission); and on the functions and limitations of routers (facility that selects and provides a path for a message).

End-users should also be trained on computer programs for network management. For example, there is a Profiler program that collects information provided by the end-user. If not completed correctly by the end-user, then programs and updates due to the end-user will not be forthcoming.

The timing of the training is also important. For example, training on the applications specific to a LAN should be done before the LAN is installed or else the "shock" resulting from an unfamiliarity with the new application can be demoralizing causing a drop in productivity.

Introducing personnel to networking involves some of the same problems of introducing laymen to computers. The change has to be managed with great care, some psychology and a lot of patience. It would help if the network system, especially the interfaces, were end-user friendly. What does this mean? An example would be a system with a fast response time, tolerance of common human errors, and one that keeps the end-user fully informed. For example, if there is a system crash, breakdown or slow-down in the network, the system should acknowledge the problem and estimate the time it would take to come up again. Many end-users are tolerant and understanding of problems provided they know what is happening and what to expect.

Development of networks

Thus far we have assumed the existence of a network which must be reconfigured, made secure, accounted for, and maintained. But how about an organization without a network? Or, how about one that has a network but wants another LAN, or considers the existing LANs to be inadequate and needing to be replaced? Then we need a project which must be developed: i.e., designed and implemented. This requires a development methodology.

The methodology appropriate for a complex project like a network is the SDLC (systems development life cycle). The activities of the SDLC for a network are similar to other projects in IT: feasibility study, user requirements specification, design, implementation, and the system made ready for operations. During operations there are evaluations. If a modification is required and it is minor, then the system is maintained. If the modification required is deemed to be major, then the system is redeveloped. These activities (and their iteration and recycling) are shown in Figure 16.2. There are some differences in content with a typical IT project and these differences will now be examined.

Figure 16.2:
Development of a network

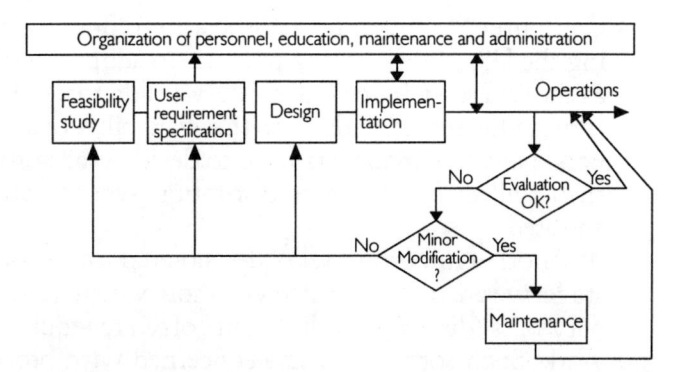

The first decision to be made is what type of network is needed. The choice is among LANs, proprietary network, ISDN, public packet switching network, and a public switched telephone network. There are also choices within these types of network, like the type of LAN that is best for the needs at hand. Also, the question of organization of the network (centralized or client–server) needs to be considered.

Another important decision in the design of a network is to decide whether the entire system is to be supported by one vendor or by many vendors and make it an open system. The advantage of having one vendor is mostly in the short-term since this will avoid the hassle when something goes wrong and one vendor blames another. With only one vendor the system is well integrated and easy to install, train on, maintain, and manage. However, not being tied to one vendor has the great advantage of being able to select the best (or cheapest) component and "plug-and-play". This is the advantage of open architecture and open systems, where there is interoperability between components available from different vendors (preferably internationally). In contrast, a closed architecture is proprietary technology developed by firms in the telecommunications and computing industry like SNA by IBM, DecNet by Digital Corporation, XNA by Xerox and those developed by governments like the DDN in the US.

The important design decision of selecting an architecture often depends on where you are and what equipment you have. If you are in the US and have IBM equipment, the chances are that you will select the SNA (Systems Network Architecture). It is one of the earliest architectures and has the most products designed for it. However, if you are in Europe you may well prefer the OSI (Open Systems Interconnection). The OSI is developed by the ISO (International Standards Organization) and is strongly supported by many countries in Europe. Europeans also support standards developed by CCITT (Consultative Committee on International Telegraphy and Telephone) and ECMA (European

Computer Manufacturers Association). But all over the world, including the US, there is strong pressure to adopt international models such as the OSI model. The OSI model will add to flexibility, reduce response time, reduce costs, and add to the availability of standard network products. Network managers have to decide what products to add so that they will cause the least disruption when a standard is ultimately adopted.

Another important set of decisions concerns software. At this design stage, we are not concerned with software required for management of networks (discussed earlier), but software required for operating a network. Such software is also concerned with protocols such as SNMP and CMIP. The SNMP is the Simple Network Management Protocol which defines systems/network management standards for primarily the TCP/IP-based networks. The TCP/IP (Transactional Control Program/Internet Protocol) is a system designed for the US Department of Defense and is a commonly used communications standard. In competition, though, is the CMIP (Common Management Information Protocol), currently the only internationally ratified network management protocol standard for the OSI. The CMIP was intended to support business at different levels (local, metropolitan and wide area networks), i.e., the LAN, MAN, and the WAN. The CMIP, however, has not yet caught on. Meanwhile, there are several network management platforms, such as OpenView, that are based on standards including SNMP and CMIP. OverView is actually a family of over 130 solutions from over 80 vendors.

Another set of important design decisions includes the selection of bridges and gateways, security features, backup and recovery procedures, transmission mode, links to carriers, switches, and even surge protection.

The implementation of a network will most likely involve acquiring ("buy" decision) some network software and the rest is developed in-house (the "make" decision). Most of the hardware needed will be acquired and only rarely made in-house. In all cases, there are well tried-and-tested procedures of resource acquisition in IT that are applicable to network development.

During operations there are evaluations. Here, the decision as to whether a modification needed is a minor one for maintenance, or a major one for redevelopment. This is an important and difficult decision. Such maintenance decisions are not unfamiliar to IT personnel, but the terms of defining a minor or major modification are different. Consider, for example, three requests for modification of a network:

1. My LAN connection worked fine for a year and is now down. Can you please help?
2. I would like a LAN connection for my assistant who now is located in Room 39 of Building 131.
3. The current network is inadequate for my needs. I think that I need a token ring network for my department. How soon can I have it?

Of the above three requests, the first is clearly a problem with maintenance and can most likely be covered by the maintenance budget and existing maintenance personnel. The second problem is minor if building 131 is wired for a LAN and is connected to the corporate LAN. Otherwise, it is a major problem of modification and may well require redevelopment. This request needs further investigation and is categorized under "to be advised". The third request is a major modification and will require a new project development and new funding.

The problem facing network management is to clearly distinguish, and quickly as possible, which is a minor and which is a major modification. What network management needs is a set of guidelines for policy and procedures relating to maintenance of networks so that the maintenance process is clearly stated and known to all end-users.

Resources for network management

From the description of the nature and functions of network management it becomes clear that it is an important responsibility. It is also a difficult one, especially if there are hundreds if not thousands of nodes connected to the network and when the operations, and indeed the survival of the enterprise, may depend on the corporate network(s).

Hardware and software

The resources needed for network management include hardware and software. They are needed to provide information necessary for network management. What is the information that is needed? Much of it is needed for operations at the console: in an online real-time mode. The console operator should be able to see the network displayed (preferably in colour) at any level of aggregation, identifying the current and potential bottlenecks which may be flashing. The status of each crucial physical and logical component can be traced (each physical and logical unit may well be identified by its parameters such as name, state, physical location, etc.). All monitoring information and even statistics should be available that are either menu-driven or command-driven. The console operator should be able to get answers to questions like:

- What are the network loads on different sectors and at different times?
- What type of errors are occurring and where?
- What type of conflicts (like concurrency) are occurring and where?
- What channels are loaded or near-loaded and with what load factors?
- What are the waiting-line queues and to what extent are they exceeding or approaching the set thresholds?
- Where is security weak or possibly being violated?
- What printer and print driver is location 119 using? (Are they compatible?)
- What is the printer and print-queue status?

Answers to some of the above questions (and others) may come without a query. That depends on the network management systems program being run. Some systems may even have a simulation program that would give answers necessary for "smoothing" the load and increasing the efficiency of the system. What-if questions asked may include:

- What if I added a workstation (or ports) at point 119? How would this affect the service time and length of queue?
- What if I added a router on segment 5?
- How will the performance be affected by the addition of specific hardware or software?
- What is the maximum distance travelled by end-users if I were to add a workstation at point 146? (The answer to this question will require a database of floor plans, site plans, wiring closets, and equipment inventory by location.)

The answers to some of the simulation questions may be long-term solutions that are important to planning, but such capability is often useful in problem solving and decision-making for a network.

Some consoles have the ability to send and receive messages with the receiving being prioritized. Some of these incoming messages are recorded and appear as reports for later analysis. Some systems have alarm filtering. Some perform functions of monitoring and reconfiguration automatically. Some systems can even predict network faults based on historical data. Unfortunately, however, there is no system that is fully integrated and provides end-to-end management, partly because different components of the system are manufactured by a proliferation of vendors. As a result, a network management centre for a large and complex system would have multiple consoles each manned by a trained operator and performing one or more functions.

Many of these problems of network management will come close to resolution as we approach a truly open system (some systems use a buffer layer to approach an open standard architecture). The open standard will not only provide flexibility in operations, but will decrease delays, improve response times, and reduce costs.

One desired feature of a network system on the wish list of many network managers is that network management systems programs be intelligent (by using AI techniques for making inferences). We already have some intelligent components like the intelligent router, which may optimally route a message between Paris and Frankfurt through New York. What we do not have are intelligent hubs (a centre and spoke configuration) and an intelligent network management system.

Personnel

To perform the functions needed in network management and to manage its resources, there is a need of a staff headed by a network manager, also called a *network administrator*. The staff can be organized either centrally or distributed. The principles involved in the selection of a central or distributed organizational configuration is no different from those relevant for a distributed IT organization. The personnel involved are, of course, different and must be grouped for functional efficiency and effectiveness. The organization will also depend on the size and complexity of the network organization, the organizational culture of the enterprise, and the personalities involved both in IT and in corporate management. In the case of a small organization, there may be just one person (carrying a screwdriver) responsible for a network; in complex networks the number of personnel involved may be in the tens.

The functions of network management have been mentioned as being reconfiguration, monitoring, and maintenance. These functions could result in the addition and subtraction of network nodes. This can be a difficult political decision in cases of a zero-sum game i.e., additions must be balanced by subtractions. Which ones go and which ones stay? A somewhat similar problem arises in assigning software and security levels. This may not be a zero-sum game, but withdrawing or not assigning high security levels to new software can cause ill feelings. Security levels can be a status symbol and if a higher level of security (or new software) is given to a subordinate on a "need-to-have" basis, but not to the supervisor, it can raise serious problems of unhappiness and loss of face.

Such decisions, along with the other decisions needed for planning, developing, and operating a network fall on the network administrator who in addition to being a technician, must be comfortable with software (especially operating systems software), have a working knowledge of hardware, be knowledgeable of accounting and budgeting practices, and also be a politician.

To perform the functions of network management, the staff must be organized. For the network of a medium-sized company one possible organizational structure is shown in Figure 16.3.

Figure 16.3:
Organization for network planning

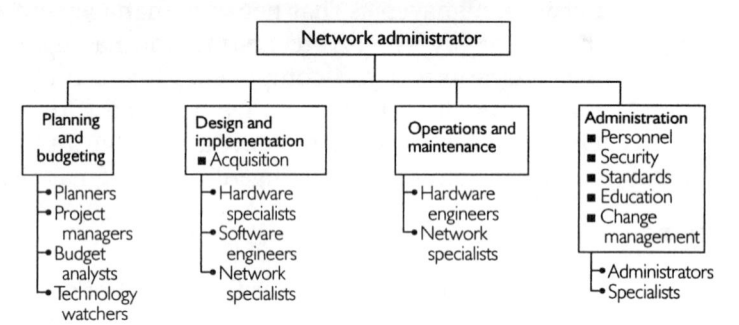

```
                        Network administrator
          ┌──────────────┬──────────────┬──────────────┐
     Planning       Design and      Operations and    Administration
       and         implementation     maintenance     ■ Personnel
     budgeting     ■ Acquisition                      ■ Security
                                                      ■ Standards
    → Planners    → Hardware        → Hardware        ■ Education
    → Project       specialists       engineers       ■ Change
      managers   → Software         → Network           management
    → Budget       engineers          specialists
      analysts   → Network                            → Administrators
    → Technology   specialists                        → Specialists
      watchers
```

Each person may represent one function or multiple functions. For example, the Librarian or the Security Officer may be part-time jobs assigned to a person most inclined and trained for the task or the assignments made in order to "smoothen" and distribute the load. Also, one person may do other jobs as the need arises. For example, a software or hardware engineer assigned to maintenance may well help out in the installation and implementation of a system and may even contribute to a feasibility study. This rotation of work is good both for the personnel involved (providing a variety of work) and for the organization (providing backup and knowledge necessary for integration).

Network management must not only be concerned with the operations of networks, but also with the planning of networks. This may include facilities planning. For example, if the organization is to build a new building, should it be wired for networks? If networking is needed after the building is built, then wring will be much more expensive. Likewise, putting cable conduits underground in order to connect buildings for networking is much cheaper and easier if planned before the buildings are built. Sometimes, such planning is not possible, but when possible, networking should be planned because such planning ahead is not only cheaper but much less disruptive for the organization.

Training is another important function of network administration. Typically, this means the training of the end-user and education in telecommunications and networking for corporate management and other corporate personnel. This is important, yet the principles involved apply to other IT functions such as those discussed in Chapter 4.

Network personnel, including the network manager and network planners, must be cross-trained on the central network console. Also important is the training and upgrading of network management staff, including the network administrator. Their field is ever-changing with developments that sometimes have organizational and social implications. Network management must keep well abreast of these developments and new networking products as they occur and, in some cases, before they occur. Some of the changes in telecommunications and network technology will now be discussed.

Historical view

We conclude this section with a historical view of networks and telecommunications which is depicted in Figure 16.4. We started off telecommunications with telephones and the PBXs while the computer equipment were stand-alone mainframes. Later, we had mainframes, minis, and PCs which were connected together by ARPANET, other private and public telecommunications networks, as well as fibre optics. This led to interorganizational interconnections.

Figure 16.4:
Evolution of networks (growth curves over time)

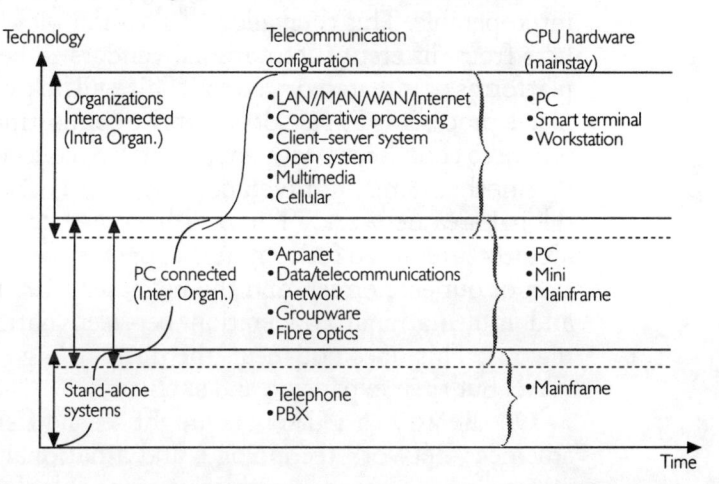

Technology	Telecommunication configuration	CPU hardware (mainstay)
Organizations Interconnected (Intra Organ.)	• LAN//MAN/WAN/Internet • Cooperative processing • Client–server system • Open system • Multimedia • Cellular	• PC • Smart terminal • Workstation
PC connected (Inter Organ.)	• Arpanet • Data/telecommunications network • Groupware • Fibre optics	• PC • Mini • Mainframe
Stand-alone systems	• Telephone • PBX	• Mainframe

Time →

We now have intraorganizational connections with computer equipment, including workstations and smart terminals but mostly PCs connected up with LANs, MANs, WANS, and the Internet (successor to the ARPANET). The newer equipment maturing in the 1990s include open systems, multimedia, and cellular phones with the integration of data, voice, graphics and video in digital form. The most common configuration, especially for PCs and workstations, is the client–server system.

Network management and the future

We conclude this chapter with a look at the future of network management. There is nothing very exciting on the near horizon as to new methodologies and aids for network management except, perhaps, better diagnostic and network management tools at the central console and software defined networks. However, there is much that network management must respond to in terms of the changing environment of telecommunications and networks. We look at these developments from two points of view: the demand side, that is the demand for more network services and the supply side, the probable availability of new technology relevant to network management.

Networks are growing at an explosive rate. By the year 2000 it is estimated that there will be over 100 million microcomputers tied into corporate networks and many of them will be using the Internet. In addition, there are minis and mainframes that use networks for daily transactions like reservations, financial services, electronic publishing, EFT (electronic fund transfer), and other commercial applications including interactive ones.

There is a great need for open systems in the hardware and software components of networks allowing them to be interchangeable and interoperable. This then allows "plug-and-play" computing with products from different international vendors to be plugged into different platforms of integrated systems. This will help cooperative and collaborative processing as part of enterprise computing allowing anyone anywhere to collaborate with anyone else on collective projects.

Another demand-driven development is the trend towards a GAN (global area network). This will be a response to the need of a better architecture suited for commercial operations, the increasing globalization of our economies, and the increase in multinational corporations and multinational cooperation between national governments and regions. This does not mean the dismantling of the LAN, MAN, and WAN but their expansion and extension.

On the way to a GAN one might see a different architecture, more advanced network technology, and a national infrastructure like the telecommunications superhighway (or information highway) in the US. There, the five channels of communications (telephone, TV, cable, satellite, and wireless cellular phones) now being opened to competition by many channels being auctioned (rather than licensed) by the government. The desire for competition and the "levelling of the field" for all players in telecommunications is also being pursued in the European Union, although through a different route: the Open Network Provision, planned for initiation on January 1, 1998.

It has been argued that we already have a GAN in the form of the Internet, which is a confederation of networks with each having its own opinion on how things should work. Each net pays its own share with the backbones being supported on a national or regional basis. Thus, in the US, the National Science Foundation was the payer; in France it is the EASInet funded by IBM and for the 18 European countries it is CERN in Geneva, Switzerland. However, there is the counter argument that the Internet is too *ad hoc* and informal. It is the outgrowth of ARPA-NET that was originally designed in the US to allow researchers and educationalists to "talk" to each other electronically. It was never designed for commercial use and is inadequate for the business and commercial needs of our modern world.

It is also possible that a network within the Internet may well grow faster than Internet. One such possibility is the World Wide Web, also called WWW, W3, or just "the Web". It is a set of servers that hold information on a massive range of topics including, of course, those of special interest to computer scientists and business computing personnel. The Web is a multimedia, hypertext-based electronic publishing system that makes it easy for anyone to navigate among the thousands of international databases that consist of text, diagrams, colour photographs, video clips and even sound tracks. The hypertext feature allows you to jump from one source to another related source merely at the click of the mouse. Many software interfaces are available for accessing the Web; the most popular graphical interfaces ("Web browsers") as of the mid-to-late 1990s are *Mosaic, Netscape* and *Internet Explorer*.

Figure 16.5:
Trends from past–current to current–future

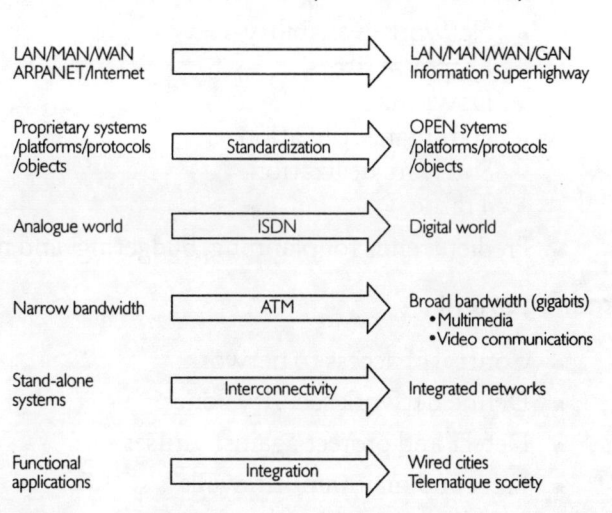

From	Via	To
LAN/MAN/WAN ARPANET/Internet		LAN/MAN/WAN/GAN Information Superhighway
Proprietary systems /platforms/protocols /objects	Standardization	OPEN sytems /platforms/protocols /objects
Analogue world	ISDN	Digital world
Narrow bandwidth	ATM	Broad bandwidth (gigabits) • Multimedia • Video communications
Stand-alone systems	Interconnectivity	Integrated networks
Functional applications	Integration	Wired cities Telematique society

Chapter 16: Network Management

Access to the Internet is of great interest to businesses because it facilitates the publication of electronic brochures and catalogues (as well as product information) quickly and seamlessly by hiding all the complexities of navigation behind buttons and objects highlighted on the screen. The Web and the Internet are also used by people who belong to *cyberculture*, move in *cyberspace*, use digital money, and work on a computer at home as a telecommuter.

Trends in computing that will affect network management are shown in Figure 16.5.

Summary and conclusions

A summary of functions to be performed by network management are listed below.

Fault/problem management

- Troubleshoot, diagnose, and predict potential:
  - Faults.
  - Outages.
- Identify, classify, analyze, and report faults/outages:
  - Initiate selected automatic "fixes" and restorals.

Performance management

- Measure/meter/monitor:
  - Network availability.
  - Response times.
  - Downtime.
  - Hardware utilization.
  - Software utilization.
  - Traffic.
- Predict trends for planning, budgeting, and maintenance.

Security management

- Control of access to network.
- Define network security zones.
- Detect and protect against viruses.
- Erect and maintain "firewalls".
- Backup and restore.
- Report unauthorized use and misuse.

Configuration management

- Initialize network entities.
- Reconfigure:
  * Systems (add/subtract/modify).
  * Rerouting of traffic through links and devices.

Account management

- Manage assets of inventory:
  * Hardware.
  * Software (application programs).
- Track and enforce licences.

User management

- Management of change:
  * Training.
- Make system end-user friendly.

Network management personnel have a virtual job that changes all the time, not only because the enterprise environment changes, but also because the technology changes. This may be said of many an IT professional, but more so for telecommunications personnel because their technology is ever-changing and changes rapidly. Telecommunications is one of the fastest-changing sectors of computer technology and the results can have profound implications – not just for the enterprise, but for the nation and, indeed, all of us.

Networking is not just networking of telecommunications and computer equipment, it is the networking of *people*. It not only brings people together through e-mail and the bulletin board, but it can facilitate group collaboration and have an impact on decision-making and problem solving.

Successful networking will require changes: changes required by corporate management and end-users as well as those required by maintenance (preventive or otherwise). Also, there is a lot of swapping of data on networks; for example, from the client to the server and vice versa. In all cases, changes should be transparent to the end-user otherwise they may feel anxious and worry about how they will be affected. The satisfied end-users are often ones who are not required to change what they do not initiate and want. Also, they do not always want to know about the bits and bytes of the system. When they need to learn about the system, they should be given the appropriate resource *when they need it*, not too much too soon and certainly not too little too late.

Just as training and education programmes need to be reactive they should also strive to be proactive. Education and training, as well as communication between the end-users and the technical personnel, are important strategies to reduce the stress of systems change. The relationship between the provider of communication services and customers of services must be reactive as well as proactive. There is often tension between the provider and customer because the customer often feels that the provider is not giving all that is possible and something is being held back. The customer and end-user may also feel that the provider can potentially reach further into their domain than they would like. The provider has more control over the customer's equipment than the customer would prefer. The customer may feel that their equipment is not restored fast enough and long after the systems performance is degraded.

There is sometimes a tension between end-users and corporate management on one side and network personnel on the other side. Why? Partly because telecommunications and networking personnel have great power since possession of information leads to power. These personnel are what Boguslaw calls the "computer elite". They have complete access to the corporate and enterprise information that enters the network. This situation arises with other IT personnel especially database personnel. But telecommunications personnel have great power of another kind. They can often start and stop any client and any server. They can "listen" into any message that comes in or goes out. These personnel may not use their power and commit computer crime but they still have access to enterprise and corporate information that they may misuse to affect decision-making and problem solving by corporate management. One way to overcome this problem is to bond all telecommunications personnel. Another approach is to build trust among the end-users and corporate management so that misuse could be contained and controlled, if not totally eliminated.

Case 16.1: Networking Parliament

Networking has made a wide range of information services instantly accessible to Members of Parliament. The parliamentary network has an FDDI (fibre distributed data interface) backbone and spans three buildings including the Palace of Westminster. The standard services include e-mail, word processing, bulletin boards and access to a CD-ROM library containing archives of national newspapers and Hansard. The system already has over 400 users but is designed for up to 4,000.

The plan for the ultimate network is still being implemented. Progress is slow because cabling through the twelve-inch-thick walls of the venerable building is extremely time-consuming. In addition, any cabling needs to allow for the future. However, some of the future services planned do not face technological problems but purely political and social ones. For example, take the implementation of videoing all the parliamentary happenings and debates directly into the Members' offices. This is technologically possible. But is it desirable? If implemented, would Members of Parliament stay in their offices rather than go to the floor?

Source: George Black. "All-party networking." *Which Computer?*

Case 16.2: Intrusions into the Internet

The Internet is the successor to the ARPANET that was designed by the US government to help researchers connect with each other. The Internet was not designed for general and extensive use by individuals and business organizations and hence no security measures for such use are in place. Internet gateway suppliers have maintained that antivirus scanning is the responsibility of the end-user.

Security measures are now being implemented and include "firewalls", electronic tokens and the PersonaCard. Meanwhile, numerous intrusions into the Internet have taken place:

- In 1988, a self-perpetuating worm virus, appropriately called the Internet worm, found its way into the University of California campus system and wriggled out of control for many days infecting and corrupting thousands of computers on the Internet.
- In 1993, the Lawrence Livermore National Laboratory in the US conceded that an employee had used its computers to distribute pornography on the Internet.
- In 1993, CERT (Computer Emergency Response Team) at the Carnegie Mellon University in the US warned network administrators that tens of thousands of Internet passwords have been stolen.
- CERT estimated that in 1993, there were 1,300 "incidents" on the Internet compared to 50 a few years earlier.

Source: *Business Week*, November 14, 1994, p. 88.

Things might get worse not better. The Internet is growing at 51–63% per year depending on the market segment. By the end of this century, it is predicted that there will be 200 million users.

Source: http://wwwe.cyberatlas.com/

Case 16.3: Analyzers at a Honda car plant

The Honda car-production plant in the US needs analyzers for maintaining its large network. Since it has a high-value-added product it cannot afford delays in its monitoring efforts and in detecting failures in its token ring network.

Management wanted probes connected to its critical LANs all the time:

> ... so we can get immediate alerts of problems and already have the diagnostic equipment in place.

The site has a LANvista system that comprises a master console with four remote token ring "slave" probes. Jeffers, at Honda, adds:

> Using the master console, we can toggle a view of any LAN, or all the LANs, to view any network activity, or perform diagnoses... Because probes are continually monitoring, we may already have data on problems – which is important if something has crashed to the point where we can't recreate the event.

Because of the client–server architecture used, network management:

> ... can make changes to the settings on the remote units, such as changing thresholds and trap requests, from the master console, can monitor and control multiple screens from a single console.

Source: Dern, Daniel P. (1992). "Troubleshooting Remote LANs." *Datamation*, vol. 38, no. 4 (February 15), pp. 53–6.

Case 16.4: Citibank with its $200 billion a day business

Citibank is one of the largest banks in the world as well as a high street bank in the US and Asia. In 1991, it began replacing its terminals with PCs to reduce paperwork and to validate the data input to its mainframe computers, of which it had 17 based in Lewisham. In 1992, Citibank began integrating all the securities functions into a single system and all the funds transfer into another function. The system is a client–server running on a Compaq SQL server cutting the end-of-day runs from three hours by a factor of six. The system is expected to:

- Handle 30,000 fund transfer transactions per day.
- Support 200 users.
- Give sub-second response times.
- Handle a business volume of $200 billion per day.

Source: George Black, "Citibank's Big Gamble." *Which Computer?* (May 1994), pp. 42–4.

References

Antaya, D. and Heile, Robert. (1992). "Digital Access Devices: Criteria for Evaluating Management Options." *Telecommunications*, vol. 29, no. 6 (June), pp. 51–2.

Boehm, W. and Ullmann, G. (1991). "Network Management." *International Journal of Computer Applications in Technology*, vol. 4, no. 1, pp. 27–34.

Briscoe, Peter. (1993). "ATM: Will It Live Up To User Expectation." *Telecommunications*, vol. 27, no. 6 (June), pp. 25–30.

Broadhead, Steve. (1992). "Network Management." *Which Computer?*, vol. 15, no. 10 (October), pp. 11–125.

Chapin, A. Layman. (1994). "The State of the Internet." *Telecommunications*, vol. 28, no. 1 (1994), pp. 13–8.

Derfler, Frank J. Jr. (1993). "An Eye into the LAN." *PC Magazine*, vol. 12, no. 1 (January 12), pp. 277–300.

Gaw, Shannon. (1996) "Signals from Servers." *LAN*, vol. 11, no. 12 (November), pp. 77–86.

Henderson, L. Brooks and Pervier, Cheryl S. (1992). "Managing Network Stations." *IEEE Spectrum*, vol. 29, no. 4 (April), pp. 55–8.

Marx, Gary T. (1994). "New Telecommunication Technologies Require New Manners." *Telecommunications Policy*, vol. 18, no. 7, pp. 538–551.

Miyatotmo, Bing. (1991). "The Growing Importance of Network Management Systems and Equipment." *Telecommunications*, vol. 25, no. 3 (March), pp. 26–30.

Muller, Nathan J. (1992). "Integrated Network Management." *Information Systems Management*, vol. 9, no. 4, pp. 8–15.

Sankar, Chetan S., Carr, Houston and Dent, William Dudley. (1994). "ISDN May be Here To Stay. But it's Still Not Plug-and-Play." *Telecommunications*, vol. 28, no. 10 (October), pp. 27–32.

Schneier, Bruce. (1994). *Applied Cryptography*. New York: John Wiley and Sons.

17 Privacy and Security

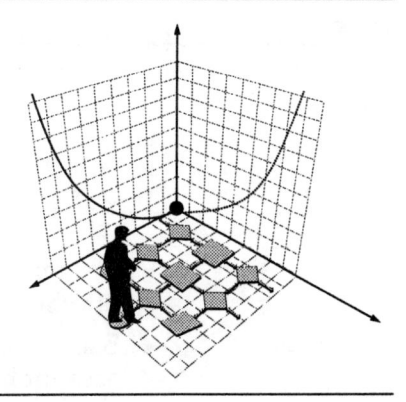

> Every new technology carries with it an opportunity to invent a new crime.
>
> *Laurence Urgenson*

Introduction

Most commercial, industrial and financial organizations process and transmit proprietary and sensitive information in the course of their daily activities. Protecting privacy and securing data from criminal access is a major concern. Equipment, software, manuals, forms and other components of computer systems are also vulnerable to wilful damage and theft. This chapter examines the issue of privacy and outlines security measures that help safeguard the security and privacy not only of data but of all computing resources. Recovery following natural disasters is also discussed. Management's responsibility in planning and implementing security is presented, and the question "How much security is essential?" is addressed.

Privacy

Issues of privacy

In modern society, data of a personal nature is collected by most business units. For example:

- Employers keep personnel records that include data on the address, age, education, work experience, salary, dependents, sick leave, capabilities and job performance of employees.
- Information on the status of customer accounts, including history of account ageing, payment record, and personal credit data, is kept in the files of organizations involved in sales.

- Patient information on health history, allergies, disabilities and prescribed medications is located in the files of doctors and hospitals.
- Insurance companies store information on the number and cost of vehicles, types, accident record and claims of clients.
- Banks keep records of loans, savings, deposits and withdrawals of account holders.

This list could go on and on. Just about every salient fact about every individual is in a computer file somewhere.

Although record-keeping has always been a part of organized society, the amount of data collected in the past was constrained. Because of access and storage problems and the inability to integrate and correlate data with speed, it was impractical to develop large databases prior to electronic processing. Nowadays, the ability of computers to process, store and retrieve vast quantities of data at high speeds has led to the collection of pools of data that constitute comprehensive personal dossiers. The data need not be centralized in a single, all-inclusive data bank. With the technology of linked databases and telecommunications networks, bank records can be integrated with medical records, employment records can be linked with government records, and so on.

Few people want the intimate details of their private lives in the public domain. They believe that they have a right to privacy, including the right to control the collection, dissemination and use of information of a personal nature. They recognize that their human rights and freedoms may be infringed when governments and other organizations have unrestricted files of personal data, for such files can be used for purposes of social control through surveillance. For example, a file listing an individual's race might be used to limit opportunity; a file listing political affiliation might be used to encourage conformity.

Concern for the "dignity and worth of the human person" underlies the historical and philosophical origins of claims to personal privacy. Some countries, like Germany, have constitutional underpinnings for the right to privacy. Most others rely on their legislators to study privacy concerns, develop codes of fair information practices and pass laws to protect citizens from the misuse of personal data.

Within Europe, *Guidelines on the Protection and Privacy of Transborder Flows of Personal Data*, published by the OECD in 1980, contributed to awareness of privacy issues. All twenty-four OECD members, including the UK, subsequently adopted these guidelines. And, in 1985, the Council of Europe's *Convention for the Protection of Individuals with Regard to Automatic Processing of Personal Data* went into effect.

Not all countries with data privacy laws follow the same legislative model. For example, the Americans have no federal watchdog agency to protect privacy like the UK's Data Protection Tribunal, and federal privacy law regulates only government handling of personal data, not corporate data banks. Some countries allow their citizens to check the accuracy and relevance of personal data in police files, which British law does not. See Table 17.1 for a summary of privacy protection provisions in Germany, Sweden, France, Canada and the United States.

Unfortunately, the existence of a legal framework for privacy legislation does not ensure that the public is being adequately protected from privacy infringement. As stated by David Flaherty, author of *Protecting Privacy in Surveillance Societies*:

> It cannot be emphasized too strongly that the incentives for the government and the bureaucracy are in the direction of invading, or at least ignoring or neglecting, privacy interests rather than protecting them. Most measures that are perceived as 'necessary' to cope with a societal problem involve surveillance through data collection. Especially in difficult economic times, the predominant goals are to improve efficiency, to reduce fraud, to cut expenditures on programs and staff, and to step up monitoring of the target population.
>
> *Flaherty*, 1989:382

A universal trait of data protection has been lax enforcement of legal provisions for audits and inspections. Complaints about misuse, or of inaccurate data are common in all countries with privacy legislation. In England, Community Charge officers were investigated for failure to comply with the Data Protection Act on Community Charge registration forms. More than 125 local councils asked unwarranted personal questions on the forms, such as the relationships between people living at the same address, dates of birth and educational details. And government leaflets failed to tell Scottish Community Charge payers how personal data was to be collected and compiled from confidential sources to form the Community Charge register. It is not enough simply to pass privacy protection laws: those charged with implementation must make the laws work.

Many westerners see the protection of privacy as a major societal issue of the 1990s. The problem is to allow organizations to collect and process personal data when they have a legitimate need to do so while at the same time protecting privacy.

Privacy in business

Every business with computerized files stores data on its employees and clients, often sensitive data of a personal nature, such as financial data,

Table 17.1 Models for protecting privacy

	Germany	Sweden	Canada	France	USA
Act	Federal Data Protection Act 1977	Data Act 1973, twice amended	Privacy Act 1982. Coupled with Access to Information law in one bill. Strengthens privacy provisions of Canadian Human Rights Act 1977	Law of Informatics and Freedoms 1978	Privacy Act 1974
Purpose	To "ensure against the misuse of personal data during storage, communication, modification and erasure (data processing) and thereby to prevent harm to any personal interests of the person concerned that warrant protection"	To prevent undue encroachment on individual privacy. Requires registration and license of databases with personal information	To regulate collection and use of personal information by the federal government. Includes principles of fair information practices	To protect data, with expanded coverage to a broad range of societal issues, with separate subcommissions on freedom to work, research and statistics, local government and technology and security	To place limits on government surveillance. Defines code of fair information practices for the collection and handling of personal data by agencies of the federal government
Organizational model	Bundestag selects a Data Protection Commissioner with advisory responsibilities to: 1. Assist in developing new data protection laws 2. Modify existing laws 3. Establish guidelines for data protection 4. Advise on policy implications for surveillance of different legislative proposals	Creates Data Inspection Board to control collection and dissemination of personal data, regulate data usages and enforce system of responsible keepers for computerized data banks. Law establishes detailed set of duties for data keepers	Creates Office of the Privacy Commissioner. Commissioner is Officer of Parliament. Acts as Ombudsman	Creates the National Commission on Informatics and Freedoms to implement law. Commission authorizes information systems and has 13 regulatory duties, including issuing deliberations, setting standards or issuing rules on security, making recommendations such as on right of access, carrying out inspections, and reporting offences	Requires that reports on new or altered information systems be submitted to Congress and the Office of Management and Budget, and the publication of these reports in summary form in the Federal Registrar. Responsibility for implementing fair information practices widely diffused
Powers of intervention	No authority for binding instructions if law is infringed, but can submit formal complaint to the competent body	Series of penalties and damages for breach of statute. But both government and legislature retain power to create data banks exempt from the Board's supervision	Commissioner has powers of investigation and auditing, but role is advisory. Oversseeing is secondary. Law makes each government institution responsible for administration of Privacy Act within the organization	Statutory burden on those being regulated to cooperate with Commission. Penal sanctions can be imposed for those who hinder the Commission's activities or refuse to supply information	Includes criminal sanctions for wilful disclosures of personal data or wilfully maintaining a record system without meeting public notice requirements. Enforcement left to officers in government agencies and individuals who can bring lawsuit to redress a grievance

Table 17.1 Models for protecting privacy (continued)

	Germany	Sweden	Canada	France	USA
Special features	Eleven states have counterparts of federal Data Protection Commissioner's office. States are mainly responsible for data privacy in education, health and police whereas the federal focus is security, defence, insurance and social security	Mandatory licensing system for information systems. In amended law, licensing requirements were modified to reduce bureaucratic burden and cost of data protection	Direct relationship between Commission and legislature through a standing committee of Parliament. Individual or privacy commission may appeal to the Federal Court-Trial Division following complaint to commissioner. Potential to reach Supreme Court of Canada. First time a country has linked laws on freedom of information and data protection in coherent manner	Part-time commissioners, many of whom are senior members of state bodies such as the administrative courts. Most are politicians with experience in government work but lacking technical competence	No privacy protection commission at the federal level. Dependence on litigation for enforcement
Model effectiveness	Federal Commissioner's advisory function well developed, but there is a risk that advice will be ignored. Lack of regulatory power for specific sensitive surveillance practices. Law needs strengthening	Sweden already is more of a surveillance society than western counterparts, which reduces scope of privacy in individual relations with the state	Data protection system suited to a federal state. Main problem: lack of implementation	Ineffective commission, bogged down in paperwork, weak leadership, inexperienced staff. Commission neglects audits, investigation of complaints and meaningful public relations. Commission highly politicized, unwilling to confront government on surveillance practices	Overseeing Privacy Act left to Office of Management and Budget which assigns low priority to this duty. Congressional committee overseeing has been limited and episodic. Loopholes in law, like "routine use" provision that allows fair use provisions to be bypassed. Yet progress is being made. Laters example: passage of the Computer Matching and Privacy Protection Act 1988

■ Source: David Flaherty, *Protecting Privacy in Surveillance Societies*. Chapel Hill, NC: University of North Carolina Press, 1989.

health status and work evaluations. Business managers have an obligation to ensure that such data are accurate, updated, secret and used for restricted purposes. Indeed, all of the data protection principles should be adopted by business as good practice, even when not mandated by law.

Data accuracy

Unfortunately, many businesses have lax data protection policies. Data accuracy, for example, may not be a priority unless accuracy is crucial to operations. To illustrate, a birth certificate is not required when applying for a bank loan or credit card since approval does not depend on the applicant's exact age. Yet a birth date mistake in bank records is important if that mistake is passed on to another organization where an accurate birth date is vital.

Most database administrators claim that they have no obligation to determine the accuracy of information that they receive from others. This is the position of TRW Information Service, a company that sells thirty-five million credit reports each year to 24,000 subscribers in the United States. Each month TRW receives computer tapes from thousands of companies containing the status of their customer accounts. TRW computers then lift, organize and store information from the tapes so that credit history can be supplied to TRW clients making credit checks. This service could not be provided if TRW were forced to check the accuracy of data elements on each tape. (It should be noted, however, that the company tries to ensure the accuracy of its files.)

Inaccuracy of files is not a trivial problem. Each year some 350,000 people register formal complaints about mistakes in TRW reports and about 100,000 of these result in change to information stored in TRW computers. How many incorrect entries are never noticed, never corrected? A business with personal data on file that are inaccurate may be responsible for:

1. Customer inconvenience and frustration. For example, a billing error may take numerous telephone calls and letters to correct.
2. The denial of goods and services to which individuals are entitled. For example, a car loan may be denied on the basis of inaccurate credit information.
3. The ruin of reputations and disruption of lives. For example, a mistake in an evaluation rating may cost a worker a deserved promotion.

One way to reduce errors in data banks is to allow individuals the right to inspect personal records and to challenge mistakes that they find. However, there is no way for the challenger to know whether mistakes were circulated prior to correction and, if so, what other databases contain the error. This explains why civil libertarians are concerned with the growth of computerized data banks and the unmonitored exchange of data.

Unfair use of personal data

Most people want control over the collection and use of personal data. They view secret files as a threat to individual freedom, and want limits placed on data collection to prevent organizations from gathering data that has no relevance to their legitimate needs. They favour *fair use* policies: for example, corporate policy stating that only personal data relevant to an organization's mission can be collected; that an individual's consent is required before stored personal data is passed from one data bank to another.

Personal information has a market value. For example, merchants can determine from such information where to direct their advertising. They can draw up lists of people who like the outdoors, to whom camping equipment might appeal, or lists of Mercedes owners, who might be attracted to diamond jewellery. By gaining access to a data bank of personal information, a mailing list of prospective customers could be prepared. Would this activity constitute an invasion of privacy?

A fair-use restriction gives individuals the right to participate in this decision. *Fair use* means that consent must be obtained before personal data in a data bank are shared with others. After all, data pools are attractive targets for all types of groups. Consider how a thief might value information regarding who goes on camping weekends or who likes diamond jewellery.

Fair use has gatekeeping ramifications as well. *Gatekeeping* is restricted access to services, privileges, benefits or opportunities. An example of gatekeeping is the point-scoring method used by many credit agencies to determine whether an individual is a good credit risk based on age, salary, duration of employment and so forth. In this case, gatekeeping serves a legitimate business interest; but gatekeeping can also be used to discriminate in ways that to most people would seem unfair. For example, suppose that doctors refused to treat all patients (and their families) whose names appeared in the database of malpractice claimants.

Guidelines for businesses

Most business mangers today are becoming sensitive to the public's concern over privacy. The following guidelines are ways to ensure that individual rights are respected when personal data are collected, maintained and used in the course of daily operations:

1. *Store only essential data.* Purge irrelevant and outdated information. This will not only reduce the danger of privacy invasion but will also diminish the information glut which plagues many firms, thereby lowering storage costs.
2. *Improve the security of data.* Periodically review and update physical safeguards and carefully screen personnel. Many computer systems in use today were designed before widespread concern over privacy issues and hence lack adequate data protection.
3. *Identify which data elements are sensitive.* Add data descriptions to these elements so they can be easily extracted from the data stream for control inspections and correction. Require management approval when use of these elements is extended to new applications.
4. *Adopt as policy that personal data should be complete, accurate and timely.* This requirement is good business, irrespective of privacy ramifications. One reason why it is difficult to isolate and assess the cost of privacy measures is that all sound information processing and control practices also serve the interests of privacy.
5. *Appoint an officer* to plan security and privacy measures, coordinate privacy policies with legal requirements and oversee privacy policy implementation.
6. *Establish procedures to implement notification and challenge rights.* Authorization forms for consent of use or release of information may be required. Appeal routines should be established. In many cases, procedures can be automated.
7. *Anticipate privacy legislation.* Design new information systems to report on sensitive data and to log and monitor use of the data: such controls will likely become law in the future. (Some privacy laws are already on the statute books, although they are not as comprehensive as many citizens would like.) Privacy features can be added to a system under development at low marginal cost, whereas adding them after a system is operational involves expensive redesign.

Cost of privacy

Two types of expenditure are involved when implementing corporate privacy policies: one-time development costs and recurring operational disbursements.

Development costs include analysis and design of procedures for privacy protection and the acquisition of equipment and software dedicated to that purpose. The main component of operations is salaries, primarily for clerks handling notification, access, challenge, correction and erasures. The cost of a manager's time to monitor procedures and standards and to resolve disputes should be added to this category, as should fees paid for legal advice. Other operational costs are for computer time, data storage, data transmission, rental or maintenance of security equipment and supplies. Operational costs peak after passage of privacy legislation, when many people exercise new rights of access and challenge and then stabilize at a lower level.

One problem in determining costs is that so many implementation strategies exist for privacy policies. Some companies require written consent from each data subject for each application. Others use a single release for all applications. If companies discontinue (or do not initiate) applications because of privacy considerations, should operational costs include estimates for degraded service?

Cost allocation is a problem when practices that affect privacy also serve other business interests. For example, security measures that protect personal data reduce the danger of lost records, guard trade secrets and circumvent sabotage of facilities. How can the cost of privacy policies be isolated from security costs?

Robert Goldstein has developed a model to simulate cost components and total costs, given different assumptions of privacy protection requirements and different management strategies. Goldstein's model is based on the premise that privacy costs do not come "out of the blue" but rather arise in response to various events. Each time one of these events occurs, certain actions are taken to comply with privacy regulations. These actions consume resources and generate costs. The model includes 22 events and 19 requirements (laws are represented as sets of requirements) and can calculate a potential of 7,500 different actions from the 18 most useful combinations of strategy variables. In spite of the complexity of this model the costs produced will not be accurate figures for any given organization because of the many unproven assumptions on which the model is based. The model's usefulness is for comparing relative costs of various strategies and for identifying variable relationships and assumptions.

Security

To ensure privacy of information, computer systems must be secure. That is, data must be protected against unauthorized modification, capture, destruction or disclosure. Personal data are not the only vulnerable data. Confidential data on market strategies and product development must be kept from the eyes of competitors. The large sums of money transferred daily by electronic fund transfer must be protected against theft. The very volume of business information processed by computers today means that the rewards for industrial espionage and fraud are of a much higher magnitude than in the past and are still increasing.

Records must also be protected from accidents and natural disasters. For example, a breakdown in the air-conditioning system may cause a computer to overheat, resulting in loss of computing capabilities. Fire, floods, hurricanes and even a heavy snowfall causing a roof to collapse can cause destruction of data and valuable equipment.

The *security* measures described in the following sections are designed to guard information systems from all of the above threats. The measures can be envisioned as providing layers of protection, as shown in Figure 17.1.

Figure 17.1:
Layers of control

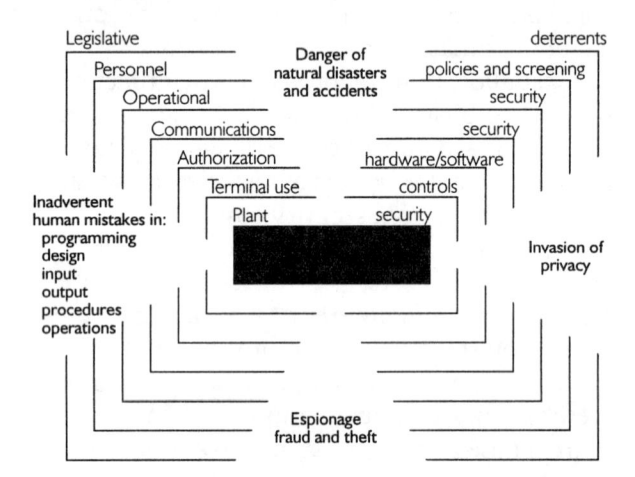

Some controls guard against infiltration for purposes of data manipulation, alteration of computer programs, pillage or unauthorized use of the computer itself. Other measures guard the physical plant, monitor operations and telecommunications and regulate personnel. Since control of inadvertent errors is the subject of Chapter 18, this chapter will focus on protection against calamities and criminal acts.

Plant security

Many protective measures can be incorporated in the construction or renovation of buildings to protect a computer from unlawful intrusion, sabotage or destructive acts of nature such as fire, floods or earthquakes: for example, locks and window grills, alarms and panic buttons, smoke detectors, earthquake-proof foundations and automatic fire extinguishers. (The fire extinguishers should be gas extinguishers, not water. Water can be almost as destructive as fire to electronic equipment, particularly to magnetic storage.)

Terminal use controls

Controlling access to terminals is a common method of guarding a system from illicit use. When all terminals are located in the computer centre, closing the centre to unauthorized personnel will provide one method of access control.

Badge systems, physical barriers (locked doors, window bars, electric fences), a buffer zone, guard dogs and security-check stations are procedures common to restricted areas of manufacturing plants and government installations where work with secret or classified materials takes place. A vault for storage of files and programs and a librarian responsible for the checkout provide additional control.

With online systems using telecommunications, security is a greater problem, since stringent *access controls* to terminals may not exist at remote sites. The computer itself must, therefore, ascertain the identity of persons who wish to log on and must determine whether they are entitled to use the system. Identification can be based on:

- What the user has, such as an ID card or key.
- Who the user is, as determined by some biometric measure or physical characteristic.
- What the user knows, such as a password.

Keys and cards

Locks on terminals that require a *key* before they can be operated are one way to restrict access to a computer. Another way is to require users to carry a *card i*dentifier that is inserted in a card reader when they want to use the computer. A microprocessor in the reader makes an accept or reject decision based on the card.

Many types of card system are on the market. Some use plastic cards, similar to credit cards, with a strip of magnetically encoded data on the front or back. Some have a core of magnetized spots of encoded data. Proximity cards contain electronic circuitry sandwiched in the card; the reader for this card must include a transmitter and receiver. Optical cards encode data as a pattern of light spots that can be "read" or illuminated by specific light sources, such as infrared. In addition, there are smart ID cards that have an integrated circuit chip embedded in the plastic. The chip has both coded memory, where personal identification codes can be stored, and microprocessor intelligence. The disadvantage of both keys and cards is that they can be lost, stolen or counterfeited. In other words, their possession does not absolutely identify the holder as an authorized system user. For this reason, the use of passwords is often an added security feature of key and card systems.

Biometric systems

Some terminal control systems base identification on the physical attributes of system users. For example, an electronic scan may be made of the hand of the person requesting terminal access. This scan is then measured and compared by computer to scans previously made of authorized system users and stored in the computer's memory. Only a positive match will permit system access.

Fingerprints or palm prints can likewise be used to identify bona fide system users. Such security systems use electro–optical recognition and file matching of fingerprint or palm print minutiae. Signature verification of the person wishing to log onto the computer is yet another security option. Such systems are based on the dynamics of pen motion related to time when the signer writes with a wired pen or on a sensitized pad.

A biometric system can also be based on voiceprints. In this case, a voice profile of each authorized user is recorded as an analog signal, then converted into digital from which a set of measurements are derived that identify the voice pattern of each speaker. Again, identification depends on matching: the voice pattern of the person wishing computer access is compared with voice profiles in computer memory.

Biometric control systems, of special interest to defence industries and the police, have been under development for many years. Although technological breakthroughs (enabling discrimination of complex patterns) have been made, pattern recognition systems are still not problem-free. Many have difficulty recognizing patterns under less-than-optimal conditions: a blister, inflammation, cut, even sweat on hands can interfere with a fingerprint match. Health or mood that changes one's voice can prevent a voiceprint match. A combination of devices, such as voice plus hand analyzers, might ensure positive identification; but such equipment is too expensive at the present time to be cost effective for most operations in business.

Authorization controls

In addition to the identification systems outlined in the preceding sections, control systems can be installed to verify whether a user is authorized to access files and databases, and to ascertain what type of access is permitted (read, write or update).

Data directory

A computer can be programmed to reference a stored *data directory security matrix* to determine the security code needed to access specific data elements in files before processing a user's job. When the user lacks the proper security clearance, access will be denied. In a similar manner, the computer might be programmed to reference a table that specifies the type of access permitted or the time of day when access is permitted.

Table 17.2 *Access directory*

User identification: 076-835-5623
Access limitation: 13 hours (CPU time for current fiscal year)
Account Number: AS5842

Data elements	Type of access	Security level	Terminal number	Time lock
Customer number	Read	10	04	08.00–17.00
Invoice number	Read	10	04	08.00–17.00
Cash receipt	Read/write	12	06	08.00–12.00

The data elements accessible from each terminal can likewise be regulated. For example, according to a programmed rule, the terminal in the database administrator's office might be the only terminal permitted access to all files and programs and the only terminal with access to the security matrix itself. A sample printout from an access directory, sorted by user identification number, is shown in Table 17.2.

Assigning access levels to individuals within an organization can be a difficult task. Information is power, and the right to access it is a status symbol. Employees may vie for clearance even when they do not require such clearance for their jobs. Managers should recognize that security measures designed to protect confidential data and valuable computing resources may antagonize loyal employees. It is important that the need for security be understood by workers and that security controls be administered with tact.

Passwords

The use of *passwords* is one of the more popular methods of restricting terminal access. One example of a password system is the required use of a personal identification number to gain access to an automated teller machine at a bank.

The problem with passwords is that they are subject to careless handling by users. Some users write the code on a sheet of paper that they carry in their wallet, or they tape the paper to the terminal itself. When given a choice, users frequently select a password that they can easily remember, such as their birth date, house number or names of pets, wives or children. Top of the list in Britain seems to be "Fred", "God", "Pass" and "Genius". Someone determined to access the computer will make guesses, trying such obvious passwords first. Even passwords as complex as algebraic transformations of a random number generated by the computer have been broken with the assistance of readily available microcomputers. Of course, the longer a password is in use, the greater the likelihood of it being compromised.

One-time passwords are a viable alternative. But systems of this nature are difficult to administer. First of all, each authorized user must be given a list of randomly selected passwords. Then there must be agreement on the method of selecting the next valid password from the list, a method that is synchronized between computer and user. Finally, storage of the list must be secure, a challenge when portable terminals are used by personnel in remote sites where security may be lax.

Recently, a number of password systems have been put on the market that generate a new password unique to each user each time access is attempted. This is done with a central intelligent controller at the host site and a random *password generator* for each user. Typically, the system works as follows. To gain mainframe access the user enters his or her name (or ID code) on a terminal keyboard. The computer responds with a "challenge number". This is input to the user's password generator. By applying a cryptographic algorithm and a secret key (a set of data unique to each password generator) to this challenge "seed", a one-time password is generated. The user then enters this password into the computer. The central controller simultaneously calculates the correct password and will grant access if a match occurs.

Such password management systems are difficult to compromise, because passwords are constantly changed. Only a short period of time is allowed for entry of the correct password. Furthermore, the control system is protocol dependent. This compounds the problems of a person trying to breach the system in a network having a variety of protocols. The advantage to the user is that the password generator is portable, usually a hand-held device, and easy to use.

In recent years, much publicity has been given to *hackers*, usually youths, who often derive malicious pleasure in circumventing access control systems. Case studies show the damage hackers have caused by secretly inserting spurious software into information systems.

Communications security

Computer processing is today closely linked with telecommunications, which allows the transfer of computer data between remote points. Protecting the confidentiality of this data at the initiating terminal, during transmission itself or when transmission is received, has required the development of sophisticated security techniques. For example, a *handshake*, a predetermined signal that the computer must recognize before initiating transmission, is one way to control communications. This prevents individuals from masquerading, pretending to be legitimate users of the system. Most companies use *callback boxes* that phone would-be users at preauthorized numbers to verify the access request before allowing the user to log on. A hacker who has learned the handshake code would be denied access with such a system. Protocols, conventions, procedures for user identification (described earlier in this chapter) and dialogue termination also help maintain the confidentiality of data.

During transmission, messages are vulnerable to wire-tapping, the electromagnetic pickup of messages on communication lines. This may be eavesdropping, passive listening or active wire-tapping involving alteration of data, such as piggybacking (the selective interception, modification or substitution of messages). Another type of infiltration is reading between the lines. An illicit user taps the computer when a bona fide user is connected to the system and is paying for computer time but is "thinking", so the computer is idle. This and other uses of unauthorized time can be quite costly to a business firm.

Operational security

Control measures to protect information systems during processing are discussed in Chapter 18. What needs to be emphasized here are general administrative strategies to protect the system as a whole. For example, empirical evidence shows that systems are particularly vulnerable to intrusion during conversion, after the new system has passed acceptance tests and is being readied for operations. Employees inexperienced with the new system are not alert to possible security infringements, while technicians, exhausted by the rigours of conversion, are often less attentive than usual. As a result, changes in procedures, data and programs may be introduced without notice. Experience has shown that it is advisable to intensify security during conversion.

During daily operations, a careful check of logs, utilization reports and irregular behaviour should be the norm. Most companies schedule periodic audits as well. Some firms hire private detectives to oversee security, although this can have an adverse effect on employee morale. There are even reported cases of companies hiring individuals on parole for programming fraud on the premise that someone who knows how to break the system also knows how to prevent security violations.

But even the best security cannot prevent natural disasters, and determined malefactors have circumvented controls too often for any guarantee of a given system's immunity to attack. Insurance will compensate for monetary losses in same cases, but an essential part of operational security is planning for *recovery* of what is lost (data, programs or hardware) and for placing the system speedily back in operation. This is a manager's responsibility. Many vendors supply customers with manuals, including checklists, to assist in reconstruction planning. In order to plan what procedures should be implemented following a disaster or system collapse, management must:

1. Determine the minimum resource configuration needed to resume operations.
2. Identify which computer records are vital.
3. Establish job priorities. (Given reduced capacity, which jobs should be run?)
4. What turnaround times are crucial?
5. Assign recovery responsibility. (Who has the authority to mobilize organizational resources and rule on conflicts of interest during recovery?)

An alternative processing site should also be planned in case the computer facility is extensively damaged. Since a backup computer in the same building might also be destroyed in the same disaster, a distant secondary facility is advisable, although this adds communication difficulties to problems of recovery. Firms with distributed processing can generally function when one network link is broken. Firms with centralized computing will require this secondary facility.

One solution is to join a mutual backup consortium or to make a mutual assistance arrangement with another firm. Each firm agrees to carry an extra workload (a third shift, perhaps) should a partner be in need. In such cases, problems of systems compatibility need to be resolved and backup files for the alternative site must be maintained.

Some auditors recommend, as part of regular auditing procedures, surprise tests to check the effectiveness of disaster planning. Certainly, planning for systems breakdown should take place in all firms, and employees should be informed what actions to take in emergencies. A simple memo may suffice or detailed handbooks may be necessary, depending on the nature or complexity of the business.

Personnel safeguards

One might expect that external threats to security would be a firm's major concern, but many studies show that users and computer personnel within an organization are more likely to breach security than outsiders. Security may be breached by terminal operators, programmers, computer operators, even vice presidents. Motives for criminal acts can be attributed to ego (the desire to demonstrate individual superiority over the system), revenge, financial gain, irrational behaviour and zealous adherence to a cause. When screening applicants, assigning duties and supervising operations, managers should be cognizant of their vulnerability to internal security violations.

One well-known organizational principle that serves security is *separation of responsibility*: no employee should perform all the steps in a single transaction. For example, record-keeping should be separated from the physical custodianship of records.

Computer systems can be divided into five basic functions:

- Programming and systems development.
- Handling input media.
- Operation of data processing equipment.
- Documentation and file library.
- Distribution of output.

It is advisable that the work assignment of no employee cross these functional lines. Separation of responsibility serves as a deterrent to crime, because a given job must pass through many hands, which facilitates many independent checks for accuracy and possible fraud. Although separation may not be feasible in small organizations because the limited numbers of employees means a single individual may have to perform many jobs, the principle should be followed whenever possible. Security can also be promoted by rotating the duties and responsibilities of employees, by unannounced audits, by establishing a climate of honesty, and by close observation of disgruntled employees. Giving publicity to security measures may serve as a deterrent to attempted systems intrusions. Employees should be trained in security risks and procedures. In addition, the appropriateness, adequacy and readiness of emergency planning should be periodically tested by drills. Many security officers state that the installation of security devices, such as alarms and detectors, is not the hard part of their jobs. What is difficult is motivating employees to be alert and sensitive to security issues.

Security in a microcomputer environment

Even though microcomputer systems process less volume of information than mainframes, they too must be protected from accidental or intentional data loss. Most of the measures described in this chapter for guarding the privacy of data and ensuring systems security are as appropriate in a microcomputer environment as in a computer centre housing minis and mainframes.

However, a number of factors do contribute to unique problems in administering a microcomputer security programme. For example, many micro users have limited computing experience and, unlike IT professionals, are not aware of, or alert to, possible security infractions. Contingency planning is frequently ignored, regular backup procedures are lacking, provisions for audit trails are uncommon, and few local networks monitor network activity. Unfortunately, the current generation of micro hardware and software does not support effective security for the most part. The low cost of micro systems, in effect, limits the amount of system resources devoted to security. What's more, microcomputer hardware seems to present a temptation to thieves, while software theft for personal use on other machines is a common problem.

One solution to the security of micros is the use of Bernoulli drives. These have removable cartridges that can store an entire database and the source code that generates that data. After use, the disks can be secured under lock and key. Passwords and encryption are two other protective measures frequently used with microcomputer systems. Ironically, one of the principal reasons for the spread of micros – to let more people benefit from computer capabilities – is the very advantage that creates so many security problems.

Who is responsible?

Figure 17.2 summarizes management's role in planning, implementing, monitoring and evaluating security measures. A firm's survival is at stake when losses must be absorbed due to sabotage or theft.

Its reputation for quality service may be imperiled and years of accumulated goodwill endangered when security proves inadequate. Although IT personnel should participate in technical control decisions, corporate management has the responsibility to identify vital data, establish security points, outline security procedures, assign enforcement personnel, allocate the necessary resources and take corrective action when security is violated.

Figure 17.2:
Security overview and action process (source: adapted from the IBM document G320–1372, 1974, pp. 42–3)

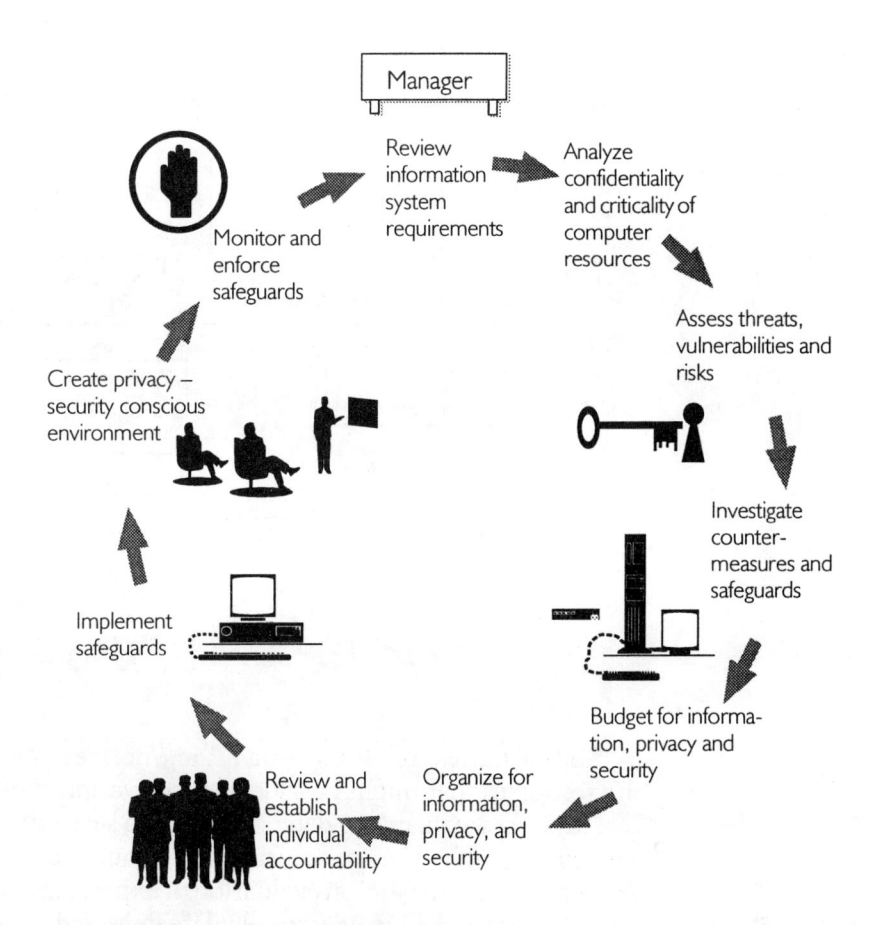

Management is also responsible for training programmes to make employees sensitive to privacy and security issues. Clearly, all security measures adopted should be flexible, effective and enforceable.

How much security?

Security is costly. In addition to the expense of equipment and personnel to safeguard computing resources, other costs must be considered, such as employee dissatisfaction and loss of morale when security precautions delay or impede operation. In deciding how much security is needed, management should analyze *risk*. How exposed and vulnerable are the systems to physical damage, delayed processing, fraud, disclosure of data or physical threats? What threat scenarios are possible?

As illustrated in Figure 17.3, systems and user characteristics should be assessed when evaluating risk.

Chapter 17: Privacy and Security

Figure 17.3:
Factors in assessing expected losses from systems intrusion

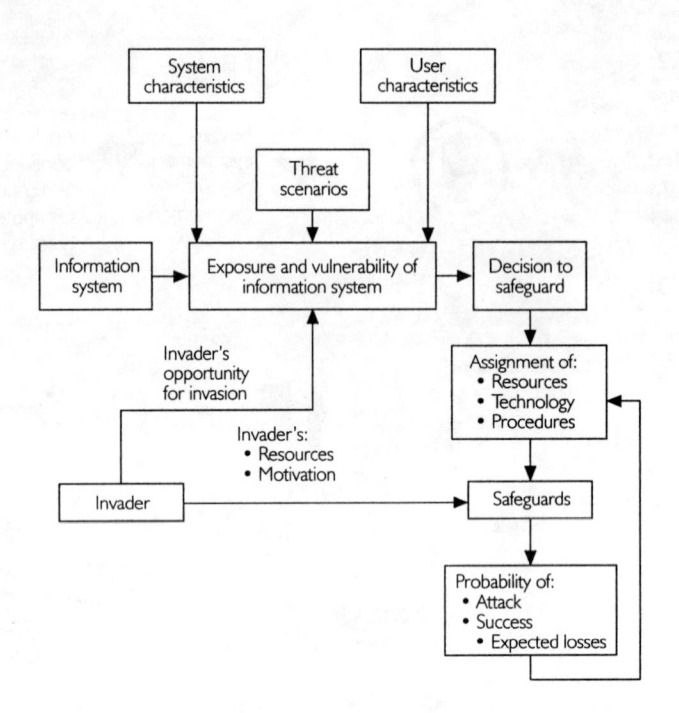

Opportunities for systems invasion, motives of a possible invader, and resources that might be allocated to invasion should be considered. The resources available to deter or counter a security breach should also be appraised. The level of security that should be devoted to a system should be based, in part, on evaluation of expected losses should the systems be breached. One way to calculate expected losses from intrusion is by application of the formula:

Expected loss = $L \times P_A \times P_B$ where:

L = potential loss
P_A = probability of attack
P_B = probability of success

An insurance company or computer vendor can help management determine the value of L. Probability values are more difficult to obtain. Rather than attempting to assign a specific value (0.045 or even 0.05 may be of spurious accuracy), relative risk (high, medium or low) should first be determined and a numerical value assigned to each of these relative probabilities (for example, 0.8, 0.5 and 0.2, respectively). The risk costs can now be calculated according to the formula. For example:

Exposure	L	× P_A	× P_B =	Expected loss
1	£500,000	1.0	0.2	£100,000
2	200,000	0.6	0.5	60,000
3	50,000	0.2	0.8	8,000
Total expected loss				*£168,000*

Loss is determined for each exposure; the sum of the expected losses is the total risk value to the system. If P_A and P_B are probabilities for the year, expected loss is £168,000 per year. The application of this formula will help management determine whether the addition of security measures is worth the cost and where the greatest reduction of expected losses could occur by improving security.

The figures derived from the formula are approximations at best. We simply do not have the data to calculate reliable probabilities, because the computer industry is too new to have a long historical record of invasions on which to base probability assessments. Furthermore, firms are reluctant to publicize how their security has been breached lest their credibility suffer, so news of security invasions is seldom broadcast. This means that data on security infractions are incomplete. More serious, is that people who design security measures are not always aware of the tricks and techniques used by perpetrators of crime to break systems security and so cannot plan countermeasures.

Security for advanced technology

Thus far, we have discussed the security considerations for layers of control in an information system, but there are many changes in the technology employed at each layer and point of control. Computer technology is well known for its many entries (and exits) of innovation. Some of these are listed in Table 17.3. Space limitations do not allow us to examine all or even some of them in any detail except perhaps one: image processing. This will illustrate the types of threat to security posed by one advanced technology. These threats include:

- Unauthorized copying and downloading of images on terminals, PCs, and workstations.
- Unauthorized release of images by users (including end-users).
- Integrity of images and unauthorized modifications made to them.
- Authenticity of images stored in documents.

- Since image processing requires large amounts of memory and fast computers, it uses minis and mainframes which are accessible through a network and telecommunications. This opens a wide set of threats. Also, the large computers necessary for image processing contribute to the temptation of using these powerful resources to break the security codes of other systems thereby increasing the threat posed to the security of the system.

Table 17.3 *Technologies affecting security of information asset*

- Image processing
- Teleprocessing
  - LANs/MANS/WANS/Internet
  - Superhighway
  - Global networks
  - PCN (personal computer networks)
  - Wireless communications
  - FAX connections
- Mechatronics (embedded computers)
- Smart cards
- NNets (neural networks)
- Laptop computers
- Palmtop computers
- Pen-based computers
- PDAs (personal digital assistants)
- Personal communicators
- Pocket pals
- Video conferencing

Each of the technologies listed in Table 17.3 present a unique set of benefits, exposures to risk, and potential losses, as well as adding the cost of implementing a response to the threat. Management must continuously evaluate the consequences of failure to protect its assets of information and the cost of updating its protection against technological changes. To achieve this, management must maintain knowledge of the technological changes and its potential impact on security; anticipate threats and vulnerabilities; and develop protective defence measures necessary to combat the threat. The anticipation aspect is important because protective measures must be instituted during the design stage of development and sometimes even earlier in the planning stage and user specification stage.

One change in technology, albeit an undesirable one, but one that can be anticipated, is the computer virus.

Computer viruses

A *computer virus* is software that, when entered into a computer system can cause it to stop or interrupt operations. It could also corrupt data, destroy data/knowledge bases, and cause errors or disrupt operations. The virus does not just appear or grow. It is inserted (knowingly and deliberately) into the system. It is definitely unauthorized.

A virus is a class of programs. Another sort of computer vermin is the *worm* which is a program that "worms" its way through a system, altering small bits of code or data when it gets access to it. A worm may also be a virus if it reproduces itself and infects other programs. In contrast, there is the *logic bomb*, which is a computer program that is set to "explode" when a specified condition is met.

The computer virus has the ability to propagate into other programs. However, the computer virus program must be run in order to reproduce or to do damage. For this to happen, a computer virus must be introduced into the system. One way a computer virus can enter the system is in the form of a *trojan horse*, which is a computer program that seems to do one thing but also does something else. But, the virus has a new and malicious twist to it. The virus can act instantly or lay dormant in the system until it is triggered by a specified date or an event such as the processing of five programs, or the logging on as a specific user, or whatever.

How does a virus operate? Zajac (1990:26) describes the Lehigh virus (named after the Lehigh University in the US). This virus consisted of seven lines of code in Pascal and was placed in a DOS command file. It operated as follows:

> ... when a user typed a DOS command, the virus would check to see if there was a non-infected... file on the system. If so, it infected it and incremented a counter that kept track of how many other disks it had infected. The virus would then execute the user's command. All this unbeknown to the user... when the infection counter hit four, it would totally erase the hard disk.

The computer virus has many objectives and can have many consequences. Some cases illustrating its variety are listed below:

- The Pakistani virus an infected untold number of PCs as it travelled around the world creating havoc and fear among PC users. The authors of this virus had the gall (or courtesy!) to announce its existence with the message "Beware of this VIRUS. Contact us for vaccination." The message was followed by a 1986 copyright date and two names (Amjad and Basit) and an address in Pakistan. The virus is also known by its generic type: the BRAIN

Chapter 17: Privacy and Security

virus, named after the volume label of an infected disk which reads "(c)BRAIN." This naming is perhaps because the authors worked for the "Brain Computer Services".

The BRAIN virus surfaced in the US at the University of Delaware in 1987 followed a month later by the Lehigh virus.

- The Cornell virus was a passive virus with the intent of collecting names and passwords. It infected thousands of mainframe computers throughout the world to enable them to be used later as deemed desirable.
- In 1987, a virus appeared in a computer network in California and interfered with the scan control on video monitors and caused one to explode.
- The Jerusalem virus followed the Delaware virus by two months and its first strain appeared in the Hebrew University in Israel.
- In the early 1990s, the "Bulgarian factory" replaced Israel as the source of viruses and over 100 viruses from Bulgaria have infected the Eastern European countries.
- A magazine publisher in Germany distributed over 100,000 disks to its subscribers. Unknown to the publisher, each disk was infected with a STONED II computer virus.
- A student in California was given a disk with a free program. She used the disk (which was infected and unknown to her) to do her homework assignments. She took the disk to her university and loaded it on the university network to continue with her assignments. Inadvertently, she infected all the students using the network and caused the system to operate incorrectly.
- An employee in a large firm used a program (not known as being infected) available externally on a public network and downloaded it to her PC. She then used this program on the firm's network thereby infecting the network and erasing many corporate files.

A "cruise" virus is similar to the Cornell virus. It is a sophisticated passive virus that could infect disks that are distributed openly. When loaded onto a system it collects information like names and passwords and can be accessed by the intruder and used for authorized access to the system.

> Once inside the system, the intruder unleashes the virus, which lurks there until an authorized individual decrypts material or enters the access sequence; the virus then attacks the material.

Dehaven, 1993:140

The "stealth" virus is named after the stealth bomber that attacked Iraq in the Gulf War. It cruises stealthily inside a system for a long time before it strikes. It is known to be designed to elude most of the anti-virus systems. Its versions include the 4096, the V800, and the V2000.

One may ask: How many viruses are around? The answer can be found in various studies. One study in 1991 estimated that there were (at that time) over 900 known viruses. Over 60% of the 600,000 PCs studied had been hit by a virus. Of the sites infected, 38% were confronted with corrupted files; 41% complained of unsolicited screen messages, interference or lockup; and 62% reported a loss in productivity (Sanford, 1993:67).

How does an end-user, or for that matter, a computer system, protect itself from these infectious and dangerous viruses? One answer lies in knowing the possible motivations and the sources of the viruses. The main motivations are: greed for money, revenge (against an employer or a firm), and "intellectual challenge" to outsmart others.

There are two main sources of computer viruses:

1. An employee (insider).
2. Openly distributed programs such as those distributed by magazine publishers and software vendors.

The employee is motivated by greed or by revenge. The intruder that uses the open distribution channels is mainly motivated by the intellectual challenge of breaking a system. This type of intruder is a professional who does not get the public media attention but nevertheless accomplishes a sinister mission. The reward for this type of intruder is a rise in ego.

The main counter strategy for (1) is to:

- Control access to programs and data/knowledge and susceptible media.
- Invest in people who are the greatest threat and also the greatest asset to security for they can often stop or at least discourage intruders.
- Monitor and control access to all "vital" computer programs as well as data/knowledge bases – *especially* access rights granted to any employees who may be unhappy with the organization.
- Control all access during the conversion phase of new systems. This is when the system has been satisfactorily tested and every one relaxes, a perfect time for the intruder to sneak a virus into the system. A strategy to prevent this is for a copy of the tested system to be locked up and used periodically to check for any unauthorized insertions.

The important controls for (2) are:
- Do not use unknown software.
- Mainframes and even PCs should have a "quarantine box" to sample check new software.
- Centralize software purchasing and purchase only from an approved list of vendors.
- Do not use freely distributed disks unless they are "reliable" and tested in a "quarantined" program.
- Control access to networks. Do not allow persons or "workstations" access without the "need" for such access. When access is allowed it is logged. This logging may not always identify the intruder but it may dissuade them.
- Regularly change the common systems passwords.
- Educate and instruct employees of the danger of viruses and their epidemics.
- Keep track of where your disks/tapes, and programs (including updates) have come from and where they have been.

Controls for both (1) and (2) are:
- Latest and frequent backups to recover, sometimes an extra generation deep.
- Anti-viral computer programs, scanners, and filters (programs that check for "signatures" of known viruses and alert the user of a possible danger).
- Keep abreast with the virus technology. One journal on the subject is *The Virus Bulletin* published in the UK.

The main danger of all these strategies is that they may lull the potential victims into a sense of being protected. The anti-viral strategies we have are against "known" viruses only. Corporate managers and end-users must recognize that intruders – especially those who are "intellectually motivated" – may be challenged by a system's control mechanism into finding a new viral strain and so add a new twist to an old threat. Determined intruders may even devise new and innovative threats just to "beat the system".

There is also a cost to all this control and strategies against viruses. There is a possible loss of morale when employees are not fully trusted. There is also a loss in efficiency. Each layer and level of security has an overhead cost and loss in productivity and performance. In addition to calculating these costs, one must estimate the probability of attack and the value of the loss entailed if the attack is successful. This analysis is necessary before a security system is designed and implemented to combat viruses.

To guard against viruses and other threats to security, a firm needs to organize for its security, the next subject of our discussion.

Organization for security

Formal organization for security is desirable when data/information/knowledge (henceforth referred to as "data") is complex, distributed, valuable, or a combination of all these factors. When data is of a simple structure, such as an inventory file of goods, its security might not be such an issue – even if the inventory was a very large data file. However, if data is complex as, for example, in a student file which has data on addresses, information on parents, personal data, and grades, then it becomes more complex to provide for the different levels of security and privacy. An example of complexity in business would be an insurance file or an income tax file containing personal, economic, and financial data.

Another reason for security may be the high value of the data such as payroll or EFT (electronic fund transfer) data. In all these cases, data may well be stored in a centralized repository with restricted access. Now consider a distributed system with data coming in and going out to different locations and to different nodes in the same physical location. Here, we not only have problems of storage but also of *flow*. We now have the problem of securing the point(s) of origin and destination (through techniques like passwords, discussed above) and securing the data flow during transmission (possibly through cryptography as discussed in Chapter 16).

In all the above cases, the problem arises as to whether the benefits of security are worth the cost. Is the protection of grades, payroll data, or financial data worth the cost of securing it? The answer should come from a risk analysis. Only if it is worth the cost should security measures be instituted, monitored, and enforced. Before the risk analysis, however, we need to take other steps, including the appointment of a security officer and identifying the assets to be secured.

All this assumes that a determination of the need for security management has been made by top management: security involves not just a financial cost but also an "organizational cost". Steps in security management are shown graphically in Figure 17.4. We shall now discuss the steps in some detail.

Chapter 17: Privacy and Security

Figure 17.4:
Organization for security

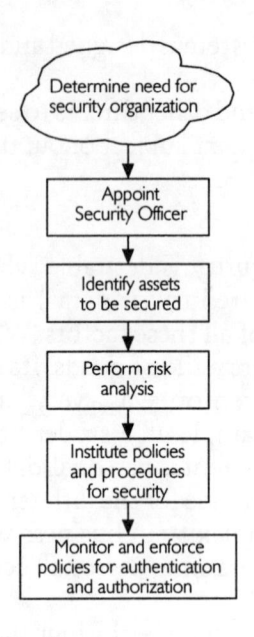

- Determine need for security organization
- Appoint Security Officer
- Identify assets to be secured
- Perform risk analysis
- Institute policies and procedures for security
- Monitor and enforce policies for authentication and authorization

Appointment of a security officer

A security officer requires skills that largely depend on the complexity, value, and distribution of data. For example, in a centralized environment the technical skills required would include an understanding of the OS (operating system) and databases. If the system is distributed, the technical skills required would include knowledge of telecommunications, clients, servers, and equipment needed in telecommunications.

Administrative and organizational skills will be needed in resolving any conflicts that arise in the demands made by distributed end-users. Rules and procedures for an orderly and secured access will have to be imposed or "negotiated". As the value and complexity of data increases, the security manager needs both skills and experience, not just in technology but in administration and management.

Identifying assets to be secured

In a small organization, securing every computing asset would be both simple and feasible. But with larger organizations, there may be a price to pay. Security in large organizations can become expensive, it can reduce turnaround times and may even add to the inconvenience of all users. It then becomes desirable to identify assets that *need* to be secured. Such assets might include hardware such as clients, servers, or peripherals which should be "locked" by time (during lunch hours?) or by control of access (for example, by password). Software can also be "locked" for types of use, such as proprietary software or those that process monetary transactions. Software can also be "locked" by type of use (i.e. read, write or modify), by user, or at any level of the database (i.e. by file, record, or even data-element). The structure of the database, the ease of navigation, and the depth of search can all affect the response time and the cost of security. Thus the identification process is not just a formality but must be comprehensive and encompass all the data elements that flow through the organization. In identifying what data is to be secured, the security officer must work closely with the DBA (database administrator).

Resources for security

Measures for the protection of security are relatively straightforward and easy to implement when assets are centralized and physical access is "closed-shop". In distributed processing there is a conflict between the concept of distributed control for operations and the desire of centralized control for security purposes. Why should control of security not also be distributed? It should be for local processing, but for corporate databases and corporate computing resources the control must be centralized and the responsibility of central administration. The security manager is responsible for the corporate rules and procedures of security that all users (including end-users) must observe. Hopefully, the observance is not a grudging one but a cooperative one. The rules may well evolve from the bottom rather than be imposed from the top. If evolving from the bottom the security manager may object to proposed rules if the centre feels that they interfere with the centre's ability to schedule and process efficiently and effectively. What is possible and desirable is largely a function of the organization, culture and management (corporate and IT) involved.

All security procedures and measures should be coordinated with the auditor who also has divided responsibility for security. The relationship between the security officer and the auditor is a horizontal one with each reporting to a different supervisor, so the relationship is a delicate one, but yet another relationship for the security manager that must be closely coordinated.

Monitoring and enforcement

The monitoring and enforcement of procedures and rules for security is the prime responsibility of the security management staff. They accomplish this largely by authorization of access and the ability to perform specific operations once access is achieved. This involves determining who can read, write, or modify a file. For example, a student may have access to the records of his/her grades but cannot change or modify them. Even an instructor may not be allowed to change a grade once assigned without approval of higher authority. Likewise, in business, authority for financial payments is restricted to different levels of management each having authority over specific amounts. So authorization becomes a matter of privilege. For security management these privileges must be carefully defined. They could involve personal feelings and prestige and must be resolved amicably without hurting feelings, whenever possible.

Another problem with monitoring is that of authentication which determines access to different computing assets. This too must be monitored and enforced to prevent unauthorized access.

Summary and conclusions

Computer technology posses a threat to personal privacy because of the speed of processing, the collection of vast data banks, instantaneous retrieval capabilities and the world-wide network of data transmission through teleprocessing and networks.

Privacy is closely linked to security. No one disputes that information systems must be guarded from unlawful intrusion, that human errors should be detected, and that damage from natural disasters must be minimized. Management's dilemma is not *whether* security is needed but *how much*.

Computer crime is increasing at an alarming rate. This can be attributed, in part, to the temptation arising from the large sums of money being transferred by electronic fund transfer and to the fact that more criminals are becoming knowledgeable about computer technology and are equipped with powerful computers to help them plan and execute their crimes. There are also individuals who are challenged simply to "beat the system".

It is generally acknowledged that crime figures are destined to rise unless the computer industry and organizations that use computers pay greater attention to security issues and devote more resources to the protection of information systems. All known protective mechanisms can be broken, given enough time, resources, and ingenuity. Perhaps the major objective of security systems should be to make intrusion too expensive (in equipment, cost, and risk) and too time-consuming (in planning effort and time needed to actually break safeguards) to make attempted violations worthwhile.

Figure 17.5: A taxonomy of flaws in software security

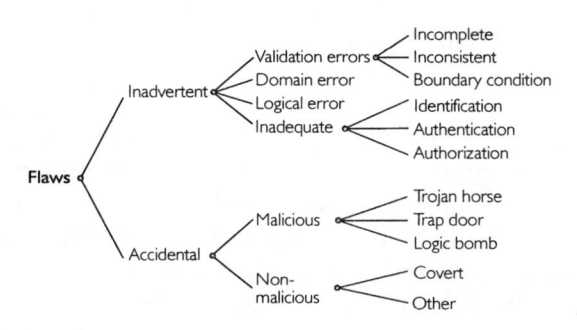

```
                            ┌─ Validation errors ─┬─ Incomplete
                            │                     ├─ Inconsistent
                            │                     └─ Boundary condition
               ┌─Inadvertent┼─ Domain error
               │            ├─ Logical error
               │            │                  ┌─ Identification
               │            └─ Inadequate ─────┼─ Authentication
       Flaws ──┤                               └─ Authorization
               │                      ┌─ Trojan horse
               │         ┌─ Malicious ┼─ Trap door
               └─Accidental           └─ Logic bomb
                         │
                         └─ Non-      ┌─ Covert
                            malicious └─ Other
```

Risk analysis and the assessment of expected losses and gains from security protection is one method of helping management determine which security strategies are most cost effective, given budgetary constraints. Security can be provided by access controls, physical safeguards, personnel screening and policies, and operational controls discussed in this chapter. Laws that act as a deterrent to computer crime also provide a measure of security. Laws relating to privacy and security are being enacted in many countries especially the UK where the 1984 Data Protection Act was revised to stay relevant to the changing computing environment.

Many security violations are due to faults in software. These are summarized in Figures 17.5 and 17.6 (an adaptation from Landwehr et al., 1994: 215–16).

Figure 17.6: Security flaws by time of location

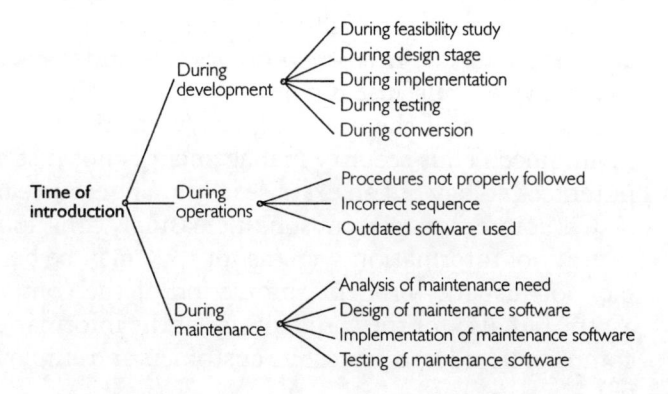

```
                       ┌─ During      ┌─ During feasibility study
                       │  development ├─ During design stage
                       │              ├─ During implementation
                       │              ├─ During testing
                       │              └─ During conversion
        Time of        │
        introduction ──┼─ During      ┌─ Procedures not properly followed
                       │  operations  ├─ Incorrect sequence
                       │              └─ Outdated software used
                       │
                       │              ┌─ Analysis of maintenance need
                       └─ During      ├─ Design of maintenance software
                          maintenance ├─ Implementation of maintenance software
                                      └─ Testing of maintenance software
```

Advances in computer technologies (like teleprocessing, wireless communication, image processing, smart cards, NNets, Internet, intranet, intelligent systems, and video conferencing) are posing new and unique problems of security. To implement effective security, IT management (and corporate management) must follow steps of appointing a security officer, planning for security needs, identifying assets to be secured, preparing risk analysis, instituting policies and procedures for security, and then enforcing and monitoring these safeguards.

In the 1970s and even early 1980s, there was great concern over privacy. In the 1990s, there is much less concern and little talk about legislation on privacy. However, concern for privacy has given way to concern for viruses. This is a problem that became public in 1984 and since then has become both troublesome and complex. Despite the growing number of scanners, immunizers, and memory-resident activity monitors that can defend against some viruses, the parasites seem to grow faster than they can be identified and information systems are compromised. Many viruses may be in their "incubation" stage and unknown to us. Also, the viruses are getting better and more ingenious making them difficult to identify let alone arrest. Furthermore, the problem has now become a global threat with potential insertions of a virus that cruises through a globally accessed network. We need informational laws and judicial systems with sufficient punitive penalties to dissuade the potential intruder. And we need better hardware, and software, and procedures to beat the intruder if he or she is not sufficiently dissuaded.

Costs and benefits of security management are often intangible. For example, the cost of access can be measured, but the cost of refusing access is intangible. A rational decision on access may well be that access should be based on a "need-to-know" basis. Often, however, the "want-to-know" is more than the "need-to-know" and refusing such access can cause bad feelings especially when the "want-to-know" by a supervisor is higher than the "need-to-know" of one under supervision. The security manager must use diplomacy and much hand-holding to diffuse such situations if the need-to-know/want-to-know discipline is to be maintained. Thus security management is not just a problem of computer technology but an exercise in human resource management.

Corporate managers must be increasingly conscious and aware of the security of information systems for they may be held legally responsible, not just for "prudent" protection of the company's information assets, but also for the "prudent use of the information available to the company in order to protect its customers and employees." (Fried, 1994: 63).

Case 17.1: Cases in hacking

- In 1991, AT&T security in the UK spotted an impostor (later known as "Berferd") on its lines and decided to follow him. In the next four months Berferd assaulted numerous organizations on the Internet including 300 in just one night. The AT&T lawyers decided to halt the monitoring fearing that they may be accused of harbouring hackers. At the time Berferd was in the Netherlands where hacking is legal. The Dutch authorities did nothing about it until Berferd attacked their machines.

- A team in Switzerland hacked into a bank account of a wealthy individual to discover how he transferred money and then defrauded him of $1 million.

- A UK shipping company paid a hacker to penetrate a competitor's database to steal competitive information on customer lists, tariff details and information on the company's planning strategies. "The company was hired by a manager and the company subsequently claimed that it had been unaware of the source of information."

Source: *Management Today*, (July, 1994:66).

Case 17.2: Examples of malicious damage

1. A "worm" has destroyed many a computer memory and database. This use of a worm is the malign mutant of the useful worm invented by John Shoch of the Xerox Corporation in California. Shoch created a worm to wriggle through large networks looking for idle computers and harnessing their power to help solve the problem of unused resources. The malign mutant now burrows holes through computer memory, leaving huge information gaps.

2. Loss of storage can also result from what is known to security specialists as "logic bombs". This happened to Dick Streeter when his screen went blank as he was transferring a free program from a computer bulletin board into his machine. Then the following message appeared: "Gotch You". Nearly 900 accounting, word processing and game files that were stored in Street's machine were erased.

3. A "trapdoor" collects passwords as they log on, giving the hacker an updated file of access codes. The technique was used to gain unauthorized access to hospital records at Manhattan's Memorial Sloan–Kettering Cancer Center.

4. A French programmer, after being fired, left a logic bomb as a farewell salute in the record-keeping software that he had been working on when fired. The bomb exploded two years later on New Year's day, wiping out all the records stored on tape.

5. A logic bomb was placed in the Los Angeles Department of Water and Power. It froze the utility's internal files at a preassigned time, bringing work to a standstill.
6. An Oregon youth in the US used his terminal to gain access to the computer of the Department of Motor Vehicles, then put the system into irreversible disarray just to illustrate its vulnerability and to prove to himself that he could "beat" the system.

Case 17.3: German hacker invades US defence files

Curiosity was aroused at the Lawrence Berekely Laboratory when Clifford Stoll, manager of a multiuser computer system at the laboratory, noticed a 75 cent accounting discrepancy. Eighteen months of detective work followed in which Stoll cooperated with law enforcement officers to track down a hacker who used 75 cents of unauthorized time. The hacker was subsequently arrested by German authorities under suspicion of espionage.

Stoll was able to monitor the hacker's activities and observe that he methodically invaded files in some three dozen US military complexes to sift out information on defence topics. But the hacker's identity remained a mystery until Stoll's girlfriend suggested setting up a trap. A fictitious file on the Strategic Defense Initiative (also known as "Star Wars") was inserted by Stoll in the Lab's computer. The hacker, whose interest was piqued when he spotted the file, stayed online long enough to be traced.

German authorities believed that they cracked a major ring that had been selling sensitive military, nuclear and space research information to the Soviets.

Source: Fritzgerald, Karen. (1989). "The Quest for Intruder-Proof Computer Systems." *IEEE Spectrum*, vol. 24, no. 8, pp. 22–6. See also the delightful book by Clifford Stoll: *The Cuckoo's Nest: Tracking a Spy through the Maze of Computer Espionage*, NY: Doubleday.

Case 17.4: Buying the silence of computer criminals

A computer industry research unit in the UK reports that the practice of offering amnesties to people who break into their computers and steal funds is widespread. Rather than prosecute, corporations keep silent on the crimes if part of the money is returned and the swindler reveals how the fraud was carried out. Employers fear that business might be lost if customers learn of such security breaches.

In one such case, a programmer who diverted $8 million to a Swiss Bank account gave back $7 million for a non-disclosure agreement protecting him from prosecution. According to a member of Scotland Yard's fraud squad, employers who make such agreements may end up in court themselves, prosecuted for preventing the course of justice.

Source: Nicolle, Lindsay and Collins, Tony. (1989). "The Computer Fraud Conspiracy of Silence." *The Independent*, (June 19), p. 18.

Case 17.5: The computer "bad boy" nabbed by the FBI

Ken Mitnick was long known for burrowing his way into the most secret silicon nerve centres of telephone companies and corporate computer centres. He even invaded the North American Defense Command computer and DEC stealing $4 million worth of software. In 1989 Mitnick was caught, convicted and put into in a low security jail. The judge ordered Mitnick to participate in a treatment program for compulsive disorders. Then Mitnick was on parole and escaped. He was back violating sensitive computer systems. His first mistake was to invade and steal software from Shimomura, a computational physicist, of all days on Christmas day. Mitnick's second mistake was to taunt Shimomura by mocking voice-mail messages. This angered Shimomura (30) who then cooperated with the FBI in search of Mitnick (31). Also cooperating with the FBI was the Well network of 11,000 users. Mitnick had violated Well's system in January 1995. Then on February 16 1995, Mitnick entered a system 5,000km away in California and wiped out all the accounting records of one of Well's subscribers. It was later learned that Mitnick had made a typing error and accidentally destroyed the accounting records. But Well's management did not know that and they decided that they could take not survive any more of Mitnick and had to cut him off (and thereby warn him) or risk their entire business. They tried to contact the FBI but the FBI was on its way to arrest Mitnick and had shut off their cellular phones for fear of alerting Mitnick. Soon thereafter, at 1.30 am, the search ended in Mitnick's flat where he was arrested.

Mitnick faces thousands of dollars in fines and decades in prison – without parole. The FBI is pushing for a harsh sentence to deter future computer criminals.

Source: *US News & World Report*. (1995). Vol. 118, no. 8 (February 27), pp. 66–7, and *International Herald Tribune*, (February 18–19, 1995), p. 3.

Case 17.6: Case on virus offender caught and punished

Robert Morris is the son of a well respected computer expert in the US. Robert inserted a virus in a computer network that impacted negatively on over 6,000 users. He was caught and tried. He was sentenced to a three-year probation, 400 hours community service and fined $10,000.

Source: Stair, Ralph M. (1992). *Principles of Information Systems*. Boston: Boyd and Fraser.

References

Bates, Regis J. (1995). "Security Across the LAN." *Security Management*, vol. 39, no. 1 (January), pp. 47–50.

Baskerville, Richard. (1993). "Information Systems Security Design Methods for Information Systems Development." *ACM Computing Surveys*, vol. 25, no. 4 (December), pp. 375–414.

Bird, Jane. (1994). "Hunting Down the Hackers." *Management Today*, (July), pp. 64–6.

Chaum, David. (1992). "Achieving Electronic Privacy." *Scientific American*, vol. 267, no. 2 (August), pp. 96–101.

Dehaven, John. (1993). "Stealth Virus Attacks." *Byte*, vol. 18, no. 6 (May), pp. 137–42.

Fagan, Peter. (1993). "Organizational Issues in IT Security". *Computers and Security*, vol. 12, no. 8, pp. 710–715.

Felker, Phillip C. (1994). "User's Privacy along the Information Superhighway." *Computer Security Journal*, vol. X, no. 2, pp. 47–54.

Flaherty, David. (1989). *Protecting Privacy in Surveillance Societies*. Chappel Hill, NC: The University of Carolina Press.

Fried, Louis. (1994). "Information Security and New Technology." *Information Systems Management*, vol. 12, pp. 57–63.

Guynes, Era. (1994). "Privacy Considerations along the Information Highway." *Computers and Security*, vol. 24, no. 3 (September), pp. 16–19.

Hafner, Katie and Markoff, John. (1991). *Cyberpunk: Outlaws and Hackers of the Computer Frontier*. Hemel Hempstead: Simon and Schuster.

Hurford, Chris. "Computer Fraud – The UK Experience." *Computer Bulletin*, Series III (May 1989), pp. 19–20.

Kephart, Jeffrey O. and White, Steve R. (1993). "Computers and Epidemiology." *IEEE Spectrum*, vol. 30, no. 5 (May), pp. 20–26.

Kohr, Robert L. (1994). "Put Security to the Test." *Security Management*, vol. 38, no. 12 (December), pp. 64–95.

Landwehr, Carl E. and Bull, Alan R. *et al*. (1994). "A Taxonomy of Computer Program Security Flaws." *ACM Computing Surveys*, vol. 26, no. 3 (September), pp. 211–54.

Lunt, Teresa F. (1996). "Inside Risks: Securing the Information Structure." *Communications of the ACM*, vol. 39, no. 6 (June), p. 130.

Murray, William H. and Farrell, Patrick. (1993). "Toward a Model of Security for a Network of Computers." *Computer Security Journal*, vol. IX, no. 1, pp. 1–12.

Nash, John C. and Nash, Mary M. (1992). "Matching Risk to Cost in Computer File Back-Up Strategies." *The Canadian Journal of Information Sciences*, vol. 17, no. 2 (July), pp. 1–15.

Peukett, Herbert. (1991). "Enhancing the Security of Network Systems." *Siemens Review* – H & D Special, pp. 19–22.

Price, Wyn. (1990). "Data Security." *The Computer Bulletin*, vol. 2, no. 9 (September), pp. 10–11.

Sanford, Clive C. (1993). "Computer Viruses: Symptoms, Remedies, and Preventive Measures." *Journal of Computer Information Systems*, vol. XXXIII, no. 3, pp. 67–72.

"Special Issue of Internet Security." *Internet World*, vol. 6, no. 2 (February 1995), pp. 32–72.

Sherizan, Sanford. (1992). "The Globalization of Computer Crime and Information Security." *Computer Security Journal*, vol. VII, no. 2, pp. 13–20.

Smith, H. Jeff. (1993). "Privacy Policies and Practices: Inside the Organizational Maze." *Communications of the ACM*, vol. 36, no. 12 (December), pp. 104–22.

Somerson, Ira S. (1994). "Information: What it Costs When It's Lost." *Security Management*, vol. 38, no. 10 (October), pp. 61–6.

Tuerkheimer, Frank M. (1993). "The Underpinnings of Privacy Protection." *Communications of the ACM*, vol. 36, no. 8 (August), pp. 69–73.

Ware, Willis H. (1993). "The New Faces of Privacy." *The Information Society*, vol. 9, pp. 195–211.

Wylde, John O. D. (1993). "The Life Cycle of Security Managers." *Information Systems Journal*, vol. 10, no. 3, pp. 62–7).

Zajac Jr. Bernard P. (1990). "Computer Viruses: Can They be Prevented." *Computers and Security*, vol. 29, no. 1, pp. 25–31.

18 Controlling Quality and Performance

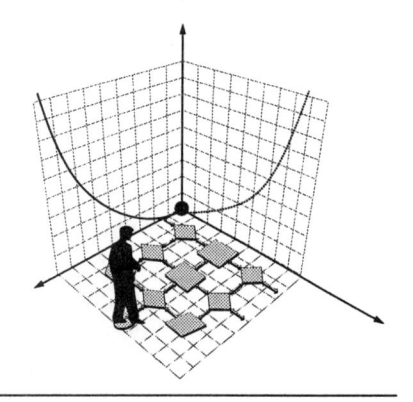

> The perfect computer has been developed. You just feed in your problems – and they never come out again.
>
> *Al Goodman*

Introduction

In order to ensure quality computing, the performance of an information systems department should be regularly evaluated. This evaluation, called *computer performance evaluation*, consists of a comparison of actual performance with desired performance in resource utilization, operations, and service, as shown in Figure 18.1.

Figure 18.1: *The process of performance evaluation*

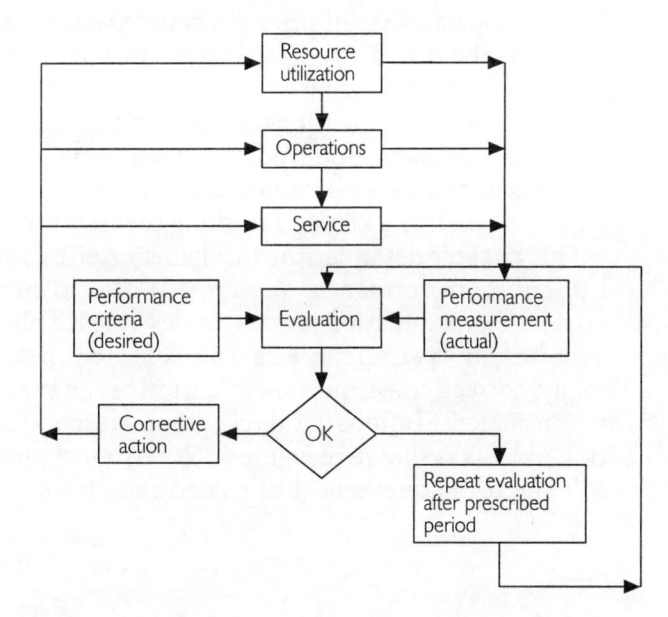

Introduction

When performance fails to measure up to prescribed standards, corrective action followed by reevaluation is required. A satisfactory performance evaluation indicates no immediate need for change but is no grounds for complacency. Computing is not a static field. New technology, an altered business climate, increased load, a change in users, demand for new applications, or delays in new systems development can suddenly turn contented clients into frustrated users. For this reason, evaluations should be scheduled at regular intervals so that systems weaknesses can be identified and rectified before they become chronic. Evaluation should also be initiated whenever problems arise.

Performance evaluation is, in effect, a control mechanism. Surprisingly, many information systems departments that design and maintain financial and performance reporting systems for the organizations they serve treat performance evaluation of their own operations casually. This occurs even though improved computing performance would have a multiplier effect, enhancing the performance of other departments in turn. After all, an information system is a service function that exists to better the effectiveness of a firm's line functions. Systems are installed because they promise to deliver benefits that equal or exceed their cost. It follows, therefore, that any gain in the effectiveness of the information-providing function would be magnified for the organizations as a whole.

There are also financial reasons to focus on improved performance of computer operations. Information systems departments consume from 1 to 5% of the revenue generated by most manufacturing concerns. As much as 20% of operating costs can be attributed to information systems for service organizations and public agencies that deal in information. What company would not welcome a way to reduce such expenditure? Performance evaluations lead to cost savings by identifying computing inefficiencies and tracking the results of corrective action.

This chapter describes the mechanisms of performance evaluation. First, critical performance variables that need to be evaluated are identified, and then evaluation criteria are described. This is followed by a discussion of how performance data are collected, measured, and analyzed. Finally, corrective action and evaluation of the evaluation process itself are considered. Sections in this chapter correspond to steps in the evaluation process as shown in Figure 18.2. Personnel, timing, and evaluation tools and techniques will be discussed at each step when relevant.

Figure 18.2: *Steps in evaluation*

```
1. Identify what is to be evaluated
2. Establish evaluation criteria
3. Organize for evaluation
4. Gather data on performance (measurement)
5. Maintain historical record
6. Analyze data on performance
7. Develop recommendations
8. Take corrective action
9. Evaluate evaluation process
```

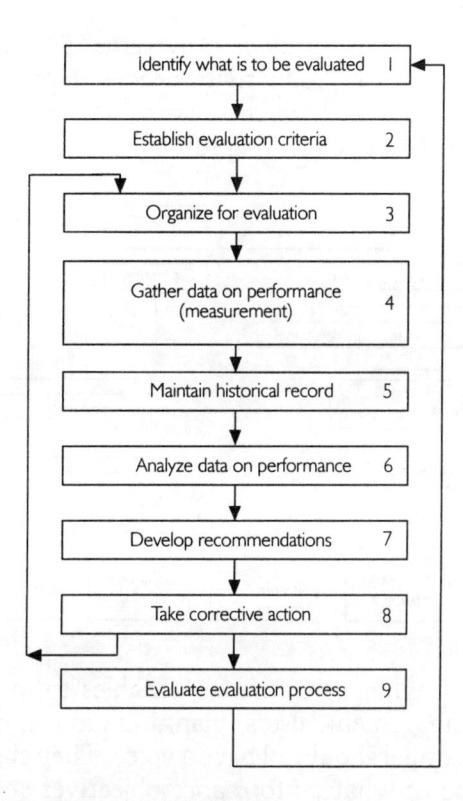

Identify what is to be evaluated

In computing, there are four key performance areas:

- *Financial management* – management of the monetary resources allocated to the information systems function.
- *Applications management* – control and reporting of the design, implementation, and maintenance of applications systems.
- *Productivity/operations management* – ensuring availability and managing utilization of computers.
- *Human resource management* – productivity of personnel assigned to information systems.

An organization that wants to improve its information function should collect performance variables in each of these four areas for analysis. The problem is to decide exactly which variables to collect and how to organize collected data for evaluation. Should data be gathered on expenditures by object of expense (salaries, supplies, and services)? By activity? By the cost to run, maintain, and enhance applications programs? By customer? What aspects of production should be measured?

Establish evaluation criteria

On time/within budget delivery of systems? Resource consumption? Is an analysis of human productivity needed in order to evaluate performance, or would a study of the distribution of the workload and skill improvements through training suffice?

Figure 18.3:
Performance components to be evaluated

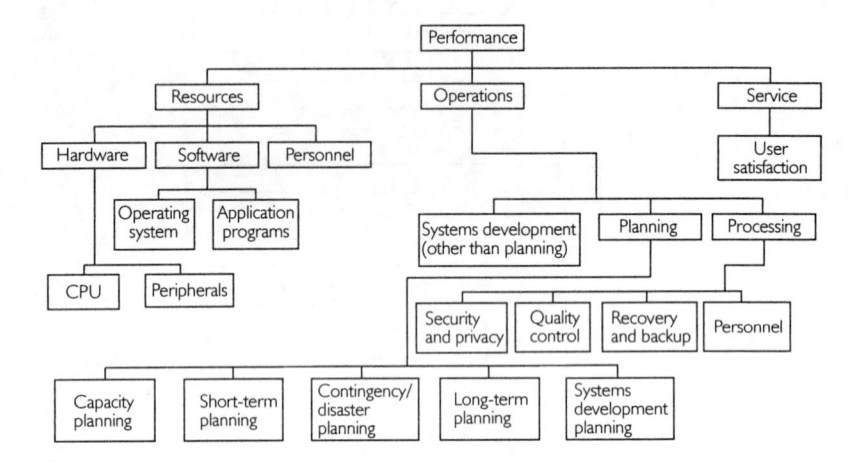

In deciding what performance variables to monitor and evaluate, corporate management, users, planning groups, data administrators, and EDP personnel should all have a voice. They should also participate in discussions of what performance objectives should be. Figure 18.3 shows commonly evaluated components of the information systems function.

Establish evaluation criteria

Efficiency of operations and effectiveness of product are basic evaluation criteria. Historically, information systems departments have focused on the computing process to ensure a high ratio of output to input (efficiency). Today, however, more emphasis is placed on effectiveness of the information function. The real issue, according to many corporate managers, is what level of service is being provided to computer users by the information systems department.

Let us now turn to a discussion of evaluation criteria in the two categories of efficiency and effectiveness.

Efficiency

Efficiency (η), a concept used in production management, is the ratio of output (O) to input (I) as expressed in the formula $\eta = O/I$. Unfortunately, the benefit of output in computing cannot always be calculated in tangible units. How can one measure the monetary value of a timely report, accuracy, or the absence of fraud? By keeping input constant, however, a change in output can be noted: if output increases, efficiency is increased; if output decreases, efficiency is decreased. Efficiency is generally measured in terms of throughput, productivity, resource utilization, and costs.

Throughput

The design of equipment, in part, determines computer *throughput*, the amount of work that can be performed during a given period of time. Throughput is advertised, known to the buyer at the time of purchase. Central processing unit (CPU) throughput may be measured in thousands of operations per second (KOPS) or millions of instructions per second (MIPS). Unfortunately, these measurements are not as standardized as horsepower or kilowatt hours, so one cannot always compare the throughput of computers sold by different vendors.

CPU throughput, however, is rarely the prime processing constraint. Rather, efficiency is limited by peripheral devices used in pre- and post-processing, such as optical recognition equipment, printers, and routing equipment. Such peripheral devices advertise throughput as a selling feature so that competing models can be compared by the buyer. When sales claims prove unsubstantiated, the vendor can be held accountable, provided that a well-written, detailed, legally binding contract has been signed.

Productivity

Productivity is the term usually applied to throughput performance of personnel – that is, the quantity of work produced by an individual in a unit of time. For example, the efficiency of data entry operators can be evaluated by comparing number of keystrokes per hour with standard tables. Lines of code (LOC) per programmer-day can measure a programmer's productivity. Other common productivity measures are documentation pages per documentor-month, cost per defect, CPU hours per programmer-month, and test cases developed and executed per programmer-month.

The problem is that the measurement of productivity in such work units can be misleading. For example, LOC is biased in favour of programmers who do not optimize their code. This measure also penalizes high-level languages, making it harder to compare productivity between programmers. Many traditional productivity measures do not take program complexity, correctness, or reliability into account, nor whether the software is structured or not. They make little allowance for the program's size, for the organization of the programming team, or for the programmer's experience. Furthermore, some standard productivity measures are founded on unproven assumptions. As a result, the quantity of a programmer's work is somewhat discredited as a productivity measure. Many companies are in search of new ways to evaluate productivity.

One new technique that is currently attracting attention is function-point measurement, a method of characterizing the size and complexity of applications based on the amount of function delivered to the users. This method attempts to quantify the cost per function and assign a benefit to the function. Halstead metrics, another technique, counts the number of action statements (operators) and data elements (operands) in a program. It has been demonstrated that the sum of the number of operators and operands is correlated with the error rate and productivity of a program.

Unfortunately, flaws and errors in programs often take a long time to surface. A programmer who is rewarded for high productivity based on a measure such as lines of code may be writing software that requires excessive maintenance.

Utilization

Another gauge of efficiency is *utilization*, the ratio of what is used to what is available. Unused capacity is a waste of resources; however, a high utilization value may indicate that bottlenecks in processing will occur in the near future. The same utilization data that is studied during performance evaluations can be used for capacity planning and scheduling as well.

Cost

Efficiency is increased when *cost*, with constant output, drops. One way to evaluate performance is by comparing budgeted with actual expenditures and reviewing trends in cost indexes:

$$\text{Material cost index} = \frac{\text{Cost of materials}}{\text{Total cost of computing centre}}$$

$$\text{Personnel cost index} = \frac{\text{Cost of personnel}}{\text{Total cost of computing centre}}$$

$$\text{Software maintenance index} = \frac{\text{Cost of maintenance (software)}}{\text{Total cost of computing centre}}$$

In computing, inefficiency can often be traced to waste of materials (tapes, paper) and run time. Habits of waste frequently develop when user departments do not pay for computing services and computer time is not constrained. By charging for services, costs may be lowered dramatically — an example of a budgetary policy that may affect performance efficiency.

Effectiveness

Effectiveness evaluation is based on the objectives of the information function. An *effective* system is one that satisfies the expectations of users. When effectiveness is under study, the following questions are asked: Are user needs being met by the information systems department? Does the output produced by applications programs meet user requirements? Are systems user friendly? Are users satisfied with their information systems?

When an organization focuses on effectiveness, the emphasis shifts from the technical aspects of information production to the problems that the computer can solve. Information specialists take on a business orientation, working closely with end-users and corporate management to ensure that information strategies fully support business plans. Performance is measured in terms of systems availability, information quality, timeliness, accuracy, and reliability, since user satisfaction is based on these criteria.

One can also evaluate availability in absolute terms. If a job requires 300 minutes of machine time on a specific date, is that 300 minutes available when needed?

Quality

Quantitative measures of *quality* are difficult to formulate, but one can identify costs associated with quality. For example, prevention cost is a measure of the money spent to prevent errors or do the job right the first time. Appraisal costs include the money spent for reviewing and testing systems to see that they meet systems requirements. Failure costs are those associated with defective systems. Evaluation teams should study these figures as they look for ways to help improve the information function.

Generally, quality is measured in terms of end-user satisfaction. Factors that will influence this satisfaction are:

- Ease of use of computer systems and software.
- Security and confidentiality of data.
- Technical support given to end-users by computer specialists.
- Completeness, readability, and organization of documentation.
- Confidence that state-of-the-art technology is being applied.
- Ease with which systems can be maintained and upgraded.

- Portability and reusability.
- Ease with which a system can be audited and tested.

Timeliness

There are really three measures for *timeliness*: turnaround time, response time, and schedule adherence. *Turnaround time* is the period of time between job submission to the information systems department and the return of output. This is usually a measure for batch work and will be measured in hours or days. *Response time* is a way of measuring the timeliness of interactive online activities and will typically be measured in fractions of a second. *Schedule adherence* refers to the ability of a computing facility to process applications on time and to deliver new systems that are under development when promised.

Other ways to evaluate timeliness would be to study waiting time, length of queue, number of days projects are delayed, and backlogs. It may be better to have 10 projects that are each delayed one day than to have one project 10 days late.

Accuracy

Accuracy can be defined as the absence of error. But what constitutes an error? When a calculated value is 1.962256, one can truncate the number to 1.96 when the unit is pounds and pence but not when 1.962256 represents millions of pounds. A misspelled name on the mailing list for an advertising circular would be regrettable but not crucial. But suppose the misspelling were the name of the chairman of the board in a firm's annual report?

These examples illustrate that accuracy must be carefully defined when evaluating systems effectiveness. The permissible magnitude of error should be established, rate of acceptable error defined (for example, one in 1 million calculations), and error limits set in absolute terms (for example, number of allowable errors per month). Degree of accuracy should be set not only for computer processing but for peripherals, telecommunications, and data entry as well.

Since errors usually result in reruns, rerun data is one way to measure performance accuracy.

Reliability

Reliability is an elusive concept although many formulas have been published to measure it. The problem is that too many variables in reliability calculations cannot be precisely measured. The relative importance of these variables in contributing to *systems reliability* is also difficult to impute. For example, what role do sickness, absenteeism, turnover, training, and operator motivation play in system reliability?

Should reliability be based on the effort, cost, or time required to keep a system operational?

Software reliability (a function of the complexity of the software, the competence of programmers, and viability of a given development approach) is also difficult to assess. The problem of identifying software errors compounds the difficulty of measuring systems effectiveness in terms of reliability. Systems may appear to function smoothly but be producing inaccurate output due to inherent, undetected software errors. Users are generally interested not in a technical measure of reliability (involving statistics and probability theory) but rather in availability. They want to know whether they can rely on the computer being operational when they need to use it.

Conflicts between evaluation criteria

Before concluding this section, a word should be said about the interrelationships that exist between performance criteria. In many cases, a high evaluation rating for one criterion precludes a high rating for another. For example, lowering response-time may raise costs, and vice versa.

Figure 18.4: *Response-time–cost curve*

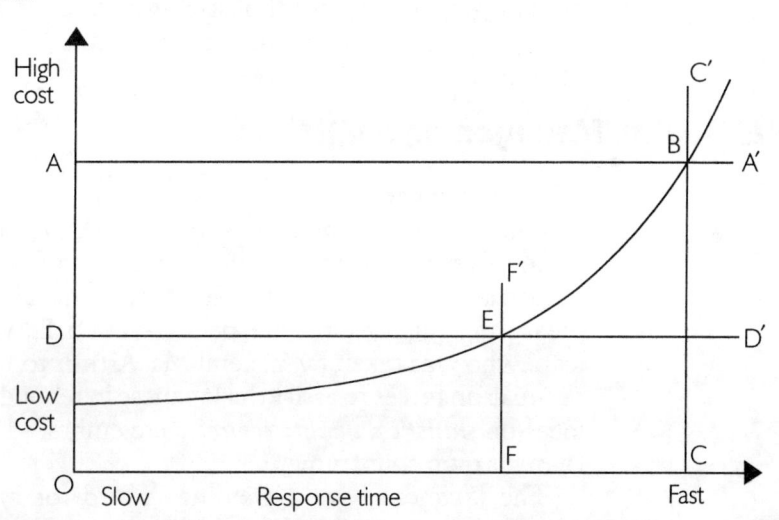

Suppose the response-time–cost curve for a given firm is as illustrated in Figure 18.4, with OC an acceptable response time according to management and OD an acceptable cost. Compromise is necessary since they yield different points on the curve. That is, both performance objectives cannot be met at the same time. At Point E, for example, the cost corresponds to DD´ but the response time OF corresponding to FF´ is slower than CC´. At Point B, the response time corresponds to CC´

but the cost AA´ is higher than DD´. One of the two variables has to give, or both may be compromised somewhat to fall within points E and B on the curve. This means either a slower response-time or higher cost than desired by management.

The same type of conflict may exist between other variables, such as quality and cost or quality and timeliness, as shown:

$$
\begin{array}{rllll}
\text{Quality control} \rightarrow & \text{Quality} & \uparrow\rightarrow & \text{Desirable} & \bigg] \text{Conflict} \\
& \text{Costs} & \uparrow\rightarrow & \text{Undesirable} & \\
\text{Quality control} \rightarrow & \text{Quality} & \uparrow\rightarrow & \text{Desirable} & \bigg] \text{Conflict} \\
& \text{Timeliness} \downarrow\rightarrow & & \text{Undesirable} &
\end{array}
$$

Indeed, more than two criteria may be in opposition in a given situation. Management must then search for a satisfactory or acceptable mix of controllable factors and set performance standards that minimize the effect of conflicts. This is not an easy task. One approach to this problem is not to look at individual quality control variables but to look at all of managing quality in a "holistic" way. Such an approach at looking at the total problem is sometimes referred to as TQM (Total Quality Management).

Total Quality Management (TQM)

TQM is a revival of interest in quality. In industry, there has been a long-standing interest in *quality assurance* (QA). In software development, there were quality metrics developed by software engineers. Among industrial engineers and statisticians there has also been great interest in measuring quality. One such person was Dr. Edward Deming, an American, who was taken by General MacArthur to Japan as part of the US occupation forces to assist the Japanese in rebuilding their industry. His ideas on *statistical quality control* were embraced more by the Japanese than his own countrymen.

The Japanese have a Deming Award for high productivity. The Americans have a Malcolm Baldrige Award. Other countries and international organizations also have their own awards. Whatever the award for quality and whatever the product being considered, if it is part of TQM, a more comprehensive and deliberative approach to quality management, then there is a process to be followed.

Total Quality Management (TQM)

Process for Total Quality Management

The process starts with the decision to commit the resources needed and then plan for quality management. The first step would be to determine the criteria for quality and then devise a strategy for measuring quality. In parallel, one needs to develop and set up procedures for the collection of information on measurement of quality. The necessary information is collected, analyzed, and the strategy for improving quality is implemented. However, this is not the end of the process since quality is not a static concept but varies over time. Thus, the quality is evaluated as part of the *continuous quality management* (CQM) process and, when necessary, the entire process is repeated. This cycling and continuous process is shown graphically in Figure 18.5 and will now be discussed in some detail.

Figure 18.5: *Processes for TQM*

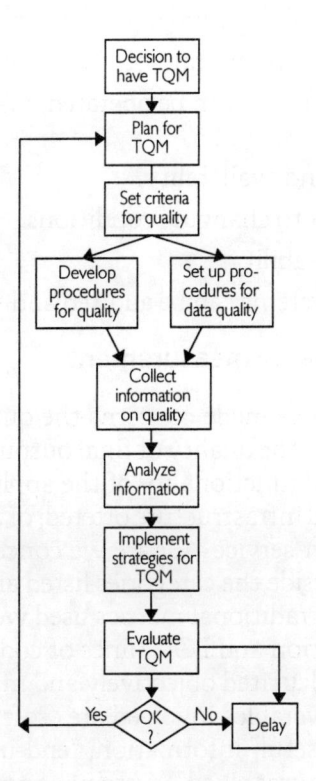

Criteria for quality

There are some strategies and practices that will improve quality whatever the product. These include:

- Educate and train; educate again and train again.

Chapter 18: Controlling Quality and Performance

- Drive out fear. Create a climate for innovation.
- Eliminate obtrusive exhortations for work.
- Learn the capabilities of processes and how they can be improved.
- Encourage self-improvement.
- Remove barriers that rob people of pride in their workmanship.

With applying quality management to information systems and computing there is a need for additional factors appropriate for computing and its management. These are:

- Ease of use of systems.
- Security and confidentiality of data/knowledge.
- Technical support given by computer specialists.
- Completeness, readability, and organization of documentation.
- End-user confidence in the state-of-the-art technology being used.
- Ease with which systems can be operated, maintained and enhanced.
- Easy accessibility and availability.
- Flexibility to adjust to changing conditions.
- Portability and reusability.
- Ease with which systems can be audited and tested.

Measures and procedures for quality measurement

One determination to be made concerns the quality that we are after. Are we concerned with the quality of final output and information generated; the quality and functionality of the applications; the quality of operational service and infrastructure offered; or are we interested in the quality of the end-user service? Or are we concerned with some other criterion, inside or outside the categories listed above?

In computing, the traditional metrics used were throughput, cost of MIP, capacity, utilization and LOC (lines of code). All these are "hard" metrics that can be calculated objectively and mathematically. In quality, however, the deliverables involved are "soft" and often subjective, such as "good" and "useful" information, "end-user satisfaction," "end-user friendly," and "humanized" systems. Some variables are partly "soft" but can be hardened like timeliness, accuracy, robustness, and reliability. The problem lies not only in identifying the criteria, but also measuring them in metrics that are useful to quality management. Special instruments and procedures are needed to calculate these metrics.

Some statistical tools are available and include: histograms, correlation charts, run charts, flow charts, Pareto charts, fishbone charts, and process simulators.

Gather data on performance (measurement)

Once performance criteria are specified and variables identified, data on the values must be collected for analysis. This can be done by logging, using monitors, or canvassing users, as illustrated in Figure 18.6.

Figure 18.6:
Sources of data for performance evaluation

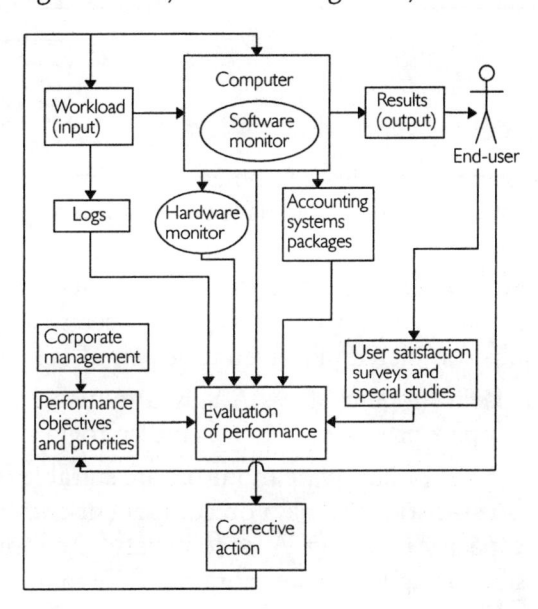

Logs

In many computer centres, manual *logs* are kept by operators. These logs are a source of information when evaluating performance. For example, data on the length of downtime for maintenance might be determined from an operator's log.

One disadvantage of such log use is that keeping logs around and drawing information from a log is time consuming: a simple calculation, such as percentage of jobs delivered on schedule, requires someone to search logs for relevant data. And human error is always possible in the calculation itself. Job accounting programs can replace manually collected statistics in some areas, but cost again is a factor, albeit much less so.

Monitors

Computer performance can also be measured using hardware and software monitors (see Figure 18.7).

Figure 18.7:
Types of monitor

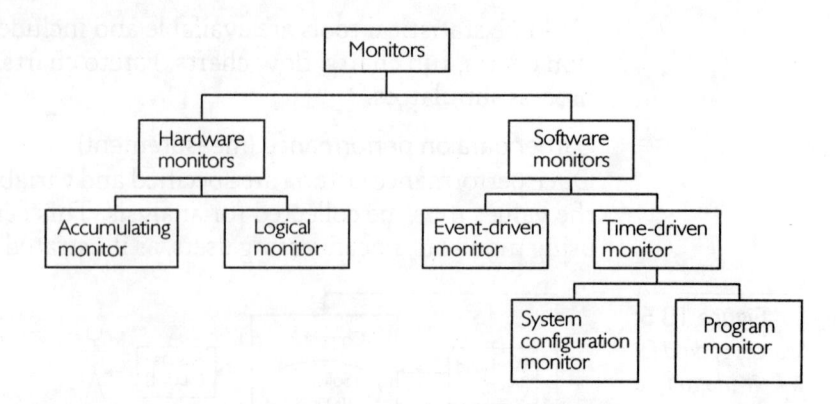

- **Hardware monitor:** equipment with input sensors and output channels, record desired data on instrument panels or on tape for later analysis.
  - An *accumulating monitor* is a counter used in simple computational environments. It might be used to count the number of jobs completed in a given time period, for example.
  - A *logical monitor* is essentially a minicomputer used in more complex processing, such as multiprogramming.

  Both types of hardware monitors are suitable for collecting utilization statistics and data on component conflicts – data needed for capacity planning. A wide variety of counting measures are possible using hardware monitors. The monitors can accurately report data on short-term activities and measure systems overhead. However, hardware monitors are costly, have a long setup time, and require skilled personnel to operate. Probes and connections can be accidentally dislodged, damaged, or incorrectly connected, resulting in false data.

- **Software monitor:** an application program that is part of the operating system or stored internally. The software contains a data collector that takes time counts and gathers data by reading internal tables, status registers, memory maps, operating system control blocks, and so on. Then an analyzer/reporter reads the data and reduces, orders, groups, summarizes, and computes values of interest. Finally, the information is displayed on a terminal screen. Software monitors are of two types:
  - An *event-driven monitor* interacts with the operating system's interrupt-handling mechanism and can monitor almost every occurrence of the event being studied.

- A *time-driven monitor* is a periodic sampling system activated at user-specific intervals. It is subdivided into system *configuration monitors* (which generate information on system components) and *program monitors*.

Software monitors can generate utilization figures, as hardware monitors do, and can also report on the performance of systems and application programs. They are easy to use, low in cost, and allow flexibility in choosing options for data collection. However, the monitors may not be able to monitor concurrent events. The cost of CPU and storage overhead is also a disadvantage. In addition, these monitors generally have low priority for CPU access, and the software must be reprogrammed when changes are made to operating systems.

User surveys

Data on user satisfaction with the performance of information systems can be collected in *user surveys* using questionnaires and interviews. The problem is designing relevant questions and framing them in a manner so that they are not misunderstood and resisted. In addition, the respondent must be motivated to reply candidly.

Questions should be neutral (no implicitly "correct" answers), and non-threatening. Otherwise, respondents will distort their replies for self-protection. That is, users must perceive their work environment as one in which they will not be penalized for making critical responses. Questions might be asked on the following topics:

- Timeliness of operations and reports.
- Validity and completeness of reports.
- Achievement of predetermined acceptable levels of operations.
- Frequency of errors.
- Response time to meet users' requests.
- Protection of privacy.
- Data and systems security.
- Systems reliability.
- Achievement of long-range technology.
- Training availability and effectiveness.
- Quality of output and service.
- Lines of communication with IT personnel.

This list is essentially a restatement of efficiency and effectiveness criteria described earlier in the chapter. Sample questions that might be used in evaluating systems performance appear in Figure 18.8.

Figure 18.8:
Questions from user satisfaction survey

1. Please express your overall satisfaction with the service you receive from the computer centre.

   ☐ Very good
   ☐ Good
   ☐ Fair
   ☐ Poor
   ☐ Very poor

2. For Report #20 (Cost Distribution by Department), please express your satisfaction in each of the areas listed on a scale of 1 to 10. (Low satisfaction would be indicated by a 1; high satisfaction by a 10.)

	For cost analysis	For fund management	For cost estimation	For decision making
Format				
Content				
Amount of detail				
Timeliness				
Overall rating				

3. How do you evaluate the charging policies for service at the data centre?

   ☐ Very reasonable
   ☐ Reasonable
   ☐ Unreasonable
   ☐ Outrageous

4. Please express how charging policies affect your use of the computer centre.

   ☐ No effect
   ☐ Discourage use
   ☐ Encourage use

5. Which of the following charging policies would you consider reasonable?

   ☐ Service at no cost
   ☐ Service at marginal cost
   ☐ Service at full cost
   ☐ Service at a cost that is competitive with external computing facilities

It is helpful if questionnaires are designed so that answers can be mark-sensed or read by optical scanning equipment. A terminal might also be used, with answers collected by one-stroke responses or by touch-sensitive screens.

Collecting information on quality

Some of the data that is needed for TQM may have to be collected by special instruments. Some data may already be available to the organization. This may have been collected by monitors for performance evaluation or operational control, historical records, and data available in logs or in the corporate database. For example, logs for maintenance may contain data on breakdowns and failures. Such data may reveal clues about the likelihood of breakdowns in quality. Frequency of breakdowns and other statistics could identify poor, or degrading levels of quality. Likewise, an analysis of complaints and requests for maintenance can yield valuable data on quality of services offered.

Another source of information is surveys. Note that such surveys are called "user" surveys not "end-user" surveys because there are many non end-users who are significant clients of computing and hence need to be included in surveys on satisfaction. Surveys can be time consuming and expensive but may be the only way to get at satisfaction – especially that of the end-user. In selected cases, in-depth interviews may have to be conducted which could reveal deep-seated resentment and anger harboured by end-users. Once these emotions have been identified, the underlying quality issues can be addressed.

Sometimes, external information is necessary to assess quality of information services. This may include information on competitive offerings, state-of-the-art technology available or in the R&D labs, and information on suppliers and vendors.

Maintain historical record

When evaluating performance data, it is useful to compare current performance with records from the past. For this reason, historical records need to be maintained. Performance data stored in a data bank should help with longitudinal analysis, setting standards, identifying performance trends, and calculating moving averages.

Analyze data on performance

Without analysis of collected performance data, the collection effort is wasted. Yet, too often, sheaves of performance data are stacked on an evaluator's desk waiting for analysis that never takes place. Time must be set aside to review and interpret data.

Analysis usually starts with a glance-check at data to see if the values of variables are reasonable. This may be followed by a trend analysis and a check to see how performance measures up to local, national and industrial standards. For example, let us look at the sample figures on

CPU utilization listed in Figure 18.9. If the 95% value was for three shifts, excluding preventive maintenance (often 5%), the computer would be running near full capacity. The person evaluating these figures would recognize that the figures indicate a need for system expansion or the acquisition of a larger system.

Figure 18.9: *Data on performance for analysis of CPU utilization*

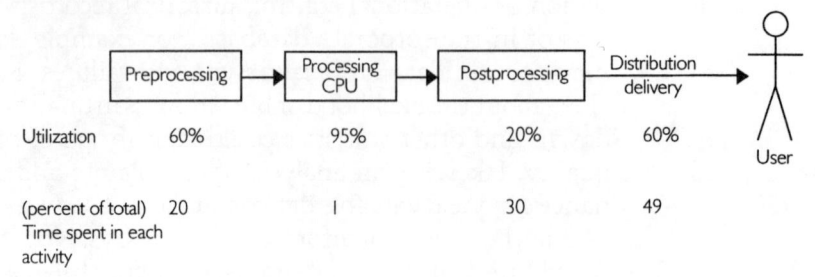

	Preprocessing	Processing CPU	Postprocessing	Distribution delivery	User
Utilization	60%	95%	20%	60%	
(percent of total) Time spent in each activity	20	1	30	49	

The 60% utilization figure for preprocessing and 20% for postprocessing is within an acceptable performance range. (The person who evaluates these figures should be well informed on standard performance statistics.) However, these figures may hide bottlenecks at specific equipment, so disaggregated data should be collected – for example, utilization statistics on all channel ports as well as utilization figures for tapes, disks, and other input/output devices. The 49% figure for distribution activities in this sample may be high compared with other computer systems. The evaluator would see this as one area of performance that could be upgraded if delivery procedures were changed.

Implementing TQM

In implementing TQM, work procedures and tasks may have to be redesigned and/or changed, and change frequently provokes resistance. One approach to such resistance of quality enhancements is to have the change introduced by a peer such as a retired person with relevant experience (not necessarily from the same company). Accepting suggestions from a retired person seems to reduce resistance especially if the change is fundamental, which it often is. Deming argues that 90–94% of waste:

> ... is built into the system and can be eliminated through fundamental changes initiated by management.
>
> *I/S Analyzer*, February 1991, p. 6.

The second problem is that quality varies with industries and even with products within an industry. Also, quality is not static. It varies over time. Thus, management of quality improvement is often unique to each situation and continuous; referred to as CQI, (continual quality improvement).

The QA plan for continuous quality improvements involves continuous education in TQM; identifying and reducing waste and redundancies; developing personal skills required for working with people and in teams; pilot projects to implement quality programs; and large projects to implement comprehensive quality programs. One proven route to TQM is the *Quality Team* approach. The teams should include people who are creative and productive as well as process-oriented and target-oriented. Also, the team members should include those who are close to the problems of quality and those who will be involved in the improvement of quality and the implementation of TQM. A TQM team should be led by a someone who is knowledgeable about the business and its processes, as well as knowledgeable about quality and statistical quality control. Sometimes, this person is a retired professional hired from outside the corporation so that he/she may be able to persuade, cajole, plead, and convincingly sell the program.

Quality control of operations

Approaches to quality control are not always "total" and attention may focus only on operations where most of the faults and errors occur. Control is instituted at strategic points in the operations of computing. These control points are shown in Figure 18.10.

Figure 18.10:
Stages of processing (boxes) and quality control locations (circles)

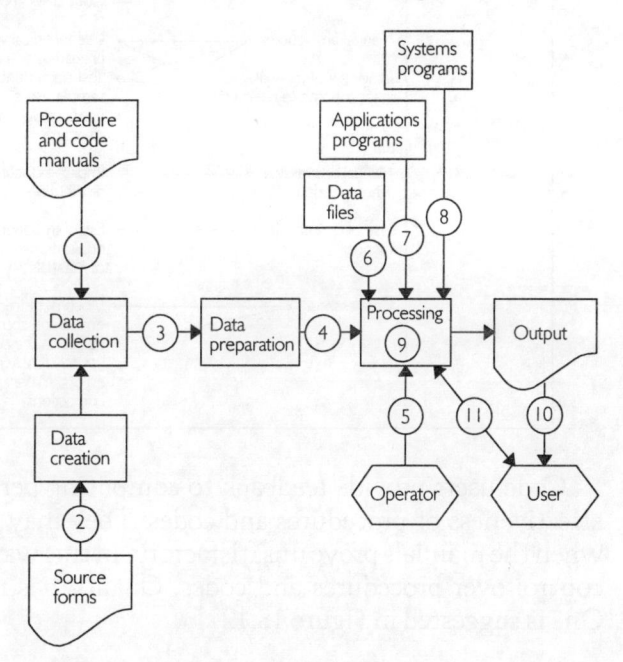

Quality control of operations

The errors, their causes and their possible solutions for each of the control points can be estimated. As an illustration, this has been done in Figure 18.11 for the control point 1 (of Figure 18.10), that of controlling procedures and manuals. Discussing the causes of potential errors and their possible solutions for all the control points in Figure 18.10 will distract us from the present topic; instead, they are displayed in Supplement 18.1 at the end of this chapter.

Control locations

Control of procedure and code manuals (circle 1)

Fig. 18.11 summarizes common sources of error when using procedure and code manuals and suggests control solutions. In many firms, the database administrator (DBA) or someone on the DBA's staff is responsible for establishing codes at the request of users and for coordinating assignment of codes so that redundant coding schemes do not occur. Publication, maintenance, and distribution of uniform code manuals are also delegated to this individual.

Figure 18.11:
Control of manuals

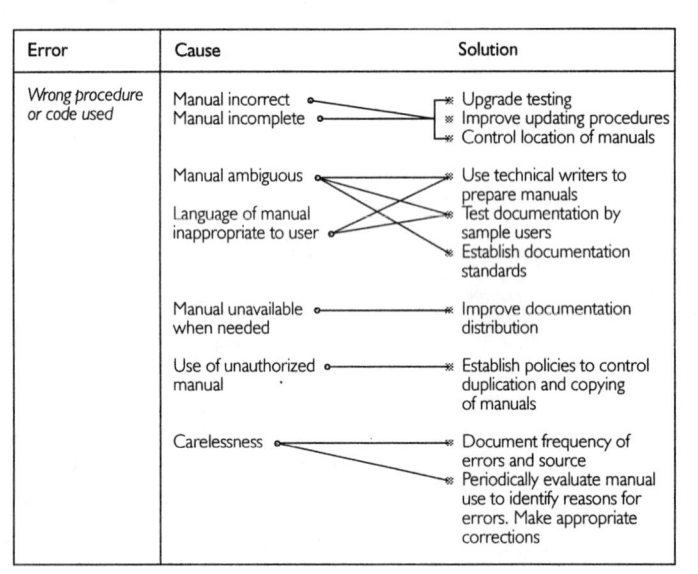

Error	Cause	Solution
Wrong procedure or code used	Manual incorrect Manual incomplete	Upgrade testing Improve updating procedures Control location of manuals
	Manual ambiguous Language of manual inappropriate to user	Use technical writers to prepare manuals Test documentation by sample users Establish documentation standards
	Manual unavailable when needed	Improve documentation distribution
	Use of unauthorized manual	Establish policies to control duplication and copying of manuals
	Carelessness	Document frequency of errors and source Periodically evaluate manual use to identify reasons for errors. Make appropriate corrections

Code users provide feedback to computing personnel regarding the effectiveness of procedures and codes. They may also initiate changes when the manuals prove unsatisfactory. In this way, users contribute to control over procedures and codes. Quality has many classifications. One is suggested in Figure 18.12.

Figure 18.12:
Criteria for quality

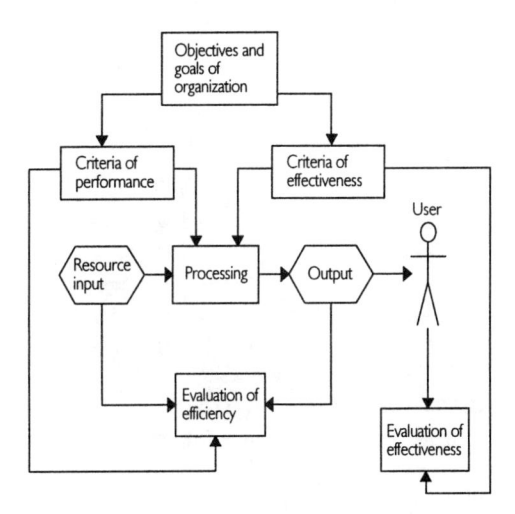

One approach to controlling quality is TQM; another approach is ISO 9000 which is a set of procedures for different stages of production and development in computing which, when adopted, will assure quality. Since this is an international standard it has a stamp of quality certification.

TQM and maintenance can support each other: improvements in quality can reduce maintenance and good maintenance can improve quality. Also, information on quality can come from maintenance activities. The major problem in TQM is not the technical aspects but the *human* issues because TQM is about *people* as well as process and objects; essentially, TQM is concerned with values and behaviour. What may be needed is a change in attitudes and habits towards work and quality. Employees must be motivated. If there is resistance then that must be transformed into a commitment for quality. This requires leadership on the part of the corporation and IT. Some corporations do this through a QA plan and a QA officer (or QA champion) appointed to shepherd the plan through.

Summary and conclusions

Performance objectives are set by corporate management. To make sure that an information systems department meets performance objectives, periodic evaluations should be scheduled; they should also be triggered when problems arise. Evaluation begins by identifying what is to be evaluated and setting evaluation criteria. The number and nature of evaluation criteria will vary from firm to firm and depend on managerial preference and processing maturity. In most organizations, both effi-

Summary and conclusions

ciency of operations and systems effectiveness are evaluated. Figure 18.13 lists common evaluation criteria in each of these two categories.

Figure 18.13:
Components of performance

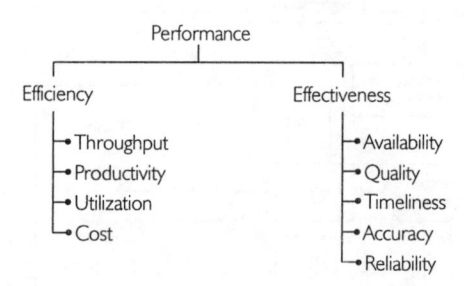

```
                    Performance
                   /           \
            Efficiency      Effectiveness
            • Throughput    • Availability
            • Productivity  • Quality
            • Utilization   • Timeliness
            • Cost          • Accuracy
                            • Reliability
```

An information systems department can run efficiently, yet still be ineffective, and vice versa. For example, the process of generating information may cost very little but deliver output that fails to meet user needs. On the other hand, the department may provide quality information that improves the productivity of employees throughout the organization. However, it might be so expensive (in computer-processing time) to *generate* the information that its cost is *greater* than any productivity gain derived from using it. The difference between efficiency and effectiveness as performance measures is illustrated in Figure 18.14.

Figure 18.14:
Efficiency and effectiveness evaluation

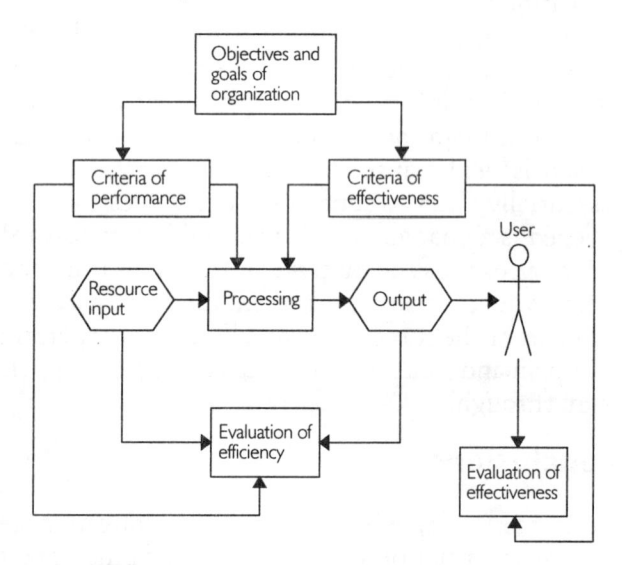

Once performance criteria have been established, performance data in these areas are collected. The data are gathered primarily by logs, user questionnaires or interviews, and hardware and software monitors. It is the responsibility of the evaluator to study performance data in order to identify performance weaknesses and to report these weaknesses to management. Which recommendations are actually adopted or implemented is for management to decide.

The evaluation process should itself be evaluated. A report listing problems and mistakes as well as successful strategies of evaluation will be useful when the evaluation cycle is repeated. The evaluation process should be periodically scheduled and should also be initiated when major performance problems arise.

Case 18.1: Quality control at Kodak

Kodak, an $18 billion company, appointed a corporate director of quality in 1983. Its corporate information systems department has an information systems executive council (ISEC) that meets four or five times a year to consider how to use IT throughout the company and identify areas of major improvement.

The key areas identified in 1993 were IT infrastructure, standards, strategies, policies, employee development, communications, and corporate data structure. One director is to apply the:

> ... quality leadership process to IT policies, including disaster recovery, control and access to global networks, the use of IT resources within the company, and so forth... Kodak's quality program insists that internal and external customer needs are clearly identified and that metrics are established to verify those needs are met or exceeded.

Kodak uses many of the tools Deming recommends such as Pareto charts, fishbone diagrams, etc. A lesser known tool is "force field analysis": a general qualitative tool to identify *driving* forces and *restraining* forces. The analytical approach uses "statistical methods and other problem solving tools, data-based analyses drive decisions."

Source: *I/S Analyzer*, February 1991, pp. 8–9.

Case 18.2: Quality at CIGNA

CIGNA is a $16 billion insurance company. Some of its 11 divisions have their own quality programmes. One division, the P&C with over 12,000 employees, has a Director of Quality Development reporting to a Vice President for Quality Development.

P&C at CIGNA has a top-down approach to quality driven by the assumption that understanding the customer and the market will improve profitability, and returns will subsequently follow. A management council was established that formulated its mission of process improvement not necessarily quality control. Process improvement teams were also created with people who could best address the quality issues. They were to work closely with their information systems department whose operational role now changed to a strategic role, the goal to keep pace with business changes, based on end-users' specifications and needs:

> In keeping with the quality initiative, the information systems organization measures itself by response to customer needs, not simply size or significance of the application it's building.

Source: *I/S Analyzer*, February 1991, pp. 10–11.

Supplement 18.1: Causes of errors and their solutions

This supplement is a series of summary tables showing causes of error and possible solutions. Errors can occur at various points within an information system – as shown in Figure 18.10. Many computing environments will have their own unique set of errors, their causes and solutions. In this supplement, we suggest a generic set of errors. A table of selected error-types suggests reasons for the error and offers possible solutions.

Each table is associated with a specific control point in the processing. The lowest significant digit of the table identification number corresponds to a control point in Figure 18.10. For example: in Table 18-10.2 the lowest digit is "2" and corresponds to point 2 in Figure 18.10.

Table 18–10.2: *Form control (for procedures and manuals)*

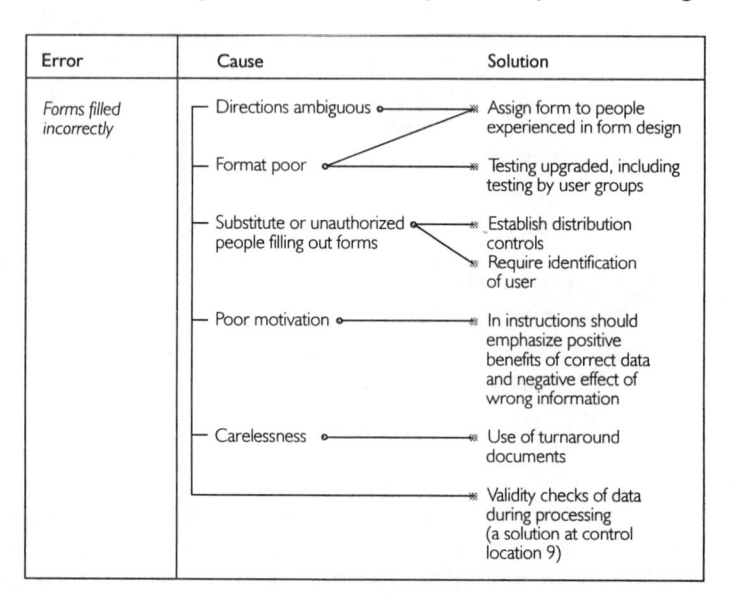

Error	Cause	Solution
Forms filled incorrectly	Directions ambiguous	Assign form to people experienced in form design
	Format poor	Testing upgraded, including testing by user groups
	Substitute or unauthorized people filling out forms	Establish distribution controls; Require identification of user
	Poor motivation	In instructions should emphasize positive benefits of correct data and negative effect of wrong information
	Carelessness	Use of turnaround documents
		Validity checks of data during processing (a solution at control location 9)

Supplement 18.1: Causes for errors and their solutions

Table 18–10.3: Data creation control

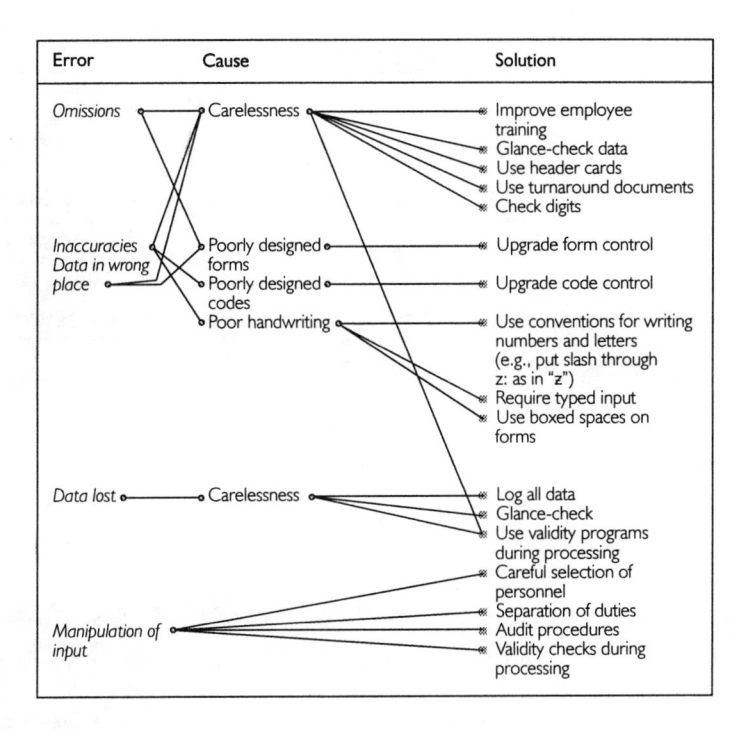

Error	Cause	Solution
Omissions	Carelessness	Improve employee training Glance-check data Use header cards Use turnaround documents Check digits
Inaccuracies Data in wrong place	Poorly designed forms Poorly designed codes Poor handwriting	Upgrade form control Upgrade code control Use conventions for writing numbers and letters (e.g., put slash through z: as in "z") Require typed input Use boxed spaces on forms
Data lost	Carelessness	Log all data Glance-check Use validity programs during processing
Manipulation of input		Careful selection of personnel Separation of duties Audit procedures Validity checks during processing

Table 18–10.4: Summary of data preparation errors and solutions

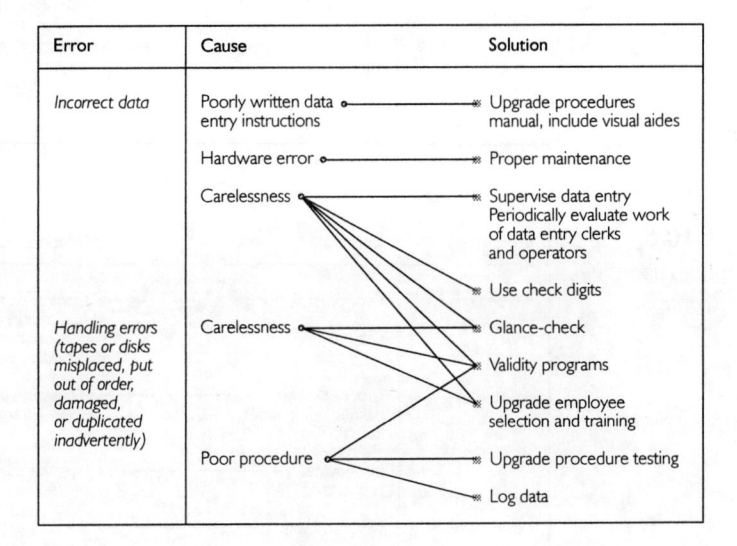

Error	Cause	Solution
Incorrect data	Poorly written data entry instructions	Upgrade procedures manual, include visual aides
	Hardware error	Proper maintenance
	Carelessness	Supervise data entry Periodically evaluate work of data entry clerks and operators Use check digits
Handling errors (tapes or disks misplaced, put out of order, damaged, or duplicated inadvertently)	Carelessness	Glance-check Validity programs Upgrade employee selection and training
	Poor procedure	Upgrade procedure testing Log data

Chapter 18: Controlling Quality and Performance

Supplement 18.1: Causes for errors and their solutions

Table 18–10.5:
Control of operations

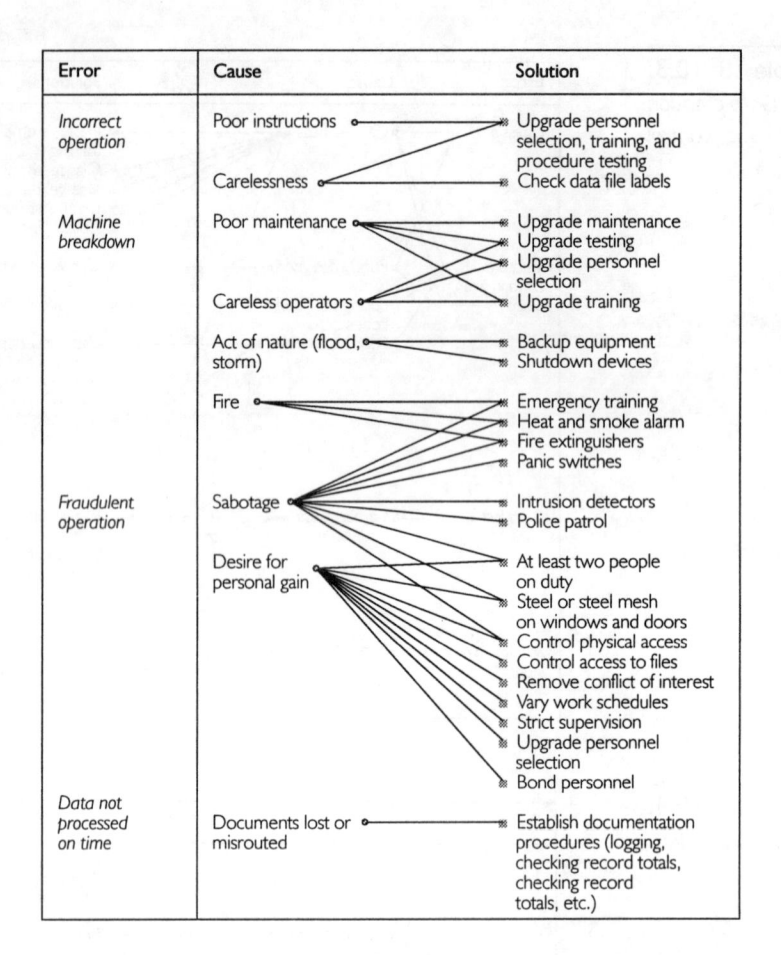

Error	Cause	Solution
Incorrect operation	Poor instructions	Upgrade personnel selection, training, and procedure testing
	Carelessness	Check data file labels
Machine breakdown	Poor maintenance	Upgrade maintenance
		Upgrade testing
		Upgrade personnel selection
	Careless operators	Upgrade training
	Act of nature (flood, storm)	Backup equipment
		Shutdown devices
	Fire	Emergency training
		Heat and smoke alarm
		Fire extinguishers
		Panic switches
Fraudulent operation	Sabotage	Intrusion detectors
		Police patrol
	Desire for personal gain	At least two people on duty
		Steel or steel mesh on windows and doors
		Control physical access
		Control access to files
		Remove conflict of interest
		Vary work schedules
		Strict supervision
		Upgrade personnel selection
		Bond personnel
Data not processed on time	Documents lost or misrouted	Establish documentation procedures (logging, checking record totals, checking record totals, etc.)

Table 18–10.6:
Summary of data file controls

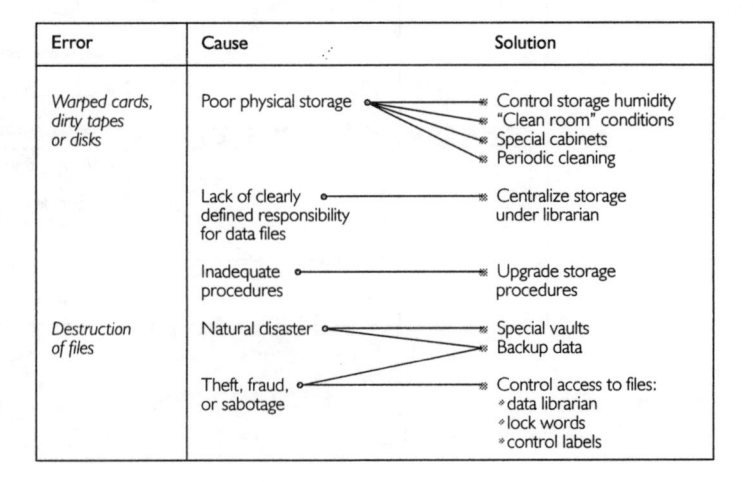

Error	Cause	Solution
Warped cards, dirty tapes or disks	Poor physical storage	Control storage humidity
		"Clean room" conditions
		Special cabinets
		Periodic cleaning
	Lack of clearly defined responsibility for data files	Centralize storage under librarian
	Inadequate procedures	Upgrade storage procedures
Destruction of files	Natural disaster	Special vaults
		Backup data
	Theft, fraud, or sabotage	Control access to files: • data librarian • lock words • control labels

438

Supplement 18.1: Causes of errors and their solutions

Table 18–10.7-8:
Programming controls

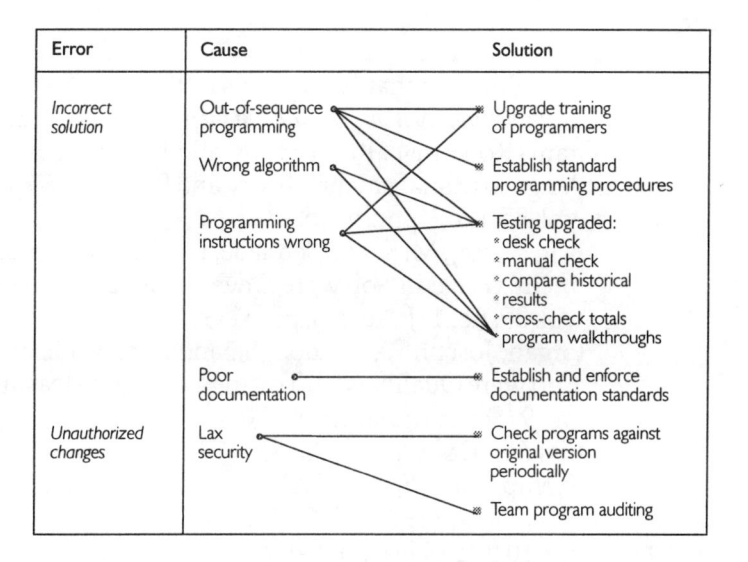

Error	Cause	Solution
Incorrect solution	Out-of-sequence programming	Upgrade training of programmers
	Wrong algorithm	Establish standard programming procedures
	Programming instructions wrong	Testing upgraded: * desk check * manual check * compare historical * results * cross-check totals program walkthroughs
	Poor documentation	Establish and enforce documentation standards
Unauthorized changes	Lax security	Check programs against original version periodically
		Team program auditing

Table 18–10.9:
Processing controls

Error	Cause	Solution
Records lost	Carelessness	Validity checks Upgrade training of personnel Log jobs
Use of incorrect file	Carelessness	Use of standard labels for all files Use program to automatically generate updated data
Lack of necessary supplies	Carelessness	Upgrade planning and inventory control

Table 18–10.10:
Output control

Error	Cause	Solution
Inaccurate output	Processing errors	Audits Validation programs Interfile comparison Defer large-volume printing until proof data checked Sample check of output with corresponding input
	Operation error	Sight check
Incomplete output	Operation or processing error	Check page counts Check control totals for each process or report

For a detailed discussion of each table, see Hussain and Hussain, 1992: 191–206.

Chapter 18: Controlling Quality and Performance

References

Esichaikul, Vatchara *et al.* (1994). "Problem-Solving Support for TQM." *Information Systems Management*, vol. 11, no. 1, pp. 47–52.

Grant, Robert M., Rami Shani, and Krishnan, R. (1994). "TQM's Challenge to Management Theory and Practice." *Sloan Management Review*, vol. 35, no. 2, pp. 25–35.

Haag, S., Raj, M. K. and Schkade, L. L. (1996). "Quality Function Deployment Usage in Software Development." *Communications of the ACM*, vol. 39, no. 1 (January), pp. 41–9.

Horgan, Joseph R., London, S., and Lyn, Michael R. (1994). "Achieving Software Quality with Testing Coverage Measures." *Computer*, vol. 27, no. 9 (September), pp. 60–70.

Hussain, Donna and K. M. (1992). *Information Management*. Hemel Hempstead: Prentice Hall International (UK) Ltd.

I/S Analyzer. (1993). "TQM in IS: Defining User Expectation." Vol. 31, no. 10 (October), pp. 1–16.

Prince, E. Ted. (1993). "Human Factors in Quality Assurance." *Information Systems Management*, vol. 10, no. 3, pp. 78–80.

Powell, T. C. (1995). "Total Quality Management as Competitive Advantage: A Review and Empirical Study." *Strategic Management Journal*, vol. 16, no. 1 (January).

Ragozzino, Pat P. (1990). "IS Quality – What is it?" *Journal of Systems Management*, vol. 41, no. 11 (November), pp. 15–20.

Ray, Darrel W. (1994). "The Missing T in TQM." *Journal for Quality and Participation*, vol. 17, no. 3 (June), pp. 64–9.

Rowe, Joyce M. and Neal, Ralph D. (1993). "TQM is Systems Development – A Paradigm without a Sound Foundation." *Journal of Systems Management*, vol. 44, no. 5 (May), pp. 12–17.

19 Project Management

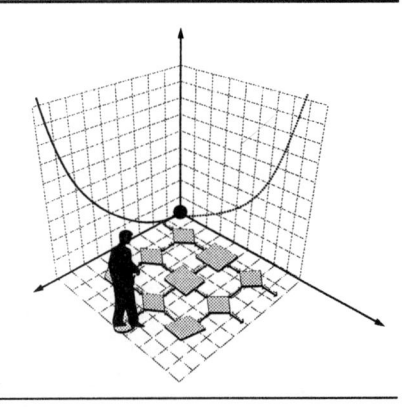

Introduction

A *project* is a temporary assemblage of resources (equipment, software personnel, and procedures) to solve a one-shot problem. Planning, organizing, and controlling these resources is called *project management*. To ensure the development of information systems within time and funding constraints, formal project management is advisable for all except simple and small systems.

Project management begins with the selection of a project manager and a development staff often referred to as a development team. It entails the definition of tasks, their desired and viable sequence, and the formulation of time estimates for *project milestones* (important points where many activities converge or diverge). Scheduling, resource allocation, amendment control, progress evaluation, and quality control are responsibilities of a project manager. For certain projects, like those involving the integration of the new system with existing systems, a *systems integrator* performs the tasks of a project manager.

The effectiveness of project control can be enhanced by good project organization and by the use of computer program output designed specifically for project management. We discuss in some detail the use of computer programs for project development largely because there is a common misconception that because we use computer programs the results are accurate and correct. The truth is that the computer profession often has no more control of its projects than any other profession does. The best hope we have for a successful development project is to nurture the critical success factors for project management and to follow a set of rules of good project management that have been developed over the years based on mistakes and errors made. Each of the stages for the organization of project management will be discussed in this chapter along with the factors of success and failure of computer systems projects and rules for good project management.

Characteristics of project management

What distinguishes project management from ongoing management? Usually, projects have the following characteristics:

- They have a specific objective; for example, the development of a sales order-entry system.
- They must be developed within a specific time period.
- Development must be accomplished within a given budget for capital expenditures and operating expenses of the project.
- An *ad hoc* team is assigned to the project. Some members will be part-time, depending on the need for their skills.

From this list, the management of a project appears to be straightforward and to involve fewer elements than ongoing management. Why then, do so many systems development projects fail to meet users' needs? Why are time and cost overruns for development projects so common? One reason is that project objectives are frequently ill-defined at the start of a system development project. Many users are unable to explain clearly and concisely what computer system is needed and what functions it should perform. Most system failures (60–80%) can be traced to an inadequate understanding of user requirements by analysts and users at the start of the project.

In addition, project deadlines are often unrealistic, arbitrarily imposed by administrative decree on the basis of external events. Even information processing managers and analysts with experience in systems development sometimes have difficulty estimating realistic time and costs at the start of a project. Generally, schedules need to be readjusted and costs recalculated after a development project is under way and problems are encountered. Furthermore, staffing for a development project is often determined by availability rather than technical competence.

To these complications, one must add the fact that information systems can be highly complex. Many development projects incorporate advanced technology. Many explore "uncharted territory". The detailed steps to be taken cannot be identified at the outset of the project, and progress cannot, therefore, be realistically assessed. The development of an information system at the frontiers of knowledge has a high risk of failure. None of the above factors, in isolation, present insurmountable obstacles to project management. But taken together, they can sorely test the skill of a project manager when an information system is under development.

Selection of a project manger

The *project manager*, a key resource in successful project management, is appointed once the development of an information system has been approved by corporate management. In the life cycle approach to development, this appointment follows management approval of the project (see Box 10, Figure 19.1). Formerly, choice of a project manager was based on the technical knowledge of candidates. But today, managerial skill – in particular, interactive personnel skills and business experience – is valued as well. It is recognized that a project manager needs to be a leader, able to direct and motivate a team chosen from different functional departments and status levels within the organization. A project manager must be able to coordinate the various aspects of development and to interact with users, often in the role of counsellor. After all, the real economic value of a computer system depends upon its effectiveness in meeting user needs. Both technical and managerial directions are needed to make that happen.

Figure 19.1: *Steps leading to project management*

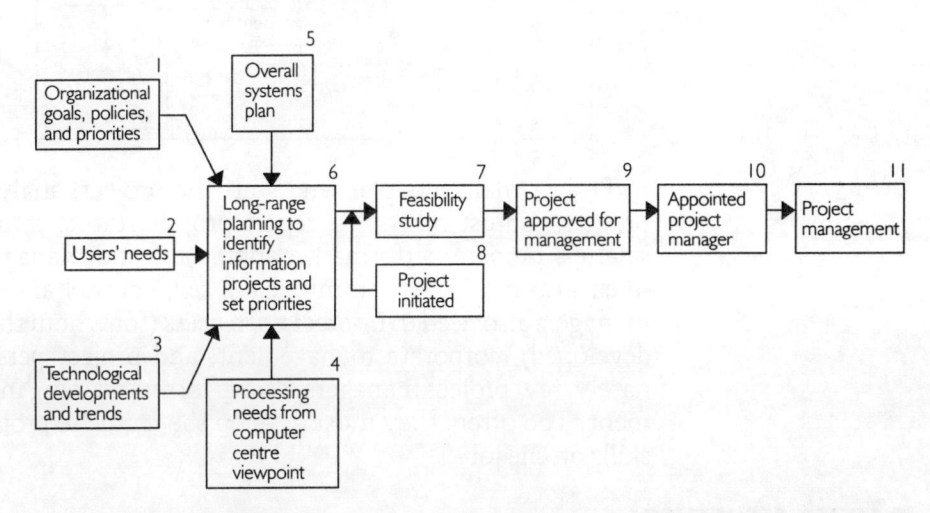

Project managers generally report to a special committee appointed by corporate management to oversee the project. This committee may have a variety of names: for example, Project Review Committee, Steering Committee, or User and Administrative Committee. Its function is to assist the project manager in interpreting the firm's policies, to clarify user's needs, and to monitor the progress of the project.

Chapter 19: Project Management

The project manager will also have input and support from corporate management, the database administrator, and the computer centre director in a staff relationship, as illustrated in Figure 19.2. End-user representatives and technical personnel will have a line relationship. Consultants and accounting department representatives assigned to the project may also fall in this latter category. Typically, 70% or more of the total resources needed for a project must be within the project manager's direct control for a successful project.

Figure 19.2:
Project organization

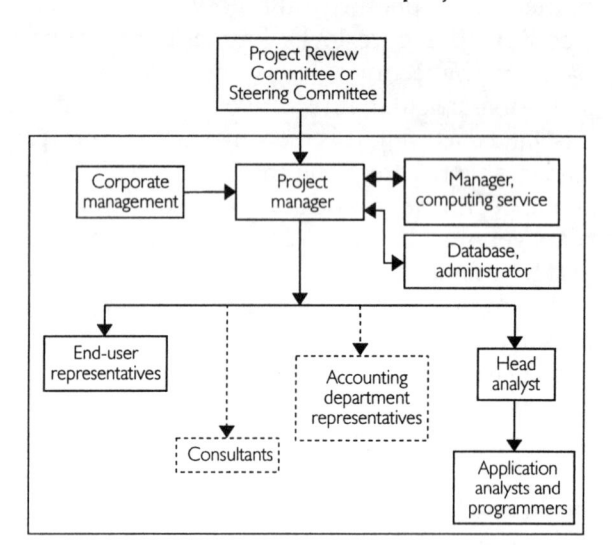

Project managers plan and staff the project, analyze risk, monitor progress, adjust schedules, report project status, control budgets and salaries, prepare performance appraisals, and manage changes. They must also motivate, communicate, sell, counsel and delegate. Project managers also need to interact with users (for whom the system is being developed), corporate management, and project personnel. Unfortunately, few project managers receive formal training in project management. Too often, they must develop the requisite project management skills on the job.

Team structure

One of the first acts of a project manager is to structure the project development team.

Approaches

Several approaches to the organization of such teams are possible: organization by function, project organization, and matrix organization.

Function organization
Function organization generally keeps traditional line-staff relationships, with a vertical flow of authority and responsibility. For some projects, this type of organization does not work well because the project requires the cooperation and use of resources from many line units. In fact:

> The essence of project management is that it cuts across, and in a sense conflicts with the natural organization structure... Because a project usually requires decisions and actions from a number of functional areas at once, the main interdependencies and the main flow of information in a project are not vertical but lateral. Projects are characterized by exceptionally strong lateral working relationships, requiring closely related activity and decisions by many individuals in different functional departments.
>
> *Stewart, 1969:295–6*

Project organization
Project organization is the creation of a unit with responsibility for all aspects of project development. In this schema, professional, technical, and administrative staff are hired for the duration of the project. When systems development projects are organized in this manner, serious problems can arise in attracting competent personnel. Many computer professionals are unwilling to join projects that offer no job security, and they dislike jobs of this nature because of a fluctuating workload.

Matrix organization
Matrix organization combines *functional* and *project* approaches to project management. The staff is "borrowed" from functional divisions. In the case of a developmental team, members might be drawn from accounting, marketing, operations research, and data processing departments. Which employees are borrowed is negotiated by the project manager with functional department heads. The choice is usually based on the availability of personnel and the qualifications demanded by the project. Sometimes, department heads are reluctant to release competent personnel. However, most recognize that having staff members assigned to the development team can be advantageous to them. Departmental interests are protected by having staff representatives on the team, and staff experience in the development process will be beneficial when future information systems for the department are planned.

One problem with matrix organization is that project members have two bosses. They are responsible to the project manager for work assignments, yet their permanent supervisors retain jurisdiction over personnel matters such as salary and promotions. The two bosses may clash in values and objectives, with the project member caught in between. Such potentially explosive situations can be defused if, before the team is constituted, ground rules are negotiated between the project manager and functional heads regarding shared authority and responsibility over project members. In summary, a matrix organization is advantageous because it:

- Allows a project manager to cut across vertical organizational divisions.
- Involves functional departments and is responsive to their needs because representatives are on the project staff.
- Has access to the resources in all functional departments (on a negotiated basis).
- Provides a "home" for project personnel after the completion of the project.
- Does not permanently disrupt organizational subgroupings or the continuity of seniority, fringe benefits, and so on.

An example of matrix organization shown in Table 19.1 illustrates the concept that both individuals and departments may be assigned to development teams and participate in several projects simultaneously.

Table 19.1 *A sample matrix organization for project management*

Personnel assigned / Project:	B19	B20	P5	P7	...	S3	K9
■ End-user requirements							
⁃ Manufacturing department	X		X				X
⁃ Marketing department		X	X				
⁃ Finance department	X		X			X	X
⁃ R & D department						X	
■ Support personnel							
⁃ Lead analyst							
• Alex Wheeler	X		X	X		X	
• Rene Kinney			X				X
⁃ Programmer							
• 3GL/4GL		X	X	X		X	
• Simulation						X	
■ Knowledge engineer							X
■ AI specialist		X					X
■ Consultant	X	X					
■ OR/MS specialist						X	X
■ Consultants		X					

Management style may be one factor in the choice of project organization. As shown in Figure 19.3, a functional organization is appropriate when people are the primary concern of a project manager.

Figure 19.3:
Choice of project organization

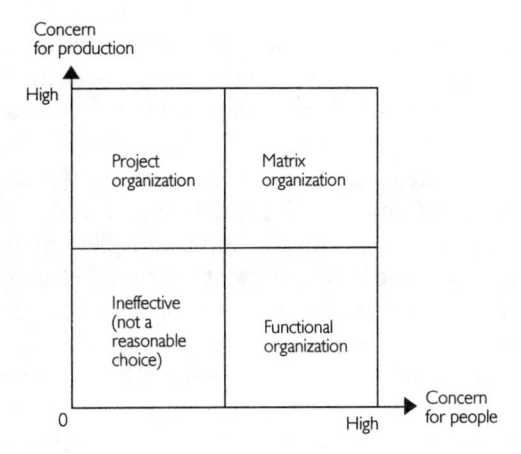

Project organization is appropriate when more importance is placed on production than on people. Matrix organization balances high concern for people *and* production. There is much anecdotal material on teams but little hard data identifying environmental variables that affect team performance. This section has suggested some team structure factors that affect development efforts, but wide disagreement exists on what makes a project, especially programming projects, successful. It is a generally accepted axiom that adding people to late projects only tends to make the project later. In addition, crash development teams also have a high cost as a result of lower productivity, overtime, overcrowding, and so on. Figure 19.4 shows the relationship of cost and efficiency to time of completion, based on past experience.

Figure 19.4:
Relationship between cost, efficiency and completion time

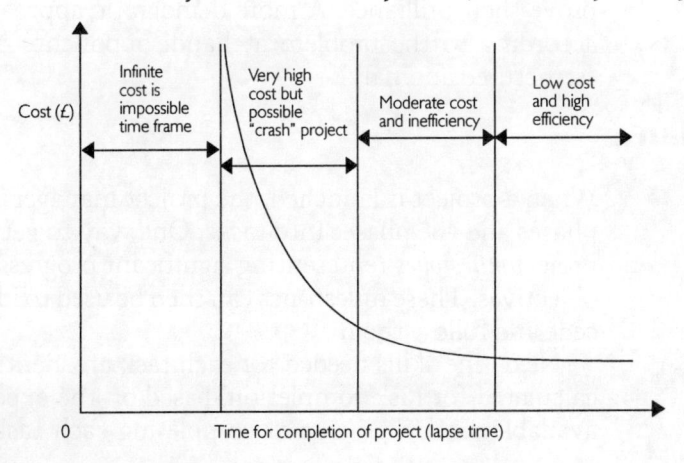

Team size

Once team structure is decided, team members are appointed. A decision on optimal team size has to be made at this juncture. This problem plagued operations research workers as far back as the 1940s and 1950s and still haunts projects. Studies in group dynamics have suggested that the optimum team size is in the range of five to seven members and that as the team size increases, job satisfaction drops, with absenteeism and turnover increasing. But some computer development projects are far too complex to have such small teams. The design of software for IBM's System 360, for example, required 5,000 man-years for completion. Teams need to be large enough to complete a project within a reasonable time frame. And should completion by a specific date be a constraint, a large rather than small team may be needed in order to have sufficient workdays of effort to complete the project on time.

Regardless of size, teams should have a balance of theoreticians and practitioners, idealists and realists, scientists and humanists, and generalists and specialists. The problem with small development teams is that they may be unable to achieve such a balance.

Once team size is determined, working groups of programmers, analysts, and users can be organized for specific tasks. The exact organization and size of each group will depend on the project. For programming teams, some project managers organize programmers under a chief programmer who is the master designer and architect of the system, who supervises structured walkthroughs and formal reviews of design and coding. This type of organization reportedly achieves high technical standards and produces programs that are simple, obvious, and transparent. The team effort minimizes problems with egocentric programmers who want to save a millisecond here and an instruction there to prove their brilliance. A more democratic approach rotates leadership according to the problem at hand; opponents of this system call it "structured anomaly".

Project plan

When a project is launched, the project manager divides the work into phases and the phases into tasks. One way to get started is to identify project *milestones* representing significant progress toward the project's objectives. These milestones can then be used to identify tasks that precede and follow them.

Next, the skills needed for each task are identified and the effort is calculated for task completion, based on the expected performance of available staff. The cost of completing each task (or group of tasks) should then be estimated by the individual or group responsible for completing it. Task definition is the basis of a detailed *project plan*; it specifies the activities that need to be completed, together with the sequence in which they should be undertaken. It states what end-product is expected, designates which individuals (or departments) are responsible, and estimates "time to complete" and project cost.

The plan should be as comprehensive as possible, since schedules and budgets are based on it. It is also used in tracking project progress. The omission of tasks in the plan is a common cause of project time and cost overruns. Frequently overlooked or underestimated are project orientation, training, validation and review, production of reports, and correction of errors and omissions. It is wise to add a contingency factor to allow for unexpected tasks or amended user requirements during the course of the project.

When making the project plan, useful information can be gleaned from project control records of past projects. Such records may provide information on how long it took to produce program specifications, ratios of elapsed time to expended effort for different activities, and data on programmer productivity related to lines of code. Many project managers keep a day-to-day log, a mine of information on systems development events, problems, and decisions that can serve as a useful reference when other projects are being planned.

Scheduling

On the basis of the system plan, a project schedule is prepared and resources are assigned to each activity. Some scheduling is straightforward sequencing, but when parallel activities are scheduled, care must be taken to ensure that adequate resources are available. For example, if two software activities are scheduled for simultaneous development, will an adequate number of programmers be available? The schedule should also keep employees working, avoiding lulls in activity with personnel being idle. Minimizing peaks and troughs of worker demand is known as *manpower levelling*. Such levelling does not mean merely juggling numbers (employees in the aggregate), because special skills may be needed for a given task. It does no good to assign a programmer who knows only FORTRAN to a project to be written in COBOL.

Project time completion and total project cost are recalculated once scheduling is complete to see if they fit within the time/cost constraints in the project authorization document. If not, rescheduling is necessary, dropping desired, but not essential, activities and reshuffling resources. In some cases, the constraints themselves may be reviewed and revised. Project managers can also acquire software packages to generate reports for project control. The types of reports that most project managers desire are:

- Activity status reports sorted by:
  - Organizational units.
  - Activity.
  - Overruns.
  - Time.
  - Cost.
- Budget:
  - Standard.
  - Exceptional.
  - Comparisons.
  - Costing.
  - Loading.
    * Personnel.
    * Equipment.
- Work schedules sorted by:
  - Start date.
  - Finish date.
  - Float/slack.

With the aid of these computer-generated reports, the project manager can identify potential bottlenecks or problems. The output can also provide information that the manager uses in solving problems. For example, budgetary reports provide a powerful cost control capability, identifying how much has been spent by each person or organizational unit and for what task. The project manager can then compare these expenditures with the target budget. Some computer-generated reports are sent to project personnel and users to keep them informed on the status of the project.

Project reviews

In general, the schedules for most systems development projects need constant updating and revision during the life cycle of the project. It is important to have a formal *review process* for evaluating the progress of development. Review sessions serve a number of other purposes as well; they also:

- Compare development against project objectives to make sure that the project is on track.

- Interject general-management awareness, concern, and support.
- Reaffirm the correctness and completeness of current plans and schedules.
- Identify potential problems and assign responsibility and deadlines for resolution.
- Foster cooperation and communication among project staff and users.
- Create a sense of enthusiasm, cohesiveness, and importance.

How often such reviews are held depends on the nature and length of the project. For projects longer than six months, biweekly reviews at the project team level are recommended. Formal review with top management should be held at least monthly.

The project leader should also receive periodic progress reports. For example, at the end of each week, team members might hand in time sheets reporting which tasks have been completed with estimates regarding the amount of time necessary to complete partially finished tasks. These reports can be compiled in numerical summaries, bar charts, written reports, or some other fashion. A full progress report should be prepared at least once a month.

Slippage

In spite of reviews and reports, vast discrepancies often exist between estimations of the time and cost of a project and the actual completion date and development cost. A number of factors can contribute to this situation. Sometimes, activities are so innovative that no one with expertise is available in-house to make accurate time estimates. Sometimes, excessive pressure to keep to schedules and budgets make teams members hesitant to report stumbling blocks. Sometimes, no clear guidelines exist for assessing the degree of completeness of a given task. Sometimes, the scope of a project is changed midstream. Time and cost estimates will also require revision when system specifications change.

Of all project development activities, software preparation (both systems and applications software) has the worst record for accuracy in time estimates, even though many formulas exist for calculating needed programming time. One formula, proposed by Lawrence Putnam, is:

$$t_d = \frac{S_s}{C_k K^{1/3}}$$

where:

t_d = development time

S_s = number of end product lines of source code delivered
C_k = state of technology constant
K = life cycle in man-years

Although experts disagree about how to measure programming time variables and about the relationship between these variables, such formulas do help to identify what variables should be considered.

When a record exists of past productivity of employees on development projects, a project manager can use such data in making target estimates. But with the high mobility of analysts and programmers, new personnel of untested ability will always be assigned to projects, and even known workers will not necessarily have stable productivity. Studies have shown that productivity may vary by as much as a factor of 10, even among experienced programmers. A few software firms with permanent staff that use standard methodologies have completed up to 88% of their projects within 20% of their time/cost estimates but firms not specializing in software are doing very well to come even close to this performance. At best, team members can only approximate the time needed for activity completion. The project manager must be prepared to revise the project completion date as a development moves forward.

In many projects, schedule slippage is unavoidable. However, in all projects, a point is reached when specification and design should be frozen and no further modifications allowed. It is important that project managers have the authority to overrule users (even high-ranking users who would otherwise outrank the project manager) who wish to add system features after the cutoff date.

To ensure that development progress is being reported by the project team as accurately as possible:

- Precise criteria for what constitutes task completion should be provided.
- More severe penalties should be imposed for misreporting progress than for reporting slippage or other problems.
- Guidelines should be provided for the proportion of effort to be allocated to standard tasks.
- The project manager should occasionally participate in team review sessions to ensure that task completion estimates are taken seriously.
- When a wide variance exists between estimates and actual time and cost figures for a given task, the figures of related tasks should be carefully reviewed to ensure that they, too, have not been underestimated.

The proper response of a project manager to schedule slippage should be to try to determine ways to make up for lost ground. Alternatives might include the reordering of task sequences and priorities. Functions may be deleted and "gingerbread" features eliminated. Another option is to introduce additional resources, such as extra staff or more computer run time during testing. Perhaps overtime work is an answer: perhaps workloads can be readjusted to make teams more productive.

The temptation to do a less thorough job should be strenuously avoided. If there is no way to make up for schedule slippage, a project manager should reluctantly accept the inevitable: a deadline should never take precedence over quality. If saddled with intense pressure to meet an impossible delivery date, the first responsibility of the project manager is to protect the development team from destructive pressure; the second is to get top-level management and users to negotiate a compromise. If system requirements are reduced, with some of the expected benefits excised, perhaps the deadline can be met. Perhaps a minimal system can be implemented on time, with additional subsystems added later. Another alternative is throwaway code, a temporary system to meet user demand. If, after explaining the problems of development and the reasons for delay, an unrealistic deadline is still imposed, the project manager should consider asking to be reassigned to another project. One manager is this situation told his boss: "If you think the project can be done in less time than I estimate, you may be a better person for this job." An end-users' steering committee might be formed to evaluate the design. A user might be assigned as either project leader or second in command. It is wise to distribute minutes of all key design meetings to users.

In such projects, however, network analysis may be of little value. Tasks that appear simple at the start of the project may be found to be complex once analysts begin work on them. For this reason, the use of formal planning techniques may be inappropriate at the start of the project, and it may not be possible to make accurate time and cost estimates using these techniques early in the cycle of development.

Project organization

Slippage can be reduced and the effectiveness of project management can be increased in many other respects by good project organization, the use of computer programs, by appointing a systems integrator, by encouraging the critical success factors for project management, and by following "rules" of good project management. All these topics are examined later.

Table 19.2 *Project organization as a function of software*

Lines of code (LOC), (K= 1,000)	Project organization
1 to < 5K	Individual Programmer
5K to <25K	Team of programmers
25K to <100K	Large team of programmers
100K to <1,000K	Several teams of programmers
1 million to <10 million	Several companies collaborating
10 million to <100 million	National collaboration

The organization of the project management personnel is a function of project complexity. One measure of the complexity of a project is the size of the software requirements for the project. The choice of different project organizations for different sizes of projects is shown in Table 19.2. Examples of large projects are Case 19.1 and other governmental systems like the Air Defense System of North America. Whatever the size of the project software, all projects for information systems are developed by a project team. That team's composition must be given careful consideration and is our next topic of discussion.

Project team design

Information systems projects of any complexity are carried out by project teams. Assembling and managing a project team is not a new problem. It was faced in the 1950s by projects in OR. Since then, team design (when applied to information systems and software development) has been based on principles, organizational paradigms and experiences of project managers in the field. It is these principles, paradigms and experiences that we shall now examine.

There are five principles of software staffing as enunciated by Boehm (1981:667–672):

1. *Principle of Top Talent* recommends fewer but better people.
2. *Principle of Job Matching* "fits" and matches the skills and motivations available to the task at hand.
3. *Principle of Team Balance* recommends that there needs to be a balance between the technical skills, knowledge and personality characteristics of team members.
4. *Principle of Phase Out* acknowledges that there will inevitably be a misfit on the team resulting in "unhealthy results in the long run."

Getting the misfit out may not be easy but must be done with adequate time, thought and sympathy.

5. *Principle of Career Progression* recommends bringing out the best of one's self by helping people to "self actualize."

These principles for team construction must be applied within an *organization paradigm* which is the set of assumptions constituting the basis for the structure and operations of the organizational unit. Constantine (1993) suggests four organizational paradigms and they are summarized in Table 19.3. Constantine hastens to comment that:

> ... none of the reference paradigms is ideal for software development projects. Software projects typically involve a combination of complex problem solving with the need for a certain amount of innovation, yet much of software development is also routine and calls for dependable, predictable tactical performance... By understanding the fundamentals of organization paradigms, a carefully conceived combination of models can be constructed. A promising example is the structured open teamwork model... that combines closed... elements and open... ones, with a sprinkling of random teamwork. It uses formal structures to promote flexibility along with more efficient problem solving.
>
> *Constantine*, 1993:41

Whatever organization paradigm is selected and for whatever reason, there are many recommendations and suggestions made by people experienced in the project management of information systems. These recommendations and observations relate not just to team management but sometimes to project management. They are:

- Remember the advice of Henry David Thoreau: *simplify, simplify, simplify*.
- Planning should proceed top-down until the work is divided into small manageable modules and tasks.
- A crucial decision will be related to how to break up a large project so that the dependency of subprojects on context is minimized.

> Experienced designers recognized that customers may not understand the true nature of the requirements at the beginning of the project.
>
> Walz *et al.*, 1993:63

> More than half the cost of the development of complex computer-based information systems (IS) is attributable to decisions made in the *upstream* portion of the software process; namely requirements specification and design.
>
> Quoted from W. Myers in Walz *et al.*, 1993:63

Table 19.3 Organizational reference paradigms

Organizational paradigm	Closed	Random	Open	Synchronous
Organizational representation	(triangle/hierarchy)	(scribble/cloud)	(circle)	(arrows converging upward)
Characteristics	■ Traditional hierarchy of authority	■ Independent creative free-wheeling individualism	■ Adaptive and collaborative communication	■ Harmonious alignment with common vision
Strengths	■ Stable security ■ Preserves resources	■ Creative ■ Inventive ■ Promotes personal best	■ Information sharing ■ Practical adaptation	■ Smooth operation ■ Quiet efficiency
Weaknesses	■ No genuine innovation ■ No full use of individuals	■ No dependable stability ■ No efficient resource use	■ Not necessarily smooth, simple or efficient	■ Not too responsive to change
Best applications and examples	■ Routine tactical projects e.g. governmental bureaucracies	■ Creative breakthroughs e.g. R&D and developing new technologies	■ Complex problem solving e.g. several IS projects	■ Where there is sustained unified action and shared knowledge e.g. Amish communities
Characteristics	■ Loyal ■ Committed ■ Action-oriented ■ Respond to leadership	■ Independent thinkers ■ Intellectual ■ Artistic	■ Good interpersonal skills ■ Sensitive to "people issues"	■ Somewhat introvert ■ People sensitive

> Customer iteration is a powerful team design technique. When we can produce an idea, develop it, test it with customers, prototype it, test it with customers, and validate, modify or discard it within 48 hours, we can stabilize a design very quickly.
>
> *Holtzblatt and Beyer*, 1993:102

- Project teams must be organized based of sound principles as well as varying project objectives and needs.
- Matching team members to the organization paradigm and team model can lead to high performance.
- Specifics of team culture should fit circumstances and personalities without compromising on principles.
- Building a team consistent with the team culture can result in a quick peak performance.

> A cohesive team cannot tolerate extremist mavericks. One of our most difficult realizations was that some talented individuals cannot flourish in a team-oriented environment.
>
> *Hyman*, 1993:59

> "Adding manpower to a late software projects makes it later." This is advice by the "father" and project manager for the then revolutionary IBM 360.
>
> *Brooks*, 1975

- As team size grows, stability can become a problem.

> Order and simplicity are not the norm, chaos and complexity are the rule... The true objective is to take the chaos as given and learn to thrive on it.
>
> *Hyman*, 1993:60

> The department's challenges were new resource management, co-ordination, communication, and most important, ownership... Management of resources required constant negotiation and prioritization across functional lines... Coordination and communication now required formal channels. Even with the formal channels, we found that information was filtered and interpreted between levels, reducing the effective flow.
>
> *Hyman*, 1993:58

> There is no royal road to software sizing. There is no magic formula that will provide an easy and accurate substitute for the process of thinking through and fully understanding the nature of the software product to be developed.
>
> *Boehm*, 1981

Past experience, creative skills, and knowledge of structured approaches to systems development lead to successful estimation of the time required for project activities. Creating a climate and environment where the discovery or exposure of problems is *rewarded* not punished or swathed in threats.

> Team members let go of ideas more easily when they see users react badly to them than when another team member rejects them... Ideas not chosen are not lost in developing each idea, the groups are expected to pull together the best parts of all ideas.
>
> *Holtzblatt and Beyer*, 1993:101–2

Successful team and project leadership should fit the style and form of the organization paradigm used. Project organization and management is not hardware and software, but *peopleware*.

Many failures of information systems projects do not occur because there are inadequately skilled personnel on project teams to implement the system but because these skilled personnel do not work together; or because they are badly managed; because the original concept of the system was flawed, too large or too complex; because the choice of software package and hardware platform was wrong; because the systems were underfunded; or, because there was no good support from computer programs for project management.

Use of computer programs

Managing complex projects may require support software that runs on minis or mainframes and in the right hands many of these programs are powerful management tools. Many programs are capable of more than just the basic project management activities of manpower and resource levelling and the optimization of cost, time or manpower effort (some programs allow on-screen editing of PERT charts).

Whether using graphics or entering data via a keyboard it is also possible to ask "what if" questions and simulate changes to project-management parameters. For example, what would be the effect on resource consumption and time of project completion if the sequence of specific activities were changed or the time estimates of an activity were altered? Such simulation results can be important to project management. Whatever hardware or software is used there are some things that cannot be performed by any computer program. Such as:

- It cannot guarantee correct input. It can check for obvious errors such as time of completion being before time of start or the pessimistic time being smaller than the optimistic time of completion of an activity. However, if the time estimate or cost estimates are

within specified bounds but incorrect, then there is no way that the PERT program (or any other project management software) will catch the error. Such errors can be disastrous.
- No computer program can guarantee that projects using it will complete the project on time and within budget. It is hoped that information supplied to the project management staff (in a timely fashion) will reduce the likelihood of time and budget overruns but the extent of this would depend on how and when the information is used.
- Computer software cannot identify activities that are incorrectly sequenced, included or excluded.

The solution of the PERT algorithm requires simple arithmetic and many comparisons of calculated values. The numerous reports generated all need multiple copies because, in a typical project, many people are involved. And all this must be done promptly for it is no good knowing about zero slacks and bottlenecks when is too late to do anything about it. So, there is a lot of paperwork – an ideal application for a computer program but highly dependent on good input.

The operation of the project management software is mostly clerical work providing the resource (time, personnel, equipment and materials) estimates for each of the activities. The demanding tasks are upfront: the identification of the activities, establishing task dependencies and sequencing them correctly, assigning resources to activities and estimating all the task times. These tasks must be performed by the project management staff. They also must decide when to update and to whom to communicate the updating. Too often could be unnecessarily costly and too seldom could be harmful to the management process.

The project management staff are also responsible for the decision on whether or not to use computer software. The rule of thumb is that if there are over 100 activities then software should be considered. The number would go as low as 20 if a project manager has multiple projects that are being implemented simultaneously. Another important decision is to determine who gets which reports and when. Overloading reports can be worse than no reports. Also, slick reports can give the dangerous impression that everything is completely under control just because the current situation is monitored by "a computer report".

In the last resort, project management depends much on people using their judgment, experience in project management, and skills in estimation. These are not a hardware or software problem but a people problem. These include getting the project team members to work together productively and creatively. Computer programs can help identify bottlenecks and even provide information of the activities where there is a surplus and shortage of resources. Reallocating resources with the least disruption of time, cost and morale of team members (and without any reduction in the quality) is the function of the project manager and the project management staff.

Most projects for information systems development will use PERT (Program Evaluation and Review Technique) because it requires three estimates (optimistic, pessimistic, and most likely) for each activity and because of the probabilistic nature of the activities in the development of information systems.

There is a well accepted PERT algorithm that generates much basic information including:

- The critical path.
- Time of project completion.
- Slacks for each activity.
- Earliest and latest time of start for each activity.
- Project management software can do the following:
  - Provide basic information on scheduling (as listed above).
  - Provide validity checks for obviously incorrect data input on time estimates.
  - Identify schedule conflicts when a resource is assigned to a multiple simultaneous tasks.
  - Identify loops in sequencing.
  - Identify slippages in activities as well as potential slippages.
  - Provides information in different sortings and orderings.
  - Integrates accounting data and project data with the corporate database if desired.
  - Provides relevant information to the person responsible.
  - Offers ease of replanning and adapting quickly and easily to real-time changes.
  - Graphics capability allows Gannt charts, PERT charts, project networks, histograms and work breakdown schedules. Colour capability can identify different responsibilities and resource consumptions in colour codes.

There are many computer programs for project management. In 1995, there were well over 100 project management software packages for the PC alone.

Systems integrator

Integration tasks that involve complex logical relationships and sophisticated hardware (including telecommunications), can demand special resources such as a *systems integrator*. This could be a vendor that provides a project manager and staff who are well experienced and knowledgeable about information processing and integration. They accept responsibility for a project for which the client firm may not have the time or personnel. They allow the client firm's IS staff to devote their time to operations and applications that require a greater understanding of end-user needs and organizational priorities. Systems integrators have the project management skills and may also possess software that could be useful to the project.

Due to their volume of business, systems integrators can get the client firm a quantity discount on purchases of equipment and other such resources. Systems integrators, like consultants, keep abreast of technology and are expected to be objective. This objectivity is very useful in many situations of corporate mergers especially when closely-related or identical industries are involved – such as the merger of two airlines or two banks. With such mergers there are (initially) two sets of resources: hardware, software and personnel when only one set is necessary. What gives? For compatibility, a development approach or even a programming language must go. For economy, some senior staff must go. And what if two managers like their jobs but there is only room for one of them? This is where the objectivity of a systems integrator can be crucial. The result is often not only a rational one but the "loser" can save face without resulting in hard feelings.

Concomitant with the advantages of a systems integrator there are disadvantages. The corporation may loose control in decision-making and authority over the project. The IS staff may feel slighted at not being given the complex project but being assigned to more mundane tasks instead. Hiring people from outside may lead to a loss of morale among the IS staff, which would be very bad news because, eventually, the IS staff have to maintain and support the newly-integrated system. Their active participation and cooperation may be (or become) essential to the successful completion of the project.

The systems integrator could be a source for loss of proprietary information. This danger and the fear of losing control of the project may well prevent the systems integrator from being hired for mission critical projects. Also, if hired, the systems integrator may take the experience to another customer, possibly a competitor. This danger can be safeguarded against by a clause in the contract that prevents such a transfer of technology. The contract must contain terms and clauses to ensure that the *client* has controlling authority when determining the choice of resources – *especially* when the vendor sells such resources. The vendor can also be made to provide the staff of the client with training on the project. The client's role and share of work in implementation (up to 50% is quite typical), as well as the client's expectations, constraints, and responsibilities must be carefully spelled out. There have been numerous cases in facility management contracts that had to be interpreted in court. This may be avoided by a well-prepared contract that is written in global terms of structures and responsibilities with flexibility and yet no ambiguity.

Part of the contract could be the specification of a system integrator who must be chosen with care. The system integrator must of course know the methodologies involved, be able to manage and work with professional computer personnel, and be experienced in managing projects (with, perhaps, around 15 years' experience). Being a good listener helps but understanding the local procedures and corporate culture (as well as having the confidence of top management) can be very helpful. Being able to break up a project into manageable tasks and bridge them together is important for developing and installing large, complex, and unique projects.

Table 19.4 *Summary of advantages and disadvantages of a systems integrator*

Advantages	Disadvantages
- Accepts responsibility for completion of deliverables (as stated in contract) - Has knowledge of complex and diverse technologies - Has depth of experience in integrated projects - Has well developed project management skills - Assumes risks and relieves client of risks of completion - Access to packages - Access to purchasing discounts due to high volume of other projects - Quick access to services on time-critical projects - Will train user and offer a transfer of technology - Can arbitrate objectively between internal competing parties	- Danger of loss of control of decision-making and authority over IS staff (very bad for mission-critical projects) - IS staff may feel slighted and hence resentful with morale going down because they are being assigned to simpler projects - Resentment against "hired gun" with no knowledge of organization. Can be very bad since IS staff must maintain system - Can bring bias towards its products (hardware of software) - Danger of loss of proprietary information to competitor who could later be another client of the systems integrator

Systems integrators often need a staff and this is to be found with firms that are large hardware vendors, accounting and consulting firms, as well as aerospace firms. One large computer hardware vendor has over 18,000 employees working for their Systems Integration Division. It is important that the vendor's personnel should "fit" with the client IS staff, have their confidence and know their functional business.

A systems integrator is not for all projects because it can become very expensive: around 1/3 of the total cost of the project. It may well be a once-in-a-life choice (a top management decision) when the system is very large, unique or extremely complex.

A summary of the advantages and disadvantages of a systems integrator is shown in Table 19.4.

Critical success and failure factors

There is much empirical data on success factors considered vital to project management. But within the collective body of knowledge lies a tremendous breadth of experience which has lead to the voicing of many opinions on precisely what constitutes a *critical* success or failure factor. The author's list is shown below.

Critical success factors

- Support from top management especially for projects that cut across organizational units.
- Selection of a competent project manager (or systems integrator).
- Authority empowered to the project manager to select the best team for project management.
- Discipline for enforcing the "freezing" of specifications requested by end-users and corporate management.
- Use of project management tools in controlling projects.
- Frequent monitoring of project status (for time and costs) and comparing it with plans and schedules.
- Good reporting of progress at milestones.
- Good communication within the project team and with all others involved in the project.
- Identify deviations early enough to take necessary corrective actions.
- Follow recognized standards for project management.

Failure factors

- Absence of success factors relevant and critical to project.

- Incorrect scheduling of activities.
- Unrealistic assignment of time estimates for activities.
- Inadequate resources for the project.
- Bad balance of human resources on project team in terms of knowledge and skills needed.
- Bad communication between project team members.
- Slow and late control of project.
- Failure to monitor and measure project progress.
- Having an overrun may be unavoidable but not recognizing an overrun before it escalates can be avoided.

Rules for project management

We conclude this chapter with rules for project management as formulated by Louis Fried in a letter to his daughter who just got an assignment as project manager (Fried, 1992:71–4). The rules listed below are the one-liners without Fried's explanations but with the author's annotations.

Rule 1: You can't estimate large projects.
Rule 2: It is impossible to control large projects.
- You can't control people.
- Project control must be built in, not added on.

Rule 3: The task is not done until it is done.
- Most tasks depend on other tasks.
- Tasks produce products: the only real evidence of task completion.

Rule 4: People are not immortal.
Rule 5: Completion of each task establishes a requirement for the next task.
Rule 6: Sooner or later you have to stop designing the system.
- With large projects, the resulting system never satisfies the user.

Rule 7: Any task that takes more than 10 people can't be done.
Rule 8: You can't separate data from processes.
Rule 9: In large development efforts, configuration management is not possible.
Rule 10: There are always alternatives and risks.
- There are always trade-offs.

Rule 11: Management controls are intended to increase productivity.

Rule 12: Measurement intervals must be smaller than task completion intervals.
Rule 13: If it's not documented, it does not exist.
Rule 14: Don't do anything that you don't have to do.
- You have to build quality assurance into the project.

Rule 15: You can't get there unless you have a map.
Rule 16: Its never too early to plan.
Rule 17: No project is ever perfectly organized.
Rule 18: The objective of a project is to implement the requested system.

Summary and conclusions

Project management attempts to bring order and control to projects. An important step in project management is the appointment of a project manager. The choice of a project manager in the development of information systems is not just based on technical competence in computing and information systems or even in the functional application area of the project but rather on communication skills, sensitivity to group dynamics, business knowledge and organizational ability.

As illustrated in Figure 19.5, the work of a project manager falls into three categories: planning, scheduling, and control. In each category, the project manager must serve as a negotiator, coordinator, and counsellor as well as a technical adviser and manager.

Figure 19.5: *Project management staff*

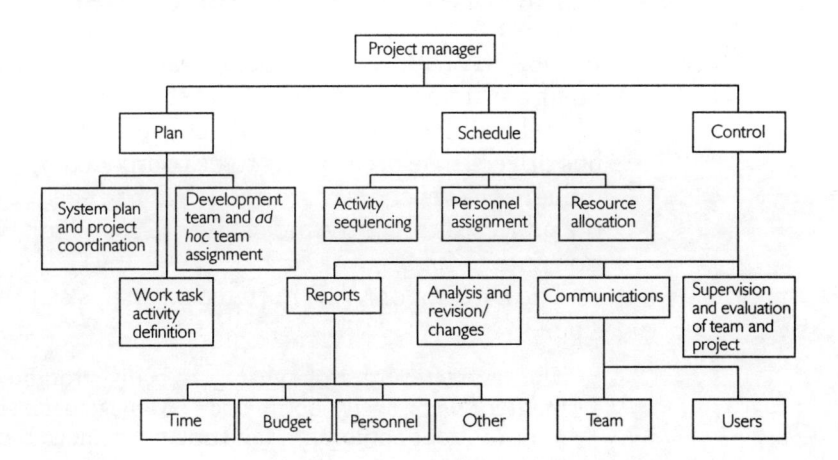

The project manger and the project management team have responsibility for planning, scheduling and control. A great aid in project management are the many computer programs available that generate valuable information in identifying bottlenecks, slacks in activities, on manpower levelling and in resource allocation to prevent cost and time overruns. However, no computer program can identify, let alone correct, an incorrect sequence of activities or poor input – especially of time estimates. Computer programs for project management are no substitute for the experience and judgement of the project management staff.

Project management is successful not because of luck or a unique expertise, but rather through well-tested practices, adequate resources (financial, personnel and time), and a well-developed plan for project management, the main activities of which are shown in Figure 19.6.

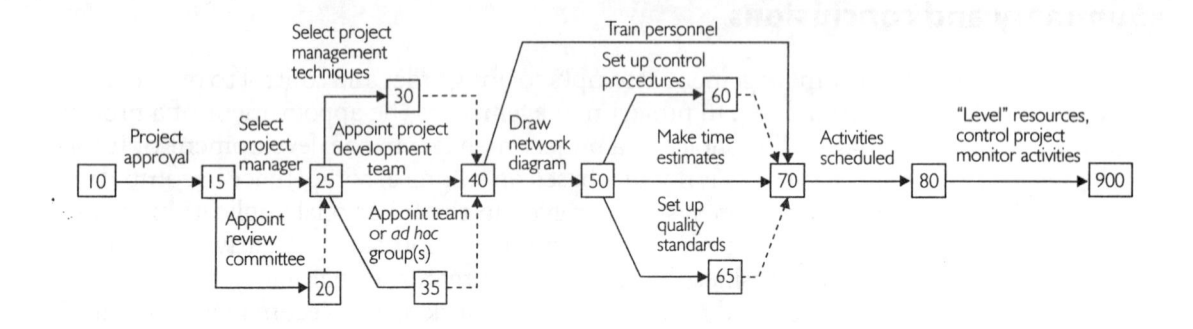

Figure 19.6

Case 19.1: Project failure at MVD, California State

In 1987, MVD (Motor Vehicles Department) of California started developing a system for maintaining records of more than 38 million vehicles, 31 million drivers, and 232,500 occupational licences for workers such as bus drivers. The project was to be completed by 1993 at a cost of $28.5 million. However, by that time MVD had spent over $44.3 million and the projected cost of the project was $185 million with a revised completion date of 1998.

The Director of MVD initiated an analysis of the project which concluded:

> The impracticalities of what was being promoted by the technical industry were overly optimistic... Management should have taken a more cautious approach... (and not) succumbed too readily to industry hype.

The report also blamed the primary contractor involved, Tandem Computer Inc., for touting capabilities for its equipment that could not be achieved. Tandem, a hardware company, claimed that they did what they were asked to do and the failure of the project was due to the failure of software.

Other criticisms of the project include the inability of the MVD management to supervise the technocrats on the staff and the fact that people in key positions on the project left state government to join Tandem or companies close to it and in some cases they returned to state government. There was also criticism of the MVD management culture that allowed the technical staff a free rein without adequate checks and controls.

Source: *Sacramento Bee*, vol. 275 (May 26, 1994), p. A5.

Case 19.2: Project disaster at AMR

In 1988, AMR (parent company of American Airlines) went into partnership with Hilton Hotels, Marriot Hotels and Budget Rent a Car company with the intention of developing a $50 million CONFIRM information system that was to leapfrog existing technology and integrate the hospitality industry. Five years later, AMR took a $165 million write-off loss and is facing damages of more than $160 million. It has already made out-of-court settlements with former partners (Marriot, Hilton and Budget) for undisclosed amounts. In the process, at least 8 project managers were dismissed with one manager who sued for defamation and the others who reached a settlement with AMR.

The disputes started with AMRIS (AMR Information Services) suing its partners in September 1992 for breach of contract for:

> ...sabotaging the system by submitting thousands of change requests long after the development plan had been completed... and attempting to exploit a fixed price contract by trying to force AMRIS essentially to create systems for each partner instead of one common system.
>
> *Business Week*, 1994:36

In defence, the partners fired back and argued that AMR had admitted that it was 18 months behind an already-delayed June schedule. The defence argued that AMRIS knew of the woes including a report in April 1989 which concluded that the CONFIRM project was "in dire need of more critical action by AMRIS management". The defence argued that AMR repeatedly failed to inform the partners of the report and their woes and they were now stuck with the project even though they had the right to opt by September 1989.

AMR maintains that its partners had 130 employees working on the project and so concealment of any woes, the "report", and potential delays would have been impossible.

Source: *Business Week*, no. 3354, (January 17, 1994), p. 36.

Case 19.3: Systems integrator at USAA

The United Services Automobile Association (USAA) was an $11 billion insurance company with volumes of paper for over 1.8 million clients. It needed to reduce the 39,000 square feet of space used for record keeping and reduce its staff by at least 100 people. One possibility was to assemble and install a complete imaging system on optical disk.

USAA put the project for bid and selected IBM from its five bidders, even though IBM did not have the best scanners on the market. IBM was attracted to the project because they wanted to incorporate the new systems into its vast product line.

Once selected IBM did assemble the best equipment like the scanners built by Bell & Howell and its own magnetic disks.

Arthur Andersen & Co., a consultancy company, got permission to assign (free of charge) two of its consultants on the project just for the experience.

Source: *Computer Decisions*, vol. 20, no. 1 (October 1988), p. 45.

Case 19.4: Systems integrator at Mölnlycke

Mölnlycke is a $115 million business which makes disposables such as hospital disposables and tissue products. Its IT manager, Mr. Baker, has a permanent staff of five. Mr. Baker faced the problem of converting its HP graphical terminal applications from PCs to Mac computers. Normally, Mr. Baker would go a nationwide computer dealer for services but instead chose the systems integrator. Mr. Baker did not think that his computer dealer was bad:

> ...but to them we were just a small fish in a big sea...We wanted a more personal touch. We approached HG because they were responsive to our needs... It's not that we lack the technical skills, but there's so much going on. We like our people to remain business-focused. We use companies like HG to help with the technical side, because it's easier to define... It's in our interest to know your integrator, then try to form longer-term relationships, so they know your business better.

HG works with Mölnlycke on small contracts less than $50,000 and supplies preconfigured systems in addition to consultancy on Oracle.

Source: Paul Bray, "Systems Integrator", *Which Computer?*, vol. 17, no. 7 (August 1994), p. 49.

References

Boehm, B. W. (1981). *Software Engineering Economics*. Englewood Cliffs, N. J.: Prentice Hall Inc.

Brooks, Frederick. (1975). *The Mythical Man-Month*. Reading: Addison Wesley Pub. Co.

Constantine, L. L. (1993). "Work Organization: Paradigms for Project Management and Organization." *Communications of the ACM*, vol. 36, no. 10. (October 1993), pp. 35–43.

Fried, Louis. (1992). "The Rules of Project Management." *Journal of Information Systems Management*, vol. 9, no. 3 (Summer 1992), pp. 71–4.

Henderson, John C. and Soonchul Lee. (1992). "Managing I/S Design Teams: A Control Theories Perspective." *Management Science*, vol. 18, no. 6 (June 1992), pp. 757–77.

Holtzblatt, Karn and Beyer, H. (1993). "Making Customer-Centered Design Work for Teams." *Communications of the ACM,* vol. 36, no. 10 (October 1993), pp. 93–103.

Hyman, Risa B. (1993). "Creative Chaos in High Performance Teams: An Experience Report." *Communications of the ACM*, vol. 36, no. 10 (October 1993), pp. 56–61.

Marchewka, Jack T. (1995). "Portfolio Theory Approach for Selecting and Managing IT Projects." *Information Resources Management Journal*, vol. 8, no. 4, pp. 5–15.

McKeen, James D., Guimaraes, Tor and Wetherbe, J. (1994). "A Comparative Analysis of MIS Project Selection Mechanisms". *Database*, vol. 25, no. 1 (February 1994), pp. 43–59.

Raz, T. (1993). "Introduction of the Project management Discipline in a Software Development Organization." *IBM Systems Journal*, vol. 32, no. 2, pp. 265–77.

Rettig, Marc and Simmons, G. (1990). "A Project Planning and Development Process for Small Teams." *Communications of the ACM*, vol. 36, no. 10, pp. 44–56.

Stewart, M. (1969). "Making Project Management Work" in *Systems Organizations, Analysis, and Management: A Book of Readings* by D. I. Cleland and W. R. King, (eds.) New York: McGraw Hill.

Stokes, Stewart L. Jr. (1990). "Building Effective Project Teams." *Information Systems Journal,* vol. 7, no. 3, pp. 38–45.

Thamhain, Hans J. (1991). "Developing Project Management Skills". *Project Management Journal*, vol. XXII, no. 3, pp. 39–44.

Vasudevan, Venu. (1994). "A Monitoring Approach to Active Project Management." *Proceedings of the ACM National Annual Conference*, 1994, pp. 257–63.

Wallace, Ron and Halverson, Wayne. (1992) "Project Management: A Critical Success Factor or a Management Fad?" *Industrial Engineering*, vol. 24, no. 4, pp. 48–50.

Walz, Diane B., Elam, J. and Curtis, B. (1993). "Inside a Software Design Team: Knowledge Acquisition, Sharing and Integration." *Communications of the ACM*, vol. 36, no. 10, pp. 62–77.

Ward, James A. (1994). "Productivity through Project Management." *Journal of Information Systems Management*, vol. 11, no. 1, pp. 16–21.

Ware, Robert. (1991). "Project Management Software: Project Panacea?" *Journal of Information Systems Management*, vol. 8, no. 1, pp. 79–83.

Williams, Iwan. (1990). "Project Management Software." *Which Computer?*, vol. 13, no. 4, pp. 81–93.

Postscript: What Lies Ahead?

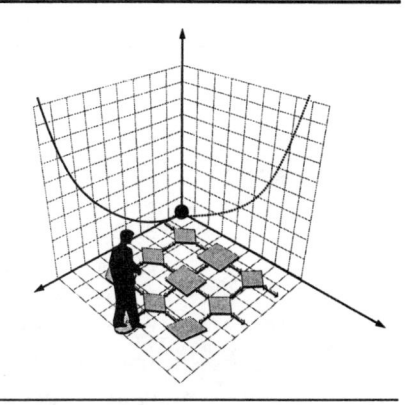

Many new technologies will shape tomorrow. For example, circuit lines 0.18 micron thick (a human hair is 100 microns thick) are predicted for the end of this decade. With such microminiaturization, "superchips" will dramatically increase the power of all computers. These "superchips" are expected to contain a self-repair capability: that is, spare parts to overcome flaws introduced in manufacturing, and hard-wired software able to detect non-functioning elements and then reconfigure the circuitry to bypass the fault. Such chips will increase the useful life of computing equipment as well as improve computer reliability and robustness. These chips will be supported by faster and more powerful input devices especially voice processors and optical scanners, and by advanced peripherals including the ability to store holographic patterns where data can be read and written in parallel.

What is currently an experimental design or fledgling technology may soon become an "essential accessory" and part of our way of life. From a technological point of view, this will include hand-held computers with built-in scanners connected by international networks to anyone around the world, flat high-resolution screens, continuous-speech recognition, speech synthesis, use of natural language for computer interfaces, language translation by computer, intelligent peripherals, secure user identification, as well as efficient and end-user friendly computing.

In terms of applications, the future portends shopping, banking and reading the daily newspaper from our computer at home. We may see libraries replaced by interactive videotext; multimedia distance-learning supplanting education and training at fixed sites; using e-mail instead of visiting friends; using digital money instead of cash, and even travelling to far-off places by virtual reality.

Future applications are moving away from the legacy applications of processing data to the processing of real-time data, text, voice, and images. Processing needs are shifting from desktop networking to enterprise-wide strategic computing; from store-and-forward computing to strategic computing; from offline computing to real-time computing; from local processing to remote processing; and from analogue to digital transmission. Networking is being transformed from the early environment of military systems tied to private networks that were switched mechanically, to the digital devices of today with broadband fibre-optically transported messages that are electronically switched by sophisticated software and intelligent network systems.

Advances in artificial intelligence will also be incorporated into intelligent computer systems of the future. (Artificial intelligence is the ability of a computer to imitate certain actions or skills associated with human intelligence, such as problem solving, voice and image processing, learning, and decision-making.)

Businesses are becoming less centralized and more distributed. Businesses are no longer operating exclusively within their national boundaries but going global where physical boundaries are no longer an issue. Traffic in telecommunications is shifting from a LAN to a metropolitan MAN and to a wide-area WAN or the Internet.

The Internet has shown explosive growth. The number of users has doubled every year since 1988. A doubling of growth is not uncommon in the computer industry, even sustained growth like the doubling of microprocessor capabilities every 18 months over twenty-five years. The periodic doubling of growth is mind-boggling if one considers the following problem: What would be your assets at the end of one month if you were given one penny on the first day and doubled the amount you have on each of the following days? Precisely £5,368,709.12.

With anything like such growth on the Internet it is no wonder that we are having problems with messages like "the server is not responding" or data getting trapped in loops or just getting lost, and Web sites that are slow to be accessed, if at all. The system is overloaded. But this is a managerial problem: better prediction of load and allocation of resources to sites where and when needed. The real problem with the Internet is a technological one: making it secure enough for personal and commercial transactions using a credit card or a bank account number. Funds (including personal funds) should be transferable by electronic means quickly, cheaply and safely.

The future of IT will see much integration. The integration will be partly technological: the logical integration within an enterprise and the integration of all media: data, text, sound, video, images and animation. Such deployment of multimedia technology will be on a platform of intelligent interactive processing. The other dimension of integration is largely organizational and may come from strategic partnerships, joint ventures, acquisitions, or by hostile takeovers. Resulting corporate conglomerates are partly designed to bring within one firm's jurisdiction all the necessary informational infrastructure, which includes:

- Technologies (including digital telecommunications).
- Very large client bases:
  - Television and cable (one-way and high capacity).
  - Telephone subscribers (two-way but low capacity).
- Content programming including educational programmes, video and movies.
- Software for program navigation.
- High capacity transmission and switching abilities (including satellite and fibre optic systems) to deliver full informational services to all customers.

Such integration could well lead to the electronic office, the automated plant, the wired city and eventually perhaps to a telematique (telematic in English) society. Communications will take place in cyberspace on an electronic highway initially with an NII (national information infrastructure) and later with an III (international information infrastructure). Access of information will be to businesses, individuals, libraries, educational and training programs, and databases. The convergence of computers, communication structures and programming media will no longer be dependent on location but can take place anywhere, for anything and by anyone, and may even be in a visual environment or in virtual reality. Computing will not only be democratized but it will offer the consumer more choices and will be end-user-friendly.

The speed of technological and organizational changes will require adjustment of consumer behaviour and still possibly be pro-competitive. If there are important restraints (actual or perceived) to competition, then there will most likely be regulation by governments. In any event, our telematique future will require a redefinition of work, leisure, home and community. Along the way we will edge towards a cashless and paperless society. We may well see a blend of national, regional and private networks with governments agreeing to the interoperability of national networks, to provide open access to corporate players, universal service to consumers, and promote cultural and linguistic diversity in traffic. It would be desirable for national governments to provide ramps to the information superhighway and enforce international standards for the protection of data and intellectual property, as well as allow the free flow of transborder data and information.

Not all predictions made in this postscript will come to pass. Some goals of the fifth and sixth generation computers may prove to be technologically infeasible, or too expensive to implement. Limited resources, government regulatory schemes, interference (unfavourable tax policies, for example), high risk of realizing capital investments, product development priorities in other fields, lack of markets, legal restrictions, and user resistance, are all factors that may affect the speed and direction of change.

The rapid pace of change in our information age confuses our ability to predict the future. However, we must be aware of the caution expressed by the *Librarian Emeritus* of the US Congress Library, Daniel Boorstin:

> We have created and mastered machines before realizing how they may master us.

Since business and IT managers often serve in a leadership role in their communities as well as at work, they will have a prominent role in shaping our telematic society. Planning must now begin for the computerized society that is to come. As stated by Montague and Snyder:

> Many deplore the computer and some even fear it as more monster than machine. Whatever we think of it, however, we must adjust to it. This does not imply resignation, but rather that we must understand the true nature of this latest of man's inventions and learn how its powers can be combined with our own abilities to be used to the best advantage for humanity.
>
> *Montague and Snyder*, 1972:1–2.

The author hopes that this book will help you to prepare for the challenges and opportunities ahead.

References

Bell, Gordon and Gemmell, J. (1996). "On-ramp Prospects for the Information Superhighway Dream." *Communications of the ACM*, vol. 39, no. 7, pp. 55–61.

Forester, Tom. (1992). "Megatrends or Megamistakes? Whatever Happened to the Information Society?" *Computers and Society*, vol. 22, nos. 1–4, pp. 2–11.

Hayashi, Alden, M. and Varney, Sarah E. (1996). "Six Technologies for the 21st Century." *Datamation*, vol. 42, no. 14, pp. 68–72.

Knorr, Eric. (1990). "Software's Nest Ware: Putting the User First." *PC World*, vol. 8, no. 1, pp. 134–43.

Levy, Steeve. (1994). "E-Money: That's What I want." *Wired*, vol. 2, no. 12, pp. 174–7 and 213–15.

Lowry, Michael R. (1992). "Software Engineering in the Twenty-First Century." *AI Magazine*, vol. 13, no. 9, pp. 71–87.

Malhotra, Yogesh. (1994). "Controlling Copyright Infringements of Intellectual Property: Part Two." *Journal of Systems Management*, vol. 45, no. 7, pp. 12–7.

Montague, Ashley and Snyder, S. (1972). *Man and the Computer*. Philadelphia: Auerbach.

Nash, Jim. (1993). "State of the Market, Art, Union and Technology." *AI Expert*, vol. 8, no. 1 (January), pp. 45–51.

Niederman, F., Brancheau, J. C., and Wetherbe, J. (1991). "Information Systems Management Issues for the 1990s." *MIS Quarterly*, vol. 15, no. 4, pp. 475–502.

Reed, Sandra R. (1990). "Technologies in the 1990s." *Personal Computing*, vol. 14, no. 1, pp. 66–90.

Rheingold, Howard. (1991). *Virtual Reality: The Revolution of Computer Generated Artificial World–and How it Promises and Threatens to Transform Business and Society*. New York: Summit Books.

Rockhart, John F. and Short, James E. (1989). "IT in the 1990s: Managing Organizational Independence." *Management Review*, vol. 30, no. 2, pp. 7–12.

Seitz, Konrad. (1991). "Creating a Winning Culture." *Siemens Review*, vol. 58, no. 2, pp. 37–9.

Selker, Ted. (1996). "New Paradigms for Using Computers." *Communications of the ACM*, vol. 39, no. 8, pp. 60–69.

Spence, Malcolm D. (1991). "A Look into the 21st. Century: People, Business and Computer." *Information Age*, vol. 12, no. 2, pp. 91–9.

von Simpson, Ernest. (1993). "Customers will be the Innovators." *Fortune*, vol. 128, no. 7, pp. 105–7.

Toffler, Alvin. (1980). *The Third Wave*. New York: William Murrow.

Thompson, Tom. (1996). "What's Next?" *Byte*, vol. 21, no. 4, pp. 45–54.

Tatsuno, Sheridan. (1986). *Technopolis Strategy: Japan, High Technology, the Control of the Twenty-First Century*. N.Y.: Prentice-Hall Press.

Appendix: Glossary in Prose

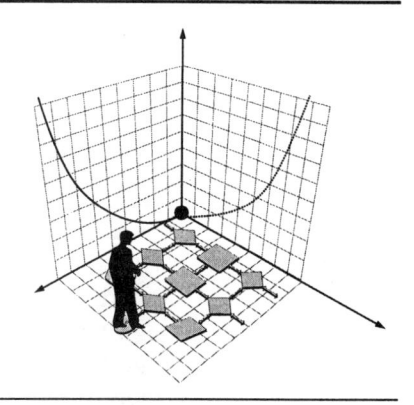

A problem in studying any subject relating to computing is that it often involves a whole new set of definitions and acronyms. Reading a text without a mastery of such terminology can be a frustrating experience. One approach to this problem is to master (or at least get acquainted with) these unique terms and acronyms before starting the text. Facilitating this approach is the purpose of this appendix. While familiarizing the reader with the terminology, this appendix also provides various subject overviews and indicates the way in which many of the basic terms relate to each other.

The definitions, when given, are informal and designed to give the reader an intuitive appreciation and understanding of computers and the management of computing resources. The basic terms used in this appendix are shown in **bold** print. Detailed definitions are left to the text of the book.

Information is processed data where **data** is usually a fact or observation. The **processing** is done by a computer under the instruction of a computer **program**.

Information is a derivation of data and makes no value judgement. In business and industry we often need data and information that allow us to make judgements and inferences. These can be made if we had **heuristics** or **rules of decision-making** that are often simple rules of thumb based on experience and common sense. Thus we can have a heuristic which says that a sweet-toothed person likes chocolate. Now couple this with a fact that Kristi is sweet-toothed. Combining the fact with the heuristic we then have the **knowledge** that Kristi likes chocolate. We can then take actions based on that knowledge which, in this case, may be taking chocolates as a present to Kristi's birthday party.

The relationship between facts and decision-rules that allows us to make **inferences** and take **actions** is called a **decision table**. It is a representation of the knowledge that enables us to make judgements akin to those made by a human expert. Such a system is called an **expert system** (**ES**). It is also known as a knowledge-based information system (**KBIS**).

The ability to make inferences gives us an important characteristic: the faculty of **intelligence**, and hence is of great interest to the researcher in **artificial intelligence, AI**. Other areas of interest to AI are **pattern recognition**, which is essential in the optical recognition of text, voice recognition and even the comprehension of natural language; all topics of great interest to the end-user. The **end-user** is the ultimate recipient of results from an information system as distinct from other **users** of computing such as the **programmer** who uses the computer to generate programs but is not an end-user of its results.

Use of AI is a more recent type of information system. The earliest was a **transactional system** that processed transactions such as a payroll cheque based on the **data** for time worked and the salary rate, or producing an invoice for payment based on data for the quantity sold and the price of the product. Early transactional systems used data that were numeric and were referred to as **data processing** or **EDP** (**electronic data processing**). Later processing was not just on data but also on text (**word processing**), as well as on graphics (**graphics processing**) and was referred to as **information processing**. Such processing along with the technology needed for the processing is referred to as **IT, information technology**.

Transactional systems are used by operational personnel and operational management. At higher levels of management the operational data must be processed for purposes of control management. Such processing may require models of decision-making as for inventory control and production control. These models are the expertise of **OR/MS** (**operations research/management science**) personnel. An information system using such OR/MS models is the **DSS** (**decision support system**) which generates information for the control of operations. This information is passed on to higher levels of management who use the information for planning. Here too models are used, but often these are simpler models like a **spreadsheet**. These systems are the **EIS, executive information system**.

Transactional systems, DSSs, EISs, and ESs can all be developed, operated, and managed separately, but this can lead to redundancies, inefficiencies, and even bad and inconsistent output. It is logical then to collect all the data/knowledge necessary for the entire organization (enterprise) at one time, process it in one place, and then share the results. Such a methodology is referred to as **integration**. When integration is achieved at any one level for all functions it is called **horizontal integration** and when achieved at all levels for any one function it is **ver-**

tical integration. If achieved at all levels and for all functions it is then **total integration**: an ideal **MIS**, management information system. Total integration for an organization is called **enterprise computing**.

Integration is difficult when part of the enterprise is distributed over space. Then we have **DP**, distributed processing, or **DDP**, distributed data processing. In contrast, when processing is not distributed we have **centralized processing**. In the large, real-world systems we have a combination. In many cases, however, we have processing which is distributed, controlled, and managed by the end-user. Such systems are called **EUC, end-user computing**. The feasibility and viability of end-user computing is partly the consequence of the end-user becoming **computer literate** and willing to take the responsibility of developing and managing localized systems. It is also the result of technological developments of the PC and their **interconnectivity** through **networks** and **telecommunications**.

The **PC, personal computer**, and its more powerful cousin, the **workstation**, are becoming just as powerful and robust (but much lower in cost) as the **mainframe** computers of most earlier computer systems. Somewhere in between the PC and the mainframe sits the **mini**, short for **minicomputer**. The PC (and workstation) now act as a **client** to a computer system where a larger computer acts as a **server** in a computer paradigm called the **client–server system**. Through a client computer an end-user can share/access the data, knowledge and application programs that reside on a server computer; a server that might be specially designed and optimized for the serving activity. (The server might be a mainframe or minicomputer.)

For convenience of the end-users and for technological reasons the clients and the servers are often dispersed. To connect them we need a telecommunications **network** which, when localized, is called a **LAN**, (local area network); when restricted to a building or a metropolitan area is called a **MAN** (metropolitan area network), and when extended over a wide area is called a **WAN** (wide area network).

Advances in hardware, software, and organizational configurations (like client–server) led to a need for greater integration, not just horizontal and vertical, but for the enterprise using **groupware**: software that allows for collaborative computing (and group communications). For example, colleagues who are working on the same project will need good communications facilities and might want to share particular resources – such as a group database.

Further integration between local enterprises within a city is referred to as a **wired city**. The integration of regional technopolises (technologically oriented cities) is a **technopolis strategy**. When the regions are limited to a country we have an **NII, national information infrastructure**, also referred to as the **super information highway**. Further integration between regions of the world is referred to as the **telematique society**.

The telematique society, known in English as the **telematic** society, is a term coined by two French administrators (Norma and Minc) who were asked by the French President to evaluate the societal impact of computers and telecommunications. Prominent French politicians of the time were very concerned that the American dominance in computing/telecommunications would reduce France to a "McDonald" society. In their study, Norma and Minc concluded that the confluence of computers and telecommunications will be so significant that it would create a new society, one that they dubbed the **telematique society**.

The telematique society has many technological, economic, social, and political implications that are yet to be resolved. Meanwhile, there is an informal global network in the **Internet**. Until mid-1996, it was an independent, autonomous, and informal organization self-regulated by its computer-oriented users. The Internet is actually a set of servers that hold information and other resources – including software and images of fine art. The Internet also facilitates global communication through **e-mail**, electronic mail, via its millions of host servers.

The Internet owes much of its technology to the first network: the **ARPANET**, which was founded in 1969 and by 1971 had only 15 nodes and 23 hosts. ARPANET was designed for communications between researchers and academics working on US defence projects and was not designed for business. Today, the Internet is used by businesses which advertise on their **home pages**. However, one cannot sell products freely on the Internet until we resolve **security** issues that surround the unauthorized use of funds.

An **intranet** is a private network using the Internet by observing all its **protocols** (rules of engagement). The intranet needs a stripped version of the PC called the **NC, network computer**. For an online glossary of Internet terms, go to the Internet site:

    http://www.mattise.net/files/glossary.html

Electronic security is not just an issue on the Internet but is also an important and serious issue for other users of information systems. In transactional systems the security issue also concerns funds as well as the integrity of data. The transfer of funds between banks is efficiently (and fairly securely) processed through **EFT, electronic fund transfer**.

In a DSS and EIS, the security problem is one of protecting confidential and proprietary data. In centralized systems, security is achieved largely through locking-up the system to unauthorized users. In distributed systems, or in centralized systems with **remote access**, there are many security measures that include **access control** through **passwords**, together with the more experimental systems such as **voice recognition**, **handwriting recognition**, and **biometric** security through the recognition of patterns or the shape of the hand.

Security in telecommunications can be achieved partly through controlling access at the origin and destination of a message being transmitted but also through message **encryption** (coding).

A recent threat to the security of information systems comes from computer **viruses**: unauthorized computer programs that cause systems to **crash** (breakdown); cause the destruction or erasure of databases, or otherwise disrupt normal system functions – sometimes with catastrophic results. There are many commercially available anti-viral computer programs but new viruses are always appearing (together with mutations and variations of existing viruses). New viral strains include the **worm**, the **logic bomb**, and the **trojan horse**. Protecting a system against these threats is an ongoing task for computer system managers. Security of an information system can also be approached at each component level of an information system: hardware, software, data, and personnel. We shall now consider each of these components.

Hardware

Hardware is equipment which includes the electronic circuits for the processor and the support equipment peripheral to the processor, called the **peripherals**. The processor is called the **CPU**, an acronym for **central processing unit**. The CPU has three parts: the **ALU** (**arithmetic and logic unit**) that performs the calculations; the **internal memory unit** that temporarily stores information; and the **control unit** that selects the order of operations and coordinates other units. The support equipment that is peripheral to the CPU includes the input and output devices as well as the external memory. Common examples of external memory devices are disks and tapes. **Tapes** are **sequential** while **disks** are **random**. Random, in the context of memory, means to permit any word in the memory to be accessed and not necessarily in sequence.

Peripherals are **online** when they are under the direct control of a CPU. Conversely, devices that are not under the direct control of the CPU are called **offline** and are **stand-alone**. Peripherals are much slower than the CPU and are considered **compute-bound**. The speed of the earliest computers was measured in **milliseconds** (thousandths of a second). As computers developed, the time of operations was reduced to **microseconds** (millionths of a second), then to **nanoseconds** (billionths

Appendix: Glossary in Prose

of a second), and now speed of computers is measured in **picoseconds** (a thousandth of a nanosecond). Another measure of operational speed is **MIPS** (**millions of instructions per second**).

Software

In contrast to hardware, physical objects that can be touched, there is **software** written as programs stored on an input medium such as tape and disks to be used when needed. A **program** instructs the computer on the algorithm to be used: a specific computer procedure to achieve the desired results and the sequence in which the operations are to be performed.

Programmers are individuals who write programs instructing the computer what to do. The computer only recognizes electronic pulses, so programs are written in a manner necessary to generate these pulses. One way to do that is in **machine language**, a programming language in which instructions are written as numbers. It is a **low-level language** because it is conceptually close to the machine. Machine language contrasts with languages such as BASIC because BASIC is a **high-level language** and is conceptually close to human language. There is a wide spectrum of programming languages; many are **procedural** languages because they state the procedure for computations. **COBOL** and **RPG** are common in business and commerce. For scientific computing, **FORTRAN**, **Pascal**, and **Ada** are popular in the US while **ALGOL** is favoured in Europe. Some languages serve dual purposes, being popular in both business and scientific programming. Examples are **PL/1** and **BASIC**. Languages like **APL** are **conversational** or **interactive languages**. Of interest to managers in business (and used in DSSs) are simulation languages like **Simula**, **SIMSCIPT** and **GPSS**. For AI applications, **LISP** is common in the US and **PROLOG** is popular in Europe and Japan. Generally speaking, a language name is displayed in upper-case letters when it is an acronym (e.g. FORTRAN) and in mixed upper- and lower-case letters when it is named after a person (e.g. Ada and Pascal).

Procedural languages are third generation languages and referred to as **3GLs**. Dialogue and conversational languages operate at a higher level of human friendliness and are referred to as the **4GLs**.

Data

As implied above, programs are a set of instructions for processing data. The data must be organized and managed so that it can be processed efficiently and effectively. This is known as **data management** or **file management**. Organized data is a **database**, also called a **data bank**, consisting of integrated files. A **file** is a set of records; a **record** is a set of data, where **data** are facts or observations.[1]

Data is stored in computer memory as bits (**bi**nary digi**t**) when representing one character or as **bytes**, a set of bits. A data element is the lowest level of data that an end-user can typically manipulate. Each data element is defined in a **data element dictionary** (**DED**). It is used by a set of computer programs to structure, access, and manage the database. This is known as the **database management system** (**DBMS**).

Information systems

Hardware, software, and data are the three basic components of an information system and these components must be harnessed, brought together and **developed** to generate desired results and information.

Information systems are developed in **stages**, each comprised of a set of tasks called **activities**. Activities are performed in a specific sequence as part of a systems life cycle, called the **SDLC, systems development life cycle**. The SDLC methodology is commonly used in large and complex information systems development **projects**. It begins with a **feasibility study**, where alternative approaches to producing information within constraints of the organization are considered, where a **constraint** is a factor that places a limit on what is possible.

Once a project has been selected by management, the next stage is to define informational needs specifically in order for the system to be designed to meet these needs. This stage is one of analysis and is referred to as the **end-user specification stage**. The design is then implemented through programming and organizing other resources needed for successful operations. The system is then **tested**, **documented**, and then **converted** with the old system being **phased out** and the new system made **operational**.

Prototyping is another development methodology in common use today for *ad hoc* systems such as planning in an EIS and for control as in a DSS. A prototype can be a tentative system, based on interaction between analyst and end-users, or one built as a preliminary solution to a problem. Prototyping can be used in conjunction with an SDLC.

Information processing

Computer operations have many **modes** of operation. One is **batch processing**, in which jobs are collected together into a **batch** before they are

---

1. Everyday language uses the word "data" to describe *one or more* facts or observations. Strictly speaking, a *datum* is a *single* piece of information or *a* fact, and *data* is the plural of *datum*.

Appendix: Glossary in Prose

processed. Another is **time-sharing**, where users take turns being served. The very fast processing speeds of modern computers means that users are serviced almost instantly, giving each user the illusion of being the only individual online; of having the machine **dedicated** solely to one's own use. Time-sharing systems are used largely by programmers and users of scientific computations. Some businesses require a **real-time system** in which the system searches the database, updates it, and gives results in time to affect the operating environment. **Remote processing**, processing through an input–output device that is distant from the CPU, can be combined with the above-mentioned processing modes.

Sometimes a firm has to hire a **facilities management** vendor to operate its computing resources instead of assigning the responsibility to **in-house** personnel. Another option is a **computer utility**. Instead of contracting with a client for a specific service, the computer utility provides services on request, offering continuous service in somewhat the same manner as an electric utility company. The computer utility uses a **telecommunications network** so that computer power can be accessed from a distant **node** if regional facilities are overloaded. Yet another option is to contract their processing to a **service bureau**. Some of the data preparation work (and programming) is contracted out; this is called **outsourcing**.

The availability and low cost of PCs has led to **end-user computing**: programming and operation of computers by **end-users** (who use the output but are not necessarily computer "experts") instead of data processing and computer professionals.

To provide support to end-users, **information centres** are being established in many firms. These centres are either service centres providing consulting, solution centres, resource centres, or support centres. They are staffed by computer personnel to help improve the self-sufficiency of end-users and to help improve end-user's computing efficiency and effectiveness.

To run a computer centre and to staff information centres requires the services of professionals and support personnel. Amongst them is the **systems analyst**, a technician who studies processing problems and decides which procedures, methods, or techniques are required to realise the solution to a particular problem. **Programmers** write and test the instructions that tell the computer what to do. Processing itself is done by **operators**. Large and complex databases require a **DBA (database administrator)** to keep files **updated** and to monitor and control data usage. Examples of other support personnel are **data entry clerks, security officers, communication analysts, data analysts, problem analysts**, and **technical writers**. It is management's responsibility to decide what tasks are needed in a given computer environment and to write **job descriptions** (for each position identified) that can be used in hiring and evaluation of personnel. Job descriptions are also used to establish **career ladders** so that employees can advance within the computer field.

During operations, the system is controlled for quality of information. **Controls** are also designed to protect the systems from intentional tampering, computer theft and computer crime, as well as errors that are unintended or accidental. However, security is not always completely successful. Part of the problem is that design procedures and training for control do not keep up with advances in technology. This is particularly relevant to hardware developments and the need for **privacy**: the protection against unauthorized use and distribution of "personal" data.

All information systems should be regularly evaluated to check their efficiency and effectiveness. **Efficiency** refers to the relationship between input and output, while **effectiveness** refers to the successful achievement of critical factors of performance set by the end-user and corporate management. Examples of critical factors in **performance** are **accuracy**, a specified percentage of freedom from error; **timeliness**, the **availability** of information when needed; and **completeness**, the availability of all relevant data and information.

The computer environment

Within the computer industry IBM dominated hardware first through the mainframe and later through its PC. However, other manufacturers produced PCs and operating systems that have robbed IBM of its dominance. The industry is no longer monopolistic or even oligopolistic. It is highly fragmented with many sectors including telecommunications, peripherals, chip manufacturers, and the service sector of **training** and **consulting**.

The segmentation of the computer industry has given the consumer (firm and individual) greater choice in product and performance, but increased choice also complicates the resource-acquisition process.

With advances in technology applications have expanded. Many corporate managers today use an EIS or a DSS to assist in planning and control. Such systems have altered the accepted methods of decision-making. Computers and information systems have changed the tasks of corporate management. They must now be familiar with computer terminology and understand how information systems are developed and implemented to effectively use computers in their work.

Corporate management must also know how to effectively (and efficiently) manage computer resources *and* be knowledgeable about the law as it relates to computing. Management must be aware of "human factors" and "ergonomics" and how these relate to humanizing the information systems environment. Although these terms have similar meanings, **ergonomics** emphasizes the *physio*logical aspects of computing whereas **human factors** refers to the *psycho*logical aspects of human–machine relationships.

The success of an information system may well depend on managerial (IT and corporate) sensitivity to employee concerns and the establishment of a climate receptive to **change**: computerization alters the structure and interpersonal relationships within a firm. Such a management of change should encourage **critical success factors** (**CSF**) and try to reduce the **causes of failure and abandonment** of information systems.

Index

A

Abbey National 88
Abraham Maslow 86
Adhocracy 102
AI (Artificial Intelligence) 2, 3, 29, 55, 66, 86, 126, 273, 472
  AI language 75
  defined 472, 478
  frames 315
Alvin Toffler 102
American Airlines
  SABER 141
Andersen Consulting 59
Apple Computer 62
APT 83
ARPANET 365, 367, 371
AT&T 187, 234
Auditors 58, 93, 97

B

Banks 111
  Bank of Boston 88
  Bank of Montreal 344
  Citibank 344, 372
  database organization example 19
  Meritir Savings Bank 234
British Aerospace 234
British Computer Society 153
Bulletin board 102

C

Canadian Tire Corp. 169
Career development 81–2
CASE (Computer-Aided Software Engineering) 137, 144, 196, 336
  available tools 137–8
  problems with 139
  reengineering 242
  training 139
Centralization
  and decentralization 16
Chief Executive Officer 66, 76, 110
Chief Information Officer 66, 76, 110
Client–server system 5
  advantages 339
  compared to host computing 329
  components 329
    server 333–5
  database processing 335
  navigation through 343
  obstacles 340
  Olympic Games example 343
  organizational impact 337
  query processing (SQL) 331
  resources needed 328
  schema 328
  system components
    client 330–1
    networks 332
    user 330
  X terminal 332
COBOL 70, 137, 159–60, 186, 196, 310
Codd, Dr. E. F. 310
CODASYL (Conference on Data System Languages) 310
Complexity
  effect on costs 241
Component engineering 175
  abstraction 176
  SDLC 178
Computer department
  typical personnel 98

Index

Computer Science Corporation 234
Computer systems
  evolution of 5
  history of 14
Computer utilities 55
  and service bureaux 55
Computing resources
  selecting a location 14
Computing services 35
  facilities management 35
  service bureau 35
Consultants 39, 57, 61
  during systems testing 130
  finding 41
  in-house friction 40
  objectivity 40
  security 40
  selection 40
    some guidelines 41
  some conclusions 42
Contract
  (for) outsourcing 227–9
  (for) remote processing 38
  (for) resource acquisition 207–9
  (for) software maintenance 296
Cooperative processing 341–2
Corporate policy
  for computing management 93
Cost–benefit analysis
  and feasibility study 120
Costs
  and system complexity 241
Cost–value method 215
  for vendor selection 199
Cryptography 353
  and passwords 388
Custom-made software 173
Cyberculture 368
Cyberspace 368

D

Data processing
  centralized 14, 15
Data representation 307 – see also *Knowledge representation*
Database – see also *Knowledge base*
  centralized and DDP 19
  client–server processing 335
  compared to knowledge base 321
  DBA (Database Administrator) 71, 86
    functions of 72
  evolution of 323
  growth in size 323
  hybrid organizational approaches 20
  replicated distributed 19
    advantages of 20
    data redundancy 20
  segmented distributed 19
  SQL 331
DBMS (Database Management System) 71, 307
  Codd, Dr. E. F. 310
  defined 308
  models 308
    CODASYL model 308, 310
    hierarchical data model 308–9
    network data model 308–10
    object-oriented 312
    relational data model 308, 310–11
    which model? 311
DDP (Distributed Data Processing) 19, 21
  advantages and disadvantages 21–2
  definition 17
  grid analysis 23
  hierarchical distribution 18
  impact assessment 23
  implementing 22
  network configurations 17, 18
Decentralization
  and centralization 16
Deming, Dr. Edward 422
Design
  (of) information systems 123–4
  (of) interfaces 128
  logical design 126–7
  physical design 126
  (and) reengineering 252

(of) software 157–8
subsystems approach 124–5, 127
"waterfall" model 124
Development 105, 153–4
"make" or "buy" decision matrix 155
"buy" vs. "make" 154
in-house 155
  advantages 156
process automation 137
risk analysis 120
role of management 97
strategies 116 – see also *SDLC* and *Prototyping*
time saving and software reuse 173
Digital Equipment Corporation 169
R1/XCON development 142
Digital libraries 3
Distributed computer systems 17
Documentation 131
flow in development 132
(of) software 162–3
Domain analysis
and reuse strategies 176
Domain expert 123
Downsizing 328, 337, 340
DSS (Decision Support System) 27, 118, 332
programming languages for 159

E

Edgar Schein 86
EDP (Electronic Data Processing) 14, 15, 27
EIS (Executive Information System) 118
Electronic Data Systems 59, 62
E-mail 3, 102
message encryption 352–3
End-user
classification of 26
compared to user 25
computer literacy 24
definition of 24
responsibility shifts 78
End-user computing (EUC) 16, 23, 60, 77, 224
compared to outsourcing 230

critical success factors 28–9
features of 26
hidden cost 29
providing help 29
relationships in 27
research on 30
responsibility shift 27–8
shift in costs 29
shifting of responsibility 24
Environment
impact on computing 6
Ergonomics 77, 87, 276, 281 – see also *Humanizing*
European Space Agency 187
ES (Expert System) 73–4, 119
example dialogue 314
knowledge representation 313
rules 315

F

Facilities management 28, 44, 57, 233
advantages and disadvantages 44–5
compared to outsourcing 221
contracts 45–6
cost 46
security 46
Fail-safe capability 18
Fail-soft capability 18, 56
Feasibility study 116, 118
cost–benefit analysis 120
flowchart for 119
perspectives 118
reengineering 248
Financing
of resource acquisition 201
FLOWMARK 336
FORTRAN 70, 159, 313
Frames 315–6
example 316
Fred Brooks 104
Fred Herzberg 86

G

GATT agreement 232
General Dynamics 235
General Motors 59
Global outsourcing 231
GPSS 71, 157
Grid analysis
  of DDP 23
Groupware 341
GTE Data Services 187

H

Hackers 388
  Ken Mitnick 409
Hartford Insurance Group 186
Hewlett Packard 186
Hierarchical distribution 18
Hiring
  personnel 78–9
Hitachi 187
Hoare method 168
Honda 372
Hoskyns 137
Human factors 68, 77, 87, 182, 276, 281
Humanizing (of information systems) 261
  design of a workstation 281
  explanation and justification facilities 269, 271–2
  human–computer interaction 262–3
  hypertext and hypermedia 273
  image processing 267
  input–output 268
  messages 269
  natural language interface 272
  natural language recognition 273
  strategies 264–5
  technostress 262
  voice processing 267
Hypercard 274
Hypermedia 273
Hypertext 273

I

IBM 62, 234
  American Airlines and SABER 141
  birth of computer leasing 202
  RSI court case 280
IEF (Information Engineering Facility) 140
Image processing 267
  security issues 395
Implementation (of an IS)
  organizational changes 129
  testing 129
Information
  as an asset 2, 9, 396
  management of 8, 9
Information centres 28, 30, 47, 60
  future of 50
  service delivery 50
  services offered 47, 49
    consultation 47
    product support 48
    technical support 48
    training 48
  success factors 51–2
Information glut 8
Information services
  coordinating 51
  integrating 51
Information system
  development of 115
Inland Revenue 59, 234
Integration
  of information system 126
  of subsystems 126
Intellectual property 231–2
Interfaces
  design of 128
Internet 274, 333, 340, 367–8, 405, 407, 472
  Gopher 274
  misuses of 371
  worm 371
Interoperability 333
ISDN 359

Index

ISDOS (Information System Design and Optimization System) 137, 140
ISO (International Standards Organization) 333
ISO 9000 433

J

John McDermott 142

K

KBIS (Knowledge Based Information System) 66, 74
  physical and logical design 126–7
Knowledge base
  compared to database 321
  evolution of 323
Knowledge engineer (KE) 73–4, 122, 322
Knowledge representation 313
  frames 315–6
  logic 319
  object–attribute–value triplets 318
    example 319
  production rule 313
  resources needed 321
  rules 313
  semantic network 317–8

L

LAN (Local Area Network) 5, 327, 330, 347
Lawrence Putnam 451
Laws
  affecting computing 6, 7
Leasing of computer resources 202, 205–6
Library
  of reuse components 178
  of reusable software 173
Linkage
  to mainframes 20, 21
LISP 75, 126, 140, 321–2, 332

Logic
  for knowledge representation 319
Logic bomb 407–8

M

Mainframe 20, 23–4
  linkage 20–1
Maintenance 243, 256, 285
  cost of 291
  life cycle 286–7
  outsourcing 222
  priorities 297
  reengineering 239–41, 293
  reuse 294
    reduce by reuse 173
  software 285
    contract 296
    management of 295
  statistics 299
  tools for 292
  triggers for 287, 289
    external environment 288
    IT personnel 288
    output errors 287
  types 289–90
    costs affecting 291
Malcolm Baldrige Award 422
MAN (Metropolitan Area Network) 347, 330
Management
  conflicts with IT personnel 104–6
  functions of 8
  (of) information 8
  role in daily operations 98
  role in development 104–5
  strains with IT personnel 104
Manager of Technology (MOT) 76
Marvin Minsky 315
Merise 145
Merrill Lynch 234, 279
Microcomputer
  links to mainframes 21
Modularization 137

491

Index

Motorola 345
Multiview 145

N

Network management 348
  administrator 363
  analyzers 349
  choosing a network
    architecture 359
    single or multi-vendor 359
    software/protocols 360
  configuration 355
  development 358
  end-users 357–8
  fault/problem management 349
  historical view 365
  inventory control 355–6
  ISO functions 348
  message encryption 352
  monitoring 361–2
  network development 359
  performance management 350–1
  personnel needed 363
  protocols 355
  resources needed 361
  security 351–2
    firewalls 354
  software for 356
  traffic 351
    monitor 349
    poller 349
  trouble ticket 350
  viruses 354
Networks
  client–server 332
  evolution of 365
  SNA (Systems Network Architecture) 333
NobelTech 187
Nolan's growth curves 31
Northern Telecom 234

O

Object–attribute–value triplets 318
  example 319
Objectivity 123
  and systems testing 130
Object-oriented (OO) methodology 140, 145
ObjectView 336
Obsolescence
  and financing acquisition 205
OLRT (Online Real-Time) 36, 240
Olympic Games 62
  client–server example 343
Online processing 36
Operators 71
OR/MS (Operations Research/Management Science) 66
OSI (Open Systems Interconnection) 333
Outsourcing 8, 165, 221, 230
  advantages and disadvantages 232–3
  compared to end-user computing 230
  contracts 227–8
    types of 228–9
  decision matrix 225
  factors favouring 226
  intangible benefits 224
  maintenance 222
  nature and content 221
  risks and rewards 223
  security issues 231
  shifts in control 224, 225
  when to do it 225
Oversight
  of computing 92

P

Packaged software 173
  advantages and disadvantages 156, 165
  vs. custom-written 154
Passwords 387–8 – see also *Security*
Performance – see also *Quality*

effectiveness 419
  accuracy 420
  quality 419
  reliability 420
  timeliness 420
efficiency 416–7
  cost 418
  Halstead metrics 418
  productivity 417–8
  throughput 417
  utilization 418
evaluation
  choosing criteria 415–6
  conflicting criteria 421
  of information systems 413–5
response-time–cost curve 421

Personnel 66
  career development 81–2
  Chief Information Officer 66
  communication problems 263
  (of) computer department 98
  conflicts between 14
  end-user computing 26
  hiring 78–9
  Manager of Technology 65–6
  outsourcing as solution to scarcity 223
  Policy Analyst 65
  security issues 391
  security officer 402
  (for) software maintenance 295
  strains with management 104
  Technology Watcher 65
  technostress 83
  training 82–3
  turnover 80

PERT (Program Evaluation and Review Technique) 460
Piggybacking 389
PL/1 121, 160, 313
Policy analyst 75, 86
Privacy 71 – see also *Security*
  business 377
  Community Charge forms example 377
  cost of implementing 382–3

data accuracy 380
fair use policies 381
issues of 375–6
legal frameworks 377
  non-UK models 378–9
personal data
  business guidelines 381–2
  unfair use of

Problem analyst 75, 86
Problem specification 121, 123
Processing demand
  cushioning surges 37
Productivity
  mathematical formulation 103
Programmers 70
  job satisficers 80
  reducing turnover 81
  salaries 79
Programming language
  3GL 75, 159
    advantages 160
  4GL 3, 75, 159, 167, 240
  generations of 160
  selection 128, 159–60
  spectrum of languages 170
Project management 441
  characteristics 442
  failure factors 463–4
  Lawrence Putnam formula (programming time) 451
  milestones 448
  organization 453
  planning 448–9
  project manager 443–4
  project reviews 450
  reports 450
  rules of 464
  scheduling 449
  slippage 451–3
  success factors 463
  systems integrator 441, 461
    advantages and disadvantages 462
  team design 454, 457
  team size 448

team structure 444
　approaches 444
　　function organization 445
　　matrix organization 445
　　project organization 445
　use of software 458–9
　　PERT algorithm 460
PROLOG 75, 140, 321, 332
Prototype
　breadboard type 135
　partial type 135
　pilot type 135
　rapid type 135
　staged type 135
　throw-away type 135
Prototyping 115–16, 133, 135, 140, 164
　characteristics/advantages 136
　process of 134
　software development 163

Q

Quality 413, 419 – see also *Performance* and *Total Quality Management*
　Deming, Dr. Edward 422
　ISO 9000 433
　Malcolm Baldrige Award 422
Quality control
　of operations 431–2
　　control locations 432

R

R1/XCON 142
RAD (Rapid Applications Development) 140
Rank Xerox 258
Raymond Abrial 168
　B-method 168
Recovery
　disaster 390
Reengineering 239
　analysis 250
　CASE 242
　Citibank client–server example 344
　corporate strategy 247–8
　defined 244
　design 252
　dimensions of 251
　examples 259
　feasibility study 248
　getting started 249
　implementation and monitoring 253
　maintenance 241, 293
　planning 246–7
　process overview 247
　process summary 255
　reasons for 239–40
　reverse engineering 244
　success and failure factors 253–4
　taking the decision 242–4
　when to consider 241
　　relevant factors 242
Remote processing 36, 55
　cushioning demand 37
　factors to consider 38–9
　modes of 37
　reasons for 37
　selecting a service 38
　turnaround time 38
Renting
　computer resources 202
Request for proposals
　acquisition of resources 190
Resources
　acquisition approval 201
　contract negotiations 207
　　contract content 208–9
　　contract implementation 209
　financing acquisition 201
　　comparison of alternatives 211, 213
　　lease vs. lease/purchase calculations 217
　　leasing 202
　　purchase 204
　　rental 202
　　rent vs. purchase calculations 216
　procurement process 190

request for proposals 190
   sample contents 192
specifying requirements 191
vendors
   benchmarks 195–6
   briefing the vendor 191
   proposal cost elements 199
   proposal submission 193
   proposal validation 193–6
vendor selection procedures 198
   cost–value method 199, 200, 215
   matrix method 191
   weighted-score method 198, 214
vendor-supplied information 193

Reuse
approaches 185
component archiving 180
component classification 181
defined 173
domain analysis 178
library 178, 293
   adoption procedure 180
maintenance 294, 299
management of 174, 181–2
programmer incentives 182
review board 178
software factory 183–4
software library 173
strategy 176–7
   developing using SCERT 178
   domain analysis 176
   NobelTech example 176
   sequencing 177
   success stories 187

Reverse engineering 244
defined 245

Rightsizing 337
Motorola 345

RSI (Repetitive Strain Injury) 262
lawsuit example 279

S

SABER/SABRE 116, 142
SAM 196
SCERT (System and Computer Evaluation Review Technique) 177–8, 196–7
SDLC (Systems Development Life Cycle) 115–17, 140, 244
   critique of 133
   network development 358
   reuse component engineering 178
   software development 156–7, 165
   spiral effect 116, 118

Security 71, 268, 383
access to terminals 385
biometric systems 386
callback boxes 389
client–server systems 340
computer utilities 56
(and) consultants 40
data directory security matrix 387
designated personnel 392
disaster recovery 390
during an acceptance test 129
during system development 389
facilities management 45
hackers 388, 409
hacking example 406
handshaking systems 389
identifying assets 402
image processing 395–6
keys and cards 385
layers of protection 384
levels of 393
message encryption 352–3
message piggybacking 389
messages and wire-tapping 389
monitoring and enforcement 403
network firewalls 354
network management 351–2
operational 389
outsourcing concerns 231
passwords 387

Index

personnel
  responsibility separation 391
  safeguards 391
plant security 384
private detectives 389
resource allocation 393–4
risk assessment 393–5
security officer 402
viruses – see Viruses
Sema Group 62
Semantic networks 317
  example 317–8
  OAV triplets 319
Servers 333, 335 – see also Client–server system
Service bureaux 35, 52, 55, 58
  advantages 53
  computer utilities 55
  selection criteria 54
  services offered 53
SIMSCRIPT 71, 159, 332
Singapore
  Internet laws 6
SNA (Systems Network Architecture) 333, 359
Societe General 168
SODA (System Optimization and Design Algorithm) 137
Software "factory" 174, 183
Software component engineering 175
Software development 156
  design 158
  documentation 162–3
  implementation 159
  prototyping 163
  SDLC for 157
  specification 157–8
  strategies for 166
  walkthrough testing 161–2
SpectraVision 59
SQL 331
SSADM (Structured Systems Analysis and Design Method) 140, 146
SSAM (Strategic Software Asset Management) Award 169
Staff – see Personnel

Steering committee 91–2, 109, 111
  composition 93
  frequency of meetings 94
  functions of 93–4
  subcommittee types 95
Stress 83–4 – see also Technostress
  table of symptoms 84
  techniques to reduce 89
Structured methodologies 136–7, 140
  HIPO (Hierarchy plus Input-Process-Output 137
  Jackson structured design 144
  Merise 145
  Multiview 145
  RUDE and POLITE 144
  SADT (Systems Analysis and Design Technique) 137
Structured programming 136
Subcontracting – see Outsourcing
Systems analyst 24, 67–9, 122
  desirable characteristics 69
Systems integrator 461–2
Systems plan 116
Systems specification 121

T

TCP/IP 333, 360
Technical writers 73
Technology
  evolution of 3, 4
  watcher 75–6
Technostress 83–4, 261
Teleconferencing 102, 341
Testing 127, 129, 131
  acceptance testing 129
  approaches to 130
  interactions and iteration 131
  subsystems 129
  systems test 130
  unit testing 129
Texas Instruments 137
  reengineering example 256
Time-sharing 36, 55

Top-down decomposition 137
Toshiba 188
Total Quality Management 423
  data gathering 425
    logs 425
    monitors 425–6
    user surveys 427–8
  implementing TQM 430
  quality criteria 423–4
  quality measurement 424
Training 47, 82–3
  CASE 139
Transactional processing 229–30
Transactional systems
  and reengineering 241
Trojan horse – see *Viruses*
Turnaround time 420
Turnover
  of personnel 80

U

United Distillers 32
UNIX 332
US Library of Congress 59
User
  classification of 26
  compared to end-user 25
  definition of 25
  requirements 121
  specification 105, 121
    essential properties of 123
    factors to be considered 122
    importance of 123

V

V chip 6
Vendor 189, 193 – see also *Resources*
  bias 191
  packaged software 156
  selection matrix 138

(as a) source of expertise 43
Video Lottery Technologies 59
Viruses 354
  BRAIN virus 397
  Bulgarian virus factory 398
  Cornell virus 398
  infection rates 399
  Jerusalem virus 398
  Lehigh virus 397
  logic bomb 397, 407–8
  management strategies 399, 400
  Pakistani virus 397
  "stealth" virus 399
  Trojan horse 397
  worm 397, 407
Voice processing 267

W

Walkthrough 162, 166
  advantages and pitfalls 166
WAN (Wide Area Network) 330
Waterfall-based methodology
  POLITE 144
Web browsers 367
  Mosaic, Netscape and Internet Explorer 367
Weighted-score method 214
  for vendor selection 198
WIMP (Windows, Icons, Menus and Pointers) 269
World Wide Web 274, 367
Worm – see *Viruses*

X–Z

X terminal 332
X Windows 332
Xerox 59
Yourdon 145

BEYOND THE MAINFRAME
A GUIDE TO OPEN COMPUTER SYSTEMS
CONOR SEXTON

COMPUTER WEEKLY PROFESSIONAL SERIES

Credit Card Hotline Tel: (01865) 314627

On reading this book you will be able to:

- Define the term 'Client/Server Architecture' and 'Open Systems'.
- Compare the relative strengths and weaknesses of the client/server model and the traditional time sharing approach.
- Understand the developments in computer hardware, operating systems, networks and application software which have led the move to smaller distributed systems.
- Assess the opportunities presented by Client/Server and the pitfalls inherent in implementing it
- Evaluate current Client/Server application.
- Better predict future trends in distributed computing technologies
- Understand the benefits of the new computing model for your enterprise and your customers

Beyond the Mainframe aims to describe clearly the component technologies of open and Client/Server computer systems and networks and is intended to be accessible to non-specialist readers including: managers responsible for procurement of computer systems or management of them when they have been procured; managers who want to know the terminology and the main principles, as an aid to working with their colleagues; sales; pre-sale and post-sale staff working for computer manufacturers, resellers and other system vendors.

0 7506 1902 3, 300 pages, 263 x 156mm, October 1995.

EFFECTIVE MEASUREMENT & MANAGEMENT OF IT COSTS & BENEFITS

COMPUTER WEEKLY PROFESSIONAL SERIES

DAN REMENYI, ARTHUR MONEY
AND ALAN TWITE

Credit Card Hotline
Tel: (01865) 314627

For those concerned with the rocketing level of IT expenditure this book can show you how to take control and make more effective use of IT.

The rapidly increasing expenditure on IT in most organizations is one reason why IT benefits management has become an important concern.

This book provides a basic, practical framework for understanding the economic issues of information as well as some suggestions as to how a company's IT efforts may be appraised.

This book:

- Looks at the IT investment decision process
- Shows how to produce cost/benefits analysis of IT spend
- Shows how to measure benefits and how to evaluate the success of the IT function
- Includes case studies - learn by example

1995, 246 x 189mm, 285 pages, paperback
0 7506 2432 9.